Beginning Java with WebSphere

■ ■ ■

Robert W. Janson

Beginning Java with WebSphere

ISBN-13 (pbk): 978-1-4302-6301-2

ISBN-13 (electronic): 978-1-4302-6302-9

President and Publisher: Paul Manning
Lead Editor: Steve Anglin
Development Editor: Matthew Moodie
Technical Reviewer: Rohan Walia
Editorial Board: Steve Anglin, Mark Beckner, Ewan Buckingham, Gary Cornell, Louise Corrigan, Morgan Ertel,
    Jonathan Gennick, Jonathan Hassell, Robert Hutchinson, Michelle Lowman, James Markham,
    Matthew Moodie, Jeff Olson, Jeffrey Pepper, Douglas Pundick, Ben Renow-Clarke, Dominic Shakeshaft,
    Gwenan Spearing, Matt Wade, Tom Welsh
Coordinating Editor: Jill Balzano
Copy Editor: Laura Lawrie
Compositor: SPi Global
Indexer: SPi Global
Artist: SPi Global
Cover Designer: Anna Ishchenko

Distributed to the book trade worldwide by Springer Science+Business Media New York, 233 Spring Street, 6th Floor, New York, NY 10013. Phone 1-800-SPRINGER, fax (201) 348-4505, e-mail orders-ny@springer-sbm.com, or visit www.springeronline.com. Apress Media, LLC is a California LLC and the sole member (owner) is Springer Science + Business Media Finance Inc (SSBM Finance Inc). SSBM Finance Inc is a Delaware corporation.

For information on translations, please e-mail rights@apress.com, or visit www.apress.com.

Apress and friends of ED books may be purchased in bulk for academic, corporate, or promotional use. eBook versions and licenses are also available for most titles. For more information, reference our Special Bulk Sales–eBook Licensing web page at www.apress.com/bulk-sales.

Any source code or other supplementary materials referenced by the author in this text is available to readers at www.apress.com. For detailed information about how to locate your book's source code, go to www.apress.com/source-code/.

Contents at a Glance

Contents

Foreword

Java and WebSphere provide a solid base for developing large-enterprise applications. However, the training materials available often assume knowledge of object-oriented programming and system design. This text fills that gap by providing a step-by-step guide for creating and installing both client- and server-based Java applications using RAD 8, WAS 8.0, and Java 1.6.

Because more and more Java applications are moving to the server and using HTML for the user interface, there is a minimal amount of time spent exploring the Java GUI components. For the same reason, applets are almost completely ignored and AWT was chosen over Swing because of its ease of use. In addition, the detailed explanation of reference variables is delayed until Chapter 5 so that the student may get comfortable with the Java syntax and the RAD environment.

Many Java purists may decry the omitted detail on certain topics (static vs. nonstatic methods, private/protected/public, arrays, etc.). However, we have intentionally minimized these topics to concentrate on base topics that allow students to get to the server-side and database topics quickly.

About the Author

Robert W. Janson—Computer and Information Systems Instructor.

Professor Janson has developed and taught a variety of computer courses including online and blended classes and for variety of corporations and at FSCJ since 1990. Classes have covered topics such as programming languages, DBMSs, System Development and Design, and PC applications for a wide variety of computer environments (JEE, mainframe, midrange, PC).

Before working at FSCJ, Professor Janson worked for IBM at their semiconductor manufacturing center in New York. During his eight years at IBM, he held a variety of managerial and technical positions (system architect, database designer, programmer/analyst) in the IS department developing and maintaining manufacturing and logistics systems.

About the Technical Reviewer

Rohan Walia is a Software Consultant with extensive experience in Client-Server, Web-Based, and Enterprise application development. He is an Oracle Certified ADF Implementation Specialist and Sun Certified Java Programmer. He is responsible for designing and developing end-to-end Java/J2EE applications consisting of various cutting-edge frameworks and utilities. His areas of expertise include Oracle ADF, WebCenter , Spring, Hibernate, and Java/J2EE. When not working, Rohan loves to play tennis, travel, and hike. Rohan would like to thank his wife Deepika Walia for helping him to review this book.

Acknowledgments

I would like to thank the following people and institutions for their support:

Gail Gehrig and Robert Yoder, colleagues and friends, for their meticulous comments and suggestions. Thanks for all your time and concern; I appreciate it greatly.

Mike Baker, Dane Warner, John Boynton, Shane Retzer, Sarah Byrd, Lynne Sluder, Glen Orsburn, Chris Harris, and Mike Brock for their willingness (and sometimes delight) in finding typos and errors.

My employer, FSCJ, for the time and facilities to work on this text.

Of course, Brenda, for consultation on all aspects of this project and being my wife. Thanks for listening!

And then all my friends and relatives (who really like to see their names in print): Aly, Brian, Carol, Caroline, Chris, Coke, David, Dyan, Ed, Helmut, Janson, Jim, Jimmy, Joyce, Kathy, Kevin, Marc, Marty, Matt, Morgan, Pat, Peggy, Pete, Ray, Rick, Ron, Sharon, Steph, Susan, Susie, Tammy, Vivian, and Whitey.

CHAPTER 1

■ ■ ■

Java Basics

After a very short history of Java, we will jump right into Java programming. We will create and use a bare bones program to demonstrate the Java basics and the capabilities of Rational Application Developer.

After finishing this chapter, you should understand:

> Basic Java keywords and syntax
>
> Classes, methods, and variables
>
> Constructors and comments
>
> Perspectives and views

Using WebSphere, you will be able to:

> Create projects, packages, and classes
>
> Use and customize perspectives and views
>
> Write a basic Java application
>
> Run a Java application

The Java Language

Java shares many of the same characteristics as spoken and written languages such as English, Spanish, and so on. For instance, both Java and spoken languages consist of a unique set of words. In Java, these words are called **keywords**. Java also uses symbols (; , {}, (), etc.), just as written languages use punctuation marks. All of the symbols and keywords that comprise the Java language are referred to as **tokens**. (Another definition of a token is the smallest unit of the Java language.) We mention this right at the beginning of the text because error messages often cite an "incorrect token" or "token expected" as problems—not that we are expecting you to make any errors!

Programming languages also have rules of grammar that must be followed. These grammar rules are called the programming language's **syntax**. Just as a written language's grammar dictates how to combine words and punctuation into sentences and paragraphs, the Java syntax dictates how tokens are combined to create Java statements, methods, and classes.

Who makes the rules? Oracle. Sun Microsystems (acquired by Oracle in 2009) originally developed Java in the early 1990s and modeled it after the very popular C++ programming language. Java shares many of the same syntax rules and keywords as C++ but the major difference with Java is its network orientation. The Java language was designed so that graphical, two-way interactions between computing devices can be easily created.

In the early 1990s, the Internet was primarily text-based. Sun, working with Netscape, enabled the Netscape browser to download Java **applets** from another computer (called a server). The applet ran on the user's PC (known as the client), and the applet results were displayed in the browser window.

Java programs can also be stored and run on a client. These types of Java programs are called client-based **applications**. Finally, Java programs can be stored and run on a server and the results sent to the PC's browser for display. There are many different types of Java programs that can run on the server. As a group they are called a server-side (or server-based) application. However, each different type of Java program (Servlet, JSP, Bean, etc.) has advantages and disadvantages and a specific purpose in the application. We will explore this in later chapters.

Oracle/Sun has continued to work with many companies (Microsoft, IBM) and international organizations to insure that Java is compatible with all hardware and operating systems. Of course, there is also competition. Microsoft offers a number of programming languages, specifically J# (pronounced "jay sharp"), that compete with Java and an Integrated Development Environment (IDE) called .Net (pronounced "dot net") that competes with IBM's WebSphere.

Classes

Java statements are grouped into a **class**. A class is comparable to what other programming languages call a program. A class begins with a header. The **class header** identifies the Java code as a class and defines **class attributes**. For instance, a class header can include an access modifier (e.g., public, private), the keyword class, and the class name with at least one space between each. For instance, the following class header defines a class called Employee (note we still need to add a body to this class definition):

public class Employee

The words public and class are examples of keywords (also called reserved words). A keyword has a specific purpose in Java and can only be used in the manner dictated by the Java syntax. For example, class identifies the code as a class, and public means that any other class can access Employee. The access modifier public must come before the class keyword, and the keywords public or class cannot be used as the name of the class. There are many other keywords (such as if, else, do, while, return) that also cannot be used as a class name, and there are a couple other rules that must be followed. For instance, class names can consist of letters, numbers, and some special characters, however, it is strongly recommended that class names begin with an uppercase letter. Table 1-1 shows a brief list of the rules and examples.

Table 1-1.

Class name rule	Good	Bad
Begin with a letter	Sale1 Sale$	1Sales
No spaces	Tax_Calc TaxCalc	Tax Calc
No keywords	MyFirstClass Class	class do

Notice that the third row in Table 1-1 lists "Class" as a valid name but "class" as invalid. This highlights another feature: Java is case sensitive. This means that classes named Employee, EMployee, and EmployeE are all considered different classes. In addition, if you referred to employee or EMPLOYEE, the system would not find a class with that name. Be aware and careful of your capitalization! It is customary (but not required) to begin class names with a capital letter and capitalize the first letter of each "word" within the class name (e.g., MyFirstClass). This mix of upper- and lowercase letters is called "camel case."

All of the Java code following the class header is called the body of the class and is enclosed in braces, { }. Therefore, a valid class definition would be:

```
public class Employee {}
```

However, as there are no Java statements between the braces, this class does not do anything.

Java Statements

The class body is comprised of what we will refer to as **class variable** definitions and methods. Variables are categorized by their scope. This text will define class variables as those variables that can be accessed by any statement within the class. The official Java definition of class variables is much more specific and has many other variable classifications (such as instance variables). However, the distinctions between the various variable scopes are beyond this introductory discussion of Java.

Class variable definitions traditionally follow the class header. Simply stated, the purpose of a variable is to hold stuff, but we will discuss this in more depth later. Variables are also be classified by the type of "stuff" they hold. For example, the following Java statement declares (defines) a String variable called empName. String variables hold String objects:

```
String empName = new String();
```

Let's explain the various pieces of this statement. The definition begins with the variable type (String), at least one space, and the name of the variable (empName). This creates a String variable called empName. Think of this as telling the computer to reserve some space in memory and calling this space empName. Next, the equal sign assigns a value (or in Java-speak, an object) to this variable. Please note that the Java equal sign is not like a mathematical equal sign. The Java equal sign associates an object or value on its right to a variable on its left. So in this case, new String() creates an empty String object (meaning no text has been assigned), and the equal sign assigns the String object to the variable empName.

Another way to look at the statement is that everything to the right of the equal sign creates the String object and everything to the left creates the String variable empName.

Finally, there is a semicolon (;). Java statements end with a semicolon. This is a requirement. In fact, forgetting the semicolon will be your most common coding mistake. (Try not to get too frustrated the first thousand times you do it.) If you do not specify a semicolon at the end of a line, Java assumes that the statement is not finished and will look to the next line for more of the statement. For example, the empName definition above can also be written as follows:

```
String
    empName
    =

    new
            String();
```

Although perfectly valid, this is one ugly looking statement.

As mentioned, strings can be assigned text. When a String object is created, a text value can be assigned at the same time as follows:

```
String empName = new String("Joe Employee");
```

The value of a String variable can be changed very easily (which is unique for Java variables. In other words, since most other variable can't be changed as easily, don't get used to this!) The following would assign empName to a String object with text of Mary Worker:

```
empName = "Mary Worker";
```

Methods are subsections of a class that contain executable statements. An executable statement performs an action (e.g., adding two variables, printing, etc.). Methods can receive and return variables. Methods, like classes, require a header. A method header has an access modifier and the method name. In addition, the header defines what data the method expects (is receiving) and what data the method will return. For instance, the following header defines a method called salaryCalc:

```java
public double salaryCalc(int hoursWorked, double payRate)
```

The access modifier (public) comes first, is followed by a space, and then the type of variable (double) that the method will return. In this case, salaryCalc will return a variable of type double (more on this type of variable later). There is another space and then the name of the method is next. It is customary to begin method names with a lowercase letter. The method name is followed by parameters for the values that the method is expecting. The parameters must be enclosed in parentheses and separated by a comma. Parameters define **method variables** that will hold the passed values. Method variables are different from class variables because they have a more **limited scope**. In other words, class variables are considered **global** in scope because any method (within the class) can use a class variable. Method variables are **local** in scope because they can only be used in statements within the method that defines them.

Classes can contain specialized methods. For now, the two specialized methods we will discuss are the main method and a type of method called a constructor.

The main Method

When you run a class as an application, Java looks for and runs the class's main method. The following is a valid main method:

```java
public static void main(String[] args) { }
```

There must be at least one space between each keyword (public, static, void) and the method name (main). Also, the tokens must be in the order shown. You are already familiar with the purpose of the access modifier public. The keyword void means that the main method does not return anything. String[] args defines the expected data as an array of String variables called args. One nice feature of Java is that if the person running the class does not specify an array of strings, Java automatically supplies one at runtime. Finally, the method is defined as static. A static method does not need any class variables or other methods to work properly. In other words, a static method can be executed as a "stand alone method." Usually only one class within an application is coded with a main method. This single main method creates the objects that comprise the application. In other words, the main method "kicks off" the application.

Objects and Instantiation

Most classes are not run as applications; rather, most classes are **instantiated**. Instantiated is a very intimidating word. Essentially, when a class is instantiated, a copy (also called an **instance**) of the class is placed in the computer's main memory. A class instance is also called an **object**. You can actually have many instances of a class or, to say it another way, many objects of the class type.

For instance, we could instantiate two Employee objects. One object could have a pay rate of ten dollars per hour and an employee name of "Joe Smith." The other Employee object's pay rate could be twelve dollars an hour and have an employee name of "Mary Jones."

You actually have already instantiated a class (i.e., you have already created an object). A String object was created when new String(""Joe Employee"") within the following statement was executed:

```java
String empName = new String("Joe Employee");
```

If you executed the following statements, you would have two more String objects:

```
String empAddr = new String("1 Main St");
String empCSZ = new String("Albany, NY 11508");
```

Therefore, in the example, there are three unique String objects. Since an object is an instance of a class, this means that there is a String class. The String class was created by the Java developers and "comes with Java."

If you're a little confused, don't worry. We will cover instantiation and explain "what comes with Java" in greater detail in later chapters. For now, just remember that there are a number of very useful classes that come with Java and that these classes are used to build sophisticated Java applications quickly.

Constructors

When an object is created, Java runs the instantiated class's (i.e., the object's) **constructor**. A constructor is a method with the same name as the class that does not return any value. For example, the constructor method for the Employee class would be called Employee and could be defined as follows:

```
public Employee() { }
```

Notice that a return variable type is not specified. This is a rule for constructors: they cannot return any data. The example is also considered a null (or default) constructor because it does not accept data (i.e., no parameters are specified). However, a constructor can accept information. The following defines a constructor that accepts a String object, creates a String variable called name and assigns the String object to name:

```
public Employee(String name) { }
```

As mentioned, when the Employee class is instantiated, the constructor method is automatically run. In the above example, however, the constructor does nothing. Constructors are often used to initialize variables needed by the class methods. For instance, the following constructor assigns the passed String object to the class variable empName:

```
public Employee(String name) {
    empName = name;
}
```

This is similar to the algebraic statements: A=1, B=A. In the Java example: name = String object, empName = name. Therefore, name and empName contain the same value.

WebSphere

WebSphere is a group of IBM software products that includes all of the "development tools" that a programmer would need to write, debug, and install Java applications. "Development tools" is a category of software that usually includes a code editor, syntax checker, debugger, and many other useful programming utilities. In addition, WebSphere includes software that can be installed on any computer to make that computer a Java application server.

There are many "versions" of WebSphere products (Express, Standard, Enterprise, etc.). These different versions simply have different sets of tools. As of this writing, the Enterprise Editions have the most complete and powerful set of Java development tools.

We will use the development tools provided by the Rational Application Developer (RAD). We will begin with a tour of the RAD "client environment" and then demonstrate several of the "tools" used to create and run Java applications. Later in the text, we will cover the WebSphere Application Server (WAS) software.

Tutorial: Starting Rational Application Developer

Let's get started:

1. Assuming that WebSphere has already been installed, from the Windows desktop, click the Start button (in the lower left of the screen), then All Programs.

2. Within the program list find and click on the entry for IBM Software Delivery Platform, IBM Rational Application Developer, then Rational Application Developer (see Figure 1-1).

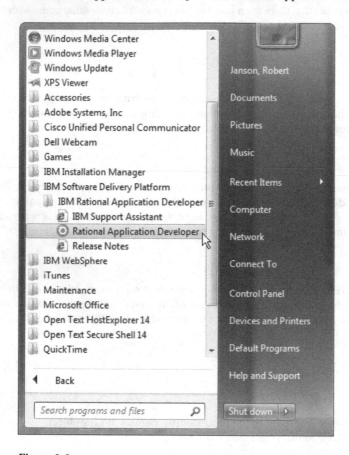

Figure 1-1.

■ **Note** If Rational Application Developer is running for the first time, this may take a little while.

---

3. You may be prompted for a location on the PC where WebSphere should store the work (see Figure 1-2). If so, specify a location (e.g., a flash drive) and click the OK button.

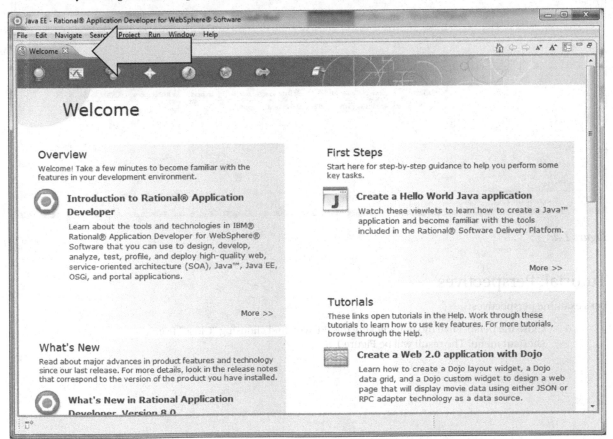

Figure 1-2.

4. Rational Application Developer (RAD) will be started and if this is the first time RAD has been run, the Welcome pane will be displayed (see Figure 1-3). Close the Welcome pane by clicking the X in the pane tab (indicated by the arrow in Figure 1-3).

Figure 1-3.

The Rational Application Developer (RAD) will be started and the default "perspective" will be displayed (see Figure 1-4). RAD provides several different "views" of Java applications. These different views are called perspectives. Each perspective provides a unique set of panes, functions, command options, tool bar buttons, and so on. Initially, the Java EE (Java Enterprise Edition) perspective is displayed. You can tell which perspectives are open by the icons on the upper right of the window. In this case, the arrow in Figure 1-4 is pointing to the Java EE icon.

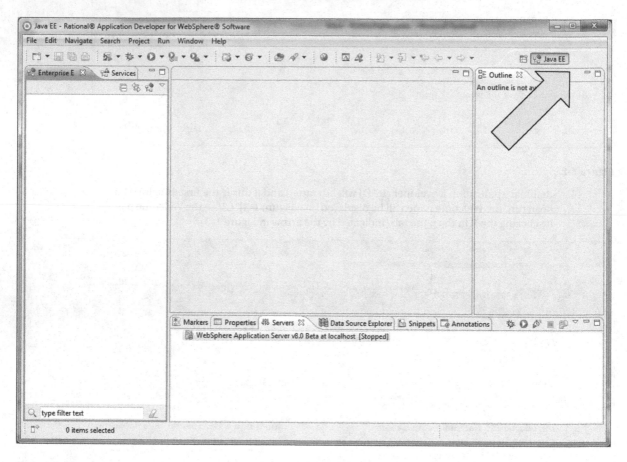

Figure 1-4.

Tutorial: Perspectives

Let's examine perspectives:

1. Close the perspective by right-clicking the JEE icon and choosing "Close" from the shortcut menu. The result will be Figure 1-5.

Figure 1-5.

2.   Click the "Open a Perspective" icon (indicated by the arrow in Figure 1-5). A shortcut menu will be displayed with an option for ""Other."" A list of available perspectives can be viewed by choosing the "Other" option.

3.   Click on the ""Other"" option. The ""Open Perspective"" window will be displayed (see Figure 1-6).

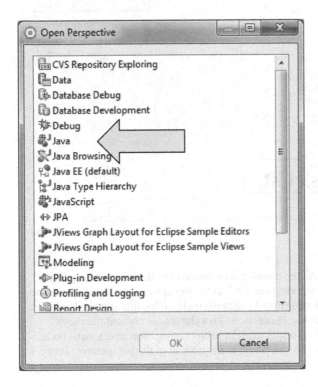

Figure 1-6.

4.   For now, simply select "Java" from the "Open Perspective" window and click the OK button. The Java perspective will be displayed (see Figure 1-7)

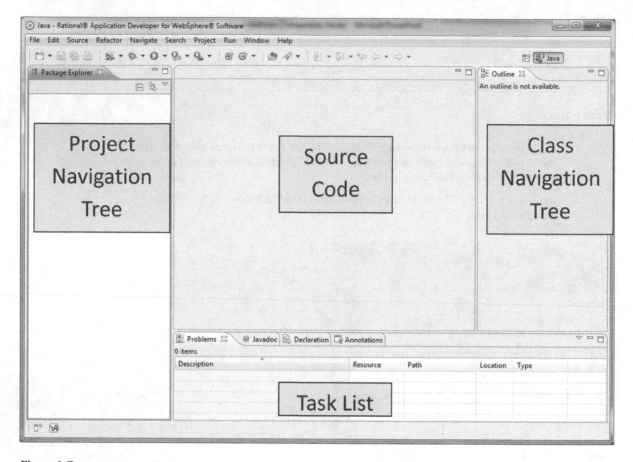

Figure 1-7.

The initial Java perspective is comprised of four panes. All the panes can be resized by clicking and dragging on their borders and some panes can contain different views. Each view has a tab at the top of the pane that displays the views name and, at least, a close button. You can switch between views by clicking on the tabs. Initially, the Package Explorer view, the editing area, and Outline view display nothing. However, as Java classes are created the views contents will change. Most of the time, these views will display (respectively) a project navigation tree, source code, and a Java class navigation tree. One of the views provided in the task pane (at the bottom of the perspective) keeps track of work (e.g., problems) that needs to be completed.

Tutorial: Creating and Deleting a Project

RAD stores everything in projects. Projects are comprised of packages and packages contain Java classes. This means that a project and package must exist before creating a Java class. (Think of projects and packages as specialized folders. In fact, a project and its packages are implemented as folders when a project is exported from RAD to a Windows environment.)

1. To create a project, click File (on the Menu bar), New, then Java Project (see Figure 1-8).

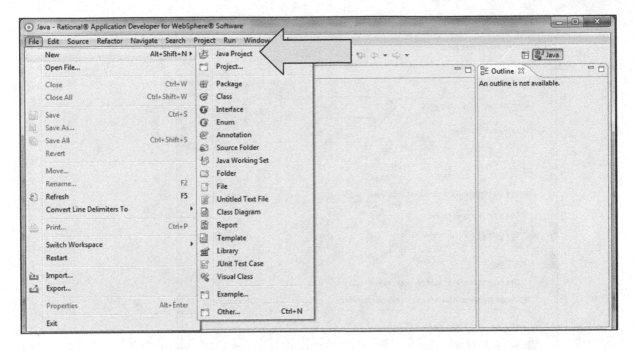

Figure 1-8.

2. The "New Java Project" window will be displayed (see Figure 1-9). At the "New Java Project" window, specify MyFirstProject and click the Finish button.

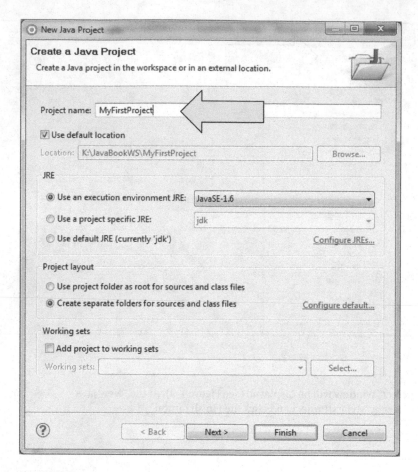

Figure 1-9.

■ **Note**   MyFirstProject now appears in the Package Explorer view.

---

3. Selecting an item in the project navigation tree results in the item name being enclosed in a rectangle with a pale blue background. Because MyFirstProject was just created, it is automatically selected by RAD. (An item can also be selected by clicking its name or icon.) Any subsequent actions you specify will be performed against the selected item. On the Menu bar, click Edit, then Delete.

4. At the "Delete Resources" window, click the "Delete project contents on disk" checkbox, and then the Yes button. The Java Perspective is redisplayed. Notice that MyFirstProject has been removed from the Package Explorer view. The delete was performed against MyFirstProject because MyFirst-Project was the selected item.

5. Perform steps 1 and 2 again to recreate MyFirstProject. The "Package Explorer" pane should look like Figure 1-10.

Figure 1-10.

Tutorial: Creating a Package

Now let's create a package:

1. On the Menu bar, click File, New, then Package to display the "New Java Package" window.

■ **Note** MyFirstProject/src already appears in the Source folder field. This is because MyFirstProject was selected in the "Package Explorer" view and RAD requires that all source code packages be in project subfolder called src (source). (RAD does a lot for the programmer but it also sometimes imposes its own unique standards.) The Browse button to the right of the Source folder field can be used to find and select a different project.

---

2. At the "New Java Package" window, specify MyFirstPackage in the Name field. Notice the message at the top of the window. Package names usually begin with a lowercase letter to make it easier to distinguish them from project names. RAD tries to warn programmers about errors and suggest good programming practices throughout the development process. This is one of the many advantages provided by a development tool such as RAD.

3. Change the name to myFirstPackage. Notice the message goes away (see Figure 1-11).

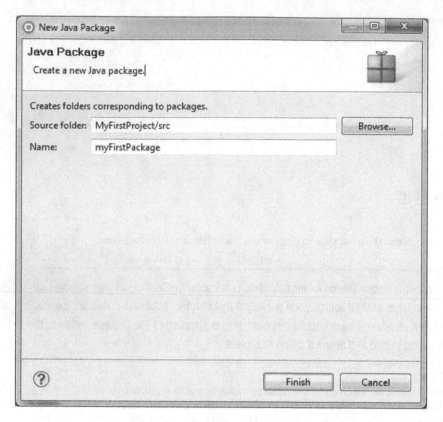

Figure 1-11.

4. Click the Finish button. Notice that myFirstPackage is selected in the "Navigation Tree" within the "Package Explorer" view and appears as a branch or subitem within src (see Figure 1-12).

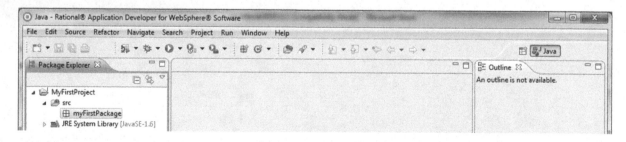

Figure 1-12.

The project navigation tree allows the programmer to easily navigate and manipulate the Java projects, packages, and their contents. Notice to the left of each item name is an icon that indicates the item type. To the left of some of the item type icons are the symbols (▷, ▲). These are expansion icons. Expansion icons appear next to items that contain other items. These icons indicate if the tree item's contents are displayed (▲) or are not displayed (▷). In this case, the contents of MyFirstProject and src are displayed, but the JRE (Java Run time Environment) System Library package's contents (created by RAD when the project was created) are not. myFirstPackage does not have an expansion icon because it was just created and is empty. You can display and close a sub-tree by clicking the item's expansion icon or double-clicking the item name or item type icon.

5. Click on the MyFirstProject expansion icon. The contents are hidden and the expansion icon is changed.

6. Click on the MyFirstProject expansion icon again. The contents are displayed and the expansion icon is changed back.

7. Double-click the project icon for MyFirstProject to hide the contents and then double-click the project name (MyFirstProject) to redisplay the contents.

Tutorial: Creating a Java Class

Do you remember all the syntax rules for defining a class header? Probably not. Fortunately, RAD will walk you through the process. In other words, just as you created a project and a package, RAD will supply a series of windows to help you easily define a class:

1. If myFirstPackage is not selected, select it by clicking its name.

2. On the menu bar, click File, New, and then Class to display the "New Java Class" window (see Figure 1-13).

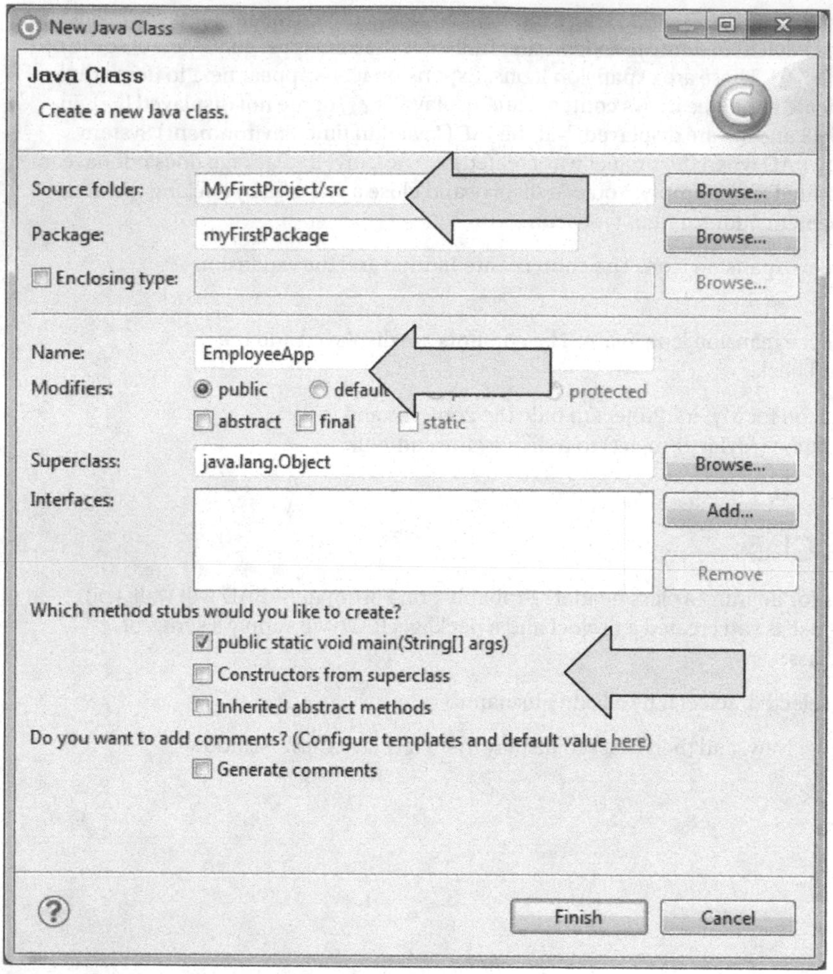

Figure 1-13.

■ **Note** The source folder and package names are already specified. Because myFirstPackage was selected in step 1, RAD assumed that was where the class should be created. A different project and package can be specified by simply entering their names in the appropriate fields or clicking the Browse buttons next to each field.

---

3. Specify EmployeeApp in the Name field. Notice that the access modifier `public` has already been selected. Other modifiers can be chosen by clicking the other modifier option's radio button or check boxes.

4. Make sure the main method option is the only method stub option selected. Since EmployeeApp will be run as an application, it needs a main method. By checking the "main method" option, RAD will automatically generate an empty main method (e.g., a stub) relieving you from having to code it.

5. Click the Finish button to create the class and redisplay the Java perspective (see Figure 1-14).

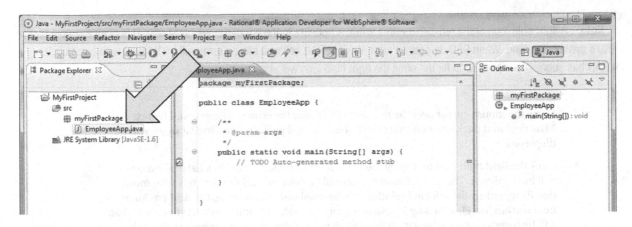

Figure 1-14.

Notice that the EmployeeApp class was stored in a file called EmployeeApp.java within myFirstPackage and that if myFirstPackage is selected it has an expansion icon. Java source code must be stored in a file that has the same name as the class and the file name extension must be **java**. RAD generates the correctly named file automatically so there is less chance of error.

Please note the following about the RAD generated Java code.

RAD has included comments in the source code. **Comments** are nonexecutable statements. This means that comments do not perform any computing function. Characters that appear within /* and */ or /** and */ are treated as comments. These comments can span multiple lines. For a single line of comments use //. Any characters that appear after // on a line are considered comments.

Comments are used to document the Java code. Generally, programmers will include their name, the date the class was created, as well as, brief descriptions about what the class does and how the various methods work. Notice that RAD generated two comment sections: a Methods comment section (in blue, right before the method header) and a Method body comment section (in green, after the method header). Each comment section has default text that will be inserted into every class and method that RAD generates. To change the comment default text, click Window, then Preferences.... At the Preferences window, expand the Java item then the Code Style item and select Code Templates. Two expandable items are displayed: Comments and Code. The Methods comment is within Comments and the Method body comment is within Code. Expand the appropriate item and then select either of comment items to display the default text. To change the text, click the Edit... button, modify the text, and then click the OK button. One would think that the default text has been changed—one would be wrong! You must click the Apply button and then the OK button to make the change permanent.

Changing comments that have already been inserted in a class is much easier. Simply select the comment text and type over it.

When a class is defined within a package, **a package statement must be included**. The package statement must come before the class header and follows the simple syntax of the package keyword followed by at least one space, the package name, and a semicolon (e.g., package myFirstPackage;). The package name actually becomes part of the file identifier. For example, if the file name is Employee and the package is myFirstPackage, the file is identified as myFirstPackage.Employee.

We'll prove that the package statement is required by "commenting it out."

6. Move the cursor before the package keyword and insert two forward slashes (//). Notice that the text changes to green. Green text indicates that Java considers the text a comment and this text will not perform any function.

■ **Note** A light bulb icon and a red circle with a white X appears to the left of the very first line. This is an example of RAD's syntax checking. When RAD detects an error, the line RAD believes has an error will be flagged with a red circle. If RAD has suggestions on how to fix the error, the light bulb icon will also appear.

7. Move the mouse cursor over the red circle to display the error message text. The text "The declared package" does not match the expected package "myFirstPackage" will be displayed.

8. Click the light bulb icon to display the possible solutions. A box with a list of solutions will be displayed. The first solution option will be selected and a yellow box with more details regarding the selected solution will be displayed. In this case, the **Add package declaration 'myFirstPackage;'** solution should be selected and the exact statement that will be inserted and where within the code it will be placed should appear to the right.

■ **Note** If you double-click a solution, RAD will make the changes to the code. In this case, the package statement is there but has been commented out so we don't want RAD to insert the statement. We will simply uncomment the statement using a RAD shortcut.

9. Click anywhere on the commented out package statement line to select it.

10. Press and hold the Ctrl key, then press the forward slash (/) key. (We will use **Ctrl-/** to indicate this action).

Notice that the two forward slashes are removed. The package statement is now executable and the error icon on the first line is gone. Statements can also be commented out quickly by selecting the line(s) and pressing Ctrl and forward slash (**Ctrl-/**). Essentially **Ctrl-/** acts as a toggle switch to comment and uncomment statements.

11. Select all the lines of the class.

12. Press Ctrl-/ to change them all to comments.

13. Press Ctrl-/ to uncomment all the statements.

14. On the menu bar, click File and then Save.

Tutorial: Entering and Editing Java Statements

Now let's do some editing:

1. Click to the right of the opening brace ({) in the main method header. The insertion cursor (a blinking vertical line) should appear at the far right of the line.

2. Press the Enter key to insert a blank line.

3. Enter the following statement on the blank line:

```
System.out.println("Howdy");
```

This statement will display the text "Howdy." Why and how this statement works is beyond your understanding right now. Accept the fact that there is a class called **System** that contains a wonderful object called **out**. The **out** object has a nice method called **println** that will display anything passed to it. This statement passes the simple text "Howdy" to the **println** method, and **println** displays the text.

The code should look like Figure 1-15.

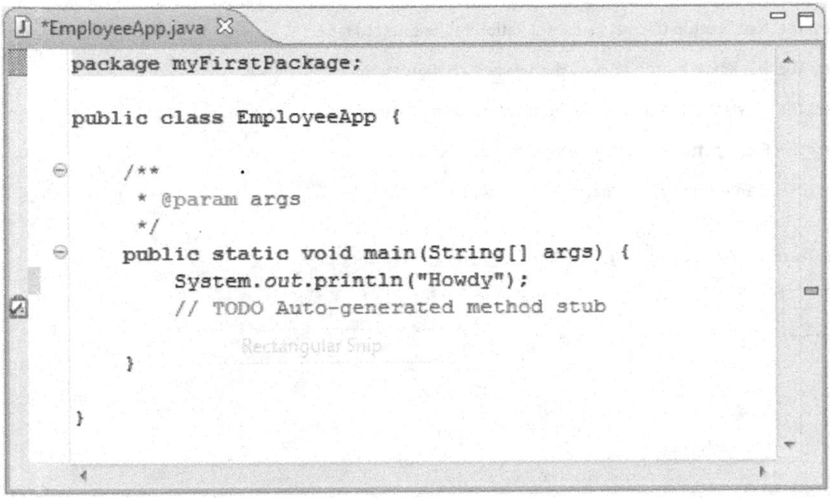

```java
package myFirstPackage;

public class EmployeeApp {

    /**
     * @param args
     */
    public static void main(String[] args) {
        System.out.println("Howdy");
        // TODO Auto-generated method stub

    }

}
```

Figure 1-15.

Notice the asterisk, to the left of the text EmployeeApp.java in the tab at the top of the content pane. This means that there are unsaved changes in the code.

4. Save the code by clicking File and then Save. (You can also click the floppy-disk icon on the tool bar.) Notice that the asterisk is no longer there.

Tutorial: Running an Application in RAD

This application simply prints out the text ""Howdy"". Within RAD, the Console view displays text and system messages. The Java perspective does not offer the Console view in any of its panes; however, perspectives can be customized by adding or deleting views.

1. Add the Console view by clicking Window, Show View, and then Console. The Console view will replace the Problem view in the Task pane at the bottom of the Java perspective window. Did you notice all the views that were listed when you clicked Show View? We will explore other views in later chapters and demonstrate many of RAD's very useful tools offered in these views.

2. On the Menu bar, click Run, and then Run Configurations.... The Run Configurations window will be displayed.

3. Select Java Application and then click the New button (see Figure 1-16).

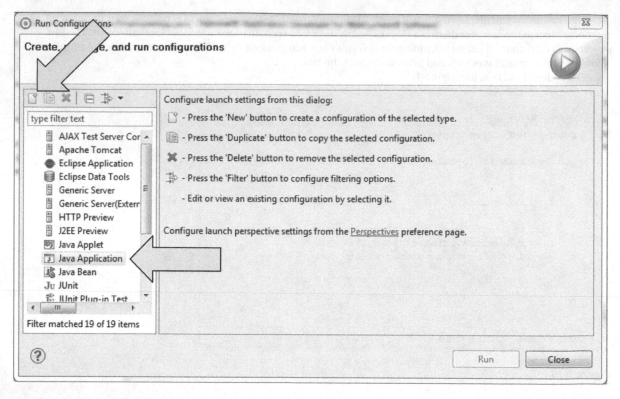

Figure 1-16.

RAD will display a "run configuration" for EmployeeApp in the "Run Configurations" window. In the future, you can simply select this run configuration to execute EmployeeApp.

    4.   On the "Run Configurations" window, click the Run button.

The first time a Java application is executed it may take a while because RAD must perform one-time configuration and setup tasks. Remember, the Console view is the default area for printed text to be displayed and, in this case, the text "Howdy" appears. This proves that **the main method is executed when a Java class is run as an application**.

The last application executed is considered the default application. To rerun EmployeeApp, simply click the Run button (⊙) on the Tool bar. (RAD runs the default application when the Run button is clicked.)

    5.   In the main method, add the following statement before the println statement:

```
String sample = new String("Howdy from EmployeeApp");
```

This statement will create a String variable called sample and associate the text "Howdy from EmployeeApp" to it. We will now change the println statement to print the text associated with the variable sample.

    6.   In the println statement, replace **"Howdy"** with **sample**. (Make sure the double quotes around the text Howdy are removed also.) The source code should look like Figure 1-17.

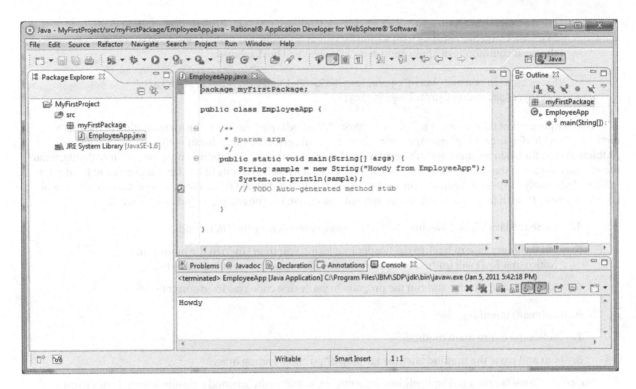

Figure 1-17.

7. Save EmployeeApp by clicking on the floppy-disk icon.

8. Click the Run button. The text "Howdy from EmployeeApp" will be displayed in the Console view.

After an application has been run (besides becoming the default application to run), the application is also added to a list of "applications to run." Instead of re-specifying an application to run, it can be selected from this list.

9. Click the black arrowhead to the right of the Run button to display the "applications to run" list.

EmployeeApp should be displayed at the top of the drop down menu. The application at the top is the default application to run. However, any application can be selected and run from the list by simply clicking it.

Tutorial: Breaking the Code

Many engineering disciplines use destructive testing to understand how a product or design will function. For instance, automobile manufacturers crash cars in walls to improve design and safety features. Programmers can do the same with Java code. Removing pieces of code will help you understand what function the code performs. In addition, producing errors highlights common programming mistakes and their associated error messages. Hopefully, by producing the errors now, you will recognize them sooner and fix them faster when you make them later.

1. In EmployeeApp, change the name of the main method to Main (capital M).

2. Click the Run drop down button and select the EmployeeApp configuration. Notice that RAD prompts you to save the EmployeeApp source code.

21

3. On the "Save and Launch" window, click the OK button. RAD will display a Java Virtual Machine Launcher window with a Fatal exception message and in the Console view one of the most common Java application error messages will be displayed:

```
Exception in thread "main" java.lang.NoSuchMethodError: myFirstPackage/
EmployeeApp.main([Ljava/lang/String;)V
```

The key portions of this message are the text "NoSuchMethodError" and then the identification of the main method—"myFirstPackage/EmployeeApp.main." Notice that the error message doesn't tell you exactly what the problem is (i.e., the Main method doesn't begin with a lowercase m), only that there is no main method. Really, what the message means is that there is no main method **coded exactly as it is needs to be**. The main method header has to be coded exactly as specified earlier. Any deviation will result in the above error. When you get this error, you will have to figure out which picky Java syntax requirement was violated in the main method and correct it.

4. Close the Java Virtual Machine Launcher window by clicking the OK button.

5. Put the lower case m back in the header by clicking Edit then Undo in the menu bar. Notice that RAD will undo the change even though the source code was saved.

6. Save the source code, and run the program to verify that code was fixed correctly.

Now, let's break something else!

7. Select the entire main method.

8. Cut and paste the method after the EmployeeApp class' ending brace.

Notice that there is now a red squiggly line under the class and main 'method's closing braces. Like a word processor, this is another way RAD indicates that there is an error. Again, we'll ignore 'RAD's warnings and run the application.

9. Run the application by selecting the EmployeeApp run configuration.

10. On the Save and Launch window, click the OK button (to save the changes).

RAD tries to warn us about errors by displaying the Errors in Workspace window. (Please also notice that RAD calls "running an application" a "launch." Launches will come up later in the book.)

11. Click the Proceed button on the Errors in Workspace window to run the application.

The following error message will be displayed in the Console:

```
Exception in thread "main" java.lang.Error: Unresolved compilation problem:
Syntax error, insert "}" to complete ClassBody
at myFirstPackage.EmployeeApp.main(EmployeeApp.java:16)
```

The first line of the error message simply means there was a fundamental Java language syntax error (i.e., compilation problem). The second line tries to pinpoint the error and offer a solution (i.e., there is a syntax error because the class body was never ended with a closing brace.) The red squiggly line under the first closing brace indicates that RAD thinks that token is incorrect. If you move the cursor over that error icon or the red squiggly line, RAD will display a message saying that the token } should be deleted. However, the real problem is that the main method is outside of the class body. Obviously, RAD is not too good at identifying this particular error. The third line of text explains where the error was found. Notice it contains the package name, class name, and method name where the error was found, as well as, a hyperlink to the suspected line with the error.

12. Move the mouse pointer over the third line of the message and click the hyperlink.

The Java statement/line that RAD believes caused the error is highlighted. Every line in the source code is assigned a sequential number, but initially the line numbers are not displayed. However, you can change this (and other appearance aspects of any view).

13. Cut and paste the main method back within the EmployeeApp class body. Notice that the error icons to the left of the source code are removed but there is still an error icon in the tab at the top of the Editor pane.

14. Save the source code. The error icon in the tab is removed.

15. Click Window, then Preferences to display the Preferences window.

16. In the list on the left, expand the General item, the Editors item and then select Text Editors (see Figure 1-18).

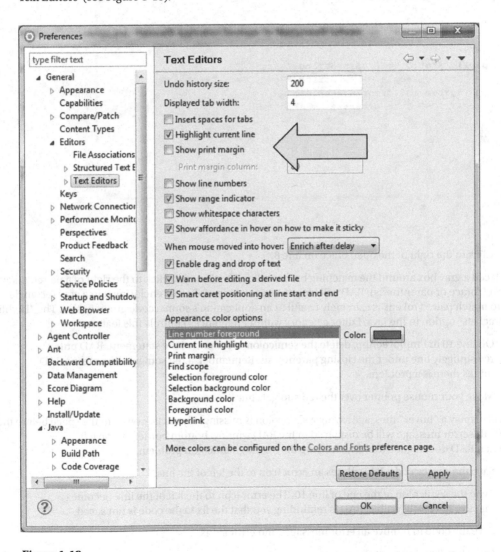

Figure 1-18.

The Text Editors pane is displayed on the right of the window. The checkboxes and text fields provide control over various options. Notice that the "Show line numbers" checkbox is not selected.

17. Click the "Show line numbers" checkbox to select it.

18. Click the Apply button and then the OK button.

The line numbers are now displayed to the left of each line (see Figure 1-19).

```
EmployeeApp.java ✕

1   package myFirstPackage;
2
3   public class EmployeeApp {
4
5       /**
6        * @param args
7        */
8       public static void main(String[] args) {
9           String sample = new String("Howdy from EmployeeApp");
10          System.out.println(sample);
11          // TODO Auto-generated method stub
12
13      }
14
15  }
16
```

Figure 1-19.

19. Click to the right of the open brace on line 8.

RAD placed a gray box around the matching brace on line 13. When you click to the right of a paired token (e.g., a bracket, brace or parenthesis), RAD will identify the matching token by enclosing it in a gray rectangle. Being able to match paired tokens is extremely useful as an application's source code grows in size. The "Highlight matching brackets" option in the Java/Editor category within Preferences controls this feature.

20. On line 10 in EmployeeApp, delete the semicolon at the end of the statement. RAD puts a red squiggly line under the closing parenthesis. Remember, a red squiggly line means RAD thinks there is a problem.

21. Move your mouse pointer over the red squiggly line.

RAD will display a "hover" message saying a semicolon is missing. If you click on or in the space before the red squiggly line, the error message will be displayed in the RAD window bottom border on the left.
Notice that RAD does a good job of identifying the missing semicolon problem.

22. Save the source code. RAD places an error icon to the left of the line.

23. Type the semicolon at the end of line 10. The error icon to the left of the line becomes inactive but is still visible. RAD is reminding you that the fix to the code is not saved.

24. Save the code to remove all error messages and error icons.

25. Go to line 9 and remove the equal sign.

A red squiggly line is placed under the text sample in line 9 and if you display the error message, you will see that RAD suggests entering a semicolon. RAD does not do as good a job identifying this error. While technically it is true that placing a semicolon after sample would make a valid statement, this is not the real source of the problem. Rather, this shows that RAD often identifies/highlights the token **before or after the real problem** and **error messages will often suggest incorrect solutions.**

Be careful. Because of the widespread use of word processing software, most people assume that whatever text is "red squiggled" is the problem. For instance, a novice programmer might think that the text **sample** is the problem and try changing it or delete it entirely (since it appears to be the problem).

Avoid compounding a mistake by thoroughly reading the error message and looking for the problem in the statement(s) or token(s) preceding or following the "red squiggled" text.

26. Replace the deleted equal sign on line 9 and run the application to verify it is correct.

27. On line 9, change the "s" in sample to a capital "S." This changes the variable name to "Sample."

Notice that line 10 is flagged as an error. There are two lessons to be learned. First, Java is case sensitive. Line 10 refers to sample but there is no variable sample, however, there is a variable Sample. For beginner programmers, incorrect capitalization is a source of countless errors. Second, sometimes RAD's first solution is correct. Click on the light bulb icon to display solutions. Notice that RAD suggests changing the variable name to Sample. This is a viable solution to remove the error indicators.

28. Copy the println statement from line 10 and paste it on line 12.

RAD flags the statements on both lines 10 and 12 as errors. If you display the solutions, RAD will once again suggest changing the variables from sample to Sample. In this case, this is not the best solution. Instead, you should change the variable definition on line 9 not the two statements on lines 10 and 12.

29. On line 9, change Sample to sample.

Notice that RAD removes both errors icons. This is an example of a cascading error. A cascading error is a single error that results in many error messages being generated. This is why you shouldn't panic if many lines of source code are flagged as incorrect. Often solving one error will clean up many error messages. This is also why you should **solve errors within the source code from top to bottom**.

30. Delete the println statement from line 12 and save the source code for EmployeeApp. The code should look like Figure 1-19.

Results of the Tutorial

Here's what we now have:

1. A new project called MyFirstProject.

2. In MyFirstProject/src, a new package called myFirstPackage.

3. In myFirstPackage, one file called EmployeeApp.java.

4. The source code in EmployeeApp should look like Figure 1-19.

Review Questions

1. What is the minimum Java source code needed to define a class?

2. What is the syntax to define a String variable?

3. Where must the package statement appear in the class?

4. In a method header, where is the keyword void specified?

5. How can you tell if there are unsaved changes in a source code file?

6. When an object is instantiated, which is done first: the constructor is executed or class variables are created?

7. Determine which of the following statements are valid and which are invalid:

```
String coolStuff
public displayCoolStuff() {}
String veryCoolStuff("ice");
string veryCoolStuff;
String extremelyCoolStuff = new String(liquid nitrogen);
```

8. What is a token?

Review Exercise

Overview

In the exercises, you will create a Java-based application for a company called TNT Salvage. TNT receives unwanted consumables (food, kitchen and laundry products, toiletries, etc.) from large retail organizations, repackages them, and sells them to smaller retail outlets at a significant discount. Throughout the chapter exercises, you will create an application that accepts information about shipments from the large retailers.

Detail

In this first exercise, you will create a Java class called ShipmentApp that creates and uses five variables to store shipment information and displays that information.

1. Start RAD and create a new Java project called ReviewEx.

2. In ReviewEx, create a package called c1.

3. In c1, create a public class called ShipmentApp with a main method.

At this point, the code should consist of:

a package statement

a class header

the opening and closing braces for the class body

a main method header

the opening and closing braces for the main method body

4.   Save the ShipmentApp source code and verify that there are no errors.

5.   Define five `String` variables in the main method called:

shipmentNum

supplierName

rcvDate

rcvTime

employeeNum

And assign the following text:

99

Costco

12/15/2011

10:25 AM

33

6.   Save the ShipmentApp source code and verify that there are no errors.

7.   Insert five println statements to display each of the `String` variables.

8.   Save the ShipmentApp source code and verify that there are no errors.

Check that the Exercise Was Done Correctly

Finally, let's check that everything was done correctly:

1.   Verify that ShipmentApp.java is in c1.

2.   Run ShipmentApp and verify that the Console displays the following:

99

Costco

12/15/2011

10:25 AM

33

CHAPTER 2

■ ■ ■

Java on a PC

In this chapter, we will expand on your knowledge of Java applications by showing how to instantiate (create) an object and demonstrating how constructors work. We will highlight the key differences between running a Java class as an application and creating an object. We will also provide a more detailed explanation of how Java "works" and "what comes with" Java. This explanation will also cover what really happened when you clicked buttons and chose RAD (Rational Application Developer) options in the previous chapter. In addition, we will explore some online documentation that explains the classes that "come with" Java.

After completing the chapter, you should understand the following:

- Instantiation and objects
- The SDK, JVM, and JRE
- Bytecode
- .java and .class files

Compiling Using WebSphere, you will be able to:

- Create Java classes that pass and receive parameters

Java Applications

In the previous chapter, the Java class EmployeeApp was created to be run as a Java application (i.e., EmployeeApp had a main method). In the real world, very few Java classes are run as applications. Most Java classes are instantiated. In other words, an instance of the class (called an object) is created. When an object is created the class variables are created and the constructor method is run. For example, if there was a class called Employee and an Employee object was created, the Employee class variables would be created and the Employee constructor would be run.

Constructors are primarily used to perform "set up" functions. This may mean initializing variables, creating objects, setting property values, establishing connections to remote resources, etc. Initially the constructor examples will seem very simple but as we expand the examples in future chapters, the real power and purpose of the constructor will become apparent.

In the previous chapter's example, we created a single Java class. In this chapter, we will create a second Java class called Employee that will be instantiated. Employee's purpose will be to display Employee information. We will modify EmployeeApp to pass an Employee name to Employee and then execute the Employee display method.

Tutorial: Passing Parameters and Formatting Source Code

Let's get started:

1. Start RAD and in the Package Explorer pane, select myFirstPackage in MyFirstProject/src by clicking on its name.

2. On the menu bar, click File, New, and then Class to display the "New Java Class" window.

Notice that the source folder and package names are already specified. Because myFirstPackage was selected in step 1, RAD assumed that was where the class should be created. A different project and package can be specified by simply entering their names in the appropriate text fields.

3. Specify Employee in the Name field.

Notice that the access modifier public has already been selected. Other modifiers can be chosen by clicking the other modifier's option radio button or check boxes.

4. Make sure none of the method stub options are selected.

Employee will be instantiated, not run as an application. Therefore, Employee does not need a main method.

5. Click the Finish button to redisplay the Java perspective.

The Employee class should appear in the Navigation tree (along with the already existing EmployeeApp) and the Employee source code generated by RAD will be displayed.

6. Click on the blank line (line number 4) that follows the class header.

7. The insertion cursor (a blinking vertical line) should appear at the far left of the line.

8. Press the Enter key to insert a blank line.

9. Define a **String** class variable by entering the following statement on the new line:

```
String empName = new String();
```

10. Press Enter to insert another blank line.

11. Define a constructor by entering the following 3 lines:

```
public Employee(String name) {
        empName = name;
}
```

The Employee method is considered a constructor because it has the same name as the class and does not return a value. The Employee constructor is defined as **public** (on line 6), meaning any class can access/use it. Notice that Employee is expecting a **String** and will assign it to a **String** variable called name. On line 7, the value associated with name will be assigned to empName (a class variable that was defined on line 5). The source code should look like Figure 2-1.

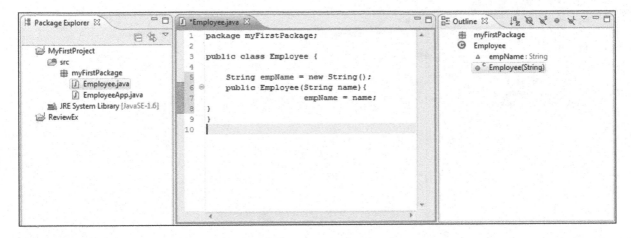

Figure 2-1.

Did you notice that when the Enter key is hit, RAD automatically indents the insertion cursor and after a token is entered, repositions the token correctly? This is done to make the code easier to understand (e.g., clearly show which statements are in a method, which brace closes a method and the class, etc.) Although RAD tried to format the code as it was entered, the code is not formatted as well as it could be. Badly formatted code can be difficult to read and therefore easier to make mistakes. Fortunately, we can make RAD reformat all the source code and even specify the formatting rules to follow.

12.   On the menu bar, click Source and then Format.

RAD will indent any nonindented or incorrectly indented class variable definitions and methods within the class. In addition, any method statements are positioned as if they were indented twice. Notice that the statement on line 7 was moved to the left and the constructor's closing brace on line 8 was indented. RAD also added a blank line to clearly separate the class variable definition from the constructor. Again, the purpose of the indentation and spacing is to make it clear where methods begin and end and which statements are contained within a method.

13.   Enter the following statements after the constructor to define a method called displayName:

```
public void displayName() {
}
```

This new method is intended to display the employee name that is associated with the variable empName. Because empName is a class variable it does not have to be passed to the displayName method (remember class variables can be accessed by any method within the class). displayName( ) is also defined as **public** (so other classes, like EmployeeApp, can access it) and **void** was specified because nothing is returned.

14.   Add a blank line after the opening brace ({) of the displayName method and then enter the following statement:

```
System.out.println(empName);
```

This statement displays the employee name by passing empName to the println method.

15.   Click Source (on the Menu bar), and then Format to reformat the source code.

The code should look like Figure 2-2 .

```
┌─ Package Explorer ⊠ ─ ─ □┐ ┌─ J *Employee.java ⊠ ─ ─ □┐ ┌─ ᵇₑ Outline ⊠  ↓ᵃ₂ ⍉ ⍉ˢ ◦ ⍉ᵗ ▽ ─ □┐
│              ᵇ ᵇ ▽│ 1  package myFirstPackage;            ▲│ │  ⊞  myFirstPackage          │
│ ▲ 🖿 MyFirstProject    │ 2                                        │ │  ◉  Employee                │
│   ▲ ⊕ src             │ 3  public class Employee {               │ │     △  empName : String     │
│     ▲ ⊞ myFirstPackage│ 4                                        │ │     ◦ ᶜ Employee(String)    │
│       ▷ J Employee.java│ 5      String empName = new String();    │ │     ◉  displayName() : void │
│       ▷ J EmployeeApp.java│ 6                                     │ └─────────────────────────┘
│   ▷ ➤ JRE System Library [JavaSE-1.6]│ 7 ⊖   public Employee(String name) {│
│   ▷ 🖿 ReviewEx        │ 8          empName = name;                │
│                       │ 9      }                                 │
│                       │ 10                                       │
│                       │ 11 ⊖  public void displayName() {         │
│                       │ 12         System.out.println(empName);│  │
│                       │ 13     }                                 │
│                       │ 14                                       │
│                       │ 15 }                                     │
│                       │ 16                                       │
│                       │                                          │
└───────────────────────┘ └──◀──────────────────────────▶──┘
```

Figure 2-2.

16. Save the source code by clicking File and then Save.

Tutorial: Defining a Java Application

We need to change EmployeeApp to create (instantiate) an Employee object and then invoke the Employee object's displayName method. Figure 2-3 shows the relationship between the user, EmployeeApp, and the Employee object.

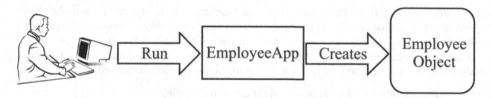

Figure 2-3.

1. In the Package Explorer pane, double click EmployeeApp to display the Java source code.

Just as EmployeeApp currently creates (instantiates) a **String** object, we will change it to instantiate an Employee object.

2. Replace the statement that creates sample with the following:

```
Employee emp = new Employee(new String("Joe Employee"));
```

Notice that the syntax for creating the Employee object and assigning it to a variable is the same as creating a **String** object. First you specify the variable type (the class name Employee) followed by at least one space and the name of the variable (emp). emp is assigned (=) a new Employee object (**new Employee**). Finally, the new Employee object's constructor is passed the **String** object it is expecting (in this case, a **String** object with the text "Joe Employee").

Let's go into a little more detail about what exactly is happening between the Employee and EmployeeApp classes.

A. When you invoke/run EmployeeApp as an application, the computer "knows" to load the statements in EmployeeApp's main method into main memory and execute them. The square in Figure 2-4 represents the main method in main memory.

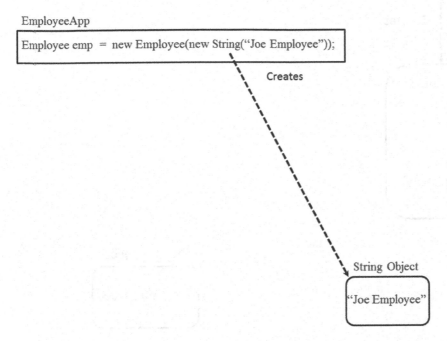

Figure 2-4.

The EmployeeApp statement is considered an assignment statement and is doing quite a bit of work. It creates two objects (one String and one Employee) and an Employee variable. It assigns the Employee object to the variable and passes the **String** object to Employee. Wow! We better look a little closer at each piece of the statement and explain what each does.

First of all, in an assignment statement everything to the right of the equal sign is executed first. Then everything on the left side of the equal sign is executed and lastly the assignment is done. If there are multiple functions within a statement, any statements in parentheses are executed first and then they are executed from right to left. So in this example:

B. The code **new String("Joe Employee")** is executed first because it is on the right side of the equal sign and in parentheses. The code creates a new **String** object (represented by the first rounded corner rectangle in Figure 2-4) with the text "Joe Employee".

C. Then the code **new Employee()** is executed. This creates a new Employee object (represented by the second rounded corner rectangle in Figure 2-5). When an object is created all the executable code from the class is loaded into main memory, the class variable statements are executed, and if there are values being passed to the new object, they are given to the constructor and the constructor is executed.

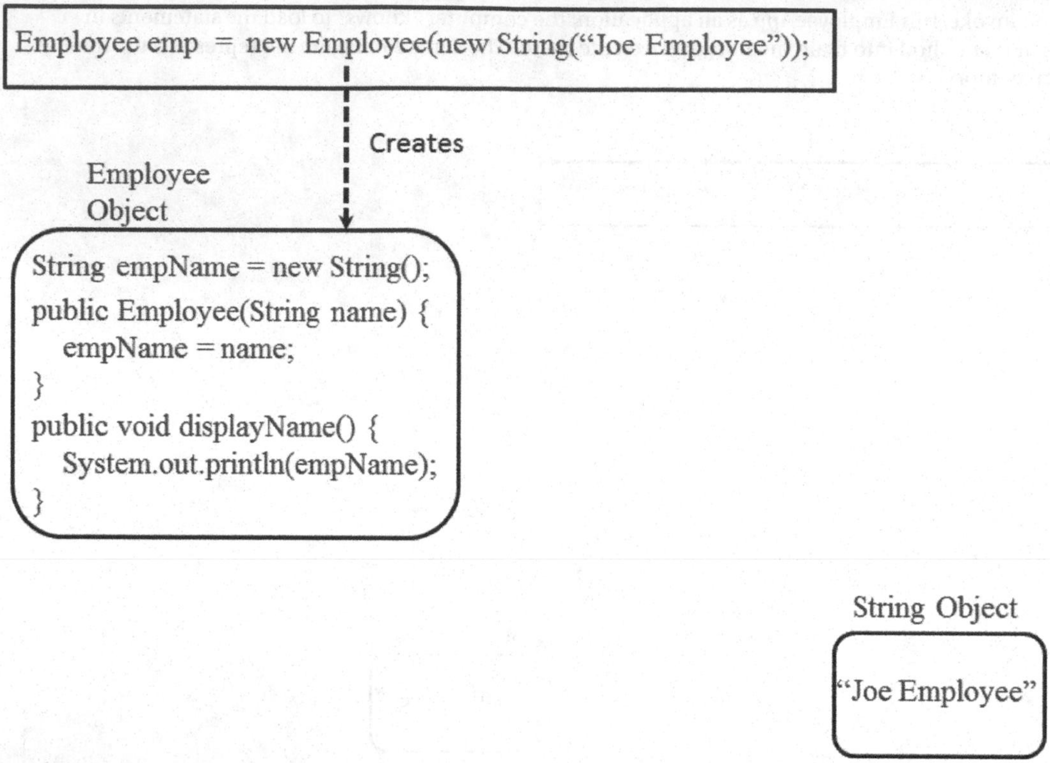

```
Employee emp = new Employee(new String("Joe Employee"));
```

Creates

Employee
Object

```
String empName = new String();
public Employee(String name) {
    empName = name;
}
public void displayName() {
    System.out.println(empName);
}
```

String Object

"Joe Employee"

Figure 2-5.

   D. In the Employee example, the first Employee statement executed is `String empName = new String();`. This is another assignment statement so the code on the right of the equal sign (`new String()`) is executed first. This creates another **String** object (represented by the third rounded corner rectangle in Figure 2-6) with no text.

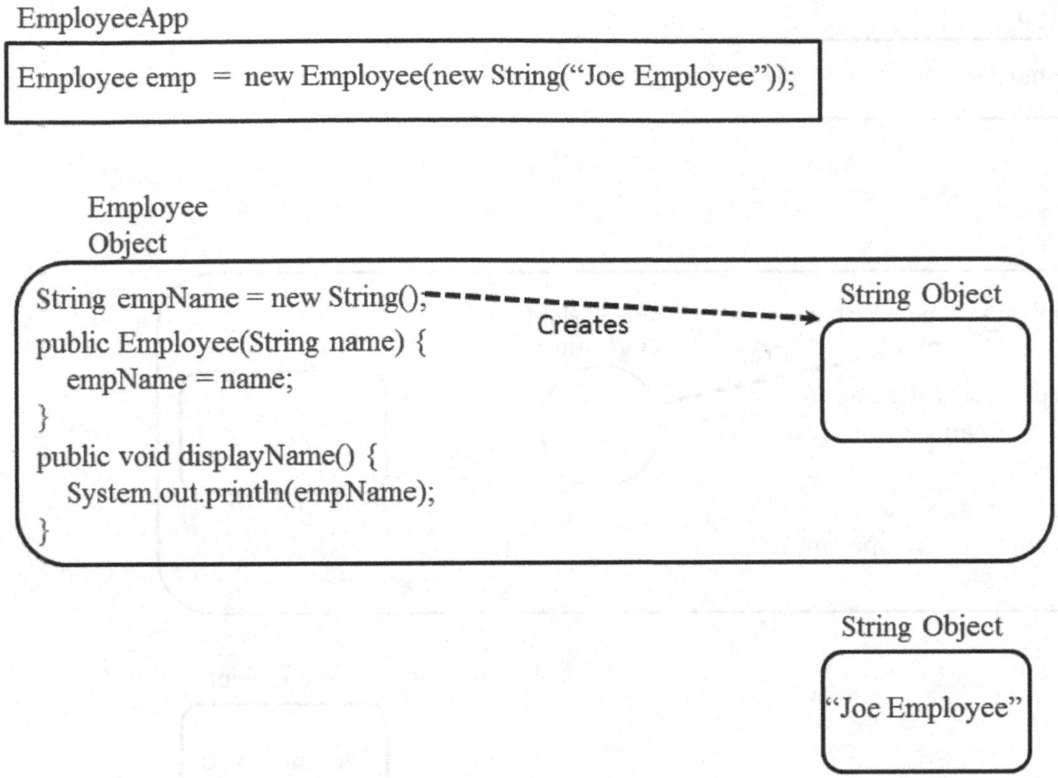

EmployeeApp

Employee emp = new Employee(new String("Joe Employee"));

Employee
Object

String empName = new String(); ------- *Creates* ------→   String Object

public Employee(String name) {
   empName = name;
}
public void displayName() {
   System.out.println(empName);
}

String Object

"Joe Employee"

Figure 2-6.

E. Next the code on the left of the equal sign (`String empName`) is executed and the variable empName is created. (This is represented by the circle in Figure 2-7.)

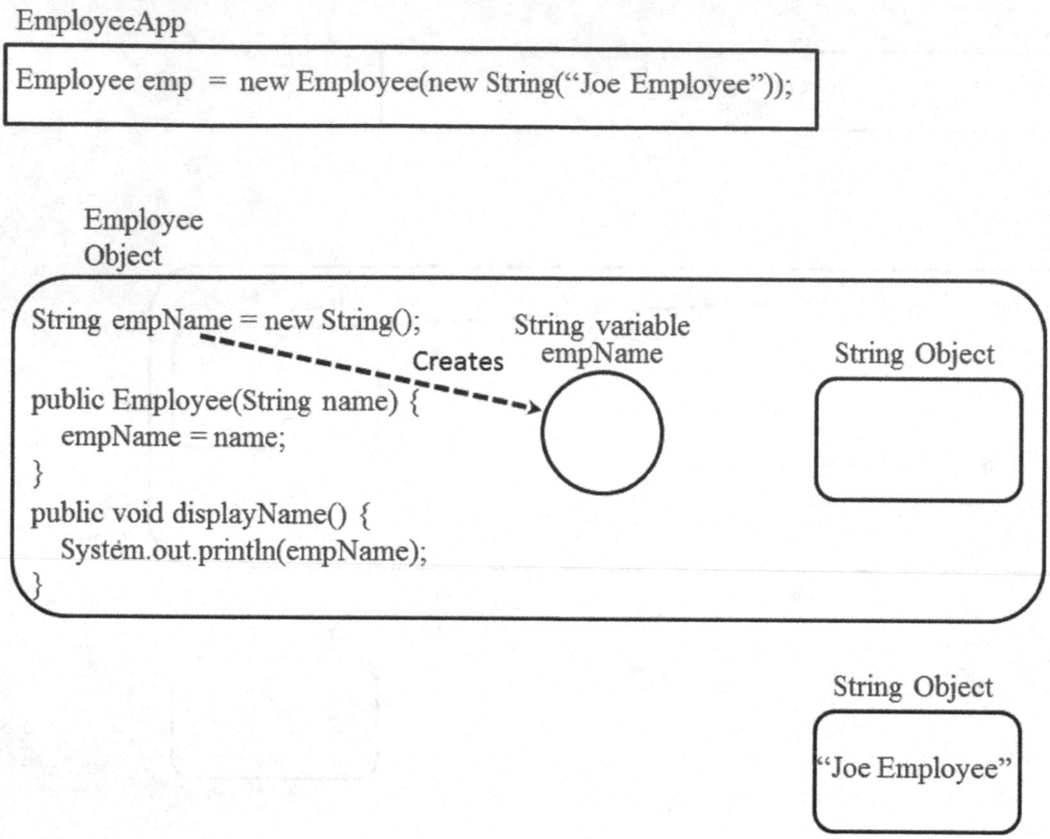

EmployeeApp

Employee emp = new Employee(new String("Joe Employee"));

Employee
Object

String empName = new String();   String variable
                                 Creates   empName   String Object
public Employee(String name) {
    empName = name;
}
public void displayName() {
    System.out.println(empName);
}

String Object

"Joe Employee"

Figure 2-7.

F. Finally the assignment is made (i.e., the equal sign is executed) that ties the variable empName to the newly created empty **String** object (see Figure 2-8).

EmployeeApp

Employee emp = new Employee(new String("Joe Employee"));

Employee
Object

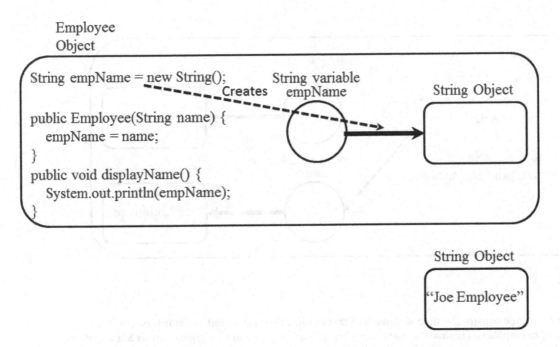

Figure 2-8.

G. Then the Employee constructor (i.e., the Employee method) is executed. The Employee method header creates a new **String** variable called name. The computer (i.e., the JRE) then assigns the **String** object with the text "Joe Employee" that was passed by EmployeeApp to this new **String** variable called name (see Figure 2-9).

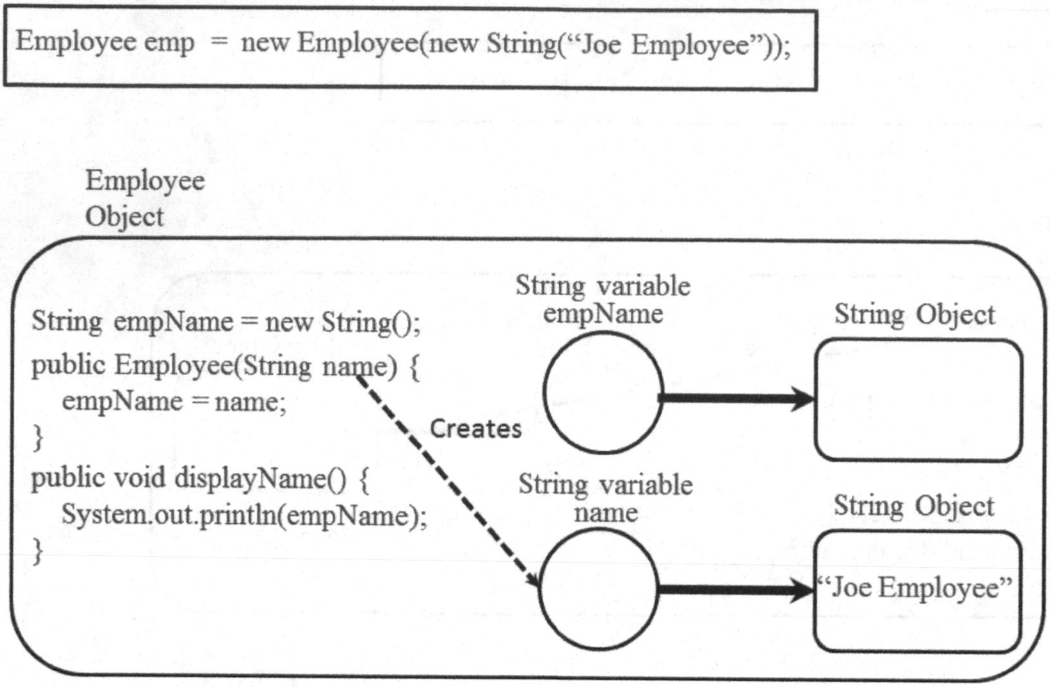

```
Employee emp  =  new Employee(new String("Joe Employee"));
```

Employee
Object

Figure 2-9.

H. The Employee constructor then assigns the **String** object that is assigned to name (i.e., the "Joe Employee" **String** object) to empName (empName = name;) See Figure 2-10. Notice that the original empty **String** object, created and assigned to empName (on line 5), still exists but is no longer assigned to any variable.

EmployeeApp

Employee emp = new Employee(new String("Joe Employee"));

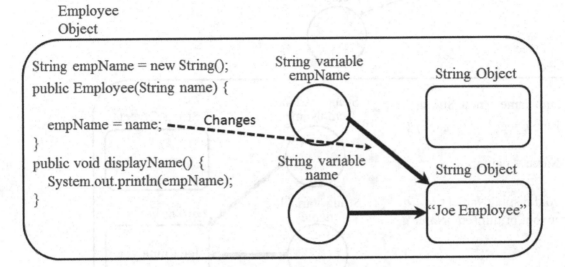

Figure 2-10.

I. The Employee constructor finishes executing (and the Employee object is complete). Execution returns to EmployeeApp's main method. The statements to the right of the assignment are complete so the statement to the left of the assignment is executed (Employee emp). This creates an Employee variable called emp (see Figure 2-11).

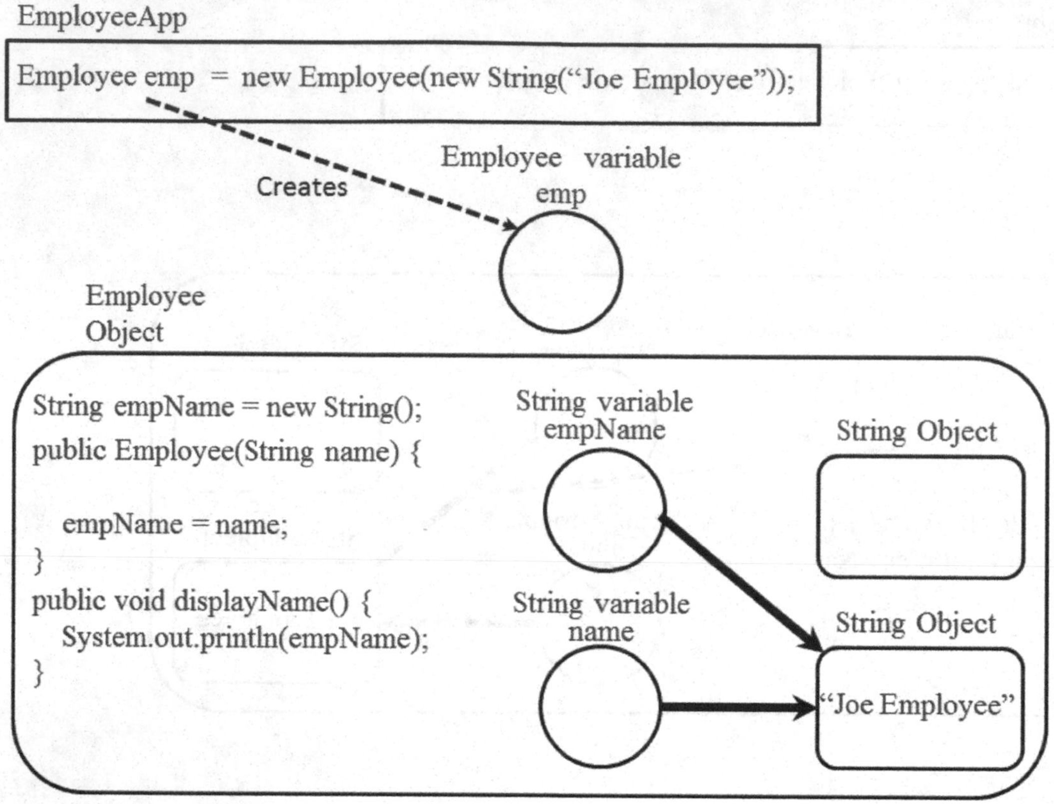

EmployeeApp

Employee emp = new Employee(new String("Joe Employee"));

Creates

Employee variable
emp

Employee
Object

```
String empName = new String();
public Employee(String name) {

    empName = name;
}
public void displayName() {
    System.out.println(empName);
}
```

String variable
empName

String Object

String variable
name

String Object

String Object

"Joe Employee"

Figure 2-11.

J. Finally, the assignment is performed and Employee object is tied to the Employee variable emp (see Figure 2-12).

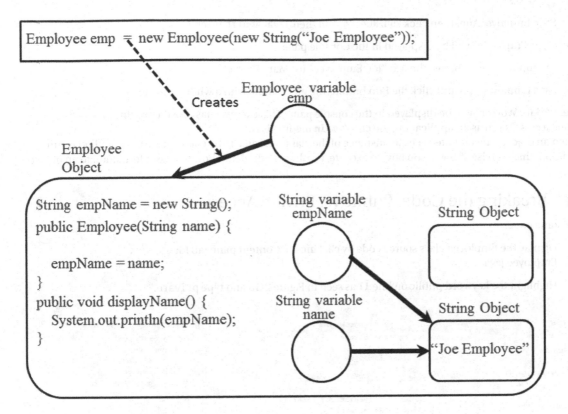

Figure 2-12.

So, the result of running EmployeeApp is three objects and three variables. Of course, there is no visible evidence of any of this activity. We need to change EmployeeApp to invoke the Employee method displayName. To invoke an object method, specify the variable name (emp) that the object is assigned to, followed by a period, the method name, parentheses and a semicolon (i.e., `emp.displayName();`). Notice that the variable name, not the class name is specified. In this example, this means you are specifying emp not Employee. If the method being called required data, that data would be specified within the parentheses.

3. Replace the println statement in EmployeeApp with the following:

```
emp.displayName();
```

The executable code should look like the following:

```
package myFirstPackage;

public class EmployeeApp {

    public static void main(String[] args) {
        Employee emp = new Employee(new String("Joe Employee"));
        emp.displayName();
    }
}
```

4. Save EmployeeApp, then click Run, Run As, and then Java Application.

The text "Joe Employee" will be displayed in the Console pane.

5. In EmployeeApp, change the text "Joe Employee" to "Mary Worker".

6. Save EmployeeApp and click the Run button (the green circle with a white arrowhead).

The text "Mary Worker" will be displayed in the console pane. This exercise has proven two things:
A. When a class is run as an application, the class's **main** method is run.
B. When an object is instantiated (i.e., an instance of the class is created), the class constructor method is run.
In addition, this exercise showed you how to execute/invoke a method and how to pass information to an object.

Tutorial: Breaking the Code, Public vs. Private Access

Let's break some code:

1. Display the Employee class source code by clicking the Content pane tab for Employee.java.

2. Highlight the keyword public on line 11 as seen in Figure 2-13 and type private.

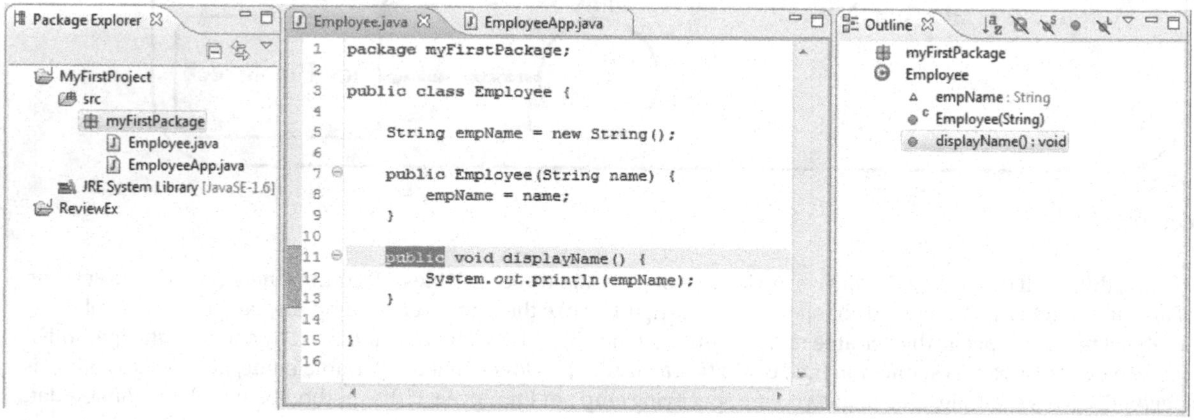

Figure 2-13.

3. Save the source code.

4. Click the Run drop down button and select EmployeeApp.

5. At the Errors in Workspace window, continue the launch by clicking the Proceed button.

Even though you are editing Employee, RAD runs EmployeeApp because that is the launch that was selected. The following error message will be displayed in the console:

```
Exception in thread "main" java.lang.Error: Unresolved compilation problem:
    The method displayName() from the type Employee is not visible
        at myFirstPackage.EmployeeApp.main(EmployeeApp.java:10)
```

If the comments have been removed from EmployeeApp, the line number 10 in the third line of the message will be 7. Because displayName's access modifier is now **private**, only methods within Employee can access displayName. In other words, EmployeeApp cannot use the private displayName method because EmployeeApp is a different class.

Notice that in the Navigation tree RAD has flagged EmployeeApp, the package, and the project as having an error.

6. Click on the Content pane's EmployeeApp.java tab to display the source code.

Notice that RAD has also flagged line 10 as in error.

We will change EmployeeApp and Employee so that the displayName method is called from within Employee not EmployeeApp.

7. In EmployeeApp, select the entire statement on line 10:

```
emp.displayName();
```

8. Click Edit and Cut to remove the line of code.

9. Redisplay the source code for Employee.java (i.e., Click the Content pane Employee tab).

10. Move your cursor to the end of line 8 and press Enter to insert a blank line after
    empName = name;

11. Click Edit and then Paste to place emp.displayName(); on line 9.

Notice that the line is flagged as an error and emp has a red squiggly line beneath it.

Because we are trying to run displayName from within the Employee class, we can't refer to the variable emp that was created in EmployeeApp. We must specify that we want to execute the displayName method within **this** (i.e., the Employee) object/class.

12. On line 9, replace emp with this so that the statement looks like the following:

```
this.displayName();
The executable code should look like the following:
package myFirstPackage;
public class Employee {
            String empName = new String();
            public Employee(String name) {
                    empName = name;
                    this.displayName();
            }

            private void displayName() {
                    System.out.println(empName);
            }
    }
```

There is a shorter and simpler syntax for identifying/running a method within the same class: simply specify the method name, parentheses, and a semicolon as in the following:

```
displayName();
```

Are you wondering, "How/why does this work?" Well, because an object is not specified (i.e., emp in **emp**.displayName( ); is not specified), the JVM assumes that the displayName method is in the same class (Employee). However, because this seems like "magic" we will continue to use the token **this** for clarity.

13. Run EmployeeApp again.

RAD will display the "Save and Launch" window listing both classes because they both have unsaved changes.

14. Click the OK button to save the changes and run EmployeeApp.

Notice that the classes no longer have errors and the employee name is correctly displayed in the console pane.

Tutorial: Breaking the Code, Parameters, and Signatures

Let's begin:

1. On line 9 in EmployeeApp, remove the text "**new** String("Mary Worker")" so that the statement looks like the following:

```
Employee emp = new Employee();
```

Notice that RAD flags the line as an error and puts a red squiggle under **new** Employee().

2. Move your cursor over the red squiggle.

The message "The constructor Employee( ) is undefined" is displayed. This brings up an interesting point. We mentioned earlier that a method has a name (for instance, Employee). However, the name does not fully identify a method. A method is fully identified by its **signature**. A method signature is comprised of both the method name and the parameters the method is expecting. In our example, we defined a method called Employee that expects one string as a parameter. With the change, we no longer specify a string, therefore, the computer tries to run a constructor method called Employee that expects no parameters. Because Employee does not have a method with this signature, an error is generated.

3. Put the text "**new** String("Mary Worker")" back in the statement on line 9.

4. In Employee on line 9, add the text "**new** String("Frank")" so that the statement looks like the following:

```
this.displayName(new String("Frank"));
```

Notice that again, RAD indicates there is an error.

5. Move the mouse cursor over the red squiggly line to display the following message:

"The method displayName( ) in the type Employee is not applicable for the arguments (String)"
Sometimes RAD's messages leave something to be desired.
Unfortunately, in Java-speak, parameters can be referred to as arguments and classes can be referred to as types (i.e., as in class type). So this message is inferring (in its own way) that there is no method with the correct signature.
Remember, the correct parameters must be passed to a method; otherwise, the statement will result in an error. We will explore parameter passing in more detail in future chapters.

6. Click Edit then Undo until the text is removed.

7. Save the source code for both EmployeeApp and Employee.

Although we have criticized RAD a little for its messages, you should drop to your knees and thank RAD for how easy it is to run applications. Here's why.

The Big Cruel Java World

RAD has hidden a great deal of the complexity of creating and running Java applications. For example, if you used Windows Explorer to display the PC file that contained the Employee class and you double clicked the file name, Windows would not know what to do with the Java statements in the file. In other words, Windows does not "speak" Java. Windows (like all operating systems) speaks **machine language**. Machine language is a set of instructions that the hardware of the computer understands. When you click on a button, select an option, hit Enter, or select a menu option, Windows interprets the action and issues the appropriate machine language instructions to the computer hardware. Because the Java classes contain Java statements, neither the computer hardware nor the operating system (Windows) can execute those statements. The Java statements need to be converted to machine language.

In Chapter 1, RAD generated the machine language for you. When you run an application in RAD, RAD generates the machine language commands and the commands are sent to the computer's central processing unit (CPU) for execution. Because there is no Java Run button in Windows, the programmer must explicitly generate the machine language and run the machine language version of the Java class. Doing this isn't difficult; it's just easier with RAD.

Java on a PC

As mentioned, Java source statements have to be translated into machine language. This is actually a two-step process comprised of compiling and interpreting. Compiling Java source code creates bytecode. Bytecode is a "language" that is neither machine language nor source code. (However, bytecode is a step closer to machine language than source code.) When a Java application is run or a class is instantiated, the bytecode is translated into machine language. You may be asking, why bother with bytecode? Translating bytecode takes less time than translating source code (because bytecode is closer to machine language). In addition, bytecode is the same regardless of the computer system. In other words, the bytecode generated from the Employee class's source code is the same on a computer running Windows, Linux, Solaris or any other operating system. This makes the bytecode portable to any computer system. When the bytecode is interpreted, the unique machine language (for the type of computer system you are working on) is generated and executed.

Oracle provides the software to compile and interpret Java (for free). There are two primary groupings of the free software called a JDK and a JRE. The JRE (Java Runtime Environment) has the interpreter (the JVM) not the compiler. As implied from the earlier discussion of converting bytecode to machine language, the JRE therefore must be unique for each computer's operating system. In other words, there is a different JRE for Windows, Linux, and Solaris.

In addition to a compiler, Oracle provides other free software tools for Java programmers. All of this software—compiler, JRE, programmer tools—is provided in a JDK (Java Development Kit sometimes also abbreviated as SDK). Early releases were simply named JSDK 1.0, JSDK 1.1, and so on. However, there are now different "editions" of Java and associated JDKs. For instance, there is a Java SE (Java Standard Edition), Java FX, and Java EE (Java Enterprise Edition). To explain the difference between them simply: SE is used to create client based applications, FX has functions for a richer client interface and alternative platforms such as mobile phones, and EE supports applications that have both server and client based components.

Each edition has a JDK included. For instance, a recent release of Java SE 6 is formally called: **Java (TM) SE Development Kit 1.6 Update 25**. However, the acronyms followed by their version and/or release numbers are used for identification. For example, the files for recent EE and SE releases have the acronyms java_ee_sdk-6u1-jdk and jdk-6u25 in their names.

However, users don't need everything in the JDK/SDK. To run a Java application all that is needed is the JRE for your operating system. The JRE contains all the classes (like **String**) that make your programming life easier, the machine language instructions that correspond to the bytecode commands, and the Java Virtual Machine (JVM). The JVM (i.e., the Java interpreter) is the software that translates bytecode into machine language.

Wasn't life so much simpler in RAD?

Figure 2-14 shows the three steps involved in creating and running a Java application on a PC and the various Java components involved.

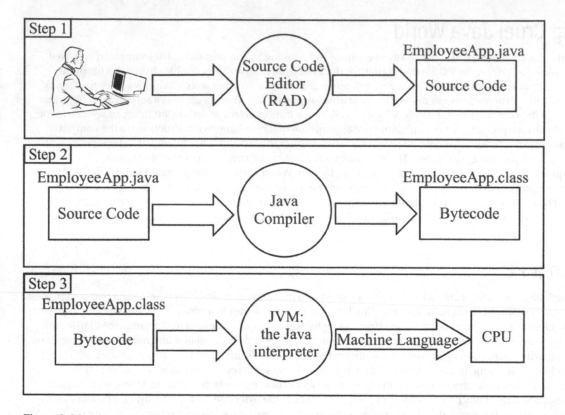

Figure 2-14.

Step 1: The programmer enters the source code

Step 2: The source code is translated into bytecode by the compiler

Step 3: The bytecode is translated into machine language by the JVM and sent to the CPU to be executed

In Chapter 1, you performed step 1 when you typed in the source code using the RAD editor. When you saved the source code, RAD performed step 2 and when you clicked the Run button RAD performed step 3.

Please notice two important items in Figure 2-14, the **.java** file and **.class** file. Source code is stored in a file with an extension of "java" (i.e., EmployeeApp.java) and bytecode is stored in a file with an extension of "class" (i.e., EmployeeApp.class). The RAD Java perspective hides the class files. However, RAD did show the Java file names both in the Content pane tabs and the Navigation tree (see Figure 2-13).

Let's take a more detailed look at the JRE using RAD and the online documentation. In addition, we'll prove that RAD does steps 2 and 3 as stated above.

Tutorial: Exploring the JRE with RAD

Now let's start exploring:

1.   If necessary, start RAD.

RAD "remembers" what was worked on last. As long as you are using the same PC and no one else has used RAD since you did, RAD will display MyFirstProject in the Java perspective and any source code that was left open in the content pane.

2. If necessary, display the contents of MyFirstProject and myFirstPackage by clicking their expansion icons in the Project Explorer view.

Notice that the navigation tree shows the file names of the two Java classes created so far.

3. If necessary, in the navigation tree, double click Employee.java to display the source code in the content pane.

The tab at the top of the content pane will show the file name along with the RAD icon that represents a Java source code file (a white sheet of paper with a blue J).

In the navigation tree, notice that there is another item within MyFirstProject called "JRE System Library". When the project was created, RAD made sure all the classes in the project had access to a JRE. As a matter of fact, RAD contains a full JDK. (In the case of the Enterprise Edition, there is a JEE JDK). You never had to worry about a JDK, JVM, or JRE because they came prepackaged. (Wasn't that nice of RAD?) These software items are further examples of what was meant by "development tools" in Chapter 1 when we said "WebSphere is an IBM software product that includes all the 'development tools' a programmer would need to write, debug, and install application software."

4. Click on the JRE System Library expansion icon.

The displayed item's text is too long to fit in the Package Explorer pane. Move the cursor over an item to display the full text in a pop-up box. Alternatively, the RAD panes can be resized. Simply move the cursor over the border of the pane, click, and drag.

5. Move the cursor over the right border of the Package Explorer pane.

When the cursor is over a border, the mouse cursor icon will change from a white, single headed arrow to a white, double-headed, horizontal, arrow.

6. Click and drag the Package Explorer pane's right border so that all the text for each item can be seen (see Figure 2-15).

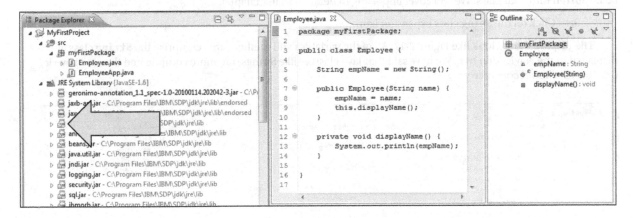

Figure 2-15.

The new items are "jar" (**j**ava **ar**chive) files. A jar file holds java resources but uses less space. (A "jar" file is actually a specialized "zip" file.) These jar files hold the packages that contain the Java classes (like **String**) that "come with Java."

7. Expand the vm.jar file (listed under the JRE System Library).

The package names within vm.jar are listed in alphabetical order and often contain the name of the organization supplying the package or class. Notice that the first several packages are from IBM.

8. Within vm.jar, expand the java.lang package and resize the Package Explore pane so that it looks like Figure 2-16.

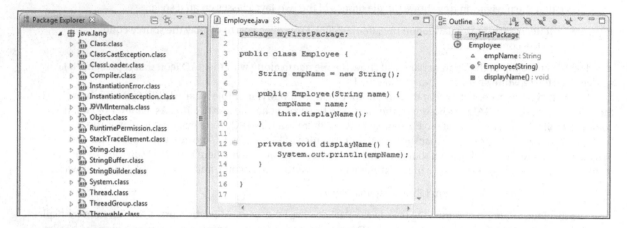

Figure 2-16.

Notice that the classes within the package are listed in alphabetical order and that the String.class file is displayed.

The java.lang package contains the basic set of classes that come with Java. In fact, the classes are so fundamental that all JREs automatically look in the java.lang package. What this means is that even though the class **String** is stored in a different package (the java.lang package) than your application, the JRE will find the class.

Try to remember: *the java.lang package is an exception.* To access any other package's classes, the package must be **imported** into your class. We will cover importing in detail in a later chapter.

9. Click on the String.class expansion icon.

The display should look like Figure 2-17. All of the variables and methods that comprise the **String** class are displayed in the Navigation tree. We have said that Java classes (like Strings) are more complicated than we have let on. This list should convince you.

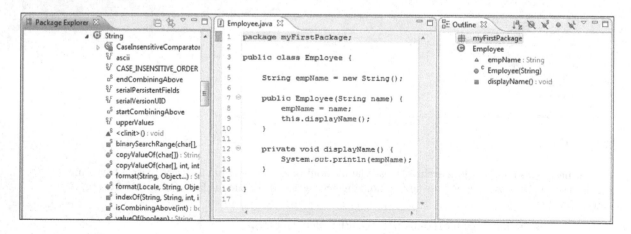

Figure 2-17.

Tutorial: RAD Icons

You may have noticed the various symbols and letters next to Navigation tree items. Each icon describes the item. For instance, a green circle (●) represents a public method, whereas an orange square (■) represents a private method. Notice in the Outline view (on the far right of the window) that the variables and methods in Employee also have icons. Can you figure out what a blue triangle with a white center (△) represents? (See the text following step 7 for the answer.)

1. Click on the beginning of line 5 in the Employee class (i.e., before the **String** keyword).

2. Type **private** and then a space.

The triangle icon changes to a red box with a white circle in the center (■). This new icon represents a private variable.

3. After the keyword **private**, type static and a space.

A red S is added to the icon. This means that the variable is static and can be accessed even if the class is not instantiated as an object.

4. Delete the keyword private.

The blue triangle is displayed and the red S remains.

5. Type the word **final** and a space before static.

A blue F is added to the icon after the red S to represent that this variable is unchangeable (more on final later).

6. Replace the keywords **final** and **static** with **public**.

The icon changes to a green circle with a white center.

7. Replace the keyword **public** with **protected**.

protected is in between **private** and **public**. Protected allows access to subclasses or classes within the same package. The blue triangle represents an access of default (or none). When no modifier is specified, access is restricted to classes within the same package.

There are couple of other RAD icons you should be familiar with. Notice that a constructor is indicated with a green C (● ᶜ) and a package has a black plus sign (+) superimposed over a square (⊞). The plus sign is the "ribbon/string" on the package icon. (Get it?). The color of the square changes depending on the view and its contents. Notice that myFirstPackage's box is gray in the Outline view but golden in the navigation tree. In addition, if the package is empty, the box will be white.

Lastly, a class header is indicated with a green circle with a white C in the center (ⓒ), see Employee in the outline view) and the class file, which holds bytecode, is indicated with a white piece of paper with a blue J, zeros, and a one (⬚), see the icon next to String.class item in the navigation window.)

8. Change the size of the source code pane so that it only displays 10 lines (see Figure 2-18).

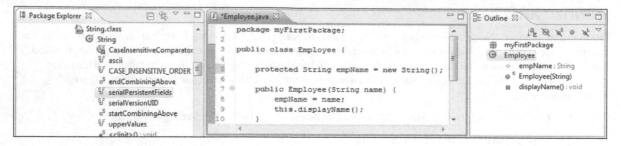

Figure 2-18.

9. In the Outline view, click on displayName( ).

Notice that the source code is shifted to display the item that was clicked (i.e., the displayName method) and the name of the item clicked is selected. In addition, in the marker bar (located to the left of the line numbers) a blue bar indicates the source code that comprises the clicked item.

In addition to quickly moving to locations within the source code, RAD allows "hiding" portions of the source code. Notice the circles with a minus sign to the left of each method header (for instance, lines 7 and 12). These lines are the start of a block of source code (or comments). Moving the mouse cursor over the circle will display a black bracket that indicates the lines "controlled" by the circle. Clicking the circle will hide the indicated lines, in this case, the body of the method. (You can tell there is hidden code because the minus sign will change to a plus sign. In addition, if you look at the line numbers, you will see that some line numbers are missing.) Again, this is a useful tool for "simplifying" the source code that is displayed.

10. Click on the green circle with the white C, next to Employee in the outline view.

Within the source code, the cursor is moved to the class name in the class header. As your classes get larger moving within the source code using the outline view is very handy.

Although icons are helpful, they do not thoroughly explain the various variables and methods. Fortunately, there is wealth of documentation available online that does.

Tutorial: Exploring the JRE through Online Documentation

There are several sites that provide a wealth of information for Java programmers. We will show a couple.

1. Start Internet Explorer and enter http://download.oracle.com/javase/6/docs/

A nice diagram is displayed that shows the various components of the JDK and JRE (see Figure 2-19). As you can see there is a lot more to both of these than we have discussed (or will discuss). You can click on any of the components in the diagram to get further information.

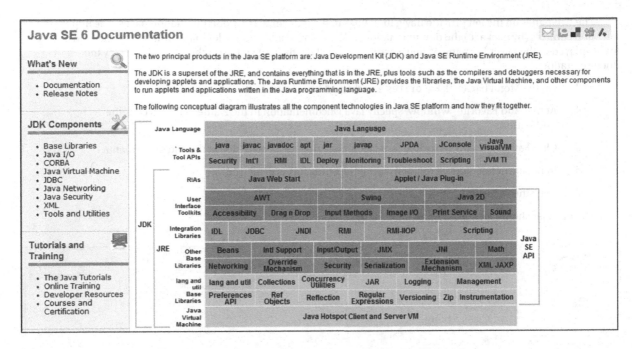

Figure 2-19.

2.   In the browser address field, add **api/** after **docs/** (i.e., the URL
     http://download.oracle.com/javase/6/docs/api/ should appear in the address) and press Enter.

API stands for Application Programmers Interface. This site has programmer documentation for all the JRE classes. The browser window should look like Figure 2-20.

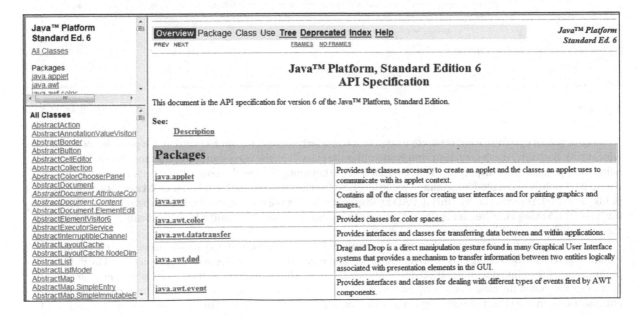

Figure 2-20.

The two panes on the left provide navigation links to the individual class documentation pages. The upper left pane controls (by package) the documentation links displayed in the lower left pane. Initially, all class links are displayed in the lower left pane. When a class link is clicked, the large pane on the right will display the documentation.

3. On the Menu bar, click Favorites and then Add to Favorites.

4. At the "Add Favorite" window, specify Java Documentation in the Name field and click the Add button.

5. Click Favorites and verify that Java Documentation has been added at the end of the menu.

6. In the lower left pane, scroll down until the String link is displayed.

7. Click the String link.

The browser should look like Figure 2-21.

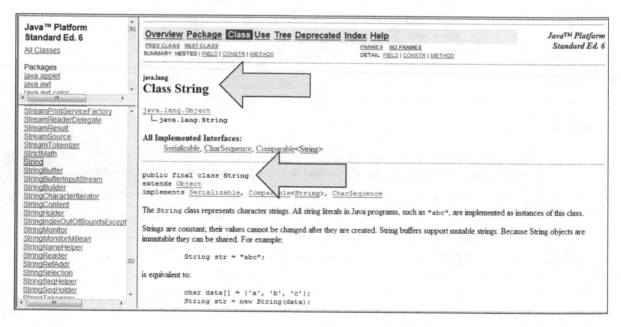

Figure 2-21.

There is a lot of information on these pages (much of which you will not understand at this point in your Java education). Basically, the first section simply identifies the class. (i.e., the class name, **String**, and the package it belongs to, java.lang, are displayed.) The remainder of the content pane has the good stuff. The second arrow in Figure 2-21 points to detailed information regarding how the class was defined. For instance, **String** is defined as public and final. You can confirm this in RAD by displaying the **String** class in the Package Explorer pane. The icon to the left of the **String** class header is a green circle with a white C in the center and a blue F indicating that the **String** class was defined as public and final.

If you compare the RAD navigation tree to the online documentation, you may notice some differences. For instance, RAD lists the **String** class's private variables and methods. Because these cannot be accessed by the programmer, the online documentation does not include them. The remainder of the online documentation will further explain what the class does and provide examples of how to instantiate the class and use its public methods. For instance, scrolling down the **String** documentation will reveal three tables. The first table documents each of the public variables in the class. The second table lists and defines the class constructors. The third table describes all the public methods. After the three tables, there are more detailed explanations of each variable, constructor, and method.

8. Scroll down to the length() entry in the method list table (the third table, see Figure 2-22).

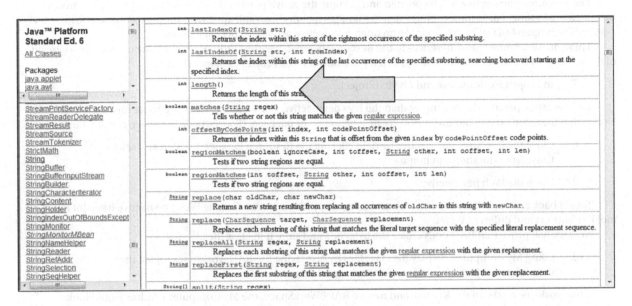

Figure 2-22.

From left to right, each method entry explains:

A. **What the method returns**. In this case, the length method returns a variable of type **int** (integer). We will discuss **int** variables in a little while.

B. **The method signature** (i.e., the method name and parameters the method is expecting). In this case, the length method expects nothing, indicated by the empty parentheses. Notice that the other methods in Figure 2-22 expect at least one parameter.

C. **What the method does**. The length method returns the number of characters assigned to the string (i.e., the length of the string).

9. Click the length method name.

The detailed documentation for the method will be displayed.

When you are having trouble understanding a class, remember this site. It has lots of useful information.

Tutorial: Changing RAD Perspectives

Now let's begin:

1. If needed, switch to the RAD session and resize the source code pane.

2. In the Package Explorer pane, scroll back to the top of the navigation tree.

3. Click the JRE System Library expansion box to close all the sub-trees.

4. Click the "Open a Perspective" icon (see Figure 1-5).

The "Open a Perspective" menu will be displayed.

5. From the short cut menu, click Other....

6. In the Select Perspective window, scroll down, click Resource and then the OK button.

The Resource perspective will be opened and become the active perspective. There can be only one active perspective at a time. For instance, notice that the Java perspective icon still appears. This means that the Java perspective is open but not active. To make an open perspective active, simply click its icon.

There are two noticeable differences in the Resource perspective: the Outline view has moved from the right side of the window to the lower left and the upper left pane now has the Project Explorer view.

7. In Project Explorer, expand MyFirstProject.

The Resource perspective is simpler than the Java perspective. For instance, there are fewer functions available. Notice that there are no tool bar buttons to create a new class or package. (Source code, however, can still be edited.)

8. Close the Resource perspective by right clicking the Resource Perspective icon and select Close from the short cut menu.

9. Open the Web perspective.

Toggle back and forth between the Web and Java perspectives. Notice that the Web perspective has a lot more tool bar buttons and different views.

Now we will prove that RAD does create the bytecode and store it in class files.

10. Using My Computer, display the class files by displaying the RAD workspace folder, then the MyFirstProject, bin, and myFirstPackage folders.

If the workspace was on the K: drive and named RAD8WorkSpace, the My Computer window would look like Figure 2-23.

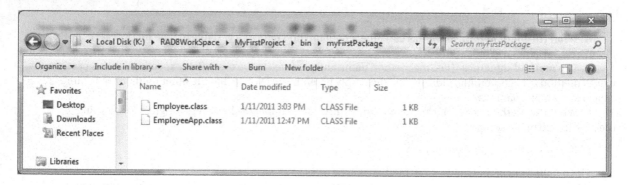

Figure 2-23.

11. Right click Employee.class and select Delete from the short cut menu.

12. In RAD run EmployeeApp.

A "no EmployeeApp class in myFirstPackage" message will be displayed. This is very true because we just deleted it in step 11. We can force RAD to generate the bytecode by resaving the source code. However, if we display either class's source code, neither the floppy disk button or the Save option (in the File menu) will be active. This is because there are no changes in the source code to be saved. An easy way to get around this is to make a simple change.

13. Display the Employee.java source code, insert a space anywhere and then delete the space.

14. Save the Employee.java source code.

Notice that **both** class files were generated even though we only saved Employee. Well, isn't RAD helpful?! Not only does RAD perform the compilation of Employee for us but because EmployeeApp creates (instantiates) an Employee object, RAD also creates the Employee.class file. Because EmployeeApp "depends" on Employee, in Java-speak, the classes are said to have a dependency relationship. This is just another example of the great help RAD provides.

Results of the Tutorial

Here's what we now have:

1. In myFirstPackage, one new file called Employee.java.

2. The executable source code in Employee should look like the following:

```java
package myFirstPackage;
public class Employee {
        public String empName = new String();
        public Employee(String name) {
                empName = name;
                this.displayName();
        }
        private void displayName() {
                System.out.println(empName);
        }
}
```

3. The executable source code in EmployeeApp should look like the following:

```java
package myFirstPackage;
public class EmployeeApp {
        public static void main(String[] args) {
                Employee emp = new Employee("Mary Worker");
        }
}
```

Review Questions

1. What is the function of the JVM?

2. Which are executable: java files, class files, or both?

3. What is a method signature?

4. What is the purpose of a jar file?

5. How does RAD indicate source code errors?

6. Explain the differences between perspectives.

7. What is the relationship between source code, machine language, and bytecode.

Review Exercise

In this exercise, a new Java class called Shipment will be created. Shipment will accept information about a shipment being received and will have a method to display this information. ShipmentApp will be modified to instantiate an object of type Shipment, assign the object to a variable named shipObj, and invoke Shipment object's display method.

1. In the ReviewEx/src, create a new Java package called c2.

2. Copy ShipmentApp from c1 to c2 by performing the following:

   A. Click on ShipmentApp.java in the Navigation tree to select it

   B. Click Edit then Copy

   C. Click on c2 to select it

   D. Click Edit then Paste

3. In c2, create a public class called Shipment without any method stubs.

4. Define five class **String** variables called shipmentNum, supplierName, rcvDate, rcvTime, employeeNum.

5. Create a constructor that:

   A. Accepts 5 strings and stores them in 5 method variables (parameters) called

      sNum, sName, rDate, rTime, eNum

      (Hint: When specifying multiple parameters they must be separated by commas.)

   B. Moves the method parameter's values to the class variables

6. Save the Shipment source code and verify that there are no errors.

7. Change ShipmentApp's main method to:

   A. Create a Shipment object and assign it to a variable called shipObj

   B. Pass the following five pieces of information to the Shipment object:

      99, Costco, 12/15/2011, 10:25 AM, 33

      (Hint: When specifying multiple parameters they must be separated by commas.)

8. In Shipment, create a public method called display that accepts nothing, returns nothing and uses System.out.println to display the five values as below:

   ```
   99

   Costco

   12/15/2011

   10:25 AM

   33
   ```

9. Change ShipmentApp to invoke the Shipment objects display method.

Check that the Exercise Was Done Correctly

Finally, let's check everything ran as expected:

1. Verify that within c2 there are two tree items called Shipment.java and ShipmentApp.java.

2. Run ShipmentApp and verify that the data is displayed in the console as specified earlier.

CHAPTER 3

■ ■ ■

Graphical User Interfaces

This chapter will explain the basic components of a graphical user interface (GUI) and how to use them in Java applications. We will begin to explore the different types of relationships between classes and document both the classes and their relationships using the Unified Modeling Language (UML).

After finishing this chapter, you should understand:

- AWT, Swing, and SWT
- Getters and setters
- Properties
- Composition
- Specialization
- Inheritance
- UML

After finishing this chapter, you should be able to:

- Create a simple frame
- Display information using labels
- Generate a UML diagram
- End an application

Introduction to GUI, AWT, Swing, and SWT

Let's face it, you didn't get into Java to enter commands at the command prompt and see the results in black-and-white text. You want Java applications with a full-color GUI (graphical user interface). A GUI is comprised of components such as frames, dialog boxes, buttons, labels, and so on. Fortunately, the JRE comes with classes that define all these components. In RAD, a programmer can create "Visual classes" that use these GUI components or create classes that are unique versions of these GUI components.

For instance, inside of the JRE there are two packages: java.awt (Abstract Window Toolkit) and javax.swing. Both of these packages contain classes for frames, buttons, labels, and so on. The main difference between the two is that the appearance of an AWT component depends on the operating system that the Java application is run on. In other words, AWT uses the operating systems windows, buttons, and so on. Swing has its own set of components that will look the same on all operating systems. In addition, the Swing components provide more functionality than AWT components. However, applications using Swing components will not look the same as other applications on that computer. In addition, because Swing does not use the operating system components, Swing applications are not as efficient as applications that use AWT. Because of these issues, a third GUI set was developed called the Standard Widget Toolkit (SWT). SWT makes use of the native operating system components as much as possible, and offers all of Swing's bells and whistles. SWT is open source (i.e., free) but it is not included in the JRE. When creating a GUI using RAD, the SWT components are always offered as an option. When you choose a SWT component, RAD makes the SWT library available to the project. The library has many jar files that contain all the SWT classes.

In general, all the components work similarly but they often do have different options, commands, and/or syntax to perform the same functions. As mentioned, the Swing and SWT components often have extra features and an added level of complexity that make them just a little harder to work with. Because of this, the examples in this chapter will use the AWT components and in later chapters, we will show some Swing examples.

Composition

One way to look at a class/object is that they are composed of many other classes/objects. To summarize the first chapter:

Classes are made up of class variables and methods. Methods contain method variables and executable statements. Variables (class or method) are defined as a class type and associated with an object of that class type.

For example, when an Employee is created a **String** object and a **String** variable named empName are created. Then the **String** object is assigned to the variable. Therefore, the **String** object assigned to empName is one component of the Employee object.

Objects, like Employee, are composed of many different objects. These objects have unique methods and information that can be utilized by Employee. Therefore, it is said that a class like Employee acquires the functionality of other classes through **composition**.

This explanation of composition may seem overly long (and painful) but it is necessary because the capabilities of frames and labels can be accessed in a different manner called **specialization**. Later in the chapter, we will explain specialization and contrast it with composition.

We want to create some GUI objects in the Employee class so that the employee name looks "pretty" when displayed. We will do this by defining a frame and label in the Employee class. In other words, just as we created a **String** object to hold the employee name, we want to create a **Frame** object and a **Label** object to display the employee name.

Visual Components

A **label** is used to display text and labels are often used in tandem with entry fields. For example, when entering a phone number on a Web page, there is an entry field to hold the information and a label (usually to the left of the entry field) with a short description of the data to be entered (e.g., the text "Phone:").

Labels must be assigned to a **container**. So, to create and use a label you need a container. **Frame**, **Dialog**, and **Panel** are all examples of container classes. Our container of choice will be a **Frame**.

Label and **Frame** objects can be created just like **String** objects - create an instance of the appropriate class and assign it to a variable. Said another way, create an object of the class type and assign it to a variable. If the explanation is unfamiliar, the syntax should not be:

```
Label empNameLbl = new Label();
```

Just like a **String**, text can be assigned when the **Label** is defined, as in the following:

```
Label empNameLbl = new Label("My First Label");
```

The value of the label can be changed. However, changing the text of a label is not as easy as changing the text of a string. For instance, the following will generate an error:

```
empNameLbl = "New Text";
```

As mentioned in the first chapter, the **String** class has all sorts of shortcuts that other classes do not. The **Label** class (like most classes) has "setter" and "getter" methods to access and change an object **property**, like a label's text. Of course, this begs the question, what is a property? A property is a private variable that represents some aspect of a class that the class user (called the client) should have control over—like the size of a label or the text that appears on the label. However, direct access to the variable that controls a property could prove disastrous. For instance, what do you think would happen if a programmer created a label and then specified the size as 16 feet? That's right, the biggest, fattest error you ever saw, and the JVM would end the entire application.

Because of this, most setter methods check the supplied property values and ensure it is valid. If a value is invalid, the setter generates an exception that the application/client (i.e., the user of the setter) should "catch." Catching the exception stops the JVM from ending the application. However, we are getting several chapters ahead of ourselves. For now, accept that you will use (and eventually create) getter and setter methods to access and control object properties.

With labels, the programmer usually specifies the text, size, and location properties. There are three setter methods to do this—setText, setSize, and setLocation. However, we can define the text when the label is created and there is another method called setBounds that allows the programmer to define both the size and location. For instance, the following:

```
Label empNameLbl = new Label("My First Label");
empNameLbl.setBounds(100, 200, 75, 20);
```

will create a **Label** object with the text "My First Label" and position the start of the empNameLbl 100 pixels from the left and 200 pixels from the top of the upper, left corner of the container to which it belongs. Lastly, the label will be 75 pixels wide and 20 pixels high. You may be asking, "How big is a pixel?" The size of a pixel depends on the computer screen's resolution setting. Earlier, we showed that many aspects of Windows' appearance are controllable. One of these aspects is the number of pixels that will be displayed on the screen (i.e., the resolution). The screens seen in all of the previous figures are set to 1024 by 768. Contrary to intuition, fewer pixels mean the GUI components will appear larger. For instance, if we changed the screen resolution to 800 × 600, one pixel would take up more of the screen; therefore, a label would look larger.

We have a label. Now we need a frame to put it on. A frame has a white content area, surrounded by a border and a title bar across the top. In Windows 7, the border and title will be light blue. As with the label, we need to create the **Frame** object and set several of its properties. Let's explore the statements needed to create a basic frame and add empNameLbl to the frame.

```
Frame empFrame = new Frame("My First Frame");
```

The first statement creates a **Frame** object and defines title text ("My First Frame") for the frame. A **Frame** variable named empFrame is created and the **Frame** object is assigned to empFrame. Notice that the syntax is the same as creating a **String** or **Label** object.

```
empFrame.setBounds(10,10,300,300);
```

This statement sets the location and size of the frame. As with a label, the first two numbers (10, 10) control the number of pixels from the left and top of the screen where the upper left corner of the frame will be placed. The second set of numbers (300, 300) defines the width and height of the frame (in pixels).

```
empFrame.setLayout(null);
```

This third statement sets the frame's layout property to null. Layouts are predefined formats that control where visual components will appear in a container. Layouts make it simpler to add and format components but impose limits on the programmer's control of the components, so we will "turn off" the property. When there is no layout defined, the programmer must define each component's location (which we already did when we defined the empNameLbl).

```
empFrame.add(empNameLbl);
```

59

This fourth statement adds the empNameLbl Label to the Frame. Pretty simple. Then you need:

```
empFrame.setVisible(true);
```

This last statement sets the empFrame property visible to true. The default value is **false**, meaning the frame will not appear on the screen. Try to remember that to see the frame you must change this property to **true**.

Notice that the **Frame** class has many setters (setBounds, setLayout, setVisible, etc.) to control the frame properties. In addition, there are useful methods, such as add, to build the frame with other components. Earlier we mentioned that the JRE contains all sorts of useful classes. Certainly all of these GUI classes can be included in that category.

Some beginning programmers are concerned that they really don't know how the **Frame** class works and that therefore they don't understand Java. The beauty and power of Java (and all object-oriented languages) is that programmers use predefined components (classes) and assemble them into unique applications. Because the programmer uses common, well-tested components, applications can be assembled quickly, will be more reliable, and are easier to change in the future. For instance, a mason doesn't know the chemical composition of a cinderblock or how cinderblocks are manufactured. He does know their properties—how much they weigh, their dimensions, how much weight they can bear. In addition, the mason can change some properties. For instance, cinderblocks can be cut down in size. The mason uses the cinderblocks (possibly changing some of their dimensions) to build a house according to the specifications of the customer.

You are doing the same thing with the Java classes. You learn the properties of the **Label** and **Frame** classes and then change the properties of individual objects to create an application that fits the customer's needs and specifications. Therefore, you really don't need to know how the **Frame** class works. Simply use the class.

Another example would be driving. Do you really need to know how the brake system works? All you need to know are the properties of the brake pedal. In other words, all you need to know is where the brake pedal is and that when you step on the brake pedal very quickly, you will stop very quickly.

Tutorial: Creating a GUI with RAD

You are going to create a new project and package, and then copy the Employee application into it. You will then modify the Employee application so that a frame and label are used to display the employee name.

Let's begin:

1. Start RAD.

2. If needed, switch to the Java perspective.

3. Create a new Java project called Tutorials and within src, a package named c3.

4. In the Navigation tree, expand MyFirstProject, src, and myFirstPackage.

5. Click on Employee.java to select it, then hold the Ctrl key and click on EmployeeApp.java to select it also.

6. Click Edit, then Copy.

7. Click on the c3 package in Tutorials to select it.

8. Click Edit, then Paste.

9. In c3, double-click Employee to display the source code.

Notice that RAD has changed the package statement to show that the class is in c3.

10. After the package statement, add the following two import statements:

```
import java.awt.Label;
import java.awt.Frame;
```

The import statements tell the JVM where to find the **Label** and **Frame** classes. As mentioned earlier, the JVM automatically looks in the java.lang package. However, if you use classes stored in any other package (even packages with the JRE), you must use an import statement to specify where the class is located. In this case, each class we identified individually; however, you can identify all the classes in a package (for example, the awt package) with the following statement:

import java.awt.*;

The * is a wild card symbol that indicates all classes in java.awt. This statement is easier for the programmer to code but it does make the program a little less efficient. By not specifying a class name, the JVM will search the package to find the class.

11. After the displayName method header, enter the following two statements:

```
Label empNameLbl = new Label("My First Label");
empNameLbl.setBounds(100, 200, 75, 20);
```

As explained earlier, these two statements create the **Label** object, assign the object to empNameLbl, define text to appear in the label, and define the label's size and location.

12. Add 2 blank lines after the setBounds statement.

13. On the second blank line, enter the following code to define the variable empFrame, define and assign a **Frame** object to the variable, and add the label to the Employee frame.

```
Frame empFrame = new Frame("My First Frame");
empFrame.setBounds(10, 10, 300, 300);
empFrame.setLayout(null);
empFrame.add(empNameLbl);
empFrame.setVisible(true);
```

14. Click on the System.out.println statement (to select it), then press and hold the Ctrl key, and then press the / key (Ctrl-/) to comment the line out.

15. Format and save the source code, then verify that there are no errors. The code should look like Figure 3-1.

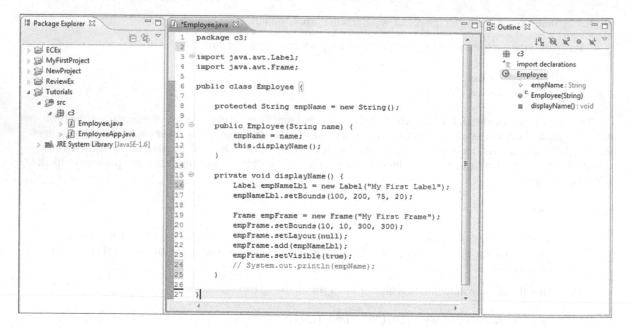

Figure 3-1.

Tutorial: Running a New Application

There are a couple of common pitfalls at this point regarding running a new application. The inclination is to simply click the Run button. However, this will run the last application, which was EmployeeApp in MyFirstProject.

1.   Display the Run menu by clicking on the down arrow to the right of the Run button.

The Run menu shows the previously defined "launches" and three menu options: Run As, Run Configurations... and Organize Favorites.... Choosing EmployeeApp from the menu will also execute EmployeeApp in myFirstPackage—again, this is not what we want. Choosing Run As... tells RAD to run the currently active Java source code. In this case, that would be c3.Employee. Running Employee as a Java application would result in an error since Employee does not have a main method. Ouch, again! (Fortunately RAD won't even let you do that.)

Because we want to run the EmployeeApp in Tutorials/c3, we can define a new launch or change the already defined EmployeeApp launch. We will change the existing EmployeeApp launch to run EmployeeApp in project Tutorials and package c3.

2.   From the drop down menu, select Run Configurations....

The Run Configuration frame will be displayed. Any previously defined launches can be found (grouped by type of configuration) in the pane on the left. If EmployeeApp is not selected, select it now. The launch's definition will be displayed as in Figure 3-2.

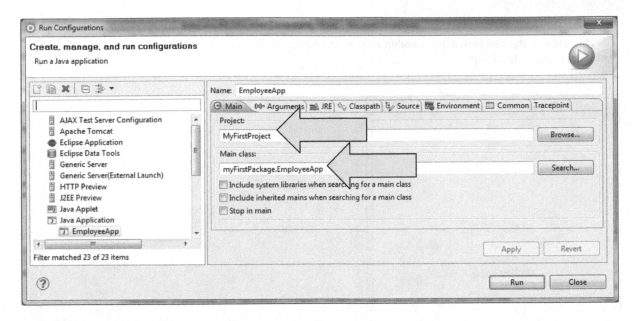

Figure 3-2.

3. Where indicated by the arrows in Figure 3-2, change the text in the project name field to Tutorials and the application name to c3.EmployeeApp so that is appears as in Figure 3-3.

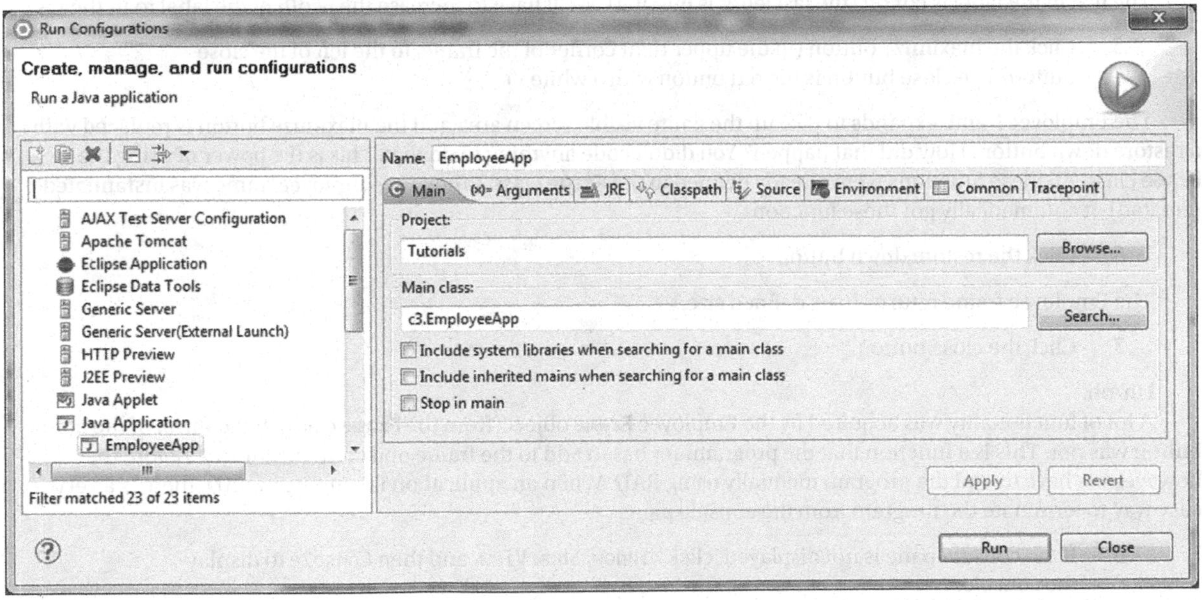

Figure 3-3.

4.   Click the Run button.

This will save the new launch information and run c3.EmployeeApp. The result should look like Figure 3-4. Notice anything not quite right?

Figure 3-4.

The text in the label is cut off (the last letter is missing). We'll have to increase the width of the label to fit the text.

5.   Click the maximize button (in the upper right corner of the frame, to the left of the close button. The close button is the red button with a white x).

The Employee frame expands to take up the entire visible screen area and the maximize button is replaced with a restore down button. How did that happen? You didn't code anything to do that. This is the power of using the **Frame** class. All these functions were already defined in the **Frame** class. When the Employee frame was instantiated (created), it automatically got those functions.

6.   Click the restore down button.

The Employee frame returns to its defined size.

7.   Click the close button.

Uh-oh.

A lot of functionality was acquired by the Employee **Frame** object (from the **Frame** class), but control of the close button was not. This is a function that the programmer has to add to the frame object (in the future). Before that, however, we have to end the program manually using RAD. When an application is running in RAD, there is a very easy way to terminate the program from the console pane.

8.   If the console pane is not displayed, click Window, Show View, and then Console to display the console.

On occasion, you will find that certain views are not displayed (whether you inadvertently closed them or not is not the issue). Simply go to the Show View menu and select the view you would like to see. The views can be moved to different locations on the window by simply clicking and dragging on the view tab.

9.   On the far left of the Console view tool bar, click the Terminate button (the button has a
     red box as an icon; see the arrow in Figure 3-5).

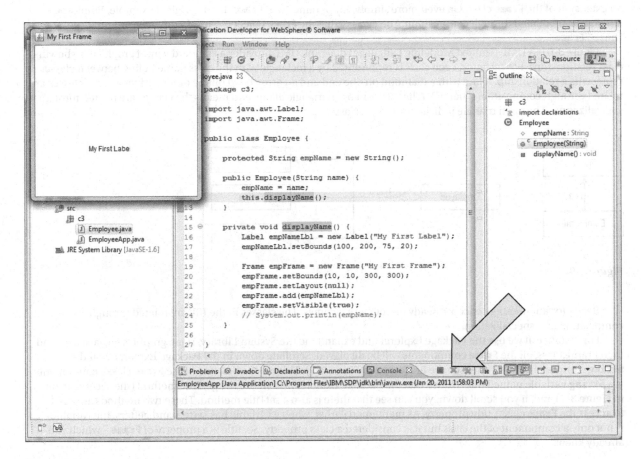

Figure 3-5.

The application will be ended and the Employee frame will disappear.

Specialization

Are you rested? This is going to get a little complicated, so you should be fresh and ready for some new, big concepts.

Besides relating many classes through composition (i.e., Employee is comprised of **String**, **Frame**, and **Label** objects), a class can be related to another class through specialization (also referred to as "extending a class"). What this means is that when you create a class, you define it as a specialized version of an already existing class.

For example, we could create a new class called EmpFrame and define it as an extension of the **Frame** class. EmpFrame is now called a subclass of **Frame**, and **Frame** is called EmpFrame's superclass. The beauty and power of specialization is that subclasses inherit all the capabilities (i.e., variables and methods) of their superclass.

Whoa, that was a mouthful. How do you feel? Do you need a glass of water?

Another way to distinguish between a composition and specialization relationship is to say whether one class "has a" class, or whether one class "is a" class. For example, EmpFrame is a kind of **Frame** but Employee has a **Frame**. So in the first case, EmpFrame and **Frame** are related through specialization. To say it another way, EmpFrame is an extension of the **Frame** class. Or, even more simply, EmpFrame "is a" **Frame**. In the original example, Employee and **Frame** are related through composition. You can say that the **Frame** object is part of Employee or Employee "has a" **Frame**.

Figure 3-6 is a UML (Unified Modeling Language) diagram. UML provides a standard way of graphically showing class relationships. For instance, each class is represented by a rectangle with the class name. A line between classes represents a relationship. A line with a diamond on one end and an arrowhead on the other end means the classes are related through composition ("has a"). A line with an open triangle at one end means the classes are related through specialization. The open triangle indicates the superclass.

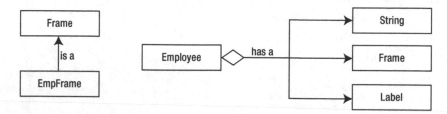

Figure 3-6.

Ready for another big concept? Ready or not, here it comes. The classes in the JRE are related through composition and specialization.

For instance, if we use the Package Explorer and expand the JRE System Library, rt.jar, graphics.jar, java.awt, and then Frame.class, all the **Frame** components will be displayed. Scrolling down in the Package Explorer would show a **String** component called title (see the first arrow in Figure 3-7). This means that one of the **Frame** class's components is a **String** variable named title. Notice that the Package Explorer also shows the getTitle method (the second arrow in Figure 3-7) and, if you scroll down, you can see that there is also a setTitle method. These two methods are used to access the **Frame** class's title property. As mentioned earlier, when a variable has setters and getters, the variable is not only a component of the class but it is considered a class property. So, title is a property of **Frame**—which you already knew!

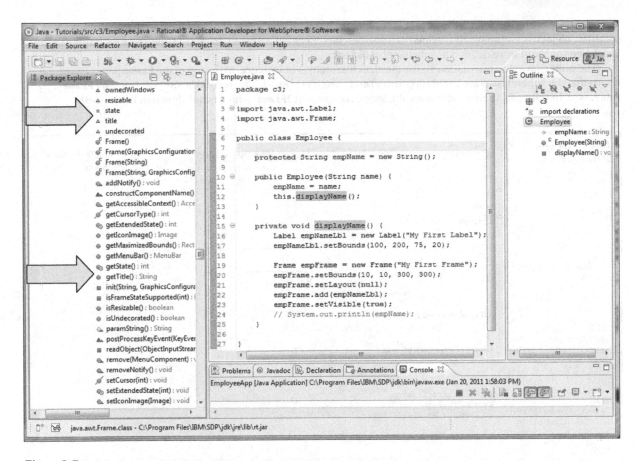

Figure 3-7.

More important, we have proven that the JRE classes are composed of many other classes/objects. In fact, every JRE class is involved in a superclass/subclass relationship and the JRE classes inherit many of their capabilities from specialization (i.e., from their superclasses). For example, Figure 3-8 shows how several of the GUI classes are related in a hierarchy. Notice that **Frame** is a type of **Window** and that a **Label** is a type of **Component**.

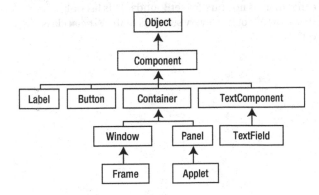

Figure 3-8.

At the top of the diagram is the **Object** class. It is the ultimate superclass. If a class is created and no superclass is specified, **Object** is automatically defined as the superclass. Because we never defined a superclass for Employee and EmployeeApp, both were defined as subclasses of **Object**.

The online Java documentation shows the class hierarchy. For instance, at the top of the **Frame** page (Figure 3-9) notice that the superclasses are listed (first arrow) and match Figure 3-8. The second arrow points to any **Frame** subclasses. In this case, there is only one—the Swing component **JFrame** (which is **not** shown in Figure 3-8).

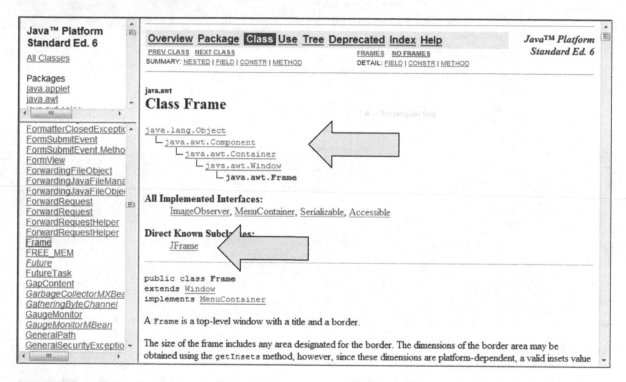

Figure 3-9.

In addition, the online documentation shows all methods inherited from the superclasses (this information follows the class method listing, see Figure 3-10). Notice that the setBounds method is inherited from the Window class. (If you scroll back to the **Frame** method list, you will see that there is no entry for setBounds. This list only includes those methods explicitly defined in the **Frame** class.) As a matter of fact, every subclass of the **Window** class inherits this method. Can you feel the power of inheritance yet?

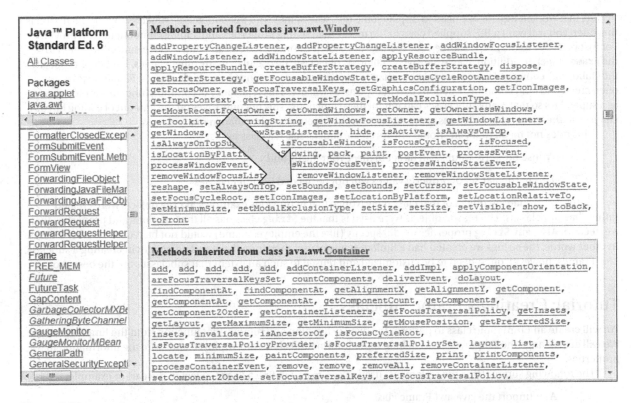

Figure 3-10.

If not, think about the options the Java programmers had when creating these classes. They could have defined a setBounds method for every visual class. When the setBounds method had to be changed, they would have to change the setBounds method in each class. Alternatively, they could create a superclass for all of the visual classes and define the setBounds method once in this superclass. All of the visual classes would be defined as extensions of the superclass and, therefore inherit the method. Not only would the programmers only write the setBounds source code once, but also any changes to the method would be made once, in one class: the superclass.

Assuming that you are now sold on the superclass/subclass relationship, maybe you would like to know how to define a superclass/subclass relationship? A class is defined as a subclass by inserting the **extends** keyword in the class header followed by the superclass name. For instance, the following would define a new class called EmpFrame as a subclass of **Frame**:

```
public class EmpFrame extends Frame {}
```

Why Use Specialization?

This is a tough question to answer simply. The short answer is the programmer has more control over a subclass than an object. Now, unfortunately, comes the long answer.

When we used a frame earlier, we:

    A.   Instantiated a **Frame** object

    B.   Modified the **Frame** object's properties (for instance, set visible to true)

    C.   Added components (like a label) to the object and modified its properties

As that worked well for our need to display some text, why bother with this superclass/subclass thing? The reason is that often you will want a JRE supplied class to "do more" than setting properties and adding components can provide. For instance, our frame needs source code to make the Close button work. You can't add a "close button" function to the **Frame** object. In addition, if an extensively "tailored" object will be useful to many other classes, it is better to specify the "tailoring" commands once in a subclass than to duplicate the commands in multiple classes. Finally, classes are often created to hold common functions that many classes will use. This repository of common functions is then used as a superclass so that many subclasses can inherit these functions. This not only saves on the amount of coding but any changes to these common functions are made once in the superclass rather than in many classes.

This does not mean that you should always create subclasses. If a class exists:

1. Whose property values can be set to meet your needs **and**

2. This particular set of property values will not be needed by other classes

simply instantiate an object of that class type. Notice that in previous examples **String** objects were created rather than subclasses. The reason objects were used is that the **String** class has all the functions and properties that we needed. Also, any **String** properties we did specify (like the employee name) would not be reused in other classes. In other words, the strings we created had a limited scope of use, therefore; there was no benefit in creating a subclass.

Frames, however, often need to be customized and reused to such an extent that subclasses are the best choice.

Tutorial: Creating a Frame Subclass

We will create an EmpFrame class to perform the display function and remove that function from the Employee class. We will also change the Employee class to hold more information about an employee and store the information in properties.

The following summarizes the statements used to create and define a **Frame** object in the earlier example:

A. Import the java.awt.Frame class

B. Create a **Frame** variable and object then assign the object to the variable

C. Define a title

D. Set the layout property to null

E. Define the size

F. Define the location

G. Make the frame visible

This time we are going to create a **Frame** subclass called EmpFrame instead of instantiating a **Frame** object. Inside the EmpFrame class, we will define all the properties thereby eliminating the need to perform steps C through G for any class that uses EmpFrame. When another class wants to use EmpFrame, they will only have to import the EmpFrame class and create an EmpFrame object (statements A and B).

1. Select c3 in Tutorials and click File, New, and then Class.

The New Java Class frame will be displayed (see Figure 3-11).

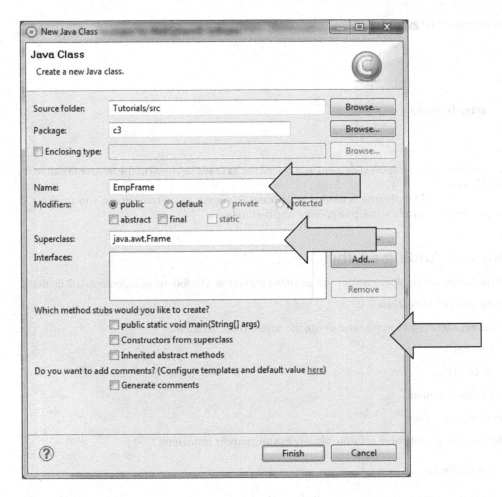

Figure 3-11.

2. Specify EmpFrame as the class name and java.awt.Frame as the superclass (as indicated by the first two arrows).

3. Make sure none of the method stub checkboxes are selected (as indicated by the third arrow), and then click the Finish button.

In addition to the comments, RAD generates the following code:

```
package c3;

import java.awt.Frame;

public class EmpFrame extends Frame {

}
```

Notice that RAD included the correct import statement and placed the **extends** keyword in the header to define EmpFrame as a subclass of **Frame**.

Congratulations; you have defined EmpFrame as a subclass of **Frame**. Of course, EmpFrame doesn't do anything, but it will after we set the properties, and add some components and methods.

Tutorial: Defining and Adding a Label

We need to create a label (to display the employee name) and add it to EmpFrame. The following statements will do that:

A. Import the java.awt.Label class

B. Create a **Label** object and variable and assign the object to the variable

C. Define the label text

D. Define the label size

E. Define the label location

F. Add the label to the frame

1. Add the following import statement after the already existing import statement:

```
import java.awt.Label;
```

We will create a label and assign it to a class variable called empNameLbl.

2. Inside of the EmpFrame class, enter the following statement:

```
Label empNameLbl = new Label("My First Label");
```

This statement does three things:

A. Creates a **Label** object with the text "My First Label"

B. Creates a **Label** variable called empNameLbl

C. Assigns the object to the variable

3. Insert the following code after the label statement:

```
public EmpFrame(Employee emp) {
}
```

This statement defines a constructor method. The primary purpose of the constructor is to "initialize" the object or said another way "to make the object useful". For EmpFrame, this means adding source code to the constructor to define the frame and its component's properties.

Notice that the constructor expects an Employee object. As mentioned, we will be changing the Employee class to hold more employee information. Passing an object, instead of individual variables, is an easy way to transfer a lot of information between two classes.

3. Inside the constructor, enter the following statement:

```
empNameLbl.setBounds(100, 150, 150, 20);
```

Notice that the length of the label was set to 150 so that all the text will be displayed. The label was also centered on the frame (100 pixels from the left and 150 from the top).

4. Add the following after the setBounds statement:

```
this.add(empNameLbl);
```

Adding the label to the frame was the last step we needed to perform. In our earlier example, the label was added to the empFrame object with the following statement:

```
empFrame.add(empNameLbl);
```

In this example, however, we do not have a frame object to manipulate. We must add the label to the EmpFrame class we are defining. The keyword **this** is used to refer to the current object/class. For example, notice that the syntax to add the labels was the same except we substituted **this** for empFrame.

You have created and added a label to EmpFrame.

The following summarizes how to create a label and which steps (that you just performed) did the required functions:

A. Import the java.awt.Label class—step 1

B. Create a **Label** object and variable and assign the object to the variable—step 2

C. Define the label text—step 2

D. Define the label size—step 4

E. Define the label location—step 4

F. Add the label to the frame—step 5

Tutorial: Defining a Functional Frame

To review, we still need to perform the following steps to create a functioning frame:

A. Define a title

B. Set layout property to null

C. Define the size

D. Define the location

E. Make the frame visible

1. Add the following statements after the this.add statement:

```
this.setTitle("New Frame Title");
this.setLayout(null);
this.setBounds(10, 10, 300, 300);
this.setVisible(true);
```

Notice that setter methods are used to define all the frame properties (Title, Bounds, etc.).

2. Format and save the EmpFrame source, then verify that there are no errors.

The executable code should look as follows:

```
package c3;

import java.awt.Frame;
import java.awt.Label;

public class EmpFrame extends Frame {
    Label empNameLbl = new Label("My First Label");

    public EmpFrame(Employee emp) {
        empNameLbl.setBounds(100, 150, 150, 20);
        this.add(empNameLbl);
        this.setTitle("New Frame Title");
        this.setLayout(null);
        this.setBounds(10, 10, 300, 300);
        this.setVisible(true);

    }

}
```

3. Run EmployeeApp.

Notice that the same old frame (empFrame) with the cut off label is displayed. This is because EmployeeApp still creates an Employee object and Employee creates the **Frame** object empFrame. We need to change EmployeeApp so that it creates an EmpFrame object and change Employee so that it does not create a **Frame** object.

4. End EmployeeApp by clicking the Terminate button.

Tutorial: Using a Frame

Now let's use the frame:

1. In EmployeeApp, add the following statement after the Employee object emp is instantiated:

```
EmpFrame ef = new EmpFrame(emp);
```

This statement:

    A.   Creates an EmpFrame object

    B.   Passes the Employee variable (emp) to EmpFrame's constructor

    C.   Creates an EmpFrame variable called ef

    D.   Assigns the EmpFrame object to ef

EmployeeApp's executable statements should look like the following:

```
package c3;
public class EmployeeApp {

    public static void main(String[] args) {
        Employee emp = new Employee(new String("Mary Worker"));
        EmpFrame ef = new EmpFrame(emp);
    }
}
```

2.   Save the EmployeeApp source code and verify there are no errors.

The following steps all concern changes to the Employee class source code:

3.   Delete the two import statements.

4.   Remove the following statement from the Employee constructor:

    `this.displayName();`

5.   Delete the displayName method.

We want to define the **String** empName as a property. As a reminder, the steps for defining a property are:

    A.   Create a private variable

    B.   Define a getter method to return the private variable value

    C.   Define a setter method to:

    accept a value for the private variable

    validate the value

    if the value is valid, set the private variable to the value passed to the setter method

For simplicity's sake, we will not define any edits to validate the data.

6.   Change the **String** empName to a private variable.

7.   Add a public setName method that:

    A.   Returns void

    B.   Accepts a **String** variable called name as a parameter

    C.   Sets the private variable empName to name

8. Specify a getName method header so that the method is:

    A. Public

    B. Returns a **String** variable

    C. Accepts nothing

9. In the getName method body, enter the following statement:

    return empName;

The keyword **return** actually passes the variable (specified after the **return** keyword) to the class that invokes the getName method. In this case, the variable empName will be sent back.

10. Change the constructor so that the setName method is invoked to assign the value to empName.

11. Format and save the Employee source code and verify there are no errors.

The executable statements should look like the following:

```
package c3;

public class Employee {

    private String empName = new String();

    public Employee(String name) {
        this.setName(name);
    }

    public void setName(String name) {
        empName = name;
    }

    public String getName() {
        return empName;
    }
}
```

12. Run EmployeeApp.

The EmpFrame should be displayed as in Figure 3-12.

Figure 3-12.

Unfortunately, we still have not solved the close button problem.

13.   From the console, terminate EmployeeApp.

Figure 3-13 shows the relationships between our three classes and the **Frame** class.

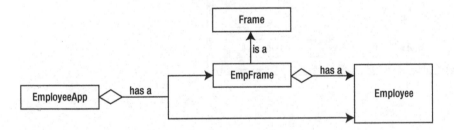

Figure 3-13.

Tutorial: Creating UML Diagrams with RAD

RAD can generate UML diagrams. There is some "diversity" regarding the symbols and line styles used in UML diagrams. Although diversity is usually a good thing, when it comes to programming, standards and uniformity are the rule because they enhance efficiency. If everyone uses the same symbols, then everyone can understand the diagrams. However, the real world is never so simple. There are a couple reasons for differences. First, there are disagreements between professionals regarding which is the best way to diagram the classes. Second, there is no way to enforce a standard. Diagramming is not like the syntax of a programming language (which has to be followed exactly) for the JVM to work. With that said, we will show (very briefly) RAD's interpretation of a basic UML diagram. Once you start developing complex applications, you will really appreciate that RAD automatically generates the UML.

1.   Click c3 in the navigation tree to select it, and then click File, New, and Class Diagram.

The New Class Diagram window will be displayed (see Figure 3-14).

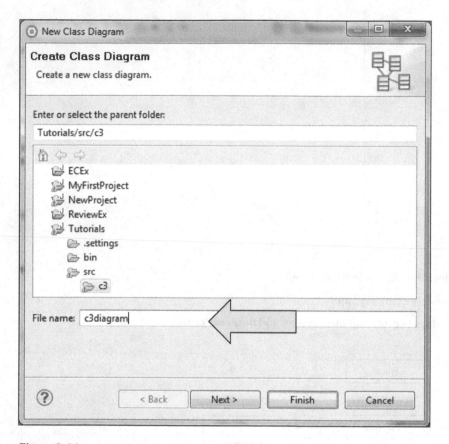

Figure 3-14.

2.   Specify c3diagram in the file name field and click the Finish button.

A file named c3diagram.dnx will be added to c3 in the navigation tree and a blank diagram will be displayed in the content pane. The diagram is blank because the classes to include in the diagram must to be specified.

3.   In the navigation tree, select the three classes by clicking on EmpFrame.java, press and hold the Shift key, then click on the EmployeeApp.java file.

All three files should be selected (see Figure 3-15).

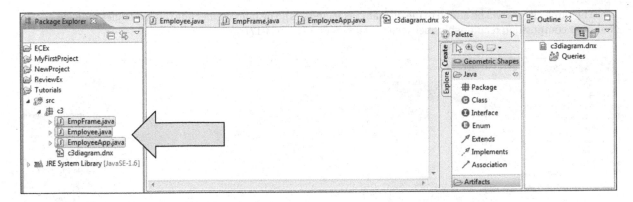

Figure 3-15.

4. Right-click on any of the selected file names in the navigation tree and from the shortcut menu, select Visualize, then Add to Current Diagram (see Figure 3-16).

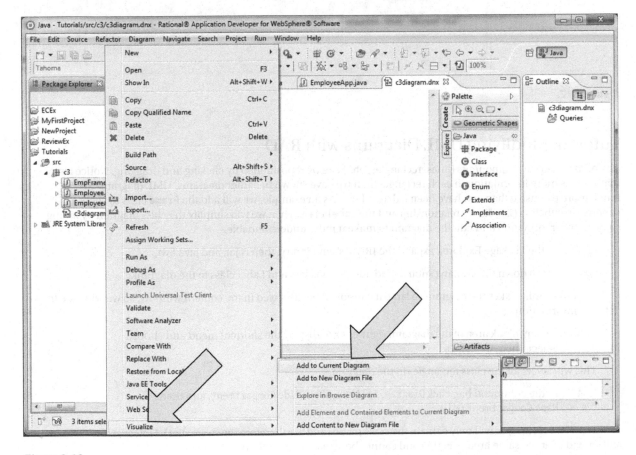

Figure 3-16.

The three classes will be added to the diagram (as rectangles). The lines connecting the rectangles indicate "has a" or composition relationships between the classes (see Figure 3-17).

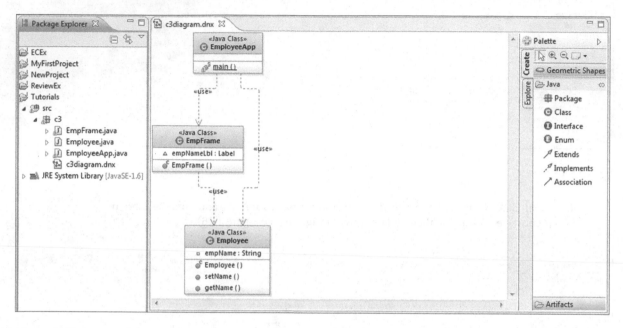

Figure 3-17.

Tutorial: Modifying UML Diagrams with RAD

Any of the diagram components (lines, rectangles, etc.) can be repositioned by clicking and dragging. Notice also that there is more information in each rectangle than we have shown in earlier diagrams. UML diagrams are much more extensive than you have been led to believe. As an example, we will add the **Frame** class to show a superclass-subclass (i.e., "is a") relationship and the **Label** class. Then we will simplify the class diagram by hiding some of the information and edit the diagram to make it more understandable.

1. In the Package Explorer, expand the JRE System Library, then rt.jar, and java.awt.

2. Scroll down the java.awt subtree and add Frame.class and Label.class to the diagram.

Of course, this makes the diagram so large it cannot all be displayed in the content window, so we will hide this detailed information.

3. On any blank area of the diagram, right-click to display the shortcut menu and choose Select, then All Shapes.

This will select all the class rectangles in the diagram.

4. In the command bar, click Diagram, Filters, Show/Hide Compartment, and then Name Compartment Only.

The class rectangles will only contain the class name (and are therefore much smaller). However, the diagram is still spread over the same area as earlier and cannot be viewed in its entirety.

5. Right-click on any class's name text and select Format, Arrange, then All.

The entire diagram will now be displayed in the content pane (see Figure 3-18).

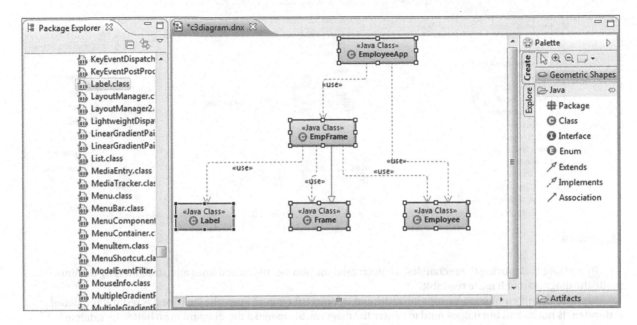

Figure 3-18.

RAD does a pretty good job arranging the diagram but sometimes you have to get in there and do it yourself. As mentioned, all of the diagram elements (i.e., the class rectangles, relationship lines, text, etc.) can be move and resized by clicking and dragging. In addition, any element can be deleted and the text can be modified. We will delete, move, align, and resize the class rectangles to make the diagram easier to read.

6. Click the EmployeeApp rectangle to select it.

7. Press and hold Ctrl then click the EmpFrame rectangle.

The order in which the rectangles are clicked is important. The last element clicked becomes the anchor. (The anchor is indicated with solid black resize handles.) When alignment functions are performed, the anchor stays in the same location and all other selected elements are moved to align with its location.

8. Right-click on the EmployeeApp rectangle and select Format, Align, and then Middle.

The EmployeeApp rectangle was moved down and is now horizontally aligned with EmpFrame but the two class rectangles overlap. As mentioned, the rectangles and lines can be resized and repositioned by clicking and dragging. We will move the EmployeeApp rectangle to avoid the overlapping.

9. Click and drag the EmployeeApp rectangle so that it is horizontally moved to the right and vertically centered over the Employee rectangle.

10. Click and drag the Frame rectangle so that it is centered above EmpFrame.

11. Drag Label and Employee rectangles under the EmpFrame.

12. Increase the Employee rectangle's width so that it is also under EmployeeApp.

13. Click and drag all the connector lines so that they are straight.

The diagram should look like Figure 3-19.

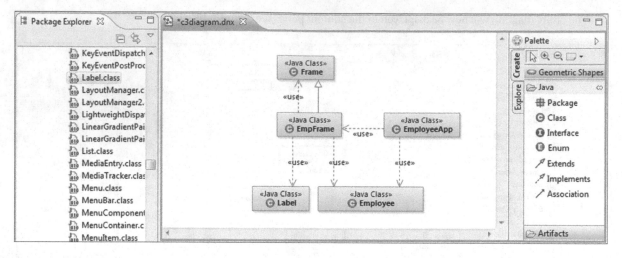

Figure 3-19.

By resizing and moving the rectangles, we decreased the number of crossed lines and straightening the lines made the diagram much more readable.

Because the different relationships are indicated by different types of lines, the "use" text is redundant. Being redundant is not so bad but it does tend to clutter the diagram. So, to make the diagram even better, let's delete these text boxes.

14. Select all five of the textboxes so that the diagram looks like Figure 3-20.

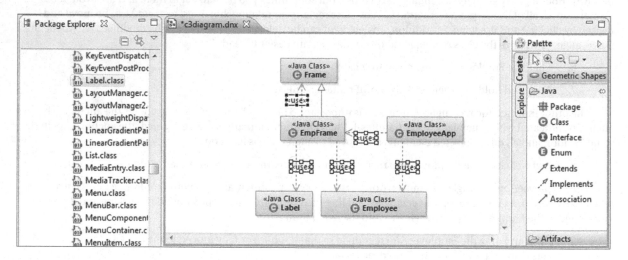

Figure 3-20.

15. Press the Delete key and save the diagram.

All of the text boxes are removed from the diagram leaving you with a very clean and crisp diagram that shows that EmpFrame is a Frame, EmpFrame has a Label and an Employee, and the EmployeeApp has an EmpFrame and Employee.

Figure 3-21 shows the final diagram.

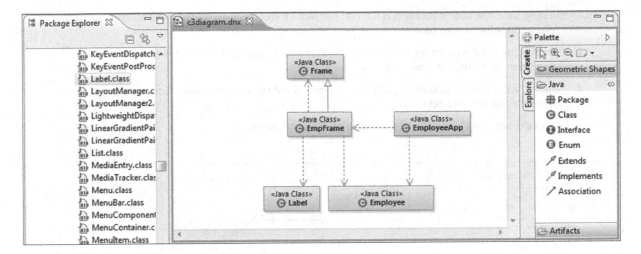

Figure 3-21.

Tutorial: Generating Getters and Setters

Currently, as shown in the following Diagram 3-1, EmployeeApp creates an Employee object and sets the one property to "Mary Worker." It also creates an Employee variable (emp) and assigns the object to the variable. The Employee variable (emp) is then passed to the EmpFrame object's constructor and the text "My First Label" is displayed.

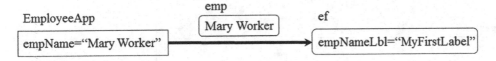

Diagram 3-1.

We want to enhance the Employee class with additional properties to hold the employee mailing address. This means that EmployeeApp has to be modified to set values for these new properties and EmpFrame must be changed to display the new property values. Diagram 3-2 shows the changes that we want to make.

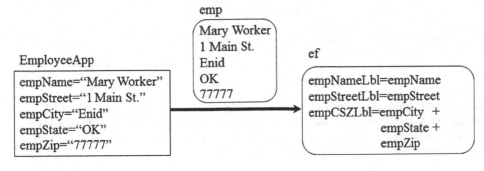

Diagram 3-2.

Unfortunately, the close button problem is too complicated for right now, so we will hold off until the next chapter to explain and solve that problem.

1. Display the Employee source code and define four new private **String** variables called empStreet, empCity, empState, empZip.

2. Right-click anywhere in the content pane and from the shortcut menu, select Source, then Generate Getters and Setters.

3. Click the Select All button (see Figure 3-22) then the OK button.

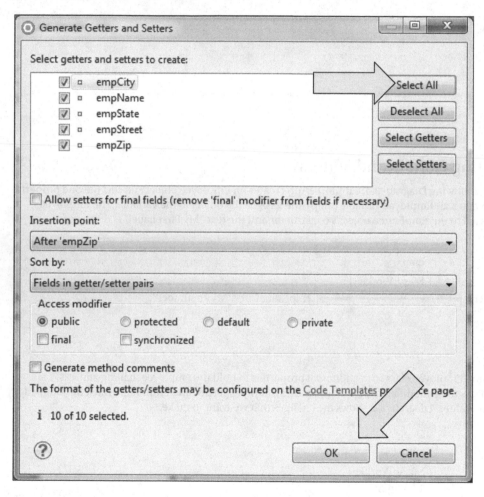

Figure 3-22.

RAD generates all ten getter/setter methods after the last class variable definition. Now, you may not be impressed because the generated code is very simple. However, the beauty and power of this feature is that it relieves the programmer of tedious and error-prone coding. Also, notice how RAD knew that private class level variables are eligible to be properties and only generated getters and setters for them.

We still must change the Employee constructor to accept all five pieces of information.

4. In Employee, change the constructor header to the following:

```
public Employee(String name, String street,
String city, String state, String zip) {
```

5. Replace the constructor body with the following code:

```
this.setEmpName(name);
this.setEmpStreet(street);
this.setEmpCity(city);
this.setEmpState(state);
this.setEmpZip(zip);
```

This code will use the setters to put the passed data into the private variables.
Finally, we need to delete the setName and getName methods we created earlier.

6. In the outline pane (far right), right-click setName and, from the shortcut menu, click Delete.

7. At the "Confirm Delete" window, click the OK button.

8. Delete the getName method, just as you deleted setName in steps 6 and 7.

9. Format and save the source code.

The executable code should look similar to the following:

```
package c3;

public class Employee {

        private String empName = new String();
        private String empStreet, empCity, empState, empZip;

        public String getEmpName() {
                return empName;
        }

        public void setEmpName(String empName) {
                this.empName = empName;
        }

        public String getEmpStreet() {
                return empStreet;
        }

        public void setEmpStreet(String empStreet) {
                this.empStreet = empStreet;
        }

        public String getEmpCity() {
                return empCity;
        }
```

```
        public void setEmpCity(String empCity) {
                this.empCity = empCity;
        }
        public String getEmpState() {
                return empState;
        }

        public void setEmpState(String empState) {
                this.empState = empState;
        }

        public String getEmpZip() {
                return empZip;
        }

        public void setEmpZip(String empZip) {
                this.empZip = empZip;
        }

public Employee(String name, String street, String city,
        String state, String zip) {
                this.setEmpName(name);
                this.setEmpStreet(street);
                this.setEmpCity(city);
                this.setEmpState(state);
                this.setEmpZip(zip);
        }
}
```

In the Package Explorer pane, notice the error icons. If you display the EmployeeApp source and then the error, it will read, "The constructor Employee(String) is undefined." The Employee source code has no errors; however, the changes to Employee are causing an error in EmployeeApp, because we no longer have an Employee constructor that accepts a single string as a parameter. This is another great feature of RAD—after a class (e.g., Employee) is changed, RAD verifies that any other classes that use the class (Employee) will still work.

10. Display the EmployeeApp source code and change the main method's first executable statement to the following:

```
Employee emp = new Employee("Mary Worker", "1 Main St.",
            "Enid", "OK", "77777");
```

11. Save the EmployeeApp source code.

Tutorial: Adding More Labels

EmpFrame needs to be modified so that all the Employee information is displayed. Perform the following steps to the EmpFrame source code.

1. After the statement that creates empNameLbl, add two new statements to create labels called empStreetLbl and empCSZLbl with the text "New label."

We will change the label's text later with the information in the Employee object.

2. In the EmpFrame constructor, before the statement that adds empNameLbl to the frame, define the two labels so that:

A. They are the same length and height as empNameLbl

B. empStreetLbl is 40 pixels beneath empNameLbl

C. empCSZLbl is 80 pixels beneath empNameLbl

If you are unsure how to do this, see the earlier discussion of the setBounds statement.

3. After the statement that adds empNameLbl to the frame, enter two statements to add the two new labels to the frame.

The executable source code should look like the following:

```
package c3;

import java.awt.Frame;
import java.awt.Label;

public class EmpFrame extends Frame {
        Label empNameLbl = new Label("My First Label");
        Label empStreetLbl = new Label("New label");
        Label empCSZLbl = new Label("New label");

        public EmpFrame(Employee emp) {
                empNameLbl.setBounds(100, 150, 150, 20);
                empStreetLbl.setBounds(100, 190, 150, 20);
                empCSZLbl.setBounds(100, 230, 150, 20);
                this.add(empNameLbl);
                this.add(empStreetLbl);
                this.add(empCSZLbl);

                this.setTitle("New Frame Title");
                this.setLayout(null);
                this.setBounds(10, 10, 300, 300);
                this.setVisible(true);
        }
}
```

4. Save the source code and verify that there are no errors.

Just because RAD is not displaying any error messages does not mean that the code is correct. You really need to test that the correct results will be produced and, if the results are not correct, find the errors. The best/easiest way to find errors is to follow the "code a little, test a little" (CALTAL) style of programming. Many beginning programmers try to enter all the source code at one time and are often then overwhelmed by all the errors. An easy way to avoid that is to test frequently after adding or changing code. Therefore, at this point, we will run the code and verify that it works correctly.

5. Run EmployeeApp.

The EmpFrame should be displayed and appear as in Figure 3-23.

6. From the Console view, end EmployeeApp.

Figure 3-23.

Tutorial: Displaying the Employee Information

EmpFrame needs to be modified so that the employee information is retrieved from the Employee object and placed in the labels. The information will be retrieved by using the object's getters (via the variable emp that was passed by EmployeeApp) and each label will be modified using its setText method.

1. Change the frame title text from "New Frame Title" to "Employee Information."

2. After the label's setBounds statements, use each label's setText method to define the label's text as "New text."

We will follow the CALTAL rules and verify that our setText statements are working.

3. Save the code and run EmployeeApp.

The frame should look like Figure 3-24.

Figure 3-24.

4. Replace "New Text" in the empNameLbl.setText statement with emp.getEmpName().

The statement should look like the following:

```
empNameLbl.setText(emp.getEmpName());
```

Remember, getters return property values. These values can be used just like a variable. So, instead of "New Text", "Mary Worker" (which is returned by the getEmpName method) is used in the setText method. Notice that the methods are executed from "inside out." This means when one statement is embedded inside another, the embedded statement is executed first. In other words, the returned value of the embedded method is used as input to the outer method.

5. Save the code and run EmployeeApp.

Verify that "Mary Worker" appears in the name label.

6. Change the empStreetLbl.setText statement to retrieve and display the employee's street address.

7. Save the code and run EmployeeApp.

Verify that "1 Main St." appears in the street label.

Now the tricky part: we need to retrieve three pieces of information, format the data (i.e., between city and state we need to add a comma, between state and zip we need to insert several spaces), and then place the final string into empCSZLbl. There are many ways to do this, but we will do it all in one statement.

8. Change the empCSZLbl.setText statement so that the following replaces "New Text":

```
emp.getEmpCity() + ", " + emp.getEmpState() + "  " + emp.getEmpZip()
```

Notice that the three getters for the employee city, state and zip are embedded in the setText method. The tricky part is how they are linked together. A plus sign between **String** variables acts as a concatenation function. Concatenation between two (or more) strings results in one string. The resulting string is comprised of the first string followed by the second string. For instance, the following concatenation, "ABC" + "DEF", results in a single string of "ABCDEF."

In our example, we are concatenating five strings: the three strings returned by the getters and the two fixed constant strings ", " (comma and a space) and " " (four spaces).

The executable code should look like the following:

```
package c3;
import java.awt.Frame;
import java.awt.Label;

public class EmpFrame extends Frame {
        Label empNameLbl = new Label("My First Label");
        Label empStreetLbl = new Label("New label");
        Label empCSZLbl = new Label("New label");

        public EmpFrame(Employee emp) {
                empNameLbl.setBounds(100, 150, 150, 20);
                empStreetLbl.setBounds(100, 190, 150, 20);
                empCSZLbl.setBounds(100, 230, 150, 20);
                empNameLbl.setText(emp.getEmpName());
                empStreetLbl.setText(emp.getEmpStreet());
                empCSZLbl.setText(emp.getEmpCity() + ", " + emp.getEmpState() + " " + emp.
getEmpZip());
                this.add(empNameLbl);
                this.add(empStreetLbl);
                this.add(empCSZLbl);

                this.setTitle("Employee Information");
                this.setLayout(null);
                this.setBounds(10, 10, 300, 300);
                this.setVisible(true);
        }
}
```

9. Save the code and run EmployeeApp.

The frame should look like Figure 3-25.

Figure 3-25.

Now, if you haven't been terminating each launch of EmployeeApp, there should be several Employee Information frames. If you go to the console and click the terminate button only the last launch will be ended.

To terminate the other frames, you must click the drop down button next to the Display Selected Console button (see the vertical yellow arrow in Figure 3-26). The currently running applications will be displayed in a drop down menu (see the horizontal yellow arrow in Figure 3-26). Simply click any of the listed items to switch the console view to that application and then click the terminate button.

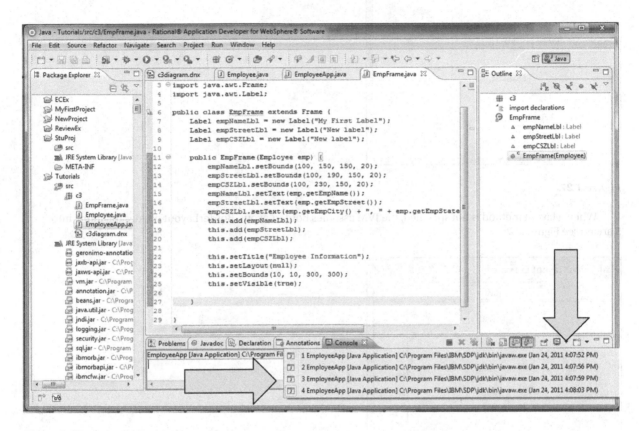

Figure 3-26.

10. End all running EmployeeApp applications.

Tutorial: Breaking the Frame Code

In the EmpFrame source code:

1. Click on the setLayout statement and comment it out by pressing Ctrl and /.

2. Save EmpFrame and run EmployeeApp.

The data should appear as in Figure 3-27.

Figure 3-27.

When a layout method is not specified, the JVM assumes BorderLayout. BorderLayout divides the frame into 5 areas (see Figure 3-28).

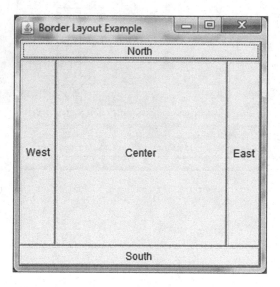

Figure 3-28.

Locations are specified as North, East, and so on, and the default is Center. However, combining component absolute locations (e.g., 100, 150) and a layout will yield unexpected results (Figure 3-27). Therefore, programmers must do one of the following:

    A.   Accept the BorderLayout defaults

    B.   Specify a layout

    C.   Specify layout as **null** and define an absolute location for each component.

3. End EmployeApp.

4. Click on the setLayout statement and uncomment the statement by pressing Ctrl and /.

For now, we will place the components manually. As you will see, this is time-consuming and error-prone.

5. Change the setBounds statement to the following (changes are in bold):

```
empNameLbl.setBounds(100, 150, 30, 20);
empStreetLbl.setBounds(100, 150, 60, 20);
empCSZLbl.setBounds(100, 150, 150, 20);
```

6. Save EmpFrame and run EmployeeApp.

The data should appear as in Figure 3-29. (To say the data is poorly formatted is a vast understatement.)

Figure 3-29.

Often when programmers are creating many components, they will simply copy another component definition and then modify the properties (i.e., change the name, size, etc.). It is very common to miss a property or two. Step 4 defined all the labels in the same location (e.g., 100, 150). In other words, the labels overlay each other. The result of this, however, is counterintuitive. The labels are added as follows: empName first, then Street, then CSZ. You would expect the CSZ label to be displayed since it is the last label added. In actuality, the first label (empName) overlays the other two. In other words, when a label is added, it "underlays" or goes "under" any existing labels. (Just to make things a little harder, this is not true when a layout is specified. For instance, in BorderLayout, labels do overlay each other, as you would expect.)

In step 4, the label lengths were modified to demonstrate the "underlaying." The empName label is only 30 pixels long, so only the first name of the employee, Mary, can be displayed. Notice how Mary overlays the other two labels text. After Mary, the text "n St." is displayed. This text resides in pixels 31 through 60 of the empStreet label. empStreet was changed to 60 pixels in length, of which, the first 30 pixels are overlaid by empName. In other words, when empStreet was added it went "under" empName, so only pixels 31 through 60 ("n St. ") are displayed. Finally, "77777" is displayed. This text resides in pixels 61 through 150 of empCSZ. empCSZ went under both empName and empStreet. Therefore, the first 30 pixels of empCSZ are overlaid by empName and pixels 31 through 60 are overlaid by empStreet, leaving only pixels 61 through 150 showing.

7. Move the add empNameLbl statement after the add empCSZLbl statement.

Can you figure out how the data will appear?

8. Save EmpFrame and run EmployeeApp.

The data should appear as in Figure 3-30. Can you explain why the data appears as in Figure 3-30?

Figure 3-30.

In step 6, the add statements were changed such that empStreet was the first and, therefore, primary label. In other words, the empStreet text will overlay any other label. Next, empCSZ was added under empStreet. Since empStreet is 60 pixels long, only empCSZ's pixels 61 through 150 are displayed (i.e., "77777"). Lastly, empName is added beneath both empStreet and empCSZ. Because empName is only 30 pixels in length, none of empName appears.

9. End EmployeeApp.

10. Move the add empName statement before the add empStreet and set the label locations and lengths back to the original values as follows:

```
empNameLbl.setBounds(100, 150, 150, 20);
empStreetLbl.setBounds(100, 190, 150, 20);
empCSZLbl.setBounds(100, 230, 150, 20);
```

11. Test that it is correct, by saving the source and running the application.

12. Comment out the **Label** import statement.

Notice that 12 errors were generated. Every statement that references a label is in error because the JVM cannot find the **Label** class. It is very common error to forget to include the import statement.

13. Uncomment the import statement and save the source.

Tutorial: Breaking the Getter/Setter Code

In Employee:

1. In the getEmpCity method, comment out the return statement.

The error message will be "This method must return a result of type String." For methods that return a result, the type of data returned must be specified in the method header and the **return** statement must specify the particular variable to return. In this case, the header specifies that a **String** variable will be returned and the return statement identifies empCity. If either of these is missing, the other will be in error.

2. Uncomment the return statement and delete "String" in the getEmpCity method header.

The error message will be "Return type for the method is missing." Remember, to return a value, the return variable type must be specified in the method header and the variable name must be specified in the **return** statement.

3. Type the text "String" before the keyword **public** in the getEmpCity method header.

Notice that the return type is still incorrect and now both the keyword **String** and the method name are highlighted as errors. The syntax for specifying the return type requires that it appear after the access modifier and before the method name. In this case, placing it before the access modifier (**public**) causes an error.

4. Delete the access modifier **public** in the getEmpCity method header.

This is a valid method header definition. An access modifier is not required because a default access modifier will be used.

5. Type the text "public " before the text "String" in the getEmpCity method header.

6. Go to the setEmpCity method and delete the keyword **void** from the method header.

The error message will say, "Return type for the method is missing." All methods except constructors must specify a return type. If a method returns nothing, then the keyword **void** must be specified as the return type.

7. Put the **void** keyword back in the method header.

8. Change the name of setEmpCity method to **p**etEmpCity and save the source code.

Because setEmpCity is invoked in the constructor, this causes an error in the Employee class.

9. Change the name of the method back to **s**etEmpCity.

10. Change the getter **g**etEmpCity name to **p**etEmpCity and save the source code.

There are no errors flagged in Employee; however, the Navigation tree shows an error in EmpFrame. It's important to realize that even though RAD says the error is in EmpFrame, in this case the error is in Employee. RAD is good at identifying errors but not so good at assigning responsibility. Do not follow the error messages and their suggestions blindly. Many times errors are caused by mismatches between classes, and the programmer will have to determine which needs to be changed.

11. Change the getter name back to **g**etEmpCity and save the source code.

Results of the Tutorials

Here are the results:

1. A new project called Tutorials.

2. In Tutorials, a new package called c3.

3. In c3, three new classes called EmployeeApp, Employee, and EmpFrame and a class diagram called c3diagram.

Review Questions

1. What does a frame's constructor method do?

2. What is a property?

3. Given the following label definitions and placements (and assuming all the code is correct for defining and displaying a frame with these labels):

```
Label lbl1 = new Label
("Col. Mustard in the library with the wrench");
Label lbl2 = new Label
("Mrs. White in the lounge with the knife");
Label lbl3 = new Label
("Prof. Plum in the kitchen with the gun");
        public ClueFrame() {
                lbl1.setBounds(10, 150, 75, 20);
                lbl2.setBounds(10, 150, 150, 20);
                lbl3.setBounds(10, 150, 250, 20);
                this.add(lbl2);
                this.add(lbl1);
                this.add(lbl3);
```

which of the following is the correct result, and why?

```
A. Col. Mustard in the lounge with the gun
B. Prof. Plum in the kitchen with the gun
C. Mrs. White in the library with the knife
D. Mrs. White in the lounge with the gun
E. Prof. Plum in the kitchen with the gun
```

4. Given the above label definitions and placements (and assuming all the code is correct for defining and displaying a frame with these labels) and with the following add statements replacing those above, which of the answers above is the correct result, and why?

```
this.add(lbl1);
this.add(lbl2);
this.add(lbl3);
```

5. List the following steps in order to create a frame such that an error message will not be generated:

   A. Add the Frames' components

   B. Create a Frame object and assign it to a variable

   C. Define the location

   D. Define the size

   E. Define the title

   F. Import the java.awt.Frame class

   G. Make the Frame visible

   H. Set layout property to null

6. What are AWT and Swing?

7. What are setters and getters?

8. Explain inheritance and why it is a benefit.

9. Would a frame and a label most likely be related through specialization or composition?

Review Exercise

In this exercise, you will modify the Shipment application to display the shipment information in a frame. Like the Employee application, you will create a new frame and have ShipmentApp pass a Shipment object with all the pertinent information.

1. In the ReviewEx project, create a new package called c3.

2. Select the ShipmentApp and Shipment classes in ReviewEx.c2, then copy and paste them into c3.

In c3/Shipment:

3. Change the five **String** variables to private.

4. Delete the display method.

5. Save the code and verify that there are no errors.

6. Using RAD, generate setters and getters for the five private variables.

7. Change the Shipment constructor so that the five setters are used to set the values of the five private variables to the parameter values.

8. Save the Shipment source and verify that there are no errors on the Shipment class.

9. Create a new class in c3 called ShipFrame, identify its superclass as java.awt.Frame, and do not have RAD generate any stubs.

The executable code should look like the following:

```
package c3;

import java.awt.Frame;

public class ShipFrame extends Frame {

}
```

10. Define the ShipFrame constructor such that a Shipment object must be passed and assigned to a variable called ship.

11. Define the ShipFrame title as Shipment Information, the size as 400 by 400, and position the frame 50 pixels from the left and top of the screen.

12. Create three labels and assign them to class variables called empLbl, dateTimeLbl, and shipLbl.

13. Define the labels' sizes and locations such that they will look like Figure 3-31 when displayed.

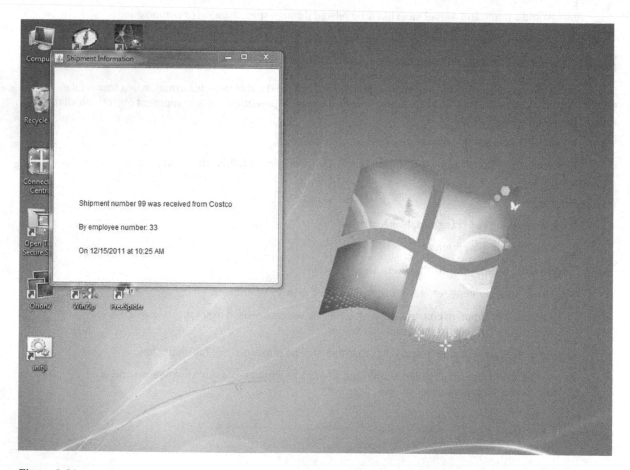

Figure 3-31.

14. Change the ShipFrame constructor such that the data is retrieved from the Shipment object and formatted to appear in the labels as in Figure 3-31.

15. Change ShipmentApp so that it does not invoke the display method but instead creates an instance of ShipFrame and passes the Shipment variable shipObj to ShipFrame's constructor.

Results of the Review Exercise

Here are the results:

1. One new package called c3 in ReviewEx project with three classes.

2. One new class called ShipFrame in c3 created as defined above.

3. Shipment and ShipmentApp modified as defined above.

Check that the Exercise Was Done Correctly

Finally, let's check the results:

1. Using RAD, verify that the new project c3 and class ShipFrame were created in the Review Exercise project.

2. Run ShipmentApp.

3. Verify that the frame is positioned and the contents displayed as in Figure 3-31.

CHAPTER 4

■ ■ ■

More GUI and the Visual Editor

This chapter will explore GUI components in more depth. We will introduce the concepts behind listeners and event driven programming. We will then, show how to implement listeners, use them to solve the "window closing" problem (from the previous chapter), and enable buttons to perform functions. In addition, we will show, in more detail, the advantages of inheritance (i.e., specialization), especially how it decreases the amount of source code that must be written by the programmer. Finally, we will introduce RAD's Visual Editor (VE). VE is a very productive tool for generating GUI classes. Through an extensive tool bar and drag and drop, VE provides a GUI for defining GUIs!

At the end of the chapter, you should understand:

> Window listeners and action listeners
>
> How to tie listeners to GUI components
>
> How and when to use specialization and composition
>
> The Visual Editor's coding standards

At the end of the chapter, you should be able to:

> Efficiently use superclass/subclass relationships
>
> Use the Visual Editor to build a GUI
>
> Enable the close button
>
> Use buttons to perform functions within an application

Listeners

We still have a big problem with our application: the close button does not work. If we installed the application on a PC, we would have to work with the Task Manager to shut the application down! This is very poor programming. There must be a better way, and there is—a listener.

Listeners are classes that implement a listener interface and that are added to visual components. In other words, just as a label is added to a frame, listeners (nonvisual classes) can be added to visual objects like a **Frame** or **Button**. You can think of a listener as a sentry. If someone approaches, the sentry asks for their ID. When the sentry hears a sound in the distance, he shouts, "Who goes there?" If no one responds, he fires a round in the air. Notice that the sentry performs different functions based on different events (or actions).

In our case, when the user performs a certain action, a specific method in the listener class will be invoked. In other words, specific methods will be called when the user clicks the close window button, when the window is opened, when a radio button is clicked, and so on. There are two catches:

- The programmer must write these methods.

- There are different types of listeners for different GUI components.

Window Listeners

Window listeners can be added to a window (and many of the **Window** subclasses like **Frame**). A window listener is on the alert for a user clicking the close window button and six other actions. For each of these possible "events" the programmer must code a unique method to handle the event. Just as the main method's header must be coded in a very specific way (name, number, and type of parameters, return value, etc.), these method headers have a specific syntax that must be followed. Another requirement is that all seven methods must be coded; if not, the JVM will return an error.

Think of the requirement in terms of the sentry example: you must tell the sentry what to do when all the possible events (in this case, seven) occur.

The following four steps must be performed to create a WindowListener:

1. Import the `WindowListener` and `WindowEvent` classes

2. Implement the WindowListener

3. Code the seven required methods

4. Add the window listener to the frame

A window listener can be created as separate class, however, a **Frame** subclass can also be defined as a window listener (i.e., it can "implement the window listener interface"). Putting the code to do this into every **Frame** subclass we create (like EmpFrame) would be very inefficient. Instead we will create a new class called UsefulFrame to hold all the "window listener code" and then make EmpFrame (and all our future frames) subclasses of UsefulFrame. In this way, all our frames inherit the window listener functionality. Sound like a good idea? I hope you said yes, because that's what we are going to do.

Tutorial: Creating a Superclass

Have you noticed that a superclass is simply a class like any other class? It's the **extends** statement (in the subclass header) that actually identifies a class as a superclass. To say it another way, it's the **extends** statement that establishes the superclass/subclass relationship.

Let's see an example:

1. In RAD, create a new package called c4 in the Tutorials project.

2. Copy the three Employee classes from c3 into c4.

3. In the Navigation Tree, click on c4.

4. On the Menu bar, click `File`, `New`, and then `Class`.

5. At the "New Java Class" window:

   - Specify the class name as UsefulFrame.

   - Specify the superclass as java.awt.Frame.

   - Do not have any other methods or stubs generated.

6. Click the Add button to begin implementing a window listener.

The "Implemented Interfaces Selection" window will be displayed. Because listeners control what happens when the user interacts with the program, the listeners are referred to as "interfaces." Instead of explicitly creating a listener object and then adding it to the GUI component (like a frame), a listener interface can be "implemented" by the GUI component class (i.e., EmpFrame). When the GUI component (EmpFrame) object is created, it is also considered a listener object. Oddly, though, you still have to add the GUI component to itself.

7.   At the "Implemented Interfaces Selection" window, start typing Window.

RAD will display a list of matching interface names.

8.   Click on **WindowListener** in the list and then the OK button.

In the "New Java Class" window, java.awt.event.WindowListener will be displayed in the Interfaces pane.

9.   On the "New Java Class" window, click the Finish button.

The source code will be redisplayed and the executable code should look like the following:

```java
package c4;

import java.awt.Frame;
import java.awt.event.WindowListener;

public class UsefulFrame extends Frame implements WindowListener {
}
```

So far, RAD has done part of step 1 and all of step 2 (of the four steps needed to enable the window listener). However, an error message is generated because step 3 has not been done. Just as we must tell the sentry what to do before he can go on guard duty, we must tell the WindowListener what to do by coding the seven methods. Each method that is not coded results in a syntax error message saying that the method must be implemented.

10.   Insert the following code before the closing brace in the class's body:

```java
public void windowClosing(WindowEvent e) {
        this.dispose();
}
public void windowClosed(WindowEvent e) {}
public void windowDeiconified(WindowEvent e) {}
public void windowIconified(WindowEvent e) {}
public void windowOpened(WindowEvent e) {}
public void windowActivated(WindowEvent e) {}
public void windowDeactivated(WindowEvent e) {}
```

Ouch, now there is an error on every line. Can you figure out the problem and solution?

As mentioned, the seven methods must be included in the class for the window listener to work. However, that doesn't mean they have to do anything. As a matter of fact, only the first method, windowClosing, does anything. To use our analogy (for the last time, I promise), we are telling the sentry/window listener to do nothing for the other six events. However, when someone clicks the close button, the frame's dispose method will be executed. The dispose method destroys (i.e., removes from main memory) the frame and all its components.

Did you figure out the cause of the error messages? Notice that the window listener passes a **WindowEvent** object to the seven methods. (Event objects contain information that can be very useful. We will use event information later when we implement multiple buttons.) The problem is that the JVM can't find the **WindowEvent** class. We must include an import statement for the **WindowEvent**.

11.   Add the following after the existing import statements (you may have to expand the code to see both import statements):

```java
import java.awt.event.WindowEvent;
```

So far, we have completed steps 1 through 3. In the constructor method, we will now add the WindowListener (UsefulFrame) to itself. You may be wondering why we do this in the constructor. Another nuance of Java is that whenever an object is created, the object's superclass constructor is automatically called by the JVM. In other words, when an EmpFrame is created, the **Frame** class's constructor method is called. We will use this feature so that all UsefulFrame subclasses automatically add the window listener and define a default size and location.

12. Add the following constructor after the class header but before the seven methods:

```java
public UsefulFrame () {
            this.setBounds(350, 200, 400, 400);
            this.addWindowListener(this);
}
```

Notice the default size is defined as 400 by 400, and the frame has been positioned at X = 350 and Y = 200 pixels, which centers it on the screen that is set at a resolution of 1024 by 768.

13. Save the UsefulFrame source code.

Tutorial: Creating a Subclass

Because UsefulFrame has all sorts of nifty code that we want included in EmpFrame, we need to define EmpFrame as a subclass of UsefulFrame.

1. In EmpFrame, change the **extends** clause from Frame to UsefulFrame.

2. Save the EmpFrame source code and run EmployeeApp.

3. Click the close button.

Pretty cool! The listener/sentry was on the job!

4. Run EmployeeApp again.

Notice that EmpFrame is not centered on the screen and does not seem to be 400 by 400. This is because EmpFrame sets the bounds as 10, 10, 300, 300. This highlights a second characteristic of the superclass/subclass relationship: subclass values and methods override inherited superclass values and methods. In other words, the EmpFrame setBounds statement overrode the superclass's setBounds statement. Let's prove that the subclass overrides the superclass.

5. In EmpFrame, comment out the frame's setBounds statement, save the source code, and run EmployeeApp.

The screen should look like Figure 4-1.

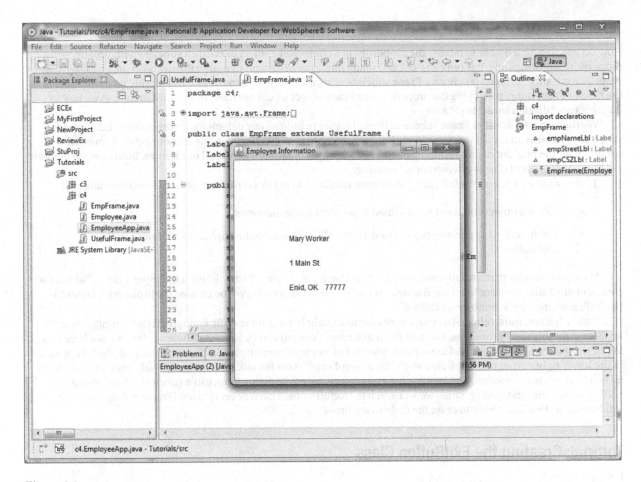

Figure 4-1.

EmpFrame inherited the size (400, 400) and location (350, 250) of UsefulFrame. Can you see how useful the superclass/subclass relationship can be? For instance, do you see any other code in EmpFrame that could go into the superclass UsefulFrame?

6. Of course, it's the setLayout statement, so add the following to UsefulFrame after the setBounds statement:

```
this.setLayout(null);
```

7. Save the UsefulFrame source code.

8. In EmpFrame, delete the setLayout statement.

9. Save the EmpFrame source code.

Specialization vs. Composition

How do you decide whether to modify the properties of a component object or create a subclass with unique properties? Unfortunately, it is not clear-cut and many times the programmer makes the decision on a case-by-case basis. For instance, should you create a **Frame** subclass or simply create a **Frame** object and modify its properties? In the case of EmpFrame, modifying the properties of a **Frame** object would not meet our requirements, so we had to define a specialized frame (EmpFrame).

We then created another **Frame** subclass (UsefulFrame) to hold all our default frame properties and methods. When we establish an "is a" (superclass/subclass) relationship between UsefulFrame and our other frames, we will cut down on the amount of programming needed and ensure consistency across all our frames. Both of these benefits are important goals of object-oriented programming.

To reiterate, we created UsefulFrame (as a **Frame** subclass) to act as a repository of source code because:

- A **Frame** object could not be modified to perform those functions

- The functions and properties defined in UsefulFrame need to be applied to all frames in the application

Have you noticed that UsefulFrame, despite its name, really doesn't do anything? It is simply a class that has the common attributes we want in all our frames. No UsefulFrame object will ever be created or displayed. Classes like UsefulFrame are known as **abstract** classes.

Unlike frames, most other GUI components (buttons, labels, etc.) are specific enough that we simply create instances, modify their properties, and add them to a frame (composition). However, there are instances where you might want to create subclasses of these components. For example, creating an ExitButton class that always appears in the lower right corner of every frame would be a useful subclass of Button. Why, you ask? Well, instead of defining an exit button's text, function, and location for every frame, we could define it once in a subclass. Then, instead of adding an exit button to every frame, we will add it to UsefulFrame. This way every UsefulFrame subclass will have an exit button and we don't have to enter the code many times.

Tutorial: Creating the ExitButton Class

Let's get started:

1. Create a new class in Tutorials/c4 called ExitButton. Define the superclass as java.awt. Button, and do not have any other methods or stubs generated.

The code should look like the following:

```
package c4;
import java.awt.Button;
public class ExitButton extends Button {
}
```

Like most visual classes, a button's location and size are set by the setBounds statement. To define the text that will appear on the button, the setLabel method is used.

2. Add the following statements to create a constructor and initialize the button:

```
public ExitButton() {
        this.setBounds(350, 370, 40, 20);
        this.setLabel("Exit");
}
```

3. Save the ExitButton source code.

To add the ExitButton to UsefulFrame (i.e., to relate them through composition), we must create an ExitButton object in UsefulFrame and then add it to UsefulFrame.

4. Add the following statement immediately after the UsefulFrame class header:

```
private ExitButton eb=new ExitButton();
```

This creates an ExitButton class variable called eb and assigns an ExitButton object to eb.

5. Add the following statement to the constructor, then format, and save the source code.

```
this.add(eb);
```

This statement adds the ExitButton object to UsefulFrame. The UsefulFrame executable source code should look like the following:

```
package c4;

import java.awt.Frame;
import java.awt.event.WindowListener;
import java.awt.event.WindowEvent;

public class UsefulFrame extends Frame implements WindowListener {
        private ExitButton eb=new ExitButton();
        public UsefulFrame () {
                    this.setBounds(350, 200, 400, 400);
                    this.setLayout(null);
                    this.addWindowListener(this);
                    this.add(eb);
        }

        public void windowClosing(WindowEvent e) {
                    this.dispose();
        }
        public void windowClosed(WindowEvent e) {}
        public void windowDeiconified(WindowEvent e) {}
        public void windowIconified(WindowEvent e) {}
        public void windowOpened(WindowEvent e) {}
        public void windowActivated(WindowEvent e) {}
        public void windowDeactivated(WindowEvent e) {}
}
```

6. Run EmployeeApp.

The frame should look like Figure 4-2.

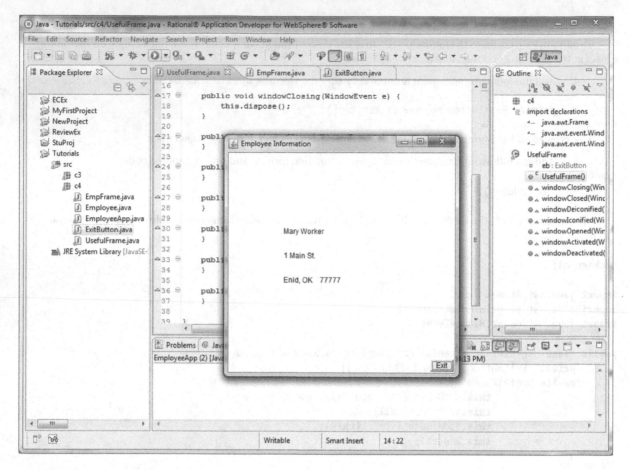

Figure 4-2.

Lookin' good, but there are some potential problems. Let's find them.

Tutorial: Making the Superclass More Flexible

Now we have to find the problems with the current code:

1. In EmpFrame, uncomment the setBounds statement.

2. Save the EmpFrame source code and run EmployeeApp.

Notice anything missing? That's right, no exit button.

3. Click and drag the lower right corner of EmpFrame to make it larger.

Notice that when the frame is enlarged, the exit button is shown (see Figure 4-3).

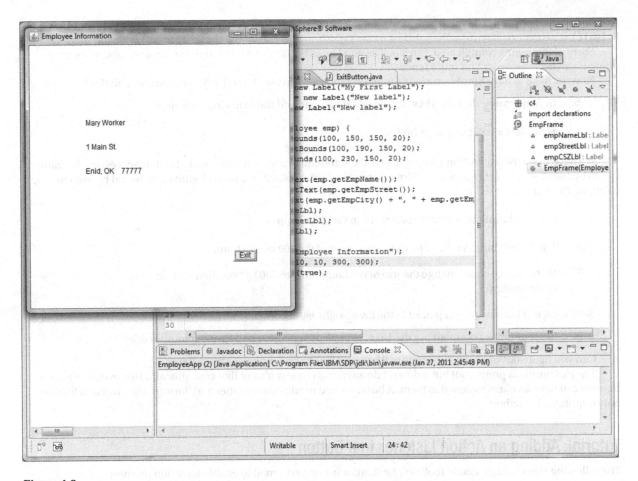

Figure 4-3.

So what happened? Because EmpFrame set the frame size to 300 by 300 and the button was placed at 350 and 370, the button was not visible. We need a method (setExitButtonLocation) to change the location of the ExitButton based on the size of each UsefulFrame subclass.

The width and height of a frame are properties (that we have set and reset many times in the examples). If a property can be set, it can also be retrieved. Can you guess the names of the methods that will return the width and height of the frame? Our new method, setExitButtonLocation, will retrieve the width and height of the frame and calculate the exit button's location as 50 pixels from the right side of the frame (the width) and 30 pixels from the bottom of the frame (the height).

4. After the UsefulFrame constructor, add the following and then save the source:

```
public void setExitButtonLocation() {
eb.setLocation(this.getWidth()-50, this.getHeight()-30);
}
```

Notice that eb's (the exit button's) location is defined with a setLocation method (which eb inherited from the **Button** class). Within the setLocation statement, we want to use the UsefulFrame subclass's size to calculate the location (instead of specifying a fixed location as we did in all past examples). This means that the setExitButtonLocation method must be executed in the UsefulFrame subclasses (so that **this** will refer to the subclass).

109

In other words, by making the subclass execute the setExitButtonLocation method, the **this.getWidth()** and **this.get Height()** statements will retrieve the subclass frame's width and height not the Useful-Frame's width and height.

Sorry, if this seems complicated, but it is. The good news is that, as you use superclasses and subclasses more often, it will become easier and more familiar.

Now we need to have EmpFrame (a UsefulFrame subclass) invoke the setExitButtonLocation method.

5. In EmpFrame, after the **this.**setBounds statement, add the following statement:

```
this.setExitButtonLocation();
```

We have to set the exit button's location after the setBounds statement because that statement resizes the frame to 300 by 300. If we place it before the setBounds statement, the default size from UsefulFrame would be used to calculate the location.

6. Save the EmpFrame source code and run EmployeeApp.

Notice that the exit button now appears in the corner of the 300 by 300 frame.

7. In the source code, change the size of the EmpFrame to 500 by 600, then save and run EmployeeApp.

Notice the exit button is again placed in the lower-right-hand corner.

8. In EmpFrame, comment out the **this.**setBounds statement and save the source code.

Can you figure out what size the frame will be now? If not, run EmployeeApp and see.

The exit button is pretty cool but it doesn't do anything! (I guess it's not that cool after all.) However, like frames, buttons can have listeners assigned to them. A button is tied to an action listener and, fortunately, an action listener only requires one method.

Tutorial: Adding an Action Listener to a Button

The following steps (which should look very familiar) must be performed to enable an action listener:

1. Import the `ActionListener` and `ActionEvent` classes

2. Implement the action listener

3. Code an actionPerformed method

4. Add the action listener to the button

This time we will perform the steps in the order of 1, 3, 2, 4. This will prevent any error messages from being generated as we enter the code. Why? When the **implements** keyword is entered (step 2), the syntax checker automatically looks for the required import statements and actionPerformed method. Therefore, we will add these statements (steps 1 and 3) before we insert the **implements** keyword (step 2).

1. In ExitButton, add the following statements:

```
import java.awt.event.ActionListener;
import java.awt.event.ActionEvent;
```

2. After the ExitButton constructor, add the following:

```
public void actionPerformed(ActionEvent e){
}
```

3. In the ExitButton header after **extends** Button, add the following:

    implements ActionListener

Notice no error messages were generated because we already coded the actionPerformed method!

4. In the ExitButton constructor, enter the following statement:

    this.addActionListener(**this**);

At this point, you have defined and assigned an action listener to the exit button. Now we need to define what should be done when the exit button is clicked. Can you figure out where to add that code?

5. In the actionPerformed method, add the following statement:

    System.exit(0);

You may not remember, but earlier we availed ourselves of the very useful **System** class. The **System** class had an object (**out**) whose method (**println**) was used to display text in the console. The **System** class also has an exit method that ends the JVM. The result of the exit method (the frame disappears) seems the same as the result of the dispose method; however, this is because our application is relatively simple. If multiple frames in the application had been displayed, exit would destroy all of them (plus any nonvisual objects). The dispose method only destroys the object it is used in.

6. Save the ExitButton source code and run EmployeeApp.

7. Click the Exit button.

Yay, a working button!

Figure 4-4 shows the Employee classes, their relationships to each other, and their relationships to some of the JRE classes. Notice the new implements relationship, shown as a dotted line and an open triangle arrowhead (e.g., between UsefulFrame and WindowListener and ExitButton and ActionListener).

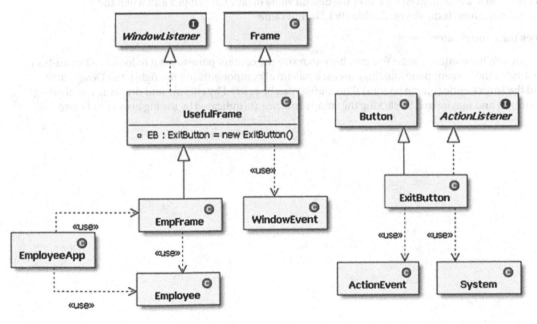

Figure 4-4.

You have done well, Grasshopper. For all your hard work, we will now use something fun, the Visual Editor (VE). In addition to being fun, VE will save you from a lot of coding and let you create GUIs faster and with fewer errors.

Visual Editor

The Visual Editor (VE) is a GUI tool that makes it much easier to define visual classes. VE will automatically be invoked when creating a visual class. You can also use VE to edit any class by right-clicking on the class in the navigation tree and selecting Open With, then Visual Editor. However, source code that does not follow VE coding standards is not easy to change with VE. So, the bottom line is that when using VE, it is best to start with a new class. In addition, VE's source code may seem very confusing at first. As with any "source code generator," the source code is more complex than is usually necessary. (For instance, if you generate a Web page using page generator, the HTML source is unbelievably complex and bewildering.) Generators do this so that the most complex enhancements can be added to the source code. So be aware that there is a downside when dealing with VE or any tool that generates source code.

Tutorial: Creating a Visual Class with VE

Let's use VE to create a new frame with some added bells and whistles.

1. Select c4 in the navigation tree, and then click File, New, and Visual Class.

The "New Java Visual Class" window will be displayed. It has all the options as the "New Java Class" window (that we have used previously) plus a Style pane in the lower left. The Style pane allows you to choose the superclass from a navigation tree. The navigation tree contains all the visual components in the three GUI sets. In this case, however, we want our new frame to be a subclass of UsefulFrame.

2. First, specify EmployeeFrame as the class name.

3. In the Style navigation tree, click Other and then click the Browse button.

4. In the Choose a type field type c4. over the default value of java.lang.Object and when the UsefulFrame item is displayed, double click UsefulFrame.

5. Click the Finish button.

VE crams a lot into the content pane. (You may have to resize the content pane to get it to look like Figure 4-5.) Essentially, VE divides the content pane into three areas: a palette of components (on the right), the Design area (at the top), and the source code (on the bottom). These areas can be resized by clicking and dragging the dividing borders or minimized and maximized by clicking the small arrowheads (indicated by the big arrows in Figure 4-5).

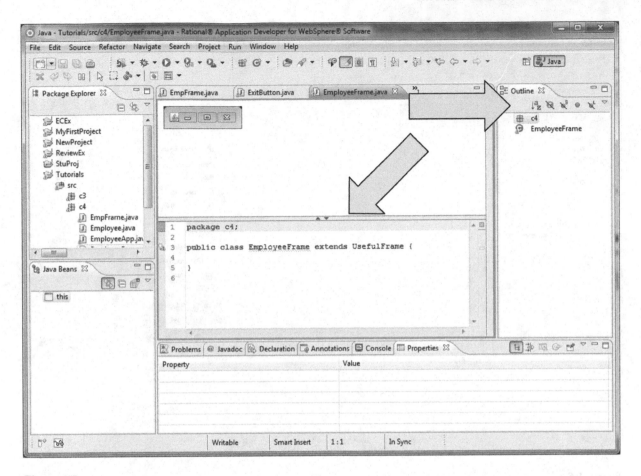

Figure 4-5.

6. Click the source code minimize arrow and the palette maximize arrow so the content area looks like Figure 4-6.

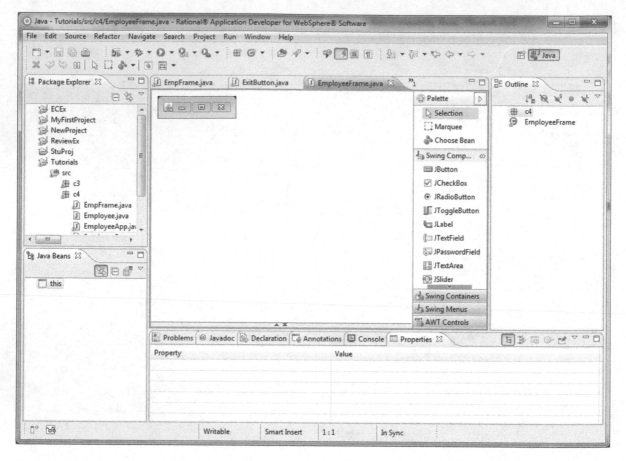

Figure 4-6.

In the component palette, there are four trays of classes indicated by a button with the name of the components (Swing Components, Swing Containers, Swing Menus, AWT Controls). Initially, the Swing Components tray is open. The various component trays can be opened and closed by clicking on the component title buttons.

7. Click the Swing Components button to close the tray, and then click the AWT Controls button to display the AWT components.

Notice that the **Label** class is listed, as well as many other components. Clicking a listed component and then clicking in the Design area will create and place the component on the frame. But, before we do that, we need to specify some EmployeeFrame properties.

8. In the Design area, click on the frame title bar to select it.

Notice that the Properties view (at the bottom of the screen) becomes active. The Properties view is very useful. We will move it where the Outline view is currently displayed so that we can easily access it.

9. Click and drag the Properties tab view to where the Outline view is currently displayed (the far right of the screen).

The Properties view displays all of the selected components properties and values. Currently you have to scroll quite a bit to the right to see the values column. The width of any column can be adjusted by clicking and dragging the column title separator (at the top of the column).

10. Adjust the Property column and the width of the Properties view so that the property names and values can be seen in Figure 4-7.

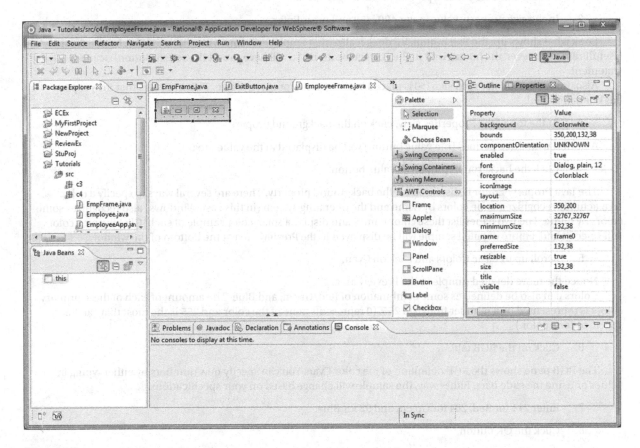

Figure 4-7.

Property values can be easily changed either by entering new values in the Properties view or by manipulating the frame in the Design area. You should be aware that the values displayed are a little misleading because VE does not capture the properties that are set in the superclass (UsefulFrame) constructor. Notice that the Properties view shows the EmployeeFrame size is 123 by 34 (this is the amount of space needed to display a minimal frame title bar). If an EmployeeFrame object were created, the size specified in UsefulFrame would override this default size. The point is that VE Design pane does not always show how the object will appear when instantiated.

Tutorial: Modifying Properties

Let's look at modifying properties:

1. In the Design pane, click and drag on the lower-right-hand corner of the frame.

Notice that the value for the size property is no longer 132, 38.

2. In the size property value, enter **400, 450** and press Enter.

Look what shows up: the Exit button. VE does realize that EmployeeFrame will inherit the Exit button from UsefulFrame; however, the button isn't in the correct location. We will have to add the setExitButtonLocation statement.

Also, notice the greater than sign (>) is placed before the size property name. This indicates that the property has been modified.

3. At the top of the Properties view, click on the background property.

A button with three periods (the value button) will be displayed in the value area.

4. Click the background property's value button.

The Java Property Editor is displayed for the background property. There are several ways to specify a color. Java actually recognizes some colors by name and the operating system (in this case Windows) also recognizes some colors by name. The two panes list these color names and display a small color sample of each. Clicking on a color will select it and a more detailed sample will be displayed in the Preview area at the bottom of the window.

5. Scroll up in Basic Colors and click on Cyan.

Notice the more detailed sample in the Preview area.

Colors can also be defined as some combination of Red, Green, and Blue. The amount of each of these primary colors is represented by a number from 0 to 255. (0 represents none of the color and 255 is the most that can be specified for a color.)

6. Click on the RGB tab.

The RGB pane shows the RGB definition of the color Cyan. You can specify new numbers by either typing in values or using the slide bars. Either way, the sample will change based on your specifications.

7. Enter 211 for Red, 204 for Green, and 92 for Blue.

8. Click the OK button.

Notice that the background property value has been changed to 211, 204, 92. That is not a very attractive color, is it? The other color tabs on the Java Property Editor window allow you to pick from a larger set of samples (Swatches) or specify the color by clicking on an "infinite" color palette (HSB).

9. Change the background property to lightGray, the title property to Employee Information and save the code.

The frame should look like Figure 4-8.

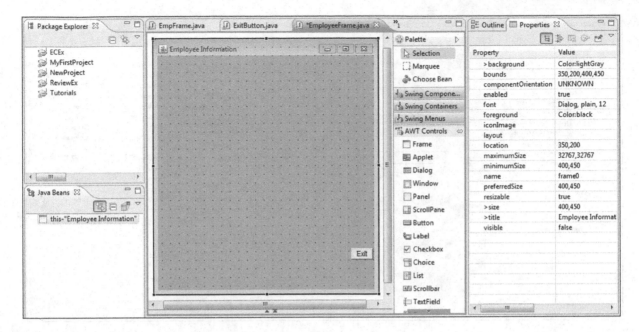

Figure 4-8.

Tutorial: Adding Visual Components

It's now time to look at adding visual components:

1. In the AWT Controls list, click on Label, and then click anywhere on the frame content area.

2. At the name window, specify nameLbl as the label name and click the OK button.

A small label will be placed on the frame (outlined, with resize handles, and the text Label). You can manipulate the size of the label by clicking and dragging the resize handles. The location can be changed by clicking and dragging on the label outline.

3. In the Properties view, change the label location to 80 by 200 and the size to 150 by 20.

The frame should look like Figure 4-9.

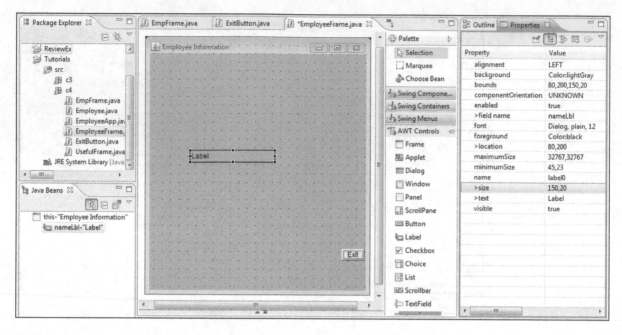

Figure 4-9.

4. At the bottom of the Design pane, click the maximize pane arrow (the arrowhead with a line across the top) to display the source code.

VE generated some comments but the following is the generated source code:

```java
package c4;

import java.awt.Dimension;
import java.awt.Color;
import java.awt.Label;
import java.awt.Rectangle;
import java.awt.Point;
public class EmployeeFrame extends UsefulFrame {

    private Label nameLbl=null;

    public EmployeeFrame() {
        super();
        initialize();
    }

    private void initialize() {
nameLbl=new Label();
nameLbl.setText("Label");
nameLbl.setLocation(new Point(80, 200));
nameLbl.setSize(new Dimension(150, 20));
```

```
this.setSize(new Dimension(400, 450));
this.setTitle("Employee Information");
this.setBackground(Color.lightGray);
this.add(nameLbl, null);

    }

}
```

Let's examine some of the VE coding standards.

Inside the constructor, VE explicitly calls the superclass's constructor (**super();**). We mentioned earlier that the JVM does this automatically. However, it is slightly more efficient to call it explicitly, so that's what VE does.

VE creates a method called initialize that sets the frame's property values and adds the components. Notice the new setter setBackground. VE added this statement when we defined the background property. The color name (Color.lightGray) brings up an interesting point regarding importing. Normally we have imported classes (e.g., **Label**, **Frame**) and then created objects of these classes. In this case, we imported the class **Color** but specified (used) a specific variable (lightGray) within the class. Obviously, lightGray is a public variable!

In the constructor, the initialize method is invoked by its name alone. We have been using the prefix "this" before all class methods (for instance, **this**.add or **this**.setSize) to clearly define what object the method belongs to. In actuality, the JVM assumes any unqualified method (or variable) names belong to the current object. So, setSize or setTitle can be used (instead of **this**.setSize or **this**.setTitle) and work correctly.

VE also uses **Point** and **Dimension** objects to hold the x, y coordinates for locations, and sizes rather then simply specify the coordinates. Lastly, notice that when adding the label component a value of **null** is also passed. When using layout managers, you can specify where components are added with an index value (e.g., in Border layout you could specify East, West, North, South, or Center). Because EmployeeFrame does not use a layout manager, RAD explicitly specifies **null**, even though **null** is assumed.

To sum up, sometimes VE is overly explicit (i.e., VE doesn't use short cuts). But, as VE is typing the code, the programmer should be able to accept RAD's little eccentricities.

5. Minimize the source code pane to redisplay the Design area.

Tutorial: Adding to the Frame

We now need to add the frame:

1. Add two more labels and accept the default names.

2. Move and resize the labels so that they look similar to Figure 4-10.

Notice the label names assigned by VE (see the arrow in Figure 4-10).

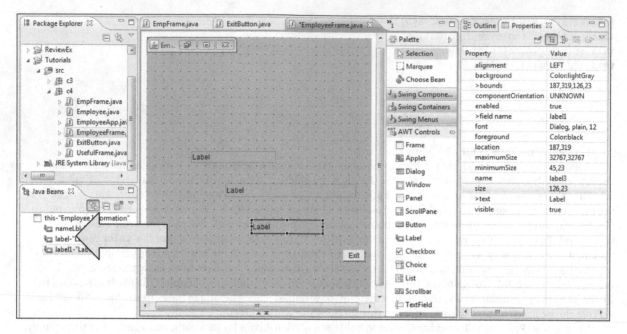

Figure 4-10.

3. Press and hold the Ctrl key, then click on each label in order from bottom to top.

The labels should all be selected and nameLbl (the top label) should be the anchor (indicated with the solid black resize handles as in Figure 4-11).

4. Click on the Show customize layout window button (indicated by the arrow in Figure 4-11).

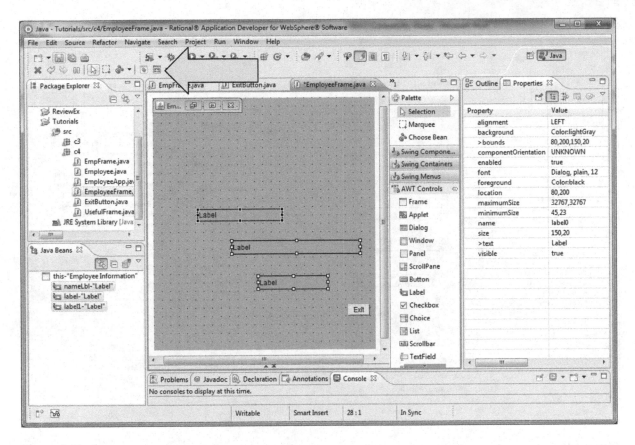

Figure 4-11.

The Customize Layout window will be displayed (see Figure 4-12).

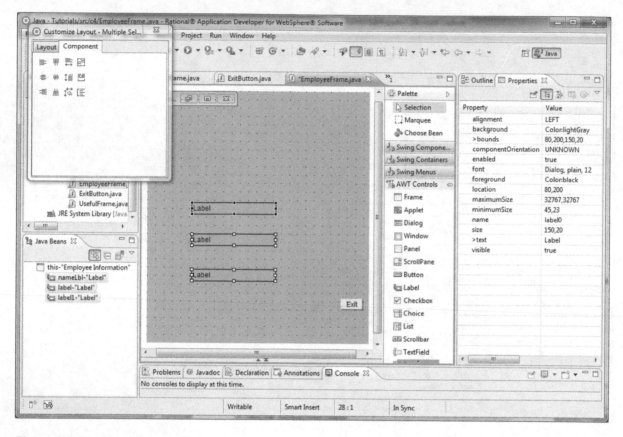

Figure 4-12.

5. If the Component options are not displayed in the Customize Layout window, click the Component tab.

Components can be quickly aligned (both horizontally and vertically) and resized by clicking on the various buttons in the Customize Layout window. For instance, we will left align all three labels, make them the same size, and evenly distribute them vertically.

6. Click on Align left (the button in the first row and first column of the Alignment window).

The two new labels will move left to align with nameLbl (the anchor).

7. Click on Match width (the button in the first row, third column).

The two new labels will be resized to match nameLbl in length.

8. Click on Match height (second row, third column).

The labels will be resized to match nameLbl in height and should look like Figure 4-12. Finally, we would like to have the same amount of vertical space between the labels.

9. Click on Distribute vertically (third row, fourth column).

Although this option does put an equal distance between the labels, it also distributes them over the entire frame. Instead, we want to spread the labels evenly over the area where they were originally defined.

10. If needed, drag the Customize Layout window out of the upper-left-hand corner of the screen, so that the Menu bar Edit option is shown.

11. Click Edit, and then Undo Typing.

The labels will be returned to their previous locations. (By the way, don't forget about Undo while working through the Tutorials. If you make a mistake on a step or several steps, simply keep selecting Undo until you are back in sync with the Tutorial.)

12. In the Customize Layout window, click the Show distribute box button (first row, fourth column).

This selects the current area occupied by the selected components as the area of distribution. The area of distribution can be changed by clicking and dragging the blue resize handles. In this case, we want to keep this default area, so we will not make any adjustments.

13. Click on Distribute vertically button (third row, fourth column) again.

This time, the labels are evenly spread over the originally defined area.

14. Close the Customize Layout window.

15. Click on the white area outside the frame to deselect all components.

We need to give the new labels meaningful names. VE provides a very easy way to rename components.

16. Right-click on the second label and select "Rename field" from the shortcut menu.

17. Specify streetLbl as the new name and click the OK button.

Displaying the source code would show that the label has been renamed throughout the class. (By the way, this is much easier than using the Find/Replace function in the source code.)

18. Change the bottom label's name to cSZLbl and save EmployeeFrame.

Tutorial: Finishing the Application

VE's GUI can only do so much. Eventually programmers have to work directly with the source code. In EmployeeFrame, we have to change the constructor to accept an Employee variable. In addition, we have to:

1. Create a class level Employee variable

2. Assign the method Employee variable to the class Employee variable

3. Add code to move the Employee object's information to the labels

4. Make the frame visible

5. Fix the location of the Exit button

6. Change EmployeeApp to create an EmployeeFrame object (instead of EmpFrame)

7. Display the source code and modify the EmployeeFrame constructor to accept an Employee variable called employee.

If you are unsure of how to do this, refer to the EmpFrame constructor as an example.

1. Create a **private** class Employee variable called emp.

2. In the constructor, assign employee to emp so that the initialize method will be able to access the Employee object.

3. In the initialize method, change the three label's setText statements so that the appropriate property values from the Employee object are displayed.

Again, if you are unsure of how to do this, refer to the EmpFrame constructor. (Note that the names of the labels in EmpFrame are different from EmployeeFrame.)

4. At the end of the initialize method, invoke the method that recalculates the exit button location.

If you are unsure of the statement syntax, refer to the EmpFrame constructor.

5. Switch back to the design pane, select the frame, and in the Properties view, change the visible property value to true.

Note where VE places the setVisible statement.

6. Save the EmployeeFrame source code.

Now we need to change the application to use EmployeeFrame instead of EmpFrame.

7. In EmployeeApp, change the last statement so that an EmployeeFrame object is created, not an EmpFrame object.

8. Format and save the EmployeeApp source code then run EmployeeApp.

The frame should look like Figure 4-13.

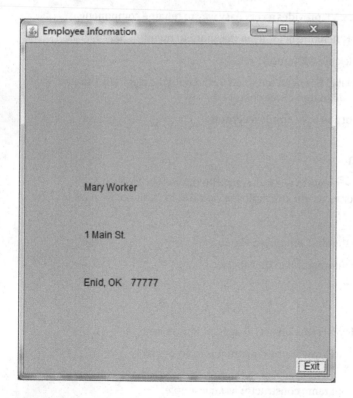

Figure 4-13.

9. Click the Exit button to shut down the application.

The EmployeeFrame executable source code should look like the following:

```java
package c4;

import java.awt.Dimension;
import java.awt.Color;
import java.awt.Label;
import java.awt.Rectangle;
import java.awt.Point;

public class EmployeeFrame extends UsefulFrame {

        private Label nameLbl=null;
        private Label streetLbl=null;
        private Label cSZLbl=null;
        private Employee emp;

        public EmployeeFrame(Employee employee) {
                super();
                this.emp=employee;
                initialize();
        }

        private void initialize() {
cSZLbl=new Label();
cSZLbl.setBounds(new Rectangle(80, 318, 150, 20));
cSZLbl.setText(      emp.getEmpCity()+", " +
        emp.getEmpState()+" " +
      emp.getEmpZip());
streetLbl=new Label();
streetLbl.setBounds(new Rectangle(80, 263, 150, 20));
streetLbl.setText(emp.getEmpStreet());
nameLbl=new Label();
nameLbl.setText(emp.getEmpName());
nameLbl.setLocation(new Point(80, 200));
nameLbl.setSize(new Dimension(150, 20));
this.setSize(new Dimension(400, 450));
this.setTitle("Employee Information");
this.setBackground(Color.lightGray);
this.setVisible(true);
this.add(nameLbl, null);
this.add(streetLbl, null);
this.add(cSZLbl, null);
        this.setExitButtonLocation();
        }
}
```

The EmployeeApp executable code should look like the following:

```
package c4;

public class EmployeeApp {

public static void main(String[] args) {
Employee emp = new Employee("Mary Worker", "1 Main
St.", "Enid", "OK", "77777");
        EmployeeFrame ef = new EmployeeFrame(emp);
}
}
```

Tutorial: Breaking the Code with VE

Not only does VE make building a GUI very easy, but because the GUI is displayed while being defined, the programmer is much less likely to make mistakes. For instance, in VE the programmer can easily see when labels overlap. When specifying locations in the source, it is very difficult for a programmer to "see" where all components are in relation to one another. In addition, it usually takes the programmer many attempts to define the component sizes and spacing so that they are visually appealing. However, even with all of VE's wonderful features, the programmer can still screw up.

1. In the EmployeeFrame Design view, drag the second label (streetLbl) so that it overlaps the first label (nameLbl) and save the source code.

Notice that VE lets you define overlapping components and doesn't even generate an error message.

2. Click Edit, and then Undo Typing.

Notice that Undo lets you reverse changes even after the source code has been saved. However, because Undo made a new change (the reversal), the code needs to be saved again.

3. Select all three labels. (The order does not matter this time.)

The style, size, and color of text can be specified for many visual components. In this case, we will change the size and color of all three labels at once.

4. In the Properties view, click on the background property to display the property value button, and then display the Java Property Editor by clicking on the value button.

5. Select Yellow and then click the OK button.

6. Display the Java Property Editor for the foreground property.

7. Select Blue and then click the OK button.

8. Display the Java Property Editor for the font property.

9. In the Size pane, select 36 for the text size and click OK.

EmployeeFrame should look like Figure 4-14. Notice anything wrong?

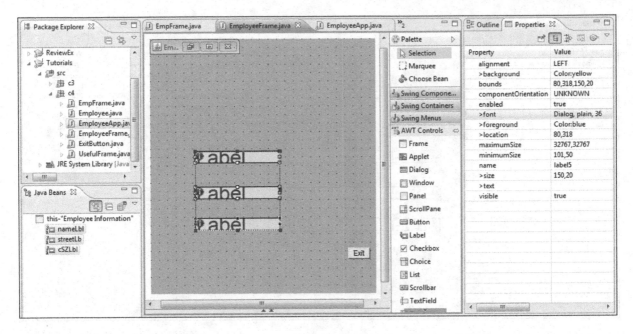

Figure 4-14.

Fortunately, we never changed the initial text (Label) in the labels, so we are able to see that the text size is too large to be entirely displayed.

10.   Run EmployeeApp.

Notice that the labels are now not long enough to fit all the text either.

11.   Click the Exit button to shut down the application.

12.   In the EmployeeFrame design view, redisplay the Customize layout window and click the Hide Distribution Box button (first row, fourth column) so that the distribution box is no longer displayed.

13.   Click and drag cSZLbl's right side middle resize handle so that the right edge of the label lines up with the left edge of the Exit button, see Figure 4-15.

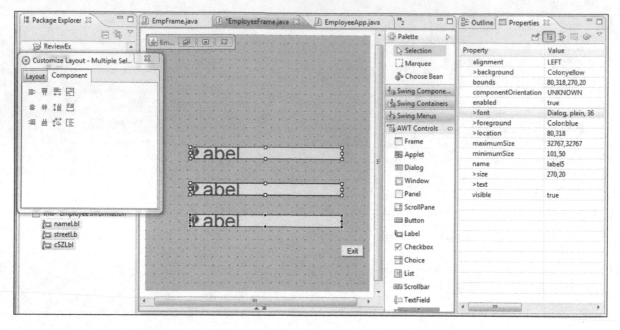

Figure 4-15.

Because all three labels are selected, all of the labels are resized.

14. On cSZLbl's the bottom edge, click the middle resize handle and drag so that the label's bottom edge almost touches the top of the Exit button (see Figure 4-16).

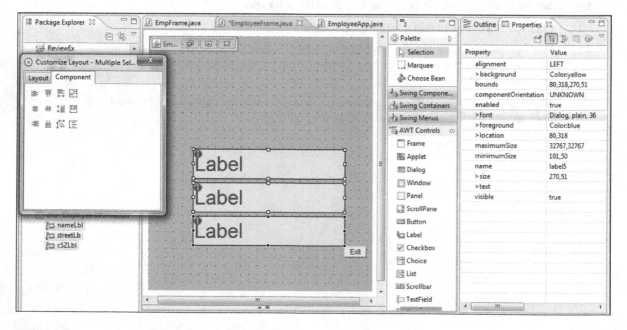

Figure 4-16.

Don't worry that the third label is so close to the Exit button. VE displays the frame according to the property values specified in the initialization method. The Exit button's location will be reset to the lower-right-hand corner of the frame in the constructor.

Now we'll test to see if the new labels are long enough.

15. Close the Customize Layout window.

16. Run EmployeeApp.

The zip text almost fits in the labels. Should we resize the labels again?

Enid is only a four-letter city. What if we tried to display Jacksonville? It probably would not fit. So really we need to decrease the font size—but by how much? Usually, a programmer would determine the largest value that must fit in the label and use that value to select the correct font size.

17. In the Design view of EmployeeFrame, click the cSZLbl label to select it and then click the label again.

An input text box will be displayed where new label text can be specified.

18. Enter "Jacksonville, FL 32246" (as seen in Figure 4-17) and press Enter.

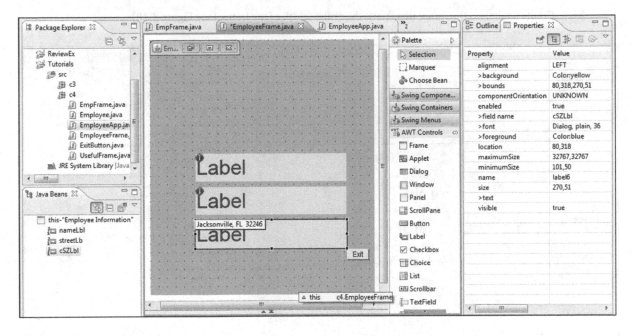

Figure 4-17.

Because none of the zip code can fit in the label, we will change the font size. This time instead of selecting a size, we will specify a size.

19. Select all three labels, display the Java Property Editor for the font property, and in the Size field type 26 over the current value of 36.

Notice that sizes not listed can be specified. This is not true for all properties. For example, for Name and Style you can only choose among the listed options.

20. In the Name field, replace Dialog with Sims and hit the OK button.

Notice that VE selected SimSun as the Font Name. Because there is no Font called Sims, VE chooses the first valid Font Name that would alphabetically follow the characters specified. In this case, SimSun is alphabetically the first Font Name that follows the characters Sims.

21.　Click Undo.

Notice that VE resets both the font name and the size.

We still have a little problem. If you look at the source code, notice that the setText statement for cSZLbl defines the static text of "Jacksonville, FL 32246" for the field. We need to change that back so the employee information is displayed.

22.　Click Undo Typing until the original setText statement for cSZLbl is inserted.

23.　Specify 26 as the font size of all three labels and save the source code.

"Jacksonville, FL 32246" will now fit, but there is one more problem. Notice that the labels are not centered horizontally on the frame. When we aligned the labels, it was in relation to each other. The labels need to be aligned in relation to the frame. It would be nice if we could include the frame in our component selection and then realign. Unfortunately, the Customize Layout window does not offer any options when a frame is selected as a component. So, we will do a little "end run" around VE.

24.　Create a label on the frame that spans the entire width of the frame (see Figure 4-18).

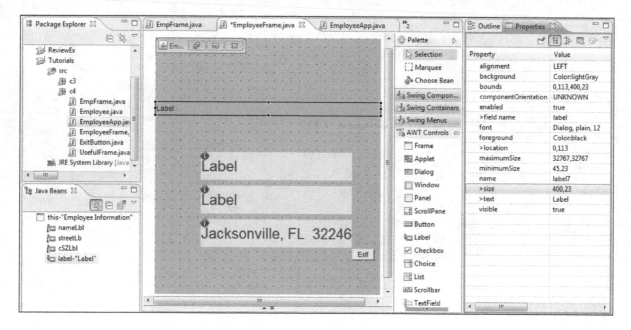

Figure 4-18.

25.　Select all four labels with the newest label as the anchor.

26.　Display the Customize Layout window and click on the Align center button (first column, second row).

Because the label was the same width as the frame, the labels will be centered on the frame (see Figure 4-19). Notice that the labels no longer align with the edge of the Exit button.

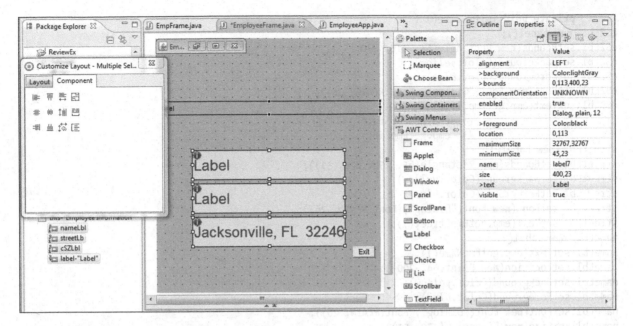

Figure 4-19.

27. Delete the new label and save the source code.

In the source code, notice that all the new setter methods that are invoked to control the appearance of the labels.
The executable code for EmployeeFrame should be the following (if your source code does not match, modify
it so that it does):

```
package c4;

import java.awt.Dimension;
import java.awt.Color;
import java.awt.Label;
import java.awt.Rectangle;
import java.awt.Point;
import java.awt.Font;

public class EmployeeFrame extends UsefulFrame {

        private Label nameLbl=null;
        private Label streetLbl=null;
        private Label cSZLbl=null;
        private Employee emp;

        public EmployeeFrame(Employee employee) {
                super();
                this.emp=employee;
                initialize();
        }
```

```
        private void initialize() {
cSZLbl = new Label();
cSZLbl.setBounds(new Rectangle(64, 318, 270, 51));
cSZLbl.setBackground(Color.yellow);
cSZLbl.setForeground(Color.blue);
cSZLbl.setFont(new Font("Dialog", Font.PLAIN, 26));
cSZLbl.setText(emp.getEmpCity()+", " +
                        emp.getEmpState()+" " +
                        emp.getEmpZip());
streetLbl = new Label();
streetLbl.setBounds(new Rectangle(65, 259, 270, 51));
streetLbl.setBackground(Color.yellow);
streetLbl.setForeground(Color.blue);
streetLbl.setFont(new Font("Dialog", Font.PLAIN, 26));
streetLbl.setText(emp.getEmpStreet());
nameLbl = new Label();
nameLbl.setText(emp.getEmpName());
nameLbl.setLocation(new Point(64, 200));
nameLbl.setBackground(Color.yellow);
nameLbl.setForeground(Color.blue);
nameLbl.setFont(new Font("Dialog", Font.PLAIN, 26));
nameLbl.setSize(new Dimension(270, 51));
this.setSize(new Dimension(400, 450));
this.setTitle("Employee Information");
this.setBackground(Color.lightGray);
this.setVisible(true);
this.add(nameLbl, null);
this.add(streetLbl, null);
this.add(cSZLbl, null);
this.setExitButtonLocation();

    }

}
```

Results of the Tutorial

Here is what we have as a result of the tutorial:

- A new package called c4, with six java files.

- EmployeeApp changed as specified in the Tutorial.

- UsefulFrame, ExitButton, and EmployeeFrame defined as specified in Tutorial.

To verify that the tutorial was done correctly:

1. Run EmployeeApp and verify the EmployeeFrame is displayed as in Figure 4-20.

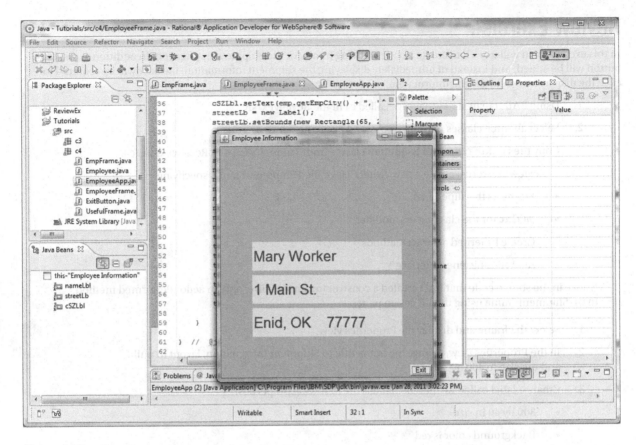

Figure 4-20.

2. Click the Exit button and verify the EmployeeFrame is no longer displayed.

3. Run EmployeeApp, click the Close button, and verify the EmployeeFrame is no longer displayed.

Review Questions

1. How does a window listener work? What other objects, methods, and/or variables does the WindowListener work with?

2. What does the VE-generated initialize method do?

3. What are the four steps for adding a listener?

4. Name at least two ways that a property value can be defined in VE.

5. What is the RGB pane?

6. What are the three VE work areas?

7. In VE, what is an anchor?

Review Exercise

In this exercise, you will use VE to create a better-looking frame for the Shipment application. In addition, a display button will be added, and instead of immediately displaying the shipment information, the user will be required to click the display button to see the information.

1. Using RAD, create a new package called c4 in the ReviewEx/src.

2. Select all three classes in c3 then copy and paste them into c4.

3. Copy the UsefulFrame and ExitButton classes from Tutorial/src/c4 to ReviewEx/src/c4.

4. In ReviewEx/src/c4, create a new visual Class called ShipmentFrame, specifying:

    *   Frame as the superclass

    *   **public** for the class access modifier

    *   Create Inherited abstract methods

    *   An ActionListener interface

Notice in the source code that RAD created a constructor, an initialize, and an actionPerformed method. In c4/ShipmentFrame using the VE design pane:

1. Select the frame and display the Properties view.

2. In the Properties view, change the frame title to Shipment Information, layout to null, and the size to 400 by 350.

3. Create a label called headerLbl that has the following properties:

    *   300 by 40 in size

    *   Background color is red

    *   Located just below the frame title bar (38 pixels from the top) and centered horizontally

    *   Contains the text "TNT Salvage"

    *   The text is centered within the label

    *   The text is Arial and 24 in size

4. In the source code, change the superclass to UsefulFrame and delete the **Frame** import statement.

5. Create and add a button called displayButton to the frame. The button's properties should be as follows:

    *   60 by 20 in size

    *   Centered horizontally

    *   Its bottom edge should align with the Exit button's bottom edge

    *   Have the text "Display" appear on the button

6. Add three labels called shipLbl, empLbl, and dateTimeLbl to the bottom half of the frame with the following properties:

- 300 by 20 in size

- Centered horizontally on the frame

- Separated from each other vertically by 10 pixels

- The last label should be separated from the displayButton by 15 pixels

- The label text color should be defined with RGB values of 0, 0, 153 and be centered

within the label

In VE, the frame should look like Figure 4-21.

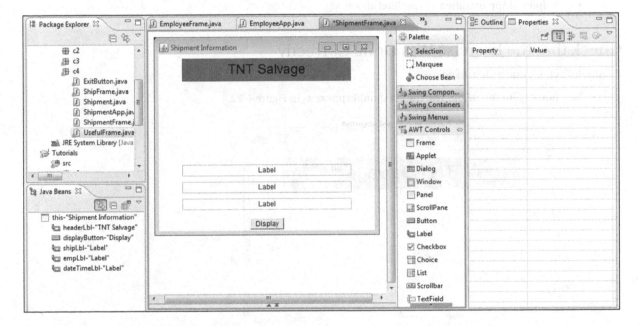

Figure 4-21.

In the ShipmentFrame source code:

1. Create a public class variable of type Shipment called ship.

2. Change the constructor so that it receives a Shipment object called s.

3. In the constructor, after the initialization method is run set ship equal to s.

4. Make the frame visible.

5. In the initialize method, recalculate the location of the Exit button.

6. Add the ActionListener to displayButton by inserting the following statement in the getDisplayButton method after the size is set:

```
displayButton.addActionListener(this);
```

7. Change the actionPerformed method to move the data from ship to the three labels (just as ShipFrame did).

In the ShipmentApp source code:

8. Change ShipmentApp so that a ShipmentFrame object is created, not ShipFrame.

Results of the Review Exercise

Now we have:

- In the ReviewEx project, one new package called c4 with six classes.
- One new visual class called ShipmentFrame specified as above.
- ShipmentApp modified as specified above.

Check that the Exercise Was Done Correctly

Finally, let's check that it all worked:

1. Run c4 ShipmentApp. The results should appear as in Figure 4-22.

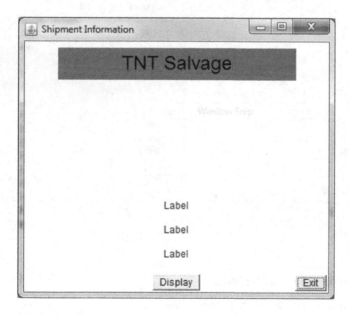

Figure 4-22.

2. Click the display button. The results should appear as in Figure 4-23.

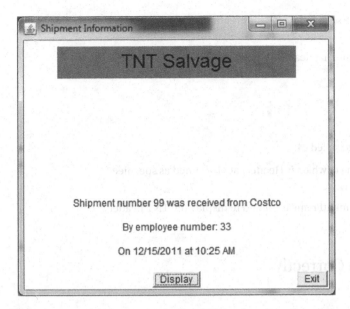

Figure 4-23.

Challenge Exercise

The ExitButton class was an example of a useful, specialized GUI component subclass. In this exercise, you will create another specialized class.

1. Create a new Java project called CE and a package called c4.

2. Copy all the classes in Tutorial/c4 and ReviewEx/c4 into CE/c4.

Don't worry about the overwrite message. The ExitButton and UsefulFrame classes were in both packages, so overwriting one with the other is not a problem here.

3. Create a new class called HeaderLabel that is a subclass of **Label** and has all the characteristics of the headerLbl (which was created in ShipmentFrame).

4. Change UsefulFrame to include a HeaderLabel component and assign it to variable hl.

5. In UsefulFrame, create a method called setHeaderLabelLocation that calculates the horizontal location of the header such that the header is centered regardless of the width of the frame.

Here's some help with that:

To calculate the horizontal position, subtract the HeaderLabel width (300) from the width of the frame and divide the result by 2. For instance, if the width of the frame is 400, the starting location is 50 or (400 – 300) / 2. If the width of the frame was 700 the starting location is 200 or (700 – 300) / 2.

OK, here's a lot of help with that. The actual method should be:

```java
public void setHeaderLabelLocation() {
            hl.setLocation((this.getWidth()-300)/2, 38); }
```

6. Change all the subclasses of UsefulFrame so that the setHeaderLabelLocation method is executed.

7. Remove all source code in ShipmentFrame that dealt with headerLbl.

Results of the Challenge Exercise

Let's check it worked:

1. One new project called CE with a package called c4.

2. CE/src/c4 should have eleven classes, one of which is HeaderLabel, defined as specified above.

3. UsefulFrame, EmployeeFrame, and ShipmentFrame modified to display the TNT header label horizontally centered on the frame.

Check that the Exercise Was Done Correctly

To finish the chapter, let's see everything:

1. Run both EmployeeApp and ShipmentApp and confirm that the TNT header label appears.

2. Change the width of either EmployeeFrame or ShipmentFrame, run the application, and confirm that the TNT header label is centered on the frame.

For instance, changing EmployeeFrame to 650 in width would result in Figure 4-24.

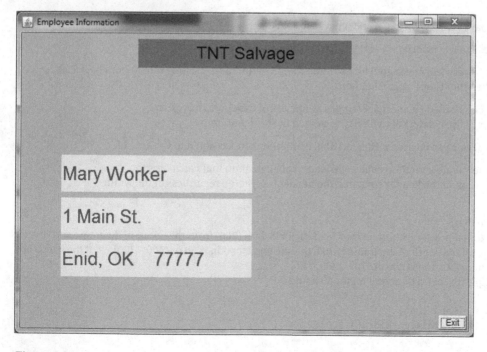

Figure 4-24.

CHAPTER 5

■ ■ ■

Variables

In this chapter, we will introduce primitive variables and compare/contrast them to reference variables. We will demonstrate how to perform math and logic functions using both primitive and String variables. A new GUI component, text field (which enables a user to input information to an application), will be demonstrated and we will revisit inheritance in more detail.

At the end of this chapter, you should understand:

> Primitive versus reference variables
>
> How to convert between variable types
>
> Wrapper classes
>
> Text fields
>
> Inheritance

After completing the chapter, you should be able to:

> Use text fields to retrieve and display information
>
> Perform calculations
>
> Convert between numeric and string information
>
> Override inherited methods

Reference versus Primitive Variables

We have hidden the full explanation of reference variables from you as long as possible. Reference variables are necessarily complex and, unfortunately, you cannot continue without understanding them.

All of the variables we have used have been reference variables and, often, we have talked about the variable and the object (assigned to the variable) as if they were the same thing. In actuality, they are two different entities. For example, we have said, "have the program pass an Employee object" or "have the method accept on Employee object" when, in actuality, an Employee variable is being passed or accepted.

When a reference variable, such as emp in EmployeeApp, is created, a small, fixed amount of space is reserved in the computer's main memory. However, when an object is created (i.e., an Employee object is instantiated), a copy of the entire class is moved into main memory. When the object is assigned to the reference variable, the storage location (address in main memory) of the object is moved into the reference variable.

Let's try a diagram. When you run EmployeeApp, the class's main method is loaded into the computer's main memory and the main method statements are executed. When the variable emp is created (Employee emp;), main memory space is allocated for that variable but the space is empty (see Figure 5-1).

Main Memory
EmployeeApp
emp

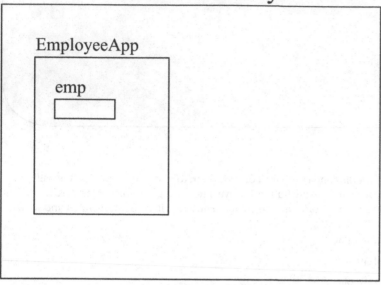

Figure 5-1.

When the object is created (`new Employee();`), the machine language version of the Employee class is moved into main memory and executed. This means the class variables are created and the Employee constructor is executed. After the constructor finishes, all of the Employee class methods and variables remain in main memory (see Figure 5-2).

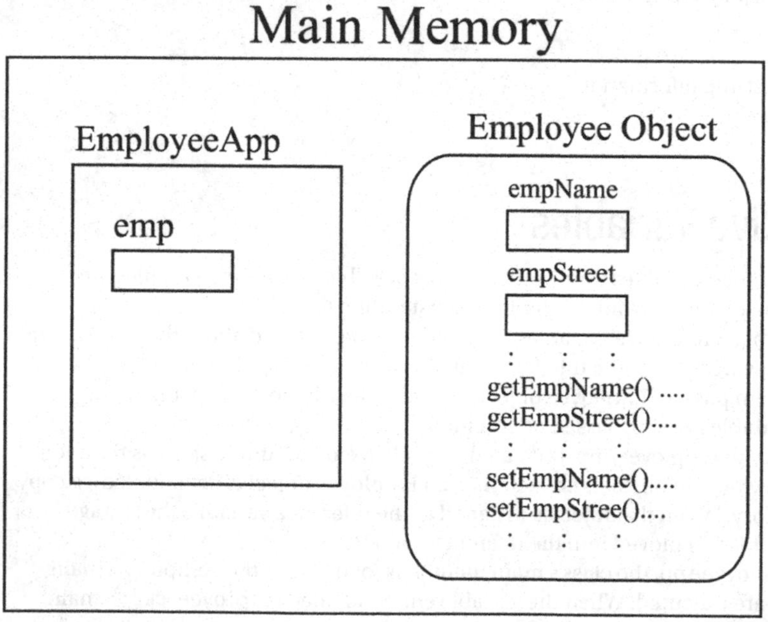

Main Memory
EmployeeApp
emp
Employee Object
empName
empStreet
: : :
getEmpName() ....
getEmpStreet()....
: : :
setEmpName()....
setEmpStree()....
: : :

Figure 5-2.

When you assign the Employee object to emp (the equal sign in the statement emp = new Employee(); does this) the main memory address of the Employee object is loaded into the variable emp. (In actuality, a number called a hash code, which is used by the computer to calculate the memory address, is loaded into emp. For simplicity's sake, we will refer to this simply as the main memory address.) The address acts as a **pointer** to the Employee object (see Figure 5-3). This is where the term **reference variable** comes from. The variable does not contain the object; the variable references the object.

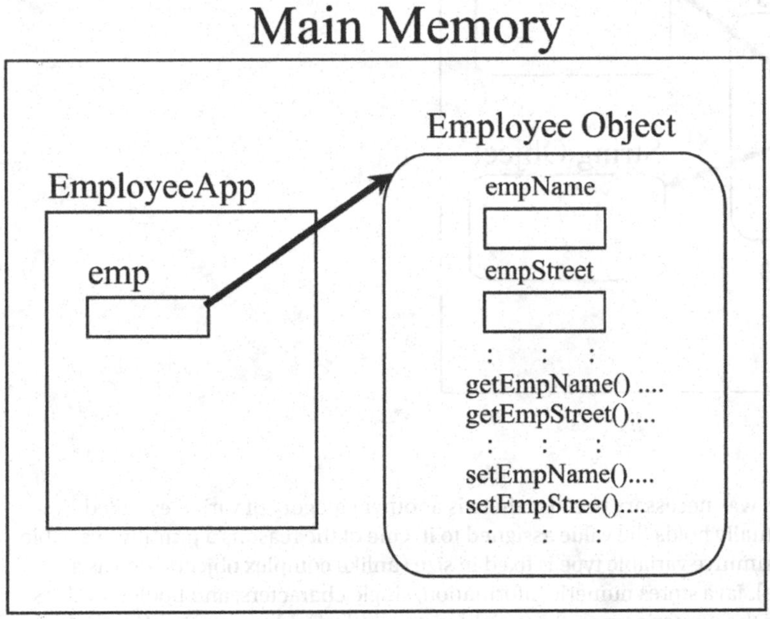

Figure 5-3.

You may be wondering why Java works like this. Well, complex objects such as Employee require varying amounts of space. For instance, when an Employee method is executed, new method variables and associated objects may be created. This means more space must be allocated for the object. In addition, the values assigned to the variables can be changed. For instance, earlier we changed the city value from Enid to Jacksonville. This type of change may also require more space for the object. Notice that the space allocated for the variable (which holds the storage location of the object); however, is a fixed amount.

For instance, the class variables empName and empStreet in Employee are reference variables. When you created these variables, (i.e., String empName = new String();), String objects were also created and assigned to the variables. A String object contains many methods and private variables. (To verify this, go to the Java online documentation and look at all the methods that comprise a String.) The String variable (empName) simply points to the String object (see Figure 5-4).

Main Memory

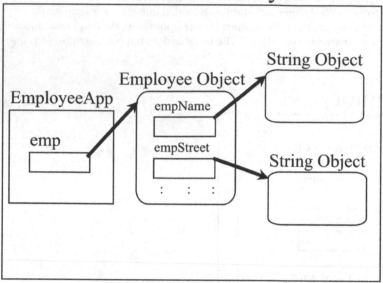

Figure 5-4.

This explanation of reference variables was necessary because there is another category of variables called primitive variables. A primitive variable actually holds the value assigned to it. One of the reasons a primitive variable holds the assigned value is because each primitive variable type is fixed in size (unlike complex objects such as a String or Employee, which can vary in size). Java stores numeric information, single characters, and Boolean values (true or false) in primitive variables. Within the numeric types, the variables store either whole numbers (integers) or floating points (numbers with decimals). A list of primitive variable types and their characteristics can be seen in Table 5-1.

Table 5-1.

Primitive Type	Value Type	Value Range	Space Allocated	Notes
boolean	logical	true or false		default is false
char	single character	any of Unicodes's 65,436 characters	16 bits	single quotes to specify value
byte	whole number	-128 to 127	8 bits	
short	whole number	- 32,768 to 32,767	16 bits	
int	whole number	-2,147,483,648 to 2,147,483,647	32 bits	
long	whole number	- 9*10**18 to 9*10**18-1	64 bits	
float	floating point	Up to 7 digits of precision	32 bits	Rounds values > limit
double	floating point	Up to 15 digits of precision	64 bits	Rounds values > limit

Most business applications only need **boolean** variables and the numeric types of **int** and **double**. In addition, most organizations try to limit the number of variable types used because working with and converting between the different types can be tricky. For instance, converting a **double** with a value of 3.75 to an **int** would result in a value of 3 for the **int** variable. Now you may say, "Big deal, .75 of something can't be that important." But, what if it were your GPA?

We will explain how to work with primitives later in the chapter. Right now, let's investigate the difference between primitives and reference variables.

Tutorial: Displaying Reference Variable Values

We will use EmployeeApp to show some of the differences between primitive and reference variables. In addition, pay attention to how EmployeeApp's main method is used as a testing tool. Main methods will often be added to classes for testing purposes. In future examples, we will quickly check the progress of our application development by using this technique.

1. Create a new package called c5 in the Tutorials project.

2. Copy the six Employee classes from c4 to c5.

In the c5.EmployeeApp source code:

3. Comment out the two statements in the main method.

We are going to substitute two statements for the first statement so that we clearly separate the creation of the Employee variable from the creation of the Employee object.

4. After the main method header, insert the following:

```
Employee emp = null;
emp = new Employee("Mary Worker", "1 Main St.",
            "Enid", "OK", "77777");
```

The first statement sets the reference variable emp to **null**. This means that emp does not reference any object. We will now insert a statement to display the value of emp after each statement.

5. Enter the following after the first statement in the main method:

```
System.out.println("emp value before the object is assigned: " +
        emp);
```

6. Enter the following statement after the last (i.e., now the third) statement in the main method and run c5.EmployeeApp:

```
System.out.println("emp value after the object is assigned: " +
        emp);
```

Running EmployeeApp would result in the following messages in the console:

```
emp value before the object is assigned: null
emp value after the object is assigned: c5.Employee@7a627a62
```

The location value you get will probably be different from 7a627a62. Notice that the second message also displays the object type—which is the package name and class name separated by a period. (The package name is part of the class/object identifier.)

Why does it work like this? The answer is, "How could it work any other way?" How could the JVM print out an object? Should the source code be printed? Or, all the variable values? Or, only the class variable values? Is there really a correct way to print an object?

In addition, don't forget that the println statements specify that the reference variable emp should be displayed, not the Employee object. Because the reference variable contains the **location of the object** (not the object), the JVM is actually being helpful. The JVM displays not only the location but also what the location contains (a c5.Employee object). You can interpret the text "c5.Employee@125e69d4" as "There is a c5.Employee object at main memory location 125e69 d4."

Tutorial: Working with Primitive Variables

Let's have a go at working with primitive variables:

1. In EmployeeApp, at the end of the main method, add the following statement:

```
int intTest = 2109876543;
```

A primitive variable is created just like any other variable: first the type (int) is specified, and then the name of the variable (intTest). Notice that an equal sign is used to assign a value, just like a reference variable. However, on the right side of the assignment things are quite different: **no object is instantiated**, a value is simply assigned.

2. Change the 0 (in the intTest value) to 4.

The error message will be, "The literal 2149876543 of type int is out of range." This number is too large to store as an **int**. Remember, whole number values greater than 2.1 billion (give or take a few million) must be stored in a larger primitive type such as a **long** variable.

3. Change intTest's value back to 2109876543.

4. At the end of the main method add the following statement and run EmployeeApp:

```
System.out.println("The value of intTest is " + intTest);
```

The result of the new println statement will be:

```
The value of intTest is 2109876543
```

No storage location is displayed because the value stored in the variable intTest is 2109876543 not a storage location, as with the reference variable emp.

5. At the end of the main method, add the following statement:

```
double doubleTest = 3210.12345678901234567890;
```

Notice that the value of doubleTest is more precise than a **double** variable can hold, yet there is no error message. This is because the JVM rounds the number so that it will fit in the variable. We'll prove this by printing out the value.

6. At the end of the main method add the following statement and run EmployeeApp:

```
System.out.println("The value of doubleTest is " + doubleTest);
```

The result of the new println statement will be:

```
The value of doubleTest is 3210.1234567890124
```

Notice that the remaining fractional value 34567890 was rounded up to 4.

7. Change the value of doubleTest to 12345678901234567890.

Notice that now there is an "out of range" error and that there is a huge difference regarding how the JVM handles a value that is too big versus a value that is too precise. (These are the kind of differences that drive new programmers crazy, so hang in there!)

8. Undo the change.

Let's drive the point home.

9. Uncomment the statement that creates the reference variable ef and add the following statement immediately after:

```
System.out.println("The value of ef is " + ef);
```

What do you think the result will be?

10. Run EmployeeApp and close the Employee Information frame.

The console should display something like the following:

```
The value of ef is c5.EmployeeFrame[frame0,350,200,400x450, invalid,title=Employee
Information,resizable,normal]
```

Are you surprised by the results? You probably thought that a storage location would be displayed (because ef is a reference variable and that is what happened when you tried to display emp).

When println is used to display a reference variable, the JVM actually calls a method named toString within the referenced object. An Employee object's (emp's) toString method returns the object's storage location. However, not all JRE classes' toString methods do that. Some JRE classes' toString methods return different information. For instance, the Frame class's toString method returns properties such as the size, location, and title (that the JVM then displays as in step 10). "Why does this happen?" you ask? The answer is inheritance.

To help explain inheritance, let's explore the toString method further.

The toString Method

To reiterate: when a reference variable is displayed with the println statement, the JVM searches for the reference variable's assigned object's toString method. The toString method returns values to the JVM that are then displayed. Now, the Great-Grandpappy of all classes, Object, has a toString method. This method specifies that the variable type will be displayed, followed by the "at sign" (@), and then the storage location. We have proven that this is what occurs (for example, with the Employee reference variable emp). However, the Object class documentation suggests that the toString method should be overridden by all subclasses.

The Component class (of which the Frame class is a subclass) does override the toString method. The Component class' toString method specifies that a Component object's size, title, and so on should be displayed, not the hash code. In other words, all Component subclasses that do not override the toString method will display this information.

Tutorial: Overriding the toString Method

Let's prove that the toString method controls what is displayed by overriding the inherited Component toString method in several of our classes.

1. Display the Employee source code.

2. Click on Source, Override/Implement Methods... to display the "Override/Implement Methods" window (Figure 5-5.)

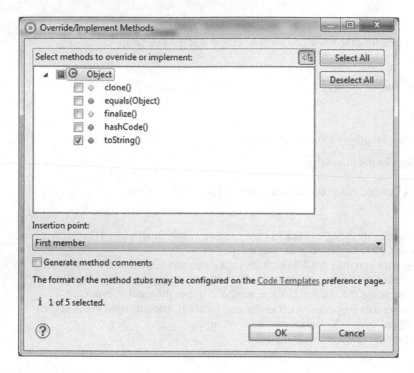

Figure 5-5.

The "Override/Implement Methods" window displays all the methods Employee inherited. Because Employee is a direct subclass of Object, only the methods inherited from Object are displayed. (Other classes, such as EmployeeFrame, will show many more superclasses and inherited methods.)

3. Click on the toString() check box as in Figure 5-5, and then click the OK button.

RAD will insert the following toString method (referred to as a stub method).

```java
public String toString() {
    return super.toString();
}
```

4. Change the return statement to the following so that the toString method returns the EmpName.

```java
return getEmpName();
```

Notice that we didn't fully identify the getEmpName method as `this.getEmpName`. Remember that the JVM assumes that a called method is for this object.

5. Save the Employee source code and run EmployeeApp.

6. Close EmployeeFrame by clicking on the Exit button.

In the console pane, notice that the memory location for emp is no longer displayed. Instead, the emp value appears as follows:

```
emp value after the object is assigned: Mary Worker
```

7. Display the UsefulFrame source code, click `Source`, then `Override/Implement Methods....`

Look at all the inherited methods! (The Oracle online class documentation also lists all inherited methods.)

8. Scroll down the list and expand Component.

Even more inherited methods!

9. Scroll down the list until toString appears, select it, and click the OK button.

10. Change the toString stub to display the frame title followed by the word "Frame" as follows:

```
return this.getTitle() + " Frame";
```

This time we fully qualified the getTitle method with the keyword `this` (even though we did not have to). Notice also how concatenation was used inside the `return` statement to build the returned string value.

11. Save the source code and run EmployeeApp.

12. Close EmployeeFrame by clicking on the Exit button.

In the console pane, the value of ef should appear as follows:

```
The value of ef is Employee Information Frame
```

In case you haven't guessed, the `String` class also overrides the toString method it inherited from Object. String. toString() returns the text value assigned to the `String` object, not the memory location. So using println to display `String` variables will display the assigned text (as you would hope), not the memory location. Wasn't this nice of the Java developers?

13. In EmployeeApp, comment out all the println statements and the statements defining intTest and doubleTest.

The executable code should look like the following:

```
package c5;

public class EmployeeApp {

    public static void main(String[] args) {
        Employee emp = null;
        emp = new Employee("Mary Worker", "1 Main St.",
            "Enid", "OK", "77777");
        EmployeeFrame ef = new EmployeeFrame(emp);
    }
}
```

Manipulating Numeric Primitives

The standard mathematical operators are used to manipulate primitive variables. Table 5-2 shows the mathematical symbols and examples.

Table 5-2.

Operation	Symbol	Example	Example result
Multiplication	*	3*2	6
Division	/	3/2	1
		3.0/2.0	1.5
Addition	+	3+2	5
Subtraction	-	3-2	1

What is going on with that first division example? No, it is not a typo. If two integers are divided, any fractional remainder is truncated (i.e., discarded). Notice that if floating point numbers (e.g., 3.0, 2.0) are specified, the fractional result is retained. Looks like a source of many future errors. The Java developers have not done anything nice here!

In addition to the standard math operations, there is a Math class that has many "higher level" mathematical functions (with a heavy emphasis on trigonometric functions such as sine, cosine, tangent, etc.). The Math class methods can be "called directly." "Called directly" means that you do not have to create a Math object to use the Math class methods. This is because the Math class methods have been defined as **static**. You may remember the keyword **static** from the main method definition. Just as the main method can be "called directly" (i.e., no object needs to be created), any static method can be called by simply specifying the class and method name. Of course, each method has a unique signature (meaning each method expects one or more specific variable types) and will return a specific variable type. Table 5-3 contains some of the more common Math class methods and examples.

Table 5-3.

Operation	Expects	Returns	Examples	Example result
Exponent	2 numbers	double	Math.pow(3.0, 2);	9.0
Random	Nothing	double (value between 0 and 1)	Math.random();	0.6051898089070796
			Math.random();	0.021619841296942277
Square Root	Number	double	Math.sqrt(3);	1.7320508075688772
			Math.sqrt(4.0);	2.0

Two other math operations that you should be aware of are increment (++) and decrement (--). Increment and decrement are specified with numeric primitive variables (e.g., intTest++; or --doubleTest;) and will increase or decrease a numeric primitive by 1. You cannot specify a different value, like 3, to increment or decrement by. For instance, assuming intTest has a value of 2, intTest++; would result in a value of 3. If intTest has a value of 2, intTest--; would result in a value of 1.

The increment and decrement operations could also be done with formulas such as intTest = intTest + 1 and intTest = intTest - 1. So, essentially, increment and decrement simply offer a shorthand method for coding these formulas. Now this may not sound like a big deal, but incrementing by one is used extensively when using loops. We will explore looping in a later chapter and you will come to appreciate this shortcut more.

The increment and decrement operation can be specified before or after the variable. For instance, if an increment is specified before the variable (++intTest), it is called a pre-increment. If the increment is specified after the variable (intTest++), it is called a post-increment. Whether the operation is a pre or post does not make a difference when the operation is specified by itself (as in the above examples). However, if the operation is embedded in another statement the results may differ.

For instance, pre operations are done before the "owning" operation is performed. In the following statement:

```
System.out.println(++intTest);
```

the pre-increment is embedded in the println operation and the println operation is considered the "owning" operation. Embedded operations are usually performed first (and the pre-increment is not an exception), then the owning operation (the println) is performed. So assuming that intTest is equal to 2, first the value of intTest is changed to 3, and then the value of intTest is displayed in the console as 3.

In the following println statement, we imbedded a post-increment:

```
System.out.println(intTest++);
```

Post-operations are performed after the owning operation. In this case, it means that first the println function is performed and then the post-increment. Again, assuming that intTest is equal to 2, the above statement will first display the value of intTest as 2 in the console and then the value of intTest will be incremented to 3.

Yikes! Isn't math fun? The only words of advice I can offer are, "If you don't like pre and post operations, don't use them." (Nevertheless, you should be able to read them in case another programmer does use them.)

Finally, when combining mathematical operations, the standard order of precedence is followed:

- Multiplication and division first, from left to right
- Then addition and subtraction, from left to right

So, the following statement would result in the value 16:

```
System.out.println(4.0+3.0/2.0*8.0);
```

Are you asking, "How the heck does that equal 16?". If you think like the machine and follow the rules, the above formula is equivalent to 4.0 + ((3.0 / 2.0) * 8.0) . Why? Because multiplication and division are done first, from left to right. So the addition operation is ignored even though it is the first operation in the formula. The JVM goes from left to right and runs into the division (3.0 / 2.0) first. The division is performed, resulting in 1.5. As far as the JVM is concerned, the formula now looks like the following: 4.0 + 1.5 * 8.0. So what happens next? That's right the multiplication (1.5 * 8.0) is performed, resulting in 12. Now the JVM thinks the formula is 4.0 + 12.0. Since the addition is the only operation left, the JVM performs the addition, and the result is displayed as 16 in the console.

You can control the order in which operations are performed with parentheses. Anything enclosed in parentheses is done first, and then the normal order of precedence is followed. For instance, changing the formula to the following:

```
System.out.println((4.0+3.0)/(2.0*8.0));
```

results in the value 0.4375 being displayed. Why? Because the addition (in the leftmost parentheses) is done first, resulting in 7. Next the multiplication is done (because it is also in parentheses), resulting in 16. That leaves 7 divided by 16, which equals 0.4375.

149

Tutorial: Using Primitive Variables

For each of these tests, try to determine what the result will be (and why) before entering and executing the source code. The answer and explanation for each test will appear after the tutorial.

1. Create a new Java class in c5 called MathTestApp with a main method.

2. In the main method, define an int variable called intTest and set its value to 3, and define a double variable called doubleTest with a value of 2.0.

3. Add the following two statements after the variable definitions and run MathTestApp:

    ```
    System.out.println(++intTest);
    System.out.println(intTest++);
    ```

4. Comment out the previous println statements, add the following statements, and run MathTestApp:

    ```
    System.out.println(intTest/2);
    System.out.println(intTest/2.0);
    System.out.println(intTest/doubleTest);
    ```

5. Comment out the previous println statements, add the following statements, and run MathTestApp:

    ```
    System.out.println(Math.pow(doubleTest, intTest)/(2.0*3.0));
    ```

6. Comment out the previous println statements, add the following statements, and run MathTestApp:

    ```
    System.out.println(Math.pow(doubleTest, intTest)*3/2);
    System.out.println(Math.pow(doubleTest, intTest)*(3/2));
    ```

7. Comment out the previous println statements, add the following statements, and run MathTestApp:

    ```
    System.out.println(intTest);
    System.out.println(intTest++/2);
    System.out.println(intTest);
    System.out.println(++intTest/2);
    System.out.println(intTest);
    ```

8. Comment out the previous println statements, add the following statements, and run MathTestApp:

    ```
    System.out.println(doubleTest++ + ++intTest);
    System.out.println(doubleTest + " " + intTest);
    ```

9. Comment out the previous println statements, add the following statements, and run MathTestApp:

    ```
    System.out.println(" " + Math.pow(doubleTest++,
            ++intTest) + doubleTest++);
    System.out.println(doubleTest);
    ```

10. Print out a copy of the MathTestApp source code.

Using Primitive Variables Tutorial Answers and Explanation

The first println statement:

```
System.out.println(++intTest);
```

contains a pre-increment for intTest. The pre-increment is performed before the println operation and the value of intTest is increased from 3 to 4. The println is then performed, resulting in a 4 appearing in the console.

The second println statement:

```
System.out.println(intTest++);
```

contains a post-increment. This means the println is performed first, resulting in the value of intTest being displayed as 4 again, and then the value of intTest is incremented to 5. Result:

```
4
4
```

The next println contains a formula that divides two integers and, as mentioned earlier, any fractional result is truncated.

```
System.out.println(intTest/2);
```

So, 3 divided by 2 results in 1.5, but the .5 is dropped. The other formulas:

```
System.out.println(intTest/2.0);
System.out.println(intTest/doubleTest);
```

divide an integer by a double. When an integer is divided by a double, the integer is promoted to a double. In other words, the JVM converts the integer (2) into a double (2.0) then performs the operation. Division between two doubles will retain any fractional result, so the .5 is retained for both results. Result:

```
1
1.5
1.5
```

Now let's consider the following line:

```
System.out.println(Math.pow(doubleTest, intTest)/(2.0*3.0));
```

The multiplication is done first (because it is enclosed in parentheses, (2.0*3.0)) resulting in 6.0. The JVM now "sees" the formula as Math.pow(doubleTest, intTest)/6.0 and performs the remaining operations from left to right: Math.pow raises doubleTest (2.0) by the power of intTest (3) resulting in 8.0. Then 8.0 is divided by 6.0. Result:

```
1.3333333333333333
```

The next statement's math operations are simply executed from left to right.

```
System.out.println(Math.pow(doubleTest, intTest) * 3/2);
```

doubleTest (2.0) is raised to the third (intTest) power, resulting in 8.0. 8.0 is multiplied by the **int** value 3, resulting in 24.0. Next 24.0 is divided by the **int** value 2. The 2 is promoted to a double (2.0), and the division result is 12.0.

The second formula's division (3/2) is in parentheses; therefore, it is performed first.

```
System.out.println(Math.pow(doubleTest, intTest) * (3/2));
```

These are both int values, so the result is an int value of 1. (Remember: the fractional result is truncated in division between int values.) The Math.pow method is performed, raising doubleTest (2.0) to the third (intTest) power resulting in 8.0. 8.0 is then multiplied by the int 1, resulting in 8.0. Tricky, tricky, tricky! Result:

```
12.0
8.0
```

Now the following simply prints the initialized value of intTest (3).

```
System.out.println(intTest);
```

Next intTest (3) is divided by 2, the result (1) is printed, and then the intTest post-increment is performed, increasing intTest to 4.

```
System.out.println(intTest++/2);
```

The third of this group simply prints the value of intTest (4).

```
System.out.println(intTest);
```

Next intTest is pre-incremented, resulting in intTest being set to 5. Then intTest (5) is divided by 2, and the result (2) is printed.

```
System.out.println(++intTest/2);
```

Finally, the value of intTest (5) is printed.

```
System.out.println(intTest);
```

Result:

```
3
1
4
2
5
```

The next example has both a pre- and post-increment.

```
System.out.println(doubleTest++ + ++intTest);
```

The pre-increment is done first, setting intTest to 4. The addition of doubleTest and intTest is then performed, resulting in the value 6.0. Next, println displays the result (6.0) and, lastly, doubleTest is incremented by 1, resulting in a value of 3.0.

Next, the plus signs represent the concatenation function, because they appear between numeric values and strings.

```
System.out.println(doubleTest + " " + intTest);
```

The JVM converts the numeric to a string and concatenates the two strings. In this case, the value of doubleTest (increased to 3.0 in the previous println) is converted to a string and concatenated to a space resulting in the text "3.0". The second plus sign is also between text ("3.0") and a numeric value (intTest), so intTest is converted to a string ("4") and concatenated to "3.0", resulting in the text "3.0 4", which is then displayed in the console. Result:

```
6.0
3.0 4
```

We're onto the last group now. Notice in the first statement of this group that there are two post-increments and one pre-increment.

```
System.out.println(" " + Math.pow(double Test++, ++intTest) + doubleTest++);
```

The Math.pow operation will be performed before the concatenations. Inside of Math.pow is one pre-increment that is performed first, resulting in intTest being set to 4. The value in doubleTest (2) is then raised to the fourth power, resulting in 16.0. The post-increment is then performed on doubleTest, changing its value to 3.0. You may be confused that the post-increment is performed before the println. Post increments are done after the owning instruction is executed. In this case, the post-increment is embedded in the Math.pow instruction. Therefore, once Math.pow completes, the increment is performed. The second doubleTest post increment is not done until its owning operation (the println) is performed. Concatenations are done next (from left to right), resulting in a space being concatenated to the result of the Math.pow function (16.0). The text "16.0" is then concatenated to the value of doubleTest (3.0) resulting in the text "16.03.0". Now that the println has completed, doubleTest is incremented to 4.0.

The next println simply prints the value of doubleTest as 4.0 and proves that the first statement really did change the value of doubleTest to 4.0.

```
System.out.println(doubleTest);
```

Result:

```
16.03.0
4.0
```

The purpose of this exercise was to impress upon you the complicated nature of combining many numeric and String operations. Many programmers strive to write compact, dense instructions that use the smallest amount of source code. The small benefits of source code compactness are usually greatly outweighed by the increased testing time and errors that this hard-to-understand, complicated code generates. It is best to err on the side of simplicity and clarity when coding, even if this does result in more source code.

Converting Between Primitive Types

Working with the various numeric primitives is confusing enough; however, converting between primitives and strings adds yet another layer of complexity. Unfortunately, strings have to be discussed, because GUI components only work with text. This means any numeric data that you want to display (on a frame, window, etc.) must be converted to text. In addition, any information retrieved from a GUI component is a string. If you want to perform mathematical functions on that data, a conversion from string to a numeric primitive must be performed. First, we will deal with converting between primitives, and then bring strings into the mix.

Converting a numeric value from a smaller numeric type to a larger type is easy: simply assign the smaller type to the larger type. For example:

```
doubleTest = intTest;
```

This works for all the numeric types from smallest to largest. Assuming the following:

```
byte byteTest = 1;
short shortTest = 2;
int intTest = 3;
long longTest = 4;
float floatTest= 5;
double doubleTest = 6;
```

Running the following:

```
System.out.println(" " + byteTest + shortTest +
        intTest + longTest + floatTest + doubleTest);
```

Would result in:

```
12345.06.0
```

If we then assigned the values as follows:

```
doubleTest=floatTest=longTest=intTest=shortTest=byteTest;
```

and displayed the values as follows:

```
System.out.println(" " + byteTest + shortTest + intTest +
        longTest + floatTest + doubleTest);
```

the result would be:

```
11111.01.0
```

Notice that the assignments are made from right to left. In other words, the **byte** variable byteTest (with a value of 1) was promoted to the larger type of **short** first and then assigned to shortTest, and then shortTest was converted to **int** and assigned to intTest, and so on.

Going from a larger primitive variable to a smaller primitive type requires **casting** and is a little more complicated. The syntax for casting is: the smaller primitive variable, the equal sign, the smaller variable type in parentheses, then the larger primitive variable. For instance, assuming doubleTest equals 6.0, the following statement:

```
intTest = (int)doubleTest;
```

would set intTest to the value 6.

Casting is relatively simple until a value is too large for the smaller type. For instance, changing doubleTest's value to 9876543210987.99 and then casting to each of the smaller types yields a variety of values. For instance, the **float** variable value would be 9876543000000. Because **float** only supports 7 digits of precision, only the seven highest digits (9876543) are saved and all finer precision is lost. (This **float** value would actually display in scientific notation. Controlling the appearance of numbers is a whole other can of worms that we will cover later.)

Converting the new doubleTest value to a long variable would result in a value of 9876543210987. Long variables can handle very large whole numbers, so most of the value is saved but the fractional value (.99) is truncated.

Converting to an **int** variable would result in a value of 2147483647, the largest value an **int** variable can hold. This is really bad because the **int** value is not even close to the original **double** value. The **short** and **byte** values are equally bad at -1 and -1.

In summary, the syntax for casting is a little complicated; however, the real complication comes from trying to fit larger values into smaller variable types. Be very careful when casting because of the possibly unexpected results of moving from larger to smaller types.

Strings to Primitives and Vice Versa

The String class has a very nice set of static toString methods that will convert primitive types to strings. Again, a static method can simply be invoked without creating a String object. For instance, the following are all valid statements:

```
String byteString = String.valueOf(byteTest);
String shortString = String.valueOf(shortTest);
String intString = String.valueOf(intTest);
String longString = String.valueOf(longTest);
String floatString = String.valueOf(floatTest);
String doubleString = String.valueOf(doubleTest);
```

Converting from a string to a primitive is a little more complicated. Unlike String, primitives are not classes and do not have useful methods such as valueOf. However, the Java developers have created a series of classes for each of the primitive types that contain many useful methods. These classes are called **wrapper classes**.

Each wrapper class has the same name as the primitive type (except **int**), but the wrapper class name begins with a capital letter. For example, the wrapper class associated with **double** is Double, the **long** wrapper class is Long, but the **int** wrapper class is Integer.

You can think of the wrapper classes as helper classes: they have methods that help programmers work with primitive variables. For example, each wrapper class has a parse method that will convert a String variable to the associated primitive type. Each parse method has a unique name that begins with the text "parse" and then is followed by the primitive variable type. For instance, the following are all valid statements:

```
byteTest = Byte.parseByte(byteString);
shortTest = Short.parseShort(shortString);
intTest = Integer.parseInt(intString);
longTest = Long.parseLong(longString);
floatTest = Float.parseFloat(floatString);
doubleTest = Double.parseDouble(doubleString);
```

Notice that the **Integer** parse method is called **parseInt**, not parseInteger. In addition, the wrapper classes have static toString methods that perform the same function as the String valueOf methods (i.e., convert from primitive to string). The syntax would be as follows:

```
byteString = Byte.toString(byteTest);
shortString = Short.toString(shortTest);
intString = Integer.toString(intTest);
longString = Long.toString(longTest);
floatString = Float.toString(floatTest);
doubleString = Double.toString(doubleTest);
```

Don't forget that the JVM often does the conversion from primitive to string automatically (for instance, when displaying primitives with the println method).

Table 5-4 summarizes the conversion methods between primitive types and strings and gives an example of each.

Table 5-4.

From	To	How	Example
Smaller Primitive	**Larger Primitive**	Assignment	`doubleTest = intTest;`
Larger Primitive	**Smaller Primitive**	Casting	`intTest = (int) doubleTest;`
Primitive	**String**	String.valueOf( ) *Wrapper*.toString( )	`intString = String.valueOf(intTest);` `intString = Integer.toString(intTest);`
String	**Primitive**	*Wrapper*.parse*Xxx*( )	`intTest = Integer.parseInt(intString);`

TextField

Sorry for all this pain, but the parse method will be required to retrieve and manipulate numeric information from a GUI component. Speaking of which, our next new GUI component is a text field. A text field looks like a rectangle. Users can enter information into a text field and, like a label, information can also be displayed in a text field. You can probably guess the syntax for creating a `TextField` object, but here it is anyway:

```
TextField empNameTF = new TextField();
```

Of course, the text field must be sized and placed on the frame (like our other GUI components) and we will need to retrieve the text from the text field. Like the other GUI components, `TextField` objects have getters and setters for manipulating properties. One of a text field's properties is its text. The getText method returns the contents of the text field as characters, and the setText method places text in the text field. We will use these methods to modify EmployeeApp so that it can accept input from a user.

Until now, EmployeeApp has simply displayed "hard-coded" employee information. We will modify the application to accept employee information using a new frame called EnterEmpInfo. We will also perform a gross salary calculation and display the results.

Truly, the EnterEmpInfo frame is **not** the correct place for the salary calculation method. EnterEmpInfo should only have methods that pertain to entering employee information. Calculating an employee's gross salary really belongs in the Employee class. For right now, it is simply easier to put it in the frame. Later we will move it to Employee.

Tutorial: Inputting Data

Let's do a little data input:

1. In c5, create a visual class called EnterEmpInfo that is a subclass of Frame, implements an action listener, and has a main method.

2. In the source code, change the superclass from Frame to UsefulFrame.

You may be wondering why we originally defined the superclass as Frame and then changed it to UsefulFrame. As mentioned earlier, VE has coding standards. If a class does not follow these standards, VE does not "play well" with that class. For example, UsefulFrame was not created as a Visual class therefore, it does not follow the VE standards (i.e., it doesn't have an initialize method, a long variable called serialVersionUID, etc.) Because of this, if we define a new class as a subclass of UsefulFrame, VE cannot display the class in the Design pane. This means you cannot drag and drop components, use the Properties view, etc. and will only be able to modify the class by changing the source.

3. In the Design pane, click on the frame to activate the Properties view.

4. In the Properties view, define the frame size as 400 by 400 and place it 100 pixels from the top and left of the screen.

5. Set the frame's visible property to true and layout to null.

6. In the main method, add the following to create an EnterEmpInfo object:

```
EnterEmpInfo eei = new EnterEmpInfo();
```

7. Create five labels called empNumLbl, empNameLbl, empStreetLbl, empCSZLbl, empPRLbl with the following text:

   - Employee Number

   - Name

   - Street Address

   - City, State, and Zip

   - Hourly Pay Rate

8. Create five text fields called empNumTF, empNameTF, empStreetTF, empCSZTF, and empPRTF.

9. Size, position, and align the text fields and labels on the frame such that when the class is run as a Java application, the frame appears as in Figure 5-6.

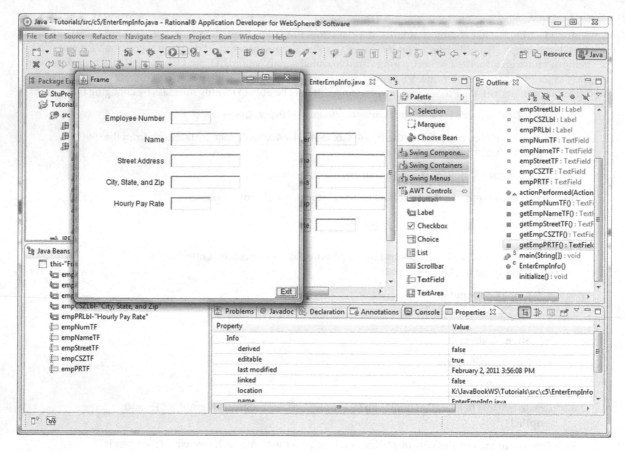

Figure 5-6.

10. Click on empCSZTF.

11. In the Properties view, define the text as "**Jacksonville, FL 322**".

This will set up a default value for the employee's city and state information. Because most of the company's employees come from the greater Jacksonville area, this will cut down on the typing needed to enter the employee's information. We defined the zip as 322 because all Jacksonville zip codes begin with 322. This will save three keystrokes when entering most employees' zip codes.

Notice that in the getEmpCSZTF() method, the following statement was added:

```
empCSZTF.setText("Jacksonville, FL 322");
```

12. Add a button called grossBtn that:

- Displays the text Gross

- Is centered horizontally on the frame

- Aligns horizontally with the Exit button

13. In the getGrossBtn method, add the following statement:

```
grossBtn.addActionListener(this);
```

This will tie the Gross button to the actionPerformed method.

We now need to change the actionPerformed method so that it reads the hourly pay rate and calculates the gross pay for the employee by multiplying the hourly pay rate by 40 (the number of hours in a work week).

14. In the actionPerformed method, add the following statement:

```
String empPayRate = empPRTF.getText();
```

Ok, that's plenty of coding, let's do a little testing.

Tutorial: Testing EnterEmpInfo

Before we try to do the calculation and display the result, let's prove that we are actually retrieving the text field information.

1. In the actionPerformed method, add the following println statement (after the statement entered in step 14 above) to prove that pay rate has been successfully placed in the variable empPayRate:

```
System.out.println(empPayRate);
```

2. Run EnterEmpInfo as a Java application.

The frame should look like Figure 5-7. Dang! Even before we test, there is trouble. Notice that the city, state, zip text field isn't big enough to display the information. Also, the Gross and Exit buttons are different sizes: we obviously need to define some button standards.

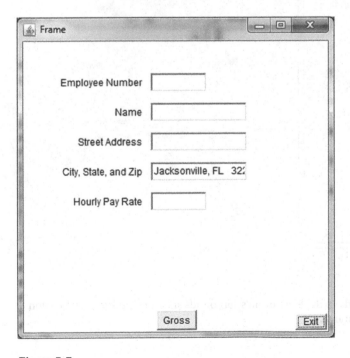

Figure 5-7.

3. Increase the length of empCSZTF to 150.

4. In c5, create a new visual class called TNTButton, and define its superclass as java.awt.Button.

5. Define TNTButton's properties as follows and save the class:

```
Size: 50, 25          Font: Tahoma, 14
```

6. In c5, change the ExitButton class so it is a subclass of TNTButton and comment out the setBounds statement.

This will ensure that the Exit button inherits the size from TNTButton.

7. In EnterEmpInfo, change the getGrossBtn method so that:

- grossBtn is defined as a new TNTButton, not as a java.awt.Button

- grossBtn does not have a setBounds or setSize statement

- grossBtn has a setLocation statement that defines the location as 177, 365

8. Save all the changes and run EnterEmpInfo as a Java application.

The frame should look like Figure 5-8.

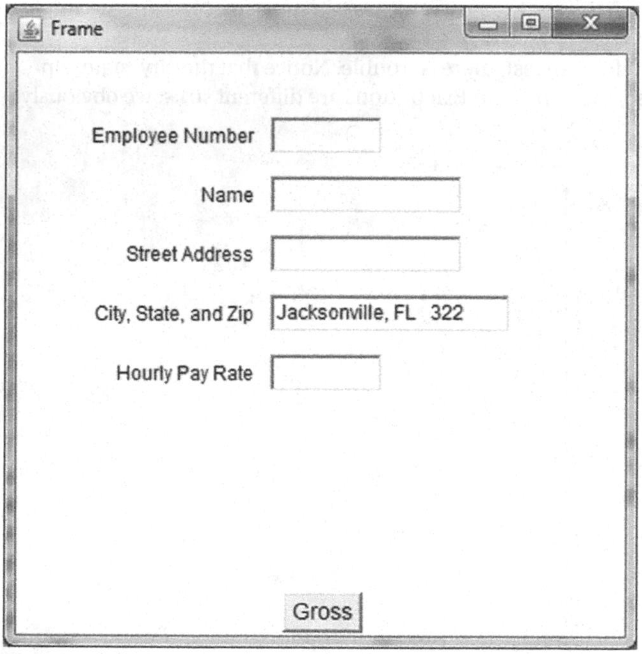

Figure 5-8.

Dang, another problem! Because we commented out the Exit button's setBounds statement, the default location was never set and the exit button isn't placed on the frame.

9. In EnterEmpInfo's initialize method, add the following to place the exit button on the frame.

   this.setExitButtonLocation();

10. Save all the changes and run EnterEmpInfo as a Java application.

Double dang! Because we changed the size of the Exit Button, its location on the frame is calculated incorrectly.

11. In UsefulFrame, change the location calculation so that the button is placed 60 and 35 pixels from the right and bottom of the frame and save the class.

12. Run EnterEmpInfo as a Java application.

The frame should look like Figure 5-9.

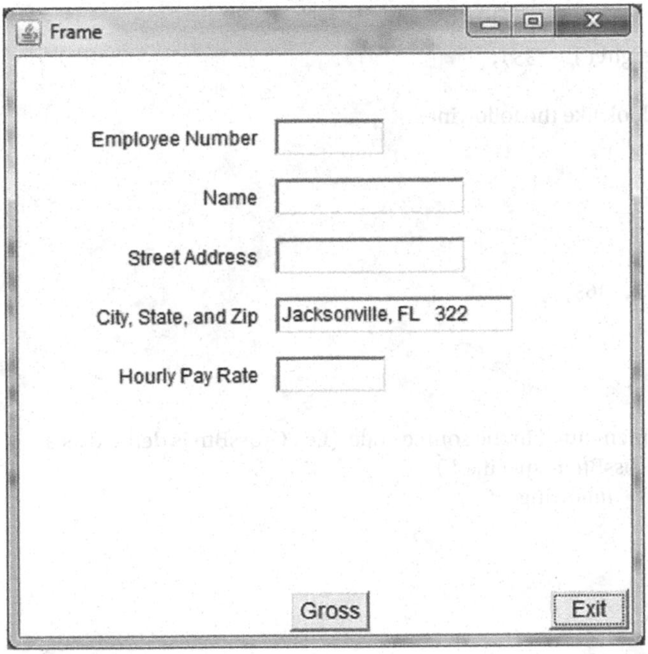

Figure 5-9.

Okay, now we're getting somewhere. We can finally test to see if the hourly rate is correctly retrieved.

13. Type 14.25 in the hourly pay rate text field and click the Gross button.

14.25 should be displayed in the console. At this point, the executable source code for TNTButton should be:

```
package c5;

import java.awt.Button;
import java.awt.Dimension;
import java.awt.Font;
```

```java
public class TNTButton extends Button {

        public TNTButton() {
                super();
                initialize();
        }

        private void initialize() {
                this.setSize(new Dimension(50, 25));
                this.setFont(new Font("Tahoma", Font.PLAIN, 14));}
}
```

Notice that the size and font properties are set as specified in step 5. The calculation in UsefulFrame (changed in step 9) should look like the following:

```java
eb.setLocation(this.getWidth() - 60, this.getHeight() - 35);
```

The getGrossBtn method in EnterEmpInfo should look like the following:

```java
private Button getGrossBtn() {
        if(grossBtn == null) {
                grossBtn = new TNTButton();
                grossBtn.setLabel("Gross");
                grossBtn.setLocation(new Point(177, 365));
                grossBtn.addActionListener(this);}
        return grossBtn;
}
```

Notice that the changes specified in step 7 were implemented in the source code. (I.e., GrossBtn is defined as a new TNTButton and only the location, not the size, of GrossBtn is specified.)

The constructor in EnterEmpInfo should look like the following:

```java
public EnterEmpInfo() {
        super();
        initialize();
}
```

Note also the setExitButtonLocation statement that was added to the initialize method. The ExitButton class should look like the following:

```java
package c5;

import java.awt.Button;
import java.awt.event.ActionListener;
import java.awt.event.ActionEvent;
```

```
public class ExitButton extends TNTButton implements
        ActionListener{

        public ExitButton () {
//              this.setBounds(350, 370, 40, 20);
                this.setLabel("Exit");
                addActionListener(this);
        }

        public void actionPerformed(ActionEvent e) {
                System.exit(0);
        }
}
```

Notice that the step 6 changes are reflected in the source code (i.e., the extends clause was changed and the setBounds statement was commented out).

Did you see that there is a warning indicated for the **import** java.awt.Button statement? Because we made ExitButton a subclass of TNTButton, there is no need to import the Button class. Although this isn't an error, it is slightly inefficient so RAD flags the statement. This warning is also in the EmpFrame class (from when we made it a subclass of UsefulFrame instead of Frame). You may have noticed that RAD displays many warnings (such as the no serialVersionUID field which, by the way, is used for version control). These are actually generated by the Java compiler, so don't shoot RAD, it's just the messenger. You can either ignore the warnings, give in to the compiler's nagging and add the field, or change your preferences to ignore the "problem."

14. Delete the import statements and generate a default serialVersionUID field (using RAD's first suggested fix) in both classes.

In the Package Explorer, the warnings icons are removed from the two classes. However, many of the other classes still are flagged with warnings.

15. Click Window and then Preferences.

16. In the Preferences windows, expand Java then Compiler (in the options tree) and select Errors/Warnings.

17. On the right of the Preferences window, close Code style and expand Potential programming problems.

Notice that the first potential problem is Serializable class without serialVersionUID and that the selected RAD option is to generate a warning.

18. Click on the option menu button, select Ignore (see Figure 5-10), and then click the OK button.

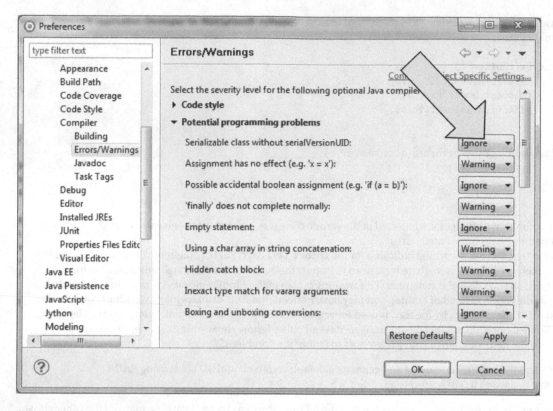

Figure 5-10.

19. At the Error/Warning Settings Changed window, click the Yes button.

Notice that the warning icon is removed from the EmployeeFrame, TNT button, and UsefulFrame classes.

Tutorial: Converting and Calculating

To calculate the gross salary of the employee, EnterEmpInfo must:

1. Convert the text in empPayRate to a numeric primitive

2. Multiply the numeric primitive pay rate by 40

3. Display the result

Inside of the EnterEmpInfo's actionPerformed method:

1. Create two double method variables called doubleEmpPR and doubleGross.

2. Use the wrapper class Double to convert empPayRate to double and then assign it to double-EmpPR as follows:

```
doubleEmpPR = Double.parseDouble(empPayRate);
```

3. Insert the following formula to calculate the gross salary:

```
doubleGross = doubleEmpPR * 40;
```

4. Change the println statement so that doubleGross is printed, not empPayRate.

5. Save the source and run EnterEmpInfo as a Java application.

6. Enter 6.50 in the Pay Rate text field and click the Gross button.

The value 260.0 should be displayed in the console. Notice that you (the programmer) have to explicitly convert the text to a double (i.e., define a double variable, parse the text, and assign it to the double variable). However, to display the double value as text, the println statement automatically converts the double to a string.

Now, the console is not the best way to display information to a user. We should create a new label on the frame to display the results.

Tutorial: Adding a Result Label

We will create a new label called resultLbl that is:

- 250 pixels in length
- Centered horizontally on the frame
- Vertically 10 pixels above the Gross button
- Not initially added to the frame

and when the Gross button is clicked:

- The label is added to the frame
- The label text shows the value of doubleGross as follows:

```
The Gross Salary is: $260.00
```

Let's get started:

1. In the design pane, add a label and set its name to resultLbl.

Notice that a resultLbl variable has been added and that an add statement was inserted in the initialize method.

2. In the Properties view, define the label's length as 250, location as 75, 332, and alignment as CENTER.

3. In the initialize method, cut out the add label statement (that puts the resultLbl on the frame) and paste it into the actionPerformed method (after the calculation is performed).

This means that the label is added to the frame after the Gross button is clicked. Notice in the design pane that resultLbl now appears outside of the frame. This means the component is part of the class but initially is not on the frame.

4. In the actionPerformed method after the add label statement, add the following setText statement:

```
resultLbl.setText("Gross Salary is: $" +
        doubleGross + "0");
```

This statement defines the resultLbl's text as "Gross Salary is: $", concatenated to doubleGross, concatenated to the character zero (0).

5. Save the source and run EnterEmpInfo as a Java application.

6. Enter 6.5 in the Pay Rate text field and click the Gross button.

The frame should look like Figure 5-11.

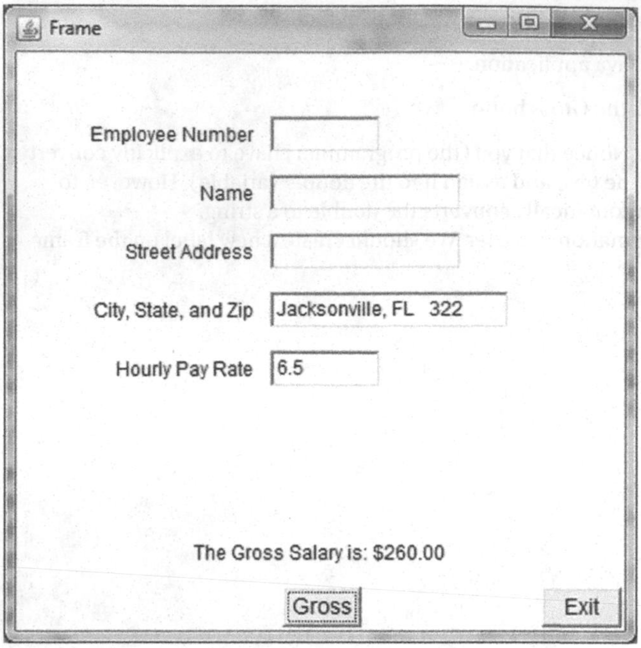

Figure 5-11.

You should note a couple of things about this tutorial. The EnterEmpInfo's main method has been used as a means to test the frame. Currently there is still no way to access the frame from the Employee application. Second, the formatting of the gross salary value was very "coarse." By this, we mean that manipulating a String object is very limited, and only simple formatting can be done easily. For instance, if the number had been over a thousand dollars, inserting the comma would have been much more difficult. Later in the text, we will cover some easier methods for formatting common numeric information such as currency, dates, and times.

The "resultLbl code" in the initialize method should look like the following:

```
resultLbl = new Label();
resultLbl.setText("Label");
resultLbl.setAlignment(Label.CENTER);
resultLbl.setBounds(new Rectangle(75, 332, 250, 23));
```

The actionPerformed method should look like the following:

```
public void actionPerformed(ActionEvent e) {
        String empPayRate = empPRTF.getText();
        double doubleEmpPR, doubleGross;
        doubleEmpPR = Double.parseDouble(empPayRate);
        doubleGross = doubleEmpPR * 40;
        this.add(resultLbl, null);
        resultLbl.setText("The Gross Salary is: $" +
                    doubleGross + "0");
        System.out.println(doubleGross);
}
```

Results of the Tutorial

Let's review what we have:

1. In the Tutorials project, a new package called c5 with three new .java files called MathTestApp, EnterEmpInfo and TNTButton.

2. A printout of the MathTestApp source code.

3. The source code in the three files should match the tutorials.

4. Running EnterEmpInfo should generate the same results as the "Adding a Result Label" tutorial steps 5 and 6.

Review Questions

1. What is casting?

2. What is a wrapper class? Give an example.

3. What is concatenation?

4. What do concatenation and addition have in common?

5. Explain "pre-" and "post-" increments.

6. Describe the appearance and function of a text field.

7. Explain the difference between primitive and reference variables and give an example of each.

Review Exercise

In this exercise, you will create an Enter Shipment Information frame re-using much of the code in ShipmentFrame.

1. In the ReviewEx/src, create a new package called c5.

2. Select all six classes in ReviewEx.c4, then copy and paste them into c5.

3. In c5, right-click on ShipmentFrame and select copy.

4. Right-click on ShipmentFrame again and select paste.

5. At the Name Conflict window, specify EnterShipInfo as the new name.

In the c5.EnterShipInfo source code:

6. Change the constructor to receive no parameters (instead of a Shipment object).

7. Delete the statement that assigns *s* to *ship*.

Using VE, change c5.EnterShipInfo as follows:

8. Add two more labels (above the three existing labels), and change their foreground colors to blue.

9. From top to bottom, name the five labels to empNumLbl, shipNumLbl, dateLbl, timeLbl, supplLbl.

10. Change all five labels so that:

    - They are 120 in length

    - Their text is right justified

    - They are right aligned to each other

    - They are distributed evenly vertically between the header and the button

    - They are 74 pixels from the left

11. Change the text for each label to the following:

    - Employee Number:

    - Shipment Number:

    - Date Received:

    - Time Received:

    - Supplier Name:

12. Add five text fields called: empNumTF, shipNumTF, dateTF, timeTF, supplTF with lengths of 50, 50, 75, 75, and 150, then left-align them to each other.

13. Align each text field horizontally with the appropriate label and separate them by 10 pixels.

14. Rename the button enterBTN and change the button label to Enter.

The design pane should look like Figure 5-12.

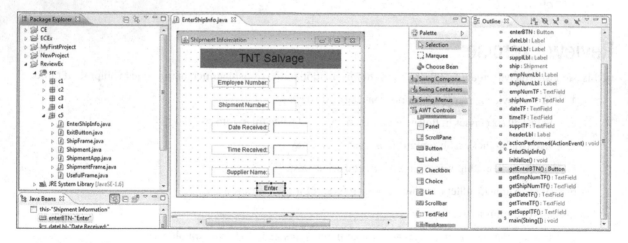

Figure 5-12.

In the source code, change the initialize method to:

15. Create a Shipment object with blanks for all the properties and assign it to the class variable ship.

In the source code, change the actionPerformed method to:

16. Read each text field and set the appropriate Shipment object property.

17. Create a new ShipmentFrame object and assign it to a variable called sf.

In ShipmentApp:

18. Comment out the two statements in the main method.

19. Add a statement to create a new EnterShipInfo object and assign it to a variable called esi.

Results of the Review Exercise

Here's what we've got after the review exercise:

1. In the ReviewEx project, one new package called c5.

2. One new visual class called EnterShipInfo specified as above.

3. ShipmentApp modified to create an EnterShipInfo object.

Check that the Exercise Was Done Correctly

Now we can test:

1. Run ShipmentApp and verify the Enter Ship Information frame appears.

2. Enter information into the text fields and click the Enter button.

3. The Shipment frame should be displayed.

4. Click the Display button, and the information entered on the Enter Ship Information frame should be displayed in the three labels with the appropriate text. As an example, see Figure 5-13.

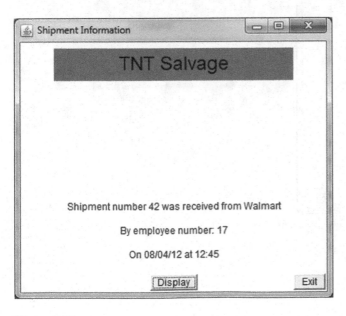

Figure 5-13.

169

Challenge Exercise

After a shipment is received, each individual item in the shipment needs to be recorded and placed into a sorted box/carton. The box/carton will hold many items of the same product type and, eventually, will be put into the inventory stockroom. For now, we will create a Sort Item frame to identify which shipment the item came from and the box number the item is placed in. In addition, the frame will keep a running total of the number of items in the shipment.

1. In the CE/src, create a new package called c5.

2. Copy the following into CE/c5 and overwrite any duplicate classes:

   - All the classes in CE/c4

   - ReviewEx/c5.EnterShipInfo

   - ReviewEx/c5.ShipmentApp

   - Tutorial/c5.EnterEmpInfo

   - Tutorial/c5.TNTButton

   - Tutorial/c5.ExitButton

3. In CE/c5, change the UsefulFrame exit button location calculation as you did in the tutorial.

4. Create a new visual class called SortItem that is a subclass of UsefulFrame and looks like Figure 5-14 when first displayed.

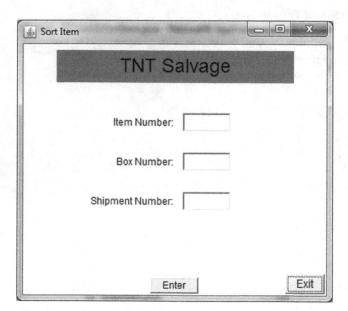

Figure 5-14.

5. Write the source code so that after entering information and pressing the Enter button, the Item Number and Box Number text fields are blank and a message saying how many items have been specified are displayed.

The application logic should correspond to Figure 5-15.

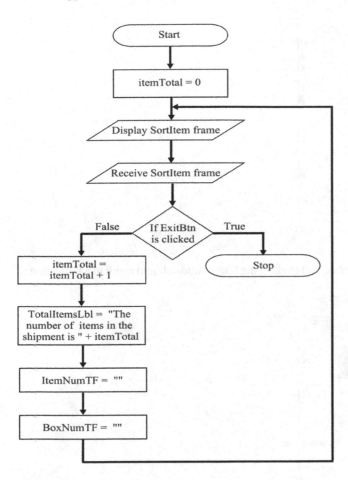

Figure 5-15.

For instance, entering 99 for item number, 1 for box number, 2 for shipment, and clicking the Enter button should result in a frame that looks like Figure 5-16.

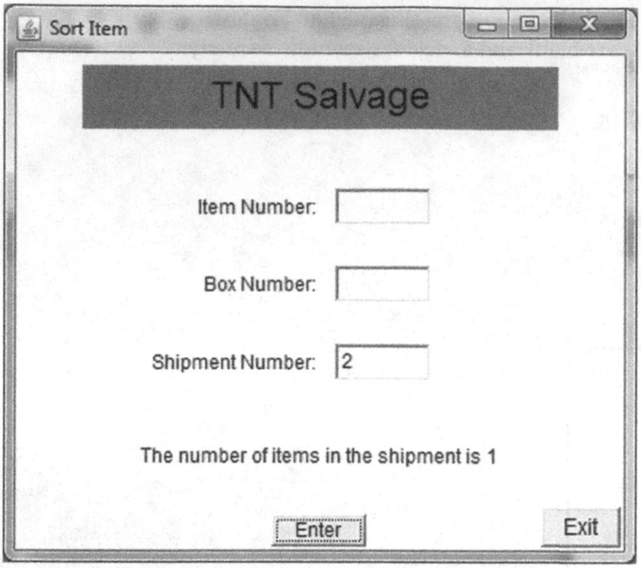

Figure 5-16.

Then, entering 47 for item number, 8 for box number, and clicking the Enter button should result in a frame that looks like Figure 5-17.

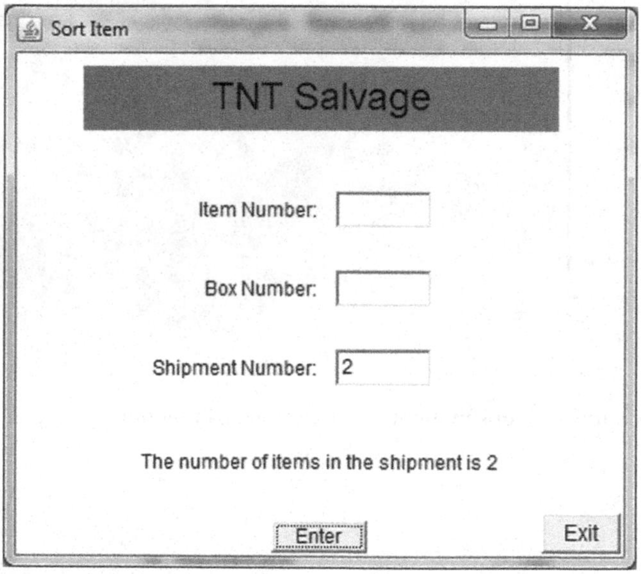

Figure 5-17.

6. Ensure that clicking the Exit button closes the frame.

Results of the Challenge Exercise

Here is what we have after the challenge exercise:

1. UsefulFrame modified to correctly position the Exit button.

2. CE/c5 should contain 15 classes, one of which SortItem is defined as specified above.

Check that the Exercise Was Done Correctly

Run SortItem and verify that the frames displayed match Figures 5-16 and 5-17.

CHAPTER 6

■ ■ ■

Conditional Logic and Checkboxes

In this chapter, we will tackle conditional logic. Conditional logic, also called "If Then Else" logic, is used extensively in programming. It has probably been used in almost every "real-world" program ever written! We will use conditional logic to enhance our applications so that frames can perform multiple functions and execute calculations that are more realistic. (Conditional logic can be a little baffling to first-time programmers but I have confidence in you!) In addition, we will cover some new GUI components, item events, and delve deeper into comparison operators.

Because our application logic will be getting much more complex, we will also begin working with the Debug perspective to find and resolve errors in the source code.

In this chapter, you will learn about:

> Comparisons
>
> Conditional logic
>
> Events
>
> Checkboxes
>
> Checkbox groups
>
> Dispose versus System.exit

After this chapter, you should be able to:

> Use an if/else statement
>
> Use an ItemEvent
>
> Check a component's state
>
> Build compound conditions with *ands* and *ors*
>
> Set breakpoints
>
> Step through statements in the Debug perspective

Conditional Logic

The term "conditional logic" sounds imposing but the concept is very simple: a statement is performed only if a condition is true. Another way to say it is: **If** condition is true **then** perform this action. You use conditional logic every day. For instance, when you are driving: **If** traffic light is red **then** stop. Or said another way, the function *stop* is only performed when the condition is true. Pretty simple, right?

Every high-level programming language provides commands to execute statements conditionally. Java uses the keyword **if** and optionally the **else** keyword to perform conditional logic.

Let's use an example. Our gross salary calculation (pay rate * 40) is not very useful. For instance, most organizations need a net salary calculation that takes into consideration income tax. The tax rate is dependent on how much is earned. For instance, if an employee's weekly salary is less than $50, no taxes are withheld. However, if the weekly salary is greater than $50, then the tax is 12 percent on all income above $50 up to $150. If the weekly salary is greater than $150, then the tax is $12 (that's 12 percent of the salary from $50 to $150) plus 15 percent of all income over $150 up $550. (These salary numbers and tax percentages are, of course, fictional.)

Of course, there are exemptions. For each declared exemption, $60 of the gross weekly salary is not taxed. If you think I'm making things unnecessarily complicated, I'm sorry, but this is really a very simplified version of the tax calculation. For instance, we aren't taking into consideration: state, province, or city taxes, FICA, pretax retirement deductions, pre-tax medical deductions, pre-tax tuition deductions, and so on.

We'll use the following rules for our new calculation.

Salary >	Tax +	Percentage	Of amount over
$50	$0 +	12%	$50
$150	$12 +	15%	$150
$550	$72 +	25%	$550
$1,150	$222 +	28%	$1,150

Another way to depict the calculation is shown in Figure 6-1.

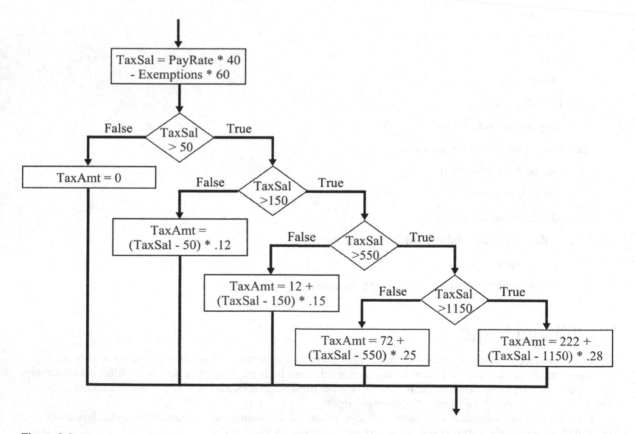

Figure 6-1.

Notice that we slipped in a new symbol, > (greater than). The greater than symbol is an example of a comparison operator. We spoke earlier about mathematical operations and their symbols, such as +, -, or *. Comparison operations (also called logical operations) are also represented by symbols. Comparison operators are at the heart of a condition. Many conditions are comprised of two fixed constants or variables (operands) separated by a comparison operator. When a condition is encountered, the computer compares the values on either side of the comparison symbol and returns a Boolean value of **true** or **false**. (This Boolean value can then be used as the basis for an **if** statement.) The following table shows the various comparison symbols, an example using primitive values in a condition, and the condition example results.

Symbol	Function	Example	Result
<	less than	1 < 2	**true**
>	greater than	1 > 2	**false**
>=	greater than or equal to	1 >= 2	**false**
<=	less than or equal to	1 <= 2	**true**
==	equal	1 == 2	**false**
!=	Not equal	1 != 2	**true**

Please note that the equal operator is represented by two equal signs! A common rookie mistake (that happens to pros too!) is to use a single equal sign when trying to define a condition. A single equal sign is the assignment operator. For instance, trying to assign 2 to 1 (1 = 2) makes no sense and not only does not result in a Boolean value of **true** or **false** but will result in an error message.

Tutorial: Comparisons

Let's have a go at comparisons:

> In the Tutorials project, copy the c5 package.

> Paste the c5 package into Tutorials/src with the new name c6.

> Create a new class in c6 called CondTestApp that has a main method stub.

Enter the following statement in the main method:

```
System.out.println(1=>2);
```

You should get an error (i.e., a red squiggly line beneath the >). Can you figure out what the problem is?
The "greater than or equal to" comparison must have the greater than symbol first and then the equal sign. Yes, the JVM is that picky! The same is true for the "less than or equal" comparison.
Change the comparison to >=, save the source, and run CondTestApp as a Java application.
Notice the Boolean value that is displayed. Just like an addition operation, the computer performs the comparison operation and returns the result. In this case, instead of adding two numbers and returning the sum, the comparison operation is performed/evaluated and the Boolean result is returned. The result (in either the addition or comparison case) is then displayed by the println method.
Comment out the println statement and add the following statement.

```
System.out.println(1=2);
```

Another red squiggly line! Notice the error message says that a variable must be on the left-hand side of an assignment. Remember, the single equal sign represents an assignment not a comparison.

Add a second equal sign to make an equal comparison, save the source and run the application.

The evaluation is performed and **false** is displayed because 1 is not equal to 2.

Tutorial: Ifs

The **if** statement syntax is: the keyword **if**, followed by the condition in parentheses, and the statement to be executed when the condition is true. It is customary to indent the executable statement(s) on the line following the condition. The indentation signifies that the statement is dependent on the condition.

1. In CondTestApp, comment out the println statement, add the following statements, save the source, and run the application.

    ```
    double doubleSalary = 6.50 * 40;
    if (doubleSalary > 550)
            System.out.println("The tax rate is 25% or higher");
    ```

Are you surprised by the result? Does Figure 6-2 help?

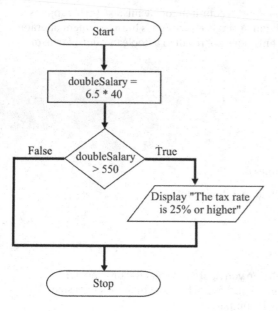

Figure 6-2.

Because doubleSalary is less than 550, nothing is displayed in the console and it seems that the application does nothing. In actuality, the calculation of doubleSalary and the comparison were performed. Let's prove it.

2. Add the following statement after the println statement, save the source, and run the application.

    ```
    System.out.println(doubleSalary);
    ```

Notice that the value of doubleSalary (260.0) is displayed, proving that the calculation is being performed. Why was the doubleSalary value displayed but not the text **"The tax rate is 25% or higher"**? Because only one statement is tied to the condition (see Figure 6-3). To associate more than one statement to a condition, the statements must be enclosed in braces. Because we did not have the println statement inside braces, the value is displayed whether the condition is true or false.

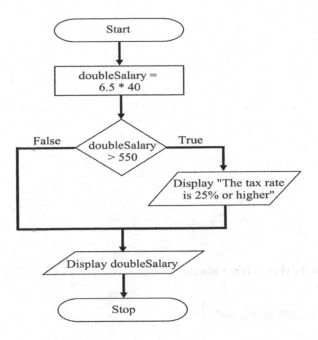

Figure 6-3.

3. Change the source code so that there is an opening brace after the condition and a closing brace after the last statement (see below).

```
if (doubleSalary > 550) {
        System.out.println("The tax rate is 25% or higher");
        System.out.println(doubleSalary);
}
```

Notice that it is customary to place the closing brace on the line following the executable statements and to align the closing brace with the **if** keyword.

4. Save the source and run the application.

Nothing appears again! Well, that's right, because the condition is still false. Our logic flow (as seen in Figure 6-4) still dictates that nothing is done when the condition is false. Let's code an **else** clause so that when the condition is false, something happens.

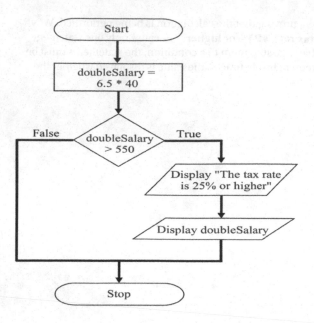

Figure 6-4.

5.   Change the source so that an **else** clause follows the closing brace as follows:

```
if (doubleSalary > 550) {
        System.out.println("The tax rate is 25% or higher");
        System.out.println(doubleSalary);
} else {
        System.out.println("The tax rate is 15% or lower");
        System.out.println("Somebody needs a raise!");
}
```

Again it is customary (but not required) to slightly indent the **else** to denote that the else is associated with the **if**. This makes the code much easier to understand, especially when there are multiple ifs and elses. Multiple statements can also be tied to an **else**. Just as with the **if**, simply enclose the statements in braces. The logic flow can be seen in Figure 6-5.

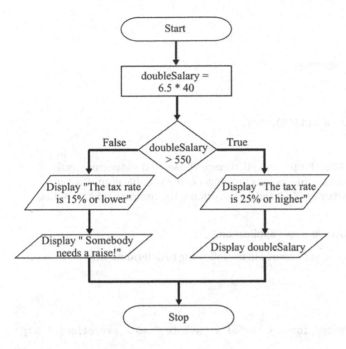

Figure 6-5.

6. Save the source and run the application.

Notice that the **else** statements are executed.

7. Change the calculation so that the pay rate is 15.50, save and print the source code, and run the application.

Notice that the appropriate statements are executed when the condition is true.

Tutorial: Tax Calculation—Part I

In Tutorial/c6.Employee:

1. Create two private class variables of type **double** called taxAmt and taxSal.

2. Create a new public method called fedTaxCalc that returns the variable taxAmt and expects 2 parameters: a **double** variable called payRate and an **int** variable called exemptions.

3. Based on the taxSal calculation in Figure 6-1, in the fedTaxCalc method, enter the formula to calculate the value of taxSal.

4. Inside the fedTaxCalc method, enter an **if** statement that sets taxAmt to zero if taxSal is less than or equal to 50 but 100 if taxSal is not less than or equal to 50.

Okay, that's enough coding; let's test a little.

5. Add a main method.

6. In the main method, add the following statements:

```
        Employee emp;
emp = new Employee("","","","","");
        System.out.println(emp.fedTaxCalc(15.50, 2));
```

Can you explain what these statements do?

The first statement creates a reference variable of type Employee called emp. The second statement creates an Employee object (with blank values for all its properties) and assigns the object to the variable emp. The third statement invokes the fedTaxCalc method using a payRate of 15.50 and 2 exemptions. The returned taxAmt is then displayed in the console.

7. Save the Employee source and run Employee as a Java application.

The result 100.0 should be displayed. If not, compare your source to the following to determine where the mistake is.

```
private double taxAmt;
private double taxSal;
public double fedTaxCalc(double payRate, int exemptions) { taxSal = payRate * 40 - exemptions * 60;
    if (taxSal <= 50) {
        taxAmt = 0;
    } else {
        taxAmt = 100;
    }
    return taxAmt;
}

public static void main(String[] args) {
    Employee emp;
    emp = new Employee("","","","","");
    System.out.println(emp.fedTaxCalc(15.50, 2));
}
```

Compound Conditions versus Nested Ifs

There are actually several ways to code the tax calculation. We will cover two methods: one using compound conditions and the other using nested ifs.

The condition examples so far have been simple conditions: one comparison operator and two values. You can actually build a condition with multiple comparisons by linking the comparisons with && (and) and || (or) operations. For instance, if you were searching for employees with pay rates less than $10 and exemptions greater than 5, the condition could be written as follows:

```
if ((payRate < 10) && (exemptions > 5))
```

Notice that the entire condition is enclosed in parentheses. The individual comparisons do not have to be in parentheses but for clarity purposes, we have done so. You can use many &&'s and ||'s in any combination within a single condition; however, the logic becomes very tricky, so be careful.

We could write the tax calculation code using the && operation and four **if** statements as follows:

```
if (taxSal <= 50)
        taxAmt = 0;

if ((taxSal > 50) && (taxSal <= 150))
        taxAmt = taxSal - 50 * .12;

if ((taxSal > 150) && (taxSal <= 550))
        taxAmt = 12 + taxSal - 150 * .15;

if ((taxSal > 550) && (taxSal <= 1150))
        taxAmt = 72 + taxSal - 550 * .25;
else
        taxAmt = 222 + taxSal - 1150 * .28;
```

Figure 6-6 shows this logic.

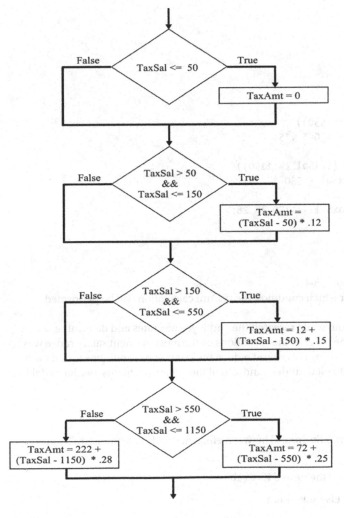

Figure 6-6.

This solution is clear and concise but not efficient. For instance, if the taxable salary amount is less than 50, the tax amount is set to zero but the three succeeding **if** conditions are still executed. We want the computer to ignore the other comparisons after the tax amount is determined. This can be done by nesting the ifs.

Nesting ifs means that an **if** statement is placed within another **if** statement. In this case we will add **else** keywords to the first three **ifs** and place each succeeding **if** inside the previous **else** clause. For instance, the first **if** condition checks if the amount is less than 50. Only if this condition is false do we want the computer to check the other conditions. So we add an **else** clause and place the next **if** inside the **else** as follows:

```
if (taxSal <= 50)
       taxAmt = 0;
else {
       if ((taxSal > 50) && (taxSal <= 150))
              taxAmt = taxSal - 50 * .12;}
```

Now, only when the tax salary amount is greater than 50 will the second condition be tested. We also only want to check the third condition when the second is false and the fourth condition only when the third is false. So, we will nest those **ifs** as follows:

```
if (taxSal <= 50)
       taxAmt = 0;
else {
       if ((taxSal > 50) && (taxSal <= 150))
              taxAmt = taxSal - 50 * .12;
       else {
              if ((taxSal > 150) && (taxSal <= 550))
                     taxAmt = 12 + taxSal - 150 * .15;
              else {
                     if ((taxSal > 550) && (taxSal <= 1150))
                            taxAmt = 72 + taxSal - 550 * .25;
                     else
                            taxAmt = 222 + taxSal - 1150 * .28;
              }
       }
}
```

This source code matches the logic shown in Figure 6-1.

Notice how the indentation helps identify under which condition the taxAmt calculation will be performed. This will help when trying to debug the application.

If you were really trying to improve efficiency, you would research the employee pay rates and determine which salary ranges were the most prevalent and arrange the order of the conditions so the most frequent salary range was checked first, then the second most, third most, and so on. This would reduce the number of conditions tested even further. Of course, the code would be much more difficult to understand and, if there were problems, harder to debug.

Tutorial: Tax Calculation—Part II

With the above discussion in mind, we will take the middle ground between efficiency and understandability and implement the nested **ifs** as above.

1. Replace the **if** condition in fedTaxCalc with the nested **ifs** as above.

2. Click to the right of the brace on the first **else** statement.

Notice that the matching brace 13 lines below is outlined in gray. Because Java uses so many braces and parentheses, this is an extremely helpful RAD feature.

3. Move the cursor before the brace.

Notice that the matching brace is not highlighted anymore. To display a paired symbol's matching symbol, the cursor must be placed after the symbol.

4. In the following statement, click to the right of the last parenthesis:

```
if ((taxSal > 50) && (taxSal <= 150))
```

Notice that the matching parenthesis after the **if** is outlined in gray.

5. Move the cursor one character to the left.

The parenthesis following the && is now highlighted.

Great, we have the calculation, now we need to test that it is correct. We will code a series of "test cases" in the main method. Once we are satisfied that the calculation is correct, we will then modify the rest of the application to use this new feature.

6. After the println statement in the main method, add these four statements:

```
System.out.println(emp.fedTaxCalc(15.50, 0));
System.out.println(emp.fedTaxCalc(30.75, 0));
System.out.println(emp.fedTaxCalc(7.75, 0));
System.out.println(emp.fedTaxCalc(7.75, 3));
```

There are many strategies for testing. A simple one is to ensure that every condition and calculation is tested at least once. These added pay rates will test many of the conditions but not all.

7. Save the Employee source and run Employee as a Java application.

Based on the results, is the application ready? Can you explain the results?

Debugging

There are many different types of errors: syntax errors, compilation errors, and runtime errors. RAD will identify the first two types but is not smart enough to catch the third type of error. Runtime errors can occur for many different reasons: logic errors, user input errors, missing resources (e.g., a required data file is not available), and security (e.g., the application doesn't have authority to a required data file) are only a few of the possibilities. Fortunately, most source code editors provide two tools to find logic errors: breakpoints and stepping.

Breakpoints are statements that when reached during program execution will temporarily halt program execution. Once a breakpoint is reached, stepping allows the programmer to control when the next statement(s) will be executed. Both of these capabilities are provided by RAD in the Debug perspective.

In case you didn't notice, there is a major problem with the test results: the values are all incorrect. For instance, the very first test is for a pay rate of 15.50 per hour. For a forty-hour work week this results in a gross salary of $620 per week. Our calculation is returning a tax amount of $489.50. That seems a little steep, don't you think? On top of that, the example is for two exemptions, which decreases the taxable amount by $120 for a total taxable amount of $500. So, our calculation is saying that $489.50 of the taxable $500 is going to taxes.

Why get out of bed to go to work?

Tutorial: Debugging

We'll use the Debug perspective to look at what is going on within the calculation.

1. In the fedTaxCalc source code, define the taxSal calculation statement as a breakpoint by double-clicking the marker bar (the vertical light blue area to the left of the line numbers) next to the taxSal calculation line number.

A blue circle (indicated by the arrow in Figure 6-7) will be placed in the marker bar to indicate a breakpoint has been defined for the statement.

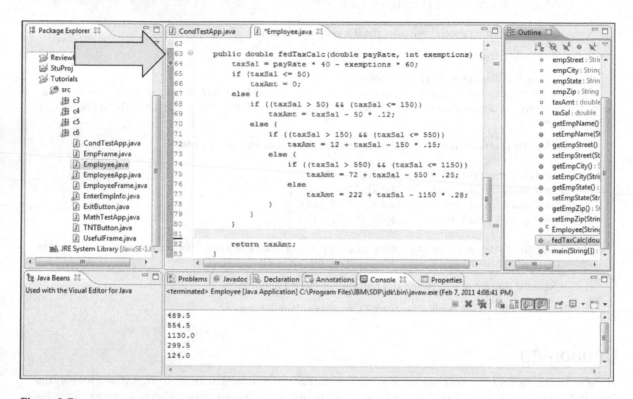

Figure 6-7.

2. To open the Debug perspective, click on the Debug button (the button with the bug icon, to the left of the Run button), and answer yes to the Confirm Perspective Switch prompt.

The Debug perspective will be displayed (see Figure 6-8). To start finding the problem, the programmer first determines if the processing (up to the breakpoint) was correct. By examining the variable values, the programmer can usually determine if the processing was correct. (Fortunately, variable values are easily displayed in the Debug perspective.) If the processing was not correct, then the programmer has narrowed down where the problem lies (e.g., the statements before the breakpoint probably contain the error(s)). If the processing was correct, then the statements after the breakpoint probably contain the error(s).

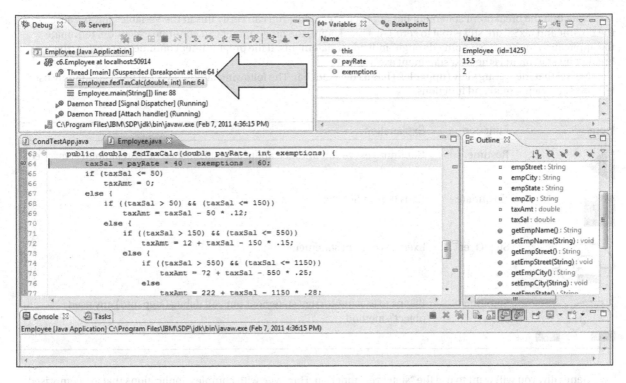

Figure 6-8.

The default Debug perspective is broken up into five panes, several of which support multiple views. We will cover the default views.

The upper left pane (the Debug view) displays the "thread stack." The thread stack allows you to trace the path of execution through the various objects and methods up to the breakpoint. At the top of the stack will be an entry displaying the breakpoint line number and method. Additional entries will be for the previous methods that were executed (and the specific line within each that called the next method). In Figure 6-8, notice the first (and highlighted) stack entry for the breakpoint statement (Employee.fedTaxCalc method, line 64) and then the entry for line 88 in the Employee.main method, which invoked the fedTaxCalc method. Essentially, the thread stack shows that the main method was executed first, then the fedTaxCalc method. This "trace of the methods executed" is very helpful for finding logic errors. In this case, the path in the stack trace is the path that we expected the application logic to follow. (Beware: even if the processing flow is correct, there can still be errors in particular statements.)

The upper right pane shows the Variables view. It displays the current method's parameters and the object (i.e., Employee). Click on the object's expansion icon (to the left of the green circle) to display the object's variables and their values.

You can change a variable value by right clicking the variable name, choosing Change Value, and entering a new value.

3. Click on the Employee object's expansion box and adjust the Variables view to display the five properties, all the variables, and their values.

The final three panes provide the same functions as in the Java perspective. At the bottom, the Console view shows the results of println statements. The Outline view displays a tree of all the object's variables and methods and allows you to traverse the source code by clicking the tree items. Finally, the source code pane displays the object's source code and allows the programmer to modify the source. One difference with the Debug source pane is that the next executable statement is highlighted, in this case, the breakpoint statement (i.e., line 46).

Note that the breakpoint statement has not been executed. (You can verify this in the Variable view because the taxAmt and taxSal are still equal to zero.) At a breakpoint, the programmer can continue execution, terminate the application, or begin "stepping through" individual statements. If the programmer continues execution, the breakpoint statement is the next statement executed.

Notice that the Debug view (upper left) has its own tool bar. The following table shows the most commonly used buttons (i.e., their icons) and functions.

Icons	Function	Explanation
	Resume	Continues execution until the application is finished or a breakpoint is reached
	Terminate	Ends the application
	Step Over	Executes current statement
	Step Into	Begins to execute current statement but will debug (step into) any used object's method

Generally, you will want to use the "step over" function. However, with complex applications that are comprised of many objects, you may need to use "step into." Step into will "bore into" any other object used in the current statement. For instance, stepping into a statement that used a `String` object would mean the `String` class's source statements would be executed one at a time. Usually the Java-supplied classes are not the source of problems, so you will not want to step into these.

Looking in the Variable view, we see that the payRate and exemptions values have been correctly set. This tells us that the processing up to the breakpoint was correct, so the problem probably lies in or after the breakpoint statement. Therefore, we want to continue program execution until we find a statement that generates an incorrect value.

4.   Click the "step over" button.

The breakpoint statement is executed, the next statement (line 65) is highlighted in the source code and listed in the stack trace (meaning it is the current statement), and the new value for taxSal (calculated in line 64) is displayed in the variable pane (see Figure 6-9).

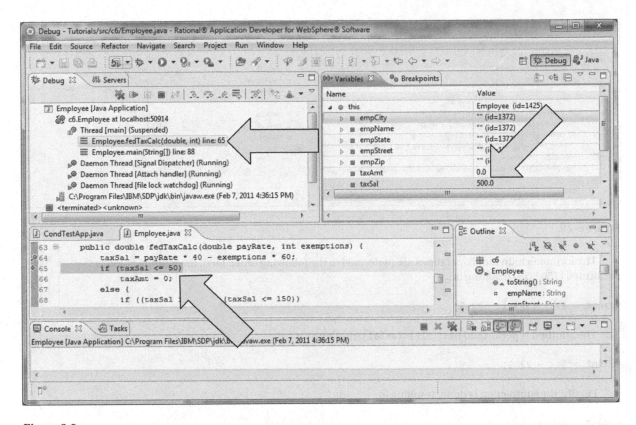

Figure 6-9.

Again, the programmer must determine if the processing was correct. Because the taxSal value of 500 is correct, we will step to the next statement.

5. Click the "step over" button.

Notice that the condition in line 65 was evaluated and the current statement is now line 68. This means that the condition in line 65 was false and processing proceeded to the **else** clause. This is just as we expected.

6. Click the "step over" button.

Again the condition was false, and processing proceeded to the **else** clause, just as we expected.

7. Click the "step over" button.

This time the condition is true, so the taxAmount calculation should be performed. Once again, this is exactly as expected.

8. Click the "step over" button.

The calculation is performed (as expected) but the value (489.50) is incorrect (see Figure 6-10). We have found the culprit! Take a closer look at the calculation and try to figure out what is wrong.

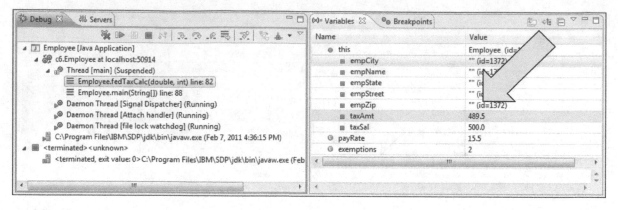

Figure 6-10.

The formula's individual operations are performed in the following order. First, the multiplication is performed (150 * .15) resulting in:

```
taxAmt = 12 + taxSal - 22.5;
```

The addition is performed next (12 + taxSal), resulting in:

```
taxAmt = 512 - 22.5;
```

Finally, the subtraction is done, resulting in:

```
taxAmt = 489.5;
```

This was not expected. The individual operations should have been executed as follows: subtract the already taxed amount (150) from taxSal, calculate the additional tax amount, and add that amount to 12 (the tax amount on the first 150 dollars of income). The formula should be:

```
taxAmt = (taxSal - 150) * .15 + 12;
```

There is actually another way that the formula can be specified. Can you figure it out?

Here's a debugging lesson that will save you a lot of time and aggravation in your programming future: if there is an error in a statement, then similar statements are highly likely to contain errors and should also be checked. In this case, it means you should review the other calculations for errors. Lo and behold, three of the other calculations are also wrong.

9. Close the Debug perspective, by right clicking the Debug perspective icon (on the far right of the window) and selecting Close from the pop-up menu.

10. Correct the formulas and save the Employee source code.

Figure 6-11 shows the alternative formula solution.

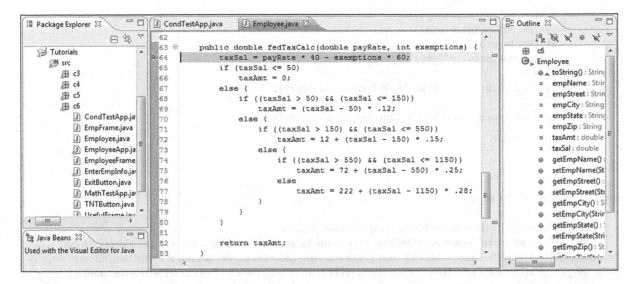

Figure 6-11.

11. Run Employee as a Java application.

The results in the console should be:

```
64.5
89.5
244.4
36.0
9.6
```

Tutorial: Comparisons between Reference Variables

Comparing primitive variables is easy. Comparing reference variables is a little more complicated. Remember, reference variables contain memory addresses not data. So, when comparing two reference variables, they must both point to the same object in storage. We will use Employee variables first and then String variables to drive this concept home.

1. Create a new Java class in c6 called StringCompApp that has a main method stub.

2. Enter the following statements in the main method to define two Employee objects and variables:

```
Employee emp1 = new Employee("Joe","1 Main St.","","","");
Employee emp2 = new Employee("Joe","1 Main St.","","","");
```

3. Enter the following statements after the string definitions:

```
System.out.println(emp1);
System.out.println(emp2);
if (emp1==emp2)
System.out.println("emp1 is equal to emp2");
else
System.out.println("emp1 is NOT equal to emp2");
```

4. Save the source, and run StringCompApp as a Java application.

The results will be:

```
Joe
Joe
emp1 is NOT equal to emp2
```

Are you surprised by the results? Can you explain these results?

emp1 and emp2 are reference variables that contain the location of two different Employee objects. These Employee objects have the same values for their name and street address properties but they are two different objects. Now, the println statements may have confused you. They both display the employee names (not the memory location) because we changed the toString method to return the Employee object name. If we comment out the toString method, you will see a little better why the two objects are not equal.

5. In c6.Employee, comment out the toString method.

6. Run StringCompApp as a Java application.

The results will look like the following (the memory addresses will probably be different from the following):

```
c6.Employee@646d646d
c6.Employee@64796479
emp1 is NOT equal to emp2
```

Notice that the addresses in the variables are different, therefore the comparison results in a value of **false**.

7. In StringCompApp, enter the following statements after the if/else statements:

```
if (emp1.getEmpName() == emp2.getEmpName())
System.out.println("emp1 name is equal to emp2 name");
else
System.out.println("emp1 name is NOT equal to emp2 name");
```

8. Save the source, and run StringCompApp as a Java application.

The results should be the following:

```
c6.Employee@7a807a80
c6.Employee@7ac87ac8
emp1 is NOT equal to emp2
emp1 name is equal to emp2 name
```

Notice that the comparison between the name values was equal. This is the same as comparing two character strings.

9. Comment out all the main method statements.

10. Add the following statement after the main method header:

```
System.out.println("Joe" == "Joe");
```

11. Save and run the application.

The result will be the Boolean value **true** in the console. This same comparison was done between the different objects' name values. The Employee name getters returned two identical character strings that were compared and found to be equal.

Unfortunately, comparing strings gets a little complicated.

Tutorial: Comparisons between String Variables

Now let's try to compare string variables:

1. Comment out the current main method statement and add the following:

```
String name1 = new String("Joe");
String name2 = new String("Joe");
System.out.println(name1 == name2);
```

2. Save the source and run the application.

As you probably expected, the result is false. We compared two String variables that point to two different String objects (just as we did with the Employee variables earlier).

3. Comment out the current main method statements, add the following, and run the application:

```
String name1 = new String("Joe");
String name2 = name1;
System.out.println(name1 == name2);
```

This result is true because we set name2 equal to name1. In this case, both String variables point to the same object.

4. Comment out the current main method statements, add the following, and run the application:

```
String name1 = "Joe";
String name2 = "Joe";
System.out.println(name1 == name2);
```

This produces the surprising result of **true**. Using the shorthand notation to define the strings activates a JVM feature called "string optimization." Explaining in detail what happens in the first two statements will clarify "string optimization".

The first statement does the exact same thing as the first statement in steps 1 and 3: a String object is created and name1's value is set to the String object's memory location.

The second statement, because it does not explicitly tell the JVM to create a new object, activates "string optimization." The JVM searches for any already existing String object that contains the same value (Joe). If there is an already existing object, the memory address of the already existing object is assigned to name2 (as in step 3).

This is done rather than creating a new object and assigning the new object's memory address to name2 (as in step 1). In other words, step 4 saves memory space because only one object is created (as in step 2) instead of two objects (as in step 1).

Now that we have opened up this can of worms, we need to explain another String "feature" regarding changing values. If you change the value of a String, the JVM creates a new String object and changes the variable to point to the new object. The old String object still resides in memory: however, no String variable points to it.

5. Comment out the current main method statements, add the following, and run the application:

```
String name1 = new String("Joe");
String name2 = name1;
System.out.println(name1 == name2);
name1 = "Mary";
System.out.println(name2 + " " + name1);
```

The results will be as follows:

```
true
Joe Mary
```

The fourth statement (name1 = "Mary";) creates a new object (just as if you had specified name1 = new String("Mary");) and the old object, with the value "Joe", is still in memory. We know this because name2 is still pointing to it. If we added a statement to change name2 to "Sam", a new object would be created, name2 would be set to point to the new object, and the original object with "Joe" would be in memory with no variable pointing to it.

Intuitively most people think that strings should work the same as primitives (i.e., a new value simply replaces the old value in the original memory location), as seen in Figure 6-12:

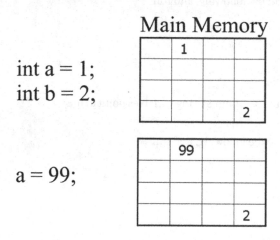

Figure 6-12.

The new value 99 replaces the old value 1.

However, when a new value is assigned to a string, a new object is created and the old object stays in main memory. The memory allocation looks like Figure 6-13.

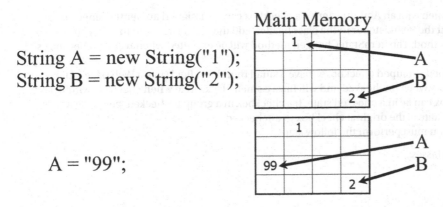

String A = new String("1");
String B = new String("2");

A = "99";

Figure 6-13.

Notice that the object holding the original value of "1" is still in memory and that there are actually three objects. If we then set A equal to B and assigned B a new value of "50", memory would look like Figure 6-14.

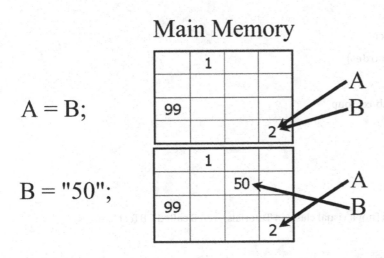

A = B;

B = "50";

Figure 6-14.

Yikes! Once again, this topic may seem unnecessarily complicated. However, the purpose is to show that String objects are more complicated than they appear and that you should be careful when comparing and changing their values. When using strings you should strive for simplicity and try to avoid complicated value assignments.

Checkboxes

A checkbox appears as a small square text field, with a label to the right. A checkbox is like a toggle switch: it has two states. A toggle switch can be on or off, and a checkbox can be checked or unchecked. Clicking on a checkbox will change the state from unchecked to checked or from checked to unchecked. When in the checked state, the checkbox's small text field will contain a checkmark and when in the unchecked state, the text field is empty.

Just as a button can be associated with an ActionListener, a checkbox can be assigned an ItemListener. To use an ItemListener, simply implement the ItemListener in the class header, add the ItemListener to the checkbox, and code an itemStateChanged method. The itemStateChanged method will be executed whenever the checkbox's state is changed.

Checkboxes can also be grouped. Grouped checkboxes have a small round text field (like a Web page radio button). The checkbox will be empty when unchecked and will have a small black circle when checked. Within a checkbox group, only one checkbox can be in a checked state. If a checkbox in a group is checked, checking any another checkbox will change the state of the original checkbox to unchecked.

To create a checkbox group, you must perform the follow steps:

A. Import the following classes:

- Checkbox

- CheckboxGroup

- ItemListener

- ItemEvent

B. Add an itemStateChanged method

C. Implement the ItemListener

D. Define at least one Checkbox object

E. Add the ItemListener to the checkbox(es)

F. Create a CheckboxGroup object

G. Add the checkbox(es) to the checkbox group

H. Add the checkbox(es) to the frame

Tutorial: Coding a Checkbox

Now let's code the checkbox:

1. Using RAD, create a new Java class (not a visual class) in Tutorials/src/c6 called CBTestApp as follows:

- c6.UsefulFrame is the superclass;

- an ItemListener interface is implemented; and

- main and inherited abstract method stubs are created.

The source code should look like the following:

```
package c6;
import java.awt.event.ItemEvent;
import java.awt.event.ItemListener;

public class CBTestApp extends UsefulFrame implements ItemListener {

    public void itemStateChanged(ItemEvent e) {
    }
```

```
    public static void main(String[] args) {
    }
}
```

So far, part of step A and all of steps B and C (from above) have been coded. Because we coded a little, let's test a little.

2. Add the following constructor:

```
public CBTestApp() {
        setVisible(true);
}
```

3. Add the following statement to the main method:

```
CBTestApp cbta = new CBTestApp();
```

4. Save the source and run CBTestApp as a Java application.

A very boring frame should be displayed. This boring frame, however, proves that everything has been coded correctly, so let's not ridicule it too much.

5. Click the Close button to close the frame.

6. After the existing import statements, add the following statements:

```
import java.awt.Checkbox;
import java.awt.CheckboxGroup;
```

This finishes step A.

7. Add the following statement to create a class variable of type Checkbox called empAppCB and assign a new Checkbox object with the text "Employee Application" to empAppCB.

```
private Checkbox empAppCB = new Checkbox("Employee
                Application");
```

This starts step D.

8. In the constructor, before the frame is set visible, add the following statements.

```
empAppCB.setBounds(94, 62, 148, 23);
empAppCB.addItemListener(this);
add(empAppCB);
```

The first statement finishes the checkbox definition (as specified in step D). The second statement adds the ItemListener to the checkbox (as specified in step E). The third statement adds the checkbox to the frame (as specified in step H). So far, we have done steps A through E and step H. This is enough code to test that the checkbox appears on the frame and that the ItemListener has been added correctly.

9. Add the following statement to the itemStateChanged method:

```
System.out.println("Checkbox was clicked!");
```

Can you explain why/how this new statement tests that the ItemListener has been tied to the checkbox?

10. Save the source and run CBTestApp as a Java application.

11. On the frame, click the checkbox four times and click the Window Close button.

The text from the println statement should appear four times in the console. In addition, the check mark should have appeared and/or disappeared each time the checkbox was clicked. Notice also that clicking anywhere on the checkbox (the label or the tiny text field) changes the state.

Tutorial: Coding a Checkbox Group

We need to add a couple more checkboxes, define a checkbox group (step F), and then add the checkboxes to the checkbox group (step G).

1. Define two more checkboxes by placing each of the following statements in its correct location within CBTestApp:

```java
private Checkbox shipAppCB = new Checkbox(
"Shipment Application");
private Checkbox sortAppCB = new Checkbox(
"Sorting Application");
shipAppCB.setBounds(94, 142, 148, 23);
add(shipAppCB);
shipAppCB.addItemListener(this);
sortAppCB.setBounds(94, 222, 148, 23);
add(sortAppCB);
sortAppCB.addItemListener(this);
setExitButtonLocation();
```

Let's test that you added the statements in the right places.

2. Save the source and run CBTestApp as a Java application.

If you added the statements correctly, the frame should appear as in Figure 6-15.

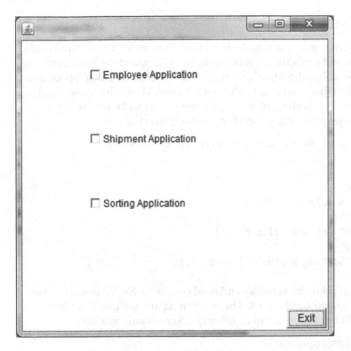

Figure 6-15.

3. Click the Exit button to close the application.

Now we need to perform steps F and G.

4. Add the following statement to create a CheckboxGroup object and class variable:

    private CheckboxGroup cbg = **new** CheckboxGroup();

Can you explain what this statement does?

5. Add each of the following statements after the appropriate checkbox's setBounds statement:

    ```
    empAppCB.setCheckboxGroup(cbg);
    shipAppCB.setCheckboxGroup(cbg);
    sortAppCB.setCheckboxGroup(cbg);
    ```

6. Save the source and run CBTestApp as a Java application.

Notice that the checkboxes are now round, indicating they are in a checkbox group.

7. Click the shipAppCB checkbox, then empAppCB, then sortAppCB, then the Exit button.

Notice that clicking one checkbox unchecks the previously clicked checkbox and that the itemStateChanged method is being called each time any checkbox is clicked.

Tutorial: Working with an ItemEvent and States

Until now, we've glossed over events by simply saying they are passed to the itemStateChanged (or actionPerformed) methods. Events are objects and have useful methods and properties. For example, we have added the ItemListener to three checkboxes. Wouldn't it be nice to be able to tell which checkbox has been clicked? Well, it just so happens that the ItemEvent's getSource method will return the object that was clicked. Alternatively, checkboxes have a method called getState that returns a Boolean value. If the checkbox is checked, the state value is true, and it is false if not checked. We will show how to use both methods to determine which checkbox has been selected.

1. Replace the source code in the CBTestApp itemStateChanged method with the following nested ifs:

```
if (empAppCB == e.getSource()){
System.out.println("Employee App was selected!");}
else if (shipAppCB == e.getSource()){
        System.out.println("Shipment App was clicked!");}
else if (sortAppCB == e.getSource()){
                System.out.println("Sorting App was clicked!");}
```

The earlier **if** examples had comparisons between primitive variables and fixed constants. Notice that this time we are comparing the reference variable empAppCB to the object returned by the ItemEvent's getSource method. When the objects match, the appropriate message will be displayed and no other checkboxes will be tested.

2. Save the source and run CBTestApp as a Java application.

3. Click the shipAppCB checkbox, then empAppCB, then sortAppCB, then the Exit button.

Notice that the appropriate message was displayed each time. Now we'll use the getState method in the **if** conditions to determine which checkbox is selected.

4. Comment out the code in the itemStateChanged method, add the following nested ifs, and run CBTestApp:

```
if (empAppCB.getState())
System.out.println("Employee App was selected!");
else if (shipAppCB.getState())
            System.out.println("Shipment App was clicked!");
        else if (sortAppCB.getState())
                    System.out.println("Sorting App was clicked!");
```

5. Click the shipAppCB checkbox, then empAppCB, then sortAppCB, then the Exit button.

Again, the appropriate message is displayed each time.

Tutorial: VE and Checkboxes

1. In Tutorials/c6, create a new Java visual class called AppOptions that defines:

- c6.UsefulFrame as the superclass;
- an ItemListener interface; and
- main and inherited abstract method stubs.

2. In the Design pane, click the frame to display the Properties view.

3. Modify the frame properties so the title is "Application Menu" and the size is 300, 300.

4. Drag and drop three checkboxes onto the frame and name them empAppCB, shipAppCB, and sortAppCB.

5. Modify the checkboxes such that when displayed they will look like Figure 6-16.

Figure 6-16.

Now comes the tricky part. A checkbox group is not a visual component; therefore, it does not appear in the AWT (or any GUI) list of components.

6. At the top of the Palette, click on Choose Bean.

The "Choose a Bean" frame will be displayed. A bean is a Java class that has a default constructor and a getter and setter method for each property. (By requiring beans to have getters and setters, it is easy for RAD [and other IDEs] to determine what a bean's properties are and create an appropriate property pane.) Beans are an important concept that will be covered in much more detail in later chapters. However, for something that has received so much hype they are pretty simple!

7. On the "Choose a Bean" frame, begin typing checkboxgroup (see Figure 6-17).

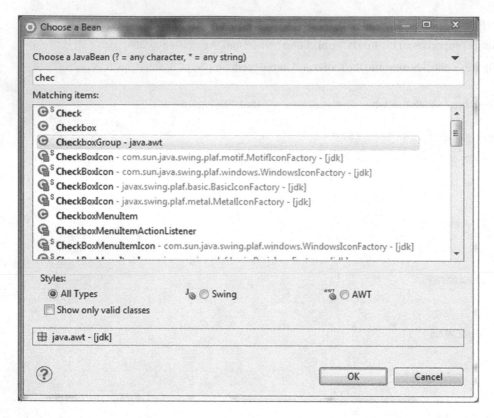

Figure 6-17.

A list of matching class names will be displayed. You must select the component and then add it to the design view (just as you would to select a label or checkbox). RAD, however, requires that the checkbox group icon be added outside the frame.

8. In the class list, click on CheckboxGroup

9. Click the OK button.

The checkbox group has been selected. It must now be added to the class.

10. Move the cursor over the frame.

Notice the cursor changes to the universal "no" symbol. This is because a checkbox group is a nonvisual component and cannot be added to a visual component (the frame). You must add the checkbox group to the Design pane but outside the frame.

11. In the Design pane, click anywhere to the right of the frame and specify appOptsCBG as the name.

The name of the variable and the icon for a Java bean will be placed in the white area to the right of the frame. See Figure 6-18.

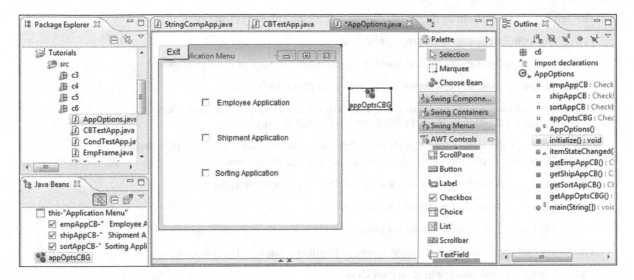

Figure 6-18.

Because the CheckboxGroup is a nonvisual component, VE does not "work" well with it. For example, in the Properties view you can't specify appOptsCBG in the checkboxGroup property value area. (Very strange.) So, we will have to enter the source code by hand.

12. In the getEmpAppCB method, add the following code to assign the empAppCB checkbox to appOptsCBG.

```
empAppCB.setCheckboxGroup(this.getAppOptsCBG());
```

13. Update the getShipAppCB and getSortAppCB methods so the other two checkboxes are added to appOptsCBG.

All of the checkboxes are now round indicating they are part of a group.

Tutorial: Tying the Frames Together

We now must finish modifying the application so that the AppOptions frame is displayed first. Then, based on the checkbox selected, the correct application frame will be displayed. In other words, we'll create a new class called TNT that displays the AppOptions frame. If someone checks the Employee Applications checkbox, we'll then display the EnterEmpInfo frame.

1. Create a new Java class called TNT that has a main method.

2. Enter the code to create an AppOptions object assigned to a variable called **ao**.

3. Save the TNT source code and run TNT as a Java application.

Why doesn't anything happen? Because the AppOptions frame's visible property was never set to true, nothing was displayed.

4. In AppOptions, set the visible property to **true**.

5. In AppOptions, add the source code to reset the Exit button location.

6. Save the AppOptions source code and run TNT as a Java application.

The AppOptions frame will be displayed with the Exit button correctly positioned.

7.   Click the Exit button to end the application.

8.   In the AppOptions source code, add the ItemListener to each of the checkboxes.

9.   In AppOptions, add the nested ifs to check each checkbox's state.

10. Add the source code such that if empAppCB is checked the EnterEmpInfo frame is displayed. (Define the EnterEmpInfo variable name as **eei**.)

11. Add the source code such that if either of the other checkboxes is selected, the message "Sorry that application is not available" is displayed in the console.

12. Save the AppOptions source code and run TNT as a Java application.

The "Application Menu" frame should be displayed.

13. Click the Sorting Application checkbox.

The "Sorry that application not available" message should be displayed in the console.

14. Click the Employee Application checkbox.

The "EnterEmpInfo" frame should be displayed.

15. On the EnterEmpInfo frame, click the Exit button.

Notice that both the AppOptions and EnterEmpInfo frame disappear. This is because the Exit button uses the System.exit() statement, which shuts down the entire JVM.

16. Run TNT as a Java application, click the Employee Application checkbox, and, on the EnterEmpInfo frame, click the window close button in the upper right of the frame.

Notice that the AppOptions frame is still displayed. This is because EnterEmpInfo frame's windowClosing method (which it inherited from UsefulFrame) uses the dispose method, not System.exit(). The dispose method only deletes the current object (the EnterEmpInfo frame), whereas System.exit() ends the JVM, thereby deleting all objects.

Tutorial: Swing

Earlier we mentioned that there are other GUI component sets available. Swing is one of them and now is a good time to demonstrate how Swing and AWT are different yet similar. We will duplicate the frame we just created using Swing components.

1.   In c6, create a new visual class called AppOptionsSwing.

2.   On the New Java Visual Class frame, in the Style pane, specify the superclass by expanding Swing and selecting Frame.

3.   Also, on the New Java Visual Class frame, implement an AWT action listener, create a main method stub, and have stubs for the inherited abstract methods.

4.   In the Visual Editor, click on the JFrame title and display the properties view.

Notice that JFrame properties are almost exactly the same as a Frame. However, some of the default values are different, for instance, the background color.

5.   Display the JFrame source code.

Components are not placed directly on a JFrame. Instead, a JFrame must have a content pane on which the components are added. Notice that there is a JPanel variable called jContentPane (defined on line 14) and that in the initialize method (line 49) the JContentPane property is set to the JPanel object (created and returned by the getJContentPane method). So, a JFrame is a little more complicated than a Frame because it needs a content pane. However, the Visual Editor hides this from the programmer by creating a JPanel and assigning it to the JFrame's content pane property.

6. In the Visual Editor Design pane, watch the properties view and click on the content pane area (center of the JFrame).

Notice that the properties change. This is because the JFrame and JPanel are two different classes with different properties.

7. In the Swing Components tray, click on JCheckBox and move the mouse cursor over the panel.

Notice how the panel "lights up" with various sections. This occurs because the JPanel has a default layout of BorderLayout (just like Frame).

8. In the Properties view, change the JPanel Layout property to null and press Enter.

9. Place a JCheckBox on the panel and accept the default name.

Notice that there are quite a few more JCheckBox properties than there are AWT checkbox properties. Many of these properties are very useful. For instance, flyover text can be defined (the toolTipText property) or a keystroke shortcut can be assigned (the mnemonic property).

10. Specify "Starts Shipment Application" for the toolTipText property.

11. Click on the mnemonic property to display the Java Property Editor button.

12. Click on the Java Property Editor button to display the Java Property Editor.

You can scroll through the list of options and select a key. Selecting a key as a shortcut means that the selected key when pressed with the Alt key will automatically select the check box.

13. From the list, select B.

14. Click the OK button and save AppOptionsSwing.

15. Create a Java class called TNTSwing that creates an AppOptionsSwing object and assigns it to variable aos.

16. Run TNTSwing.

Nothing happened—why? We never changed the AppOptionsSwing's visible property to true!

17. Change the AppOptionsSwing's visible property to true and run TNTSwing.

18. Move the mouse cursor over the JCheckBox.

Notice the flyover text is displayed.

19. Press and hold the Alt key and then press the B key.

Notice that the checkbox has been checked.

20. Close the JFrame.

Tutorial: Swing versus AWT

JCheckBoxes can be grouped just like Checkboxes, however, the class is ButtonGroup not CheckBoxGroup. Again, the Swing implementation of a checkbox group is very similar to AWT but there is a twist: the checkboxes do not become round in Swing. Now this may sound minor, but it is a standard that radio buttons (round check boxes) are used to indicate that only one item can be selected from the group. So, to abide by this standard, we need to use JRadioButton, not JCheckBox.

1. In the Visual Editor, delete the JCheckBox and add three JRadioButtons called empAppRB, shipAppRB, sortAppRB with the same text and positioning as the checkboxes in AppOptions.

    Notice that the class has a new warning message. Even though you deleted the checkbox from the frame, RAD left the import JCheckBox statement in the source code. Since the JCheckBox is never used, the import statement is not needed and RAD flags the statement with a warning. (One would think that because RAD is smart enough to know that the statement isn't needed, it would have been smart enough to delete the statement. Oh well.)

2. Assign the same mnemonic and toolTipText property values to shipAppRB that were assigned to the deleted JCheckBox in steps 10 and 13 above.

3. In the Visual Editor palette, click on Choose a Bean.

4. In the Choose a Bean window, begin typing ButtonGroup and when it appears in the Matching types pane, click on it to select it.

5. Click the OK button.

6. In Visual Editor, click to the right of the JFrame and accept the default name.

    The variable buttonGroup will be placed in the Design pane. As with AWT checkboxes, you will have to add code to tie the radio buttons to the button group. However, instead of changing each checkbox's property, the JRadioButtons are added to the ButtonGroup.

7. In the getButtonGroup method, make the radio buttons part of the button group by adding the following after the ButtonGroup object is assigned to the variable buttonGroup.

    ```
    buttonGroup.add(empAppRB);
    buttonGroup.add(shipAppRB);
    buttonGroup.add(sortAppRB);
    ```

8. In the getJContentPane method, after sortAppRB is added to the content pane, make the button group part of the content pane by adding getButtonGroup();.

9. Run TNTSwing.

    Click the radio buttons and prove that only one can be selected.

    To finish the Swing implementation, we must tie the action listener to the radio buttons and write the code for the actionPerformed.

10. Add the action listener to each button by inserting the following statements in the appropriate getXXXAppRB method:

    ```
    empAppRB.addActionListener(this);
    shipAppRB.addActionListener(this);
    sortAppRB.addActionListener(this);
    ```

In the actionPerformed method, we want to display the EnterEmpInfo frame if the first radio button is clicked. When the other two buttons are clicked, display text saying that the other applications are not available. To determine which radio button was clicked we will use the action event's getSource method to retrieve the radio button object that was clicked and compare it to the three radio buttons. This was also very similar to one of the techniques we used with the AWT checkboxes.

11.　In the actionPerformed method, add the following code:

```
if (empAppRB == e.getSource()) {
EnterEmpInfo eei = new EnterEmpInfo();}
else if (shipAppRB == e.getSource())
System.out.println("Sorry the ship app is not available");
        else if (sortAppRB == e.getSource())
            System.out.println("Sorry the sort app is not available");
```

12.　Run TNTSwing and click the Employee Application radio button.

Notice that a Swing-based object (AppOptionsSwing) can create an AWT-based object (EnterEmpInfo) and vice versa. Mixing AWT and Swing components is considered bad design because the application lacks a consistent "look and feel." However, the purpose of this exercise was not to demonstrate good design but to show how similar yet different the two GUI component sets are. Remember, the AWT components are easier to use but the Swing components have extra functions/features.

Tutorial: Using the New Calculation

Let's use the new calculation:

1.　Change EnterEmpInfo frame as follows:

- Set the Title to "Enter Employee Information"

- Change the names of empCSZlbl to cityLbl and empCSZTF to cityTF

- Change the text of cityLbl to "City"

- Change the text of cityTF to "Jacksonville"

2.　Create three new labels:

- exmpLbl with the text "Exemptions"

- stateLbl with the text "State"

- zipLbl with the text "Zip"

3.　Create three new textfields:

- exmpTF (accept the default size)

- stateTF with the text "FL" (accept the default size)

- zipTF with the text "322"

4.　Create two new TNTbuttons called dispBtn and taxBtn as follows:

- Same size as the Gross button

- Labels that say "Display" and "TaxAmt"

5.　Adjust the position of the components so that the frame looks like Figure 6-19.

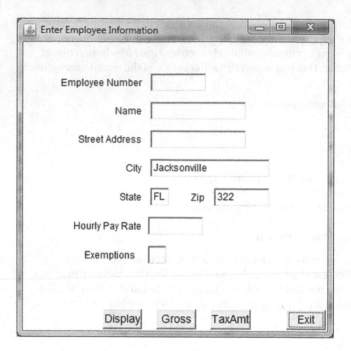

Figure 6-19.

6. Change the source code to add the ActionListener to the two new buttons.

7. In the actionPerformed method, comment out the println statement.

8. In the actionPerformed method, enter a nested **if** that uses the ActionEvent's getSource method to determine which button was clicked and perform the following logic:

If the Display button is clicked
Create an EmployeeFrame object with the text field information from the EnterEmployeeInfo frame and assign it to a variable called **ef.**
Else Add the result label to the frame
If the Gross button is clicked
Calculate doubleGross and set the result label's text
Else If the TaxAmt button is clicked
Run the Employee fedTaxCalc method and set the result label text to "The Federal Tax amount is: $" concatenated to the amount returned by fedTaxCalc
The flowchart for this logic can be seen in Figure 6-20.

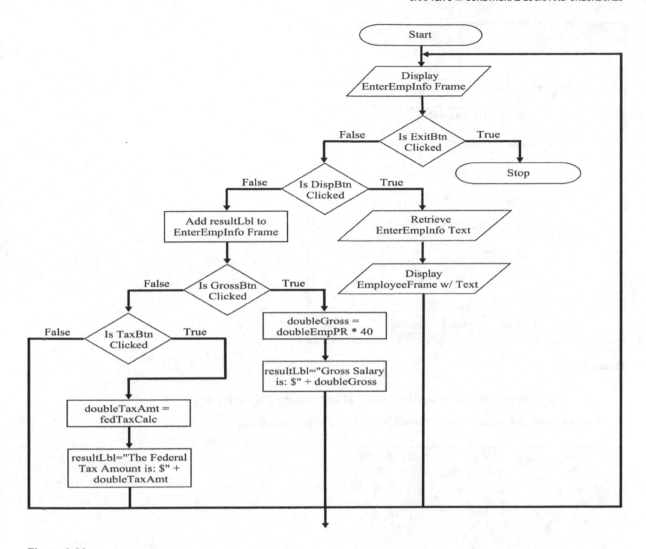

Figure 6-20.

9. Save the source code.

10. Test that the tutorial was done correctly by running TNT as a Java application and then select Employee Application.

The Enter Employee Information Frame should appear as in Figure 6-21.

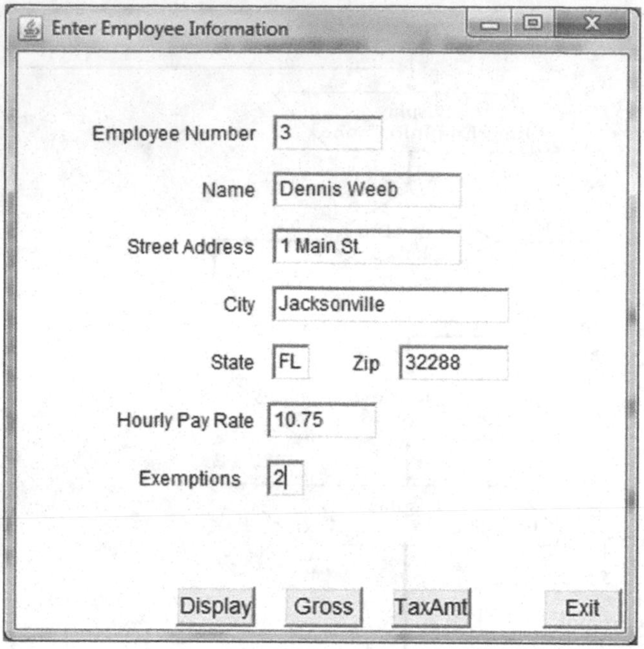

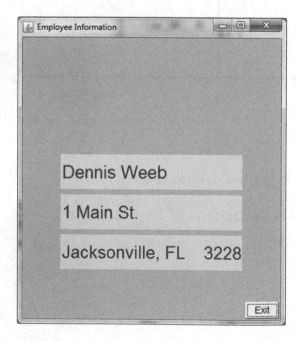

Figure 6-21.

11. Enter the information as seen in Figure 6-21 and click the Display button.

The Employee Information frame should be displayed as in Figure 6-22.

Figure 6-22.

12. On the Employee Information frame, click the Window Close button.

13. On the Enter Employee Information frame, click the Gross button.

The message "Gross salary is: $430.00" will be displayed.

14. On the Enter Employee Information frame, click the TaxAmt button.

The message "The Federal Tax amount is: $36.00" will be displayed. Congratulations, you have created a full-fledged Java application!

The EnterEmpInfo actionPerformed method should look similar to the following:

```java
public void actionPerformed(ActionEvent e) {
String empPayRate = empPRTF.getText();
double doubleEmpPR, doubleGross;
doubleEmpPR = Double.parseDouble(empPayRate);

if (dispBtn == e.getSource()){
        Employee emp =
        new Employee(empNameTF.getText(),
                    empStreetTF.getText(),
                    cityTF.getText(),
                    stateTF.getText(),
                    zipTF.getText());
    EmployeeFrame ef = new EmployeeFrame(emp);
}
else {
        this.add(resultLbl);

        if (grossBtn == e.getSource()){
            doubleGross = doubleEmpPR * 40;
             resultLbl.setText("Gross Salary is: $" +
            doubleGross + "0");
        }
        else {
            if (taxBtn == e.getSource()){
                    Employee emp =
                        new Employee("","","","","");
                    String exmp = exmpTF.getText();
                    int intExmp = Integer.parseInt(exmp);
                    double doubleTaxAmt =
                        emp.fedTaxCalc(doubleEmpPR, intExmp);
                    resultLbl.setText("The Federal Tax amount
                                is: $" + doubleTaxAmt + "0");
            }
        }
}
//          System.out.println(empPayRate);
}
```

Tutorial Results

Let's go over the results:

1. In the Tutorials project, a new package called c6.

2. In c6, new classes called CondTestApp, StringCompApp, CBTestApp, AppOptions, TNT, AppOptionsSwing, and TNTSwing.

3. A new method in Employee called fedTaxCalc.

4. Changes to the EnterEmpInfo class as explained in the tutorials.

5. A printout of the CondTestApp and StringCompApp source code.

Review Questions

Here are the review questions:

1. Explain the difference between the System.exit and dispose methods.

2. What is the difference between the following two operators =, = = ?

3. What is the thread stack?

4. What is a runtime error? Give examples of what could cause a runtime error.

5. What does an event's getSource method do?

6. Explain the relationship between an ActionListener, a Button, an ActionEvent, and an actionPerformed method.

7. What are the differences between stand-alone checkboxes and checkboxes that have been assigned to a checkbox group?

8. Explain the difference between primitive and reference variable comparisons.

9. Describe the function of the plus sign (+) when used with numeric values versus character values.

10. What are the advantages and disadvantages of using AWT versus Swing?

Review Exercise:

In this exercise, you will create two new frames called EnterShipNum (see Figure 6-14) and Ship-Options (see Figure 6-15). ShipOptions will provide choices to enter or display shipment information. When a user chooses the Display Shipment Information option, they will be prompted to supply the shipment number (i.e., the EnterShipNum will be displayed). When someone chooses the Enter Shipment Information option, the EnterShipInfo frame will be displayed.

The flow between the new and old frames can be seen in Figure 6-23. (Note that thumbnail images of the new frames appear to the right of the I/O operation that displays the frame.)

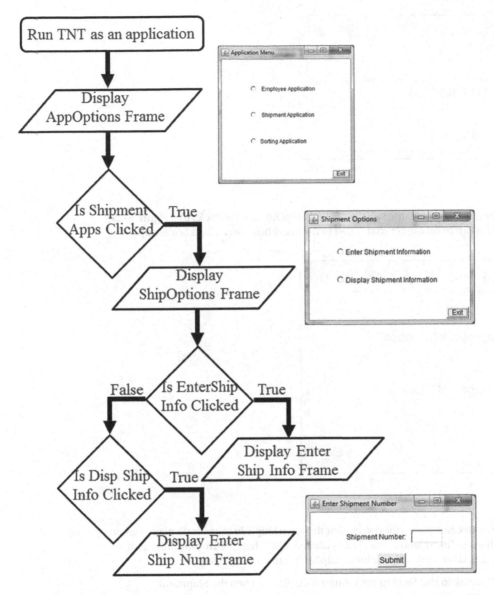

Figure 6-23.

In the ReviewEx project:

1. Create a new package called c6.

2. Select all the classes in ReviewEx's c5 package, then copy and paste them into c6

3. From Tutorials/c6, copy the Java files AppOptions, Employee, EmployeeFrame, EnterEmp- Info, TNT, and TNTButton into ReviewEx/c6.

4. Create a UsefulFrame subclass called EnterShipNum that looks like Figure 6-24, implements an ActionListener that is tied to the Submit button (which is a TNTButton), and has an actionPerformed method. The text field name should be shipNumTF.

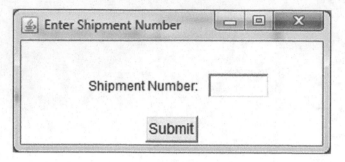

Figure 6-24.

5.　Create another new UsefulFrame subclass called ShipOptions that looks like Figure 6-25 and implements an ItemListener that is tied to the checkboxes in a checkbox group.

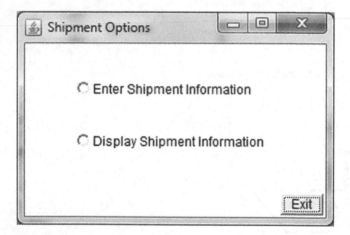

Figure 6-25.

6.　Code an itemStateChanged method such that the EnterShipInfo frame is displayed when the Enter Shipment Information checkbox is clicked, and when the Display Shipment Information checkbox is clicked, the EnterShipNum frame is displayed.

7.　Modify AppOptions so that ShipOptions frame is displayed when the Shipment Application checkbox is clicked.

8.　Arrange the frame locations so they appear as in Figure 6-26.

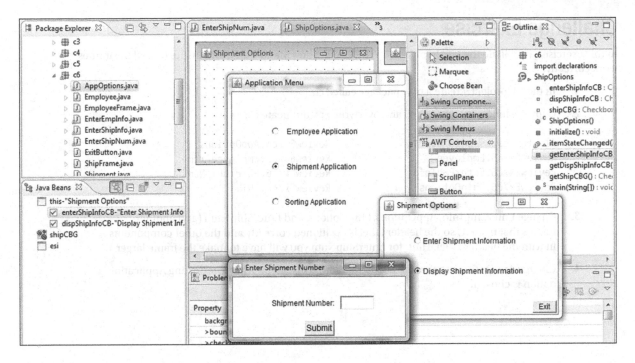

Figure 6-26.

Results of the Review Exercise

Let's go over the results:

1. A new package called c6 in the ReviewEx project.

2. Two newly coded classes in c6 (of 15 total classes) called ShipOptions and EnterShipNum that perform as specified above.

3. AppOptions modified to display ShipOptions.

Check that the Exercise Was Done Correctly

Time to check that we did everything correctly:

1. Run TNT and verify that the Enter Employee Info frame and the Shipment Options frame are displayed when the appropriate Application Menu checkbox is clicked.

2. On Shipment Options, verify that the Enter Shipment Info frame and Enter Shipment Number frame are displayed when the appropriate checkbox is clicked.

Challenge Exercise

In this exercise, you will tie the SortItem frame to the Application Menu frame and insure that all the frames work correctly.

1. In the CE project, create a new package called c6.

2. Copy the following into CE/c6 and overwrite any duplicate classes:

   ```
   All the classes in CE/c5          ReviewEx/c6.AppOptions
   ReviewEx/c6.Employee              ReviewEx/c6.EmployeeFrame
   ReviewEx/c6.EnterEmpInfo          ReviewEx/c6.EnterShipNum
   ReviewEx/c6.ShipOptions           ReviewEx/c6.TNT
   ```

3. Change EnterEmpInfo, AppOptions, ShipOptions, and EnterShipNum (and another frames that need it) so the header label is positioned correctly and the other components fit with the header label. Hint: for EnterShipNum you will have to make the frame larger.

4. Change AppOptions so that the SortItem frame is displayed when the Sorting Application option is chosen.

CHAPTER 7

■ ■ ■

Application Improvements

In this chapter, we will add functions to not only make our application easier to use, but also decrease the chance of "runtime" errors. For instance, we will begin using choice components to insure that only valid data is supplied to the Java application. In addition, we will "catch" errors before the user sees them. Once an error is caught, the application will either resolve the error or tell the user (in much clearer/simpler language than the JVM error messages) what the problem is and how to solve it. We will also explain the concept of iteration (looping) and show how programmers incorporate iteration to increase efficiency.

We will also introduce some new Java formatting classes that make displayed information easier to read, understand, and produce and, finally, demonstrate a powerful Java technique: method overloading.

In this chapter, you will learn about:

     Editing and auditing data

     Formatting numeric, date, and time data

     The StringBuffer class

     Exceptions

     try and catch keywords

     The Choice class

     Iteration (looping)

     Method overloading

After this chapter, you should be able to:

     Define, throw, and catch an exception

     Create, populate, and read selected text from a Choice object

     Define a loop

     Control the format of numeric, date, and time data

     Use and manipulate string buffers

Exceptions

Exceptions are "thrown" by the JVM when a problem is encountered during execution of a Java application. Again, there can be many reasons for a "run time" exception: user error, system error, security violation, network problems, and so on. The JVM tries to identify the problem and puts this information in an Exception object. The Exception object contains information such as the type of exception that was encountered, an error message, and the **stack trace**. When a problem is encountered, the JVM's standard procedure is to display the Exception object and end the application.

You have seen what this looks like. (See the console pane in Figure 7-1 at the end of the next tutorial if you need a reminder.) How do you think a user would react to receiving these types of messages? This is why it is a good programming practice to anticipate what errors may occur (i.e., what exceptions may be thrown) and stop the JVM from responding (i.e., catch the exception within the application program). Once the ugly JVM message is stopped from being displayed (i.e., the application catches the exception), the application should either resolve the problem or display a user-friendly message with information so that the user can resolve the problem.

Tutorial: Exceptions

Let's look at exceptions:

1. In Tutorials/src, create a new package called c7.

2. Copy all of the following classes from c6 to c7:

AppOptions	Employee	EmployeeApp
EmployeeFrame	EnterEmpInfo	ExitButton
TNT	TNTButton	UsefulFrame

3. Run c7.TNT as an application.

4. Select Employee Application

5. Enter "$9.50" (including the $ in the text field) for Hourly Pay Rate, "six" for Exemptions, and click the Gross button.

The result should look like Figure 7-1. The text in the console pane is the JVM's printout of the Exception object. Notice that the first line contains a general error message that identifies the type of exception (NumberFormatException) and the offending piece of input ($9.50). The remaining lines show the **stack trace**. Most of the stack trace is unintelligible because you don't know how the supplied classes (Frame, String, Double, etc.) work internally. For example, the Double class's parseDouble method creates objects and invokes methods of which you are blissfully unaware. The second line in the console pane shows that the readJavaFormatString method in the FloatingDecimal class (of which you know nothing) was actually where the error occurred.

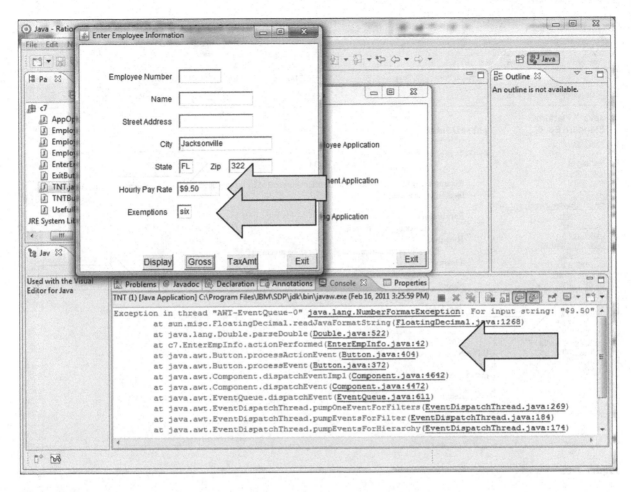

Figure 7-1.

However, some of the stack trace will make sense to you. In this case, it is the fourth line that indicates that line 42 within c7.EnterEmpInfo (in the actionPerformed method) was the statement that triggered the problem.

Now, was it really the Java statement that caused the problem, or was the data passed to the statement the problem? It was the data. Because the value being parsed contained a text character ($), the parse method failed. So what is a programmer to do? Fortunately, programmers can add code to handle (i.e., catch) exceptions when they occur (i.e., are thrown).

Identifying an Exception

Programmers can determine which exceptions may be generated (thrown) through testing. In other words, a programmer could type in a variety of incorrect information to generate exceptions. However, this is a very time consuming technique and not very thorough.

Fortunately, the online documentation for class methods lists the exceptions that can be thrown (i.e., generated). Figure 7-2 shows the online documentation for the Double class's parseDouble method. (Notice that the lower-left-hand pane shows that the Double class was selected and in the right-hand pane, we have scrolled down to the parseDouble method.) The exceptions that can be thrown are identified in both the method header and the text explanation below the header. So, based on the documentation, we now know that every parseDouble statement can generate a NumberFormatException object.

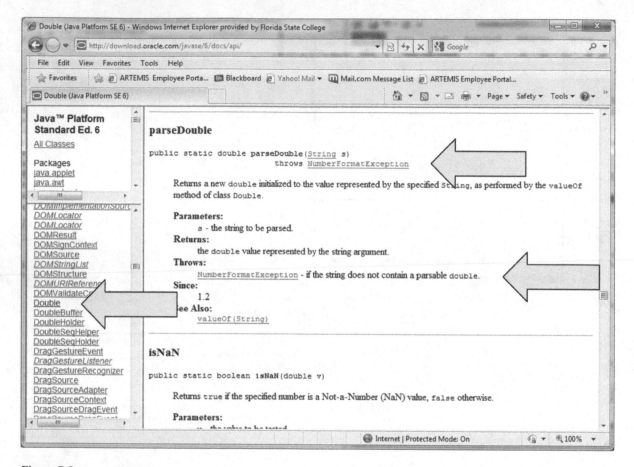

Figure 7-2.

In addition to the online documentation, RAD has a very nice feature that will figure out the exceptions that can be thrown by a statement. More on that a little later.

Tutorial: Catching an Exception

The two keywords try and catch are needed to catch an exception. A **try** block identifies the Java statements that may throw an exception. The **try** block consists of the keyword try followed by braces that enclose the statements that can throw the exception.

Following the **try** block are **catch** blocks. Each **catch** block identifies the exception to be handled and contains executable statements. If an exception is thrown and there is a **catch** for the thrown exception, the JVM will execute the statements specified in the **catch**. In other words, the JVM ignores the exception (i.e., the JVM does **not** stop the application and display the exception information).

For instance, we know that the parseDouble statement on line 42 is throwing a number format exception. We will enclose that statement in a **try** and then code the **catch** to display a user-friendly message asking the user to specify the pay rate in the correct format.

1. In the c7.EnterEmpInfo actionPerformed method, select the statement that parses empPayRate, click Source, Surround With, then Try/catch Block.

The resulting code will be:

```
try {
        doubleEmpPR = Double.parseDouble(empPayRate);
} catch (NumberFormatException e1) {
        // TODO Auto-generated catch block
        e1.printStackTrace();
}
```

Notice that RAD knew which exception(s) could be thrown and inserted the correct catch block(s). However, putting the parseDouble statement into the **try** block caused new errors. The JVM is smart enough to know that a statement in a **try** block may not be executed (because of an exception). If the parseDouble statement is never executed, no value will be assigned to doubleEmpPR. Therefore, statements that use doubleEmpPR are flagged with an error.

To avoid this error, we will initialize the variable to negative one. (Later in the application we determine if we should continue processing by checking if the pay rate value is still –1 or not.)

2. In actionPerformed, change the variable's definition statement to the following:

```
double doubleEmpPR = -1, doubleGross;
```

3. Change the catch block to the following:

```
catch (NumberFormatException error) {
                empPRTF.setText("");
                resultLbl.setForeground(Color.red);
                resultLbl.setText("Pay rate must be a numeric " +
        "value: 1, 2, 3...");
}
```

The first statement clears the invalid value in the empPRTF field. This makes it harder for the user to reenter the incorrect value. The second statement changes the result label's text color to red (so that the message will be more noticeable and because red is the universal color for errors), but notice that the statement has an error. The value red that was specified is not just simple text. It is actually a variable stored in the class Color. Because of this, we must include an import statement for the class Color.

4. Click on the text Color so the insertion point is in the text.

5. Press and hold the Ctrl and Shift keys, and then press the M key.

After clicking on a class name, Ctrl-Shift-M is a RAD shortcut for adding the correct import statement. In this case, import java.awt.Color; is added. (If there are classes with the same name in different packages, a window will be displayed with the available options to select from.)

Finally, notice that the third statement in the catch block displays a "matter of fact" message that identifies the field that had the incorrect value and provides examples of valid values. Most organizations will have their own standards for error messages (i.e., their color, content, etc.) and these standards could dictate much more elaborate messages. For instance, an error message could include instructions for resolving the error, provide a contact person for help, contain a hyperlink to more detailed error information, etc. However, this is an example of a good simple error message.

After parsing (and the **try/catch** blocks), we only want to keep processing if a valid value for pay rate has been entered. So, we need to check if the pay rate is still –1. If pay rate is still –1 (meaning invalid data was entered), we want the JVM to redisplay the frame. In other words, we don't want the remaining statements in the method to be executed. To stop the statements from being executed, we will surround the statements in the following if statement:

```
if (doubleEmpPR != -1) {
        remaining method statements
}
```

6. Select all the remaining statements in the method (but not the last closing brace) and click Source, Surround With, then 3 if (if statement).

RAD surrounds the statements with the if statement but doesn't know what condition should be coded. So, the placeholder text "condition" is put in the parenthesis as follows:

```
if (condition) {
        remaining method statements
}
```

7. Replace the text "condition" with:

```
doubleEmpPR != -1
```

Now, when the pay rate value is invalid (i.e., doubleEmpPR's value was not changed from –1), this if prevents the remaining statements from executing. We have coded a little, so it's time to test a little.

8. Save and run the application.

9. Try to calculate tax amounts for the following pay rate and exemptions values and notice all the errors.

Pay Rate	Exemptions
Ten	4
10	four
10	4
10.33	4

You should have noted the following "problems":

A. The error message is not always displayed

B. The tax amount is not always formatted correctly. For example:

    a. it is displayed in red

    b. it has too many decimal places

C. The message does not always fit in the label

D. Entering an invalid exemptions value results in an exception being thrown that is not being caught. In addition, the previous message remains on the frame thereby indicating there is no problem or incorrectly identifying the problem.

Tutorial: Solving Program Errors

Problem "A" is an example of a logic problem. Logic errors are the most difficult to solve because the reason and location of the error is totally unknown. For instance, if the application generated an incorrect tax amount, you would probably examine the calculation statement(s). If the calculation looked good, you would then try to verify that the values entered by the user were actually being used in the calculation. Ninety-nine percent of the time, this would result in finding the mistake. However, with the error message not appearing, there is no obvious starting point or procedure to find the error. For instance, is the setText statement wrong, or is the text erased somewhere in the code, or is the label never defined, or..., or..., or...? Even if you stepped through the source code statements in the Debug perspective, the error would not be obvious.

The cause of this problem is that the result label is added to the frame in the actionPerformed method after it is determined that a button other than the display button has been clicked. In other words, when the incorrect values are entered the first time, the add statement is never reached. This is an example of poor program structure. The initialize method (that RAD created) is the correct place to specify all of the frame's components. The result label should have been added to the frame in initialize not in the actionPerformed method.

1. Cut the following statement from the actionPerformed method and paste it at the end of the initialize method.

```java
this.add(resultLbl);
```

2. Save the source and run the application with the test data again.

Well, problem "A" is solved (because the error message is now being displayed). However, a new problem (which we will call problem "E") has been uncovered: when the frame is initially displayed, the result label has the text Label. Dang, another error!! (Changes can often have unintended results and this is why you should test, test, and then test again.) Can you figure out how to fix this?

This is an excellent example of a "soft" error. "Hard" errors are program failures, incorrect results, etc. Problems "A" and "D" are examples of hard errors. This new error is considered a soft error because it does not produce incorrect results; however, soft errors may confuse a user. As mentioned earlier, red text traditionally indicates an error. So, if correct results are displayed in red (as in problem "B1"), the user may think that the results are incorrect. Problems "B" and "C" are considered soft errors because the results are correct but poorly formatted.

Soft errors are usually fixed after the hard errors are resolved. However, we will use a new visual component to solve problem "D." Since the new component will require an explanation, we will instead solve the soft problems ("B1", "C" and "E") now, and then solve problem "D." Problem "B2" is also a soft problem, but formatting is a topic that needs an explanation, so we will also tackle it later in the chapter.

3. In the actionPerformed method, after the double variables are defined, add the following statement:

```java
resultLbl.setForeground(Color.black);
```

This will set the result label text to black each time the actionPerformed method is executed. If the label color was previously changed to red, this will reset the color to black.

4. In the initialize method, change the label's text to blanks, length to 350, and horizontal location to 25 (see the following):

```java
resultLbl.setText("");
        resultLbl.setSize(new Dimension(350, 23));
        resultLbl.setLocation(new Point(25, 332));
```

5. Run the tests again to prove that problems "B1", "C", and "E" have been resolved.

The Choice Component

One way that we could cut down on data entry errors (like an incorrect value for exemptions) is to always check the user-entered values and make sure it is numeric. However, an even better technique is to provide a "list" of correct values and only allow users to select and submit values from the list. A Choice component looks like a text field with a small rectangular button on the right. When the button is clicked, a drop-down menu containing text is displayed. The text displayed in the drop-down menu can be defined in the application and when a user clicks one of the values, the application can retrieve the selected value.

Because there are a limited number of correct values, the exemptions value is a good candidate for a choice. Other data, for instance pay rate, are not good candidates because there are thousands of correct values (e.g., 10.50, 10.75, etc.) We will delete the exemptions text field and add a Choice component.

1. In Visual Editor, click the exemptions text field and press the Delete key.

A statement in the actionPerformed method will be flagged with an error because it references the exemptions text field. We will fix this (a little later) by replacing the statement with one that will work with the choice we are about to add.

2. In the component palette, click on the AWT Choice component then click on the frame location where the exemptions text field was.

3. Specify the name as exmpChoice and then change exmpChoice:

    So it aligns with the text fields and exmpLbl

    Resize to 46, 21

We now need to put some values into the choice's drop-down menu. Values are added to a choice with the component's add method.

4. At the end of the getExmpChoice method, insert the following statement that adds the value zero to the drop-down menu:

```
exmpChoice.add("0");
```

5. In the actionPerformed method, replace the flagged statement that retrieved the exemption text field value with the following (which retrieves the choice's value):

```
String exmp = exmpChoice.getSelectedItem();
```

Let's test and make sure the value appears.

6. Save the source and run the application.

When the frame is displayed, the value 0 should appear in the choice.

7. Click on the choice field button.

A very small drop-down menu with the single value 0 should be displayed.

8. Press the exit button to end the application.

Obviously, the choice needs more values. We could add 10 more add statements for the values one through ten, but this would not be very efficient. Instead, we will define a **loop** so that the same add method will be performed 11 times with a different value each time.

Iteration

The ability to perform loops (i.e., iteration) is a basic function provided by all programming languages, and there are usually several different types of loops that can be defined. For example, a loop can be defined to run a set number of times or a loop can have a condition that controls when the loop is performed or discontinued. We will examine three types of Java loops: **while**, **do while**, and **for**.

To define a **while** loop, use the keyword while followed by a condition in parentheses, and then with in braces, the statements to be executed. For instance:

```
while (condition) {
        statements to be repeated;
}
```

The **while** loop checks the condition at the beginning of the loop. This means that if the condition is initially false, none of the statements to be repeated will be executed.

On the other hand, a **do while** loop checks the condition at the end of the loop. This means that the statements to be repeated will be executed at least once. The **do while** loop syntax is the keyword do, followed by the statements to be repeated in braces, then the keyword while, followed by a condition in parentheses and a semicolon. (Beware: forgetting the semicolon after the while condition is a common mistake!) For instance:

```
do {
        statements to be repeated;
} while (condition);
```

The **while** and **do while** loops are conditional loops. Both of these loops can be defined to execute a fixed number of times but the **for** loop makes that type of processing easier.

The **for** loop begins with the keyword for. Next, in parentheses, are an initialization, a condition, and an update. The initialization and condition are followed by semicolons. Finally, in braces, the statements to be repeated are specified. For instance:

```
for (initialization; condition; update) {
        statements to be repeated;
}
```

The initialization defines and/or sets a value for a **control variable**. The control variable is usually a primitive variable of type int and is commonly called **ctr** (i.e., the counter). The condition is based on the counter value, and the update changes the counter by a set value. For instance:

```
for (int ctr = 1; ctr <= 10; ctr = ctr + 1) {
        statements to be repeated;
}
```

Tutorial: Iteration

Let's take more time to go over iteration:

1. In c7, create a new Java class called LoopTestApp with a main method.

2. In the main method add the following:

    ```
    for (int ctr = 1; ctr <= 10; ctr = ctr + 1) {
            System.out.println(ctr + " little");
    }
    ```

3. Save and run LoopTestApp as a Java application.

In the console, there should be 10 lines with the counter (ctr) value followed by the word "little." Please note a couple of the **for** loop's nuances. For example, the value 1 is displayed on the first line. Even though the increment of ctr is defined at the beginning of the loop, the increment is not performed until the end of the loop. Essentially the increment is implemented as if it were a statement at the end of the **for** loop. Because of this, you could have specified a pre-increment (++ctr) or post-increment (ctr++) and they both would have worked the same as ctr = ctr + 1.

The initialization (which is only performed once) and the condition check are performed before the statements to be repeated are executed. Finally, because ctr was defined in the initialization, ctr can only be used by statements within the **for** loop. In other words, ctr is a local variable with a *scope* of the **for** loop. If ctr was defined as a class variable and initialized in the for statement, ctr would be accessible by any statement in any method in the class. In other words, the variable would have a class *scope*.

If you were to create a flow chart for the **for** loop, it would look like Figure 7-3.

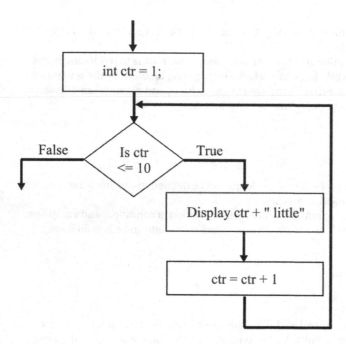

Figure 7-3.

4. Comment out the **for** loop and add the following while loop:

```
while (ctr <= 10) {
        System.out.println(ctr + " little");
}
```

RAD displays two errors because the variable ctr has not been defined. The while statement does not allow a counter variable to be defined or initialized, therefore the counter must be defined before the while statement.

5. Add the following statement before the while loop:

```
int ctr = 1;
```

This statement defines and initializes a counter but we have not defined a counter update. Because the counter is never updated, the condition will always be true and the println statement will execute endlessly. What we have created is called an **endless** (or **infinite**) **loop**. Do I need to tell you that this is a bad thing?

If you were to run the application now, it would run until you either terminated it from the Console view or closed RAD.

We definitely need to update the ctr so that it reaches 10 and the loop is ended.

6. After the println statement, add the following:

```
ctr = ctr + 1;
```

7. Save and run LoopTestApp.

The results will be the same as the **for** loop: 10 lines with the counter (ctr) value followed by the word "little."

8. Comment out the **while** loop (don't comment out the ctr definition).

9. Add the following **do while** loop after the ctr definition:

```
do {
        System.out.println(ctr + " little");
        ctr = ctr + 1;
} while (ctr <= 10);
```

10. Save and run LoopTestApp.

Once again, the same results will be displayed. You may be wondering why there are three methods for defining loops. Unfortunately, you do not have enough programming experience to appreciate the subtle differences between the three methods. When we change our application to access a database, your appreciation of loops will grow considerably.

Tutorial: More About Iteration

The keywords break and continue are often used with loops. A break statement ends the loop. This means that the first statement following the loop will be executed. A continue statement bypasses any remaining statements within the loop but does not end the loop. A **continue** statement in a **for** loop results in the counter being updated, and the next iteration is performed. In **while** and **do while** loops, a continue forces the JVM to perform the condition test and either perform another iteration or end the loop.

Both keywords are usually used within an if statement to stop looping or to skip the remaining statements in one iteration of a loop. Let's try to skip the "5 little" text.

1. In LoopTestApp, comment out the **do while** loop (don't comment out the ctr definition).

2. Add the following **do while** loop and run the application:

```
do {
        System.out.println(ctr + " little");
        if(ctr == 5) {
                break;
        }
        ctr = ctr + 1;
} while (ctr <= 10);
```

Only five lines are displayed as follows:

```
1 little
2 little
3 little
4 little
5 little
```

If you changed the break to a continue, an endless loop would be created. Why, you ask? Because the continue occurs before the increment, ctr will never be incremented beyond 5. This means that the condition will always be true. So, after displaying the first 4 lines, the application endlessly displays "5 little."

This "skipping the 5th line" is a tough nut to crack!

We want to be sure that the update is always performed but that the println is not performed. So, we need to rearrange the statements such that the increment is done first and then the println is performed. We will then put the **if** statement (with the continue) before the println statement.

3. Comment out the **do while** loop (don't comment out the ctr definition).

4. Add the following **do while** loop:

```
do {
        ctr = ctr + 1;
        if(ctr == 5) {
                continue;
        }
        System.out.println(ctr + " little");
} while (ctr <= 10);
```

5. Save and run LoopTestApp.

This time the results don't include the "5 little" line. However, notice that the "1 little" line does not appear at the beginning and that there is now an "11 little" line at the end.

Because the increment is done at the beginning of the loop, the initial value of 1 is never displayed. To fix this we will have to change the ctr initialization to 0. The "11 little" line, however, is displayed because the condition check is performed at the end of the loop. When ctr is equal to 10, the condition is true and control passes to the top of the loop. ctr is then incremented to 11 and the "11 little" is displayed. So, to fix this we need to change the condition to continue processing when ctr is less than or equal to 9.

6. Change the ctr definition from 1 to 0 and the condition from 10 to 9.

7. Save and run LoopTestApp.

Finally, nine lines are displayed, with the 5 line being skipped.

There are occasions where you will want to nest loops (i.e., have loops within loops). For instance, we will build an initial nested loop and then add continue and break statements to display the classic "Ten Little Indians" song.

8. Comment out the **do while** loop (don't comment out the ctr definition).

9. Change the ctr definition back to 1.

10. Add the following nested loops:

```
while (ctr <= 10) {
        for (int i = 1; i <= 3; i++) {
                System.out.print(" " + ctr + " little");
```

```
            ctr = ctr + 1;
            System.out.print(",");
        }
        System.out.print(" Indians");
        System.out.println("");
    }
```

In this case, the **while** loop is referred to as the outer loop and the **for** loop is called the inner loop.

11.   Save and run LoopTestApp.

The results will be the following:

```
1 little, 2 little, 3 little, Indians
4 little, 5 little, 6 little, Indians
7 little, 8 little, 9 little, Indians
10 little, 11 little, 12 little, Indians
```

Close, but no cigar.

We need to break out of the inner loop before the third comma on each line is printed. In addition, we want to break out of the inner loop when the counter reaches 10. To do this we need to set up a compound **if** statement that checks for the inner counter (i) value of 3 and the outer counter (ctr) value of 10. When either of these conditions is true, a break should be performed.

12.   Add the following if condition after ctr is incremented but before the print of the comma:

```
if (ctr > 10 || i == 3){
break;
}
```

13.   Save and run LoopTestApp.

The results will be the following:

```
1 little, 2 little, 3 little Indians
4 little, 5 little, 6 little Indians
7 little, 8 little, 9 little Indians
10 little Indians
```

Not bad. The first three lines are good, but the last line should say "Indian boys" not "Indians." So, we will insert an outer loop break when ctr is greater than 10. We will also add a print statement outside the outer loop to display "Indian boys" as the last line.

14.   Add the following **if** condition before the print "Indians" statement in the outer loop:

```
if (ctr > 10){
break;
}
```

15.   Save and run LoopTestApp.

The results will be the following:

```
1 little, 2 little, 3 little Indians
4 little, 5 little, 6 little Indians
7 little, 8 little, 9 little Indians
10 little
```

16. Add the following statement after the outer loop:

```
System.out.print(" Indian boys");
```

17. Save and run LoopTestApp.

The results will be the following:

```
1 little, 2 little, 3 little Indians
4 little, 5 little, 6 little Indians
7 little, 8 little, 9 little Indians
10 little Indian boys
```

18. Print out a copy of the LoopTestApp source code.

The LoopTestApp executable source code should be the following:

```
package c7;
public class LoopTestApp {
        public static void main(String[] args) {
                int ctr = 1;
                while (ctr <= 10) {
                        for (int i = 1; i <= 3; i++) {
                                System.out.print(" " + ctr + " little");
                                ctr = ctr + 1;
                                if (ctr > 10 || i == 3){
                                 break;
                                }
                                System.out.print(",");
                        }
                        if (ctr > 10){
                         break;
                        }
                        System.out.print(" Indians");
                        System.out.println("");
                }
                System.out.print(" Indian boys");
        }
}
```

Now this may seem like a childish example, but please don't think that nested loops are childish. You will have many occasions in your programming career to use them.

Tutorial: Finishing the Choice

You will now use your newfound looping skills to add the choice exemption values using only one add statement.

1. In the EnterEmpInfo's getExmpChoice method, add a **for** loop (around the ExmpChoice. add statement) to go from zero to ten, incrementing by one as follows:

```
for (int ctr = 0; ctr <= 10; ctr = ctr + 1) {

}
```

2. Change the add statement to add ctr as follows:

```
exmpChoice.add(ctr);
```

Notice the error stating that the add method expects a String and ctr is an int. We must convert ctr to a String. We will use the String class's valueOf method.

3. Change the add statement to the following:

```
exmpChoice.add(String.valueOf(ctr));
```

4. Save EnterEmpInfo source and run as an application.
5. Click the choice button.

The values 0 through 10 should be displayed.

6. Select 3 for exemptions, enter 15 for pay rate, and click the tax amount button.

The tax amount displayed will be $52.50. Notice that the values are listed in the order they are added to the choice. A good programmer/analyst would determine the most common number of exemptions and define that value as the default for the choice. A default value is specified with the choice's select method.

7. Click the Exit button and in the EnterEmpInfo's getExmpChoice method, after the **for** loop, add the following statement:

```
exmpChoice.select("2");
```

Notice that the default value is simply passed to the select method. When the frame is displayed, the default value will already be selected in the choice. If the drop-down menu is shown, the values will still appear in the order in which they were added, and the default value will still be selected.

8. Save EnterEmpInfo source and run as an application.

"2" should be displayed in the choice. The choice source code should look like the following:

```
private Choice getExmpChoice() {
        if (exmpChoice == null) {
                exmpChoice = new Choice();
                exmpChoice.setBounds(new Rectangle(195, 299, 46, 21));
                for (int ctr = 0; ctr <= 10; ctr = ctr + 1) {
                        exmpChoice.add(String.valueOf(ctr));
                }
```

```
                exmpChoice.select("2");
        }
     return exmpChoice;
}
```

9. Click the Exit button.

The choice has solved problem "D" because the user cannot enter an invalid value.

Formatting

Several very useful classes provide greater control over character and numeric data. The first one we will explore is `StringBuffer`.

A string buffer acts just like a string but has more methods for content manipulation. For instance, the append method allows you to easily concatenate strings, numbers, or constant text to a string buffer.

Another useful string buffer method is insert. The insert method allows the programmer to insert text anywhere within the string buffer. The programmer must supply the insertion location within the string buffer, and you should be aware that the beginning of the string buffer is position 0 not position 1.

The substring method lets you extract a range of characters (i.e., a substring) from within a string buffer. With substring you must specify the starting and ending locations (separated by a comma) of the substring within the string buffer.

Finally, the replace method lets you substitute characters within the string buffer. Again, you must specify the range (i.e., location) of the characters to be replaced and the new text. Note that the number of new characters can be smaller or larger than the number of characters being replaced.

Assuming the following:

```
StringBuffer a = new StringBuffer("abc");
String b = new String("def");
```

The following table shows these four methods with examples.

Method	Example	Result
.append	`a.append(b);`	abcdef
	`a.append(55);`	abc55
	`a.append("xyz");`	abcxyz
.insert	`a.insert(0, b);`	defabc
	`a.insert(1, 55);`	a55bc
	`a.insert(2, "xyz");`	abxyzc
.substring	`a.substring(0, 1);`	a
	`a.substring(0, 2);`	ab
	`a.substring(2, 3);`	c
.replace	`a.replace(0, 2, b);`	defc
	`a.replace(1, 3, b);`	adef
	`a.replace(2, 3, "xyz");`	abxyz

The NumberFormat class provides numeric formatting functions; however, you cannot instantiate an object of type NumberFormat. Instead, the getInstance method, which returns a NumberFormat object, is used. The following is an example of the syntax:

```
NumberFormat nf = NumberFormat.getInstance();
```

Of course, the NumberFormat class must also be imported as follows:

```
import java.text.NumberFormat;
```

Once the number formatter has been created, you can modify its formatting properties. For example, the following sets the number of displayed decimal digits to 2.

```
nf.setMaximumFractionDigits(2);
nf.setMinimumFractionDigits(2);
```

If you now used nf to format numbers, they would be rounded to two decimal digits. For instance, the following statements:

```
System.out.println(nf.format(10/3));
System.out.println(nf.format(34.565));
System.out.println(nf.format(34.5651));
```

Would result in the following values being displayed:

```
3.00
34.56
34.57
```

You may be a little surprised by the results. Note that the first calculation is between two integers so the result is truncated to 3 before the formatter even gets the results. The next two numbers demonstrate the formatter's rounding feature. Any fractional value of .5 or lower (beyond the maximum number of digits) is rounded down. In this example, the second number's fractional value beyond the 2 fractional digits is .5 but the third number's is .51. So the first number is truncated (or rounded down) and the second is rounded up.

Another very useful formatter is the currency formatter. Once again, use the NumberFormat class to create and return an instance as follows:

```
NumberFormat cf = NumberFormat.getCurrencyInstance();
```

If we then formatted and displayed the following two numbers:

```
System.out.println(cf.format(34.565));
System.out.println(cf.format(34.5651));
```

The results would be:

```
$34.56
$34.57
```

Other formatting options can be specified such as the type of currency symbol or decimal symbol to use. However, because these options are used less frequently, we will leave you to explore them in the online documentation for the NumberFormat class.

Finally, we need to cover date and time formatting. It cannot be overemphasized how important dates and times are in business applications. Not only are there many important dates (due date, payment date, birthday, hire date, etc.), but every transaction that occurs in an organization is documented and stored in a database. A very important piece of this stored information is the date and time of the transaction. Reports, information retrieval, and editing, are all performed and generated according to these "date/time stamps."

Most organizations develop a standard format for all dates and times so that there is consistency across all reports. In addition, a standard makes programming simpler because the programmer never has to figure out what format to use. However, there are many different standards; for instance, universal (i.e., 24 hour) time versus HH:MM am/pm, and some countries have their own standards. In addition, there is a SQL standard for storing dates and times in a database. Java supports many standards and allows you to create your own display "pattern." We will first look at some predefined formats and then show how to define a pattern.

Tutorial: Date and Time Formatting

Java comes with a Date class that, when instantiated, contains the current date and time (retrieved from the operating system). The Date object stores the current date and time as the number of milliseconds since January 1, 1970. Not a very useful number for programmers; however, when displayed, the date is converted into a user-friendly format. The DateFormat class has predefined formats that can be used and the SimpleDateFormat class allows programmers to define their own date format patterns. To define a date (like due date or birthday), a Calendar object is needed.

1. Create a new Java class called DateTimeApp with a main method in c7.

2. In the main method, add the following statements to create and print a Date object:

```
Date d = new Date();
System.out.println(d);
```

Notice that the first line is identified as an error. You must import the Date class.

3. Add the following import statement:

```
import java.util.*;
```

This will also insure the JVM can find the Calendar class, which we will use later.

4. Save and run DateTimeApp as a Java application.

The date and time will be displayed as a three-letter day of the week, three-letter month, two-digit day of the month, the time in universal format (HH:MM:SS), a three-digit time zone, and a four-digit year. For instance:

```
Thu Feb 17 14:30:48 EST 2011
```

Although complete, rarely will the date and time be stored or displayed in this format. To display the current date or time in a different format, use the DateFormat class to get a date formatter or time formatter instance (i.e., object) for a particular format.

5. Add the following import statement so that the DateFormat class can be accessed:

```
import java.text.*;
```

6. At the end of the main method, add the following to define date and time formatter objects:

```
DateFormat dfShort = DateFormat.getDateInstance(DateFormat.SHORT);
DateFormat dfMedium = DateFormat.getDateInstance(DateFormat.MEDIUM);
DateFormat dfLong = DateFormat.getDateInstance(DateFormat.LONG);
DateFormat dfFull = DateFormat.getDateInstance(DateFormat.FULL);
DateFormat tfShort = DateFormat.getTimeInstance(DateFormat.SHORT);
DateFormat tfMedium = DateFormat.getTimeInstance(DateFormat.MEDIUM);
DateFormat tfLong = DateFormat.getTimeInstance(DateFormat.LONG);
```

7. At the end of the main method, add the following statements to display the date and time in the various formats:

```
System.out.println(dfShort.format(d));
System.out.println(dfMedium.format(d));
System.out.println(dfLong.format(d));
System.out.println(dfFull.format(d));
System.out.println(tfShort.format(d));
System.out.println(tfMedium.format(d));
System.out.println(tfLong.format(d));
```

The current date and time will appear in the following formats:

```
Thu Feb 17 14:32:50 EST 2011
2/17/11
Feb 17, 2011
February 17, 2011
Thursday, February 17, 2011
2:32 PM
2:32:50 PM
2:32:50 PM EST
```

8. Comment out the statements added in steps 6 and 7.

We are going to create a SimpleDateFormat object and define a unique pattern (format). We will then modify the pattern.

9. Add the following statements (after the println statement, in the main method), to create two SimpleDateFormat objects:

```
SimpleDateFormat sdf = new SimpleDateFormat("MM/dd/yyyy");
SimpleDateFormat stf = new SimpleDateFormat("hh:mm:ss a");
```

A pattern is defined with "date format symbols" and constant text. The following is a partial list of the various date format symbols and the data each symbol represents. As always, upper- and lowercase letters make a difference.

Symbol	Data	Example
y	Year	yy : 12
		yyyy : 2012
M	Month	MM : 01
		MM : 10
		MMM : Oct
		MMMM : October
d	Day of month	d : 1
		d : 31
		dd : 01
H	Hour (0-23)	H : 1
		H : 23
		HH : 01
h	Hour (0-12)	h : 1
		h : 12
m	Minutes	m : 1
		m : 59
		mm : 01
s	Seconds	s : 1
		s : 59
		ss : 01
a	AM/PM	a : PM

10. Add the following two statements to display the date and time in the defined patterns:

```
System.out.println(sdf.format(d));
System.out.println(stf.format(d));
```

11. Save the DateTimeApp source code and run as an application.

The results should be the current date and time in the default format and the two new patterns:

```
Thu Feb 17 14:37:56 EST 2011
02/17/2011
02:37:56 PM
```

12. Comment out the statements added in step 10.

To set a date such as a due date or birth date, you would first create a Calendar object and then set its month, day, and year. You can then use the Calendar object's getTime method to retrieve a Date object with the defined date.

13. Insert the following statements to define a birthday of January 23, 1991 and display it in the SimpleDateFormat pattern (sdf) defined earlier:

```
Calendar cal = Calendar.getInstance();
cal.set(1991, Calendar.JANUARY, 23);
Date bday = cal.getTime();
System.out.println(sdf.format(bday));
```

Notice in the second statement that the date is specified as year, month, and then day and that the Calendar object's static fields (JANUARY, FEBRUARY, etc.) are used to specify the month. You can use numbers instead of the month fields but beware: the numbers to specify the individual months begin at 0 and end at 11 (i.e., 0 for January, 1 for February, 11 for December). Boy, oh boy! Is that numbering sequence a potential source of error and confusion or what?! That's why it is best to use the month fields.

14. Save DateTimeApp and run as an application.

The results should be:

```
Thu Feb 17 14:42:02 EST 2011
01/23/1991
```

15. Change the calendar set statement to the following and run the application.

```
cal.set(1988, Calendar.FEBRUARY, 30);
```

Bet you weren't expecting that. The calendar property lenient controls whether the date specified is validated. The default is not to check (i.e., lenient is true), so we will change that.

16. Change the calendar lenient property by adding the following on the line after the calendar is created but before the date is set.

```
cal.setLenient(false);
```

17. Run the application.

Notice in the console that an IllegalArgumentException was generated for the Month field.

18. Change the day of the month to 29 and run the application.

Notice that 29 is valid for February 1988. This proves that Calendar takes into account leap years.

As you can probably tell, working with dates and times is a little awkward. This is a prime area for a company/organization to create their own date and time classes to simplify and standardize formatting.

19. Print out a copy of the DateTimeApp source code.

Tutorial: Formatting Currency

So far, we have been unsuccessful in using concatenation to format the employee salary and tax values. Let's apply our newfound formatting knowledge to fix the application. First, we need to determine where the formatting should be done. We had been formatting in EnterEmpInfo but formatting should be performed in Employee. Why? The philosophy of object-oriented programming is to store all related data and functions in one object, in this case, Employee. The EnterEmpInfo object's function is to receive and validate information about an Employee, not store the information or provide Employee functions. Calculating the gross salary and tax amount has nothing to do with entering employee information. These functions should be in Employee not EnterEmpInfo.

So, we will move the gross salary calculation from EnterEmpInfo into Employee where it belongs. In addition, we will create new methods to return the information as formatted strings.

1. In Employee, add the following import statement:

```
import java.text.NumberFormat;
```

2. In Employee at the end of the class variable definitions, add the following statement to create a currency formatter object called cf:

```
NumberFormat cf = NumberFormat.getCurrencyInstance();
```

3. In Employee, after the fedTaxCalc method, create a new method called fedTaxCalcFormatted as follows:

```
public String fedTaxCalcFormatted(double payRate,int exemptions) {
        String taxAmt = new String();
        taxAmt = cf.format(this.fedTaxCalc(payRate, exemptions));
        return taxAmt;
}
```

Notice that this method doesn't duplicate the fedTaxCalc function. Rather, it uses the fedTaxCalc method to perform the tax calculation and then simply formats the result. We need to change EnterEmpInfo to call this new method and use the returned string.

4. In EnterEmpInfo, at the beginning of the actionPerformed method, enter the following statement to create a string called stringTaxAmt that will hold the formatted tax amount:

```
String stringTaxAmt = new String();
```

5. In EnterEmpInfo's actionPerformed method, change the following statement:

```
double doubleTaxAmt =
emp.fedTaxCalc(doubleEmpPR, intExmp);
```

to:

```
stringTaxAmt =
emp.fedTaxCalcFormatted(doubleEmpPR, intExmp);
```

6. In EnterEmpInfo's actionPerformed method, change the following statement:

```
resultLbl.setText("The Federal Tax amount is: $" +
        doubleTaxAmt + "0");
```

to:

```
resultLbl.setText("The Federal Tax amount is: " +
stringTaxAmt);
```

7. Save EnterEmpInfo and run as an application.

8. Enter 10.3338 for the payRate and 4 for the number of exemptions.

9. Click the TaxAmt button.

The result will be the message: "Federal Tax amount is: $15.50".

10. Click the Gross button.

The result will be the message: "Gross Salary is: $413.3520." So, the tax amount is being formatted correctly, but we now need to format the gross salary amount.

11. Click the Exit button and in Employee, add the following statement at the end of the class variable definitions, to create a new class variable called doubleGrossSalary:

```
private double doubleGrossSalary;
```

12. In Employee, after the fedTaxCalc method, create two new methods called grossSalary Calc and grossSalaryCalcFormatted as follows:

```
public double grossSalaryCalc(double payRate){
        doubleGrossSalary = payRate * 40;
        return doubleGrossSalary;
}

public String grossSalaryCalcFormatted(double payRate) {
        String grossSalaryFormatted = new String();
        this.grossSalaryCalc(payRate);
        grossSalaryFormatted = cf.format(doubleGrossSalary);
        return grossSalaryFormatted;
}
```

13. Save the Employee source code.

14. In EnterEmpInfo's actionPerformed method, replace the following statements:

```
doubleGross = doubleEmpPR * 40;
resultLbl.setText("Gross Salary is: $" +
doubleGross + "0");
```

with:

```
Employee emp = new Employee("", "", "", "", "");
resultLbl.setText("Gross Salary is: " +
                emp.grossSalaryCalcFormatted(doubleEmpPR));
```

Notice that this removes the gross salary calculation and substitutes a call to the Employee object's (emp's) grossSalaryCalcFormatted method.

15. Save EnterEmpInfo and run as an application.

16. Enter 10.3338 for the payRate and 4 for the number of exemptions.

17. Click the Gross button.

The result will be the message: "Gross Salary is: $413.35." Notice that the currency formatter rounded the result to two digits.

The actionPerformed method should look like the following:

```java
public void actionPerformed(ActionEvent e) {
String stringTaxAmt = new String();
String empPayRate = empPRTF.getText();
double doubleEmpPR = -1, doubleGross;
resultLbl.setForeground(Color.black);
try {
        doubleEmpPR = Double.parseDouble(empPayRate);
} catch (NumberFormatException Error) {
        empPRTF.setText("");
        resultLbl.setForeground(Color.red);
        resultLbl.setText("Pay rate must be a numeric " +
"value: 1, 2, 3...");
}

if (doubleEmpPR != -1) {
        if (dispBtn == e.getSource()) {
         Employee emp = new Employee(empNameTF.getText(),
empStreetTF.getText(), cityTF.getText(), stateTF.getText(), zipTF.getText());
         EmployeeFrame ef = new EmployeeFrame(emp);
        } else {
                if (grossBtn == e.getSource()) {
                        Employee emp = new Employee("", "", "", "", "");
                        resultLbl.setText("Gross Salary is: " +
                         emp.grossSalaryCalcFormatted(doubleEmpPR));
                } else {
                        if (taxBtn == e.getSource()) {
                                Employee emp = new Employee("", "", "", "", "");
                                        String exmp = exmpChoice.getSelectedItem();
                                        int intExmp = Integer.parseInt(exmp);
                                        stringTaxAmt = emp.fedTaxCalcFormatted(doubleEmpPR, intExmp);
                                        resultLbl.setText("The Federal Tax amount is: " + stringTaxAmt);
                        }
                }
        }
//                              System.out.println(empPayRate);
}
}
```

Tidying Up Our Messy Method

We have incrementally added source code to EnterEmpInfo with very little thought about the eventual scope and function of the application. Whoa, that's a big statement! Essentially it means that we have been adding on to a house room by room instead of first designing the house (i.e., flowcharting the class's function) and then building the needed foundation, walls, plumbing, and so on (i.e., class variables, methods, and method variables). Because of this, we have redundancy and inefficiency in our class.

For instance, notice in the actionPerformed method that the method variable emp is defined three separate times and assigned three different Employee objects. We should have created one class variable and Employee object. In addition, we created several method variables to hold information from the frame. We already had a perfect place to store this information: the Employee object.

We will change the Employee class to include new properties for pay rate and exemptions and define getter and setter methods for the properties. We will also allow the user to specify different parameters when instantiating an Employee object by using a technique called **method overloading**.

Method overloading takes advantage of the fact that a class can contain many methods with the same name. Methods within a class must have a unique signature (the method name and expected parameters), not a unique method name. Therefore, methods can have the same name as long as they expect a different set of parameters.

Method overloading is used to make a class's interface (i.e., public methods) easier to use. For instance, the String class uses method overloading for the valueOf method. If you look at the String documentation, you will see several methods named valueOf. However, each valueOf method expects a parameter of a different type (int, double, long, etc); therefore, each method has a different signature. Overloading makes converting primitives to strings easier because the programmer only has one method name to remember, valueOf. The JVM determines the correct valueOf method to execute based on the parameter variable type.

All I can say is, "Thank you, JVM."

Tutorial: Method Overloading

In Employee, we will create overloaded calculation and constructor methods to make the class easier to use. Yes, you can overload constructors. Have you noticed how every time we try to create an Employee object, we had to pass five empty strings? We are going to create a null constructor: a constructor that does not expect any parameters. The null constructor makes it easier to create an "empty Employee" object but still ensures that the object and class variables are created.

In Employee:

1. Add the following statements to define new private class variables:

    ```
    private int exemptions;
    private double payRate;
    private String stringTaxAmt;
    private String stringGrossSalary;
    ```

    These class variables will be used for the employee's new properties and take the place of the method variables used in the calculations.

2. Click on the first statement you just added to select it.

3. Click Source then Generate Getters and Setters...

4. At the "Generate Getters and Setters" window, click on the payRate check box and make sure that exemptions is selected.

    The bottom of the window should say 4 of 16 selected.

5. Click the OK button.

    Four new methods will be generated: two getters and two setters.

6. Before the constructor, add the following null constructor:

    ```
    public Employee(){}
    ```

That wasn't too hard was it? Notice that the null constructor does nothing. However, the class variables, defined before the constructor will be created.

7. In the fedTaxCalcFormatted method, remove the statement that defines taxAmt and change the two other references to taxAmt to stringTaxAmt. The method should look like the following:

```
public String fedTaxCalcFormatted(double payRate,
int exemptions){
        stringTaxAmt = cf.format(this.fedTaxCalc(payRate,
exemptions));
        return stringTaxAmt;
}
```

Essentially, we substituted the global (i.e., class) variable stringTaxAmt (created in Step 1) for the method variable taxAmt. We will now put it to good use in a new method.

8. Before the already existing method of the same name, add the following method:

```
public String fedTaxCalcFormatted(){
        this.fedTaxCalcFormatted(this.payRate, this.exemptions);
        return stringTaxAmt;
}
```

Notice that this method expects no parameters. Instead, the method uses the Employee object's payRate and exemptions properties (i.e., to supply those values to the fedTaxCalcFormatted method). Also, notice that no variable is needed to receive the result (a string) returned by the fedTaxCalcFormatted method. Because these methods are within the same class, the global variable stringTaxAmt can hold the result and be returned by both methods.

9. In the grossSalaryCalcFormatted method, remove the statement that defines the string grossSalaryFormatted and change the two other references to grossSalaryFormatted to stringGrossSalary.

The method should look like the following:

```
public String grossSalaryCalcFormatted(double payRate) {
    this.grossSalaryCalc(payRate);
    stringGrossSalary = cf.format(doubleGrossSalary);
    return stringGrossSalary;
}
```

We created a global variable stringGrossSalary earlier and have substituted it for the method variable grossSalaryFormatted.

10. Before the already existing method of the same name, add the following method:

```
public String grossSalaryCalcFormatted() {
        this.grossSalaryCalcFormatted(this.payRate);
        return stringGrossSalary; }
```

As with the fedTaxCalcFormatted method, we used the Employee object's properties and a global variable (instead of a method variable) to simplify using this class. Now we need to change the EnterEmpInfo class to use the new methods.

Tutorial: Tidying Up Our Messy Method

In addition to using the new and improved Employee class, we want to organize EnterEmpInfo better and use a few global (class) variables instead of many local (method) variables. In addition, when actionPerformed is executed, the frame information should be retrieved and placed in an Employee object. However, currently actionPerformed creates an Employee object. This means a new Employee object is created each time the user clicks a button. This is not very efficient. Instead, a single global Employee variable (and object) should be created and its properties changed each time actionPerformed is invoked (i.e., each time the user clicks a button). So, the Employee variable (emp) will be changed to a class (global) variable and assigned an Employee object only once.

The source code to retrieve the text field values and assign them to the Employee properties will be placed in a private method called setEmployeeProperties. (Creating a new private method allows other methods in the class to invoke this function.) The setEmployeeProperties method will be invoked from the actionPerformed method. In EnterEmpInfo:

1. Add the following new class variable definition:

    ```java
    private Employee emp = new Employee();
    ```

2. Before the main method, add the following method that retrieves the various text field values and assigns them to the appropriate Employee property:

    ```java
    private void setEmployeeProperties() {
            emp.setEmpName(empNameTF.getText());
            emp.setEmpStreet(empStreetTF.getText());
            emp.setEmpCity(cityTF.getText());
            emp.setEmpState(stateTF.getText());
            emp.setEmpZip(zipTF.getText());
            emp.setPayRate(Double.parseDouble(empPRTF.getText()));
            emp.setExemptions(Integer.parseInt(exmpChoice.getSelectedItem()));
    }
    ```

The first five statements are relatively easy. We simply used each text field's getText statement as a parameter in the appropriate property setter method. Notice that we eliminated the need for a method variable by using the result of the getText method as the setter parameter. This efficiency becomes even more apparent in the last two statements. In addition to retrieving the text, these statements also parse the text into a primitive. Earlier three statements and two method variables were used as follows:

```java
String stringPayRate = EmpPRTF.getText();
double doubleRate = Double.parseDouble(stringPayRate);
emp.setPayRate(doubleRate);
```

3. In actionPerformed, add the following as the first statement so that the setEmployeeProperties method is invoked:

    ```java
    this.setEmployeeProperties();
    ```

Notice that many of the remaining statements set up method variables. We have eliminated the need for many of these by using an Employee object and the setEmployeeProperties methods.

4. Delete the statements that define the method variables stringTaxAmt, empPayRate, double-EmpPR and doubleGross.

This will cause several syntax errors to be flagged in the source code.

5. Delete the following statement (contained in the **try** block):

```
doubleEmpPR = Double.parseDouble(empPayRate);
```

This statement is no longer needed because setEmployeeProperties retrieves and parses the pay rate.

6. In the **if** statement, after the catch block, replace doubleEmpPR with emp.getPayRate() as follows:

```
if (emp.getPayRate() != -1) {
```

Originally, doubleEmpPRwas initialized to –1 so that we could ensure that a valid numeric pay rate value had been retrieved from the frame. However, we really should use a separate and more descriptive variable to indicate an error. In addition, we should add further validation checks on the pay rate value. For instance, do you think that a pay rate of 99 cents is valid?

To summarize, we need to do two important things:

A. Check for the number format exception when the text is parsed

B. Validate that the pay rate value is valid

One of these functions should be included in the setEmployeeProperties method, and the other should be in the Employee class. Can you identify which function should go where?

The number format exception check should be in EnterEmpInfo's setEmployeeProperties method. Because setEmployeeProperties retrieves text data and parses the text to a primitive, it is the logical place to perform the check.

Data validation is one of the key functions of a setter. Therefore, the validation that the pay rate is within a certain range should be in the setPayRate method of Employee class. We will code the setter data validation in the next section.

7. Cut and paste the try and catch from actionPerformed to setEmployeeProperties and change the code it so that the setPayRate and setExemptions appears as follows:

```
try {emp.setPayRate(Double.parseDouble(empPRTF.getText()));
             emp.setExemptions(Integer.parseInt(exmpChoice.getSelectedItem()));
}
catch (NumberFormatException error) {
             resultLbl.setForeground(Color.red);
             resultLbl.setText("Pay rate must be a" +
"numeric value: 1, 2, 3...");
}
```

8. After the catch header but before setting the foreground color to red, add the following statements to erase the incorrect pay rate from the textfield and set pay rate to -1:

```
empPRTF.setText("");
emp.setPayRate(-1);
```

The beginning of the actionPerformed method should look like the following:

```
public void actionPerformed(ActionEvent e) {
     this.setEmployeeProperties();
     resultLbl.setForeground(Color.black);
     if (emp.getPayRate() != -1) {
```

Notice that in the code that follows the above (which is executed when the Display button is pressed) an Employee object is created and passed information from the frame. This is no longer needed as setEmployeeProperties now performs this function.

9. Delete the statement that creates the Employee object.

The code should look like the following:

```
if (dispBtn == e.getSource()) {
        EmployeeFrame ef = new EmployeeFrame(emp);
```

In the next set of code (executed when the Gross button is pressed), another method variable and Employee object was created. Because we created a global Employee variable and object, we don't need this statement anymore.

10. Delete the statement that creates the Employee object when the Gross button is pressed.

The code should look like the following:

```
if (grossBtn == e.getSource()) {
            resultLbl.setText("Gross Salary is: " +
                    emp.grossSalaryCalcFormatted(doubleEmpPR));
```

The statement setting the result label should be changed because it tries to calculate the gross salary with the doubleEmpPR variable. This local variable's value is no longer set because the Employee object's pay rate property is used to hold the value (set in setEmployeeProperties). To calculate the gross salary, simply execute the grossSalaryCalcFormatted method.

11. Change the statement to the following:

```
resultLbl.setText("Gross Salary is: " +
        emp.grossSalaryCalcFormatted());
```

Finally, the code that executes when the tax amount button is pressed tries to read the text and parse it. This is redundant because setEmployeeProperties is performing this function.

12. Delete the first four statements and change the fifth statement to the following:

```
resultLbl.setText("The Federal Tax amount is: " +
                emp.fedTaxCalcFormatted());
```

13. Save EnterEmpInfo and run as an application.

14. Enter 10.3338 for the payRate and 4 for the number of exemptions.

15. Click the Gross button.

The result will be the message: "Gross Salary is: $413.35." Notice that the dollar value is formatted as currency and rounded to two digits. At this point, a good programmer would run tests to ensure that the tax amount calculation works and that the numeric value validity check is working for pay rate.

16. Run tests to ensure that the tax amount is correct and only numeric values can be entered for pay rate and then click the Exit button.

You should have discovered another soft error: the error message does not appear in red. We always want to reset the color to black when we start actionPerformed. Remember that the error color is set to red in setEmployeeProperties, and we called setEmployeeProperties before the color is reset to black.

17. Move the setForeground statement before the setEmployeeProperties statement.

The actionPerformed method should look like the following:

```java
public void actionPerformed(ActionEvent e) {
resultLbl.setForeground(Color.black);
this.setEmployeeProperties();
if (emp.getPayRate() != -1) {
if (dispBtn == e.getSource()) {
            EmployeeFrame ef = new EmployeeFrame(emp);
     } else {
            if (grossBtn == e.getSource()) {
                resultLbl.setText("Gross Salary is: " +
                        emp.grossSalaryCalcFormatted());
            } else {
                if (taxBtn == e.getSource()) {
                 resultLbl.setText("The Federal Tax amount is: "
             + emp.fedTaxCalcFormatted());
                }
            }
     }
  }
}
}
```

Now, isn't that a cleaner method? In addition, this method is much more efficient because we eliminated almost all the method variables and all the duplicate Employee objects.

Tutorial: Throwing Exceptions

Up until now, we have only caught exceptions thrown by the system. Not only can your Java classes throw exceptions but the messages can be customized. For instance, no employee can make less than $6.50 an hour, nor is there any employee who can earn more than $35.00 an hour. The setter should check that the value supplied is within this range, and if not, an exception should be thrown. We will throw an InvalidValue exception and customize the message based on the invalid value.

After making this change to setPayRate, any method that uses the setPayRate method must be changed to check for the exception. So, we will add **try** and **catch** blocks to the setEmployeeProperties method in EnterEmpInfo.

1. In Employee, add the following import statement.

   ```java
   import org.omg.CORBA.DynAnyPackage.InvalidValue;
   ```

As usual, we must first import the class before we can use it.

Method headers must specify which exception(s) can be thrown. Exceptions are identified in the method header with the throws keyword.

2. Change the setPayRate method header to following:

   ```java
   public void setPayRate(double d) throws InvalidValue {
   ```

3. Change the setPayRate method body to the following:

```
if (d < 6.5 || d > 35) {
        throw new InvalidValue("The value for a pay rate " +
        "must be at least $6.50 but no more than $35." +
        " Please reenter the pay rate.");
} else {
        this.payRate = d;
}
```

This statement checks if the value is outside the valid range. If so, an InvalidValue exception is created with a descriptive message and then thrown. If not, the employee pay rate is set to the parameter value that was passed.

4. Save the Employee source code.

The EnterEmpInfo source code should have errors in the setEmployeeProperties method because InvalidValue is unhandled. We need to change setEmployeeProperties to catch the InvalidValue exception.

5. In the EnterEmpInfo source code, add the following import statement.

```
import org.omg.CORBA.DynAnyPackage.InvalidValue;
```

The exception class must be imported even if the program is only catching the exception.

6. In the setEmployeeProperties method, add the following catch after the already existing catch and save the source code:

```
catch (InvalidValue e) {
        empPRTF.setText("");
        resultLbl.setForeground(Color.red);
        resultLbl.setText(e.getMessage());
}
```

This solves one of the errors. However, the statement that sets empPayRate to –1 is still an error because –1 is an invalid value for pay rate. We were using the –1 value as an **error flag** within the actionPerformed method. This is really a misuse of the empPayRate variable. Instead, we will create a boolean variable called inputError and, if the pay rate value is invalid, set inputError to true. We'll change actionPerformed to check inputError, not empPayRate. In addition, we need to reset inputError to false each time actionPerformed is executed.

7. In the EnterEmpInfo, add the following statement to create a class boolean variable called inputError.

```
private boolean inputError = false;
```

8. In the setEmployeeProperties method, replace emp.setPayRate(-1); with the following statement:

```
inputError = true;
```

9. In the InvalidValue catch block, add the following statement:

```
inputError = true;
```

10. In actionPerformed, change if (emp.getPayRate() != -1) { to the following:

    if (inputError == false) {

11. Add the following else block to the above if:

    else {
            inputError = **false**; }

This statement resets inputError back to false because setEmployeeProperties removed the invalid value from the text field.

12. Save EnterEmpInfo and run as an application.

13. Enter 39 as the pay rate value and click the Gross button.

The EnterEmpInfo frame should look like Figure 7-4. Obviously, the message is too large to fit in the label. We need to go back and fix that.

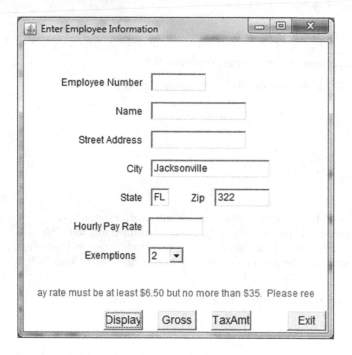

Figure 7-4.

14. In Employee's setPayRate method, change the message to the following:

    throw new InvalidValue("Please re-enter a pay rate " +
            "between 6.50 and 35.");

15. Save EnterEmpInfo, run as an application and verify that the message is correct.

Results of the Tutorial

Let's examine the results of the tutorial:

1. In Tutorials, a new package called c7 with 11 classes, two of which are the new classes LoopTestApp, and DateTimeApp.

2. Printouts of the LoopTestApp and DateTimeApp source code.

3. The EnterEmpInfo frame should have a choice for exemptions that displays the values zero through ten using a loop.

4. EnterEmpInfo should check that the pay rate value is numeric.

5. Employee's setPayRate method should verify that a pay rate value is between $6.50 and $35.00.

6. EnterEmpInfo's actionPerformed method should look like the following:

```java
public void actionPerformed(ActionEvent e) {
resultLbl.setForeground(Color.black);
this.setEmployeeProperties();
if (inputError == false) {
        if (dispBtn == e.getSource()) {
                EmployeeFrame ef = new EmployeeFrame(emp);
        } else {
                if (grossBtn == e.getSource()) {
                        resultLbl.setText("Gross Salary is: " +
emp.grossSalaryCalcFormatted());
                } else {
                        if (taxBtn == e.getSource()) {
                                resultLbl.setText(
                                "The Federal Tax amount is: " +
emp.fedTaxCalcFormatted());
                        }
                }
        }
}
else {
        inputError = false;
}
}
```

7. EnterEmpInfo's setEmployeeProperties method should look like the following:

```java
private void setEmployeeProperties() {
emp.setEmpName(empNameTF.getText());
emp.setEmpStreet(empStreetTF.getText());
emp.setEmpCity(cityTF.getText());
emp.setEmpState(stateTF.getText());
emp.setEmpZip(zipTF.getText());
try {
emp.setPayRate(Double.parseDouble(empPRTF.getText()));
emp.setExemptions(Integer.parseInt(exmpChoice.getSelectedItem()));
}
```

```
catch (NumberFormatException Error) {
empPRTF.setText("");
        inputError = true;
        resultLbl.setForeground(Color.red);
        resultLbl.setText("Pay rate must be a " +
"numeric value: 1, 2, 3...");
}
catch (InvalidValue e) {
        inputError = true;
empPRTF.setText("");
        resultLbl.setForeground(Color.red);
        resultLbl.setText(e.getMessage());
}
}
```

Review Questions

1. What are formatters?

2. What is the difference between the String and StringBuffer classes?

3. What is the purpose of the try and catch keywords and how do they work together? How does an exception object fit in with these two keywords?

4. Describe the function of the Choice class.

5. What are the three primary types of iteration and what are their differences?

6. What is method overloading, and why would a programmer use method overloading?

7. What are the functions of the break and continue keywords?

Review Exercise

In this exercise, you will create six new classes that are subclasses of the Choice class. These new classes will display the current date and time and will replace the EnterShipInfo frame's date and time text fields. You will also create a new method to retrieve the information from the frame, verify that information has been supplied for all fields, and then populate a Shipment object.

1. In the ReviewEx/src, create a new package called c7.

2. Copy all the classes from c6 into c7

3. From Tutorials/src/c7, copy the Java files EnterEmpInfo and Employee into ReviewEx/src/c7.

We want to replace the older versions copied from c6 in step 2, so click Yes To All when the system prompts you with an overwrite message.

4. Create three new visual Java classes that are subclasses of the AWT Choice class called MonthCh, DayCh, and YearCh.

5. In MonthCh's initialize method:

6. Set the size to 44, 21

7. Set the values to 1 through 12 using a loop.

8. In MonthCh, add the following statements to get a Calendar object, retrieve the current month, and set the selected value to the current month.

```
Calendar c = Calendar.getInstance();
select(String.valueOf(c.get(Calendar.MONTH)+1));
```

Because Java always assigns a value of zero to the first item in a group (i.e., the first character in a string is at location zero, not location one), you must add 1 to the returned value to obtain the correct value for the current month. In other words, the value of MONTH during January is zero. (Ouch!) So, the "trick" to get the commonly accepted month number is to add 1 to the returned value. We placed the get inside of the select statement so that the correct value will be selected when the choice is first displayed.

9. In DayCh:

    - Set the size to 44, 21

    - Set the values to 1 through 31 using a loop

    - Retrieve the current day (the DAY_OF_MONTH field in a Calendar object)

    - Make the current day the selected value

10. In YearCh:

    - Set the size to 51, 21

    - Retrieve the current year (a Calendar object's YEAR field)

    - Set the values to the previous year, the current year, and the next year using a loop

    - Make the current year the selected value

11. Create 3 new visual Java classes that are extensions of the Choice class called HourCh, MinCh, and AMPMCh and set all their sizes to 44, 21.

12. In HourCh:

    - Set the values to 0 through 12 using a loop.

    - Retrieve the current hours (the HOUR_OF_DAY field).

The HOUR_OF_DAY field contains a value between 0 and 23, so you will need to change any value greater than 12 to the correct value before selecting it in the choice. The logic for doing this is as follows:

    - if the current hours is less than or equal to 12 select the value in the choice values

    - else subtract 12 from the value and select the result in the choice values

13. In MinCh:

    - Set the values to 0 through 59 using a loop.

    - Retrieve the current minutes (the MINUTE field).

    - Make the current minutes the selected value.

14.   In AMPMCh:

   •   Set the values to AM and PM.

   •   Retrieve the current hour.

   •   Using an if statement select AM if the returned value is less than 12 else select PM.

In EnterShipInfo:

15.   Replace the dateTF text field with MonthCh, DayCh, and YearCh components called monthCh, dayCh, and yearCh. (Hint: In the VE palette, select the Choose Bean option, and specify c7.MonthCh, then c7.DayCh, etc.)

16.   Replace the TimeTF text field with HourCh, MinCh and AMPMCh components called hourCh, minCh, and aMPMCh.

The fields should look like Figure 7-5 when displayed.

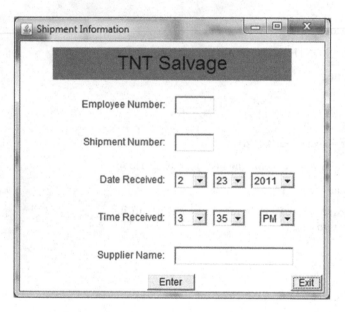

Figure 7-5.

We will now change the application to check that data is entered in all the text fields and, if data is missing, issue a message specifying which fields must be supplied. We will also retrieve and format the information from the frame components.

17.   Move the components so that a new label field (called msgLbl that will be used to display messages) can fit beneath the Supplier Name and above the Enter button. Set the length to 290, the initial text to blank, center the label and define the alignment as CENTER.

18. Create a new private method (after actionPerformed) called setShipmentProperties that does the following for each text field:

    - Retrieves the value of the text field

    - Checks that the length of the value is greater than zero (use the String method length)

    ```
    if (length is not greater than zero)
    ```

19. Define an error message in the msgLbl field stating which field value must be entered

20. Set an error flag (a boolean variable called isDataEntryError) to true

21. Create several new private class variables to help with the formatting as follows:

    A. Two new SimpleDateFormat class variables called sdf and stf and assign SimpleDateFormat objects with the following formats to the variables

    ```
    MM/dd/yyyy              hh:mm a
    ```

    B. One new Calendar variable called cal and assign a calendar instance as follows

    ```
    private Calendar cal = Calendar.getInstance();
    ```

22. Create a **Date** variable called shipDateTime and assign null to it as follows:

    ```
    private Date shipDateTime = null;
    ```

23. Create an int variable called shipHour.

24. In setShipmentProperties, if the error flag (isDataEntryError) is false, execute the following source code to retrieve and format the date and time choice field's values, create a shipment object called ship, and set the shipment object's properties:

```
shipHour = Integer.parseInt(hourCh.getSelectedItem());
if (aMPMCh.getSelectedItem().equals("PM")&& shipHour < 12){
        shipHour = shipHour + 12;
}
if (aMPMCh.getSelectedItem().equals("AM")&&shipHour == 12){
        shipHour = 0;
}
cal.set(
        Integer.parseInt(yearCh.getSelectedItem()),
        Integer.parseInt(monthCh.getSelectedItem()) - 1,
        Integer.parseInt(dayCh.getSelectedItem()),
        shipHour,
        Integer.parseInt(minCh.getSelectedItem())
);
shipDateTime = cal.getTime();
ship = new Shipment(
        shipNumTF.getText(),
        supplTF.getText(),
        sdf.format(shipDateTime),
        stf.format(shipDateTime),
        empNumTF.getText()
);
```

The first statement retrieves the selected text for the hour choice, parses the value to an int, and assigns it to the variable shipHour. Because the Calendar object needs an hour value from 0 to 23, we need to calculate this by checking if AM or PM was selected. The if statements retrieve the aMPMCh value and checks the hour value. If PM was selected and the hour value is less than 12, 12 is added to the hour value. (E.g., if 12 && PM, then 12 is correct. If 1 && PM, then 13 is correct.) Similarly, if the user specified 12 and AM, the correct hour value for the calendar object is 0.

Next, the Calendar object (cal) is set to the values specified in the other choice fields and the calculated shipHour value. Notice that for each choice, the selected value must be parsed to int. Also, the month value must be decreased by one. (Because cal uses 0 to represent January, 1 to represent February, etc., we need to change a user specified 1 to a 0, a 2 to a 1, etc.)

We then use cal to get a Date object (for the date and time specified) and assign it to the Date variable.

The last statement assigns the values from the text fields and the formatted date and time values to ship's properties.

25. Change the actionPerformed method to do the following:

```
Execute the setShipmentProperties method
Check the error flag
If (error flag is true)
Set error flag to false
Else
        Create a ShipmentFrame object (passing ship)
```

26. Save the EnterShipInfo source code.

Results of the Review Exercise

Here are the results:

1. A new package called c7 in the ReviewEx project.

2. Six newly coded classes in c7 (of 21 total classes) that are subclasses of Choice and that display the current date and time.

3. EnterShipInfo has:

    A new method called setShipmentProperties that uses the new classes

    Several new private class variables to work with dates and times

    A new label to display messages

Check that the Exercise Was Done Correctly

Finally, let's check everything went as planned:

1. Run TNT and ensure that the EnterShipInfo frame can be accessed.

2. Verify that EnterShipInfo initially displays the current date and time in the choices.

3. Verify that EnterShipInfo ensures that information is entered in the text fields and if not, displays an error message in the new label.

4. Enter several different dates and times and verify that ShipmentFrame displays the information in the correct format.

CHAPTER 8

■ ■ ■

Servlets

So far, we have focused on client-based (desktop) applications. In this chapter, server-side (Web-based) applications are introduced, and the advantages and disadvantages of client versus server-based applications will be explained. There will be a short tutorial on HTML (Hypertext Markup Language) and then we will show how easy it is to create Web pages using RAD's Page Designer rather than entering HTML. We will then explain and create a Java servlet (i.e., a Web-based Java class), demonstrate how to tie a Web page to a servlet, and show how to pass information from a Web page to a servlet using a form.

In this chapter, you will learn about:

> HTTP
>
> HTML
>
> Forms
>
> The Web Perspective
>
> Application Servers
>
> Requests and Responses
>
> Page Designer

After this chapter, you should be able to:

> Create a Web page with a form
>
> Create a servlet that retrieves and displays information from a Web page
>
> Run Web pages and servlets on RAD's application server

What is a Server?

A server, of course, is a computer. However, that simple definition is like saying a coin is metal. True, a coin *is* metal, but a coin is much more than metal. Saying that a server is a computer describes only one aspect of a server (and not a very illuminating aspect), because not every computer is a server. What makes a computer a server is software, specifically, server software. Of course, the computer has to be "connected" to the Internet and to add a server to the Internet; the "Internet overseers" must be paid. However, we will leave a detailed discussion of how to set up a server for a different text and instead concentrate on how to create Java programs for a server.

To make things a little more confusing, there are many different types of Internet servers. For instance, email servers, Web page servers, and application servers are three different types of servers. What makes each server different is the type of information that is transferred and the protocol (or rules) that are followed to transfer the information. As a matter of fact, the Internet is really just a collection of protocols that specify how to send information. The Internet is not some specific network; rather, the Internet is comprised of those communications that follow an Internet protocol over any network. In other words, the network hardware used to transmit information does not define the Internet.

Is this hurting your brain? Maybe an alternative look at the Internet is needed.

Internet 101

The majority of Internet users don't clearly understand what the Internet is. For example, it is a common misconception that the World Wide Web (WWW, or the Web) and the Internet are the same thing. The Internet actually encompasses many methods of communicating over a network, and the WWW is only one of these communication methods. In other words, the WWW is just one piece of the Internet.

For instance, using a telephone to call someone is not communicating over the Internet. But, if you hook the phone line into a computer and send an e-mail message, you are communicating over the Internet. The same is true if you have a cable or satellite television connection. Hook the cable to your TV and you are receiving communications over the TV network. However, if you order Internet access from a cable or satellite company and connect the cable to a PC, you will be able to access Web pages. Notice that the network hardware (phone lines, coaxial cable, or satellite dish) does not determine whether the network is part of the Internet. Rather, it is the *type of communication* that determines if it is an Internet communication.

Of course, communicating over the Internet is not quite as easy as attaching a phone line or cable to the computer. You actually need software to communicate over the Internet, and there are separate software applications to support the different types of communication. For instance, communications over the WWW follow the rules called HTTP (Hypertext Transfer Protocol). Or, said another way, HTTP dictates how information in the form of Web pages is transferred over the Internet. Some other examples of Internet protocols are POP (Post Office Protocol) and SMTP (Simple Mail Transfer Protocol), both of which define the rules for transferring information as e-mail; and FTP (File Transfer Protocol), which defines the rules for transferring files between computers. If you use the Internet frequently, you may be bewildered because you have never heard these terms before (even though you can probably send e-mail and look at Web pages with the best of them!). This is because people use software applications that format the information according to the various protocol rules. In other words, the software does all the heavy lifting.

To communicate over the WWW, there are two primary pieces of software involved: the browser and the server software. The browser (such as Microsoft Explorer, Firefox, Chrome, etc.) is on the client computer. The server software (such as IBM's WebSphere Application Server, Apache Tomcat, and Microsoft's Internet Information Services) resides on the server (the computer that manages the Web pages).

One of the "rules" of HTTP is that every Web page is identified with a unique "address." Also, every server is assigned a unique address called an IP (Internet Protocol) address. IP addresses consist of a very long number broken up into four parts, with each part separated by a period (e.g., 123.218.76.4). This is not a very user-friendly way to locate information on the WWW. Therefore, URL (Uniform Resource Locator) addresses were created." URLs consist of at least a server (host) address—a series of words separated by periods such as www.spam.com. Sometimes the server address is followed by a directory path and the file name of a specific Web page (web.fccj.org/~rjanson/cgs1062/JIorderpage.html).

When you specify a WWW address (either IP or URL) and press Enter, the browser builds a Web page **request** and formats the request so that it is routed (sent) to the correct server. You can compare this to writing a letter (building the Web page request) and then addressing an envelope to send the letter in (formatting the request). In the case of a Web page request, the address follows the rules of HTTP.

The server receives the request, retrieves the appropriate Web page, packages the Web page (again, think of it as addressing an envelope), and sends the page to the browser. The browser receives and displays the Web page.

Wow, there's a lot going on! Just like the telephone system, communications over the WWW are very complex and do not happen by magic. It is the browser and server software that makes the WWW seem simple.

E-mail works very similarly. The user has client e-mail software (Microsoft's Outlook) that requests mail from the e-mail server software. When you send an e-mail, Outlook formats the note according to the rules of SMTP and, through the magic of the Internet; the e-mail is routed to the correct mail server. FTP, the other protocol listed earlier, also requires client and server software.

Fortunately, there is server software that supports many protocols. Therefore, instead of installing many different server software applications, companies purchase a single application (like WebSphere) that supports all of these protocols.

In addition to the browser and server software, another important part of the WWW is Web pages. (All that software is not much use if there aren't any pages to look at!) Simple Web pages are defined with a language called HTML (Hypertext Markup Language). HTML "tags" define the content and appearance of a Web page. Many HTML tags are paired. This means that there is one tag that marks the beginning of a page area and another tag that marks the end of the area. In addition, most tags start with a < and end with a >. For instance, a Web page begins with the "start HTML" tag (<HTML>) and ends with an "end HTML" tag (</HTML>). In addition, each Web page is usually broken up into a header area and the Web page body. The header section contains information about the page and the body contains the actual content of the page. These sections are also defined by start and end tags.

Tutorial: Using HTML to Create a Web Page

We will now go through the pain of entering HTML code to define a Web page so that you will appreciate RAD's Page Designer later.

1. In the Tutorials/src, create a new package called c8.

2. In the Navigation pane, click on c8 to select the package.

3. To create a file to hold the HTML, click File, New, and then Other.

The New frame will be displayed.

4. Scroll down the list and expand the Web item.

5. Scroll down the list and select Web Page (as in Figure 8-1).

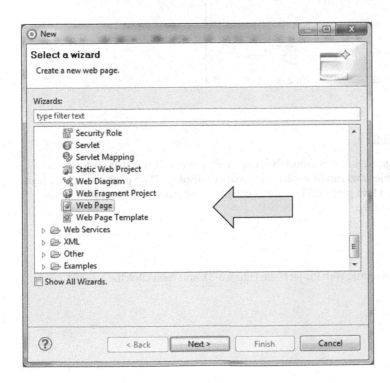

Figure 8-1.

6. Click the Next button.

The New Web Page frame will be displayed (see Figure 8-2).

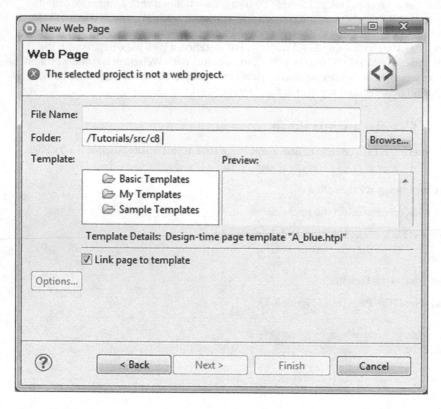

Figure 8-2.

7. Specify /Tutorials/src/c8 as the folder name.

Notice that RAD displays an error message, saying that Tutorials is not a Web project. This is true, Tutorials is a Java project. This means the project contains files that run on a client. To create or display a Web page (or create a Java class to run on a server), the files cannot be in a Java project. There are several types of projects that support server based files; the easiest to work with is a Web project.

8. Close the New Web Page frame.

9. Click File, New, and then Project.

10. At the New Project frame, select Dynamic Web Project (see Figure 8-3), and then click the Next button.

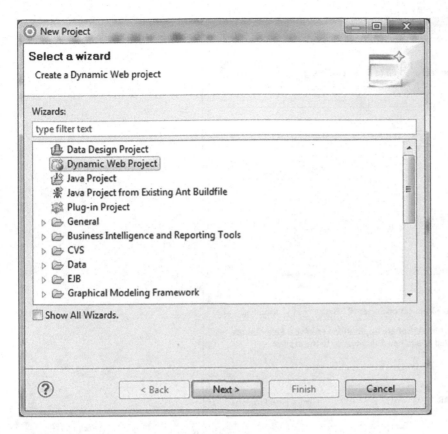

Figure 8-3.

The New Dynamic Web Project frame will be displayed (see Figure 8-4). At this screen, you can specify what type of server the application will run on. Notice that RAD has identified the latest WebSphere Application Server version, in this case 6.1, as the target. Also, RAD assumes you want to package this project in an EAR (Enterprise ARchive file). Just as JARs provide an easy way to package client-based applications, EARs hold applications that have both server and client-based components. The EAR contains JARs that contain the client components and WARs (Web ARchive files) that hold the server-based components (Web pages, servlets, JSPs, etc.). If you don't want RAD to generate an EAR, simply uncheck the option.

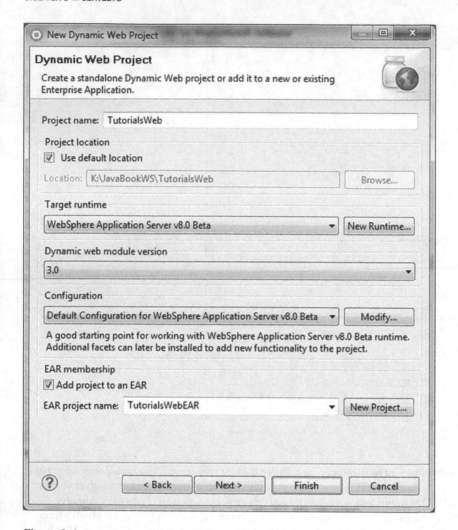

Figure 8-4.

11. At the New Dynamic Web Project frame, specify TutorialsWeb as the project name (see Figure 8-4) and click the Finish button.

You will be prompted to switch to the Web Perspective.

12. Click the Yes button.

Notice the new Web Perspective icon (a globe) in upper right hand of the RAD frame.

13. In the Navigation pane, display the contents of the TutorialsWeb project by clicking on its expansion icon.

Dynamic Web projects work differently than Java projects. Servers require that a server-based application's components (Web pages, java classes, etc.) be stored in specific folders. For instance, html files must reside in the WebContent folder. Generally, you don't have to worry about this, because:

A.   RAD automatically builds the correct folders when the Web project is created.

B.   When you create a file in a Web project, RAD will put the file in the correct folder based on the file type.

Let's prove it.

14.   Select TutorialsWeb and then perform steps 3 through 6 from above.

Notice that RAD has already specified WebContent as the folder to hold the file.

15.   At the New Web Page frame, select HTML/XHTML (beneath Basic Templates), specify Howdy as the File Name (see Figure 8-5), and click Finish.

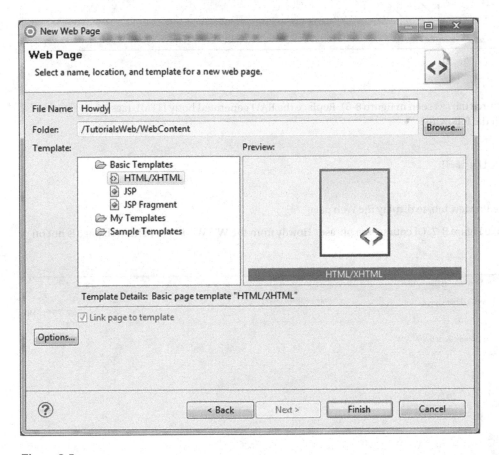

Figure 8-5.

A blank Web page is created and displayed. What this means is that RAD created the Howdy.html file in the WebContent folder then generated and stored the HTML that defines the Howdy Web page in the file. RAD then started Page Designer and displayed the Howdy page in the Page Designer Design view.

Page Designer has four views for Web pages: Design, Source, Split (the default view), and Preview. The view can be changed by clicking the view tabs at the bottom left of the content pane (see Figure 8-6). We will demonstrate the tools available in Design view later. Right now, we will simply enter the HTML code in the Source view.

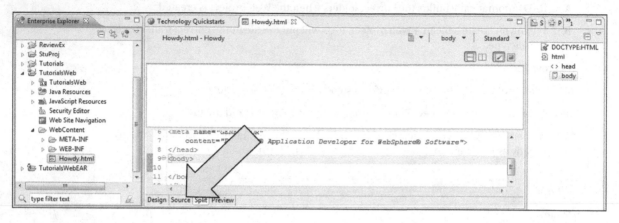

Figure 8-6.

16. Click the Source tab (as seen in figure 8-6). Replace the RAD generated body HTML tags in Howdy with the following:

```
<body>
Howdy from the WWW!
</body>
```

17. Click on the Preview tab, to display the Web page.

RAD should look like Figure 8-7. Of course, the phrase "Howdy from the WWW!" is a lie. The Web page is not on the WWW, it is in RAD.

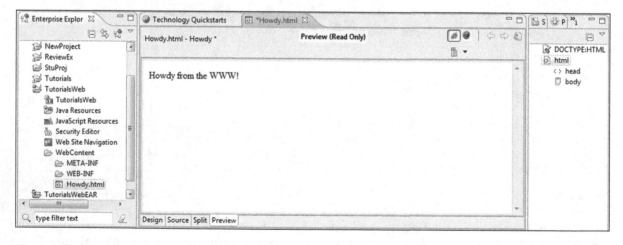

Figure 8-7.

18. Save Howdy.

19. Click File, then Export.

20. At the Export frame, expand General, select File System, and then click the Next button.

21. In the Export frame's right pane, make sure that the Howdy file's check box has been selected (see figure 8-8).

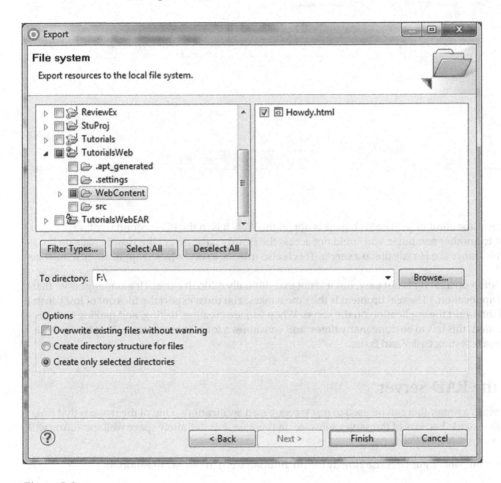

Figure 8-8.

22. Specify a secondary storage drive (e.g., C:\ or F:\).

23. Make sure the "Create only selected directories" option is selected and click the Finish button.

24. Using "My Computer" in Windows, display the contents of the drive that Howdy was exported to in step 23.

25. Double-click the Howdy file.

Windows will automatically start the PC's default browser and display the Howdy file as in Figure 8-9. You might not have known this, but in addition to looking at Web pages on the Internet, browsers can be used to view local files (i.e., files that are stored on your PC).

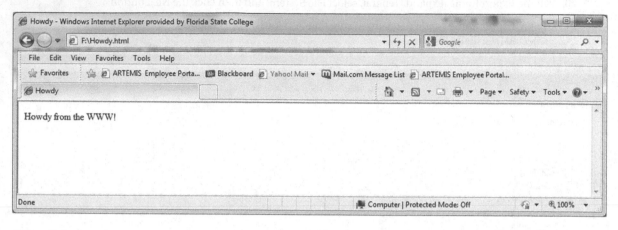

Figure 8-9.

Of course, Figure 8-9 is just another lie! The Web page is not on the Web, it is in the PC's secondary storage. For instance, if you went to another computer, you could not access the Howdy page. To get the Howdy page on the World Wide Web, you must move the Howdy file to a server. This is also true for a server-based application: it must be installed on a server.

Installing an application on a server is not easy, but it is not exceptionally difficult either. (It's actually easier than installing a client-based application.) The real problem is the time it takes. You must export the files out of RAD, install them on the server, and then start the application on the server. When you are creating, testing, and making changes to a server-based application, this has to be done many times, and consumes a lot of valuable time. That is why RAD has a built-in server: to make testing easier and faster.

Tutorial: Using the RAD Server

As mentioned, RAD provides a server that can be used to test server-based applications. One of the reasons that RAD takes up so much PC disk space is because of the server software. In this case, it is definitely space well spent. You will now use the RAD server to display the Howdy page.

1. In the Navigation pane, right-click the Howdy file (in TutorialsWeb) to display the shortcut menu.

2. From the shortcut menu, select Run as, and then Run on Server (see Figure 8-10).

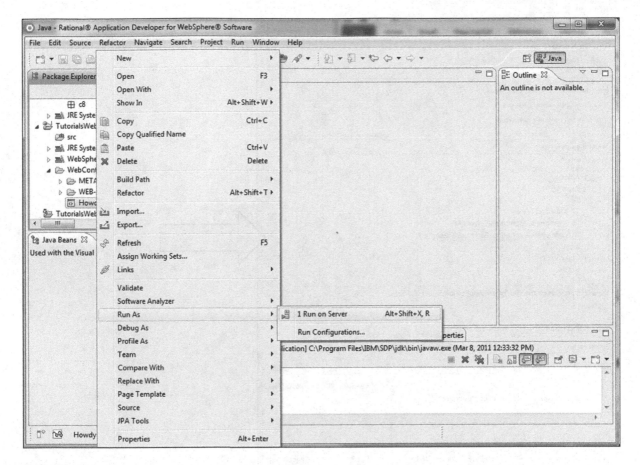

Figure 8-10.

If a server has already been created, the Run On Server frame will be displayed with the "Choose an existing server" radio button checked and a default server already selected. Simply click the Finish button and the server will be started.

If this is the first time the RAD server has been used, the Server Selection frame will be displayed with the "Manually define a new server" option selected (see Figure 8-11). A server must be created before it can be run. RAD offers several different server types and versions. Make sure the latest WebSphere version's Test Environment server is selected (i.e., 8.0) and then click the Finish button. After being successfully created, the server will be started.

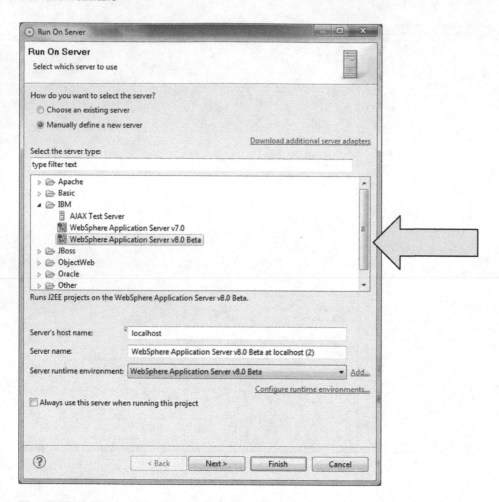

Figure 8-11.

Starting the server may take some time (depending on the speed of your computer) and many messages will be generated in the console. After the final message is displayed in the console, a browser pane with the Howdy Web page will be displayed (see Figure 8-12).

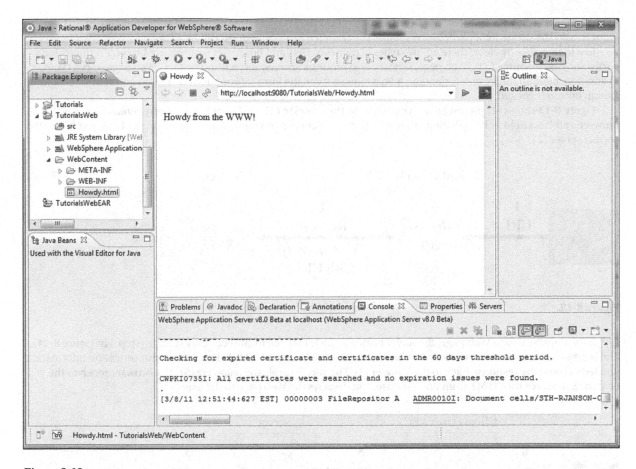

Figure 8-12.

Servlets

Servlets are Java classes that reside on a server and can be accessed with a browser. Servlets can perform any Java command but, more importantly, servlets can send HTML back to a browser. To explain how the servlet does this we need to go into a little more detail about how the browser and server work.

Up until now, we have only used the browser to view a Web page. However, instead of specifying a Web page URL (i.e., `http://My.Website.com/Howdy.html`) a servlet URL can be specified. The servlet URL consists of the RAD server's (i.e., the host's) address, which resides on the PC you are working on and is identified in the URL as `http://localhost:9080`. Then, after the host address, specify the project name (/**TutorialsWeb**) and the name of the servlet (i.e., /**MyFirstServlet**) separated by forward slashes. The ability to access servlets also highlights why Web addresses are called Uniform **Resource** Locators, not Uniform **Web Page** Locators: URLs can identify more than just HTML files.

Rather than specifying a servlet's URL, servlets can also be invoked from a **form**. A form is an area of a Web page that contains a submit button and components where information can be entered. (If you have ever bought anything on the Internet, you have filled out a form that has at least "name," "address," and "credit card number" text fields.)

When you specify a Web page (e.g., you enter a URL and press Enter or you click on a hyperlink), the browser sends a request to the server for that Web page. This type of request is called a **Get request**. If you are using a form and click the submit button, the same thing happens—a request is created and sent to the server. However, in this case a **Post request** is created and sent, not a Get request. A Post request contains the form information and, like a Get request, asks the server for a particular resource. The resource in a Post request can be a servlet.

Just to be perfectly clear: there are two types of requests, Gets and Posts. Get requests are browser requests for a particular Web resource (e.g., Web page, servlet). Post requests also request a resource (e.g., Web page, servlet) but, in addition, contain the form information. A Post request (with the form information) is created and sent when a form submit button is clicked.

Figure 8-13 shows (1) the user supplying a URL to the browser. (The URL could have been entered in the browser's address field or be specified in a form.) The browser creates a request and, based on the URL, sends it to the correct server (2).

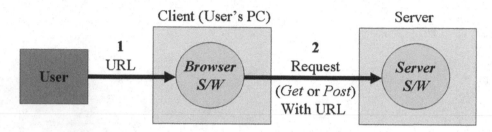

Figure 8-13.

If the request is for a Web page, the server retrieves the HTML file from secondary storage (step 3 in Figure 8-14). The server then creates a response and embeds the web page (i.e., the HTML) along with communication information needed to route the response back to the browser (4). The server sends the response (5). The browser receives the response, retrieves the HTML from the response, and displays the Web page to the user (6).

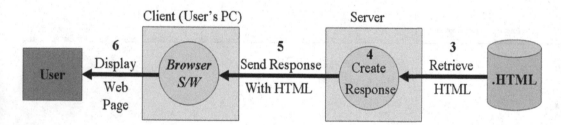

Figure 8-14.

If, instead, the request is for a servlet, the server creates a response object but does not embed any HTML (see step 3 in Figure 8-15). The servlet class file is retrieved from storage, and an object of that class type is instantiated (4). Then either the servlet's doGet or doPost method is executed. (Can you guess what decides which method is executed? Yes, if the browser's request was a Get, the servlet's doGet method is invoked. If the request was a Post, the servlet's doPost method is executed.) The Server passes both the request (actually a HTTPServletRequest) object and the just created response (HTTPServletResponse) object to the doPost or doGet methods (5).

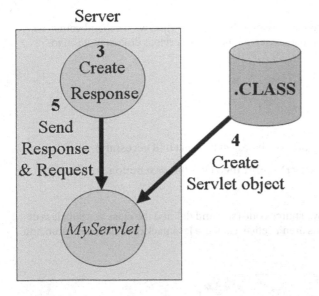

Figure 8-15.

A servlet can do many things. For instance, a servlet can embed HTML into the response object. When the servlet ends, the server will send the response object back to the browser, and the browser will display the HTML created by the servlet. However, the servlet does not have to echo back static HTML. A servlet can perform any function a Java class can perform. For instance, the servlet could run other Java object methods, redirect the browser to a different Web page, or pass the request and response objects to other objects for processing. In addition, if a Post request was passed, the servlet can retrieve and process the form information.

Figure 8-16 depicts a servlet embedding HTML into the response object and passing the response back to the server (6). The server then sends the response back to the browser (7). The browser then retrieves the html from the response and displays it (8).

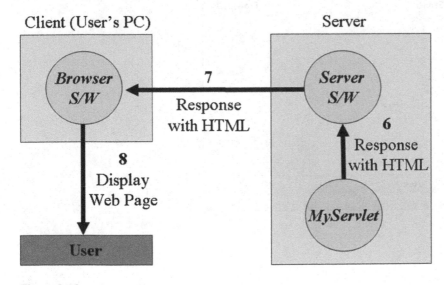

Figure 8-16.

Wow, there sure is a lot going on at the server!

We will create a simple servlet with a doGet method that processes a Get request. Then we'll expand your Web page knowledge and create a form. Lastly, we'll tie the form to a servlet and code the servlet's doPost method to process the form information.

Tutorial: Creating a Simple Servlet

Let's have a go at a servlet.

1. In the Enterprise Explorer pane, click on the TutorialsWeb project to select it (if necessary).

2. Click File, New, Other, expand the Web folder, select Servlet then click the Next button.

3. Specify MyServlet as the class name.

Notice that RAD has specified the folder to hold the Java source code (src) and defined the class as a subclass of HttpServlet (see Figure 8-17). (If the Next and Finish buttons aren't active, click the Java package's Browse button and select the default package.)

Figure 8-17.

4. Click the Finish button.

The servlet source code will be displayed in the Editor.

5. In TutorialsWeb, expand Java Resources/src/(default package) to show where MyServlet.java was placed in the project.

In the source, notice that RAD has generated import statements (for the classes the servlet needs) and there are constructor, doGet, and doPost method stubs. Note that the doGet and doPost methods expect both request and response objects.

6. In the body of the doGet method, insert the following statement:

```
System.out.println("Howdy from MyServlet");
```

7. Save the source code.

When the source code is saved, RAD automatically generates the servlet class file. However, the RAD server does not have this new resource. In other words, the servlet has to be installed on the server. There are several ways to do this however restarting the server is easy to do and forces the entire project (all the Web pages, servlets, etc.) to be loaded onto the server.

8. Click the Servers tab, (to the left of the Console tab, see the first arrow in Figure 8-18).

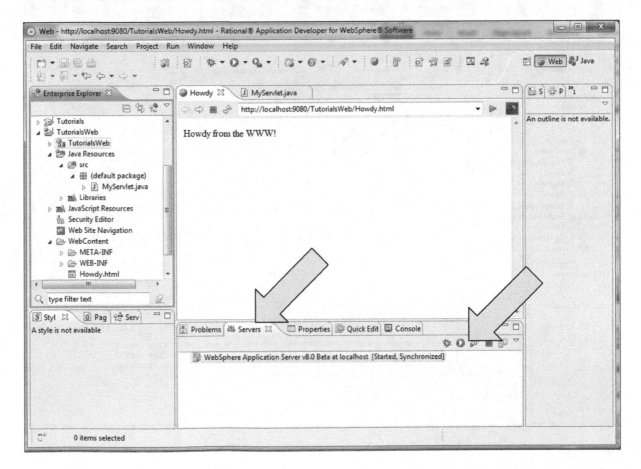

Figure 8-18.

The Servers view displays all defined RAD servers and their status. In the upper right of the Servers pane are buttons that allow you to perform a variety of server functions. For example, you can stop, start, or restart a server. (To activate the buttons, select a server by clicking on it.) The Restart button is the second button (see the second arrow in Figure 8-18).

9. Make sure the correct server is selected in the server pane, and then click the Restart button.

The server will be stopped and then started. This may take a minute or two.

10. In the Enterprise Explorer pane, expand the new TutorialsWeb folder (within the TutorialsWeb project) and then the Servlets folder to display the MyServlet.class file.

11. Right-click MyServlet to display the shortcut menu, then choose Run As, and then Run on Server.

12. On the Run On Server frame, click the Finish button.

The Console should show the message, "Howdy from MyServlet," as seen in Figure 8-19. (If nothing appears in the console, click the Refresh button in the Browser window; see the arrow in Figure 8-19.)

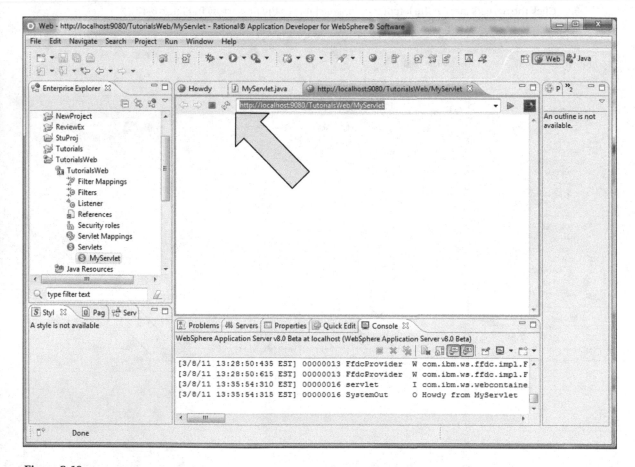

Figure 8-19.

This example proves that the doGet is called when the servlet is requested by the browser. However, the servlet did not insert any HTML into the response object; therefore, the RAD browser window displays a blank page. Our next step is to change MyServlet to insert HTML into the response object.

Working with Response Objects

As mentioned, response objects can hold HTML. However, there are syntax rules that must be followed and we will need several objects to change the response object. Fortunately, we can import one of the Java classes we'll need and the response object comes with several useful methods that will help us with the other requirements.

Response objects have a property called content type. Content type is used by the browser to determine how to handle the response. For instance, if the content type indicates that the response contains HTML, the browser will read the HTML and display it. If the response's content type specified an Access database file, the browser would prompt to see if the user wanted to display or download the file.

So, for our example, the servlet needs to set the content type to indicate HTML. The content type property is modified by the response object's setContentType method. The correct syntax is:

responseVariable.setContentType("text/html");

Once the content type has been specified, we can start writing the HTML to the response object. We will need two objects to do this: a `PrintWriter` and an `OutputStream`. A print writer converts primitives and reference variables into text. For example, a `String` variable points to a `String` object. If you pass a `String` variable to a print writer, the print writer will extract the text from the `String` object. Similarly, the print writer will convert primitive variables to text values (see Figure 8-20). Getting the information into text format is only half the battle. The text has to be converted into a binary stream (i.e., a set of zeros and ones that the browser can recognize). An `OutputStream` object converts the text to a binary stream and this binary stream is written to the response object.

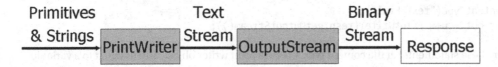

Figure 8-20.

Now, the tricky part.

When a print writer is created, an `OutputStream` object must be passed to the print writer. This means that an output stream must be created before the print writer. Response objects have a getOutputStream method that creates an output stream that is already associated with the response object (i.e., the output stream will automatically write to that particular response object). In other words, you don't have to create an output stream and then tie it to the response object. The following statement:

```
PrintWriter out = new PrintWriter(resp.getOutputStream());
```

will:

- Get an output stream from the response object
- Create a `PrintWriter` object
- Pass the output stream to the print writer
- Assign the print writer to a `PrintWriter` variable called "out"

Of course, we must also import the `PrintWriter` class with the following statement.

```
import java.io.PrintWriter;
```

That was the hard part. All you need to do now is write the HTML to the response object using out's (the print writer's) println method.

Tutorial: Working with a Response Object

Let's look at the Response object:

1. In MyServlet.java, add the following import statement:

   ```
   import java.io.PrintWriter;
   ```

2. In the doGet header, select the variable request, right-click on it, choose `Refactor`, and then Rename.

3. Specify req as the new name and press Enter.

4. In the doGet header, rename response as resp.

5. In the doPost header, rename the variables to req and resp also.

6. In the doGet method, replace the System.out.println statement with the following statements:

   ```
   resp.setContentType("text/html");
   PrintWriter out = new PrintWriter(resp.getOutputStream());
   ```

As explained earlier, these statements set the content type, create a print writer object, and assign it to a variable called out.

7. At the end of the doGet method, add the following statements to define a Web page's header and title:

   ```
   out.println("<HTML>");
   out.println("<HEAD>");
   out.println("<Title>MyServlet Get Response</Title>");
   out.println("</HEAD>");
   ```

8. At the end of the doGet method, add the following statements that define a Web page's body and content:

   ```
   out.println("<BODY>");
   out.println("Howdy from MyServlet's doGet method!");
   out.println("</BODY>");
   out.println("</HTML>");
   out.close();
   ```

Notice that the print writer's close method is called. The close method "flushes" the output stream and releases any resources allocated to the output stream. Essentially, flushing ensures that the binary stream is written to the response. (If you do not close the print writer, the response may not contain the HTML and a blank page would be displayed.)

9.   Save the source code and run MyServlet on the RAD server.

The browser should look like Figure 8-21. If it doesn't, click the refresh button.

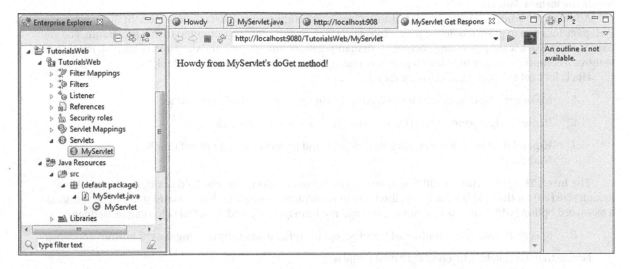

Figure 8-21.

10.   In the browser's address field, replace MyServlet with Howdy.html and press Enter.

The Howdy page will be displayed.

11.   In the browser's address field, replace Howdy.html with MyServlet and press Enter.

The browser should again look like Figure 8-21. Notice that you were able to run the servlet from the browser. The point being: browsers can be used to access more than just Web pages and, as described, the application server finds and executes class files, and then sends the response back to the browser. In addition, notice that the file extension (.class) did not have to be specified in the servlet's URL. (With most Web pages, the extension .html must be included.)

Of course, using servlets to display static text is way too much work for the programmer. Simple Web pages can do this with much less effort. However, retrieving user-specified information and then displaying it would be worthy of a servlet.

Tutorial: Defining Form Components

To retrieve user information, we will create a form for data entry and then code the servlet's doPost method to retrieve and display the information.

1.   In the Enterprise Explorer pane, click on TutorialsWeb project to select it.

2.   To create a file to hold the form, click File, New, and then Other.

3.   On the New window, expand the Web item, select Web Page, and click the Next button.

4.   On the New Web Page window, select HTML/XHTML, specify EnterEmpInfoForm as the File Name, and click the Finish button.

A blank page will be displayed in the Split view. We will use the Design view's GUI to build the Web page this time instead of typing the HTML code.

HTML supports many of the same GUI components as Java but, unfortunately, has different names for many of the components. A form is similar to a Java frame in that it is usually comprised of many GUI components. The two major differences with a form are that a form must include a submit button and the form components are defined before the form is defined.

Adding form components is similar to adding Java frame components: select the component then click on the Web page location to paste it onto the page. However, a Web page is more text-oriented than a Java frame. The Web page is more like a word processing document, so manipulation through click and drag is very limited. For instance, to move a component lower on the Web page you must press the Enter key and insert blank lines.

Heck, let's get to it instead of talking about it.

5. Make sure the Design view is selected and then type the text Employee Name.

6. In the far right pane, change from the Outline view to the Palette view.

7. Expand the Form Tags tray, click Text Field, and then click to the right of Employee Name text.

The Insert Text Field window will be displayed. This is used to specify the text field attributes. Notice that a default size (20) for the field is already specified. There is also a maximum length parameter that can be specified, a password option (which means that entered text will not be displayed), and an initial value can be defined.

8. Specify the Name as empNameTF and accept the other defaults by clicking the OK button.

Notice that a text field is inserted right next to the text.

9. Press the left arrow key to move the cursor between the text and the text field.

10. Press the spacebar once to insert a space.

Pressing the spacebar a second time will not insert another space.

11. Click Insert, then Non-breaking Space to insert another space between the two components.

The text field can be dragged to the next line by clicking on the border and dragging, but this is the extent of the click and drag capability (at this time). There are also resize handles on the text field but they will only control the field's length not its height.

12. Change the text "Employee Name" to "Employee Number."

13. Display the text field's properties by right-clicking on the text field then select Properties.

14. In the Properties view, change the field Name to empNumTF and the size (Columns) to 6.

15. Select the text "Employee Number."

Notice that the properties view now displays the text's properties.

16. In the Properties view, click on the font tab (on the left side) and specify the font properties as seen in Figure 8-22.

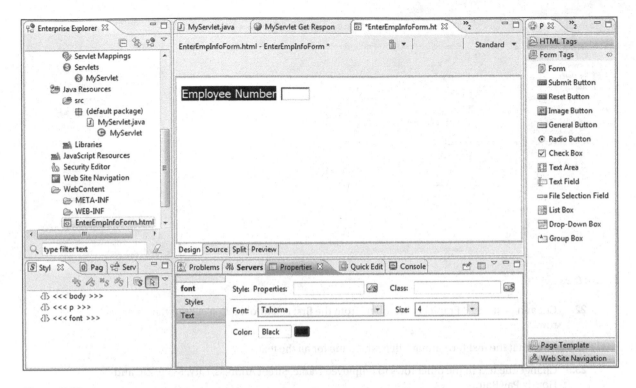

Figure 8-22.

17. Click anywhere on the Design page to deselect the text field.

As mentioned earlier, Web pages are much more text oriented than frames. For example, specific location coordinates can be specified for frame components. Web page components can be aligned (on a particular line) but to position a component vertically, blank lines must be inserted or deleted. One of the secrets to Web page design, however, is using an invisible table to control the location of page components.

18. Move the cursor after the Text Field component and click `Table`, then `Insert Table`.

19. At the Insert Table frame, specify 6 rows and 2 columns and click the OK button.

20. Cut and paste the text into the table's first cell in the first row.

21. Cut and paste the text field into the table's second cell in the first row.

The page should look like Figure 8-23.

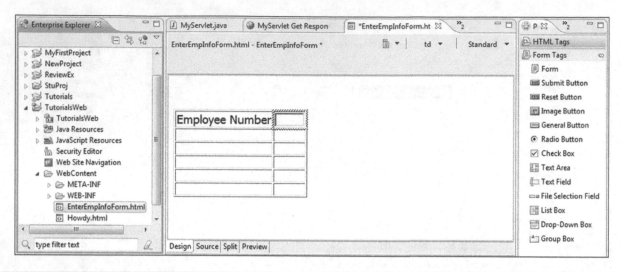

Figure 8-23.

22. Cut and paste the "Employee Number" from the first cell into the first cells in the other rows.

This ensures that the text formatting will be the same for all the text.

23. Change the text in the other rows to Employee Name, Street Address, City, State, Zip and Hourly Pay Rate.

Oops, we're one row short.

24. Move the cursor to the last row and click Table, and then Add Row Below.

A new row will be inserted at the end of the table.

25. Paste the original text into the new row's first cell, then change to "Hourly Pay Rate."

26. Select all the cells in the first column.

27. In the Properties view, select right for the align Attribute (as in Figure 8-24).

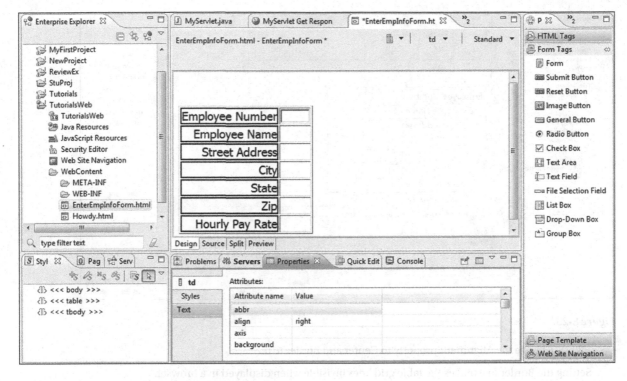

Figure 8-24.

All the text in the first column will be right justified within the cells.

28. Insert text fields into the other six cells with the following names and lengths:

empNameTF	20
streetAddrTF	20
cityTF	13
stateTF	13
zipTF	6
hPRTF	8

29. Select the table by clicking anywhere to the right of the table in the Design area.

The table and the Properties view should appear as in Figure 8-25.

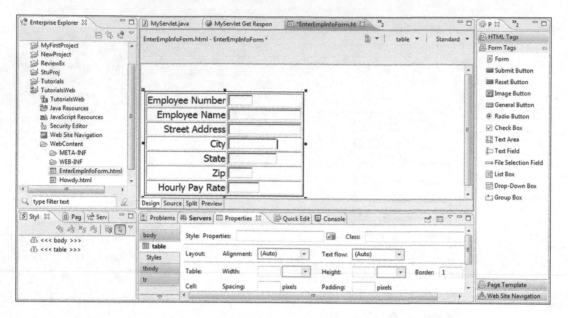

Figure 8-25.

30. Change the Alignment property to Center and Border to 0.

Setting the Border to 0 makes the table grid lines invisible when displayed in a browser.

31. In the content pane, click the Preview tab.

The Web page should appear as in Figure 8-26.

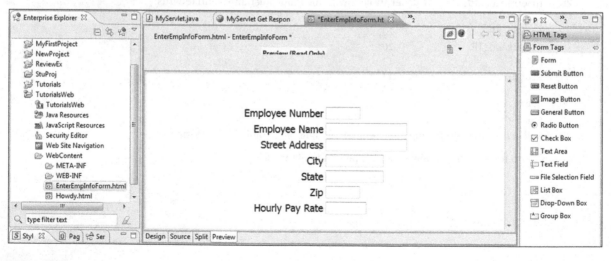

Figure 8-26.

There are many other Web page formatting functions and good design practices; however, they are not within the scope of this text. So, we will leave behind Web page formatting and get down to business: defining a form and tying the form to a servlet.

Tutorial: Defining a Form

As mentioned earlier, a form must have a submit button. So we will add a submit button and then define a form.

1. Change back to Design view.

2. In the Forms Tag tray, click Submit Button then, in the Design view, click on the line after the table.

3. At the Insert Submit Button window, specify submitBtn as the name, Submit as the label text, and click the OK button.

The submit button will be inserted beneath the table.

4. Click to the right of the submit button.

This selects the entire line. Now we will center the button on the page.

5. In the Properties view, change the alignment property to center.

Adding components from a tool bar is an alternative to the adding from the palette. To define the form this way, we must first display the "Form and Input Fields" toolbar.

6. Click Toolbar and then Form and Input Fields.

Buttons representing the most commonly used components from the Form Tags tray will be added to the right of the toolbar print button. The first new button is the Insert Form button (see Figure 8-27).

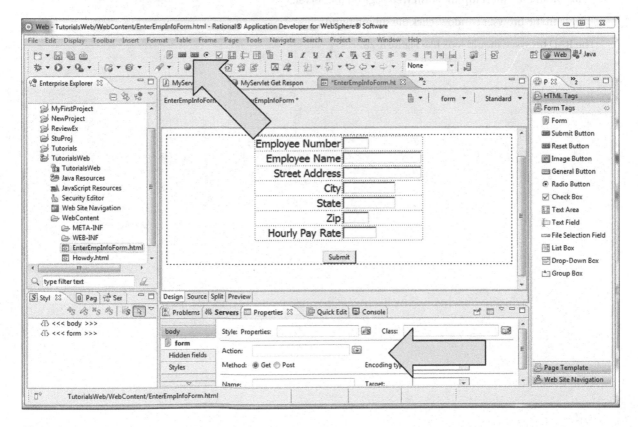

Figure 8-27.

7. Select all the components on the page (i.e., the table and submit button).

8. Click the Insert Form button.

The table and submit button will be enclosed in a dashed line box. The box indicates the form. In the Properties view, the form tab is selected and its attributes/properties are displayed.

9. In the Attribute pane, click the Action Browse button and select servlet from the shortcut menu (see Figure 8-27).

10. At the Select Servlet window, select MyServlet and click the OK button.

The Properties view will display /TutorialsWeb/MyServlet in the Action field.

11. In the Properties view, click the Post method checkbox to ensure that a Post request is generated when the submit button is clicked.

12. Save the source code.

The Web page is now tied to the servlet. Let's prove it. We'll put some code in the doPost method, run the page on the server and submit the form. If the doPost code is executed, then everything is good.

13. In MyServlet, copy all the statements from the doGet method into the doPost method.

14. In doPost, change the title to "MyServlet Post Response" and the page content to "Howdy from MyServlet's doPost method!"

15. Run the EnterEmpInfoForm Web page on the server.

16. In the browser window, click the submit button.

The RAD browser should look like Figure 8-28.

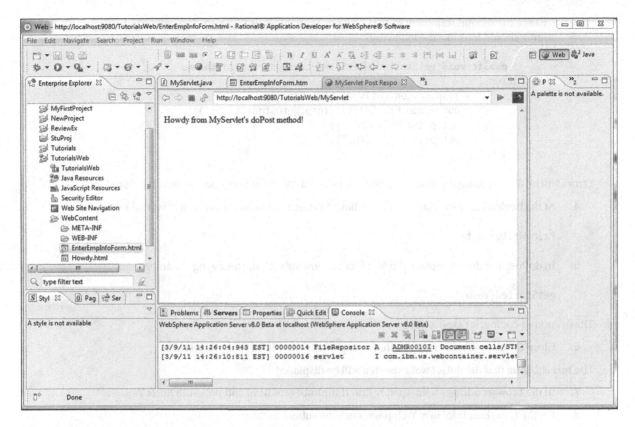

Figure 8-28.

Although this proves that the EnterEmpInfoForm Post request does invoke the doPost method, doPost doesn't really do much. Let's modify doPost so that the form information is retrieved and then redisplayed.

Tutorial: Retrieving Form Information

In addition to enhancing the function of the servlet, we will also improve its structure. Notice that there is duplication in MyServlet. For example, both do methods create print writer variables and set the response context. Couldn't the context be set once and shouldn't we use one class print writer variable instead of two method variables? We will create a new printer writer class variable and a new method called getStarted that will perform the common functions.

1. Create a new method at the end of the class as follows:

```
public void getStarted(HttpServletResponse resp) throws
IOException {
        }
```

The header must throw an IOException because the getOutputStream method (which we will use in this method) can throw an IOException. Notice that the method also requires that the response be passed.

2. Copy the first 4 statements from the doPost method into getStarted method.

3. Change the second statement so that a new out variable is not created. The getStarted source should look like the following:

```
public void getStarted(HttpServletResponse resp) throws
IOException {
        resp.setContentType("text/html");
        out = new PrintWriter(resp.getOutputStream());
        out.println("<HTML>");
        out.println("<HEAD>");
}
```

Errors will be displayed saying that out cannot be resolved. We need to create out as a class variable.

4. At the beginning of the class, add the following statement to create out as a class variable:

```
PrintWriter out;
```

5. In doPost and doGet, replace the first four statements with the following statement:

```
getStarted(resp);
```

That's enough coding, let's test a little.

6. Close the any browser windows that are open and run MyServlet on the server.

The text showing that the doGet was executed will be displayed.

7. In the browser address field, specify EnterEmpInfoForm.html and press the Enter key.

8. On the EnterEmpInfoForm Web page, click the submit button.

In the console, the text indicating that the doPost was executed will be displayed. This means that you successfully tidied up the class. Now, we'll add code to retrieve and display the form data. The request (passed to the servlet) contains the form's text field values as parameters. The values can be retrieved (as strings) using the request's getParameter method. The getParameter method simply requires that you specify which component's text to retrieve.

9. In doPost, replace the statement that displays the static text with the following:

```
out.println("Employee Number " + req.getParameter("empNumTF"));
```

10. Save the source code and run the EnterEmpInfoForm page on the server.

11. On EnterEmpInfoForm, enter 123 as the employee number and click the submit button.

The text "Employee Number 123" will be displayed in the browser.

Think of the implications to our application! If the servlet created an employee object and the Web page offered options to calculate gross salary, tax amounts, and so on, then:

A. All of the employee functions could be available from any computer that had access to the Web.

B. We would not have to install the application on multiple (thousands? millions?) of PCs, thereby saving a good deal of time, effort, and confusion.

C. Modifications would be made to a single set of programs on the server, not to multiple copies of the programs on each PC.

Of course, if a computer's Internet connection isn't working, the Web page and servlet can't be accessed and, if the server malfunctions, no one can access the functions. So, there are some disadvantages to server-based applications.

Notice that to display results, servlets require the programmer to enter the HTML; there is no GUI to generate the HTML. For professional looking Web pages, this is not a trivial amount of coding. Fortunately, there is an alternative to servlets called **Java Server Pages**. JSPs make defining a result page much easier. We will cover JSPs in the next chapter.

Results of the Tutorial

Time to go over the results:

1. In Tutorials, a new package called c8.

2. A new project called TutorialsWeb, with the following four files (that you created):

   ```
   MyServlet.java          MyServlet.class
   Howdy.html              EnterEmpInfoForm.html
   ```

3. A copy of the Howdy.html file on one of the secondary storage drives (e.g., C:\ or G:\)

4. When run on the server:

   - Howdy.html will display static text

   - EnterEmpInfoForm.html displays fields to enter employee information and, when the submit button is pressed, invokes MyServlet

5. When specified in the browser address field, MyServlet will display static text.

6. When invoked from EnterEmpInfoForm, MyServlet will display static text and the employee number from EnterEmpInfoForm.

7. MyServlet's source code should look like the following:

```java
import java.io.IOException;
import javax.servlet.ServletException;
import javax.servlet.annotation.WebServlet;
import javax.servlet.http.HttpServlet;
import javax.servlet.http.HttpServletRequest;
import javax.servlet.http.HttpServletResponse;
import java.io.PrintWriter;

public class MyServlet extends HttpServlet {
        PrintWriter out;
        private static final long serialVersionUID = 1L;

        public MyServlet() {
                super();
        }

        protected void doGet(HttpServletRequest req,
                HttpServletResponse resp)
                throws ServletException, IOException {
            getStarted(resp);
            out.println("<Title>MyServlet Get Response</Title>");
```

```
                out.println("</HEAD>");
                out.println("<BODY>");
                out.println("Howdy from MyServlet's doGet method!");
                out.println("</BODY>");
                out.println("</HTML>");
                out.close();
        }

        protected void doPost(HttpServletRequest req,
                    HttpServletResponse resp)
                    throws ServletException, IOException {
                getStarted(resp);
                out.println("<Title>MyServlet Post Response</Title>");
                out.println("</HEAD>");
                out.println("<BODY>");
                out.println("Employee Number " +
                req.getParameter("empNumTF"));
                out.println("</BODY>");
                out.println("</HTML>");
                out.close();
        }

        public void getStarted(HttpServletResponse resp)
                    throws IOException {
                resp.setContentType("text/html");
                out = new PrintWriter(resp.getOutputStream());
                out.println("<HTML>");
                out.println("<HEAD>");
        }
}
```

Review Questions

1. What is a servlet?

2. What is a server?

3. What is a protocol?

4. What is HTTP?

5. How are the Internet and the World Wide Web related?

6. What are the advantages of server-based applications over client-based applications?

7. What does a server pass to a servlet?

8. What are the two primary methods in a servlet?

9. What is the relationship between a form and a servlet?

10. What are HTML tags?

Review Exercise

In this exercise, you will create a Web page and servlet to enter and display shipment information (probably not a big surprise).

1. Create a Dynamic Web project called ReviewExWeb and an EAR called ReviewExWebEAR.

2. Create a Web page called ShipInfoForm that looks like Figure 8-29 and name the input text fields empNumTF, shipNumTF, dateRcvdTF, timeRcvdTF, and suppNameTF.

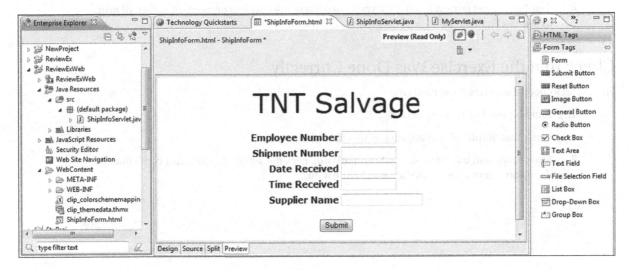

Figure 8-29.

3. Create a servlet called ShipInfoServlet that will read the shipment information from a request and display that data, as seen in Figure 8-30.

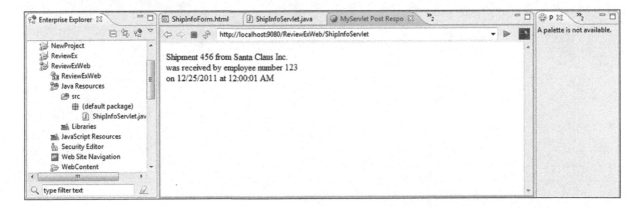

Figure 8-30.

4. In ShipInfoForm, create a form that will invoke the servlet ShipInfoServlet and pass the text field data.

Results of the Review Exercise

Here are the results:

1. A new project called ReviewExWeb and ReviewExWebEAR.

2. In ReviewExWeb, one Web page called ShipInfoForm and one servlet called ShipInfoServlet.

3. ShipInfoForm invokes ShipInfoServlet.

4. ShipInfoServlet retrieves and displays the shipment information entered on ShipInfoForm, as seen in Figure 8-30.

Check that the Exercise Was Done Correctly

Finally, let's check that it was done correctly:

1. Run ShipInfoForm on the server.

2. Verify that ShipInfoForm appears as specified above.

3. Enter Shipment information into ShipInfoForm, click the submit button, and verify that the information appears as shown in Figure 8-30.

CHAPTER 9

■■■

Java Server Pages

In this chapter, we will make your programming life easier by introducing Java Server Pages (JSPs). In addition to making it easier to build a GUI interface, JSPs can use JSP tags and Expression Language (EL) instead of Java statements. JSP tags (and EL) are very useful because their syntax is much simpler than Java statements.

This chapter will also demonstrate how to create and use Java beans. We will then explore the Model-View-Controller (MVC) architecture and show how JSPs, beans, and servlets fit into the MVC framework. In addition, we will expand your knowledge of Web page components and introduce several very useful objects and functions that the server provides to applications.

In this chapter, you will learn about:

> JSPs
>
> Scriptlets, Expressions, Declarations, and Directives
>
> JSP tags and Expression Language
>
> Java Beans
>
> Implicit Objects
>
> Drop-down Menus and List Boxes
>
> Redirect and RequestDispatcher

After this chapter, you should be able to:

> Create a JSP
>
> Invoke JSPs from servlets
>
> Define and use beans in JSPs and servlets
>
> Use JSP tags and Expression Language

Tutorial: What is a JSP?

JSPs are Web pages that have Java code mixed in with HTML statements that define the page. The advantage of the JSP is that instead of writing a servlet, that laboriously embeds HTML statements into a response; a programmer can use a GUI tool to generate the HTML (that defines a Web page) and then enter the much smaller amount of Java code that performs the desired functions. Of course, an example is worth a thousand words of explanation.

1. In the Web Perspective, click the TutorialsWeb/WebContent folder to select it.

2. Click File, New, and then Folder.

3. At the New Folder frame, specify c9 as the folder name and click the Finish button.

4. With the folder c9 still selected, click File, New, and then Web Page.

5. At the New Web Page frame, expand the Basic Templates item, and select JSP.

6. Specify HowdyJSP for the file name and click the Finish button.

The JSP file will be created and an edit session will be started. Notice that the initial page is the same as when creating a Web page and, like the Web page, the JSP can be modified from either the Design or Source views.

7. In the Design view, type: Howdy from the JSP!

8. Click before the "H" in "Howdy" to position the cursor before the text.

9. Click JSP, and then InsertScriptlet.

A scriptlet icon (a scroll) will be inserted before Howdy.

In the Design view, embedded Java statements are specified in the scriptlet's Properties view. In this case, we will insert a for loop so that the text is displayed five times. We will need one scriptlet before the text (containing the beginning of the for loop) and one scriptlet after the text (to finish the for loop).

10. In the Properties view, enter the following in the jsp:scriptlet: input area:

```
for (int i = 0; i < 5; i++) {
```

11. In the Design view, click after the text to position the cursor at the end of the line.

12. Click JSPand then InsertScriptlet.

13. In the jsp:scriptlet input area, enter an ending brace (}) to finish the **for** loop.

14. Save the source and run HowdyJSP on the server.

The result should look like Figure 9-1.

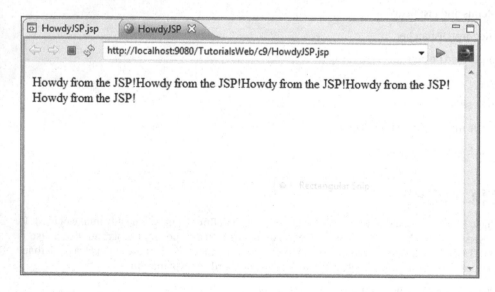

Figure 9-1.

15.   Change the view by clicking on the Source tab in the Content pane.

The result should look like Figure 9-2.

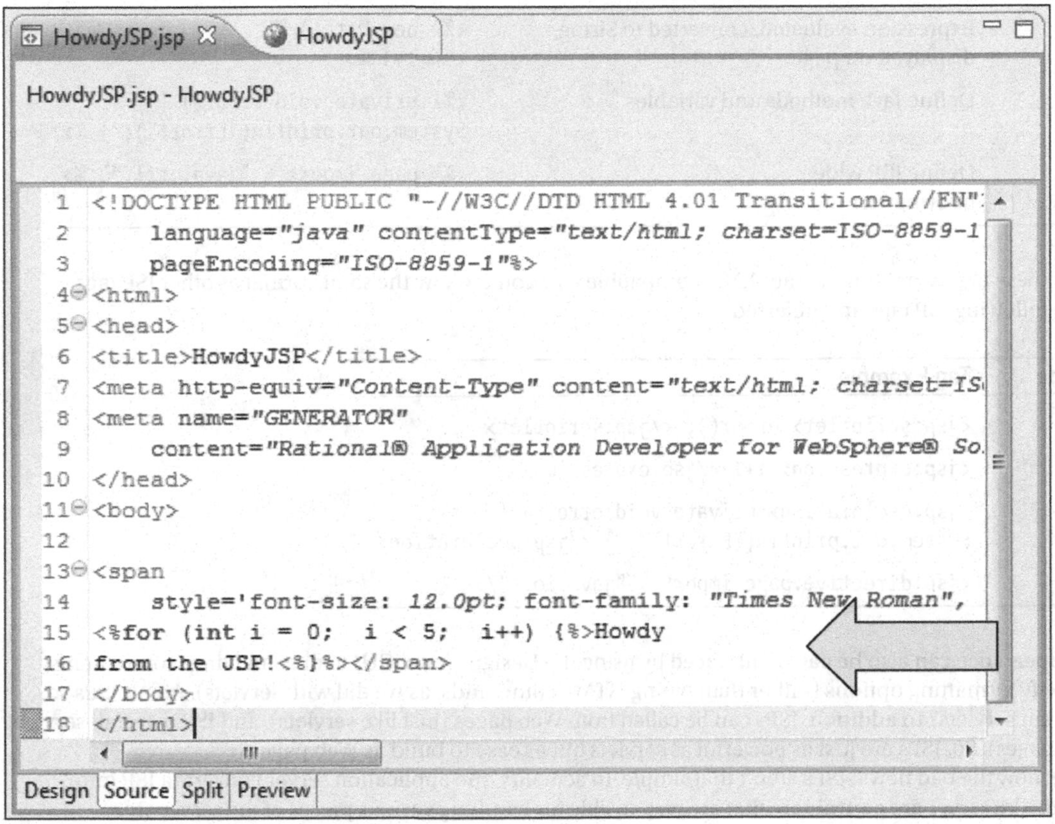

```
 HowdyJSP.jsp  ✕      HowdyJSP

HowdyJSP.jsp - HowdyJSP


 1  <!DOCTYPE HTML PUBLIC "-//W3C//DTD HTML 4.01 Transitional//EN":
 2      language="java" contentType="text/html; charset=ISO-8859-1
 3      pageEncoding="ISO-8859-1"%>
 4 <html>
 5 <head>
 6  <title>HowdyJSP</title>
 7  <meta http-equiv="Content-Type" content="text/html; charset=IS
 8  <meta name="GENERATOR"
 9      content="Rational® Application Developer for WebSphere® So.
10  </head>
11 <body>
12
13 <span
14      style='font-size: 12.0pt; font-family: "Times New Roman",
15  <%for (int i = 0;  i < 5;  i++) {%>Howdy
16  from the JSP!<%}%></span>
17  </body>
18  </html>

Design  Source  Split  Preview
```

Figure 9-2.

More About JSPs

JSPs can contain four major types of Java "scripts:" scriptlets, expressions, declarations, and directives. Notice in Figure 9-2 that even though the Java scripts and HTML statements are mixed together, the Java is differentiated by **tags**. Each type of script has its own unique tags. As you can see in Figure 9-2, scriptlets begin with a <% tag and end with a %> tag. The following table shows each of the four major tag types, its purpose, and an example.

Statement Type	Purpose	Tag Example
scriptlet	Perform Java snippets or statements	`<% error(); %>` `<% ctr = ctr + 1; %>`
expression	Expression evaluated, converted to String, displayed on page	`<%= new Date() %>` `<%= 1+1 %>`
declaration	Define Java methods and variables	`<%! private void error() {` `System.out.println("Error!"); } %>`
directive	Define JSP wide information	`<%@ page import = "java.util.*" %>`

Although these tags work, they are not XML-compatible and don't follow the same format as other JSP tags. Therefore, the following JSP tags are preferred.

Statement Type	Tag Example
scriptlet	`<jsp:scriptlet> error(); </jsp:scriptlet>`
expression	`<jsp:expression> 1+1 </jsp:expression>`
declaration	`<jsp:declaration> private void error() {` `System.out.println("Error!"); } </jsp:declaration>`
directive	`<jsp:directive.page import = "java.io.*"/>`

A JSPs' appearance can also be easily enhanced by using the Design views' GUI to drag and drop components, as well as, specify formatting options (rather than typing HTML commands, as we did with servlets). Aren't JSPs so much easier than servlets? In addition, JSPs can be called from Web pages (just like servlets), and JSPs can call servlets (just like Web pages). So, JSPs are just as powerful as servlets but as easy to build as Web pages.

Of course, now the bad news: JSPs aren't that simple. In actuality, the application server converts a JSP into a servlet. Within the server are **containers** that are responsible for handling various pieces of the server-side application. (A container is simply a subsection/piece of the application server software.) For example, there is a container that manages all servlets and JSPs. Part of this container's responsibility is to take all the HTML and Java source code in a JSP and create a servlet. When a JSP is accessed for the first time, it will often take a long time to be displayed because the container translates the JSP into a servlet, compiles the servlet source code, and then runs the generated class file.

Tutorial: JSP Standard Tag Library (JSTL)

There are actually many JSP tags and programmers can even create tags. Tags are better than Java scripts because of their simpler syntax. In addition, using tags makes the code more standard. One very popular set of tags, JSTL tags, provide the function of many commonly coded Java scripts. For example, instead of coding the Java for statement in a scriptlet, the JSTL **forEach** tag can be used. As an example, we will change the HowdyJSP to use the **forEach** tag.

JSTL comes with RAD. As a matter of fact, in the Design view palette, there is a tray for JSP Tags that includes JSTL tags.

1. In the JSP Tags tray, scroll down the options and click on the For Loop to select it.

2. In the Design view, click on the line after the second scriptlet to insert the **forEach** tag.

The For Loop icon will be displayed.

3. Switch to the Source view and notice that the following tags were inserted:

```
<c:forEach items=""></c:forEach>
```

Just like HTML tags, many JSTL tags have an open and close tag. The JSTL syntax is a little more involved than the HTML tags but we can easily avoid the syntax by using RAD's Properties view. First, we will add the text we want and then delete the scriptlets.

4. In between the **forEach** start and end tags, add the following text, "Howdy from the forEach tags!"

The tags and text should look like the following:

```
<c:forEach items="">Howdy from the forEach tags!</c:forEach>
```

5. In the source, delete the two scriptlets and the old text.

6. Switch to the Design view.

Notice that the scriptlet icons and the old text are no longer displayed.

7. Click on the **forEach** icon and switch to the Properties view.

RAD should look like Figure 9-3.

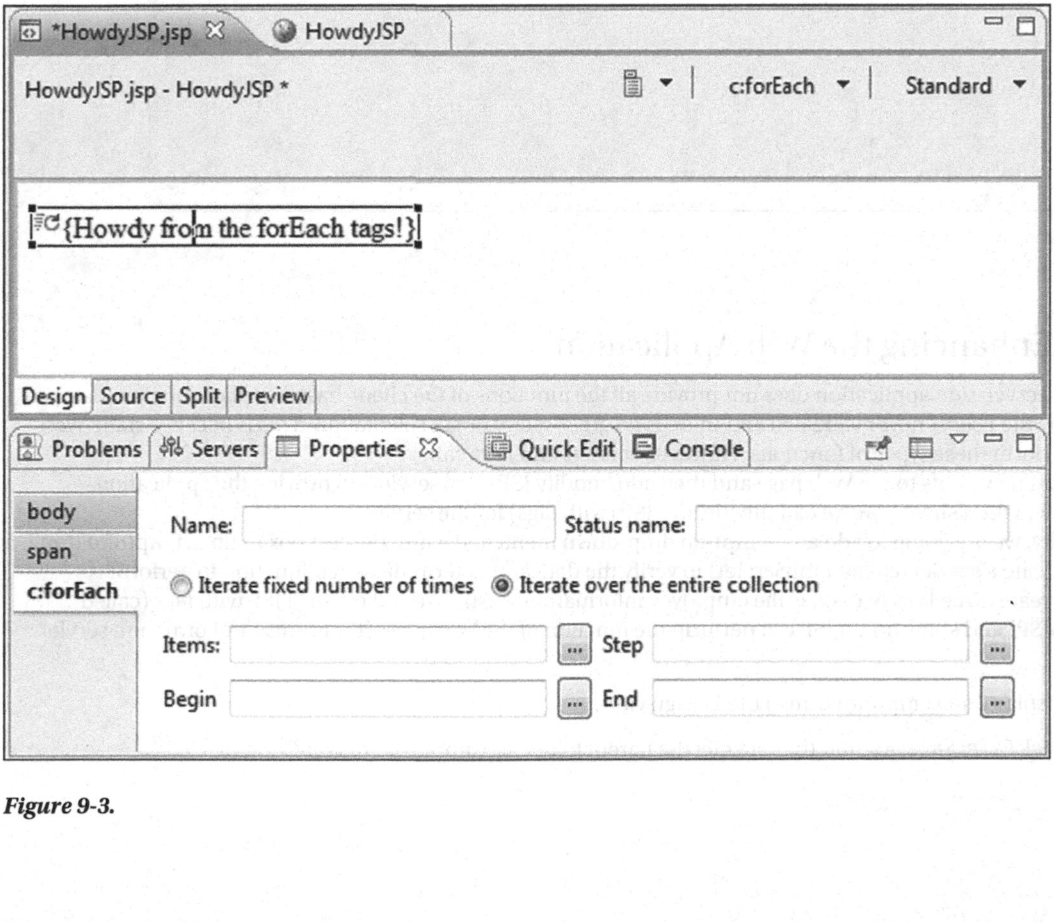

Figure 9-3.

293

You can control many **forEach** properties. For instance, you can define a counter variable such as ctr (in the Name property) or specify an increment value (i.e., the step property). However, to run a fixed number of iterations only begin and end values are needed.

8. In the Properties view, click on the Iterate fixed number of times radio button to select it.

9. Specify 1 for the Begin value and 5 for the End value.

10. Switch to the Source view.

Look at the simplicity of the tag syntax compared to the scriptlet—no semicolons, parentheses, braces, or variable definitions! Are you a tag fan yet?

11. Save the HowdyJSP source code and run on the server.

The results should look like Figure 9-4.

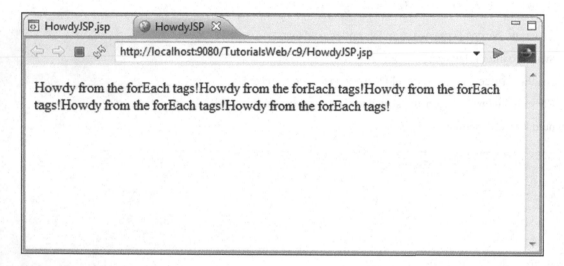

Figure 9-4.

Tutorial: Enhancing the Web Application

Currently, our server-side application does not provide all the functions of the client-based application. For instance, data entered by the user is never validated and there is no gross salary or tax calculation. This is because static Web pages can't perform these types of functions. However, servlets and JSPs can.

We will add new fields to the Web page and then add/modify JSPs and servlets to provide the application functions. We will then show how we can substitute a JSP (with tags) for the servlet.

Specifically, we are going to add an exemption drop-down menu and a function list box to EnterEmpInfoForm. We will then create a servlet (called EmpServlet) to verify the data and determine which function to perform. Then we will create three JSPs to display the employee information. Lastly, we will create a JSP with tags (called EnterEmpInfoJSP) and show how a JSP can perform the function of the Web page (EnterEmpInfoForm) and servlet (EmpServlet).

1. Display EnterEmpInfoForm in the Design view.

2. Click File, Save As, and then specify the parent folder as TutorialsWeb/WebContent/c9.

This will create a new copy of the page in the c9 folder.

3. Move the cursor to the last row of the table and press Ctrl+Shift+z to add a row beneath the last row.

4. Add another row beneath the row you added in step 3.

5. Copy the text "Hourly Pay Rate" into the first cell of each new row.

This ensures that the new cells have the correct text formatting.

6. Change the text in the first cell of the first new row to Exemptions and in the second new row to Function.

7. In the Palette's Form Tag tray click on Drop-Down Box then click the cell to the right of the Exemptions text.

8. At the Insert Drop-Down Menu window, specify exmpDDM as the name.

9. Add a drop-down menu value by:

   - Clicking the Add button

   - Specifying "zero" for the value name

   - Specifying "0" for the value

10. Add values 1 through 10 with the appropriate names.

11. Change value two's Selected property to "true" and click the OK button.

This will ensure that 2 is automatically selected when the page is displayed. Notice in the Design view that zero is displayed. To see the default value, you must save the file and switch to Preview view.

12. In the Palette's Form Tag tray click on List Box then click the cell to the right of the Function text.

13. At the Insert List Box window, specify functionLB as the name.

14. Add the following three values "Display," "Gross," and "TaxAmt" (with names that are the same as the values) to functionLB, then click the OK button.

15. Click the Preview tab.

The display should look like Figure 9-5. Notice that the default value two is displayed in the drop-down menu.

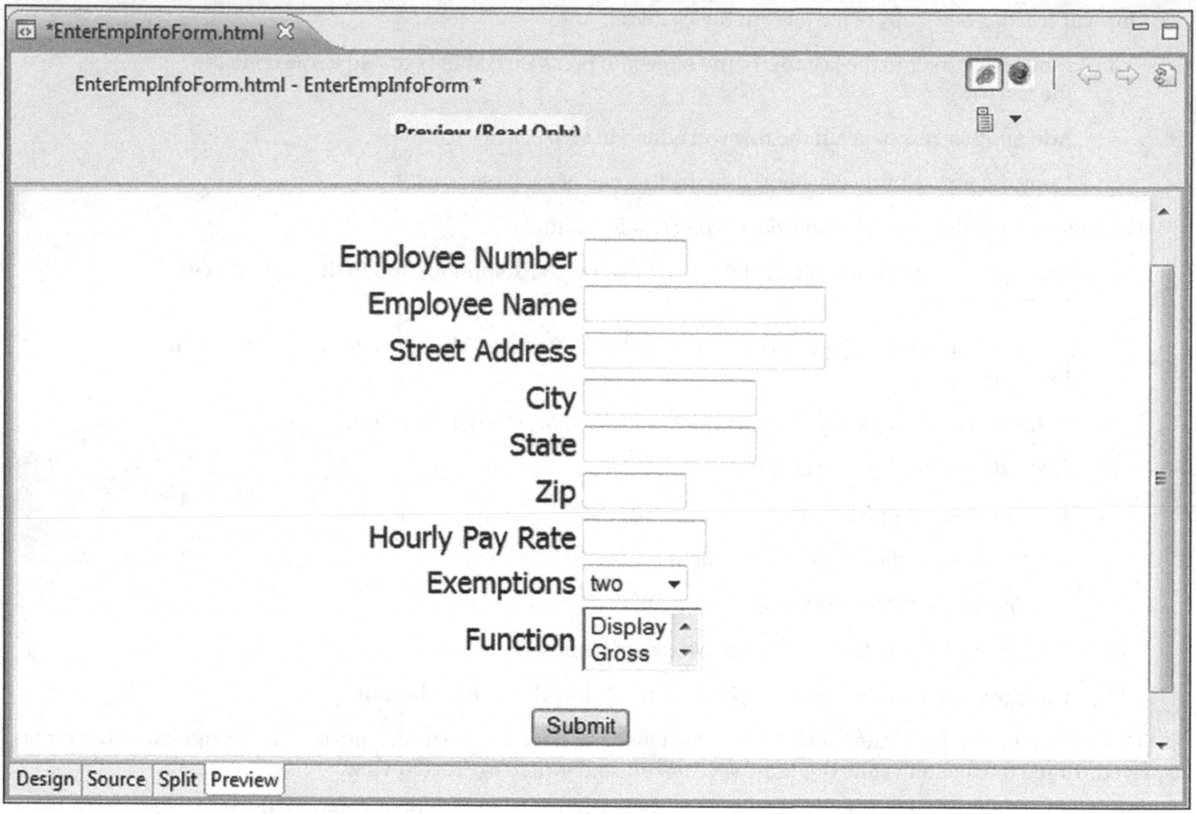

Figure 9-5.

Tutorial: Creating a Servlet for

It's now time to create the complementary servlet.

1. Create a new servlet in TutorialsWeb/Java Resources/src called EmpServlet.

2. In EmpServlet's source code, change the request and response variable names to req and resp.

3. In the doPost method, add the following statements:

```
String function = req.getParameter("functionLB");
System.out.println(function);
String exmp = req.getParameter("exmpDDM");
System.out.println(exmp);
```

The println statements will simply test that the servlet is retrieving the values from the new Web page components. After we have verified that the values are being retrieved, we will remove the println statements.

4. Return to the EnterEmpInfoForm and, if needed, change back to the Design view.

5. Display the form's properties.

6. Change the Action property to the servlet EmpServlet.

7. Run EnterEmpInfoForm on the server, select Gross, and click the Submit button.

A blank page will be displayed in the browser pane but the function and number of exemptions will be displayed in the console as follows:

```
[3/9/12 12:40:42:994 EDT] 0000002c SystemOut O Gross
[3/9/12 12:40:42:994 EDT] 0000002c SystemOut O 2
```

(Of course, the date/time information displayed at the beginning of each line will be different for you.) This proves that the Web page is tied to the servlet, that the doPost is invoked, and that the information entered in the new page components can be accessed. Notice that even though the exemption value names (one, two, three, etc.) are displayed on the Web page, the values (1, 2, 3, etc.) are returned in the request. Please remember that the values (1, 2, 3, etc.) are still strings and will have to be parsed into primitives before being used in calculations.

We will now change doPost to invoke the correct JSP based on the selected function.

8. Replace the last three statements in doPost with the following:

```
if (function.equals("Display")) {
        resp.sendRedirect("DispEmpInfoJSP.jsp");
} else {
        if (function.equals("Gross")) {
                resp.sendRedirect("DispEmpGrossJSP.jsp");
        } else {
                if (function.equals("TaxAmt")) {
                        resp.sendRedirect("DispEmpTaxAmtJSP.jsp");
                }
        }
}
```

The response's sendRedirect method tells the browser to submit a new request, in this case, for a particular JSP based on the function selected by the user. In other words, the name of the JSP file is inserted into the response and the server sends the response back to the browser. The browser then creates another request (for the JSP) and sends the new request to the server.

This is not an efficient way to access the JSPs but it is syntactically simple. In the next section we will use a more "system efficient" technique that is, unfortunately, more complicated for the programmer.

In addition, we have some work to do because these JSPs don't exist.

Tutorial: Creating JSPs

At first, we will code the three JSPs to print static text. This will allow us to test/prove that the browser is requesting the JSPs (i.e., this will prove that the servlet's redirects work). We will then use a RequestDispatcher object to forward the request and response directly to the JSPs rather than have the browser make a new request for the JSPs.

1. Click on the TutorialsWeb project to select it, and then click File, New, and Web Page.

2. At the New Web Page frame, specify DispEmpInfoJSP as the file name, JSP as the Template, and click the Finish button.

3. In the Design view, specify "Got to DispEmpInfoJSP." as the text to be displayed.

4. Create two more JSPs called DispEmpGrossJSP and DispEmpTaxAmtJSP.

5. Change the text of the two JSPs to "Got to DispEmpGrossJSP." and "Got to DispEmpTaxAmtJSP."

6. Save all the changes to the servlet and JSPs and run the EnterEmpInfo Web page on the server.

When a new JSP is created, RAD updates the server's directory and the JSP can be accessed immediately. This is not the case with servlets. When creating a servlet you have to restart the server to get the servlet information into the directory. Advantage JSP. More about this later.

7. In the Function list box, select Display and click the submit button.

Verify that "Got to DispEmpInfo JSP" is displayed.

8. Use the browser pane's "back arrow" to redisplay EnterEmpInfo.

9. Select the other functions and confirm that the other JSPs are accessed.

You might have noticed a little wait for the JSP text to be displayed. One of the reasons for this delay is that we are taking the "long way around" to the JSPs by using the redirect command. It is more efficient to have the servlet get a RequestDispatcher object and use its forward method to send the request and response directly to the JSP. This eliminates the "round trip" between the client and server.

10. Display the EmpServlet source code.

11. Add the following import statement:

```
import javax.servlet.RequestDispatcher;
```

12. Add the following statement to create a class RequestDispatcher variable:

```
RequestDispatcher dispatcher;
```

We now need to create a RequestDispatcher object and associate it with the variable dispatcher. Like a number formatter, a RequestDispatcher object is retrieved, not created. The ServletContext class provides a getRequestDispatcher method to do this. ServletContext has many useful methods that allow the servlet to communicate with the servlet container (i.e., the server). In addition, the getRequestDispatcher method allows you to associate the RequestDispatcher with a particular JSP. Of course, you must first get a ServletContext object before executing its getRequestDispatcher method. Fortunately, servlets inherit a getServletContext method from the HTTPServlet superclass.

The syntax to create the RequestDispatcher object is as follows:

```
dispatcher = getServletContext().getRequestDispatcher("xxx.jsp");
```

There is quite a bit happening with this statement, so we'll go through the statement step by step.

The getServletContext method is the first part of this statement executed. The getServletContext method, as its name implies, returns a ServletContext object that is not assigned to a variable. Instead, its getRequestDispatcher method is invoked and passed the JSP name. The getRequestDispatcher method returns a RequestDispatcher object and that object is assigned to the variable dispatcher.

13. In each **if** statement, replace the redirect statement with a statement that creates a Request Dispatcher object for each JSP and assigns it to the dispatcher such as the following:

```
dispatcher =
getServletContext().getRequestDispatcher("DispEmpInfoJSP.jsp");
```

14. After the nested **ifs**, add the following statement:

```
dispatcher.forward(req, resp);
```

The RequestDispatcher object's forward method will send the request and response directly to the JSP that was specified in the **if** statements. By invoking the JSPs from the servlet, we have taken the browser "out of the loop" thereby speeding up access to the JSPs.

The EmpServlet source code should look like the following:

```java
import java.io.IOException;
import javax.servlet.ServletException;
import javax.servlet.annotation.WebServlet;
import javax.servlet.http.HttpServlet;
import javax.servlet.http.HttpServletRequest;
import javax.servlet.http.HttpServletResponse;
import javax.servlet.RequestDispatcher;
public class EmpServlet extends HttpServlet {
        private static final long serialVersionUID = 1L;
RequestDispatcher dispatcher;
public EmpServlet(){
super();
}
protected void doGet(HttpServletRequest req,
                HttpServletResponse resp)
throws ServletException, IOException {
}
        protected void doPost(HttpServletRequest req,
                    HttpServletResponse resp)
throws ServletException, IOException {
                String Function = req.getParameter("functionLB");
                if (Function.equals("Display")) {
dispatcher =
getServletContext().getRequestDispatcher("DispEmpInfoJSP.jsp");
                } else {
                    if (Function.equals("Gross")) {
                            dispatcher =
getServletContext().getRequestDispatcher("DispEmpGrossJSP.jsp");
                    } else {
                        if (Function.equals("TaxAmt")) {
                                dispatcher =
getServletContext().getRequestDispatcher("DispEmpTaxAmtJSP.jsp");
                        }
                    }
                }
                dispatcher.forward(req, resp);
    }
}
```

15. Save the EmpServlet source code.

16. Run c9/EnterEmpInfoForm on the server and verify that all three JSPs are displayed as expected.

Tutorial: Adding Function to the Server-Based Application

We will expand the server-side application to provide the same functions as the client-based application. As a matter of fact, we will reuse the client code that performs these functions. In addition, we will define a new property for employee number in the Employee class.

    1.   Create a new folder in TutorialsWeb/Java Resources/src called c9java.

Because Employee class contains most of the application's functions, wouldn't it be a lot easier to simply include Employee in the server-based application rather than code a servlet or JSP to perform the same function? I hope you said, "Yes, it would," because that's what we're going to do.

    2.   Copy Tutorials/c7/Employee.java into c9java.

    3.   In c9java/Employee.java, add a new class level private String variable called empNum.

    4.   Have RAD generate a getter and setter for empNum and save the source code.

This is all that was needed to add a new property to Employee. If this were a client-based application, making this change to the application would require that the new Employee class be installed on many PCs. With a server-based application, only the one class file on the server needs to be reinstalled. This is one of the advantages of a server-based application.

However, just copying the class into the project does not include Employee in the server-based application. The application needs to do two things:

    A.   Get the data from EnterEmpInfoForm into an Employee object

    B.   Have the JSPs access the Employee object

We will solve the first part with a new class called EmpExtractor. EmpExtractor will retrieve the employee data from the request and create an Employee object whose properties hold the request data.

    5.   Click on c9java to select it.

    6.   Click File, New, and then Class.

    7.   At the New Java Class window, specify EmpExtractor as the class name, then click the Finish button.

An edit session will be started.

We want EmpExtractor to create an Employee object, retrieve the form information from the request, and set the Employee object's properties. The Employee object will then be passed to the JSPs. Each JSP will use the appropriate Employee object's method(s) to perform the requested function (Gross, TaxAmt, or Display) and display the results.

    8.   Click Source, Generate Constructors from Superclass...., and then the OK button.

This will generate a null constructor.

    9.   In EmpExtractor, add the following import statements:

```
import javax.servlet.http.HttpServletRequest;
import org.omg.CORBA.DynAnyPackage.InvalidValue;
```

The HttpServletRequest class has to be imported because the class is going to receive a request object (from the JSPs) and create a method variable to reference the request. The InvalidValue class needs to be imported because the setPayRate method in the Employee class can throw an InvalidValue exception.

10. Add the following to define a class variable and Employee object:

```
Employee emp = new Employee();
```

11. After the null constructor, add the following to define a new method called getEmployeeInstance:

```
public Employee getEmployeeInstance(HttpServletRequest request){
        return emp;
}
```

Notice that the method expects a request object. We will now add the code to retrieve the information from the request object and set emp's properties.

12. Before the return statement in getEmployeeInstance, add the following statements:

```
emp.setEmpName(request.getParameter("empNameTF"));
emp.setEmpStreet(request.getParameter("streetAddrTF"));
emp.setEmpCity(request.getParameter("cityTF"));
emp.setEmpState(request.getParameter("stateTF"));
emp.setEmpZip(request.getParameter("zipTF"));
try {
emp.setPayRate(Double.parseDouble(
request.getParameter("hPRTF")));
} catch (NumberFormatException Error) {
System.out.println("Pay rate must be a numeric" +
"value: 8 or 7.25");
} catch (InvalidValue Error) {
        System.out.println(Error.getMessage());
}
emp.setExemptions(Integer.parseInt(
request.getParameter("exmpDDM")));
```

Does this source code seem familiar? This is the same logic that's in EnterEmpInfo's setEmployeeProperties method. The difference is that setEmployeeProperties retrieved the information from a frame's text fields, whereas getEmployeeInstance is retrieving the information from a request object. Even though EmpExtractor and EnterEmpInfo are very similar, we had to create them because the client and server-side applications use two different interfaces to gather the Employee information: AWT (for the client-side application) versus a Web page (for the server-side application).

Notice that regardless of the interface, however, the core logic of the two applications (i.e., the Employee class) is the same. Separating the client-based application's core logic (creating the Employee class) from the interface (i.e., the frame classes) was a very wise decision. Because of this, we are able to reuse the Employee class with a different interface (e.g., the Web page in our server-based application). As a matter of fact, if we wanted to provide alternative interfaces for PDAs, cell phones, or holograms (just kidding), Employee could still be used. We will talk more about this "application architecture" later in the chapter.

Tutorial: Enhancing the JSPs

The JSPs must be modified to call EmpExtractor and then use the returned Employee object to perform the requested functions. We will modify DispEmpInfoJSP first.

1. In the Design view, edit DispEmpInfoJSP so that it contains text and a table like Figure 9-6.

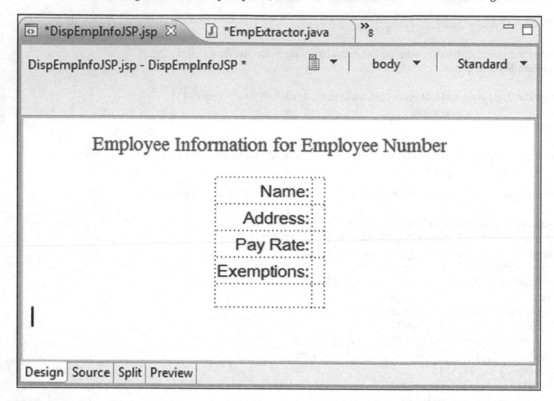

Figure 9-6.

2. Change to the Source view.

3. Add the following statement to the end of DispEmpInfoJSP's page directive (the page directive is toward the beginning of the source code):

```
import="c9java.*"
```

Because DispEmpInfoJSP will be using Employee and EmpExtractor objects, we have to import c9java. (If Employee and EmpExtractor were in the default package of the JavaResources folder, no import statement would have been required.)

4. After the page directive, add the following scriptlet:

```
<jsp:scriptlet> Employee emp;
EmpExtractor ee = new EmpExtractor();
emp = ee.getEmployeeInstance(request);
</jsp:scriptlet>
```

This scriptlet creates:

A. An Employee variable called emp

B. An EmpExtractor variable called ee

C. An EmpExtractor object

The scriptlet also assigns the EmpExtractor object to the variable ee.

Finally, the scriptlet invokes the getEmployeeInstance method and sends the request object referenced by the variable request. Hey, where did the variable request come from? In fact, where did the request object come from? There was no import statement for the Request class nor was a request object passed from the server to the JSP! Are you starting to wonder what's going on?

The variable request is another example of the server making your programming life easier. The JSP container provides what are called **JSP implicit objects**. Essentially, these are predefined variables and objects that all JSPs can access. (In addition to the request, there is also a response object and a variable named response that can be used by JSPs.) Not having to write the Java code to define and pass these variables is one more reason why JSPs are so much easier to use than servlets.

5. Change back to the Design view.

6. Put a space after the first line of text and click JSP, then Insert Expression.

7. In the Properties view, add the statement as seen in Figure 9-7.

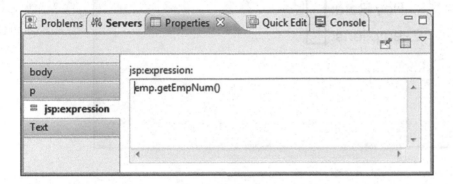

Figure 9-7.

8. As done in step 7, add the following expressions in the appropriate cells of the table's second column:

```
emp.getEmpName()
emp.getEmpStreet()
emp.getPayRate()
emp.getExemptions()
```

The Design view should look like Figure 9-8.

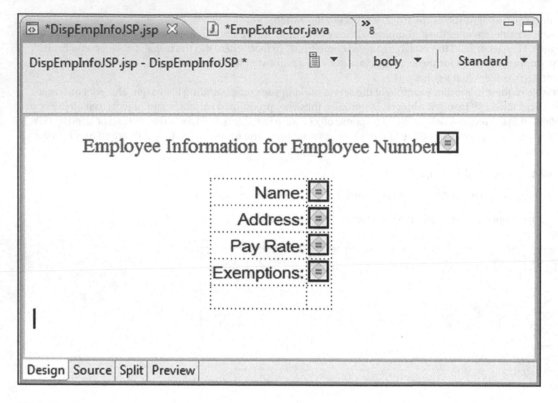

Figure 9-8.

Currently, the address cell only displays the street information. We need to modify the cell contents to include the city, state, and zip code.

9. Insert a new line in the address cell (click to the right of the expression icon that retrieves the employee's street address and press the Enter key).

10. Change to the Source view and insert a new line after the line break tag (<br>).

We switched to the Source view because sometimes it is easier to enter the Java source code rather than use the GUI.

11. At the new line enter the following and save the source code:

```
<%=emp.getEmpCity()%>, <%=emp.getEmpState()%> <%=emp.getEmpZip()%>
```

It's important to include the three spaces after the comma and the four spaces between the employee's state and zip code so that the information is formatted correctly.

Time to test!

12. Run c9.EnterEmpInfoForm on the server.

13. In the browser pane, enter the information as in Figure 9-9.

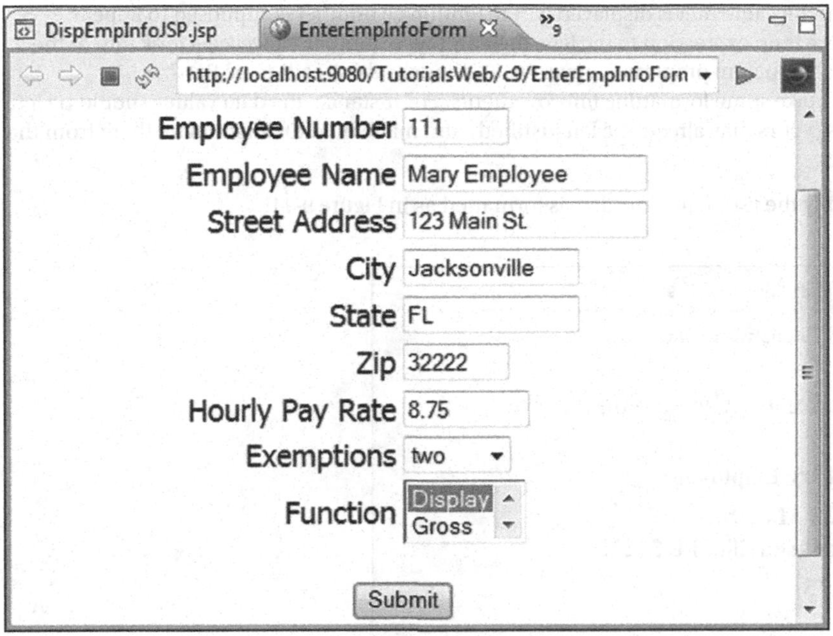

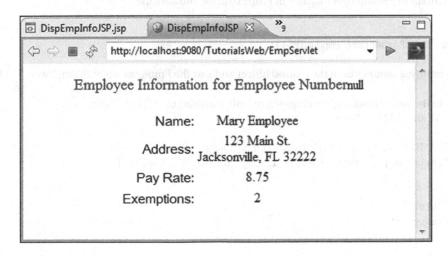

Figure 9-9.

14. Click the Submit button.

The result should appear as in Figure 9-10. Notice anything wrong with Figure 9-10?

Figure 9-10.

The most noticeable error is that the value null is displayed where employee number is supposed to appear. A look at the JSP code shows that there is an expression to retrieve the employee number, however, a look into at the EmpExtractor source code shows that empNum property is never set. Obviously, this needs to be fixed.

Although not errors, we should make some formatting improvements. For instance, the data values should be left justified so they are nearer the labels (yours may already be left justified) and made bold to differentiate them from the labels and emphasize them as results.

15. In the Design view, modify the JSP so that the data is formatted as in Figure 9-11.

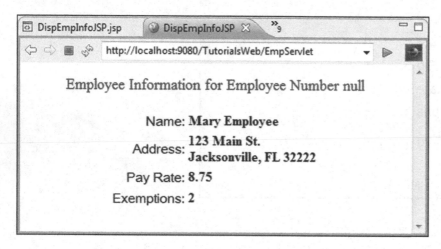

Figure 9-11.

16. Add the following statement to getEmployeeInstance in EmpExtractor and save the source code:

```
emp.setEmpNum(request.getParameter("empNumTF"));
```

This statement retrieves the employee number from the request object and sets the Employee object's employee number property.

Steps 15 and 16 should result in the page displaying the employee number instead of null as in Figure 9-11. The source code for DispEmpInfoJSP should be as follows:

```
<!DOCTYPE HTML PUBLIC "-//W3C//DTD HTML 4.01 Transitional//EN"><%@page
language="java" contentType="text/html; charset=ISO-8859-1" pageEncoding="ISO-8859-1"
import="c9java.*"%>
<jsp:scriptlet> Employee emp;
EmpExtractor ee = new EmpExtractor();
emp = ee.getEmployeeInstance(request);
</jsp:scriptlet>
<html>
<head>
<title>DispEmpInfoJSP</title>
<meta http-equiv="Content-Type" content="text/html; charset=ISO-8859-1">
<meta name="GENERATOR"
content="Rational® Application Developer for WebSphere® Software">
</head>
```

```html
<body>
<p align="center"><font size="4" color="blue"> Employee
Information for Employee Number <%=emp.getEmpNum()%></font> </p>
<center><table border="0">
<tbody>
        <tr>
<td align="right"><font face="@Arial Unicode MS">Name: </font></td>>
                <td align="left"><b><%=emp.getEmpName()%></b></td>
        </tr>
        <tr>
                <td align="right"><font face="@Arial Unicode MS">Address:</font></td>
                <td align="left"><b><%=emp.getEmpStreet()%><br>
<%=emp.getEmpCity()%>, <%=emp.getEmpState()%> <%=emp.getEmpZip()%> </b></td>
        </tr>
        <tr>
                <td align="right"><font face="@Arial Unicode MS">Pay Rate:</font></td>
                <td align="left"><b><%=emp.getPayRate()%></b></td>
        </tr>
        <tr>
                <td align="right"><font face="@Arial Unicode MS"> Exemptions:</font></td>
                <td align="left"><b><%=emp.getExemptions()%></b></td>
        </tr>
        <tr>
                <td align="right"></td>
                <td align="left"></td>
        </tr>
</tbody>
</table></center>
</body>
</html>
```

If you are a little confused about all the pieces in our server-based application, Figure 9-12 contains a diagram showing how the user and the various components interact.

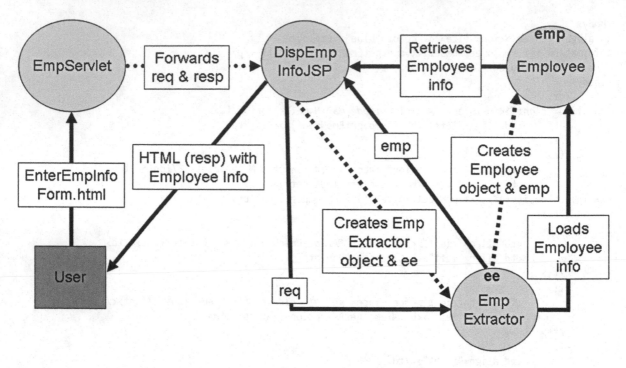

Figure 9-12.

We still need to modify the other JSPs to display the employee gross salary and tax amounts.

17. Add the statements to DispEmpGrossJSP and DispEmpTaxAmtJSP that were added to DispEmpInfoJSP in steps 3 and 4.

18. Replace the current text in DispEmpGrossJSP with "The gross salary for" and DispEmpTax-AmtJSP's current text with "The tax amount for."

19. Center the text on the pages.

20. In DispEmpGrossJSP and DispEmpTaxAmtJSP, add an expression so that the employee's name appears after the text.

21. In DispEmpGrossJSP and DispEmpTaxAmtJSP, add an expression so that the appropriate value appears in bold and centered beneath the text.

22. Test by entering the information in Figure 9-9 and selecting the Gross and TaxAmt functions.

The results should look like Figures 9-13 and 9-14.

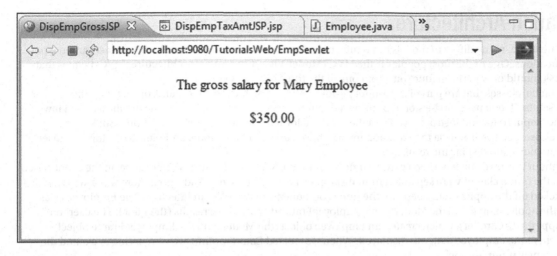

Figure 9-13.

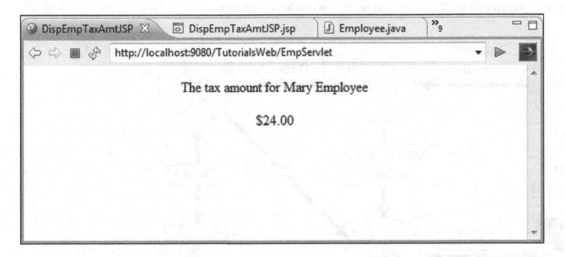

Figure 9-14.

Of course, a professional Web site would never display such plainly formatted information as seen in Figures 9-13 and 9-14. In addition, a good Web page would include navigation buttons, graphics, hyperlinks, etc. However, these additional components have more to do with Web site design than with Java. Even though WebSphere provides many Web page design tools, Java programmers generally don't use them. This is because most organizations hire lower-salaried Web page designers to create and format pages rather than have higher-priced Java programmers perform these tasks. This "economic factor" is another reason companies separate the application logic from the interface and also a reason that this application architecture is very popular.

Application Architecture

In the Java literature, many different models or architectures have been proposed to handle the most common types of Java applications. One of the most popular is the **MVC (Model-View-Controller)** architecture. MVC dictates that any Java class should only perform functions from one of the three MVC categories.

For instance, classes that are part of the **Model** perform application business logic and/or maintain the application's data. If data needs to be stored or retrieved, only classes in the Model access the database. The **View** classes gather input (data and instructions) from the user and format and display the application results. The **Controller** classes receive input via the View and invoke those portions of the Model and View to perform the user requested functions and display the results.

Throughout this text, you have been gently guided toward the MVC architecture. For instance, in the client-based application, the frame classes were separated from the application logic classes. In addition, there was always a Java class that kicked off the application. These are the three components of the MVC architecture. The Employee class performed the application logic (the Model). The EmployeeFrame displayed the results (the View). The user ran EmployeeApp (the Controller), which created an Employee object (the Model) and the EmployeeFrame object (the View) where the employee data was displayed. When we created EnterEmpInfo, we were trying to expand the view to have a new input portion.

Figure 9-15 shows the basic structure of the MVC architecture and Figure 9-16 shows how the client-based application (with the EnterEmpInfo frame) "sort of" fits into the MVC architecture.

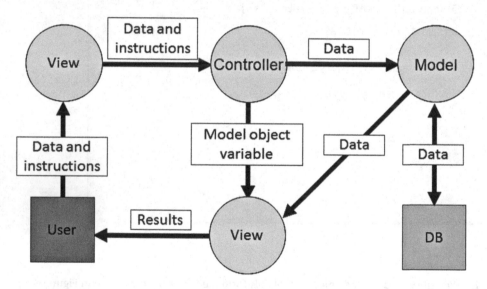

Figure 9-15.

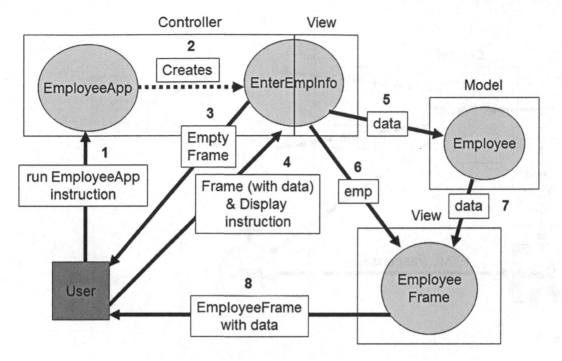

Figure 9-16.

Figure 9-16 is quite busy, so we'll walk through it step by step.

Step 1: The user starts the application. For example, a user issues the **java EmployeeApp** command or within RAD runs the EmployeeApp class as an application by clicking the Run button. Either way, the user is running a Java class that is considered part of the Controller.

Step 2: The EmployeeApp class is run and it creates an EnterEmpInfo object.

Step 3: The EnterEmpInfo frame is displayed.

Step 4: The user enters the information and clicks a button. In this case, clicking a button is how the user specifies a new instruction to the controller. The diagram assumes that the user clicked the Display button.

Step 5: Based on the button that was clicked, EnterEmpInfo snaps into action. An Employee object (part of the Model) is created, and its properties are set to the values entered in the frame.

Step 6: EnterEmpInfo then creates an EmployeeFrame object and passes the Employee variable emp. EmployeeFrame is part of the View because it will display the employee information.

(The client-based Java technology doesn't let us fully segment the classes into the MVC categories. For example, EnterEmpInfo actually has both View and Controller functions. When the empty EnterEmpInfo frame was displayed and the data returned, EnterEmpInfo was acting as part of the View. However, when it responds to the button and creates the Model component, Employee, and View component, EmployeeFrame, it is performing Controller functions.)

Step 7: EmployeeFrame retrieves the data from the Employee object and displays it.

For server-based applications, the Controller is usually comprised of servlets that are invoked from Web pages (which are part of the View). The Model is made up of Java beans, which we will explain in more detail in a later section. The View is comprised of Web Pages and JSPs. Figure 9-17 shows this architecture.

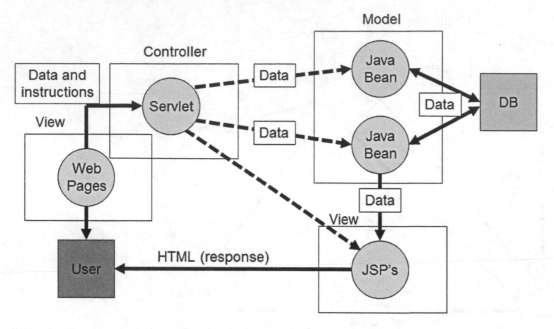

Figure 9-17.

Now there are many MVC variations. Sometimes the Model and the View are combined so that data access is faster. Or, the View interfaces with the Model instead of the Controller. This last variation is how we implemented the Employee application in TutorialsWeb. Figure 9-18 shows how the server-based Employee application fits the MVC architecture.

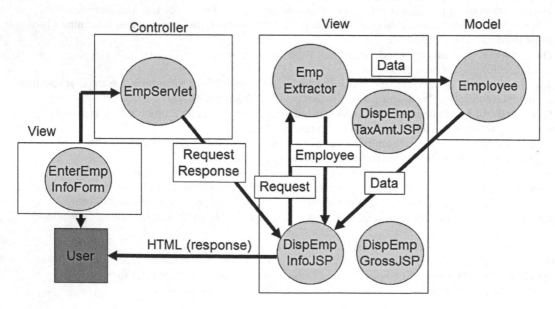

Figure 9-18.

Next, we will further explore JSP tags and show how JSP tags are much easier to code and use than scriptlets and expressions.

More JSP Tags

We are going to change our Controller from a servlet to a JSP, called EnterEmpInfoJSP, which uses JSP tags to perform the servlet's functions. We will explain the standard JSP action tags **include** and **forward** and the JSTL tags **if** and **choose**. In addition, we will introduce Expression Language (EL). EL makes using tags even easier.

In our new architecture, we want EnterEmpInfoJSP to display all the EnterEmpInfoForm fields when it is initially invoked with a get request. When the submit button is clicked, the EnterEmpInfoJSP will be invoked again but with a post request. When EnterEmpInfoJSP receives a post request, the functionLB value should be retrieved and the correct JSP invoked. Essentially the logic is:

- If request is a get

  - Display EnterEmpInfoForm fields

- If request is a post

  - Retrieve the selected function and forward to the correct JSP

Now there are two ways to create EnterEmpInfoJSP with all the required fields. We could copy EnterEmpInfoForm (i.e., the HTML code contained in the body of the page) into EnterEmpInfoJSP.jsp. This would create the form and all the components (i.e., text fields, labels, button, etc.) in the JSP. Or, we could include EnterEmpInfoForm.html in EnterEmpInfoJSP.jsp using the JSP action tag **include** and change EnterEmpInfoForm's action from EmpServlet to EnterEmpInfoJSP.

The **include** tag works as follows. When there is a request for a JSP, the container retrieves any resources specified in an **include** tag and imbeds them in the response. Any changes made to the resource since the last request will be reflected in the new request. In other words, the **include** tag allows dynamic content to be added to the JSP. For example, the following include tag will embed the EnterEmpInfo.html file into a JSP:

```
<jsp:include page="EnterEmpInfoForm.html" flush="true"> </jsp:include>
```

If we ran the JSP, it would appear as in Figure 9-19.

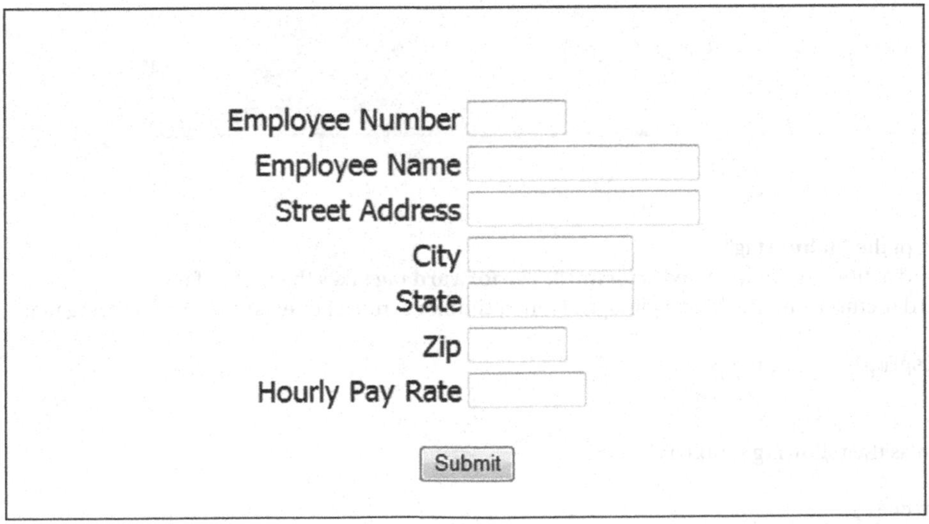

Figure 9-19.

If we had an image file that contained the TNT banner (in this example, a JPEG file called TNTBanner) and added it to EnterEmpInfo.html file with the following code:

```
<P align="center">
<IMG border="0" src="TNTBanner.jpg" width="465" height="99">
</P>
```

Running EnterEmpInfoJSP would result in Figure 9-20.

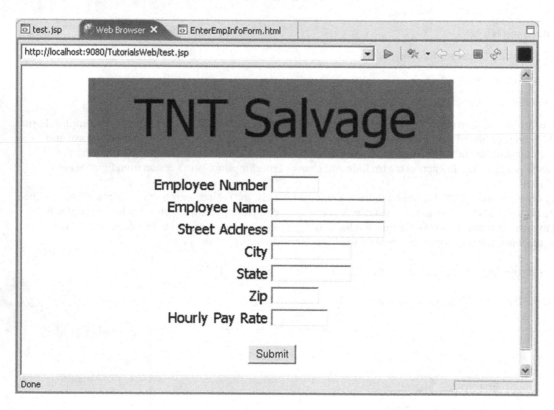

Figure 9-20.

Can you feel the power of the **include** tag?

The second JSP standard action tag we will need is **forward**. The **forward** tag takes the place of the RequestDispatcher's forward method with the big advantage of much simpler syntax. For example, the following tag:

```
<jsp:forward page = "DispEmpInfoJSP.jsp">
</jsp:forward>
```

performs the same function as the following EmpServlet code:

```
RequestDispatcher dispatcher;
dispatcher =
getServletContext().getRequestDispatcher("DispEmpInfoJSP.jsp");
dispatcher.forward(req, resp);
```

Which source code would you rather type in?

Now that know how to forward to a JSP, the trick is that we only want to forward to a JSP after the user has selected a function and clicked the submit button. In other words, if the user simply requests EnterEmpInfoJSP (with a get request), we want to display the form. When the user clicks the submit button and invokes EnterEmpInfoJSP with a post request, we want the form to check which function was selected. We will use the JSTL **if** tag to check for the request type and the JSTL **choose** tag to determine which function was selected. Both of these tags will use Expression Language (EL) to access the request object.

The **if** tag syntax is simple:

```
<c:if test='${condition}'> body </c:if>
```

The condition, of course, needs to be specified and the body contains whatever function should be performed when the condition is true. For example, inserting 1==1 as the condition and the text "Yikes it works" for the body as follows:

```
<c:if test='${1==1}'> Yikes it works </c:if>
```

would result in the text "Yikes it works" appearing in the browser. The body of the **if** tag is not limited to static text. Tags, scriptlets, expressions, or HTML can all be specified. This example also includes your first look at Expression Language (EL). Everything within the quotes of the test value is considered EL. The EL syntax dictates that any condition begin with a $ and be enclosed in braces. Not too tough to remember but it doesn't seem very useful either. The real power of EL is that it allows you to access information contained in the JSP container (like the implicit request and response objects, parameters, beans, etc.) without using the cumbersome Java syntax. Also, all the Java comparison operators (e.g., >, ==, <, etc.) can be used to define conditions. For example, in the servlet we used:

```
String function = req.getParameter("functionLB");
if (function.equals("Display")) { }
```

to get the functionLB value and check its value. Now this is a slightly unfair comparison, because in the servlet example we retrieved the functionLB value and assigned it to a variable and then used the variable in the **if** statements. A fairer comparison would be between the following **if** statement:

```
if(req.getParameter("functionLB").equals("Display")) {}
```

and the following **if** tag with EL:

```
<c:if test='${param.functionLB=="Display"}'> </c:if>
```

If we strip away the required **if** syntax in the two examples, we are left with the following Java code in the servlet:

```
req.getParameter("functionLB").equals("Display")
```

and the following EL code in the **if** tag:

```
${param.functionLB=="Display"}
```

It's pretty obvious that EL is simpler than Java.

The last piece of the puzzle is the **choose** tag. A **choose** tag is used with **when** tags, where each **when** tag identifies a different condition to test. The following is an example with two **when** tags:

```
<c:choose>
<c:when test='EL Expression'}'>
body
</c:when>
<c:when test='EL Expression'}'>
body
</c:when>
</c:choose>
```

We will use the **choose** and **when** tags to determine which function was selected and then go to the correct JSP.

Tutorial: More JSP Tags

Let's continue our application:

1. In c9.EnterEmpInfoForm source code, change the form action from EmpServlet to EnterEmpInfoJSP.jsp.

2. In TutorialsWeb/WebContent/c9, create a new JSP called EnterEmpInfoJSP.

3. In the palette's JSP Tags tray, click on the Include item and then click on design pane.

4. On the Insert JSP Include window, specify EnterEmpInfoForm.html in the File name text field.

5. Click the Flush check box in the lower left and then the OK button.

The Page Designer will display the EnterEmpInfoForm page.

So, not only are tags simpler to use, they can be easily inserted using Page Designer. It just keeps getting better!

If you switch to the Source view, you will see the **flush** parameter in the **include** tag. Previously, **flush** was a required parameter, however, in this case, it can be removed and the tag will still work. (Essentially flushing ensures that the entire contents of the included file are displayed. There are some nuances regarding the **flush** parameter, however, we will leave a detailed explanation to a more exhaustive Java text and always specify true.)

6. If necessary, switch to the Design View, and click on the If item in the JSP Tags tray.

7. Click anywhere before the EnterEmpInfoForm. (I.e., Click above the thick black line not the dashed line.)

The **if** tag icon will be placed on the Design view.

8. Display the Properties view and enter the following EL condition statement as the if condition (see Figure 9-21):

```
${pageContext.request.method=="POST"}
```

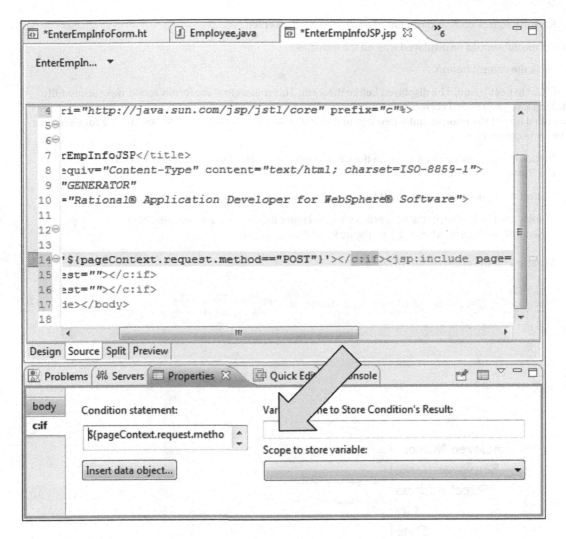

```
4  ti="http://java.sun.com/jsp/jstl/core" prefix="c"%>
5⊖
6⊖
7  rEmpInfoJSP</title>
8  equiv="Content-Type" content="text/html; charset=ISO-8859-1">
9  "GENERATOR"
10 ="Rational® Application Developer for WebSphere® Software">
11
12⊖
13
14⊖ '${pageContext.request.method=="POST"}'></c:if><jsp:include page=
15 est=""></c:if>
16 est=""></c:if>
17 ie></body>
18
```

Design | Source | Split | Preview

Problems | Servers | Properties ⊠ | Quick Edi... nsole

body

c:if

Condition statement:

Var... e to Store Condition's Result:

${pageContext.request.metho

Scope to store variable:

Insert data object...

Figure 9-21.

9. Switch to the Source view.

The following **if** tag should have been inserted:

```
<c: if test='${pageContext.request.method=="POST"}'></c:if>
```

Notice that the EL condition checks the value of the request object's method variable. This variable contains the request type (e.g., POST or GET) that invoked the JSP.

Time to test.

10. Change the body of the **if** tag as follows so that the text "Got to post" is displayed:

```
<c: if test='${pageContext.request.method=="POST"}'>
Got to post
</c:if>
```

11.   Save the source code and run EnterEmpInfoJSP on the server.

EnterEmpInfoJSP should be displayed with all the form fields.

12.   Click the submit button.

The text "Got to post" should be displayed before the form. This means that the form's action was successfully changed and the **if** tag was coded correctly.

Now we need to add the **choose** and **when** tags to determine which function was selected and the **forward** tags to invoke the appropriate JSPs.

13.   In the Design view's palette, click on the Choose item in the JSP Tags tray and click before the "Got to post" text.

This will insert the **choose** tag inside the **if** tag.

14.   Display the choose tag in the properties view and enter the following as the condition statement for the first **when** tag (see Figure 9-22):

```
${param.functionLB == "Display"}
```

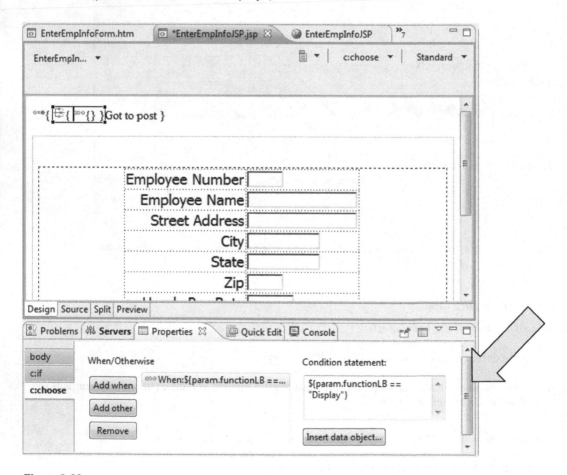

Figure 9-22.

15. In the JSP Tags tray click on Forward and then in the Design view, click between the innermost braces in the Choose icon (the innermost braces represent the **when** tags).

The Insert JSP Forward window will be displayed.

16. At the Insert JSP Forward window, click the Browse button, select File, then expand the WebContent folder, select DispEmpInfoJSP.jsp and click the OK button.

The Insert JSP Forward window will now have DispEmpInfoJSP.jsp as the Page name.

17. Click the OK button.

The forward tag should be within the **when** tag and the source code should look like the following:

```
<c:if test='${pageContext.request.method=="POST"}'>
      <c:choose>
            <c:when test='${param.functionLB == "Display"}'>
                  <jsp:forward page="../DispEmpInfoJSP.jsp">
</jsp:forward>
            </c:when>
      </c:choose>
Got to post
</c:if>
```

As you can see, you must be a bit of a sharpshooter to use the Page Designer GUI to insert within tags. Sometimes it's easier to copy the code from somewhere else and modify it.

18. Using either the GUI or cut-and-paste, add two more **when** tags inside the **choose** tag that check for values of "Gross" and "TaxAmt" and forward to the appropriate JSP.

19. Remove the text "Got to post."

The tag icons in the Design view should look like Figure 9-23.

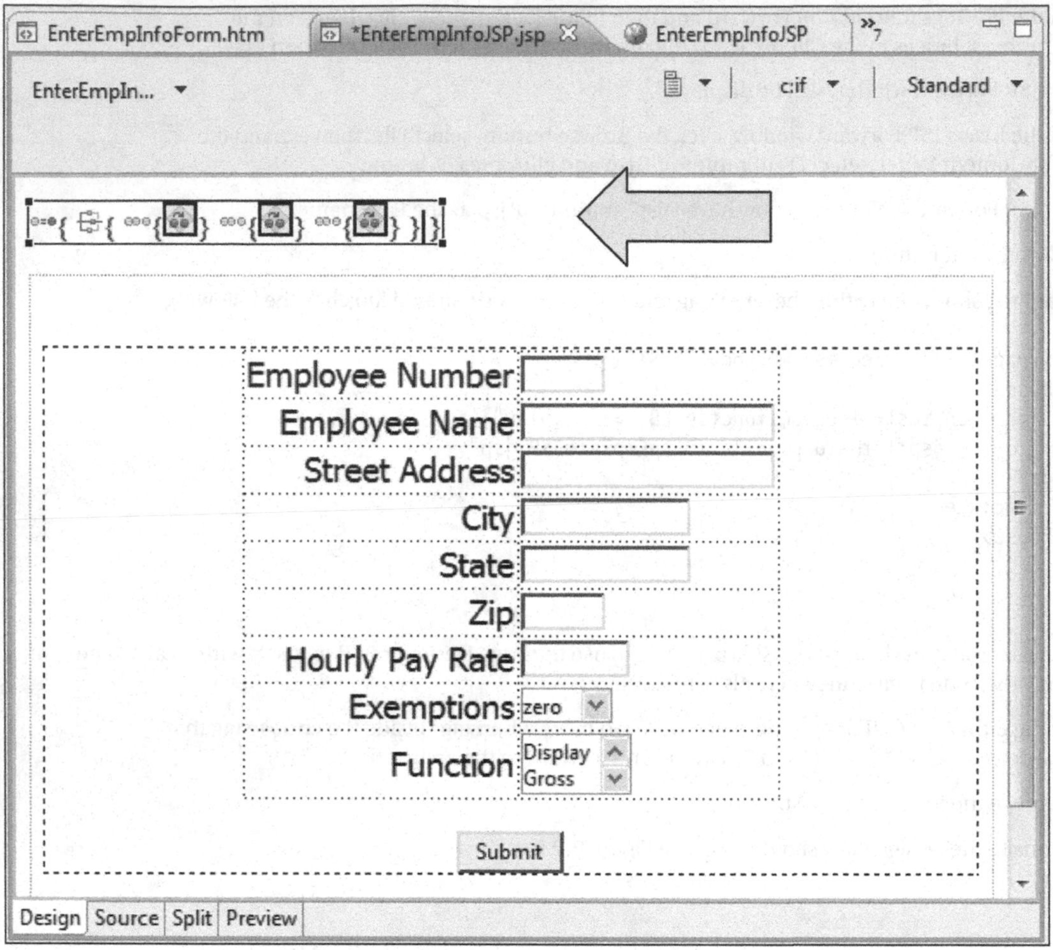

Figure 9-23.

The source code should look like the following:

```
<c:if test='${pageContext.request.method=="POST"}'>
          <c:choose>
                <c:when test='${param.functionLB == "Display"}'>
                      <jsp:forward page="../DispEmpInfoJSP.jsp">
                </jsp:forward></c:when>
                <c:when test='${param.functionLB == "Gross"}'>
                      <jsp:forward page="../DispEmpGrossJSP.jsp">
</jsp:forward></c:when>
                <c:when test='${param.functionLB == "TaxAmt"}'>
                      <jsp:forward page="../DispEmpTaxAmtJSP.jsp">
</jsp:forward></c:when>
          </c:choose>
</c:if>
```

20.   To test the application, save the EnterEmpInfoJSP source code and run it on the server.

21.   Select Display as the function and click the Submit button.

Validate that DispEmpInfoJSP is run.

22.   In the browser window click the back button, select Gross, and then click Submit.

Validate that DispEmpGrossJSP is run.

23.   Validate that DispEmpTaxAmtJSP is run when the TaxAmt function is chosen.

Java Beans

Officially, for a Java class to be declared a Java Bean it must be defined as a public class and follow a couple of simple rules:

A.   Have a public null constructor

B.   Implement the **Serializable** interface

If a bean has properties, a getter and setter should be defined for each property (so that visual tools, such as RAD, can provide easy access to the values), but it is not a requirement.

All of the visual components (buttons, text fields, etc.) are beans, and if we imported the **Serializable** class and added "implements Serializable" to the Employee class's header as follows:

```
import java.io.Serializable;
public class Employee implements Serializable {
```

Employee would be defined as a bean. (Implementing Serializable makes storing an object easier and, since beans may be stored, this is a requirement. Note that no new methods need to be coded when implementing the Serializable interface.) You should be aware that a class does not have to implement Serializable or have any getters or setters to be defined as a bean by RAD/WAS. The bean rules are for ease of use and standardization, however, RAD/WAS will let you define just about any Java class as a bean. So, even though we are going to create an Employee bean, we will not implement Serializable in Employee.

Beans may not sound like much, but server-based beans are very useful because of their "scope." In addition, using JSP bean tags makes creating objects, defining them as beans, and accessing their methods and properties much easier.

JSP Bean Tags

JSP Bean tags relieve the page designer of having to understand the Java concept of instantiation (i.e., creating objects) and the associated Java syntax to create an object. In other words, instead of creating objects and executing methods, beans are defined and properties values are assigned and retrieved. Again, the function of the tags is very similar to Java script statements but the syntax is much simpler.

For instance, the following JSP **useBean** tag creates a Java bean:

```
<jsp:useBean id="EmpBean" class="c9java.Employee"
             scope="session">
</jsp:useBean>
```

The keyword **id** identifies the name of the bean and the **class** keyword identifies the Java class to which the bean refers. The tag essentially performs the same function as the following Java scriptlet:

```
<% c9java.Employee EmpBean = new c9java.Employee();%>
```

The key difference between the useBean tag and the scriptlet is the tag's scope parameter. The **scope** keyword defines which other objects can access the bean. The four scope values that can be specified are **page**, **request**, **session**, and **application**. **Page** means that only this JSP can use the bean. **Request** ties the bean to the request that was passed to the JSP. This means that any object that can access the request can access the bean. When **session** is specified, any object created during the user's browser session can access the bean. Specifying **application** means that any object within the project created by any session (i.e., any user) can access this bean. Of course, if the server is rebooted, all beans are deleted regardless of scope.

To perform the same function of the scope parameter with Java commands we would define the new employee object as an attribute of the session, request, etc. For example, the following statements would define the variable EmpBean a session bean called EmpBean.

```
HttpSession session = req.getSession();
session.setAttribute("EmpBean", EmpBean);
```

A request object has a method called getSession, which, as the name implies returns the current browser session as an object. Session objects can have attributes and we use the session object's setAttribute method to define EmpBean as an attribute of the current session. This means EmpBean can be accessed by any other object created in the session. In other words, the programmer does not have to pass variables to share objects.

Regardless of how the bean is defined (tags or scripts), bean property values are assigned and retrieved by **setProperty** and **getProperty** tags. These tags invoke an object's getters and setters. For instance, the following setProperty tag:

```
<jsp:setProperty name="EmpBean" property="empName"
param="empNameTF" />
```

performs that same function as the following scriptlet:

```
<% EmpBean.setEmpName(request.getParameter("empNameTF")); %>
```

Notice how simple the setProperty tag syntax is compared to the Java statement. Once again, the server's JSP container is making things easy for you. When converting the JSP to a servlet, the JSP container translates the information specified in the tags into the complex Java statements. For example, because we used the keyword **param,** the container recognizes EmpNameTF as a request object parameter. (You can specify **value** instead of **param** to assign a static value to the property.) As a matter of fact, if the bean property has the same name as the request parameter (i.e., if we had called the text field empName instead of empNameTF) we could have coded the tag as follows:

```
<jsp:setProperty name="EmpBean" property="empName"/>
```

In addition, if the parameter value must be converted from one type to another type (e.g., from a primitive to string) the container automatically inserts the code to perform the conversion.

To retrieve a parameter, use a getProperty tag as follows:

```
<jsp:getProperty name="EmpBean" property="empName"/>
```

This is the equivalent of the following expression:

```
<%= EmpBean.getEmpName() %>
```

Remember, the purpose of JSP tags is to make using the Java classes that comprise the Model easier for the page designer. Notice that someone coding the bean tags doesn't need to comprehend objects, instantiation or Java's syntax rules.

Tutorial: Using JSP Bean Tags

To make full use of JSP bean tags in our application, we need to create two new properties in the Employee class for taxAmount and grossAmount. These are a little different from our previously defined properties in that they are calculated values. Earlier we mentioned that properties don't have to have getters and setters. Bean properties can be read-only or write-only and the new properties (gross salary and tax amount) are perfect examples of read-only properties. In other words, no user of the bean should be able to set these values; they should always be calculated based on the pay rate and exemptions properties.

1. In src/c9java.Employee, create two new class private variables by adding the following statements:

    ```
    private String taxAmount;
    private String grossAmount;
    ```

2. Click Source and then Generate Getters and Setters....

3. Select the options to generate only getters for the properties taxAmount and grossAmount and click the OK button.

RAD will generate two new methods that return the strings taxAmount and grossAmount.

4. Replace the code in getGrossAmount with the following statements:

    ```
    grossSalaryCalcFormatted();
    return stringGrossSalary;
    ```

5. Replace the code in getTaxAmount with the following statements:

    ```
    fedTaxCalcFormatted();
    return stringTaxAmt;
    ```

Now that wasn't too hard, was it? These getters simply invoke the methods to calculate and format the appropriate value, then return the result.

We now need to restructure the application so that EnterEmpInfoJSP creates and populates the bean. Currently this function is performed by each of the display JSPs when they invoke EmpExtractor. However, this is very redundant. The application should create the bean once and then the various JSPs should access the bean. This is a perfect function for the Controller to handle and, since EnterEmpInfoJSP is acting as the Controller, we will include the JSP tags to define and populate the bean in EnterEmpInfoJSP. We will then add the tags in the display JSPs to retrieve the correct properties.

6. In the Design view of EnterEmpInfoJSP, click on Bean in the JSP tags tray.

We want to create the bean after the user has entered the employee information and clicked the Submit button. So we need to place the **useBean** tag after the **if** tag but before the **choose** tag. Get out your sharpshooter scope.

7. Click to the right of the first open brace.

The Insert JSP Bean window will be displayed.

8. Specify the three bean parameters as seen in Figure 9-24.

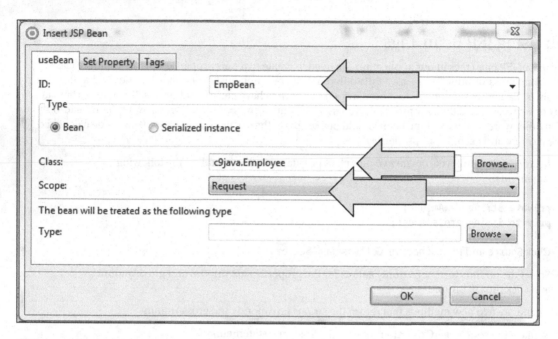

Figure 9-24.

From this information, RAD generates the following tag:

```
<jsp:useBean id="EmpBean" class="c9java.Employee" scope="request">
</jsp:useBean>
```

Now that the bean is created, the bean properties need to be set to the values entered by the user. RAD provides an easy GUI to generate the various **setProperty** tags.

9. At the Insert JSP Bean window, click the Set Property tab, and then the Add button.

The cursor will be placed in the first row's Property column.

10. Click on the options button (at the right of the cell) to display all the available properties and then select empNum (see Figure 9-25).

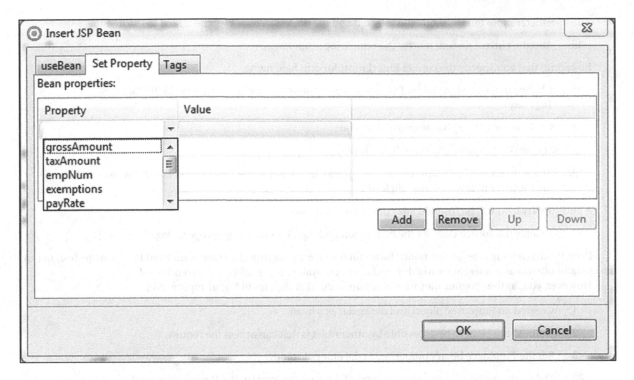

Figure 9-25.

Curiously, RAD will allow you to specify a static value for the property but not a parameter. Later, we will have to specify the **param** keyword for each **setProperty** tag.

11. Add **setProperty** tags for all the remaining properties except grossAmt and taxAmt.

12. Change to the Source view and confirm that the following tags were added to the source code after the **if** tag.

```
<jsp:useBean id="EmpBean" class="c9java.Employee" scope="request">
        <jsp:setProperty name="EmpBean" property="empNum" />
        <jsp:setProperty name="EmpBean" property="empStreet" />
        <jsp:setProperty name="EmpBean" property="exemptions" />
        <jsp:setProperty name="EmpBean" property="empZip" />
        <jsp:setProperty name="EmpBean" property="empState" />
        <jsp:setProperty name="EmpBean" property="payRate" />
        <jsp:setProperty name="EmpBean" property="empName" />
        <jsp:setProperty name="EmpBean" property="empCity" />
</jsp:useBean>
```

13. In the Source view, click on the first setProperty tag (i.e., the tag for empNum).

Notice in the Properties view that the Value radio button is already selected. This is because specifying a static value is the default. RAD, however, does provide a Parameter field.

14. Click the Parameter radio button to activate the Parameter field, enter empNumTF in the Parameter field and press Enter.

The Parameter radio button should be selected and the **param** keyword will be added to the first tag.

15. Add the correct parameters for the remaining properties.

Be careful that you specify the correct EnterEmpInfoForm field name.

16. Change to the Design view of DispEmpGrossJSP and click on Get Property (in the JSP Tags tray).

17. Click on the getEmpName expression icon.

The Insert JSP Get Property window will be displayed.

18. At the Insert JSP Get Property window, specify EmpBean as the Bean name, empName as the Property name, and then click OK.

A getProperty icon will be inserted after the expression icon.

19. Display the source code for the expression and the new entered getProperty tag.

Even though the tag is lengthier, notice how much simpler the syntax is. There is no need for the page designer to understand objects and reference variables, and, most enjoyably, say good-bye to parentheses!
However, you, as the programmer, need to understand that the tags in EnterEmpInfoJSP:

1. Created an Employee object and defined it as a bean

2. Defined the bean to be accessible by other objects that can access the request

3. Set the Employee bean's properties to the entered values

20. Delete the getEmpName expression by clicking on the icon (in the Design view) and pressing the Delete key.

Time to test.

21. Run c9.EnterEmpInfoJSP on the server.

22. Enter 999 for the employee number, select Display, and click the Submit button.

DispEmpInfoJSP should display 999 as the employee number and 2 for exemptions.

23. Change to the Source view of DispEmpInfoJSP.

24. Delete the import="c9java.*" statement from the page directive and the following scriptlet:

```
<jsp:scriptlet> Employee emp;
EmpExtractor ee = new EmpExtractor();
emp = ee.getEmployeeInstance(request);
</jsp:scriptlet>
```

25. In the Design view of DispEmpInfoJSP, replace each of the expressions with the appropriate getProperty tag and save the source code.

This is a good time to test DispEmpInfoJSP.

26. Run EnterEmpInfoJSP on the server, enter values for all the employee properties, select display, and click the Submit button.

Verify that all the data entered on EnterEmpInfoJSP is displayed by DispEmpInfoJSP.
To finish the application, we need to replace the scriptlets in DispEmpGrossJSP and DispEmpTaxAmtJSP with tags to access EmpBean.

27. In DispEmpGrossJSP and DispEmpTaxAmtJSP, remove the following statements:

```
import="c9java.*"
<jsp:scriptlet> Employee emp;
EmpExtractor ee = new EmpExtractor();
emp = ee.getEmployeeInstance(request);
</jsp:scriptlet>
```

28. In DispEmpTaxAmtJSP, replace the expression:

```
<%=emp.getEmpName()%>
```

with:

```
<jsp:getProperty name="EmpBean" property="empName"/>
```

29. In DispEmpGrossJSP, replace the expression:

```
<%=emp.grossSalaryCalcFormatted()%>
```

with:

```
<jsp:getProperty name="EmpBean" property="grossAmount"/>
```

30. In DispEmpTaxAmtJSP, replace the expression:

```
<%=emp.fedTaxCalcFormatted()%>
```

with:

```
<jsp:getProperty name="EmpBean" property="taxAmount"/>
```

Notice that neither of the JSPs defines EmpBean. They simply retrieve two EmpBean properties. Time to test again.

31. Save both JSPs and run EnterEmpInfoJSP on the server.

32. Enter Joe Programmer as the employee name, 25 as the pay rate, select Gross, and click the Submit button.

The JSP will display the following:

```
The gross salary for Joe Programmer
$1,000.00
```

33. In RAD's Web browser pane, click the back arrow to return to the EnterEmpInfoJSP.

The previously entered information should still be there.

34. Select three as the number of exemptions, TaxAmt as the function, and click the Submit button.

The JSP will display the following:

```
The tax amount for Joe Programmer
$139.50
```

Because DispEmpTaxAmtJSP used the bean created by EnterEmpInfoJSP, it proves that the bean is accessible by other JSPs.

Results of the Tutorial

Let's go over the results:

1. In the TutorialsWeb/WebContent folder, three JSP files:

    `DispEmpInfoJSP`   `DispEmpGrossJSP`   `DispEmpTaxAmtJSP`

    and two HTML files:

    `Howdy`   `EnterEmpInfoForm`

2. In TutorialsWeb/WebContent, a folder called c9 containing three files:

    `EnterEmpInfoForm.html`   `EnterEmpInfoJSP.jsp`   `HowdyJSP.jsp`

3. In TutorialsWeb/Java Resources/src, a folder called c9java containing two java files:

    `Employee`   `EmpExtractor`

4. In the TutorialsWeb/ Java Resources/src/default package, two java files:

    `EmpServlet`   `MyServlet`

Review Questions

1. What is a JSP?
2. What rules must a java class follow to be a Java bean?
3. What is the MVC?
4. How are JSPs and servlets related?
5. Why are JSP JSTL and bean tags preferred over scriptlets and expressions?
6. What are the advantages of JSPs over Java servlets?
7. Explain the difference between a response's redirect method and a request dispatcher's forward method.

Review Exercise

The Web page ShipInfoForm does not display the current date and time. So, in this exercise you will create a JSP called EnterShipInfoJSP with this information to replace the static Web page. The new date and time components will be implemented as beans. Each date and time bean will simply return HTML (as a string) to define a drop down menu with the appropriate value selected. For example, if MonthBean is accessed in April, it will return the following HTML that defines a drop-down menu with the values 1 through 12, and 4 as the selected value.

```
<SELECT name='MonthDDM'>
<OPTION value='1'>1</OPTION>
<OPTION value='2'>2</OPTION>
<OPTION value='3'>3</OPTION>
<OPTION value='4' selected>4</OPTION>
<OPTION value='5'>5</OPTION>
<OPTION value='6'>6</OPTION>
<OPTION value='7'>7</OPTION>
<OPTION value='8'>8</OPTION>
<OPTION value='9'>9</OPTION>
<OPTION value='10'>10</OPTION>
<OPTION value='11'>11</OPTION>
<OPTION value='12'>12</OPTION>
</SELECT>
```

EnterShipInfoJSP will use tags to access the various beans.

1. In ReviewExWeb/Java Resources/src, create a new folder called c9.

2. In ReviewExWeb/ Java Resources/src/c9, create a new Java class called MonthBean.

3. Replace the MonthBean default source code with the following:

```java
package c9;
import java.util.Calendar;
public class MonthBean {
        public String monthDDM = new String();
        private int currMonth;
        private Calendar c = Calendar.getInstance();

        public MonthBean() {
        }
        public String getMonthDDM() {
                currMonth = c.get(Calendar.MONTH) + 1;
                StringBuffer monthDDM =
new StringBuffer("<SELECT name='MonthDDM'>");
                for (int ctr = 1; ctr <= 12; ctr++) {
                        monthDDM.append("<OPTION value='");
                        monthDDM.append(String.valueOf(ctr));
                        if (ctr == currMonth) {
                                monthDDM.append("' selected>");
                        } else {
                                monthDDM.append("'>");
                        }
```

```
                        monthDDM.append(String.valueOf(ctr));
                        monthDDM.append("</OPTION>");
                }
                monthDDM.append("</SELECT>");
                this.monthDDM = String.valueOf(monthDDM);
                return this.monthDDM;
        }
        public static void main(String[] args) {
                MonthBean mb = new MonthBean();
                System.out.println(mb.getMonthDDM());
        }
}
```

Notice that MonthBean has a null constructor and one property, monthDDM, which can only be retrieved. In addition, the getter should look familiar because the logic is the same as the MonthCh class (in the client-based application). The difference is that the getter returns HTML that defines a Select component (i.e., drop-down menu), whereas MonthCh was a subclass of Choice. Notice also that MonthBean has two variables named monthDDM. One is a string and the other is a string buffer. The string buffer is used to build the HTML because the append function makes it much easier to manipulate the characters. However, the HTML must be returned as a string. Therefore, the string buffer's final value is converted to a string, and the class String variable monthDDM is returned. Verify that MonthBean works correctly by running the class as a Java application. The main method contains code that will create a MonthBean object and then display the text returned by getMonthDDM. Verify that the HTML returned matches the HTML shown earlier.

In the rest of the exercise, you will create beans that perform the same functions as the remaining time and date choice components from the client-based application.

4. In Java Resources/src/c9, create a new Java class called DayBean.

5. Change the DayBean source to the following:

```
package c9;
import java.util.Calendar;
public class DayBean {
        public String dayDDM = new String();
        private int currDay;
        private Calendar c = Calendar.getInstance();
        public DayBean() {}
        public String getDayDDM() {
                currDay = c.get(Calendar. DAY_OF_MONTH);
                StringBuffer dayDDM =
new StringBuffer("<SELECT name='DayDDM'>");
                for (int ctr = 1; ctr <= 31; ctr++) {
                        dayDDM.append("<OPTION value='");
                        dayDDM.append(String.valueOf(ctr));
                        if (ctr == currDay) {
                                dayDDM.append("' selected>");
                        } else {
                                dayDDM.append("'>");
                        }
                        dayDDM.append(String.valueOf(ctr));
                        dayDDM.append("</OPTION>");
                }
```

```
                    dayDDM.append("</SELECT>");
                    this.dayDDM = String.valueOf(dayDDM);
                    return this.dayDDM;
            }
    }
```

6. In Java Resources/src/c9, create a new Java class called YearBean.

7. Change the YearBean source to the following:

```
package c9;
import java.util.Calendar;
public class YearBean {
        public String yearDDM = new String();
        private int currYear;
        private Calendar c = Calendar.getInstance();

        public YearBean() {
        }
        public String getYearDDM() {
         currYear = c.get(Calendar.YEAR);
         StringBuffer YearDDM =
new StringBuffer("<SELECT name='YearDDM'>");
        for (int ctr = currYear - 1; ctr <= currYear + 1; ctr++) {
                        YearDDM.append("<OPTION value='");
                        YearDDM.append(String.valueOf(ctr));
                        if (ctr == currYear) {
                                YearDDM.append("' selected>");
                        } else {
                                YearDDM.append("'>");
                        }
                        YearDDM.append(String.valueOf(ctr));
                        YearDDM.append("</OPTION>");
                }
        YearDDM.append("</SELECT>");
        this.yearDDM = String.valueOf(YearDDM);
        return this.yearDDM;
        }
}
```

8. In ReviewExWeb/WebContent, create a new folder called c9.

9. In ReviewExWeb/WebContent/c9, create a new JSP called EnterShipInfoJSP.

Instead of recreating an entry form for the shipment information, you will copy all the components from ShipInfoForm.

10. Display the ShipInfoForm in the Design view.

11. Select all the components on the page (i.e., the text and form), click Edit, and then Copy.

12. Display EnterShipInfoJSP in the Design view.

13. Click Edit, then Paste.

EnterShipInfoJSP should look like Figure 9-26.

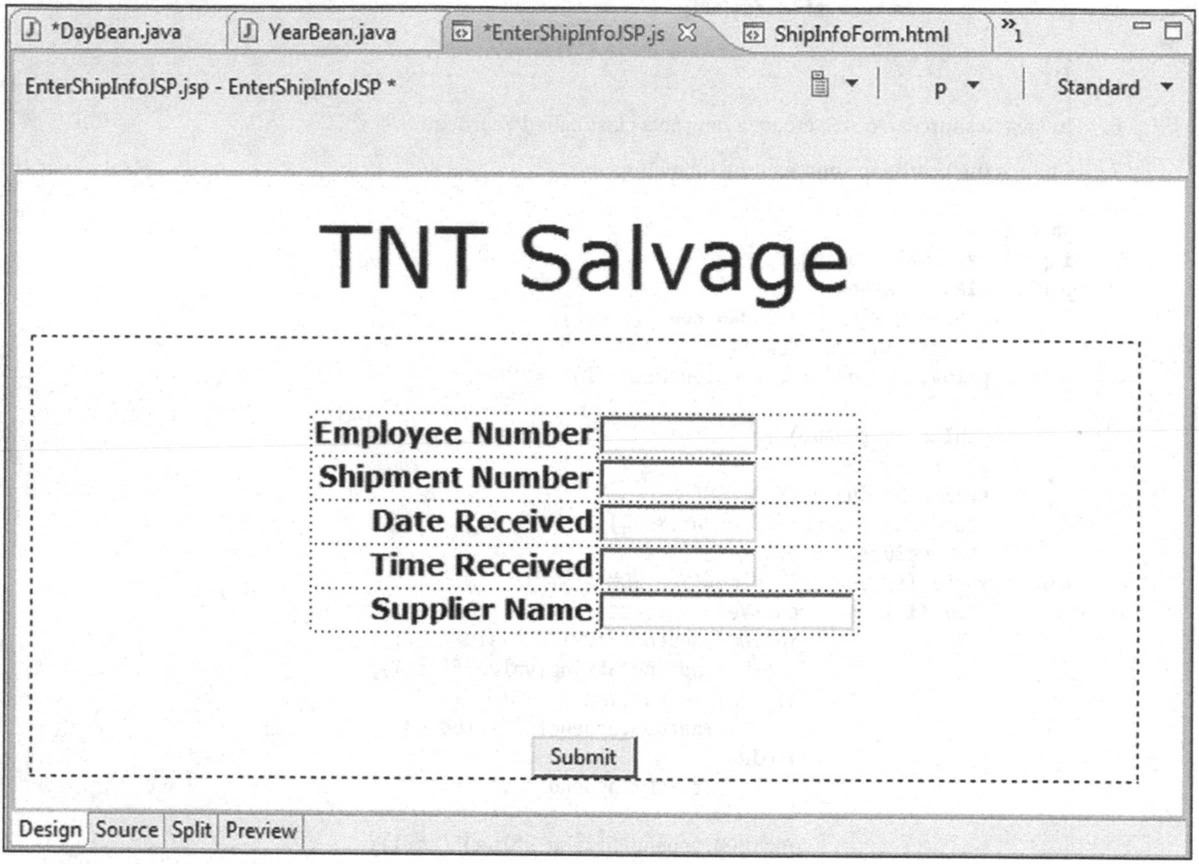

Figure 9-26.

14. Click on the form to select it and then in the Properties view click the Action button and select servlet from the pop up menu.

15. At the Select Servlet window, select ShipInfoServlet and click the OK button.

16. In the Design view of EnterShipInfoJSP, click on dateRcvdTF to select it, and then press the Delete key.

The text field should be deleted, and the cursor should still be in the table cell.

17. Click JSP, and then Insert Bean.

The Insert JSP Bean window will be displayed.

18. At the Insert JSP Bean window, specify MonthDDM as the ID then click the Class browse button (see Figure 9-27).

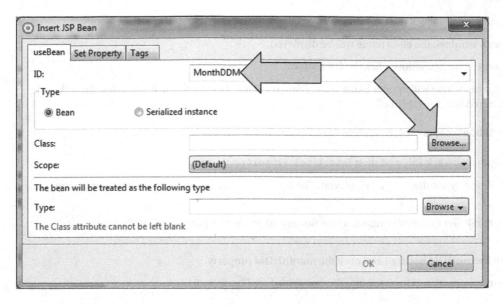

Figure 9-27.

The Class Selection window will be displayed.

19. In the Choose a class text field, start typing MonthBean.

MonthBean will appear in the Matching types pane (see Figure 9-28).

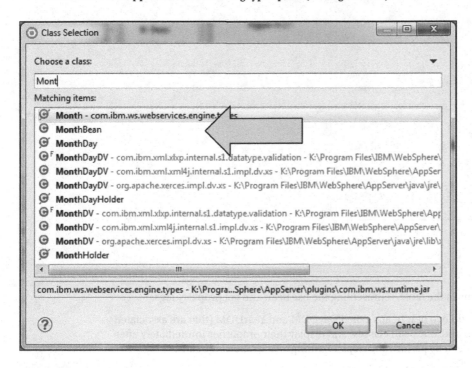

Figure 9-28.

20.   Select MonthBean and click the OK button.

In the Insert JSP Bean window, the class name will be displayed.

21.   On the Insert JSP Bean window, click the OK button.

In the Design view, a bean icon will appear in the table. Displaying the source code will show that the following JSP useBean tag was inserted into the table cell.

```
<jsp:useBean id="MonthDDM" class="c9.MonthBean"></jsp:useBean>
```

22.   In the Design view, Click JSP, and then Insert Get Property....

The Insert JSP Get Property window will be displayed. The listed items are the implicit objects supplied by the JSP container.

23.   On the Insert JSP Get Property window, in the Beans and properties pane, scroll to the end of the list.

24.   Expand the MonthDDM list item and click the monthDDM property.

Notice that the bean information is inserted into the text fields (see Figure 9-29).

Figure 9-29.

25.   Click the OK button.

There should be two icons in the table, representing the use bean and get property tags.

26.   In the table cell, add two new beans called DayDDM and YearDDM (that are associated with the DayBean and YearBean classes) and display their properties immediately after the MonthDDM bean by performing steps 17 through 25 for the new beans.

The EnterShipInfoJSP Design pane should look like Figure 9-30.

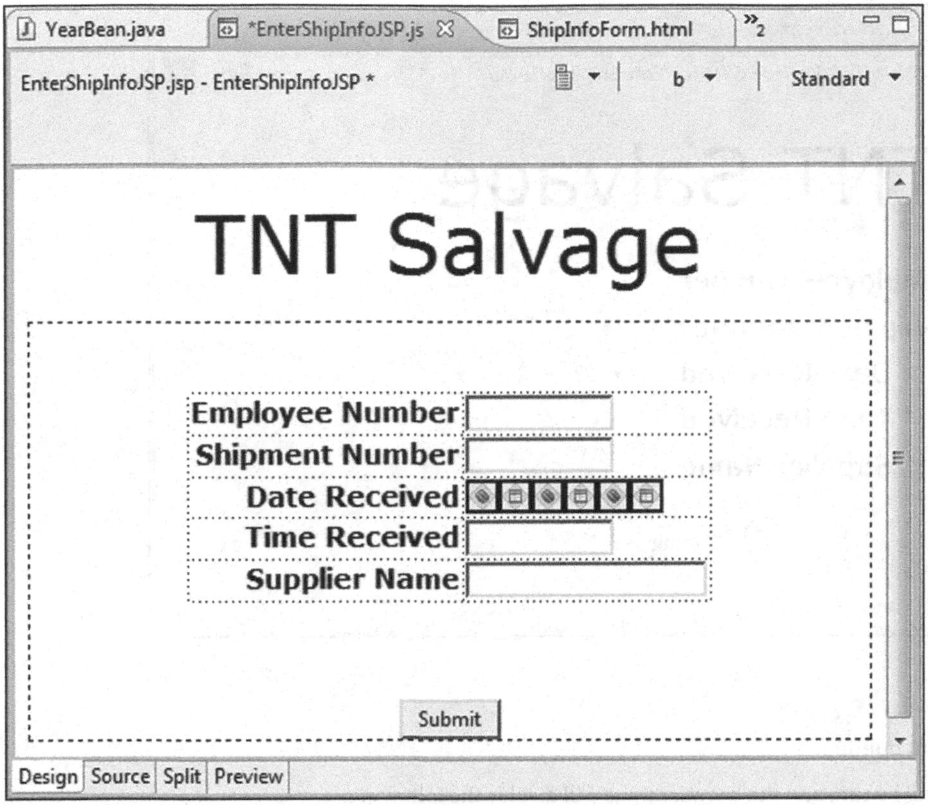

Figure 9-30.

Changing to the Preview pane will not show the new drop-down menus. To see the drop-down menus, the JSP must be run on the server. However, before we do that we must change the servlet to use the drop-down menus instead of the deleted text field, DateRcvdTF.

27. In ShipInfoServlet, replace the following statement:

```
req.getParameter("dateRcvdTF")
```

with the following statement that retrieves and formats the date information from the beans:

```
req.getParameter("MonthDDM") + "/" + req.getParameter("DayDDM")
+ "/" + req.getParameter("YearDDM")
```

28. Run EnterShipInfoJSP on the server.

The EnterShipInfoJSP should be displayed in a Web Browser (see Figure 9-31) with the current date.

Figure 9-31.

29. Click the submit button

The ShipInfoServlet will be run, and the browser pane will display the following:
Shipment from was received by employee number on 3/29/2011 at
Now the hard part.

30. Create one new class (called TimeBean) that has three getProperty methods (getHourDDM, etc.) to return HTML definitions for hour, minute, and AM/PM drop-down menus. Make sure the current time is selected in the drop-down menus.

31. In EnterShipInfoJSP, replace timeRcvdTF with useBean and getProperty tags for one new bean and its three properties. Have the component names follow the same format as the date information (i.e., HourDDM).

32. Change ShipInfoServlet to retrieve and format the time information from the drop-down menus instead of the text field timeRcvdTF.

Results of the Review Exercise

Here are the results:

1. In ReviewExWeb/Java Resources/src, a new folder called c9.

2. In c9, four new classes called:

```
MonthBean          DayBean
YearBean           TimeBean
```

3. Changes to the ShipInfoServlet to retrieve and format the date and time information from the drop-down menus instead of text fields.

4. In ReviewExWeb/WebContent/c9, a new JSP called EnterShipInfoJSP.

Check that the Exercise Was Done Correctly

Finally, let's check it all worked:

1. Run EnterShipInfoJSP on the server and click the Submit button.

2. Verify that the current date and time are displayed in the browser pane.

3. Click the submit button and verify that the current date and time are displayed and formatted appropriately.

CHAPTER 10

Database Access

In this chapter, you will learn about the objects needed to access a DBMS (Database Management System). In addition, we will cover the architectural topic of data encapsulation and use SQL as the data access language. We will then demonstrate how to configure the RAD and PC environment to connect to a DBMS and how to access the database from Java applications.

In this chapter, you will learn about:

>   JDBC

>   ODBC

The following objects:

>   Class
>   DriverManager
>   Statement
>   Connection
>   ResultSet

>   Drivers

>   SQL

>   CRUD

After this chapter, you should be able to:

>   Access an IBM DB/2, Oracle, or Microsoft Access (MS Access) database from a Java application

>   Create a database table

>   Insert, modify, retrieve, and delete information from a database table

Why Databases?

Databases hold the information most organizations need to perform their daily activities. For instance, a grocery store keeps all their prices in a database. When you go through checkout, the price for each item in the cart is retrieved and used to calculate the total amount owed. Databases are so essential that if the database is unavailable, most applications cannot function. In Java-speak this is because DBMSs provide "data persistence." Java objects do not provide data persistence. In other words, when an object is deleted any information the object contained is also deleted. With a DBMS, data is safely stored and accessible whether an object exists or not.

Applications don't have to use databases. However, without a database, applications are very difficult and time-consuming to use. For instance, would a payroll application be easy to use if all the employee's information had to be entered each time the application was run? If instead all the employee information is entered into a database once, the application can access that information at any time.

Establishing a connection to a database is a little cumbersome but, if coded wisely, only has to be specified once. In fact, a primary goal is to hide (from the programmers) the specifics of how to access a database. Organizations try to hide the specifics such that Java programmers have no idea what DBMS is being accessed or even where the database is located. This "design" goal goes by many names such as "data encapsulation," "transparency," "information hiding," and/or "implementation ignorance."

First, we will explain and demonstrate the basics for accessing a database and then show how to efficiently define and use the necessary classes/objects.

Establishing a DB Connection

Several new classes will help establish a database connection and then access the database. However, there is one piece of the puzzle, the **driver**, which does not "come with" Java. This is because the individual DBMS vendors must supply the driver software to access their DBMS. In other words, the Java developers specify how a database driver must work, but it is up to the DBMS provider (IBM, Oracle, Microsoft, etc.) to create and supply the software for Java to work with their DBMS (DB2, Oracle, Access, etc.). Most DBMS providers are very eager to supply drivers because if there is no driver, Java applications cannot use the DBMS. Of course, this means they cannot sell you their DBMS. You can tell that the DBMS providers are very eager to supply the driver software because they provide it for free! When downloaded, a driver is usually supplied as a ZIP or JAR file. (Microsoft, however, includes the driver for its Access DBMS within the Windows operating system.)

To use the driver, you must identify the driver's location (on the PC) to RAD. One way to do this is to add the driver location to the "Java Build Path." RAD uses the Java Build Path to find classes that are not in the project. Therefore, we need to add an external JAR to RAD's Java Build Path. For this discussion, we have assumed that the driver (in a JAR) is on the PC's C: drive. (Microsoft Access, however, is different. The MS Access driver must be identified when defining an Access DB as an ODBC data source in Windows.)

Once the driver is identified, the Java class must load the driver. You can think of loading the driver as creating an instance of the driver class. However, as with the formatting classes (covered in an earlier chapter), the programmer does not explicitly create the driver object. Instead, the **Class** class's forName method is used. (Yes, there is a class called **Class**!) The forName method returns an object of the class type specified. For instance, the following statement:

```
Class.forName("com.ibm.as400.access.AS400JDBCDriver");
```

returns a driver object that can be used to access a DB2 database on a Power System (an IBM midrange computer).

Next, a **Connection** object must be created. Once again, you do not directly create this object. Instead, you use the **DriverManager** class's getConnection method. The getConnection method requires the following information to create the connection:

- The **protocol** (type of driver) used to access the database.

- The **location of the database**. This will include at least the IP address or URL where the database resides. The driver type dictates what other location information is required.

- Driver **properties**. Most drivers require a user ID and password. Optional properties can be specified to control other aspects of the database interface.

A **Statement** object then needs to be created. **Statement** objects have execute methods that allow the programmer to run SQL commands that insert, retrieve, delete, or update data in the database. Again, the programmer does not explicitly create the needed object. Instead, the **Connection** object's createStatement method is used.

To review, the application environment must first be set up correctly. This means:

1. Downloading the correct database driver (not necessary for MS Access)
2. Specifying the driver

Then a Java class must do the following to access a database:

1. Load the driver with the Class.forName method
2. Create a **Connection** object using the DriverManager.getConnection method
3. Create a **Statement** object using the **Connection** object's createStatement method
4. Use the **Statement** object's execute methods to perform SQL commands

First, we will perform the generic tasks that are required regardless of the DBMS being used. Then there will be three tutorials showing how to connect to three different types of DBMSs. The way the tutorials are written, you can only do one of these. (If you do not have access to an Oracle database or DB2 on a Power System, do the "Set Up for Accessing a Microsoft Access Database" tutorial. Even though Access is rarely used for commercial applications, it is widely available and this tutorial will give you a taste of database programming.) We assume that each of these DBMSs has a database called tntdb and a table called Employee with fields that correspond to the Employee class's properties.

Let's do it!

Tutorial: Setting up the Project

The first task is to set up the project.

1. In the Java Perspective, click the Tutorials/src package to select it.
2. Click File, New, and then Package.
3. At the New Java Package window, specify c10 as the name and click the Finish button.
4. With the folder c10 still selected, click File, New, and then Class.
5. At the New Java Class window, specify DBAccess as the class name, make sure a main method is created, and click the Finish button.

A new class called DBAccess is created in c10 and the source code will be displayed.

6. Add the following source code to define a null constructor:

```
public DBAccess() { }
```

We will now add code to the **main** method so that we can test the class.

7. Add the following statement to the main method.

```
DBAccess dba = new DBAccess();
```

8. Save the source code.

Tutorial: Accessing DB2 on an IBM Power System

You must first download the driver. As of this writing, IBM offers the driver free as part of a product called JTOpen To download the driver, go to http://sourceforge.net/projects/jt400/ (see Figure 10-1) and click the link for downloading the latest version of JTOpen as a single zip file. (Be aware that the Web is constantly changing and you may have to search for JTOpen.) For this tutorial, we assume that the file was downloaded to the F: drive and named jtopen_7_3.zip.

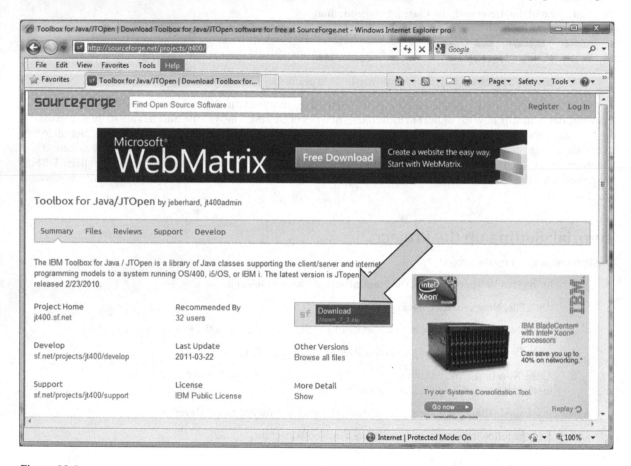

Figure 10-1.

1. Create a folder on the F: drive called jtopen

2. Unzip jtopen_7_3.zip into F:\jtopen.

This assumes you have an unzip program already installed. If not, you will have to download one. A very popular version is WinZip. To unzip, simply double-click the zip file icon, follow the prompts, and at the "unzip to folder" window specify F:\jtopen.

3. In RAD, right-click on the Tutorials project and select Properties from the shortcut menu.

4. In the left pane of the "Properties for Tutorials" window, click on Java Build Path then click the Libraries tag (see Figure 10-2).

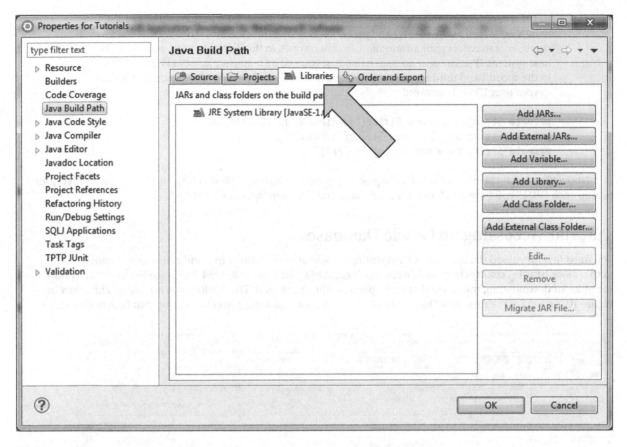

Figure 10-2.

5. Click the Add External JARs... button.

The JAR Selection window will be displayed.

6. In the JAR Selection window, drill down into F:\jtopen\lib, select the file named jt400.jar and click the Open button.

The file jt400 will appear in the Libraries pane of the "Properties for Tutorials" window.

7. On the "Properties for Tutorials" window, click the OK button.

In the Package Explorer pane, expand the Tutorials project then Referenced Libraries. If jt400.jar is listed, you have successfully added the file to the Java Build Path.

We now need four strings in the DBAccess class to hold unique information about the DB2 database.

8. In DBAccess, add the following statement to create a class **String** variable that holds the name of the driver:

```
private String driver = new
        String("com.ibm.as400.access.AS400JDBCDriver");
```

9. In DBAccess, add the following three statements that identify the location of the DB2 database, as well as the user ID and password to access the database. Then modify the statements to reflect your information. In other words, in the first statement, substitute the host systems IP address or domain name that you will be using in place of 111.22.333.444. In the second and third statements, change the user ID and password (bjanson and jeter) to your user ID and password.

```
private String url = new String("jdbc:as400:111.22.333.444");
private String userid = new String("bjanson");
private String pw = new String("jeter");
```

Notice that when specifying the URL, the protocol (jdbc:as400:) is specified before the IP address. As mentioned earlier, each DBMS will have a different protocol name and syntax for specifying the URL

Tutorial: Accessing an Oracle Database

You must first download the driver. As of this writing, Oracle offers the driver free and can be downloaded http://www.oracle.com/technetwork/database/features/jdbc/index-091264.html (see Figure 10-3). Follow the links for downloading the driver that corresponds to the Oracle and JDK versions you are using. The arrow in Figure 10-3 points at the driver for Oracle 11g Release 2. Double-click the correct driver for your Oracle system.

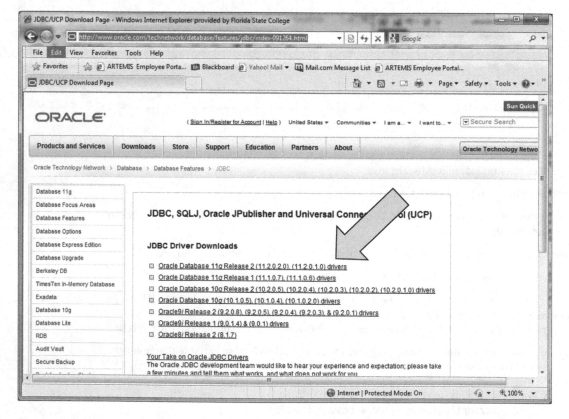

Figure 10-3.

A license agreement page will be displayed. Accept the terms. A page of JDK options will be displayed (see Figure 10-4). Oracle 11g supports many different JDK versions. RAD 8 can run at JDKs ranging up to 6.0, so choose the appropriate JDK for your installation of RAD. (Note: drivers for earlier JDK versions will work with later JDK versions. The arrow in Figure 10-4 points to a JDK 6.0 option).

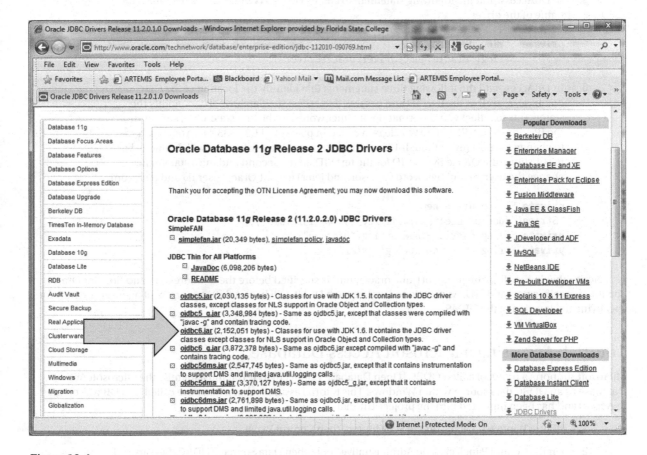

Figure 10-4.

Oracle, as with most vendors, will then require you to register with them and provide contact information. Select the option to save a zip file to a drive on your PC. For this tutorial, we will assume that the file is named ojdbc6.zip and that you saved it to the F: drive.

1. In the Package Explorer pane, right-click on the Tutorials project and select Properties from the shortcut menu.

The "Properties for Tutorials" window will be displayed.

2. In the left pane of the "Properties for Tutorials" window, click on Java Build Path, the Libraries tab, and then click the Add External JARs... button.

3. In the JAR selection window, drill down into the F: drive, select the file ojdbc6.zip, and click the Open button.

The file ojdbc6.zip will appear in the Libraries pane of the "Properties for Tutorials" window.

4. On the "Properties for Tutorials" window, click the OK button.

In the Package Explorer pane, expand Tutorials then Referenced Libraries. If ojdbc6.zip is listed, you have successfully added the file to the Java Build Path.

We will now define four strings to hold unique Oracle information.

5. In DBAccess, add the following statement to create a class **String** variable that holds the name of the driver:

```
private String driver = new
        String("oracle.jdbc.driver.OracleDriver");
```

6. In DBAccess add the following three statements that identify the location of the Oracle database, as well as the user ID and password to access the database. Then modify the statements to reflect your information. In other words, in the first statement, substitute the IP address or URL where Oracle is installed in place of 111.22.333.444. You may have to change the port (even though 1521 is the default for Oracle); but you will definitely have to substitute the Oracle System ID for the text SID. In the second and third statements, change the user ID and password (bjanson and jeter) to your Oracle user ID and password.

```
private String url = new
 String("jdbc:oracle:thin:@111.22.333.444:1521:SID");
private String userid = new String("bjanson");
private String pw = new String("jeter");
```

Notice that in the URL, the protocol (jdbc:oracle:thin) is specified before the IP address. In addition, for Oracle, you must specify a port and SID. As mentioned earlier, each DBMS will have a different protocol name and syntax for specifying the location of the DBMS.

Tutorial: Accessing a Microsoft Access Database

Microsoft supports a protocol called ODBC (Open Database Connectivity). You must identify the Microsoft Access Database as an ODBC data source within Windows. This tutorial assumes that a database called TNTDB was created in Access and has been imported into the project Tutorial

1. Within Windows 7, click on the Start button, then Control Panel.

2. On the Control Panel, click on Administrative Tools, then Data Sources (ODBC) (see arrow 1 in Figure 10-5). (If you are running 64 bit Windows 7, to see the MS Access driver you will need to run the following c:\windows\sysWOW64\odbcad32.exe.)

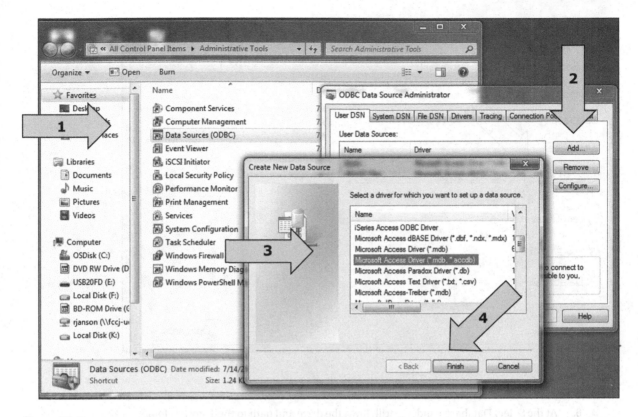

Figure 10-5.

The ODBC Data Source Administrator window is displayed. On this window, you will select the correct ODBC driver for the MS Access database.

3. At the ODBC Data Source Administrator window, click the Add button (see Figure 10-5).

4. At the Create New Data Source window, scroll down through the options and click on Microsoft Access Driver (*.mdb) to select it, and then click the Finish button (arrows 3 and 4 in Figure 10-5).

5. At the ODBC Microsoft Access Setup window, specify TNT Database as the Data Source Name and click the Select button (see Figure 10-6).

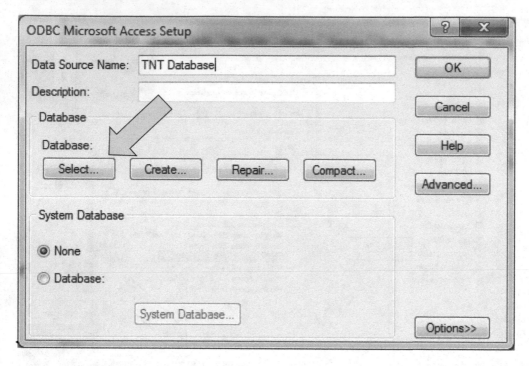

Figure 10-6.

6. At the Select Database window, drill down the drive and path to the Tutorials folder (in the Workspace folder), click on the TNTDB database (see Figure 10-7), and then click the OK button.

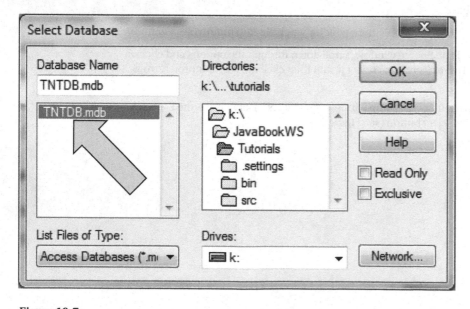

Figure 10-7.

The ODBC Microsoft Access Setup window is redisplayed with the database location and name specified.

7. At the ODBC Microsoft Access Setup, click the OK button.

The ODBC Data Source Administrator window will now show the new Data Source Name (TNT Database).

8. At the ODBC Data Source Administrator window, click the OK button to close the window.

We will now define four strings to hold the Microsoft Access DBMS information.

9. In DBAccess, add the following statement to create a class **String** variable and store the name of the driver:

```
private String driver = new
        String("sun.jdbc.odbc.JdbcOdbcDriver");
```

JdbcOdbcDriver is the driver/class we will be using to connect to the database. Fortunately, this class comes with RAD's JRE and is in every project. (You can prove this by drilling down into the JRE System Library, in the Package Explorer view. Then expand rt.jar and the sun.jdbc.odbc package to show the **JdbcOdbcDriver** class file.)

10. In DBAccess, add the following three statements that identify the location of the MS Access database, as well as the user ID and password to access the database.

```
private String url = new String("jdbc:odbc:TNT Database");
private String userid = new String("anonymous");
private String pw = new String("guest");
```

When specifying the URL (location) of the database, the protocol (jdbc:odbc:) is specified before the ODBC Data Source Name (TNT Database). Notice that the ODBC data source name is specified not TNTDB (the PC file name). Each DBMS will have a different protocol name and syntax for specifying the database location.

Tutorial: Set-Up for Accessing All Databases

The next stage is setting up access for our databases:

1. Modify the url, userid and pw strings to reflect your information. In other words, change the userid and pw strings from the values specified above to the values for the database you will be using. Also, don't forget to modify the **String** url to contain the database name/location you will be using.

2. In DBAccess, on a new line after the **package** statement, add the following **import** statement:

```
import java.sql.*;
```

This will give us access to various classes (like **Connection**) that we need to access the database.

3. Add the following statements to create three class variables:

```
Connection con = null;
ResultSet rs = null;
Statement stmt = null;
```

Next, we will create and assign objects to these variables. We mentioned earlier how the **Connection** and **Statement** objects are used; however, this is the first time a result set has been mentioned.

When information is retrieved from a database using SQL, the information is returned in the form of an object called a result set. You can think of a result set as a table that can have multiple columns (fields) and rows (records) filled with data. To retrieve the field and record information, a variety of result set getter methods are used. Each result set getter is associated with a particular data type (i.e., getString, getDouble, etc.). We'll show how to use these getters a little later.

4. In DBAccess's constructor, add the following statements to register the driver:

```
try {
        Class.forName(driver);
        System.out.println("Driver class found!");
} catch (ClassNotFoundException e) {
        System.out.println("Driver class not found: " + e);
}
```

We added **try/catch** statements because a ClassNotFoundException can be thrown by the forName method. In addition, we added println statements to help with testing and debugging. Notice that the **catch** block not only displays an appropriate message but also displays the exception object. Displaying an exception object provides extra information regarding the problem and is a good debugging practice.

5. Add the following statements to the constructor to create **Connection** object:

```
try {
        con = DriverManager.getConnection(url, userid, pw);
        System.out.println("Connection created!");
        con.close();
} catch (SQLException e) {
        System.out.println("No connection: " + e);
}
```

The constructor now performs the first two steps mentioned earlier: registering the driver and getting a **Connection** object. Notice that we also closed the connection. You can think of a **Connection** object as a link to a database just as a telephone call is a link to person. When you are done with a connection, you should close it - just as when a phone conversation is finished, you should hang up the phone so that the line is not tied up.

The last thing we need is a **Statement** object.

6. Add the following statements after the "Connection created" println statement but before the connection close statement:

```
stmt = con.createStatement();
System.out.println("Statement created!");
```

7. Save and run DBAccess as a Java application.

If the driver name and location were specified correctly, the following will be displayed in the Console view:

```
Driver class found!
Connection created!
Statement created!
```

Tutorial: Breaking the Code, Drivers, and Connections

Accessing databases can be very frustrating, especially when things go wrong because you really do not know what is going on. For instance, you use classes (like **Class** and **DriverManager**) with no idea of how they work. Often new programmers feel that if they knew how these classes worked, they could solve the problems that do occur. However, understanding how they work will not help and, trust me, you do not want to know how they work! How a connection to the database is made is complicated and understanding the process will not help solve the problems that are likely to arise. Usually things go wrong because of simple programming mistakes and typos, not because of the special database classes or the DBMS you are trying to access. We will replicate the most common mistakes and highlight some good testing techniques so you will be able to recognize and solve these common problems quickly.

1. In DBAccess, change the first letter in the text of the **String** driver from lowercase to uppercase.

2. Run DBAccess as a Java application.

The following message will appear in the Console:

```
Driver class not found: java.lang.ClassNotFoundException:
    Xxx.xxxxx.xxxxDriver
```

where Xxx.xxxxx.xxxxDriver is the incorrectly capitalized driver name.

"Driver class not found" is a straightforward message, especially in this case, because we incorrectly specified the driver class name. The lesson is: be careful of capitalization, spelling, and the use of special characters (periods, forward slashes, colons, etc.) because when problems occur, these are the usual culprits.

3. Change the first letter of the driver text back to lowercase.

4. Comment out the first six lines of the DBAccess constructor that register the driver (including the **try/catch** statements).

5. Run DBAccess as a Java application.

Notice that this time we get the error message:

```
No connection: java.sql.SQLException: No suitable driver
```

"No suitable driver" is not very descriptive, but it means that the JVM could not find the correct driver. When the connection is attempted, the JVM searches the registered drivers for the correct driver. In this case, we specified the driver name correctly but did not register it, so the JVM cannot find the driver and an exception is thrown.

6. Uncomment the six lines.

7. In the **String** url, delete the last character.

8. Run DBAccess as a Java application.

The following messages are displayed (with Xxxxxx being unique text for each DBMS):

```
Driver class found!
No connection: java.sql.SQLException: Xxxxxx
```

Notice that the driver was successfully registered but no connection was created because we did not specify the correct location. This error will also occur if the DBMS you are trying to access is not available. A DBMS may not be available for a variety of reasons. For example, the communication link between your computer and the DBMS could be down, the database could be off line for maintenance work, or the computer where the database resides is turned off. **Usually this error is generated because the programmer has simply mistyped the IP address or URL.**

9. Undo the last deletion.

10. In the **String** pw, delete the last character.

The resulting message (or lack of message) depends on the driver used and whether the database you are trying to access is password protected. (For instance, the default for MS Access databases is no password-protection but the DB2 and Oracle examples returns a "Password is incorrect" message.) A similar error will be generated for mistakes with the user ID value.

11. Undo the last deletion.

Tutorial: Using a Statement Object to Insert Data

So far, we have created all the objects needed to insert, modify, retrieve, and delete data in a database. Now we just have to use those objects and methods. This section assumes knowledge of SQL. (If you are not familiar with SQL, please see Appendix B.)

Statement objects have two primary methods (executeQuery and executeUpdate) that allow the programmer to perform SQL statements in a Java class. Each method expects an SQL statement as a string. executeQuery is used for SQL **select** statements and will return a result set with the requested database information. executeUpdate is used for SQL **insert**, **update**, and **delete** statements and does not return data from the database. However, executeUpdate does provide the option of returning the number of rows affected by the SQL statement.

Each of the statements assumes that the database (schema in SQL-speak) tntdb has been created and a connection has been established. In addition, we assume that a table named employee was created in tntdb with the following SQL statement (please note that if Oracle is being used, payrate must be defined as NUMBER not DOUBLE):

```
CREATE TABLE tntdb.employee
        (empnum CHAR(10), empname CHAR(25),
         street CHAR(15), city CHAR(12),
         state CHAR(2), zip CHAR(5),
         payrate DOUBLE, exempts INT)
```

Enough talking, let's get our hands dirty.

1. In DBAccess, before the `con.close()` statement, add the following statement:

```
stmt.executeUpdate("INSERT INTO tntdb.employee " +
        "VALUES('111', 'Mary Worker', '1 Main St.'," +
        "'Enid', 'OK', '77777', 17.50, 3)");
```

Remember, the SQL statement is simply a string parameter for the executeUpdate method. RAD does not check for SQL syntax errors and, unfortunately, the statement syntax is complex. For instance, notice that both single and double quotes are used. Double quotes surround the entire SQL statement, but single quotes surround the values being inserted into character fields.

In addition, the SQL statement must be passed as a single string. If the string spans multiple lines, each line is a separate string (surrounded by double quotes) and must be concatenated to the others. Within the SQL statement, commas separate each value and there must be at least one space after the table name. Finally, the entire string is enclosed in parentheses. Expect many mistakes typing SQL statements, and try not to get too upset at yourself.

2. Run DBAccess as a Java application.

The three messages will appear in the Console but there will be no indication that the SQL statement successfully executed.

3. Add the following to declare a class variable:

   ```
   int returnValue;
   ```

4. Comment out the statement added in step 1 and add the following immediately after the new comments:

   ```
   returnValue = stmt.executeUpdate("INSERT INTO " +
           "tntdb.employee(empnum, empname, payrate, exempts) " +
           "VALUES('222', 'Joe Programmer', 17.50, 2)");
   System.out.println(returnValue);
   ```

5. Run DBAccess as a Java application.

The following three messages and the number 1 will appear in the Console as follows:

```
Driver class found!
Connection created!
Statement created!
1
```

The one (1) indicates the number of rows affected by the executeUpdate and, in this case, proves that a row was inserted. However, a returned value of 1 does not instill a lot of confidence. So, we will prove that the data was correctly inserted by retrieving and displaying the data.

Result Sets

As mentioned, a SQL **select** statement returns data as a result set. Therefore, you must create a **ResultSet** variable and assign the **ResultSet** object (returned by the SQL statement) to that variable. Receiving the result set is only half the battle. You must then retrieve the data from the result set. Several **ResultSet** methods provide access to the data in a particular row. Which row is accessed is dictated by the result set's **cursor**. Just as a word processor's cursor indicates which line you are on in a document, a result set cursor indicates which row you are on in a table.

To retrieve data, the cursor must point to a row in the result set. The row indicated by the cursor is called the current row. Whenever an operation (like retrieving data) is executed, the operation is performed against the current row. The problem is that when a result set is returned from the SQL statement, the cursor is positioned before the first row (see Figure 10-8). The programmer must code a statement to move the cursor to the first row.

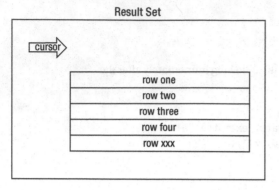

Figure 10-8.

The cursor is moved sequentially between rows with the next method. Assuming that the **ResultSet** variable is named rs, executing the next method as follows:

```
rs.next();
```

positions the cursor to the first row as seen in Figure 10-9. Each time the next method is executed, the cursor is moved to the next row. In addition, when the cursor is successfully moved to the next row, a Boolean value of **true** is returned by the next method. If the cursor is at the last row and the next method is performed, a Boolean value of **false** will be returned. This Boolean return value is very useful. For example, it can be used to determine if the result set is empty.

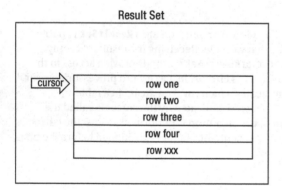

Figure 10-9.

Yes, it is possible for a **select** statement to return a result set with no rows. Therefore, to ensure that there is data to retrieve, you will want to check the returned value each time the next method is executed. Also, trying to retrieve data when the cursor is not pointing at a row, results in an SQL exception and the message "Cursor position not valid."

Once the cursor is pointing at a valid row, there is a series of **ResultSet** getter methods ::to retrieve the individual column values in the row. The programmer must use the correct getter method for the data type being retrieved and must specify which column is being retrieved. The three getters we will work with are getString, getInt, and getDouble. There are, of course, getters for the other data types. (A quick trip to the Oracle documentation website will show you all the available **ResultSet** methods.)

Again, assuming that rs is a valid **ResultSet** variable and the cursor is pointing at a row, the following would retrieve the empnum column's text data and assign it to a **String** variable called empNum:

```
empNum = rs.getString(empnum);
```

In the above example, the column was identified by the column name. You can also reference a column by its number. For instance, assuming empNum is the first column, the following statement would also work:

```
empNum = rs.getString(1);
```

Unfortunately, the column number is dependent on the select statement. For instance, if the select statement had specified the fields as follows:

```
SELECT empname, empnum FROM tntdb.employee
```

empname would be column 1 and empnum would be column 2.

Generally, specifying column numbers and retrieving the result set columns from left to right provides the fastest retrieval.

Tutorial: Retrieving Data from a Database

Let's get some data out of those databases:

1. In DBAccess, comment out the insert statement and the return value println statement.

2. Add the following statements:

```
rs = stmt.executeQuery("SELECT * FROM tntdb.employee");
System.out.println(rs.next());
System.out.println(rs.getString(1) + rs.getString(2));
System.out.println(rs.next());
System.out.println(rs.getString(1) + rs.getString(2));
System.out.println(rs.next());
```

3. Run DBAccess as a Java application.

The results will be the following:

```
Driver class found!
Connection created!
Statement created!
true
111 Mary Worker
true
222 Joe Programmer
false
```

Even though the select returned all the columns, we only retrieved data from the first two columns. This is not a terrible mistake. However, if only two columns are required, for efficiency's sake, the select should specify only those columns.

Notice how inefficient the source code is. What if we want to retrieve 50 rows? Should we perform the gets 50 times each?! That does not seem right. We need to improve our data retrieval. In fact, we will use the returned Boolean values to build a loop to access the result set. We included the Boolean value println statements to demonstrate that the first two times the next method was executed there were rows to move the cursor to and the returned value was **true**. The third time next was executed there was no row, therefore, a **false** value was returned.

4. Comment out the statements added in step 2.

5. Add the following select statement:

```
rs = stmt.executeQuery(
        "SELECT empname, empnum, payrate, exempts" +
        " FROM tntdb.employee");
```

This select will only retrieve four columns. Note that two of the columns contain non-string data.

6. Add the following code:

```
while(rs.next()){
        System.out.println(rs.getString(1) + rs.getString(2) +
                rs.getDouble(3) + " " + rs.getInt(4)); }
```

This code defines a loop that moves the cursor to each row. When there are no more rows (i.e., the next method returns a **false** value), the loop will end. For each row, the appropriate getter retrieves each column's data and the println statement displays the information.

7. Run DBAccess as a Java application.

The results will be as follows:

```
Driver class found!
Connection created!
Statement created!
Mary Worker 111 17.5 3
Joe Programmer 222 17.5 2
```

8. Comment out the statements added in step 5 and 6.

9. Add the following to display all the rows and columns:

```
rs = stmt.executeQuery("SELECT * FROM tntdb.employee");
while(rs.next()){
 System.out.println(rs.getString(1) + rs.getString(2) +
 rs.getString(3) + rs.getString(4) + rs.getString(5) +
 rs.getString(6) + rs.getDouble(7) + " " +
 rs.getInt(8));
}
```

10. Run DBAccess as a Java application.

The results will be as follows:

```
Driver class found!
Connection created!
Statement created!
111 Mary Worker 1 Main St. Enid OK7777717.5 3
222 Joe Programmer nullnullnullnull17.5 2
```

Notice the null values for Joe Programmer. In the original **insert** statement, no address information was supplied, so the DBMS assigned null values to those fields. We will rectify this by using the **update** command to change the information in the existing row for Joe Programmer.

11. Add the following code before the code added in step 9:

```
stmt.executeUpdate("UPDATE tntdb.employee " +
            "SET street = '2 Maple Ave.', " +
            "city = 'Enid', " +
            "state = 'OK', " +
            "zip = '77777', payrate = 19 " +
            "WHERE empnum = '222'");
```

This **update** command not only supplies information for the address fields (that previously had null values) but also changes the pay rate value for employee number 222. Beware: if no **WHERE** clause had been specified, all the rows in the table would have been changed and all the rows would have had the same values for the address columns and payrate. The **update** command is powerful, but dangerous if used incorrectly!

12. Run DBAccess as a Java application.

The results will be as follows:

```
Driver class found!
Connection created!
Statement created!
111 Mary Worker 1 Main St. Enid OK 7777717.5 3
222 Joe Programmer 2 Maple Ave. Enid OK 7777719.0 2
```

13. Print out the DBAccess source code.

Class Design for Data Access

Encapsulation is a design goal for Java classes. Encapsulation (also called class abstraction) tries to hide the internal workings of a class from users of the class (called clients). This means that clients cannot directly access the data or any "internal" objects used by the class to perform its function. Essentially, this means that internal variables and methods are defined as private and the encapsulated class provides easy-to-use public methods to manipulate the private variables and invoke the internal methods. These public methods define the class's **client interface**. Encapsulation is good because it simplifies using the class and cuts down on client errors.

There is no better example of the benefits of encapsulation than with a class that accesses a database. Certainly accessing a database was not easy. Connection objects, driver managers, and statement objects are enough to drive any programmer nuts! Why not hide all those objects and the required coding inside of private class methods and have clients execute relatively simple public methods to retrieve and insert to the database?

In the following example, we will also put inheritance to good use and define the various objects needed to access the database only once in a superclass. All classes that provide DBMS access will be defined as subclasses thereby inheriting the needed variables, objects, and methods from the superclass. For instance, we already created a class called DBAccess with all the needed objects. Instead of redefining the database objects in Employee, Employee will be declared a subclass of DBAccess and inherit them. (We will have to modify DBAccess a little.) If any other classes need database access, they will also be defined as subclasses of DBAccess. This is going to save you a lot of typing and errors.

Finally, we are going to modify the employee application to provide the ability to insert, update, and display employee information stored in TNTDB. When a user selects the Employee Application option from AppOptions (see Figure 10-10), the new database options will be displayed in a frame called EmpOptions (see Figure 10-11).

Figure 10-10.

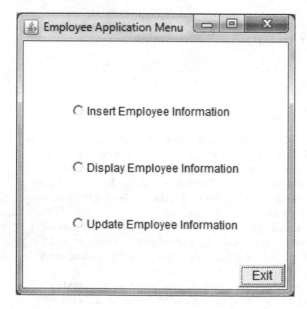

Figure 10-11.

When a user selects the display or update options on EmpOptions, a new frame, EmpNumFrame, will be displayed. EmpNum-Frame's choice box will contain all the employee numbers from TNTDB, so that the user can click on which employee's information (i.e., employee number) to update or display (see Figure 10-12). We will modify the Employee and EnterEmpInfo classes to support these new features.

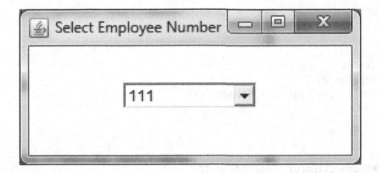

Figure 10-12.

Tutorial: Using a Database in an Application

Now it's time to use the database:

1. Copy the following classes from Tutorials/c7 to Tutorials/c10:

AppOptions	EmployeeFrame	EnterEmpInfo
ExitButton	TNT	TNTButton
UsefulFrame		

    There will be several errors displayed because c10 doesn't have an Employee class.

2. Copy the Employee class from TutorialsWeb/src/c9java to Tutorials/c10

3. In DBAccess's constructor, comment out the println statements that display the following:

    ```
    Driver class found!
    Connection created!
    Statement created!
    ```

4. In DBAccess's constructor, comment out the statements that were added in steps 9 and 11 of the last tutorial.

5. In DBAccess, comment out the close connection statement and the main method.

The executable code should look like the following (with your information substituted in the driver, url, userid and pw strings):

```java
package c10;
import java.sql.*;
public class DBAccess {
        private String driver = new String("xxx.xxx.xDriver");
        private String url = new String("jdbc:xxx:111.22.333.444");
```

```
        private String userid = new String("xxx");
        private String pw = new String("xxxx");
        Connection con = null;
        ResultSet rs = null;
        Statement stmt = null;
        int returnValue;

        public DBAccess() {
                try {
                        Class.forName(driver);
                } catch (ClassNotFoundException e) {
                        System.out.println("Driver class not found: " +
                                e);
                }
                try {
                        con =
                         DriverManager.getConnection(url, userid, pw);
                        stmt = con.createStatement();
                } catch (SQLException e) {
                        System.out.println("No connection: " + e);
                }
        }
}
```

6. In Employee, add the following in the class header:

    extends DBAccess

7. Add the following import statement:

    import java.sql.*;

8. Add the following to define a class ResultSet variable:

    private ResultSet rs;

9. In Employee, add the following code to create a new method called doSelect

```
        private void doSelect(String select) {
                try {
                        rs = stmt.executeQuery(select);
                } catch (SQLException e) {
                        System.out.println("Problem with " + select + e);
                }
        }
```

This method will be the "utility" method that executes all possible selections in the Employee class. Clients will access other public methods (like getEmpNums) to retrieve Employee information. These public methods will create the correct SQL **select** statements and invoke doSelect. Because there is no reason for clients to use doSelect (or even know that it exists), doSelect is "hidden" by being defined as **private**. Notice also that the results are assigned to the class variable rs.

10. In Employee, add the following code to create the getEmpNums method:

```java
public ResultSet getEmpNums() {
        String select =
        new String("SELECT empnum FROM tntdb.employee ");
        this.doSelect(select);
        return rs;
}
```

The method getEmpNums defines the SQL statement that will retrieve all the employee numbers. The SQL statement is assigned to the **String** variable named **select** and **select** is passed to the doSelect method for execution. The doSelect method executes the SQL statement and assigns the results to rs. getEmpNums then returns rs to the calling method (i.e., the client).

11. Create a new Java class called EmpNumFrame and enter the following code:

```java
package c10;
import java.awt.Choice;
import java.awt.event.ItemEvent;
import java.awt.event.ItemListener;
import java.sql.*;
public class EmpNumFrame extends UsefulFrame
        implements ItemListener {
    private String empNum, txType;
    private Choice EmpNumCh = null;
    private Employee emp = new Employee();
    public EmpNumFrame(String tx) {
        super();
        initialize();
        txType = tx;
    }
    private void initialize() {
    this.setSize(278, 125);
    this.setLocation(450, 303);
    this.setLayout(null);
    this.add(getEmpNumCh(), null);
    this.setTitle("Select Employee Number");
            this.setVisible(true);
    }
    private Choice getEmpNumCh() {
        if(EmpNumCh == null) {
            EmpNumCh = new Choice();
            EmpNumCh.setBounds(85, 59, 108, 21);
            EmpNumCh.addItemListener(this);
            ResultSet rs = emp.getEmpNums();
            try {
                while(rs.next()) {
                    EmpNumCh.add(rs.getString(1));
                }
            } catch (SQLException e) {
                System.out.println("No connection: " + e);
            }
}
```

```
                }
                return EmpNumCh;
        }
        public void itemStateChanged(ItemEvent arg0) {
                empNum = EmpNumCh.getSelectedItem();
                System.out.println("We are getting ready to " +
                 txType + " emp num " + empNum);
                this.dispose();
        }
    }
```

Notice that EmpNumFrame's constructor is expecting a **String** variable. The function specified by the user on EmpOptions (update or display) must be passed to EmpNumFrame. This is because if display is selected, EmpNumFrame will create an EmployeeFrame object, but if update is specified, an EnterEmpInfo object will be created. Later we will modify the itemStateChanged method to do this. For now, itemStateChanged will help us test by simply displaying the employee number specified and the function.

In addition, notice that itemStateChanged deletes the EmpNumFrame object (the dispose statement does this). This means that after the user has specified the employee number, the frame will disappear.

12. Copy Tutorials/c10.AppOptions and name the new class EmpOptions.

13. Open EmpOptions with the Visual Editor and change the name and text of the check boxes to the following:

```
insEmpCB                Insert Employee Information
dispEmpCB               Display Employee Information
updEmpCB                Update Employee Information
```

14. Resize and reposition the check boxes so all the text is displayed and they appear as in Figure 10-11.

15. Change the EmpOptions title to "Employee Application Menu."

16. Change the EmpOptions ItemStateChanged method to the following:

```
if (insEmpCB.getState()) {
 EnterEmpInfo eei = new EnterEmpInfo();}
else if (dispEmpCB.getState()){
        EmpNumFrame enf = new EmpNumFrame ("display");}
        else if (updEmpCB.getState()){
                EmpNumFrame enf =
                        new EmpNumFrame ("update");}
```

Notice that EmpNumFrame is only created if the function display or update is chosen and that the function is passed to EmpNumFrame. If insert is selected, the EnterEmpInfo frame is displayed. Now we need to change AppOptions so that it will display EmpOptions.

17. In the AppOptions ItemStateChanged method, change the following:

```
if (empAppCB.getState()) {
        EnterEmpInfo eei = new EnterEmpInfo();}
```

to:

```
if (empAppCB.getState()) {
        EmpOptions eo = new EmpOptions();}
```

Time to test.

18. Run TNT as an application.

The Application Menu should be displayed as in Figure 10-10.

19. On the Application Menu, select Employee Application.

The Employee Application Menu should be displayed as in Figure 10-11.

20. On the Employee Application Menu, select Update Employee Information.

The Select Employee Number frame should be displayed.

21. On the Select Employee Number frame, click on the choice arrow and select
employee number 222.

The Select Employee Number frame should disappear and the following should be displayed in
the Console:

```
We are getting ready to update emp num 222
```

22. Click the Exit button on the Employee Application Menu to close all frames.

Tutorial: Finishing the Employee Application, Part 1

We must add the ability to insert and update to the Employee class and modify EnterEmpInfo to invoke the correct
Employee methods based on the function selected. Remember, Employee will be performing all the database
functions. EnterEmpInfo is simply the user interface to enter the information and specify what function (insert or
update) to perform. In addition, we need to modify EnterEmpNum so that when the employee number is specified,
an Employee object is created. This Employee object should retrieve the employee information from the database
and populate the properties. EnterEmpNum will then pass the Employee object to EnterEmpInfo (for an update) or
EmployeeFrame (for a display).

First, we will add the Employee methods to retrieve, insert, and update an employee's information. Then we will
modify EnterEmpNum and EnterEmpInfo to invoke the correct Employee methods.

1. In Employee, add a new method called getEmpInfoFromRS by inserting the following code:

```
private void getEmpInfoFromRS() {
        try {rs.next();
                this.setEmpNum(rs.getString(1));
                this.setEmpName(rs.getString(2));
                this.setEmpStreet(rs.getString(3));
                this.setEmpCity(rs.getString(4));
                this.setEmpState(rs.getString(5));
                this.setEmpZip(rs.getString(6));
                this.setPayRate(rs.getDouble(7));
                this.setExemptions(rs.getInt(8));
```

```
        } catch (SQLException e) {
              System.out.println("Problem getting emp info from"
                     + " result set " + e);
        } catch (InvalidValue e) {
        System.out.println("Bad pay rate value retrieved " + e);
        }
    }
```

This will set the Employee object's properties to the information retrieved from the Employee table (which is in the result set rs). This is one of the private methods that the clients don't need to know about. In other words, clients will never have to deal with SQL statements, database-related objects (result sets, connections, etc.), or methods (getString, getStatement, etc).

2. In Employee, add a new method called getEmpInfo by inserting the following code:

```
public void getEmpInfo(String empNum) {
        String select = new String("SELECT * FROM " +
        "tntdb.employee WHERE empnum = '" + empNum + "'");
        this.doSelect(select);
        this.getEmpInfoFromRS();
}
```

This method builds the select statement, invokes doSelect to retrieve the data, and then invokes getEmpInfoFromRS to set the object's properties.

Now we will change EmpNumFrame to invoke getEmpInfo for the employee number (specified by the user) and then create an EmployeeFrame object to display the information.

3. In EmpNumFrame's itemStateChanged method, replace the println statement with the following:

```
emp.getEmpInfo(empNum);
if (txType.equals("display")) {
        EmployeeFrame ef = new EmployeeFrame(emp);
}
```

Let's test.

4. Run TNT as an application.

5. On the Application Menu, select Employee Application.

6. On the Employee Application Menu, select Display Employee Information.

7. On the Select Employee Number frame, click on the choice arrow and select employee number 222.

The Select Employee Number frame will disappear and the Employee Information frame will be displayed with the Joe Programmer information.

8. Click the Exit button on the Employee Information frame to close all frames.

Well, display was fairly easy to implement.

For updates, we must change the EnterEmpInfo frame to receive the Employee object (from EmpNumFrame), display the properties, and then update the data in the Employee table.

For inserts, the EnterEmpInfo frame must create an Employee object and then issue the command to insert the data. Oh, and we have to create methods in Employee to insert and update the information in the table.

Tutorial: Finishing the Employee Application, Part 2

Because we have put the option to display employee information on the Employee Application Menu, the display button on EnterEmpInfo isn't needed any more. What we really need is an update/insert button We will change the display button's name to actionBtn and, depending on the function selected from the menu, set the button's label to the appropriate text.

1. Open EnterEmpInfo in the Visual Editor.

2. Rename dispBtn to actionBtn and change the button text from "Display" to "Insert."

This will define the default button text as "Insert." The application must change the button text to "Update" when the user has selected update as the function. If an Employee object is passed from EmpNumFrame, EnterEmpInfo knows that the function is update. So, we need to create a new constructor that

Accepts an Employee object

Changes the button text to Update

Retrieves the information from the Employee object

Puts the Employee object's property information into the text fields

3. Add the following Java statements to start creating the new constructor

```java
public EnterEmpInfo(Employee e) {
        this();
        emp = e;
        actionBtn.setLabel("Update");
}
```

That first statement probably looks funny. The first statement executes the class's null constructor. Since all of the set-up functions still need to be performed, we simply run the null constructor instead of duplicating the code in the new constructor.

The second statement assigns the employee object (assigned to the method variable **e**) to the class variable **emp** (so other methods can access the object). And, of course, the last statement changes the button text.

Now we need to modify EmpNumFrame to send the Employee object when update is selected by the user.

4. In EmpNumFrame's itemStateChanged method, after the current if statement, add the following:

```java
if (txType.equals("update")) {
        EnterEmpInfo eei = new EnterEmpInfo(emp);
}
```

We should be able to select a particular employee for update, and when the EnterEmpInfo frame is displayed, the button should have update as the text. Let's test.

5. Run TNT, select Employee Application, Update Employee Information, and then select employee number 111.

The EnterEmpInfo frame should be displayed, and the action button text should be Update. None of the employee information is displayed, because we still must insert the code to retrieve the employee information and populate the text fields. We will create a separate method called populateTFs to do this and have the constructor invoke the method.

6. In EnterEmpInfo, insert the following code to define the method populateTFs

```java
private void populateTFs() {
    empNumTF.setText(emp.getEmpNum());
    empNameTF.setText(emp.getEmpName());
    empStreetTF.setText(emp.getEmpStreet());
    cityTF.setText(emp.getEmpCity());
    stateTF.setText(emp.getEmpState());
    zipTF.setText(emp.getEmpZip());
    empPRTF.setText(String.valueOf(emp.getPayRate()));
    exmpChoice.select(String.valueOf(emp.getExemptions()));
}
```

7. Add the following as the last statement in the **EnterEmpInfo(Employee e)** method:

```java
this.populateTFs();
```

8. Run TNT, select Employee Application, Update Employee Information, and then select employee number 111.

The Mary Worker information should be displayed in the text fields.

We will now add the insert and update functions to Employee, and then modify EnterEmpInfo to invoke those functions

9. In Employee, add the following methods:

```java
private void doUpdate(String update) {
    try {
        stmt.executeUpdate(update);
    } catch (SQLException e) {
        System.out.println("Problem with " + update + e);
    }
}
public void doInsert() {
    String insert = "INSERT INTO tntdb.employee " +
        createValuesClause();
    doUpdate(insert);
}
public void doUpdate() {
    String update = "UPDATE tntdb.employee " +
        createSetClause() + createWhereClause();
    doUpdate(update);
}

public void doDelete() {
    String delete = "DELETE FROM tntdb.employee " +
        createWhereClause();
    doUpdate(delete);
}
```

```java
    private String createValuesClause() {
        String values = "VALUES ('" +
                empNum + "', '" +
                empName + "', '" +
                empStreet + "', '" +
                empCity + "', '" +
                empState + "', '" +
                empZip + "', " +
                payRate + ", " +
                exemptions + ") ";
        return values;
    }
    private String createSetClause() {
        String set = "SET " +
                "empNum = '" + empNum + "', " +
                "empName = '" + empName + "', " +
                "street = '" + empStreet + "', " +
                "city = '" + empCity + "', " +
                "state = '" + empState + "', " +
                "zip = '" + empZip + "', " +
                "payRate = " + payRate + ", " +
                "exempts = " + exemptions + " ";
        return set;
    }

    private String createWhereClause() {
        String where = "WHERE empNum = '" + empNum+ "' ";
            return where;
    }
```

Notice that only three of the new methods are public. These public methods are the interface that clients of the Employee class use to perform the insert, update, and delete functions. Data encapsulation dictates that the encapsulating class should provide public CRUD (Create, Read, Update, and Delete) functions for other classes to access the data. The getEmpInfo method provides the read function, and the constructors provide the create function. We just added the doInsert, doUpdate, and doDelete methods to provide the UD in CRUD.

In actuality, the three public classes simply build the SQL statement string and then pass that string to the private methods doSelect(String) or doUpdate(String) for execution. Looking even closer, you will see that we have split the creation of the **set**, **values**, and **where** clauses into separate methods. Because updates, deletes, inserts, and selects may use the same clauses, we created separate methods so we only define the clauses once. Notice that the createXxxx methods do not use the public getters and setters to access the property values, they access the private variables directly. Because the methods are private, there is no danger in modifying the private variables directly. We will now enable the Insert and Update functions in EnterEmpInfo.

10. In EnterEmpInfo's setEmployeeProperties method add the following to the beginning of the method

```java
        emp.setEmpNum(empNumTF.getText());
```

11. In EnterEmpInfo's actionPerformed method, change:

```java
    if (actionBtn == e.getSource()) {
        EmployeeFrame ef = new EmployeeFrame(emp);
```

to:

```
if (actionBtn == e.getSource()) {
        if (actionBtn.getLabel().equals("Insert")) {
                emp.doInsert();
        }
        else { if (actionBtn.getLabel().equals("Update")) {
                emp.doUpdate();
            }
        }
        this.dispose();
```

Time to test.

12. Run TNT, select Employee Application, Insert Employee Information, and then enter the following employee information

```
333
Anne Analyst
3 Logic La
Jacksonville
FL 32233
22
1
```

13. Click the Insert button.

14. At the Employee Application Menu, select Display Employee and then, from the Select Employee Number frame, select employee number 333.

    The Anne Analyst information should be displayed in the Employee Information frame.

15. Close the Employee Information frame and from the Employee Application Menu, select Update Employee Information.

16. Select employee number 333 from the Select Employee Number frame.

The Anne Analyst information will be shown on the Enter Employee Information frame.

17. Change the street address to 4 Logic La and click the Update button.

18. From the Employee Application Menu, select Display Employee Information and then, from the Select Employee Number frame, select employee number 333.

The Employee Information frame will be displayed with the Anne Analyst information and the new value of 4 Logic La for the street address.

Yay, it works!! However, there are several shortcomings with our application. For instance, deleting an employee's information is not an option on any of the frames, nor are there any checks to stop duplicate employee information from being inserted into the database. This could have been easily solved by adding the delete option to the Employee Options frame, coding the call to Employee's doDelete method, and doing a simple check before inserting the new employee information. Also, navigating the frames to access the various functions is awkward. Certainly, a Web page with links to all the functions (on the left side of the page) would be much easier. We also have not been very careful about closing the connection—which wastes system resources. Finally, the way we create and execute the SQL commands (dynamically) is very inefficient, especially for high-volume database applications. Using **PreparedStatement** objects instead of **Statement** objects is more efficient. However, adding code to overcome these shortcomings would have added to the complexity of the application and taken the focus away from the point of the chapter, which was how to access a database.

Data Access in a Complex Environment

Most large organizations have multiple DBMSs and often many different DBMS types. In these complex environments, tables are often moved between the DBMSs, database locations are changed, and there are constant changes to the structure of tables (i.e., adding and deleting fields, changing field sizes, etc.) These types of changes will require changes to the Java classes. Programmers can minimize the coding needed to implement these changes by using super classes and inheritance to eliminate duplicate code. In addition, abstract classes should be used to enforce standards across the different DBMS types.

As an example, we'll assume an organization has one installation of each DBMS type (DB2, Oracle, and Access). To support the DBMSs, a "DBAccess-like" class should be created for each DBMS. This means the programmer would create three Java classes (called DB2DB, OracleDB, and AccessDB) with properties to hold the unique information required to access that particular DBMS. (If the three DBMSs were of the same type, you could put the IP address or URLs of the different hosts in the Java class name (e.g., OracleDB111. 222.333.4) to distinguish between them.

The smart programmer will also implement a common interface for all the DBMSs. Our example will consist of public methods called doInsert, doUpdate, and doDelete. Regardless of the DBMS type, internally, each class should work the same way. So, we will force each class to have non-public methods called createValuesClause, createSetClause, createWhereClause, getFieldsFromRS, doSelect(String), and doUpdate(String). A superclass (called DB) will be created that defines each of these required methods as abstract. In addition, DB will have a method (called init) that creates all the needed DB objects (connection, statement, etc.) and common variables that the table classes need, such as a **ResultSet** variable called rs, a **Statement** variable called stmt, and so on.

The code for DB would be as follows:

```java
package c10;
import java.util.*;
import java.sql.*;
abstract class DB {
        Connection con = null;
        String url = null;
        String user, pw;
        Properties p = new Properties();
        String driver = null;
        public boolean conExists = false;
        ResultSet rs = null;
        Statement stmt = null;
        int returnValue;
        public void init() {
                if (conExists == false) {
                        try {
                                Class.forName(driver);
                                p.put("naming", "sql");
                                p.put("user", user);
                                p.put("password", pw);
                                con = DriverManager.getConnection(url, p);
                                stmt = con.createStatement();
                        } catch (ClassNotFoundException e) {
                                System.out.println("couldn't find driver");
                                e.printStackTrace();
                                System.exit(1);
                        } catch (SQLException e) {
                                System.out.println("couldn't connect");
                                e.printStackTrace();
                                System.exit(1);
```

```
                }
            }
            conExists = true;
    }
    public abstract void doInsert();
    public abstract void doUpdate();
    public abstract void doDelete();
    abstract String createValuesClause();
    abstract String createSetClause();
    abstract String createWhereClause();
    abstract void getFieldsFromRS();
    abstract void doSelect(String string);
    abstract void doUpdate(String string);
}
```

Notice that before creating a connection object the init method checks to see if a connection object already exists. This will cut down on the overhead of creating and maintaining multiple connections. Of course, each individual "table class" will have to invoke the init method to ensure that the connection is created at least once.

Notice also that the init method uses a **Properties** object. Instead of dealing with all the individual property variables, a **Properties** object is defined to hold many of the values and then passed to the **DriverManager**. Lastly, note all the abstract methods. The various "table" subclasses of DB will be required to define these methods.

We need the "database classes" AccessDB, DB2DB, and OracleDB. As mentioned, each will contain the information unique to that DBMS. The source code for each is:

```
package c10;
abstract class AccessDB extends DB{

    public AccessDB () {
            driver = "sun.jdbc.odbc.JdbcOdbcDriver";
            url = "jdbc:odbc:TNT Database";
            user = "anonymous";
            pw = "guest";
    }
}
package c10;
abstract class DB2DB extends DB{
    public DB2DB () {
            driver = "com.ibm.as400.access.AS400JDBCDriver";
            url = "jdbc:as400:111.22.333.444";
            user = "bjanson";
            pw = "jeter";
    }
}
package c10;
abstract class OracleDB extends DB {
    public OracleDB () {
            driver = "oracle.jdbc.driver.OracleDriver";
            url = "jdbc:oracle:thin:@111.22.333.444:1521:SID";
            user = "bjanson";
            pw = "jeter";
    }
}
```

Notice that each of the DB classes is defined as abstract and extends DB. Because they are abstract, they do not have to implement the abstract methods defined in DB. However, all of the abstract methods will have to be defined in Employee and the ones that are currently defined as **private** will have to have the access modifier removed. Because DB defines the methods as **protected**, Employee can't define them more restrictively as **private**. Speaking of changes to Employee, Employee must call the init method (to establish the connection to the database) and we need to implement a getFieldsFromRS method. We could rename getEmpInfo-FromRS to getFieldsFromRS, however, it's simpler to code getFieldsFromRS to invoke get-EmpInfoFromRS. Finally, of course, you would substitute all your connection information for the example information above.

In Employee, we would change the constructor to invoke init as follows:

```
public Employee(){
       init();
}
```

If there are multiple constructors, all must invoke the default constructor. In Employee, there is a constructor that accepts five strings. It would be modified to the following:

```
public Employee(String name, String street, String
       city, String state, String zip) {
       this();
       this.setEmpName(name);
       this.setEmpStreet(street);
       this.setEmpCity(city);
       this.setEmpState(state);
       this.setEmpZip(zip);
}
```

As mentioned, each of the **private** methods headers must be changed as follows:

```
String createValuesClause() {...
String createSetClause() {...
String createWhereClause() {...
void doSelect(String select) {...
void doUpdate(String update) {..
```

and getFieldsFromRS can be coded as follows:

```
void getFieldsFromRS() {
       getEmpInfoFromRS();
}
```

Assuming Employee is currently in the DB2 database, the Employee class header would look like the following:

```
public class Employee extends DB2DB{...
```

and the class diagram would look like Figure 10-13. Now comes the magic of inheritance.

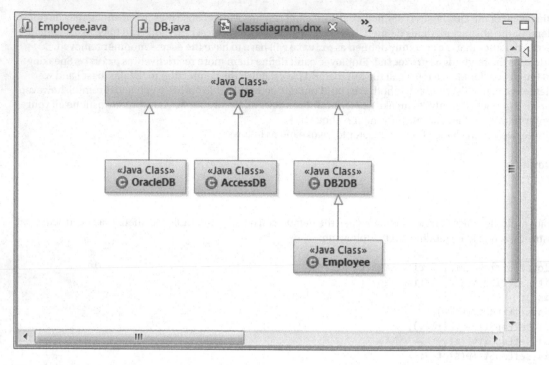

Figure 10-13.

If the Employee table is moved to the Oracle DBMS, all a Java programmer would have to change is the Employee header to extend the OracleDB class as follows:

public class Employee **extends** OracleDB{...

And, as you probably guessed, if the Employee table were moved to the Access DBMS, the Employee header would be changed to:

public class Employee **extends** AccessDB{...

Because we specified the DBMS information in separate classes (e.g., OracleDB, AccessDB) rather than in the "table classes" (e.g., Employee) and built a superclass/subclass relationships (so that the required objects, methods, and variables are inherited), physical changes to table locations have a minimal impact on the Java classes. In addition, if the DBMS was moved to a different host or a password was changed, only the DBMS classes (containing the URL address and password) would need to be changed. Even if the Java technology for accessing a database changed (e.g., connection objects were replaced), only the DB class' init method would be affected.

A great deal of the advances in Java (Java Server Faces (JSFs), Enterprise Java Beans (EJBs), etc.) are in the area of working with databases. In the next chapters, we will examine some of these new technologies.

Results of the Tutorial:

Let's look at the results:

1. In the Tutorials project, a new package named c10.

2. In Tutorials/c10, the following new Java classes:

   DBAccess   EmpNumFrame   EmpOptions

3. A printout of the DBAccess source code.

4. In Tutorials/c10, the following Java classes copied from c7 and c9:

   AppOptions   Employee   EmployeeFrame
   EnterEmpInfo   ExitButton   TNT
   TNTButton   UsefulFrame

5. The employee application can now insert, display, and update employee information in a database.

Review Questions

1. What is a result set?

2. What is a driver?

3. In a result set, what is the function of the cursor?

4. What is the purpose of data encapsulation?

5. What is SQL's function regarding databases?

6. What is the purpose of the result set's next method?

7. What is CRUD?

8. Explain the term "data persistence"?

Review Exercise

You will modify the Shipment application to insert, update, display, and delete shipment information in a DBMS. In addition, the Enter Shipment Information frame will offer the capability to delete and update shipment information.

To perform all this, the ShipOptions class must be modified to pass the selected function to EnterShipNum. EnterShipNum will receive the shipment number entered by the user and create a Shipment object for that shipment number. EnterShipNum will pass the selected function and the Shipment object to EnterShipInfo. EnterShipInfo will display the correct button text (insert, delete, etc.). The Shipment class will accept a shipment number, access the database for that shipment's information, and populate the Shipment object's properties with the database information. Shipment will also be modified to provide all the CRUD functions.

1. In ReviewEx, create a new folder called c10.

2. Copy all the files in c7 into c10.

3. Copy the following Employee application files from Tutorials/c10, into ReviewEx/c10:

   AppOptions   DBAccess   Employee
   EmpNumFrame   EmpOptions   EnterEmpInfo

4. At the Confirm Overwriting window, click the Yes To All button.

5. If you are accessing a DB2 or Oracle DBMS, add the External JAR to point to the appropriate driver. If you are accessing an Access table, import the TNTDB DB from Tutorials into ReviewEx.

6. Run TNT and verify that the Employee application works correctly.

7. In the Shipment Options frame, add checkboxes called updShipCB and dltShipCB to the frame and checkbox group. Shipment Options frame should look like Figure 10-14.

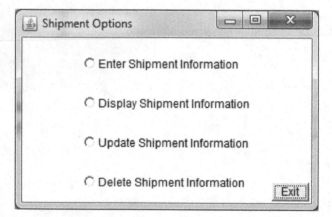

Figure 10-14.

8. Add the item listener to the two checkboxes by adding the following statements in the appropriate getter methods (hint: if unsure of how to do this, look at the other checkboxes' getter methods):

   ```
   updShipCB.addItemListener(this);
   dltShipCB.addItemListener(this);
   ```

9. In AppOptions, change the following statement in the ItemStateChanged method:

   ```
   else if (shipAppCB.getState())
           System.out.println("Sorry that application is not " + "available");
   ```

   to:

   ```
   else if (shipAppCB.getState()){
           ShipOptions so = new ShipOptions();}
   ```

This means that the Shipment Options frame will be displayed when that option is selected from the Application Options frame

10. In Shipment, create a new null Constructor.

11. In Shipment, create a Constructor that receives a **String** variable called sNum by adding the following code:

```
public Shipment(String sNum) {
}
```

12. Save the Shipment source code.

13. In EnterShipInfo, add a constructor that expects a Shipment variable called ship and a **String** variable called func. In addition, invoke the null constructor.

The code should look like the following:

```
public EnterShipInfo(Shipment ship, String func) {
        this();
}
```

By accepting a Shipment object, EnterShipInfo will be easier for other classes to use.

14. In EnterShipNum, add the ActionListener to the Submit button and add the following statement to create a class **private String** variable called function.

```
private String function;
```

Since we will change EnterShipNum to perform deletes and updates, the user selected function needs to be passed to EnterShipNum and stored in this class level variable.

15. Change EnterShipNum's constructor so that a **String** variable called func is received and the class variable function is set to func.

The source code should look like the following:

```
public EnterShipNum(String func) {
        super();
        initialize();
        function = func;
}
```

16. Change EnterShipNum's actionPerformed such that:

a. A **String** variable called sNum is created

b. The shipment number is retrieved from the text field and assigned to sNum

c. A shipment object is created for the shipment number and assigned to a variable called shipment

    d.   If the function is update or delete, create an EnterShipInfo object and pass the variables shipment and function

    e.   If the function is display, create a ShipmentFrame object and pass the shipment variable

    f.   Delete the EnterShipNum frame

The code should look like the following:

```java
public void actionPerformed(ActionEvent e) {
        String sNum = shipNumTF.getText();
        Shipment shipment = new Shipment(sNum);
        if (function.equals("Display")) {
            new ShipmentFrame(shipment);
        } else {
            new EnterShipInfo(shipment, function);
        }
        this.dispose();
}
```

Notice that neither the EnterShipInfo nor the ShipmentFrame objects are assigned to a variable. Because we will never reference the objects in the source code, there is no need to assign variables to them.

17.   In ShipOptions, create a **private** class **String** variable called function by adding the following:

```java
private String function;
```

18.   Change ShipOptions' itemStateChanged method such that:

    A.   If the enter option is chosen, the EnterShipInfo frame is displayed

    B.   If display, update, or delete are selected, the EnterShipNum frame is displayed

    C.   If display is selected, pass the string "Display" to EnterShipNum

    D.   If update is selected, then pass "Update" to EnterShipNum

    E.   If delete is selected, then pass "Delete" to EnterShipNum

To do this, change the source to the following:

```java
if (dispShipCB.getState())
        function = "Display";
 else {
     if (updShipCB.getState()) {
            function = "Update";
     } else {
            if (dltShipCB.getState()) {
                    function = "Delete";
            }
     }
 }
```

```
if (enterShipCB.getState()) {
        EnterShipInfo esi = new EnterShipInfo();
} else {
        EnterShipNum esn = new EnterShipNum(function);
}
```

So far the steps you have performed have defined "the plumbing" necessary for the classes to communicate correctly. The next steps will add the CRUD methods to Shipment and change EnterShipInfo and EnterShipNum to invoke the appropriate Shipment methods. We assume that the Shipment table was created in TNTDB with the following SQL command:

```
CREATE TABLE tntdb.shipment
            (empnum         CHAR(10),
            shipnum CHAR(10),
            rcvmon         CHAR(2),
            rcvday         CHAR(2),
            rcvyear        CHAR(4),
            rcvhour        CHAR(2),
            rcvmin         CHAR(2),
            rcvampm        CHAR(2),
            supplier       CHAR(20))
```

19.   Make Shipment a subclass of DBAccess.

20.   In the Shipment class, add the following **private String** variables along with getters and setters for each:

      rcvMon   rcvDay   rcvYear
      rcvHour   rcvMin   rcvAMPM

21.   Copy the five doXxxx and three createXxxx methods from Tutorials.c10 Employee into Shipment. We will edit these methods to fit Shipment instead of entering them in from scratch. This will cut down on errors especially with the SQL commands.

22.   If needed, in the Shipment class, add the import statement for the SQL Exception class.

23.   In the appropriate Shipment class doXxxx methods, replace the references to the employee table with shipment table. (Be careful: this step and the following seven steps require specifying the correct field and table names, as well as, the correct data types, button names, and text fields for the Shipment class and table.)

24.   In the Shipment class createXxxx methods, replace the references to the employee properties with the shipment properties (i.e., the **private** variables).

25.   Copy the getEmpInfoFromRS and getEmpInfo methods from Employee into the Shipment class.

26.   Change the Shipment class method names (copied in the step above) to getFieldsFromRS and getShipInfo.

27.   Change the two new methods to use Ship information and the appropriate Shipment methods not the Employee information and methods.

28.   Delete the catch for invalid value in getFieldsFromRS. (This was needed in Employee because of numeric data but is not needed for the shipment information.)

29. Modify the Shipment constructor that receives the ship number string so that the shipment number is moved into the class variable shipmentNumber and getShipInfo is invoked as follows:

```java
public Shipment(String sNum) {
        this.setShipmentNum(sNum);
        this.getShipInfo(sNum);
}
```

30. In EnterShipInfo, change the name of the enterBtn to actionBtn.

31. In EnterShipInfo, change the definition of the class variable ship from:

```java
public Shipment ship;
```

to:

```java
private Shipment ship = new Shipment();
```

and, in the initialize, method comment out the following:

```java
ship = new Shipment("","","","","");
```

32. In EnterShipInfo, create a populateTFs method (as was done in EnterEmpInfo) so that the Shipment text fields and the choice values from the Shipment object are displayed.

33. Change EnterShipInfo's constructor that accepts a Shipment and a **String** variable (as follows), so that the shipment information is put in the labels and the button has the correct text:

```java
public EnterShipInfo(Shipment ship, String func) {
        this();
        this.ship = ship;
        populateTFs();
        actionBtn.setLabel(func);
}
```

34. In the EnterShipInfo setShipmentProperties method, after the new shipment object is created also set the six individual properties that make up the receiving date and time.

35. Change EnterShipInfo's actionPerformed method so the correct doXxxx methods are called for the functions insert, update and delete and that appropriate message text is displayed for each operation.

36. Change EnterShipInfo's actionPerformed method so that a ShipmentFrame object is created when the display function has been selected.

37. Save all the source code.

Results of the Review Exercise

Below are the results:

1. In ReviewExWeb/Java Resources, there is a new folder called c10.

2. c10 should contain 24 classes.

3. Modifications to Shipment such that the CRUD functions are available.

4. Changes to the Shipment application such that inserts, deletes, and updates can be performed on the shipment table and shipment information is displayed on ShipmentFrame.

Check that the Exercise Was Done Correctly

Let's check if everything is working:

1. Run TNT and insert the following information for a shipment: employee 222, shipment number 1000, supplier Fred Meyers, and the current date and time.

2. Choose the display function, specify shipment number 1000, and verify the information is displayed.

Notice that the message text does not fit in the labels and there are extra spaces following the shipment number. These problems will be addressed in the Challenge Exercise.

3. Close the ShipmentFrame window.

4. Choose the update function, specify shipment 1000, and change the employee number to 111.

5. Choose the display function, specify shipment 1000, and verify that employee number 111 is displayed.

6. Close the ShipmentFrame window.

7. Choose the delete function and specify shipment 1000.

8. Choose the display function and specify shipment 1000. The following message should be generated:

```
Problem getting ship info from result set java.sql.SQLException: Xxxxx xxxxx.
```

Because shipment 1000 was deleted, the result set returned by the **select** is empty. When Shipment tries to read the result set (to put the values in the properties), we should check to see if the result set is empty. This is another deficiency the Challenge Exercise will correct.

Challenge Exercise

Finally, let's try a challenge:

1. Copy ReviewEx/c10 into CE (and, if using Access, copy TNTDB from ReviewEx).

2. Change EnterShipInfo's empNumTF to a choice called empNumCh and have EnterShipInfo populate the choice with Employee numbers from the employee table. (Hint: copy the code from the EmpNumFrame class and modify as needed.)

3. Change Shipment's getFieldsFromRS method to check if the shipment was found in the database. If the shipment is not in the database, display the following message (where the actual shipment number is display instead of xxxxx) in the Console:

    ```
    Shipment number xxxxx does not exist in the database.
    ```

4. In EnterShipNum, check if the shipment was retrieved from the database and if not, do not display ShipmentFrame.

There are several reasons the shipment information is not displayed correctly:

A. The first label is too small.

B. If a string value does not fill a table's column, the database "pads" the value with blanks.

(In other words, if the month value is 4, the retrieved value will be "4 " - the character 4 followed by a blank space. This results in the spacing being "off". In addition, because of the blank space, trying to parse "4" will result in a number format exception being thrown.)

5. Change the Shipment class's getFieldsFromRS method so that the fields RcvDate and RcvTime are built and use the **String** class's trim method on all the data fields retrieved from the result set that may be padded with spaces.

6. Change the Shipment class's setRcvDate(String) and setRcvTime(String) methods so that the six individual properties (hour, minute, day, month, etc.) values are also set.

7. In ShipmentFrame, make the first label wider so that all the text will appear.

Check that the Exercise Was Done Correctly

Perform the same tests as were done for the Review Exercise and confirm that the problems have been resolved.

CHAPTER 11

Custom Tag

This chapter will demonstrate how to create custom tags and use them in JSPs. This will require a more detailed explanation of how tags work, as well as covering new topics such as XML and tag libraries. The database access classes (created in Chapter 10) will be used in the server-based application to insert, display, and delete information from a database. We will also demonstrate how the MVC architecture makes incorporating these functions immensely easier.

At the end of this chapter, you should understand:

> XML
>
> Tag libraries
>
> Tag handlers
>
> URI
>
> The Web Deployment Descriptor
>
> Arrays

At the end of this chapter, you should be able to:

> Create and use custom tags
>
> Create and use custom visual components
>
> Access a database from a server-based application

Tags

JSTL and JSP tags are very easy to use. Just as driving a car doesn't require knowing how an internal combustion engine works, using a tag does not require understanding how tags work. This is precisely how tag creators meant it to be! Tags were created so that page designers can easily invoke complex functions. In the previous examples, however, the number of bean tags required was quite large and beyond what a page designer should be required to know. Custom tags will be used to eliminate this problem by further simplifying what the page designer must code. However, creating a tag requires a deeper understanding how tags work.

Tags actually invoke a type of Java class called a "tag handler. Tag handler classes are usually defined as a subclass of either the **TagSupport** or **BodyTagSupport** classes. The examples in this chapter will define tag handlers as subclasses of **TagSupport**. As the **TagSupport** name implies, the tag handler will inherit many variables and methods that do much of the "tag work."

As mentioned earlier, JSP and JSTL tags come with RAD. What this means is that RAD ensures that the Java classes (i.e., the tag handlers that perform the tag functions) are accessible to the JSPs. For example, the tag handlers for JSP tags are stored in a file that RAD will automatically check when the JSP is run. This means that to implement a JSP tag (like the **include** tag) the programmer simply inserts the tag into the source code. RAD will find the correct tag handler class.

JSTL tags are not as simple. When a JSTL tag is added, RAD not only inserts the tag into the source code but also inserts a taglib (tag library) directive. The directive identifies the file (i.e., tag library) that contains the tag definition. The tag definition specifies which tag handler class should be invoked for the tag. For instance, when the JSTL **if** tag was added to the JSP, RAD added the following taglib directive:

```
<%@taglib uri="http://java.sun.com/jsp/jstl/core" prefix="c"%>
```

The URI (Uniform Resource Identifier) value can be an actual file within the project such as /WEB-INF/tls/TNT. tld or an alias. In this chapter, you will create a folder named tls in WEB-INF and then, within tls, a tag library file called TNT.tld. A tag library URI (i.e., an alias) of http://www.tnt.com/taglib will then be created and associated with /WEB-INF/tls/TNT.tld. This association is defined in a project file called the **Web Deployment Descriptor**.

Notice that the taglib directive also defines a prefix of c for the JSTL tags. This means that when a JSTL tag (that is defined in the jstl/core tag library) is inserted in the page, the JSTL tag keyword must begin with the letter c followed by a colon. In other words, the prefix identifies which directive the server should use to locate the tag library associated with this tag.

In fact, RAD inserted the following JSTL tags when the **if** tag was added to the JSP:

```
<c:if test=""></c:if>
```

The actual JSTL tag keyword is **if** but notice that it is preceded by c:. So, in this example, the c: tells the server that the tag library is located at http://java.sun.com/jsp/ jstl/core. The server then goes to the Web Deployment Descriptor to get the actual location of the tag library.

Got it? Let's recap. When the server encounters a JSP tag in the page, the server:

A.   Reads the tag prefix

B.   Within the JSP, finds the tag library directive associated with the tag prefix

C.   Using the directive's URI, goes to the Web Deployment Descriptor and retrieves the tag library file name and location

D.   Goes to the taglib file and retrieves the name and location of the tag handler class associated with the tag

E.   Runs the tag handler class

With the **if** tag, the tag handler evaluates a condition. If the condition is true, the body of the tag will be embedded into the response object. For example, if the body contained the text "Yowser!" and the condition was true, the text "Yowser!" would be embedded in the page and appear in the browser.

Who cares? Well, we do. We need a simple tag to create and populate the Employee bean from the JSP fields. In addition, we are also going to create a tag that creates a specialized state choice field that limits the user to only valid state abbreviations. By creating a state field tag, we will be able to use it on multiple JSPs rather than defining a state choice field for each JSP. More important, if a state must be added to or deleted from the list, only the tag handler will have to be changed, not every JSP that displays the state value. Finally, the application will be modified to display the tax amount and gross salary for an employee on the same page as all the other employee information.

Creating a Custom Tag

As mentioned, we will create a custom tag (getEmp) to replace the following bean tags in EnterEmpInfoJSP:

```
<jsp:useBean id="EmpBean" class="c9java.Employee" scope="request">
<jsp:setProperty name="EmpBean" property="empStreet"
                 param="streetAddrTF" />
<jsp:setProperty name="EmpBean" property="exemptions" param="exmpDDM" />
```

```
<jsp:setProperty name="EmpBean" property="empState" param="stateTF" />
<jsp:setProperty name="EmpBean" property="empNum" param="empNumTF" />
<jsp:setProperty name="EmpBean" property="empName" param="empNameTF" />
<jsp:setProperty name="EmpBean" property="empZip" param="zipTF" />
<jsp:setProperty name="EmpBean" property="payRate" param="hPRTF" />
<jsp:setProperty name="EmpBean" property="empCity" param="cityTF" />
</jsp:useBean>
```

We will do this by creating:

- A tag handler class called CrtEmpBean that is a subclass of **TagSupport**. CrtEmpBean will perform the same functions that the bean tags did (i.e., create and populate an Employee bean). CrtEmpBean will use the EmpExtractor class to create the Employee object and then define the Employee object as a Java bean with a scope of request.

- A folder called **tls** (tag libraries) in WEB-INF.

- Within tls, a tag library file called TNT.tld with an entry to associate the custom tag getEmp and the tag handler class CrtEmpBean

- An entry in the Web Deployment Descriptor to define the URI http://www.tnt.com/taglib and tie it to /WEB-INF/tls/TNT.tld

We will then use the custom tag in EnterEmpInfoJSP, by inserting:

- A taglib directive that defines the prefix TNT and ties it to the URI http://www.tnt.com/taglib

- The custom tag with the prefix TNT (`<TNT:getEmp/>`)

Tutorial: Creating a Custom Tag

Let's try it

1. In the TutorialsWeb project, click on the WebContent folder to select it.

2. Click File, New, Folder, specify c11 as the new folder name, and click the Finish button.

3. From the WebContent/c9 folder, copy EnterEmpInfoJSP.jsp and EnterEmpInfoForm.html into c11.

4. In c11/EnterEmpInfoForm.html, ensure that the form action is specified as EnterEmpInfoJSP.jsp. If it isn't, change it to EnterEmpInfoJSP.jsp.

5. In TutorialsWeb/Java Resources/src, create a folder called c11.

6. From c9java, copy Employee and EmpExtractor to c11.

7. In src/c11, create a Java class called CrtEmpBean with a super class of **TagSupport** and no method stubs.

The following source code will be inserted in CrtEmpBean and displayed in Page Designer:

```
package c11;
import javax.servlet.jsp.tagext.TagSupport;
public class CrtEmpBean extends TagSupport {
}
```

Although the generated code is not very impressive, the variables and methods inherited from **TagSupport** will make this class function as a tag. However, at least one inherited method has to overridden and coded to perform the needed application functions.

The Tag Handler

As mentioned, CrtEmpBean inherits many methods from **TagSupport**. We will focus on the **doStartTag** and **doEndTag** methods that are inherited from **TagSupport**. It was stated earlier that when the tag is encountered in the JSP, the server runs the associated tag handler class. Specifically, when the start tag is encountered, the server runs the doStartTag method and when the end tag is encountered, the doEndTag method is run.

In the example, we want the doStartTag method to:

A.   Run EmpExtractor's getEmployeeInstance to create an Employee object from the request

B.   Define the returned Employee object as a bean with a scope of request

Several things will be needed to do this. First, private variables of type Employee and EmpExtractor are required. Second, the **HttpServletRequest** class needs to be imported into CrtEmpBean. This is required because getEmployeeInstance is expecting an **HttpServletRequest**, but the request object is of type **ServletRequest**. So, the **ServletRequest** object must be cast as an **HttpServletRequest**. Finally, we will be using the ever-helpful **PageContext** object (provided by the server) to get the request and define the Employee object as a request bean (or, said another way, define the Employee object as an attribute of the request).

The code to get the request object is:

```
pageContext.getRequest()
```

Because the returned request must be cast into an **HttpServletRequest**, this statement should be preceded with the following to cast the request:

```
(HttpServletRequest)
```

This results in:

```
(HttpServletRequest)pageContext.getRequest()
```

Then the **HttpServletRequest** needs to be passed to EmpExtractor. Do this by embedding the above statement in the method call as follows (where ee is the EmpExtractor variable):

```
ee.getEmployeeInstance(
(HttpServletRequest)pageContext.getRequest());
```

To define the returned Employee object as a request bean, we need to get the request again (using the page context's getRequest method again). Then use the request's setAttribute method to define the employee object as a bean called EmpBean. The statement to do that is as follows (where emp is the Employee variable):

```
pageContext.getRequest().setAttribute("EmpBean", emp);
```

Tutorial: Defining the Tag Handler Class

Time to define the tag handler class:

1. In CrtEmpBean, add the following import statement after the existing import statement:

   ```
   import javax.servlet.http.HttpServletRequest;
   ```

2. In CrtEmpBean, add the following statements to create a class Employee variable called emp and both an EmpExtractor object and EmpExtractor class variable called ee.

   ```
   private Employee emp;
   private EmpExtractor ee = new EmpExtractor();
   ```

3. In CrtEmpBean, click Source, then Override/Implement Methods...

4. At the Override/Implement Methods window, click on the doStartTag() checkbox to select it.

5. Make sure the insertion point option is After 'ee" and click the OK button.

RAD creates a doStartTag method. Notice the return statement. Even though we are overriding the superclass' doStartTag method (to create and populate the Employee bean), the superclass' doStartTag method is still executed. This is because the superclass' doStartTag method performs many functions we still want to occur. For instance, the doStartTag method returns a value indicating success or failure of the method. This still must occur for the tag to work. Therefore, the superclass' doStartTag method is executed and its return value is returned as our doStartTag method's return value.

6. Before the return statement, add the following two statements to create the Employee object, populate its properties from the data in the request, and define the Employee object as a bean called EmpBean:

   ```
   emp = ee.getEmployeeInstance((HttpServletRequest)pageContext.getRequest());
   pageContext.getRequest().setAttribute("EmpBean", emp);
   ```

The code should look like the following:

```
package c11;
import javax.servlet.jsp.JspException;
import javax.servlet.jsp.tagext.TagSupport;
import javax.servlet.http.HttpServletRequest;
public class CrtEmpBean extends TagSupport {
  private Employee emp;
  private EmpExtractor ee = new EmpExtractor();
  public int doStartTag() throws JspException {
          emp = ee.getEmployeeInstance((HttpServletRequest)
  pageContext.getRequest());
          pageContext.getRequest().setAttribute("EmpBean", emp);
          return super.doStartTag();
  }
}
```

7. Save CrtEmpBean.

Defining a Tag

The tag handler class (CrtEmpBean) has been created but the tag has not yet been defined. A tag is defined in a tag library. A tag library is a file with an extension of **tld** (tag library descriptor) that contains XML (Extensible Markup Language). XML is fast becoming the glue that holds the Internet together. XML is a markup language just like HTML is a markup language. However, HTML is limited to defining Web pages. XML can be used to define any type of information: data, documents, file locations, etc. Really, XML is a language that allows a programmer to define a language. However, we will be using XML in a much more limited capacity.

In the case of a tag library, the server expects the XML to identify a tag and its associated tag handler class. There are other optional XML statements and we will look at one of these later in the chapter. The server also requires that the tag library file (of type tld) be in the WEB-INF folder.

Tutorial: Defining a Tag

Let's define a tag:

1. In the Project Explorer, expand the WebContent folder and select WEB-INF.

2. Click on File, New, and then Folder.

3. At the New Folder window, specify tls as the Folder name.

The folder tls should appear in the Enterprise Explorer and be selected.

4. Click on File, New, and then File. (If File isn't an option, select Other, expand the Simple option, select File, and then click the Next button.)

5. In the file name, specify TNT.tld and click the Finish button.

RAD will display the empty file.

6. Enter the following XML:

```
<taglib>
      <tag>
              <name>getEmp</name>
              <tagclass>c11.CrtEmpBean</tagclass>
      </tag>
</taglib>
```

This defines the tag (getEmp) and the tag handler (c11/CrtEmpBean) that will be run by the server when the tag is encountered.

7. Save TNT.tld

8. In EnterEmpInfoJSP source code, add the following taglib directive before the existing JSTL core taglib directive:

```
<%@taglib uri="/WEB-INF/tls/TNT.tld" prefix="TNT"%>
```

9. In EnterEmpInfoJSP, replace the following tags:

```
<jsp:useBean id="EmpBean" class="c9java.Employee" scope="request">
<jsp:setProperty name="EmpBean" property="empNum" param="empNumTF" />
<jsp:setProperty name="EmpBean" property="empStreet"
        param="streetAddrTF"/>
```

```
<jsp:setProperty name="EmpBean" property="exemptions" param="exmpDDM"/>
<jsp:setProperty name="EmpBean" property="empZip" param="zipTF"/>
<jsp:setProperty name="EmpBean" property="empState" param="stateTF"/>
<jsp:setProperty name="EmpBean" property="payRate" param="hPRTF"/>
<jsp:setProperty name="EmpBean" property="empName" param="empNameTF"/>
<jsp:setProperty name="EmpBean" property="empCity" param="cityTF"/>
</jsp:useBean>
```

with these start and end tags for the custom tag:

```
<TNT:getEmp>
</TNT:getEmp>
```

Remember, the bean tags are being deleted because CrtEmpBean's doStartTag method will perform these functions (with the help of the EmpExtractor and **PageContext** objects).

10.   Save EnterEmpInfoJSP.

Time to test.

11.   Run c11/EnterEmpInfoJSP on the server.

12.   Specify the employee name as joe, pay rate as 10, select Display and click the Submit button.

The browser window should look like Figure 11-1.

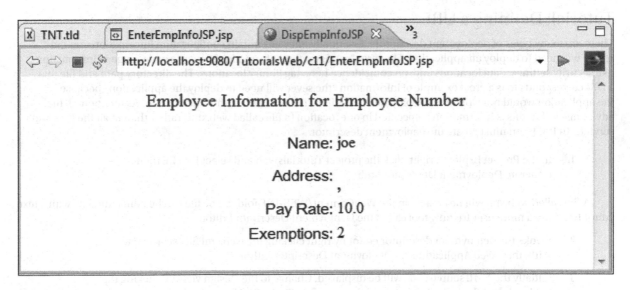

Figure 11-1.

Although not very pretty, this proves that the Employee bean was created and that DispEmpInfoJSP was able to access the bean. More important, this means that the custom tag, getEmp, worked!

When to Create Custom Tags

Does this seem like a lot of work to duplicate what can be done with already existing tags? Well, it's not as much work as it may seem. Some of the work was set-up that will not have to be repeated (e.g., creating the tls folder and the tld file). In addition, although the custom tag didn't save you, the programmer, any time, the number of tags needed in the JSP was cut down substantially and will save the page designer time. Also, all those bean tags and parameters are difficult for a non-programmer to understand and use; therefore the chance of error was greater and the time to implement longer.

So, when should a custom tag be used? Obviously, if there are no tags to supply the needed function, a custom tag is needed. If the amount of coding in the JSP, whether tags or scriptlets, is beyond the capability of the page designer, the programmer should create a custom tag(s). Also, if the required function is needed in many pages, there are two advantages to using the custom tag. One, the function is coded only once, in the tag handler class (i.e., the page designer does not enter all the bean tags in multiple pages). Two, any changes to the function are made only once in the tag handler class. If the bean tags needed to be modified, the designer would have to change every page that contained the bean tags. So, the bottom line is that if a function is not available, used on many pages, or very complex, a custom tag should be created.

In the above example, we short-stepped the custom tag implementation process. We specified the tag library and path in the directive rather than defining a URI in the Web Deployment Descriptor and using the URI in the directive. The advantage to using a URI is that if the tag library is moved or renamed, only the Web Deployment Descriptor needs to be modified. If the actual path is specified in the directive, every page that uses that tag library has to be updated.

So, we will create a URI for the tag library. In addition, a new custom tag for a state drop-down menu will be created. We will then create new JSPs to use the custom tag and show how a custom tag is easily reused and modified. Finally, we will demonstrate how to pass information to a tag handler using a **tag attribute**.

Tutorial: Defining a URI

There are many types of deployment descriptors. Essentially, they all contain configuration information that the server will need to deploy an application. The term "configuration information" covers a wide range of information like security settings, data locations and, no coincidence here, tag library locations. The directory path and file that a URI corresponds to is a great example of information "the sever will need to deploy the application" because the application would not work if the deployment descriptor did not contain this information. As mentioned, the advantage is that this is information is specified in one location (a file called web.xml) rather than in all the JSPs and servlets. In RAD, you must create the deployment descriptor.

1. In the Project Explorer, right-click the project TutorialsWeb and select Java EE then Generate Deployment Descriptor Stub.

A file called web.xml will be created in the WebContent/WEB-INF folder. The file can be edited directly with a text editor but there a more user friendly tool called the Deployment Descriptor Editor.

2. Invoke the deployment descriptor editor by right clicking the web.xml file, select Open With, then Web Application 3.0 Deployment Descriptor Editor.

3. Initially the XML source code will be displayed. Change to the Design view by clicking the Design Tab in the lower left corner of the pane (see Figure 11-2).

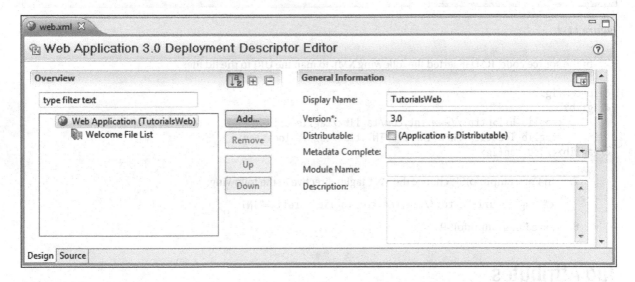

```
  1  <?xml version="1.0" encoding="UTF-8"?>
  2  <web-app xmlns="http://java.sun.com/xml/ns/javaee" xmlns:xsi="http://www.w3.org/2001/XMLSche
  3      <display-name>TutorialsWeb</display-name>
  4      <welcome-file-list>
  5          <welcome-file>index.html</welcome-file>
  6          <welcome-file>index.htm</welcome-file>
  7          <welcome-file>index.jsp</welcome-file>
  8          <welcome-file>default.html</welcome-file>
  9          <welcome-file>default.htm</welcome-file>
 10          <welcome-file>default.jsp</welcome-file>
 11      </welcome-file-list>
 12  </web-
 13
```

Figure 11-2.

The Design view makes the Deployment Descriptor look very organized (see Figure 11-3). In actuality, the Deployment Descriptor (the web.xml file) simply contains a lot of XML.

Figure 11-3.

We will use the editor's Variable view to insert the XML that maps the URI http://www.tnt.com/taglib to /WEB-INF/tls/TNT.tld.

4. To add the URI entry, click the Add button and from the Add Item window click JSP Configuration then the OK button.

5. In the Design view, JSP Configuration item will be displayed and be selected. Simply click the Add button again and select Taglib from the Add Item window.

389

The Design view will be redisplayed with a Details area.

6. Specify /WEB-INF/tls/TNT.tld as the location of the tag library, http://www.tnt.com/taglib as the URI (see Figure 11-4) and save the file.

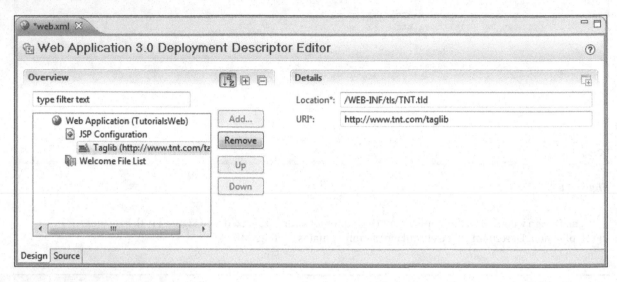

Figure 11-4.

In the source code, RAD inserted the following XML to map the URI to the tld file:

```
<jsp-config>
<taglib>
        <taglib-uri>http://www.tnt.com/taglib</taglib-uri>
        <taglib-location>/WEB-INF/tls/TNT.tld</taglib-location>
</taglib></jsp-config>
```

7. In EnterEmpInfoJSP, change the TNT taglib directive to the following:

   `<%@taglib uri="http://www.tnt.com/taglib" prefix="TNT`

8. Save EnterEmpInfoJSP.

Tag Attributes

Attributes are relatively easy to define and even easier to use. As a matter of fact, you have already used attributes in the application. (The **include** tag inserted into the JSP specified both **page** and **flush** attributes.) To define and use an attribute:

A. In the tag class, define a variable with getter and setter methods

B. In the tag library, define an attribute with the same name as the variable

C. Specify the attribute value as part of the tag in a JSP

The state drop-down menu will have an optional attribute called **selected** that allows a designer to specify a state abbreviation to be selected when the drop-down menu is displayed. The following XML code identifies the tag, tag handler, and defines the tag attribute selected.

```
<tag>
        <name>stateDDM</name>
        <tagclass>c11.TNTStateDDM</tagclass>
<attribute>
                <name>selected</name>
                <required>false</required>
</attribute>
    </tag>
```

The **required** tag is not required because attributes by default are optional. However, to define a required attribute, the "subelement" **required** must be specified and its value set to true.

An attribute must be specified in the start tag to make it available to the doStartTag method. The attribute name is specified after the tag name, separated by at least one space. For example, the following would define GA as the selected value in the custom tag stateDDM:

```
<TNT:stateDDM selected="GA"></TNT:stateDDM >
```

When the server encounters the keyword selected, the setter (in the TNTStateDDM tag handler class) will be invoked and passed the value GA. The TNTStateDDM class must check the value of the variable selected and generate the appropriate HTML such that the value is selected in the drop-down menu.

How to Generate a Visual Component

The stateDDM tag will generate a drop-down menu that has only three values to choose from FL, GA, and OK. (The tag handler c11.TNTStateDDM, of course, is actually doing all the work. In this case, the work entails inserting the HTML that defines the drop-down menu into the JSP. TNTStateDDM will do this similarly to how servlets manipulate a page. In a servlet, the programmer had to:

A. Create a `PrintWriter` object

B. Tie the print writer to the response object

C. Run the print writer's println method and embed the HTML in the response object

The tag handler (TNTStateDDM) will do the same, however, the JSP container (part of the server) makes things much easier by providing a `JspWriter` that is already associated with the JSP response object. In other words, the tag handler does not have to perform steps A and B from above. Rather the JSP writer is retrieved (using the ever-useful **PageContext** object) and the write method is executed. The following statement will do this:

```
pageContext.getOut().write("HTML to be embedded");
```

There is just one small hitch. Notice that the following HTML (which defines a drop-down menu, with the three state abbreviation options, and FL specified as the selected value) contains double quotes and that the write command above requires that the HTML be enclosed in double quotes.

```
<SELECT name="stateDDM">
        <OPTION value="FL" selected>FL</OPTION>
        <OPTION value="GA">GA</OPTION>
        <OPTION value="OK">OK</OPTION>
</SELECT>
```

As soon as the first double quote in the HTML is encountered, the RAD source editor will think that the code to be embedded is finished. In other words, if the following write statement (with the double quotes around stateDDM) is specified:

```
pageContext.getOut().write("<SELECT name="stateDDM">");
```

RAD will read this far in the statement:

```
pageContext.getOut().write("<SELECT name="
```

and think that only <SELECT name= should be embedded in the JSP. To make matters worse, RAD expects an ending parenthesis and semicolon to finish the write statement. When instead RAD runs into the remaining HTML, the entire statement will be flagged as an error.

Fortunately, RAD (and most editors) can be forced to include special characters, such as a double quote, as part of the parameter value rather than as part of the statement's syntax by preceding the special character with a backslash (\). So, each time a double quote appears in the HTML, it must be preceded with a backslash. The correct statement to insert the first line is:

```
pageContext.getOut().write("<SELECT name=\"StateDDM\">");
```

TNTStateDDM will set FL as the default selected value but must check the selected attribute to see if another value should be selected instead.

The last thing we will do is change the JSP so that it uses the new tag stateDDM. This is going to be a little tricky. Currently, we import the entire EnterEmpInfoForm.html file that includes a state text field. We no longer want to do that. Instead, we want to include the beginning of the form (up to but not including the current state field definition). Then we want to insert the new custom tag for stateDDM and then an **include** tag .for the remaining portion of the EnterEmpInfoForm.html file. Two new files called StartEEIF.html and EndEEIF.html will be created to hold the HTML needed to define the form around the new tag. We will then add the **include** tags for the new files and the stateDDM tag into EnterEmpInfoJSP.

Tutorial: Generating a Visual Component

Let's generate a visual component:

1. Close all edit and browser sessions.

2. In Java Resources/src/c11, create a new Java class called TNTStateDDM with a super class of **TagSupport** and no method stubs.

3. In TNTStateDDM, add the following statement to create a class variable called selected with a default value of FL.

   ```
   private String selected = "FL";
   ```

4. In TNTStateDDM, click Source, then Generate Getters and Setters. . .

5. On the Generate Getters and Setters window, click the check box to the left of the variable selected so that both the getter and setter are and click the OK button.

6. In TNTStateDDM, click Source, then Override/Implement Methods. . .

7. At the Override/Implement Methods window, click on the doStartTag() checkbox to select it.

8. Change the insertion point option to Last method and click the OK button.

The following source code should be in the class:

```java
package c11;
import javax.servlet.jsp.JspException;
import javax.servlet.jsp.tagext.TagSupport;
public class TNTStateDDM extends TagSupport {
        private String selected = "FL";
        public String getSelected() {
                return selected;
        }
        public void setSelected(String selected) {
                this.selected = selected;
        }
        public int doStartTag() throws JspException {
                return super.doStartTag();
        }
}
```

9. In doStartTag, before the return statement, add the following two statements to define the drop-down menu (make sure there is a blank line between them):

```java
pageContext.getOut().write("<SELECT name=\"stateDDM\">");
pageContext.getOut().write("</SELECT>");
```

These statements will be flagged as errors because the write method can throw an exception. We will have RAD generate the appropriate **try/catch**..

10. Select the statements and click Source, Surround With, and then Try/catch Block.

The **try/catch** statements will be added and the statements will no longer be flagged as errors.

Arrays

Before we go any further, we have to cover a topic that should have been covered much earlier: arrays. An array is a "structure" that can hold many primitive values or many reference variables of the same type. In other words, an array could be defined to hold multiple **int** values or multiple **String** variables. However, an array cannot be defined to hold both **int** values and **String** variables. Another way to say this is that arrays are *typed*. When the array is defined, the type of values it will hold must be specified. So for example, the following would define an array object that can hold seven **int** values:

```java
new int[7];
```

Of course, this new array of integers can't be accessed because it was assigned to a variable. To use this array, an integer array variable (e.g., myFirstArray) must be defined and the array assigned to it as follows:

```java
int[] myFirstArray = new int[7];
```

Great, we have achieved array! Maybe we should put something into the array? To reference a particular array "bucket," simply specify the bucket's index/position number and assign a value using the equal sign. For instance, the following would assign the value 42 to the fifth bucket:

```java
myFirstArray[4] = 42;
```

You can think about the array as looking like the following:

0	0	0	0	42	0	0

Are you wondering why the value 42 is where it is? Can you guess why? The first bucket has an index number of zero. In other words, the first bucket is referred to as myFirstArray[0]. So, myFirstArray[4] actually refers to the fifth bucket (or position) within the array. To reiterate, an array with a length of seven has seven buckets with position/index numbers ranging from zero to six. You can think of the array and its index numbers as looking like the following:

Index Number 0 1 2 3 4 5 6

0	0	0	0	42	0	0

Be careful, the index numbers are a source of countless errors!

Are you also wondering where all the zeros come from? The JVM inserts initial values when an array is created. For numeric arrays, that value is zero (character arrays are set to the character 0 and referenced variable arrays are set to null).

We are going to use an array to store our state values. Using an array will make adding or deleting states from the stateDDM tag much easier. For example, if we did not use an array, the following code would be needed to define the three state options in a drop-down menu:

```
<SELECT name="stateDDM">
       <OPTION value="FL">FL</OPTION>
       <OPTION value="GA">GA</OPTION>
       <OPTION value="OK">OK</OPTION>
</SELECT>
```

If we wanted to add five states, we would have to add five start and end OPTION tags with the new abbreviations specified in the body of the tags. Unfortunately, because the page designer can specify a state to be selected, it's even more complicated. The tag handler needs to check the selected variable's value and generate the appropriate HTML for that option to be selected. For example, if selected equals FL, the following HTML must be generated.

```
<OPTION value="FL" selected>FL</OPTION>
```

So, the tag handler needs several **if** statements like the following:

```
if (selected == "FL"){
 <OPTION value="FL" selected>FL</OPTION>
} else{
       <OPTION value="FL">FL</OPTION>}
if (selected == "GA"){
<OPTION value="GA" selected>GA</OPTION>
} else{
       <OPTION value="GA">GA</OPTION>}
if (selected == "OK"){
<OPTION value="OK" selected>OK</OPTION>
} else{
       <OPTION value="OK">OK</OPTION>}
```

Now when five states need to be added, the programmer must enter five **if/else** statements and ten start and end OPTION tags. That's a lot of typing and, of course, this means mistakes can easily be made. To cut down on the amount of "hard-coded" HTML, a **String** array will hold the state values and a **for** loop will:

1. Read each value in the array

2. Check if the array value is the selected value

3. Build the appropriate OPTION tags.

Tutorial: Using an Array

Now let's use an array

1. In TNTStateDDM, add the following statements to create a class String array variable called stateArray that has the following three values.

    ```
    String[] stateArray = {"FL", "GA", "OK"};
    ```

Notice that no size was specified for the array. An array can be assigned values, and the JVM will create an array of the needed size - in this case three.

2. In TNTStateDDM, add the following statements to create class **StringBuffer** variables to hold various "pieces" of the OPTION tags.

    ```
    StringBuffer optionTagStart = new StringBuffer("<OPTION value=\"");
    StringBuffer optionSelected = new StringBuffer("\" selected>");
    StringBuffer optionNotSelected = new StringBuffer("\">");
    StringBuffer optionTagEnd = new StringBuffer("</OPTION>");
    StringBuffer optionTags = new StringBuffer();
    ```

Because the HTML to define each option will be constantly changing in the loop, defining optionTags as a StringBuffer is a more computer-efficient choice than defining it as a String. However, because only Strings can be embedded into the JSP, we will need to convert the StringBuffer to a String thereby adding a little extra code.

Notice that when a state is to be selected, only the start tag is different from a non-selected state. In other words, the end tag never changes. Looking closer at the start tags, notice that non-selected and selected OPTION tags actually begin the same. The difference is the characters that follow the value attribute in the start tag. If a value is not selected, then the value in the start tag is simply followed by a double quote and a greater than sign. If the value is selected, then it is followed by a double quote, a space, the keyword **selected**, and then the greater than sign. So, two strings (optionSelected and optionNotSelected) were created to hold these two possible sets of characters.

3. In the doStartTag, between the two write statements, insert the following statements

    ```
    for (int ctr = 0; ctr < stateArray.length; ctr++) {
    optionTags.append(optionTagStart).append(stateArray[ctr]);
    if (stateArray[ctr] == this.selected) {
            optionTags.append(optionSelected);
    } else {
            optionTags.append(optionNotSelected);
    }
    optionTags.append(stateArray[ctr]).append(optionTagEnd);
    pageContext.getOut().write(String.valueOf(optionTags));
    optionTags.delete(0,optionTags.length());
    }
    ```

You should note several things. The **for** loop's counter (ctr) is initialized to zero to correspond to the index value of the array's first position/bucket. The loops test condition checks that the count is less than the length of the array. Think about that. If the array has a length of three, the largest index value in the array is two (i.e., the array has three values with index values of 0, 1, and 2). We want the **for** to execute three times for the counter values of 0, 1, and 2. So we want the **for** to only execute when the variable ctr is less than the length of the array (3).

Inside the loop, the constant text that comprises the beginning of the start OPTION tag (optionTagStart) is concatenated to the state value stored in the first position of the array (i.e., FL). This means that after the first statement in the loop, optionTags has the following value:

```
<OPTION value="FL
```

The **if** statement then compares the value in the first array position to the variable select-ed's value. Based on whether they are equal or not, either the optionSelected or optionNotSelected string is concatenated to (and finishes) the start OPTION tag. In this case, we'll assume that no attribute value was specified by the page designer and that the value of selected is the default value FL. This means that the characters stored in optionSelected are appended to optionTags resulting in a value of:

```
<OPTION value="FL" selected>
```

Next, the state abbreviation to appear in the drop-down menu (i.e., the value in position 0 of the array) and the end tag are appended to optionTags, resulting in a character string of:

```
<OPTION value="FL" selected>FL</OPTION>
```

The OPTION tag for the first state value is converted to a String and written to the JSP. The contents of optionTags is deleted and the loop begins again (the counter value is incremented by one, compared against the length of the array, etc). The loop will execute two more times and the HTML for the two remaining state values will be embedded into the JSP.

Because of the array and loop, if five states had to be added, five state values would simply be added to the array definition. No other java code or HTML statements would be needed to add the five states.

4. Save TNTStateDDM.

Tutorial: Defining and Using the Custom Tag

We can now define and use the tag

1. In TNT.tld add the following XML after the getEmp tag definition:

```
<tag>
        <name>stateDDM</name>
        <tagclass>c11.TNTStateDDM</tagclass>
        <attribute>
                <name>selected</name>
                <required>false</required >
        </attribute>
</tag>
```

2. Save TNT.tld.

3. Bring up c11/EnterEmpInfoForm.html in the Page Designer and click on the state input field.

4. Switch to the Source view.

The cursor should be positioned at the beginning of the state field's INPUT tag (indicated by the first arrow in Figure 11-5).

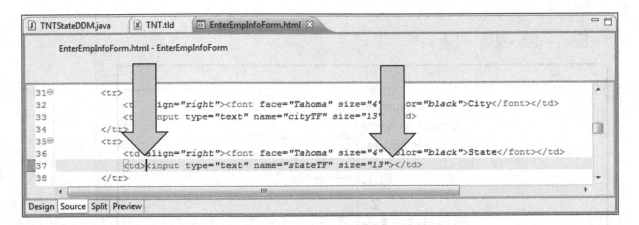

Figure 11-5.

All the HTML before the INPUT tag will be copied to a file called StartEEIF.html. The HTML after the tag (indicated by the second arrow in Figure 11-5) will be copied to a file called EndEEIF.html. In the JSP, the new stateDDM tag will be inserted and **include** tags for the new html files will be inserted before and after the stateDDM tag.

5. Copy all the HTML before the INPUT tag.

6. In WebContent/c11, create a new Web Page of type HTML/XHTML called StartEEIF.

7. In StartEEIF, select all the default code.

8. Paste the code copied from EnterEmpInfoForm over the default code and save StartEEIF.

9. In EnterEmpInfoForm, copy the HTML after the INPUT tag.

10. In WebContent/c11, create a new file called EndEEIF and paste the code just copied from EnterEmpInfoForm.

11. Save EndEEIF and at the Conflict Encoding window click Yes.

Please note that EndEEIF shouldn't be an HTML file. Because the copied HTML does not define a "complete" page, entering it in an HTML file will generate numerous source code warning messages (that we will ignore) and warnings like the encoding conflict.

12. Bring up EnterEmpInfoJSP in the Page Designer and select the **include** tag (i.e., select the form).

If the **include** tag was selected, the form should be outlined in black and the properties view will show that the jsp:include tab, on the left, is selected (as in Figure 11-6).

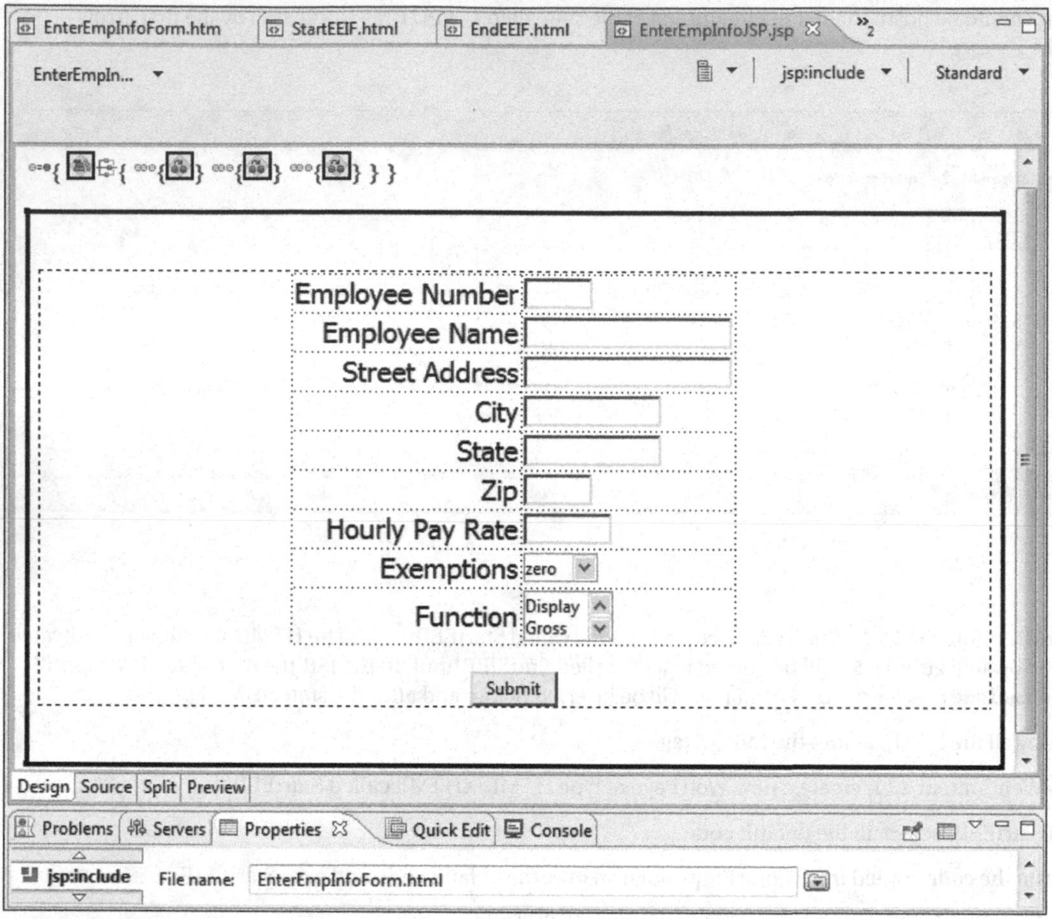

Figure 11-6.

13. Delete the tag by pressing the Delete button.

14. In the JSP tags drawer, click Include and then click beneath the tag icons.

15. At the Insert JSP Include window, specify StartEEIF.html and click the OK button.

The first half of the employee form will be displayed in Page Designer. The new state custom tag needs to be inserted after the half form.

16. Place the insertion point after the include tag by clicking anywhere beneath the half form.

17. Click JSP, and then Insert Custom. . .

Because the taglib directive is already in the JSP, RAD displays the TNT tag library and all its tags. (Click on the other tag library option if you would like to display all the tags in jstl/core tag library.)

18. At the Insert Custom Tag window, select stateDDM (as in Figure 11-7), click the Insert button and then the Close button.

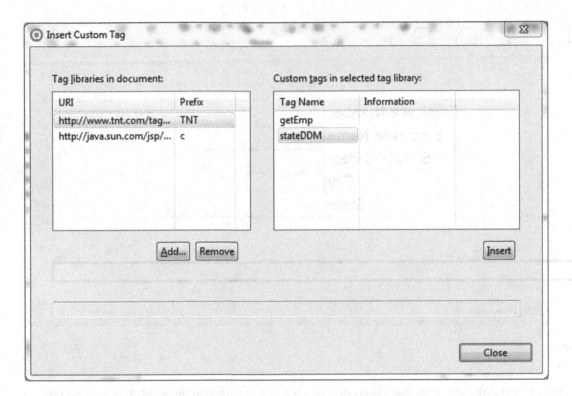

Figure 11-7.

19. In the JSP tags drawer, click Include and then click to the right of the custom tag icon

20. At the Insert JSP Include window, enter EndEEIF.html as the File name and click the OK button.

Page Designer should look like Figure 11-8.

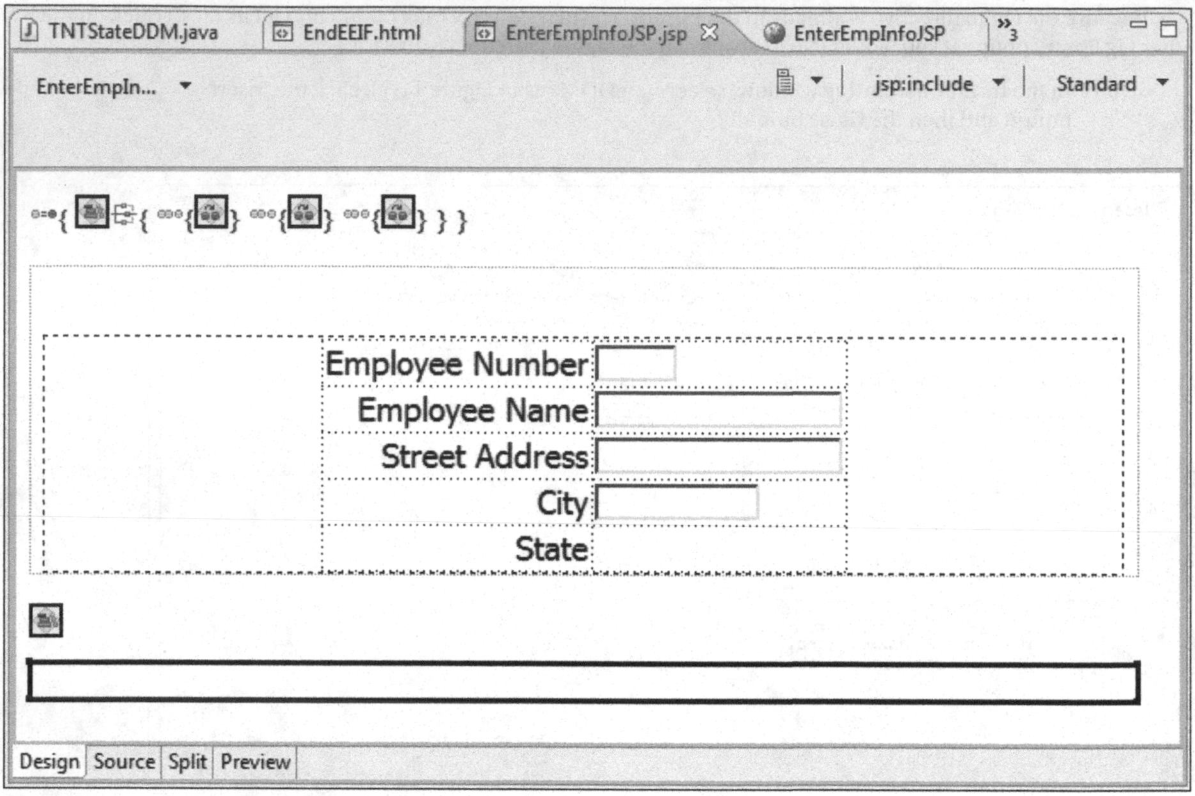

Figure 11-8.

Does Figure 11-8 surprise you? If so, then the Preview view will also be surprising! Remember the browser can only interpret HTML and scripts. Custom tags and JSP tags are resolved by the server (i.e., the server invokes the tag handler class). So, the only way to test a custom tag is to run the JSP on the server.

Tutorial: Testing the Custom Tag

We've built it, so we have to test it:

1. Run EnterEmpInfoJSP on the server.

2. In the browser session, click the refresh button.

The page should look like Figure 11-9.

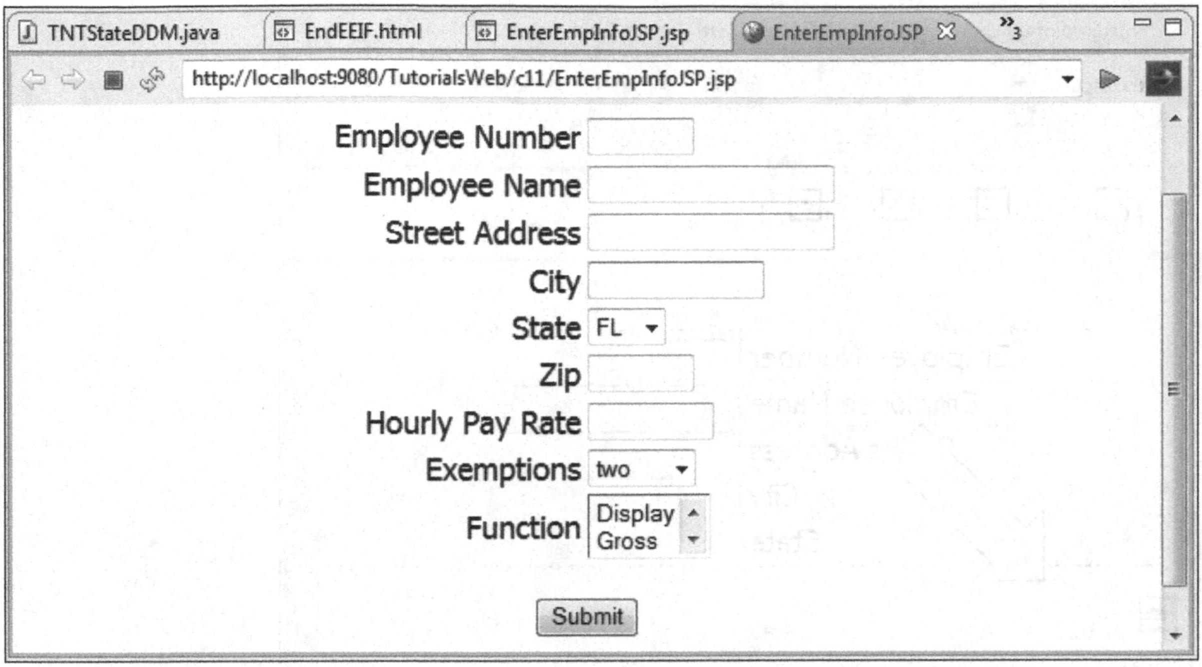

Figure 11-9.

Notice that FL appears as the default value.

3.   Click on the state field's drop-down button and verify that all the state abbreviations are displayed.

4.   Select OK as the state, 10 as the pay rate, Display as the function, and click the Submit button.

Uh-oh, no state value appears. What happened?

Well, we changed the name of the state field from stateTF to stateDDM and EmpExtractor tries to set the Employee object's state property from the value of stateTF. So, we have to change EmpExtractor.

5.   Change c11/EmpExtractor to retrieve stateDDM not stateTF.

6.   Rerun the step 4 test and verify that OK is displayed as the state.

Now we will test that the tag attribute was defined correctly and works.

7.   In the Page Designer, click on EnterEmpInfoJSP's stateDDM custom tag icon (see the first arrow in Figure 11-10).

8.   In the Properties view, enter OK as the value for the attribute selected (see the second arrow in Figure 11-10).

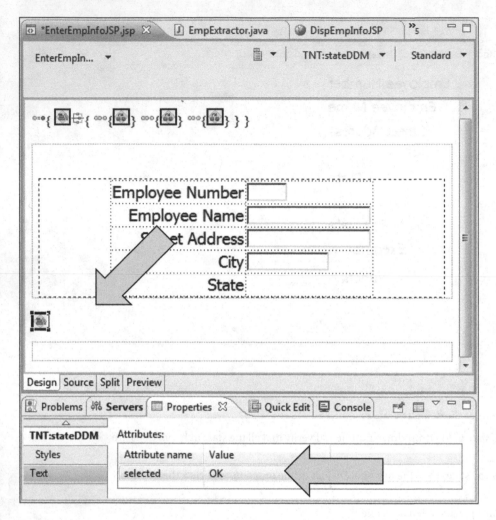

Figure 11-10.

Switching to the Source view would show that RAD has changed the start tag to the following:

```
<TNT:stateDDM selected="OK">
```

9. Save EnterEmpInfoJSP.

10. In the browser go back to EnterEmpInfoJSP and refresh the page.

OK should be displayed as the selected value in the state drop-down menu.

11. Switch to the Source view for EnterEmpInfoJSP and change the value for selected to GA.

12. Save EnterEmpInfoJSP and in the browser refresh the page to show GA is now selected.

Tutorial: Database Access with Tags

We will demonstrate the flexibility and advantages of both the MVC architecture and custom tags by changing the application to work with a DBMS. An Insert JSP (InsEmpInfo.jsp) will be created that allows a user to add employees to the database and that uses the stateDDM custom tag. Two files (StartIEIF.html and EndIEIF) will be created that define the beginning and ending of a form with all the needed data entry fields. New custom tags (insEmp, delEmp) and tag handlers (InsertEmp, DeleteEmp) will be created to perform database inserts and deletions. InsEmpInfo.jsp will use the Employee bean (created by the getEmp tag) and the insEmp and getEmp tags to insert the information.

Specifically, when InsEmpInfo.jsp is first accessed, a data entry form with the stateDDM field will be displayed. After the information has been entered and the form's submit button clicked, InsEmpInfo will be invoked again. InsEmpInfo will check to see if the request is a post and, if so, execute the getEmp tag (to create an Employee bean) and the insEmp tag (to insert the information).

StartEEIF.html and EndEEIF.html have much of the HTML we need for the new form. Therefore, we will use them as the base for StartIEIF.html and EndIEIF.html, thereby avoiding a lot of typing (and probably mistakes).

1. In c11, copy and paste StartEEIF.html as StartIEIF.html and EndEEIF.html as EndIEIF.html.

StartIEIF needs to specify the form action as InsEmpInfo.jsp so that when the button is clicked, InsEmpInfo is invoked again by the server. Also, the title should be changed to StartIEIF.html

2. In the Source view of StartIEIF, change the TITLE and FORM tags to the following:

```
<title>StartIEIF.html</title>
<FORM action="InsEmpInfo.jsp" method="post">
```

EndIEIF needs to define the remaining data entry fields and the end of the form. Because EndEEIF was copied as EndIEIF, the remaining data entry fields already exist in EndIEIF. However, the function options list box (i.e., display, tax and gross amounts) is also in EndIEIF. So, the HTML that defines the table row holding the function list box and text needs to be deleted.

3. In the Source view of EndIEIF, delete the following HTML:

```
<tr>
<td align="right">
<font face="Tahoma" size="4" color="black">
Function
</font>
</td>
<td>
        <select size="2" name="functionLB">
                <option value="Display">Display</option>
                <option value="Gross">Gross</option>
                <option value="TaxAmt">TaxAmt</option>
        </select>
</td>
</tr>
```

4. Change the Submit button's text from Submit to Insert.

The button start tag should look like the following:

```
<input type="submit" name="submitBtn" value="Insert">
```

5. Save EndIEIF.

Because EnterEmpInfoJSP has much of the code we need for InsEmpInfo, we will use EnterEmpInfoJSP as the base for InsEmpInfo and, again, save a lot of typing and mistakes.

6.   In c11, copy and paste EnterEmpInfoJSP as InsEmpInfo.jsp.

InsEmpInfo needs to be modified to include the HTML in StartIEIF and EndIEIF.

7.   In the Source or Properties view of InsEmpInfo, change the appropriate **include** tag's page attribute to StartIEIF and EndIEIF.

8.   Save InsEmpInfo.

Let's make sure InsEmpInfo looks right.

9.   Run InsEmpInfo on the server.

The browser should look like Figure 11-11. Notice that the function box is gone and the button has the text Insert. Clicking the drop-down menu button will show the three state options.

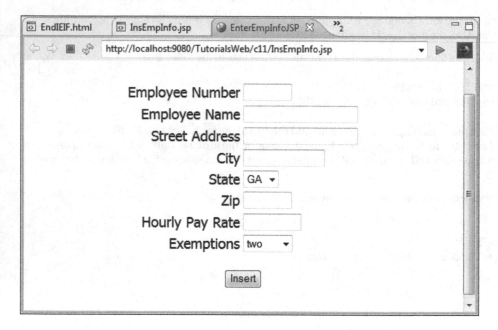

Figure 11-11.

InsEmpInfo must now be modified to create EmpBean and invoke the insert function. However, before that can be done the classes that provide the database functions must be created.

10.   Copy Employee and DBAccess fromTutorials/src/c10 to TutorialsWeb/Java Resources/src/ c11. (If you are working in a complex environment, the particular "database classes" and the DB class need to be copied instead of DBAccess.)

Because the client-based application followed the MVC architecture (i.e., the model is separate from the view and controller), implementing the database functions in a server-based application is almost as simple as copying and pasting the model classes. In other words, because the model was built independently of the view, the classes that comprise the model can be easily used in projects that use different views. If the client-based application had embedded the database functions in a **Frame** subclass (i.e., combined the view and model functions), the database functions could not have been simply copied into a server-based application.

However, just as with the client-based application, the correct database driver needs to be available for the Employee class. If DB2 or Oracle is being used, the driver must be added to the Web App Libraries in the project's Java build path.

11. If the DBMS is DB2 or Oracle, import or copy the DBMS driver file into the WebContent/WEB-INF/lib folder (if the folder lib does not exist, create it).

12. If the DBMS is Oracle, change the suffix of the driver file from .zip to .jar.

13. To prove that the driver was added successfully, right click TutorialsWeb and select Properties.

14. At the Properties for TutorialsWeb window, select Java Build Path, then expand the Web App Libraries item.

The driver file should appear as in Figure 11-12.

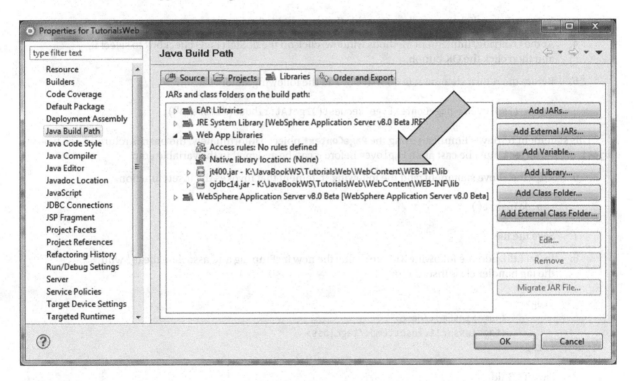

Figure 11-12.

If you are using an Access database, you will have to move the database on to the RAD test server. Access databases cannot be accessed remotely, so they must reside on the server.

15. If you are using Access, copy the TNT.mdb file to the folder containing the RAD test server. For example, if you have a standard installation of RAD with one test server, the server definition would be in C:\Program Files\IBM\SDP70\runtimes\base_v8\profiles\AppSrv01.

If you can't figure out the location of the server definition, after we create and implement the insert tag, simply run the insert JSP and try to insert an employee. The resulting error messages will display the folder location.

All that needs to be done now is to make the view (InsEmpInfo) invoke the model (i.e., the Employee class's insert function). As mentioned, a new tag call insEmp will be created to perform the insert function. The tag will be added to InsEmpInfo such that the insEmp tag is executed after the button is clicked.

Tutorial: Modifying the View

Let's make the necessary changes:

1. In Java Resources/src/c11, create a new Java class called InsertEmp with a super class of **TagSupport** and no method stubs.

2. In InsertEmp, add the following statements to define an Employee class variable called emp.

   ```
   private Employee emp;
   ```

3. In InsertEmp, click Source, then Override/Implement Methods. . .

4. At the Override/Implement Methods window, click on the doStartTag() checkbox to select it, and then click the OK button.

5. Before the return statement in doStartTag, add the following statement:

   ```
   emp = (Employee) pageContext.getRequest().getAttribute("EmpBean");
   ```

This statement retrieves EmpBean using the **PageContext** object. Unfortunately, the bean is returned as a type of **Object**. So, the **Object** must be cast as an Employee before it can be assigned to the variable emp.

6. After the above statement, add the following statement that invokes the insert function.

   ```
   emp.doInsert();
   ```

7. Save the file

8. In TNT.tld, add the following XML to define the new insEmp tag and associate the tag with the tag handler class InsertEmp:

   ```xml
   <tag>
           <name>insEmp</name>
           <tagclass>c11.InsertEmp</tagclass>
   </tag>
   ```

9. Save TNT.tld.

10. In InsEmpInfo.jsp, delete the **choose**, **when**, and **forward** tags.

This can be done by deleting the source code in the Source view or by selecting the choose icon in Page Designer (see Figure 11-13) and pressing the Delete key.

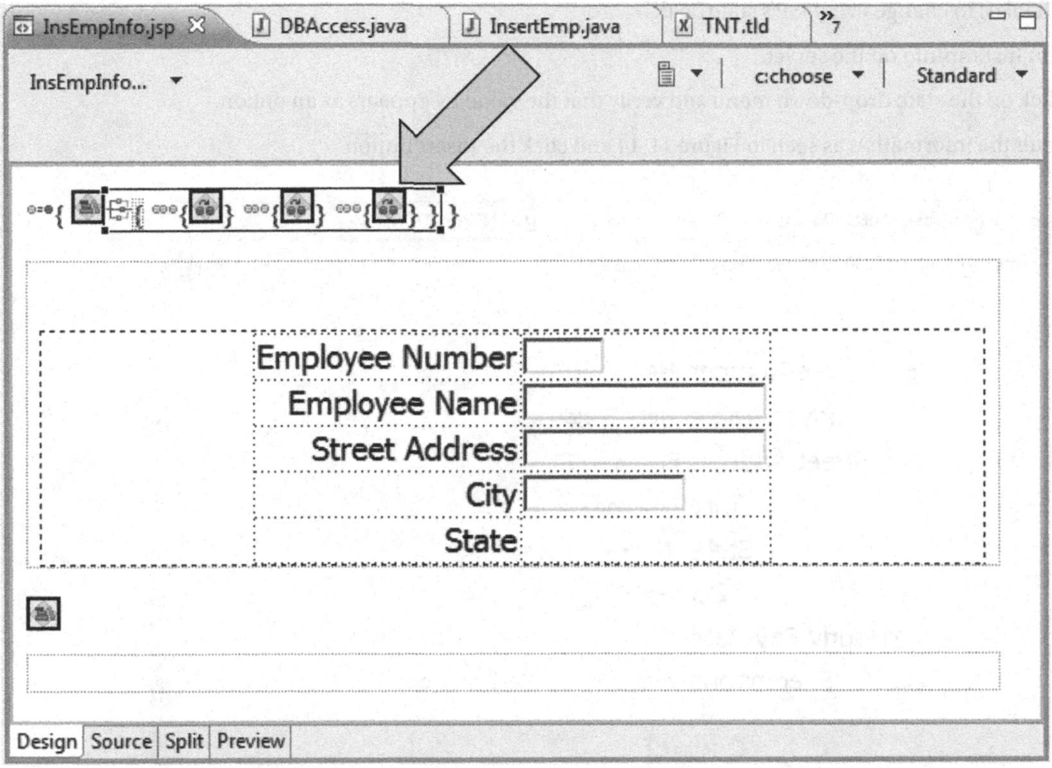

Figure 11-13.

11. After the getEmp end tag, add the insEmp start and end tags and save the file.

The **if** and custom tags should look like the following:

```
<c:if test='${pageContext.request.method=='POST'}'>
        <TNT:getEmp>
        </TNT:getEmp>
        <TNT:insEmp></TNT:insEmp>
</c:if>
```

As with most tags, the custom tags can be specified even more simply as follows:

```
<TNT:getEmp/> <TNT:insEmp/>
```

The last modification needed is to add a new state (IN) to all the state drop-down menus throughout the application. If the state drop-down menu had been defined directly in multiple JSPs, all the JSPs would have to be modified. Because the state drop-down menu is a custom visual component (implemented with custom tags), making this application-wide change means simply updating the tag handler.

12. In TNTStateDDM, add the value IN (for Indiana) to the array definition so that IN appears after GA, and then save the file.

That's all it takes to change every JSP's state field.

13. Run InsEmpInfo on the server.

14. Click on the state drop-down menu and verify that the value IN appears as an option.

15. Enter the information as seen in Figure 11-14 and click the Insert button.

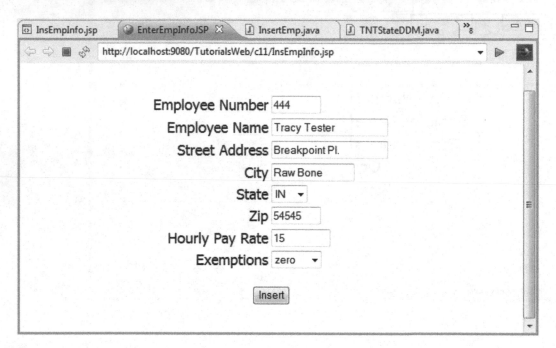

Figure 11-14.

The InsEmpInfo page will be redisplayed and all the data removed from the fields. But, did it work? Well, if you can access the database directly, display the Employee table and verify that the record was inserted. However, to prove that the insert worked, we will modify the get-Emp tag (i.e., CrtEmpBean.java) so that database information will be displayed.

Tutorial: Modifying the Tag Handler

CrtEmpBean will be modified to check the database when an employee number is entered on EnterEmpInfoJSP. If there is employee information in the database, then any information that came from the form (i.e., that is in EmpBean) will be overwritten with the database information. As before, the display page will then display the EmpBean data. We will also modify the display page to include the gross salary and tax amounts for the employee and provide the option to delete the employee information from the database.

1. In CrtEmpBean's doStartTag method, after the Employee object is assigned to emp but before EmpBean is defined, add the following statement:

```
emp.getEmpInfo(pageContext.getRequest().getParameter("empNumTF").toString());
```

This statement retrieves the employee number entered in the empNumTF field using the request object's getParameter method. Just as when page context was used to get the Employee bean, a parameter is returned as an object of type **Object**. In this case, the **Object** object is converted to a **String** using its own toString method (rather than casting it, as was done earlier). Finally, the employee number is passed to the Employee class's getEmpInfo method. This method retrieves employee information from the database and populates all the Employee object's properties. If there is no employee record, the information entered on the page will not be overwritten.

This is not the most efficient way to perform this function. For instance, the Employee object may be written to twice - once with the form data and then possibly again with the database information. For efficiency, the database should be checked before the form information is added to the employee object. Then, only if there is no information for the employee in the database, should the object be populated with the form information. However, this inefficient solution is simpler to code because only one Java statement is needed.

Notice how easy it was to access the database: one statement. Remember, this was easy because the client-based application was implemented using the MVC architecture. Following the MVC architecture not only standardizes application design, it also makes applications more flexible and easier to modify.

Tutorial: Deleting Records Using a Custom Tag

DispEmpInfoJSP needs two new fields to display the gross salary and tax amounts along with all the other employee information. All the fields will be included on a form with a delete button. When pressed, the delete button will forward the request to a confirmation JSP (ConfirmEmpDel, see Figure 11-18). If the user clicks the confirm button on the page, the request will be forwarded to a delete employee JSP (EmpDel) where the record will be deleted and a message displayed confirming the delete (see Figure 11-19). A new delete tag (delEmp) will be defined and added to the EmpDel JSP.

1. In JavaSource/src/c11, create a new Java class called DeleteEmp with a super class of **TagSupport** and no method stubs.

2. In DeleteEmp, add the following statements to define an Employee class variable.

   private Employee emp;

3. In DeleteEmp, click Source, then Override/Implement Methods. . .

4. At the Override/Implement Methods window, click on the doStartTag() checkbox to select it, and then click the OK button.

5. In the doStartTag method, before the return statement, add the following statement:

   ```
   emp = (Employee) pageContext.getRequest().getAttribute("EmpBean");
   ```

6. Add the following statement to invoke the Employee delete function and save the file:

   ```
   emp.doDelete();
   ```

Is the procedure for creating a custom tag starting to seem familiar? As a quick reminder, the steps are:

A. Create a tag support class

B. Add the XML to the tag library

C. Insert the tag library directive and tag into a JSP

Steps 1 through 6 did A. Step 7 and 8 will do B and, after creating two JSPs, steps 20 through 24 will do C.

7. In TNT.tld, add the following XML to define the new delEmp tag and associate the tag with the Java tag handler class DeleteEmp:

```
<tag>
        <name>delEmp</name>
        <tagclass>c11.DeleteEmp</tagclass>
</tag>
```

8. Save TNT.tld.

9. In WebContent/c11, create two new JSPs called ConfirmEmpDel and EmpDel.

10. In ConfirmEmpDel, insert a Form from the Form Tags tray and then insert following centered text (the font is Verdana) into the form:

```
Please confirm that employee

should be permanently deleted from the database
by clicking the Confirm button
```

11. In the JSP Tags drawer, click on Get Property and then click on the blank line (after the first line of text).

12. At the Insert JSP Get Property window specify the Bean type as session, EmpBean as the Bean name, empName as the Property name and click the OK button.

13. In Page Designer, select the Get Property tag by clicking at the end of the first line of text and then dragging the cursor to the second line of text.

This will select the tag and the line breaks (as in Figure 11-15).

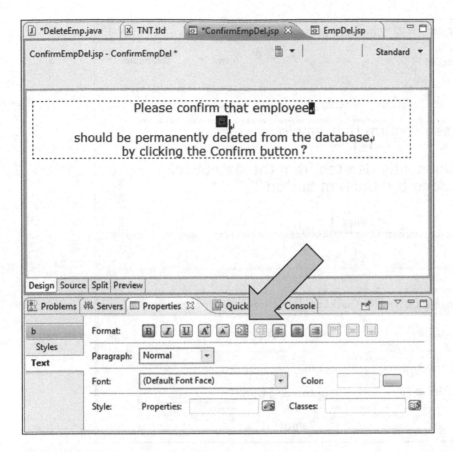

Figure 11-15.

14. In the Properties view, click the text tab (on the left) and then click the bold button (indicated by the arrow in Figure 11-15).

15. Insert a blank line after the text. Then, in the Form Tags drawer, click on Submit Button and then click on the blank line.

16. At the Insert Submit Button window, specify ConfirmBtn as the Name, Confirm as the Label, and click the OK button.

17. If needed, horizontally center the Confirm button on the page.

18. Select the form and in the Properties view, specify EmpDel.jsp as the action and select Post as the Method.

Page Designer and the Properties view should look like Figure 11-16.

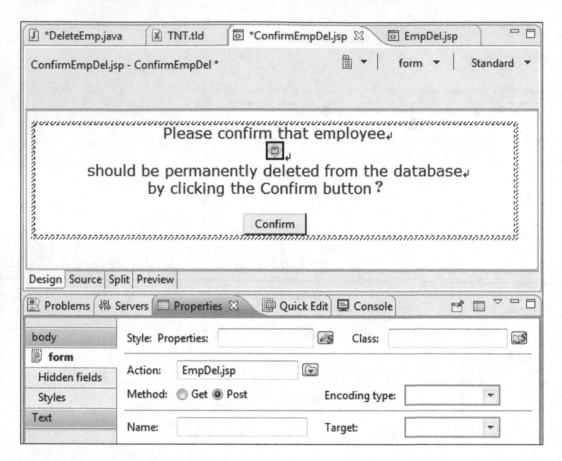

Figure 11-16.

The delEmp tag needs to be added to EmpDel.jsp and EmpDel.jsp should display a message saying the employee information has been deleted.

19. In the Page Designer view of EmpDel.jsp, click Custom in the JSP Tags drawer and then click anywhere on the page.

The Insert Custom Tag Window will be displayed with no URIs listed in the left pane or tags in the right pane. The taglib directive for the TNT tag library needs to be added to the page so that the delEmp tag can be specified.

20. On the Insert Custom Tag Window, click the Add... button.

21. Click the radio button for Show all valid URI choices and specify TNT as the Prefix

22. Scroll down the list, click the checkbox for the www.tnt.com URI name and click the OK button.

The Insert Custom Tag Window will be displayed with the TNT tag library URI displayed in the left pane and the four TNT tags listed in the right pane.

23. Select delEmp, click the Insert button, and then the Close button.

In the Source view, notice that RAD added the following taglib directive and custom tags:

```
<%@taglib prefix="TNT uri="http://www.tnt.com/taglib"%>
<TNT:delEmp></TNT:delEmp>
```

24. In Design view, click Get Property and then click to the right of the custom tag.

25. At the Insert JSP Get Property window, specify session as the Bean Type, EmpBean for the bean name, empName as the Property name, and click the OK button.

26. After the getProperty tag, add the text: has been deleted from the database.

Even though the employee information will be deleted from the database, the employee bean still exists. Therefore, we can still retrieve the name of the employee that was deleted and display it in the deletion message. We are now going to add the tax and salary amounts to the display page.

27. In the Page Designer view of DisplayEmpInfoJSP, click on the last row of the table.

28. In the Command Bar, click Table, and then Add Row Below.

There should now be two blank rows at the end of the table.

29. Add the text Gross Salary: and Tax Amount: in the first column of the two blank rows and format the text to match the existing table text.

30. In the second column of the new rows, add the appropriate getProperty tags to display EmpBean's gross amount and tax amount properties.

31. In the Form Tags drawer, click on Submit button and then, in Page Designer, click beneath the table.

32. At the Insert Submit Button window, specify DeleteBtn as the name, Delete as the Label, then click the OK button.

33. Horizontally center the button.

34. In the Forms Tag tray, click on Form then click before the first line of text. Cut and paste all the page components into the form.

35. In the Properties view, specify ConfirmEmpDel.jsp as the form action and the Method Post.

Page Designer and the Properties view should look like Figure 11-17.

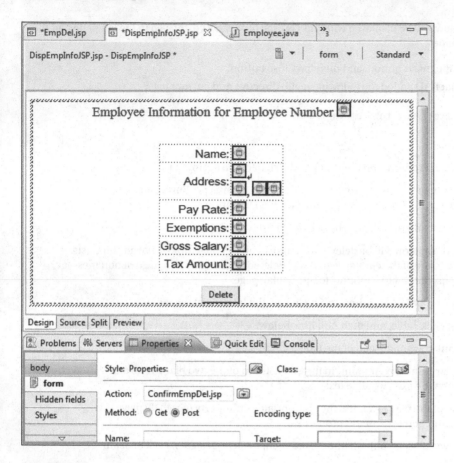

Figure 11-17.

36. Save all changed files.

Tutorial: Testing the Insert and Delete

First, we will verify that the insert was performed and then test the delete function.

1. Run c11/EnterEmpInfoJSP on the server, specify 444 as the Employee number, Display as the Function, and click the Submit button.

The Tracy Tester information and a Delete button should be displayed. This proves that the insert performed earlier worked.

2. Click the Delete button.

An error message will be displayed in the browser saying that the confirm page cannot be displayed. In the console pane, the reason for the error will be a null bean. What happened? When the Delete button was clicked (on the display page), a new request was created and forwarded to the confirm page. The new request does not have an EmpBean. "Why not?" you ask.

Because EmpBean was defined with a scope of request. Because EnterEmpInfoJSP created a new request, the EmpBean was not associated with this new request.

There are many ways to solve this problem. We will change the scope of EmpBean from request to session. The bean scope can be changed very easily because the bean is defined in only one place, the CrtEmpBean class. (If bean tags had been used, many JSPs would have had to be updated.) The statement that defines the Employee object as an attribute of the **request** will be changed to define the Employee object as an attribute of the **session**. This means that InsertEmp and DeleteEmp need to be changed to get the bean from the session not the request.

3. In CrtEmpBean, change the statement that defines the bean to:

```
pageContext.getSession().setAttribute("EmpBean", emp);
```

4. In InsertEmp and DeleteEmp, change the statement that gets the bean to:

```
emp = (Employee) pageContext.getSession().getAttribute("EmpBean");
```

Notice that the only change to these statements is that instead of invoking the page context's getRequest method, the getSession method is used.

5. Save the files.

6. In the browser, use the back button to redisplay the EnterEmpInfoJSP (444 should be specified as the Employee number and Display as the Function).

7. Click the Submit button.

Again, the Tracy Tester information and a Delete button should be displayed. This time, however, CrtEmpBean created EmpBean as a session bean.

8. Click the Delete button.

The Tracy Tester name should be displayed with the text and a Confirm button as in Figure 11-18.

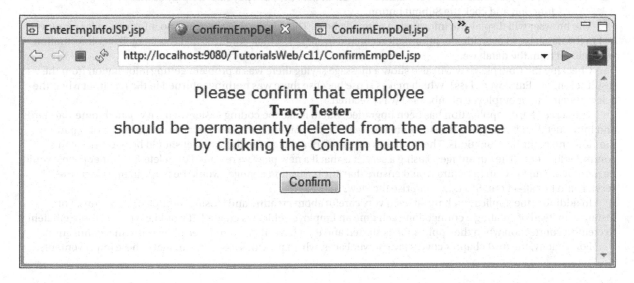

Figure 11-18.

9. Click the Confirm button.

The EmpDel JSP should be run, resulting in the employee record for Tracy Tester being deleted from the database. The browser will display the text that confirms that the record was deleted (see Figure 11-19).

Figure 11-19.

10. To verify that the record was deleted, use the browser's back button to redisplay the Enter-EmpInfoJSP with the employee number 444 specified.

11. Specify Joe as the employee name, FL as the State, 15 for the pay rate, Display as the function and click the Submit button.

The browser will display the information entered above. This means that there was no information for employee 444 in the database to override the information entered in step 11, which confirms that the Tracy Tester information was deleted from the database.

Checking the Console view will also show a message saying there was a problem getting information from the result set (in the Employee class). Which makes sense because there was nothing returned in the result set when the select statement for employee number 444 was executed.

The server-based application has been upgraded, but to make the coding easier we have violated some standards and introduced inefficiencies. One violation that we have not pointed out is that the application does not separate the view and controller functions. The JSP pages contain forward tags. Really, a servlet should be performing this controller function. The advantage to using a servlet is that if a new page were added or deleted, no other pages would be modified. The MVC architecture would ensure that any navigation changes would be made in one place, the servlet, and not affect the JSPs that comprise the view.

In addition, the application has not been very careful about creating and closing multiple connections. For instance, instead of creating a connection each time an Employee object is created, it would have been more efficient to create a connection when the application is started and then have all the employee objects use that connection.

Fortunately, the next chapter covers Java Server Faces, which provides easy tools to make these improvements.

Results of the Tutorial

Let's check our results:

1. In the TutorialsWeb project, a new package in WebContent named c11.

2. In c11, the following nine new files:

    ConfirmEmpDel.jsp

    EndEEIF.html

    EnterEmpInfoForm.html

    InsEmpInfo.jsp

    StartIEIF.htm

    EmpDel.jsp

    EndIEIF.html

    EnterEmpInfoJSP.jsp

    StartEEIF.html

3. Inside of JavaResources/src, a new folder called c11 containing the following seven Java files:

    CrtEmpBean.java

    DeleteEmp.java

    Employee.java

    TNTStateDDM.java

    DBAccess.java

    EmpExtractor.java

    InsertEmp.java

4. Modifications to DispEmpInfoJSP to display the tax and gross salary amounts and an option to delete an employee record from the database

5. The employee Web-based application can now insert, display, and delete employee information in a database using custom tags.

Review Questions

1. What is a tag handler?

2. When defining a custom tag, what is the purpose of the Web Deployment Descriptor?

3. When should a custom tag be created?

4. What is an array?

5. How is XML used to define a custom tag?

6. What is the purpose of a tag library directive in a JSP?

7. How is the **TagSupport** class used when creating a custom tag?

8. Name two methods inherited from the **TagSupport** class.

Review Exercise

The Shipment application will be modified to insert, display, and delete shipment information in a DBMS using custom tags. This will require:

A. Three new tags called crtShipBean, insShip, and delShip

B. Three **TagSupport** subclasses called CrtShipBean, InsertShip, and DeleteShip

C. Five JSPs and two Web pages to perform the View component of the application.

1. In ReviewExWeb/WebContent, create a new folder called c11.

2. In c11, create the following files:

   DispShip.jsp

   DisplayShip.jsp

   ConfirmDel.jsp

   DelShip.jsp

   ConfirmIns.jsp

   EnterShipNum.html

   ConfirmDel.html

3. Copy EnterShipInfoJSP from WebContent/c9 into c11.

4. In ReviewExWeb/Java Resources/src, create a new folder called c11.

5. In Java Resources: src/c11, create the following Java classes as **TagSupport** subclasses with no method stubs:

   CrtShipBean   InsertShip   DeleteShip

6. Copy Shipment.java and DBAccess.java from ReviewEx/src/c10 to Java Resources/src/c11.

7. In Web Content/WEB-INF/, create a new folder called tls and in tls a new file called TNT.tld.

8. In TNT.tld, add the XML to define three tags called crtShipBean, insShip, and delShip and associate them with the appropriate Java classes.

9. Add the XML to define a required attribute called **source** for the crtShipBean tag.

10. Create a deployment descriptor stub and add `http://www.tnt.com/taglib` as tag library reference URI and /WEB-INF/tls/TNT.tld as the location of the tab library.

11. In c11/EnterShipInfoJSP, change the form action from /ReviewExWeb/ShipInfoServlet to EnterShipInfoJSP.jsp.

12. In c11/EnterShipInfoJSP before the form, insert an **if** tag with a test that checks if the request type is a post.

13. Change c11/EnterShipInfoJSP, so that if the request is a post, the crtShipBean tags are executed with the **source** attribute specified as **request**. (Make sure the tags prefixes are TNT.)

14. Change c11/EnterShipInfoJSP, so that after the ShipBean is created the insShip tags are executed and a JSP **forward** to ConfirmIns.jsp is executed.

The Shipment application never had an extractor class (as the employee application did). Therefore, the CrtShipBean class will perform that function (i.e., retrieve the Shipment information from the request and populate the Shipment object properties). The Java Resources/ src/c11/CrtShipBean's doStartTag method needs to be overridden to do the following:

If the **source** attribute is equal to request:

A. Create a null Shipment object.

B. Retrieve the shipment information (from the request parameter values) and set the appropriate shipment properties.

If the **source** attribute is equal to database:

A. Create a Shipment object using the shipment number entered in shipNumTF

Then, in either case, define the Shipment object as a session attribute called ShipBean.

15. To do the above, add the following class variables definitions to CrtShipBean:

```
private String source = null;
Shipment ship;
```

16. Create a getter and setter for the variable source.

17. Override the doStartTag method and add the following statements to the doStartTag method:

```
if (source == "request"){
 ship = new Shipment();
        ship.setShipmentNum(pageContext.getRequest().getParameter("shipNumTF").toString());
        ship.setSupplierName(pageContext.getRequest().getParameter("suppNameTF").toString());
        ship.setRcvMon(pageContext.getRequest().getParameter("MonthDDM").toString());
        ship.setRcvDay(pageContext.getRequest().getParameter("DayDDM").toString());
        ship.setRcvYear(pageContext.getRequest().getParameter("YearDDM").toString());
        ship.setRcvHour(pageContext.getRequest().getParameter("HourDDM").toString());
        ship.setRcvMin(pageContext.getRequest().getParameter("MinuteDDM").toString());
        ship.setRcvAMPM(pageContext.getRequest().getParameter("AMPMDDM").toString());
        ship.setEmployeeNum(pageContext.getRequest().getParameter("empNumTF").toString()); }
if (source == "database"){
        ship = new Shipment(pageContext.getRequest().getParameter(" shipNumTF").toString()); }
pageContext.getSession().setAttribute("ShipBean", ship);
```

18. Override the Java Resources/src/c11/InsertShip doStartTag method to get the ShipBean (using the **PageContext** object) and execute its doInsert method.

19. Change ConfirmIns.jsp so that the following text and the shipment number appear as follows where XXX is the shipment number from the ShipBean.

```
Shipment XXX
has been inserted into the database
```

20. Enter the following HTML into EnterShipNum.html to display the text "Enter Ship Number:", horizontally centered, followed by a text field called shipNumTF:

```
<p align="center">Enter Shipment Number:
<input type="text" name="shipNumTF" size="20"></p>
```

21. Create a form on DelShip.jsp and DispShip.jsp and within each form:

a. Add a JSP **include** tag for EnterShipNum.html

b. Add a horizontally centered Submit button to the bottom and:

   a. In DispShip, name the button DispBtn with text of Display

   b. In DelShip, name the button DelBtn with text of Delete

c. On a post request, define the form action to return to the same JSP

d. Before the form, insert an **if** tag with a test that checks if the request type is a post.

22. In DelShip, if the request is a post, insert the crtShipBean tags with the **source** attribute defined as **database** and than a JSP **forward** tag to ConfirmDel.jsp.

Using the JSP **forward** tag means that ConfirmDel will be invoked by a post request (because DelShip was invoked by a post request not a get request). This means ConfirmDel should display the confirmation message, if the request is a post, and if the request is a get, the deletion should be performed.

23. In DispShip, if the request is a post, insert the crtShipBean tags with the **source** attribute defined as **database** and then a JSP **forward** tag to DisplayShip.jsp.

The DisplayShip JSP should display all the ship properties. Bean getProperty tags can be used to retrieve all the property values; however, formatting the retrieved date and time information is cumbersome and redundant. We will change two Shipment class methods to correctly format and return the date and time.

24. In c11.Shipment, change the getRcvDate method to format the date correctly by inserting the following statement before the return:

```
rcvDate = getRcvMon() + "/" + getRcvDay() + "/" + getRcvYear();
```

25. In Shipment, change the getRcvTime method to format the time correctly by inserting the following statement before the return:

```
 rcvTime = getRcvHour() + ":" + getRcvMin() + " " + getRcvAMPM();
```

Another formatting problem may need to be addressed. Month, day, minute, and hour values less than ten are frequently displayed as single-digit numbers in the drop-down menus. This causes formatting problems when the date and time values are displayed. For example, if the time is five minutes past noon, the value would be displayed as 12:5 PM. In addition, some DBMSs pad string values with spaces to fill up the field. For example, this means that five minutes after three o'clock in the afternoon will look like 3 :5 PM. Again, the best solution is to change the Shipment class to return the information correctly formatted. If you're having these problems, do steps 26 through 29.

26. In Shipment's getRcvHour method, change the return statement to the following so that any trailing spaces are "trimmed off":

```
return rcvHour.trim();
```

27. Change the return statements for the month and day values so that trailing spaces are also eliminated.

28. In Shipment's getRcvMin method, insert the following statement before the return so that minute values less than 10 are padded on the left with a zero:

```
if((Integer.parseInt(rcvMin.trim()) < 10)
 && (rcvMin.trim().length() < 2) ){
 rcvMin = "0" + rcvMin.trim(); }
```

29. In DisplayShip.jsp, define a table with text and JSP getProperty tags to display the ShipBean's properties as seen in Figure 11-20.

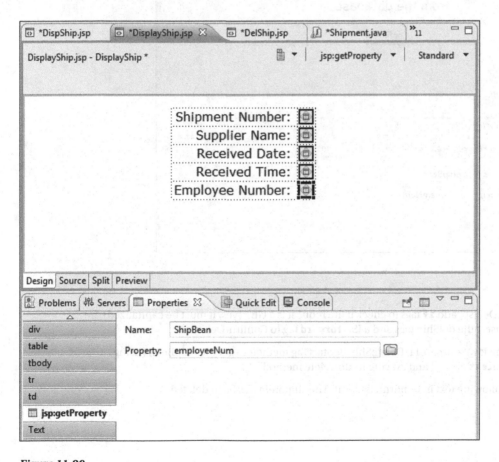

Figure 11-20.

Each of the property tags should specify ShipBean as the Name. For the date and time values, use the rcvDate and rcvTime properties, rather than the six individual properties that make up the date and time.

30. In ConfirmDel.jsp, add a form with an action of ConfirmDel.jsp when the request type is **get**.

31. In the ConfirmDel.jsp form, add text, a **getProperty** tag for the shipment number, and a confirm button (named ConfirmBtn) as seen in Figure 11-21.

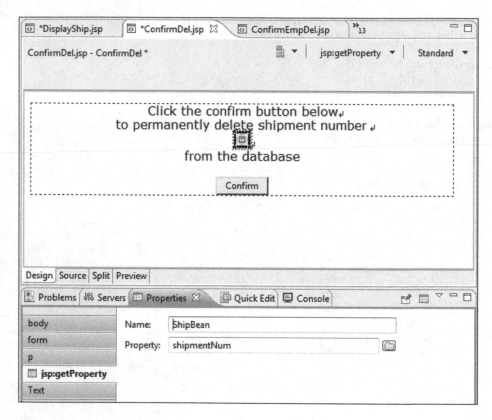

Figure 11-21.

32. In ConfirmDel.jsp, add **if** tags to check if the request is a GET (yes, it must be capitalized) and if so, insert the delShip tags and a JSP **forward** tag to ConfirmDel.html.

33. Override the JavaSource/c11/DeleteShip doStartTag method to get the ShipBean (using the **PageContext** object) and execute its doDelete method.

34. Place the following text in ConfirmDel.html: The shipment has been deleted.

Results of the Review Exercise

After the exercise, we have the following:

1. In the ReviewExWeb project, a new package in WebContent named c11.

2. In WebContent/c11, the following new files:

    ConfirmDel.html

    ConfirmIns.jsp

    DisplayShip.jsp

    EnterShipInfoJSP.jsp

    ConfirmDel.jsp

    DelShip.jsp

    DispShip.jsp

    EnterShipNum.html

3. Inside of Java Resources/src, a new folder called c11 containing the following new Java files:

    CrtShipBean.java

    DeleteShip.java

    DBAccess.java

    InsertShip.java

    Shipment.java

4. In WEB-INF, a new folder called tls and within tls, a file called TNT.tld that contains XML to define three new custom tags called crtShipBean, insShip, and delShip.

5. The shipment Web-based application can now insert, display, and delete shipment information in a database using the custom tags.

Check that the Exercise Was Done Correctly

Finally, we check that everything went as planned:

1. Save all files with changes.

2. Run c11/EnterShipInfoJSP on the server.

3. On the EnterShipInfoJSP page, insert the following shipment information into the database:

    Employee number: 333

    Shipment number: 8888

    Date: August 8th, 2012

    Time: 8:08 pm

    Supplier name: Target

The insert confirmation page should be displayed.

4. In the browser, specify the following in the URL: DispShip.jsp and press Enter.

5. Enter 8888 as the shipment number and click the Display button.

Shipment 8888's information should be displayed as in Figure 11-22.

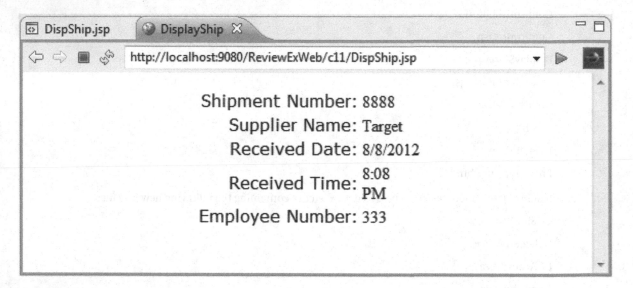

Figure 11-22.

6. Display the DelShip page, specify 8888, and click the Delete button.

The confirm deletion page should be displayed.

7. Click the Confirm button.

The confirm deletion Web page should be displayed saying the shipment was deleted.

8. Use the browser's back button to reshow DispShip and click the Display button.

The browser should show the "page cannot be displayed" message because a ShipBean could not be created with information from the database for shipment number 8888. (Actually, the error is thrown when DispShip tries to access the nonexistent 8888 shipment from the result set; specifically a null cursor exception is thrown.) Of course, the exception should be caught and handled by the application and we should fix how the time is displayed, but we will leave that for a rainy day.

CHAPTER 12

■■■

JavaServer Faces

In this chapter, we will explore the Java application framework called JavaServer Faces (JSF). In addition to learning some of the new JSF classes, the advantages of the JSF architecture will be explained and the tutorials will demonstrate how quickly a JSF application can be generated with a minimal amount of coding.

We will also introduce Service Data Objects (SDO), database connections, and scripting variables and demonstrate the advantages and limitations of using these new tools for accessing databases.

At the end of this chapter, you should understand:

> The JSF framework
>
> Facelets
>
> Pagecode classes
>
> Database connections
>
> Navigation Rules
>
> The SDO Relational Records and Relational Record Lists
>
> Scripting variables
>
> Links and parameters

You should be able to:

> Define and use a database connection

Create a JSF application that:

> displays data from a database table
>
> uses JSF components and SDO to insert and edit data in a database

JSF Overview

Do you feel that things have gotten very complicated? Well, they have! (Model, view, controller, database access and all the classes that are needed to do it, JSPs, servlets, Web pages, tags, tag libraries, Web Deployment Descriptors, URIs, etc.) It almost makes you long for the good old days of client-based applications. To simplify and standardize applications, new "frameworks" such as Struts and Java Server Faces (JSF) have been introduced. Frameworks impose a "standard" for defining and organizing an application's components (classes, Web pages, JSPs, etc.) and include new technology (i.e., Facelets, enhanced visual components, navigation rules, scripting variables) to quickly create an application. For example, both Struts and JSF come with new Java classes and tools that make implementing the MVC architecture easier and with fewer errors. Although the Struts framework is a very useful and has been around longer then JSF, the JSF framework is the direction of the future.

As mentioned, the MVC architecture dictates that an application should separate the content (i.e., the model), controller, and presentation functions (i.e., the view). JSF applications implement the model as Java beans that are subclasses of **PageCodeBase**. The class **PageCode Base** is an example of the new technology that comes with JSF. Further, the controller function is not coded in a Servlet or JSP in a JSF application, instead, the controller function is defined as a set of Navigation Rules and implemented using XML. The view is made up of Facelets (Web pages that use JSF visual components) and/or Web pages. As always, RAD's Page Designer helps the programmer build the presentation layer (i.e., the GUI) quickly and, in the case of JSF, automatically generates the model component (the pagecode classes) associated with each Facelet.

There are also a new set of components called SDO (Service Data Objects) that provide easy access to databases. RAD allows programmers to combine SDO with JSF visual components to provide data manipulation functions with a minimum of coding. The JSF framework also includes specialized tags for defining and using JSF components.

Tutorial: Creating a JSF Project

Facelets must be created in Dynamic Web Projects that are configured to support JSF. Once a project is created, a Facelet is created with a wizard (just as you have done before). To build the Facelet in Page Designer, drag and drop JSF components from the Palette onto it (just as you dragged and dropped AWT, Swing, and HTML components onto frames, JSPs, and Web pages).

1. Begin creating a new Dynamic Web Project by clicking File, New, and then Dynamic Web Project.

2. Specify TutorialsJSF as the project name, change the Configuration to JavaServerFaces v2.0 Project and then click the Modify button (see Figure 12-1).

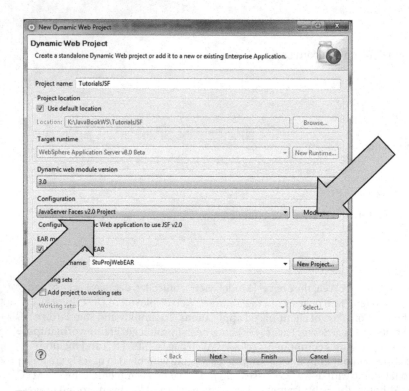

Figure 12-1.

A configuration defines what technologies/functions are included in a project. These various options are called Project Facets. Figure 12-2 shows that the JavaServer Faces v2.0 Project configuration consists of several Project Facets. You can modify the configuration by simply clicking the checkboxes. For this project, we will include JSTL.

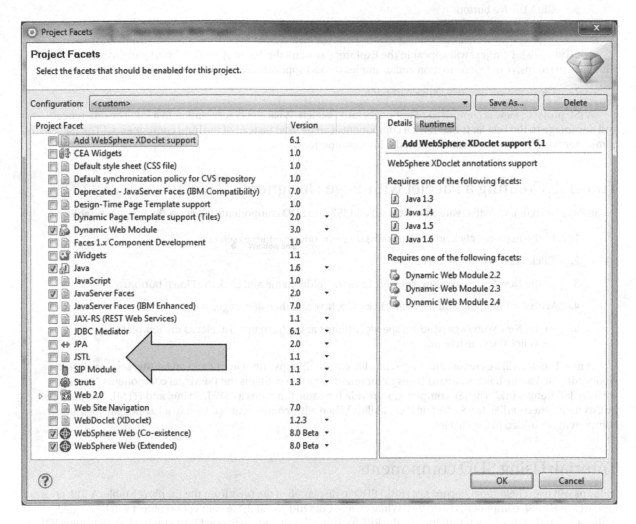

Figure 12-2.

3. Click the JSTL checkbox to select it and then the OK button.

RAD requires that each Dynamic Web Project be part of an EAR. An EAR is another type of archive file (like JAR and WAR). An EAR, however, can contain both client and server components. RAD will force you to add the project to an EAR even if only server-side components are being created. In this example, we will create a new EAR to hold the project.

4. Click the New Project button and on the New EAR Application Project window, specify TutorialsJSFEAR as the Project name then click the Finish button.

The new EAR project will be added to the Explorer pane and you will be prompted to switch to the JEE perspective. Because we are creating only server-based components, we want to stay in the Web perspective.

5. Click the No button.

6. On the New Dynamic Web Project window, click the Finish button.

The TutorialsJSF project will appear in the Explorer pane and the Technology Quickstart pane will be displayed with links to extensive help information and examples of Web application development.

7. Close the Technology Quickstart pane.

A JSF project's view is comprised of webpages and Facelets. A Facelet is very similar to a JSP. The difference and advantage to the Facelet is that JSF 2.0 components can be used instead of the html components. (The JSF components have more functionality than the html components.)

Tutorial: Creating a Facelet with Page Designer

Using Page Designer, we will create a Facelet and add JSF and SDO components to access the Employee table.

1. In the Explorer, click on the TutorialsJSF/WebContent folder to select it.

2. Click File, New, and then Folder.

3. At the New Folder window, specify c12 as the folder name and click the Finish button.

4. With the folder c12 still selected, click File, New, and then Web Page.

5. At the New Web Page window, specify AllEmps as the file name, Facelet as the template and click the Finish button.

A new Facelet will be created and stored in a file called AllEmps.xhtml in c12 and an editing session started. Notice that the Palette has a Standard Faces Components tray that contains the JSF visual components "that come with the JSF framework." The JSF components provide the same functions as AWT, Swing, and HTML components but, as mentioned earlier, have additional capability. When a JSF component is added to a Facelet, JSF tags for the component are added in the Facelet.

Tutorial: Using SDO components

AllEmps will use a Relational Record List (RRL) SDO to display all of the rows from the Employee table. A RRL creates and uses many JSF components to do this. While creating the RRL, a database connection object will be created (using a RAD wizard) which is required for the RRL to work. The advantage to creating a connection object in a JSF application is that any Facelet can access the connection. In other words, you do not have to define a connection in each Facelet or servlet.

1. In the Palette, expand the Data and Services tray and select SDO Relational Record List.

2. In the Page Designer view, click anywhere on the Facelet.

The Add Relational Record List window will be displayed. A name for the RRL must be specified in this window.

3. In the Name field specify allEmpsRRL (see Figure 12-3) and click the Next button.

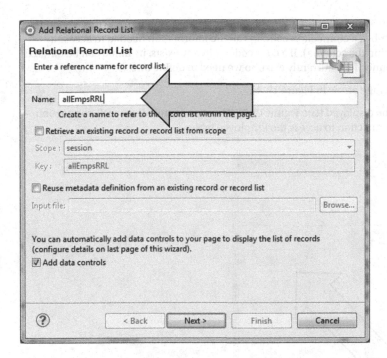

Figure 12-3.

The Record List Properties pane will be displayed (see Figure 12-4).

Figure 12-4.

An RRL needs to be associated with a particular data source—in this case, a database table. To do this, you must tie the RRL to a connection. As you may remember, a connection contains all the information needed to access a particular schema (and, optionally, a table within the schema). If a connection already exists, its name can be entered in the connection Name field. However, no connections currently exist, so we need to define one.

4. Click the New button (indicated by the arrow in Figure 12-4).

The New JDBC Connection window will be displayed (see Figure 12-5). There's a sample Derby DB connection already defined but we have to create a new connection to access the Employee table.

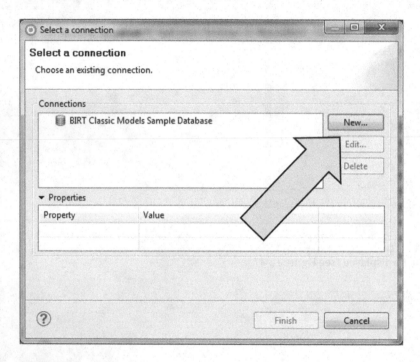

Figure 12-5.

5. Click the New button.

The New Connection window will be displayed with Cloudscape selected as the default DBMS (see Figure 12-6). There are a variety of managers that can be selected; however, notice that Microsoft Access is not one of them.

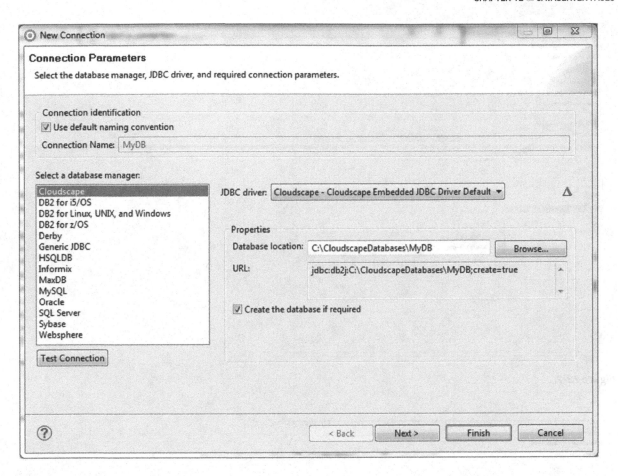

Figure 12-6.

The DBMS selected in the left-hand pane will dictate which fields are displayed and active on the right side of the window. For instance, if an Oracle DB is specified, the SID and Port number fields will be active and required (see Figure 12-7). However, if a DB2 for i5/OS database is selected, these fields will not be displayed (see Figure 12-8).

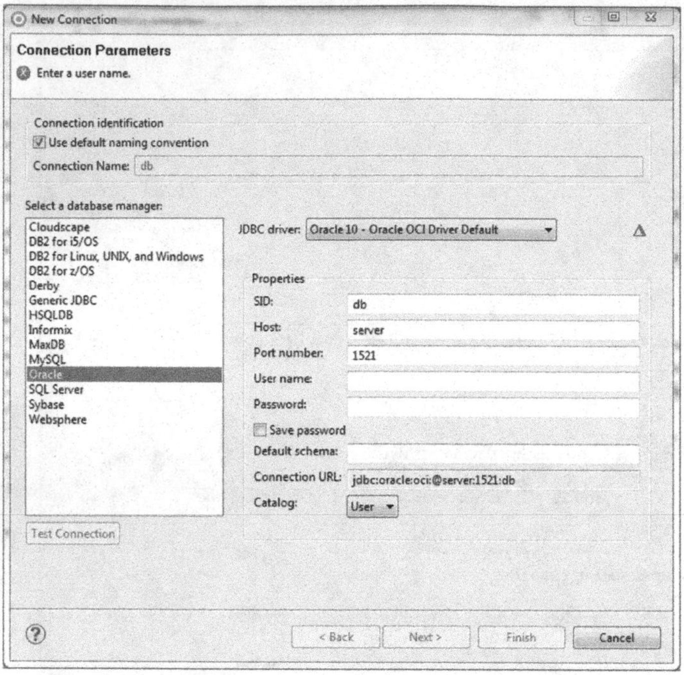

Figure 12-7.

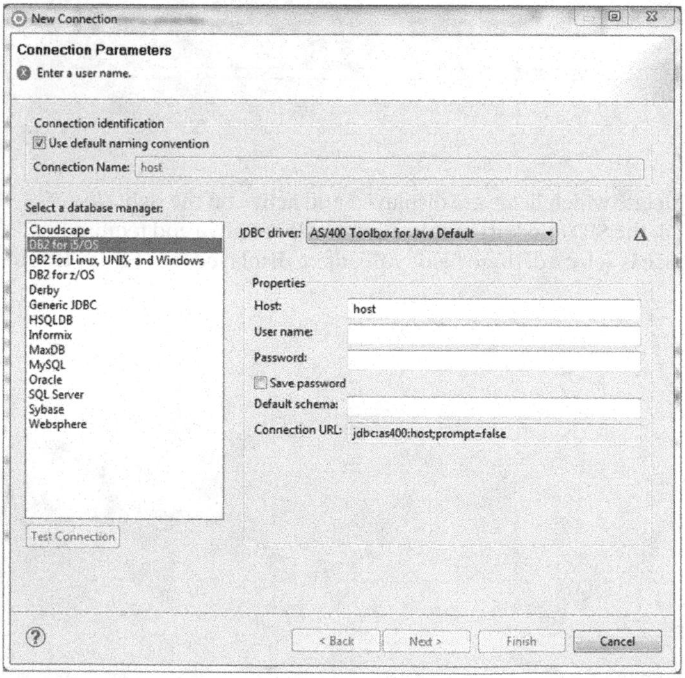

Figure 12-8.

Be careful and make sure the correct information for your database is specified in the required fields. At a minimum, the host location, user id, and password must be specified. The connection type, location of the driver, and/or a port id may be required, depending on the type of DBMS.

Notice that RAD assumes that the default naming convention will be used. The default naming convention dictates that the host address be used as the connection name. We will define a more meaningful name.

6. Select the appropriate DBMS, deselect the Use default naming convention checkbox and, in the Connection name field, enter TNT_Employee_Con.

7. Enter the values from the database chapter for the required parameters (User ID, Password, Host address, etc.) and click the Test connection button (in the lower left of the window).

If the connection information is correct, a message will be displayed saying the connection was successfully established.

8. To continue adding the relational records list, click the OK button to close the Test Connection window then click the Finish button on the New connection and the Select a connection windows.

The Add Relational Record List window will be redisplayed with the new connection name and the available database(s). This is the start of the wizard where the specific table and/or records and fields to be accessed are specified.

9. Scroll down (if needed) and expand the TNT database item, select the Employee table (see Figure 12-9), and click the Next button.

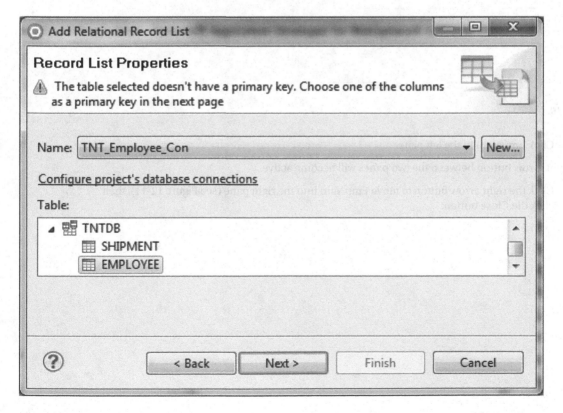

Figure 12-9.

The Add Relational Record pane is displayed with a warning message. When the Employee table was created, a key was not defined. The RRL requires a key.

There are several useful options to control both the content and appearance of the table data on this window. For example, a condition can be specified to select only certain records. In addition, the order in which the records are listed can be controlled and fields can be excluded from the displayed data.

10. Click the Modify primary key option.

The "Edit primary keys" window will be displayed (see Figure 12-10).

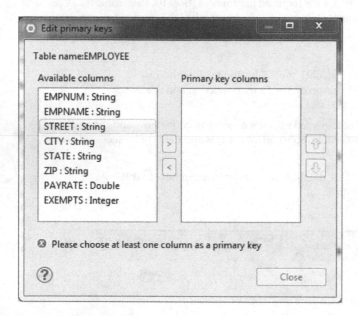

Figure 12-10.

11. Click EmpNum in the left pane.

The right arrow button between the two panes will become active.

12. Click the right arrow button to move EmpNum into the right pane (see Figure 12-11), then click the Close button.

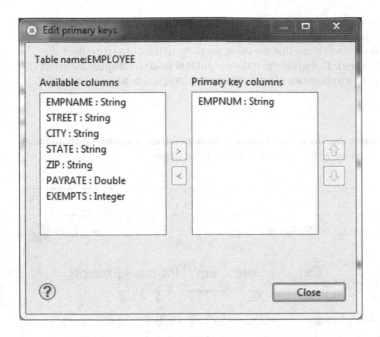

Figure 12-11.

The Add Relational Record List pane will be redisplayed and EmpNum will be defined as the key field.

13.   Click Finish.

RAD reads the Employee table's field definitions and generates a dataTable (and many other components) in AllEmps to display the Employee information (see Figure 12-12).

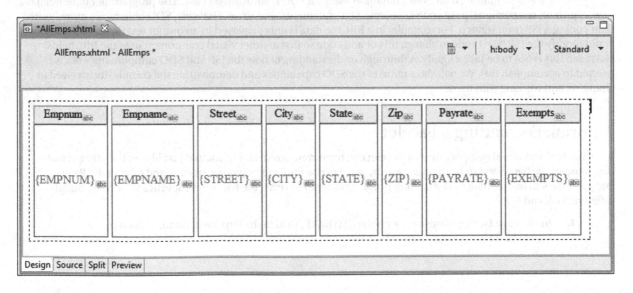

Figure 12-12.

In the dataTable, each Employee field will be displayed in an outputText field (indicated by the field name in braces). RAD has "bound" each column's outputText field to a field in the RRL. For example, selecting any of the outputText fields and switching to the Properties view will show that the value property of the outputText field contains an EL statement identifying the RRL data field. This means that the outputText field will display the value(s) from table for that field/column. We will explore the implications of binding a visual component to a data object in more detail later in this chapter.

14. Run AllEmps on the server.

The results should look like Figure 12-13. Notice that the name of the page in the address window is AllEmp.**faces** not AllEmp.**xhtml**. This will be important later when we want to navigate between the pages.

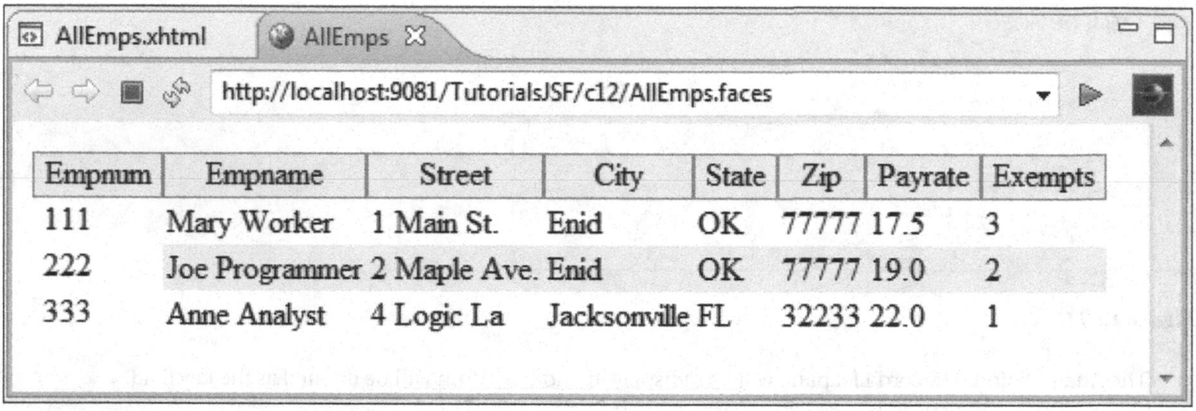
AllEmps.xhtml
AllEmps
http://localhost:9081/TutorialsJSF/c12/AllEmps.faces
Empnum Empname Street City State Zip Payrate Exempts
111 Mary Worker 1 Main St. Enid OK 77777 17.5 3
222 Joe Programmer 2 Maple Ave. Enid OK 77777 19.0 2
333 Anne Analyst 4 Logic La Jacksonville FL 32233 22.0 1

Figure 12-13.

Accessing and formatting data from a database using an SDO is surprisingly easy. The programmer does not have to worry about connections, page context objects, SQL statements, and so on. However, SDO objects are more limited than coding a JSP from scratch. For example, in a RRL the data is only displayed in an output text field. A programmer could modify the JSP/SDO code to change this or add code so that another visual component uses the RRL fields. However, this is not to be taken lightly. A thorough understanding of how the JSF and SDO components work is needed to accomplish this. We will show more of the SDO capabilities and demonstrate the complexity involved in changing and working with them.

Tutorial: Formatting a Facelet

All of the text and visual components in a Facelet can be moved, sized, and formatted just like all the other visual components we have used so far. In other words, you can use the Properties view or click and drag in the Page Designer view to manipulate the formatting property values. However, the Facelets Properties view has a slightly different look and feel.

1. In the Page Designer view, click on the {PAYRATE} field in the Payrate column, as seen in Figure 12-14.

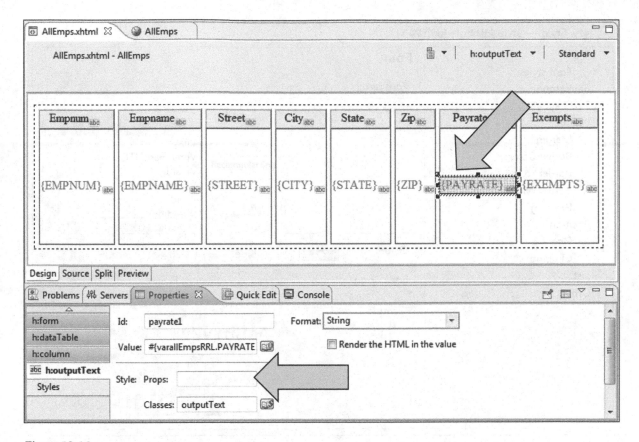

Figure 12-14.

2. Click on the Properties tab to display the Properties view.

Notice that a name (the Id property) is defined for the outputText field. The format of the data can be specified from a list of predefined formats. In this example, String is the default format; however, Payrate really should be defined as a Number.

3. Click on the Format drop-down button and select Number.

Several new Number formatting option components will be displayed.

4. Click on the Type drop-down button to display the four subtype options and select Currency.

5. Click on the Style: Props: (i.e., Style Properties) drop-down button (see the second arrow in Figure 12-14).

The New Style window is displayed with all the formatting options for the pay rate field. The appearance of the field text can be controlled, as well as, other field appearance properties such as background color and the field's alignment within the column. We'll make some simple font changes.

6. Choose the Font family, Color, and Size options as seen in Figure 12-15 and click the OK button.

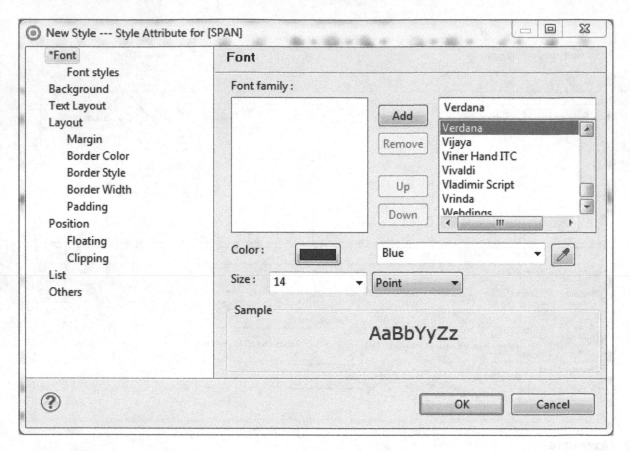

Figure 12-15.

Notice the tabs on the left of the Properties view. Instead of clicking on a visual component to select it (which sometimes requires a sharpshooters aim), you can select a component by clicking one of the tabs. For example, we could display and set the properties of the Payrate column or the entire Employee table by clicking the appropriate tabs.

For now, let's test and make sure it works.

7. Save AllEmps.xhtml and then refresh the browser.

The page will be redisplayed with the formatting changes as seen in Figure 12-16.

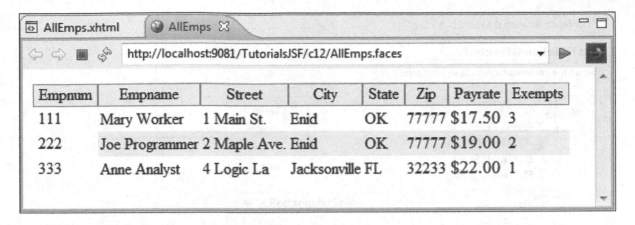

Figure 12-16.

As previously mentioned, you can control which data fields are displayed and the order of the fields. These controls are easily defined in the RRL configuration.

8. Go back to the AllEmps.xhtml edit session.

9. In the Page Data view (lower left pane, see Figure 12-17), right-click allEmpsRRL (Service Data Object) and, from the shortcut menu, select Configure.

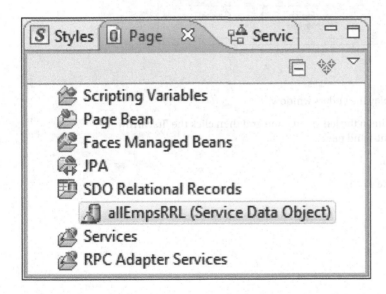

Figure 12-17.

10. At the Configure Relational Record List click the Reuse metadata checkbox, the Next button, and then at the Record List Properties pane click the Next button again.

The Add Relational Record pane will be displayed (see Figure12-18). Fields can be included or excluded from the page by clicking the checkbox next to the field name. We will specify that only employees from Oklahoma be displayed and change the sort order of the data.

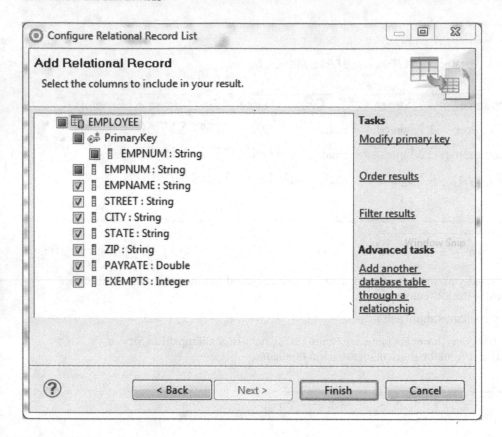

Figure 12-18.

11. Click the Order results task to display the Orders window.

12. On the Orders window, click payrate in the left-hand pane and then click the first arrow button to move the field to the right-hand pane.

13. Click the Descending radio button.

The Orders window should look like Figure 12-19.

Figure 12-19.

14. Click the Close button.

15. On the Add Relational Record pane, click the Filter results task to display the Filters window.

16. On the Filters window, start to define a filter condition by clicking the green plus sign indicated by the arrow in Figure 12-20.

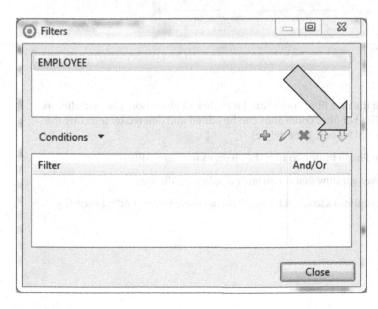

Figure 12-20.

The Conditions window will be displayed, which allows the programmer to select only certain rows from a table based on the value of a particular column (i.e., field). To specify a condition, display a list of all the column names in the table by clicking the drop down button to the right of the Column field, then select a field. Next, choose from a standard list of comparison operators (=, <, >, etc.) and, finally, define a value (or another field that contains a value) to compare the field to. In this case, we want only the rows where the state field has a value of OK.

17.   Specify the values as seen in Figure 12-21 and click the OK button.

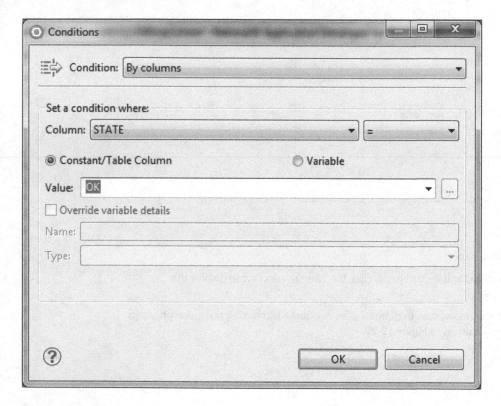

Figure 12-21.

The filters window will be redisplayed with the new filter condition. From this window more filter conditions can be added (and connected with ANDs and ORs) or filter conditions can be edited and deleted by selecting the condition and clicking the appropriate icon (pencil for edit, **X** for delete).

18.   Click the Close button and then the Finish button to save the changes to allEmpsRRL.

19.   Save AllEmps and refresh the browser window that is currently displaying AllEmps.

The browser window will display the two employees from Oklahoma and list them in descending order by payrate (as seen Figure 12-22).

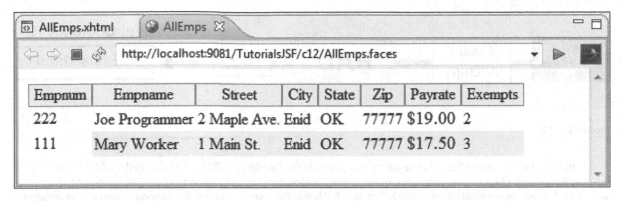

Figure 12-22.

AllEmps is now a bad name because users will naturally assume that the page displays all the employees. We could rename the Facelet but instead we'll remove the filter.

20. Display the Filters window and click on the condition.

21. Delete the condition by clicking the **X**.

22. Close the window, save the change, refresh the AllEmps page in the browser and confirm that all the employees are displayed.

Facelets and RAD

Are you amazed at how easy it was to access a data file? The SDO RAD, and the JSF components did quite a bit of work for you. To explain every object that was created or used is beyond the scope of this text. However, to modify the application, there are several classes whose function and interactions you need to understand.

First, remember that the Facelets file suffix in the browser address field is **faces**. When the resource type specified is faces, the server knows that there is an associated "pagecode" class that needs to be instantiated and defined as a bean. You may be wondering, "What is a pagecode class?"

Expanding the TutorialsWebJSF/Java Resources/src folder will reveal two folders called pagecode and pagecode. c12. RAD creates the pagecode folder whenever a Standard Faces Component, Facelet Tag, or Data and Services items is added to the first Facelet in a project. In addition, a Java class with the same name as the Facelet is created in the appropriate "pagecode" folder. In the example above, a folder, called c12 was created in WebContent and the Facelet was created inside of it. Therefore, when the RRL was added to the AllEmps Facelet, RAD created an additional folder called pagecode.c12. The classes (i.e., the pagecode classes) have the same name as the Facelets and extend the class **PageCodeBase**. The **PageCodeBase** class is one of those classes that "come with" JSF. When the PageCode folder was created, RAD also imports PageCodeBase.java into the project. (Expand the pagecode folder in JavaResources/src to see the PageCodeBase.java file.) PageCodeBase contains all the basic functions and variables for a Facelet. Because our pagecode classes extend **PageCodeBase**, they inherit these functions and variables.

Get ready. Here comes a really big concept. When a new Facelet function is defined (for instance, adding a RRL to a Facelet using Page Designer), RAD generates and inserts the methods and variables to perform that function into the pagecode class. When the Facelet tags try to access the RRL data, the server makes sure that the appropriate methods are invoked to retrieve the data.

Let's walk through, step-by-step the process that occurred when we created the AllEmps Facelet.

When AllEmps was created in c12, RAD created a new file of type xhtml. The xhtml file (in WebContent/c12) holds the Facelet (the View portion of our application). See Figure 12-23.

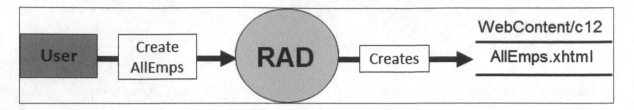

Figure 12-23.

When the first Standard Faces Component was added to the Facelet (the RRL), RAD created a folder in Java Resources/src and a java file with the same name as the Facelet. Because AllEmps was in a folder called c12, the source code folder was called pagecode.c12. The java file holds the source code for the pagecode subclass associated with the Facelet, that is, the pagecode class holds the Facelet's logic (the Model portion of the app). See Figure 12-24.

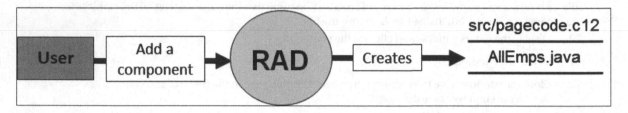

Figure 12-24.

In addition, when the RRL was added to the Facelet (and the connection was defined and assigned to the RRL), RAD generated all the Java code needed to retrieve the employee information and put that code into AllEmps.java (the pagecode class). Displaying the AllEmps.java source code will reveal many methods. The one that does most of the "heavy lifting" regarding accessing the data is called doAllEmpsRRLFetchAction().

As with all java classes, RAD also generates the pagecode class file (the bytecode file) from the pagecode source (i.e., from the .java file). In the Web perspective, the class files are hidden. To prove that they are there, use Windows My Computer to display the workspace/project folder. Then drill down into WebContent/WEB-INF/classes/pagecode/c12 and the AllEmps.class file will be shown.

RAD also put into the Facelet all the JSF and Facelet tags needed to access the pagecode bean, retrieve the data and display the data. Display the Facelet source code and see all the work RAD has done for you!

When the Facelet is requested, the server creates the pagecode object (from the class file) and defines the object as a Java bean with a scope of request. The bean name begins with the letters pc (standing for pagecode), an underscore, and then the name of the Facelet. In this example, the bean is called pc_AllEmps (see Figure 12-25).

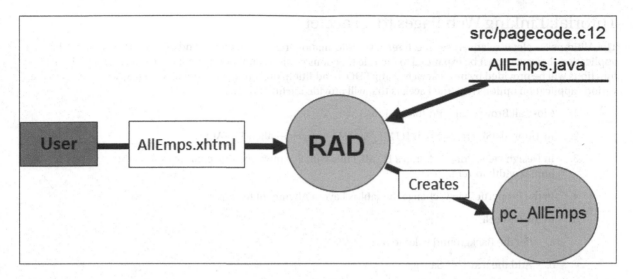

Figure 12-25.

In AllEmps Facelet, the value attribute (value="#{pc_AllEmps.allEmpsRRL}") of the dataTable tag tells the server to invoke the bean's (i.e., the pagecode subclass') getAllEmpsRRL() method. (In JSF, EL statements can begin with a $, as with JSPs, or a # as above.) getAllEmpsRRL() returns the employee information from the database as a list. The power/magic of the dataTable tag is that it will iterate through the list and generate HTML for multiple rows. The HTML and data is passed back to the server and the server sends it to the browser (see Figure 12-26).

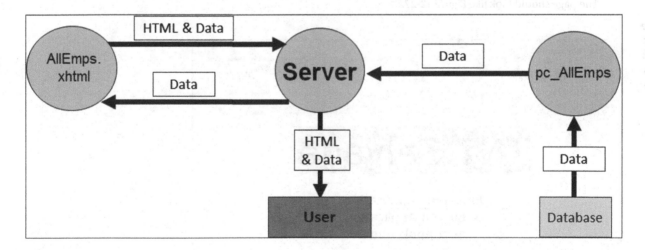

Figure 12-26.

That's enough for now.

Are you asking, "Why do I have to know all this?" Well, to enhance the application you are going to have to get your hands dirty and do some coding. (Sorry, Page Designer can't do it all for you!) In addition, to modify the code, you need to understand which classes and methods to modify, which files hold the source code, and where the files are located.

Tutorial: Linking Web Pages to a Facelet

The AllEmps Facelet is relatively simple. It retrieves information from the database and displays it on a page. The application, however, must be expanded to include functions to insert and modify employee information. These functions will be provided by new Facelets using SDO. In addition, the application needs Web pages with links to the various application options (i.e., the Facelets that will provide the functions).

1. Close all Browser and Editor sessions.

2. In TutorialsJSF, create a new HTML/XHTML web page called TNTApps.

3. In Design view, drag and drop a HTML table with five rows and one column and set the border width to zero.

4. In the Properties view, change the table's Layout Alignment to center.

5. In the first cell:

    a. Set the Background color to red

    b. Add the text TNT Salvage

    c. Set the text font to Verdana, color to black, and size to 36

6. From the Palette's HTML Tags drawer, drag and drop a Horizontal Rule into the second cell.

7. In the last three cells:

    a. Add the text Employee Application, Shipment Application, and Sort Application

    b. Bold and center the text and set the font to Verdana and color to Navy

The page should look like Figure 12-27.

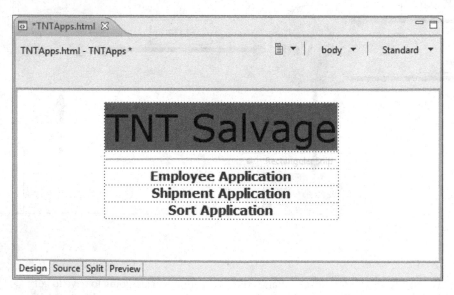

Figure 12-27.

8. Save the file.

9. Save the file again, this time as EmpApps.

10. In EmpApps, change the text in the last three cells to Display All Employees, Insert An Employee, and Update An Employee.

11. Save EmpApps.

12. In TNTApps, select the text Employee Application.

13. In the Command Bar, click on Insert then Insert Link... to display the Insert Link window.

14. At the Insert Link window, click the Browse button and select File... from the menu.

15. In the File Selection window, expand WebContent, select EmpApps.html, and click OK.

The Insert Link window will contain EmpApps.html as the URL

16. Click the OK button and save the file.

The Employee Application text should be underlined and appear in a different color then the other text.

17. Switch to the Preview view and click on Employee Application link.

The EmpApps page should be displayed.

18. In the Design view of EmpApps, highlight the text Display All Employees and click on Insert then Insert Link....

19. At the Insert Link window, click the Browse button and select File... from the menu.

20. In the File Selection window, expand the WebContent/c12 folder, click on AllEmps.xhtml, and then click the OK button.

The URL will be displayed as c12/AllEmps.faces. Even though the file name for the Facelet is AllEmps.xhtml, the resource is specified as AllEmps.faces.

21. Click the OK button.

To access a Facelet from a Web Page, we must run the Web page on the server. This is because the server must create the bean and execute the methods indicated in the Facelet.

22. Run TNTApps on the server, and then select Employee Application.

23. On EmpApps, select Display All Employees.

The AllEmps page will be displayed with the three employee records.

Tutorial: Inserting Data Using a Relational Record (RR)

Let's insert some data

1. Close all RAD sessions and, in WebContent/c12, create a new Facelet called InsertEmp.

2. In the Design view, click on SDO Relational Record (not SDO Relational Record List) in the Palette's Data and Services drawer and then click on the Facelet.

3. At the Add Relational Record window, specify empRR as the name, click on the Creating a new record radio button, and click the Next button (see Figure 12-28).

447

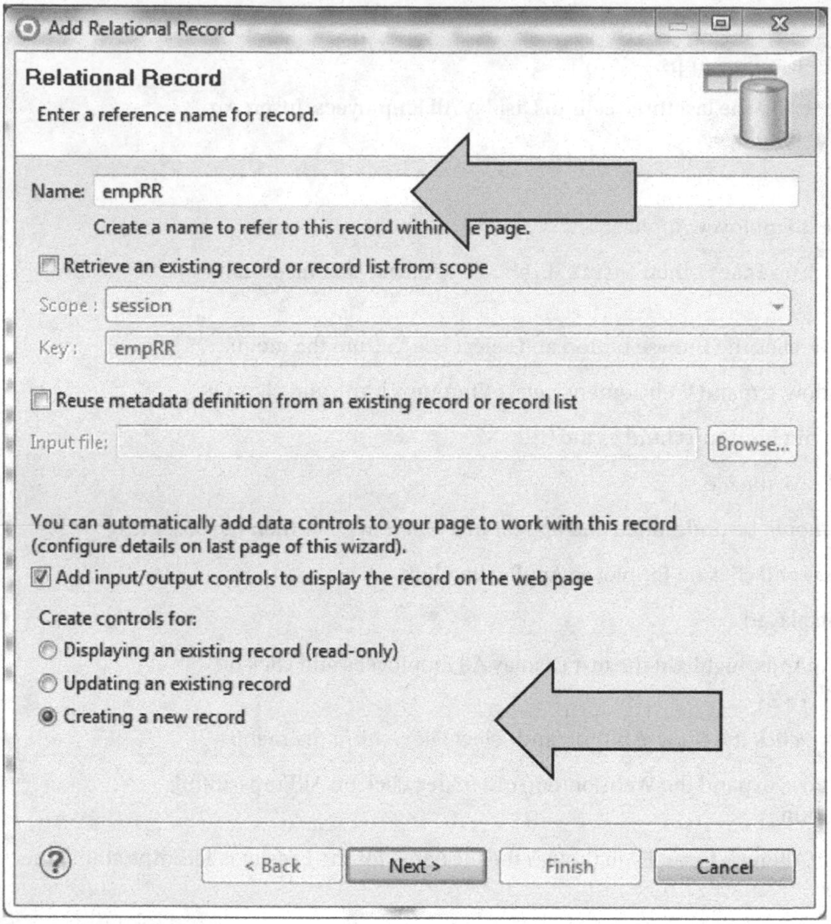

Figure 12-28.

The Record Properties pane will be displayed in the Add Relational Record window.

4. Make sure TNT_Employee_Con is specified as the connection name.

5. If necessary expand the TNTDB item, click on the Employee table, and then the Next button.

Notice that you do not have to define a connection. RAD remembers the connection information defined earlier and allows the connection to be used in any class within the EAR.

Yay, RAD!

6. On the Add Relation Record pane, click on the Modify primary key task, specify empnum as the key (just as you did earlier with the Relational Record List) and click the Close button.

7. Click the Finish button.

You have just created a Facelet that can insert a row into a database table. The InsertEmp Facelet should look like Figure 12-29. It's not very pretty but the format of the text can be modified, the table and input fields can be repositioned and resized, and so on. We are going to concentrate on the SDO data functions, not the JSF formatting options.

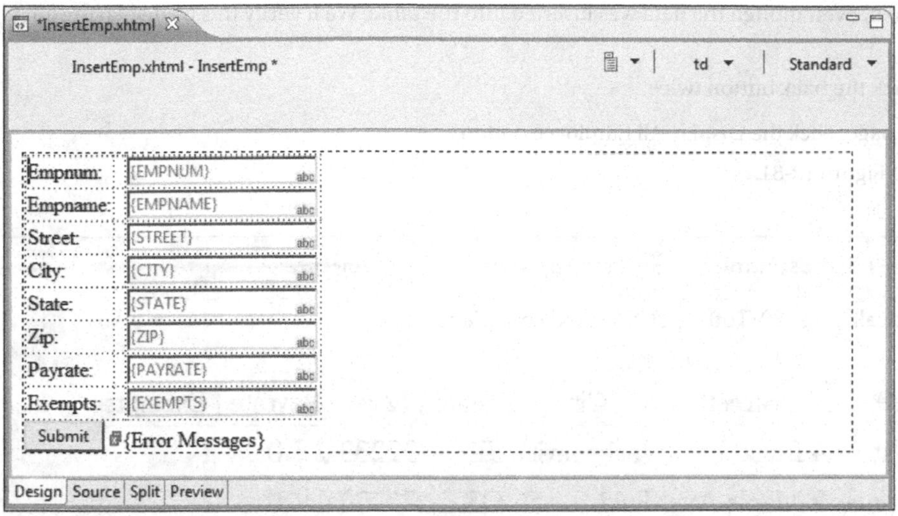

Figure 12-29.

8. Save InsertEmp.

9. In EmpApps.html, make the text "Insert An Employee" a link to InsertEmp. (When identifying the file, don't forget to specify faces as the file extension.)

10. Save EmpApps, run TNTApps on the server, and click Employee Application.

11. Click on Insert An Employee.

InsertEmp should be displayed.

12. Specify information for a new employee as in Figure 12-30 and click the Submit button.

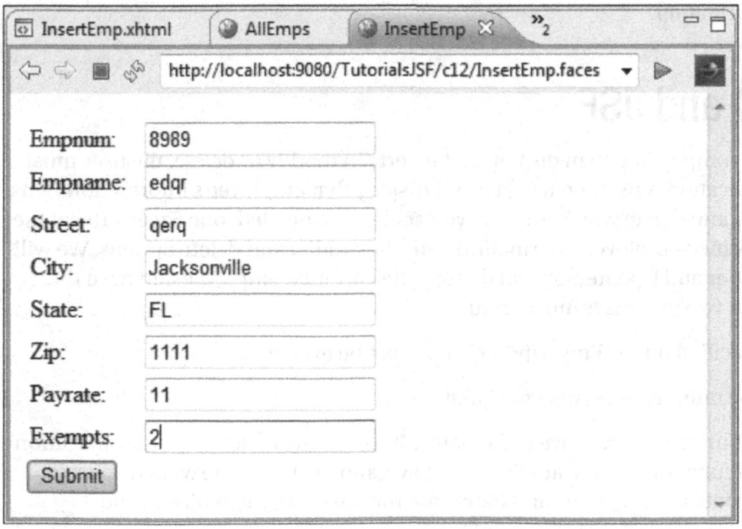

Figure 12-30.

Nothing appears to happen, even though the data was inserted into the table. We'll verify this by displaying all the employees.

13. In the browser, click the back button twice.

14. On the EmpApps page, click the Display All Employee option.

The browser will look like Figure 12-31.

InsertEmp.xhtml	AllEmps.xhtml	EmpApps.html	AllEmps

http://localhost:9080/TutorialsJSF/c12/AllEmps.faces

Empnum	Empname	Street	City	State	Zip	Payrate	Exempts
333	Anne Analyst	4 Logic La	Jacksonville	FL	32233	22.0	1
222	Joe Programmer	2 Maple Ave.	Enid	OK	77777	19.0	2
111	Mary Worker	1 Main St.	Enid	OK	77777	17.5	3
8989	edqr	qerq	Jacksonville	FL	1111	11.0	2

Figure 12-31.

Can you believe how easy it is to develop these functions using SDO and JSF? (Especially considering how long it took to code the database access functions in Chapter 10.) Of course, many niceties are missing. For example, after inserting the record, the entry fields should be blanked out and a successful insertion message should be displayed. Also, none of the entered data was validated nor can we display the gross salary or tax amounts. These functions can be coded in the pagecode class by the programmer. For now, however, we will finish the application by adding functions to update and delete employee information.

Updating Data Using SDO and JSF

Update and delete functions are a little more complicated than display and insert. To modify or delete, the user must first specify the employee to modify. The application must then retrieve and display that employee's information. This "display Facelet" must have options to modify and delete which means two Facelets are needed: one Facelet to get the employee number and one to display the specified employee information with the modify and delete options. We will create GetEmp to retrieve the employee number and UpdateEmp will display the specified employee and have the capability to update or delete. This means that two processes must occur:

1. After the employee number is specified on GetEmp, UpdateEmp must be executed.

2. GetEmp must make the employee number accessible to UpdateEmp.

To run UpdateEmp after the GetEmp submit button is clicked, we will create a JSF framework item called a navigation rule. Navigation rules comprise the controller function of a JSF application. Navigation rules define what resources should be accessed based on events and outcomes. Navigation rules eliminate the need to code redirects and forwards as in JSPs thereby separating the controller function from the view. But where is the controller function moved to? The controller function is defined in a project file called faces-config using XML (eXtensible Markup Language. We will show the XML that defines a navigation rule but more importantly, we will show how to have RAD generate the XML for us.

To satisfy number 2 (from above), we will first use a type of scripting variable called a *session scope variable*. A session scope variable is accessible by any Java object within the EAR. This variable will hold the employee number. We will use binding to ensure that GetEmp sets the variable's value to the employee number and that UpdateEmp retrieves the employee number from the variable.

Scripting variables are a very powerful tool; however, scripting variables and SDO (RRLs and RRs) do not work as smoothly together as JSF and SDO do.

Tutorial: Defining a Scripting Variable

We will go through the procedure for creating and using the scripting variable (because they are so useful) and then show how SDOs, links, and parameters can be used to perform the same function.

1. Close any open editing or browser sessions.

2. In TutorialsJSF/WebContent/c12, create a new Facelet called GetEmp.

3. Insert an HTML table with one column, three rows, and a border width of zero, and center the table on the page.

4. In the first cell, enter the following text: Enter the employee number to update and click the Submit button.

5. From the Standard Faces Component drawer in the Palette, click on the Input component and then click on the second cell in the table.

6. From the Standard Faces Component drawer in the Palette, click on the Button - Command component and then click on the third cell in the table.

7. On the left side of the Properties view, click the td tab (see Figure 12-32).

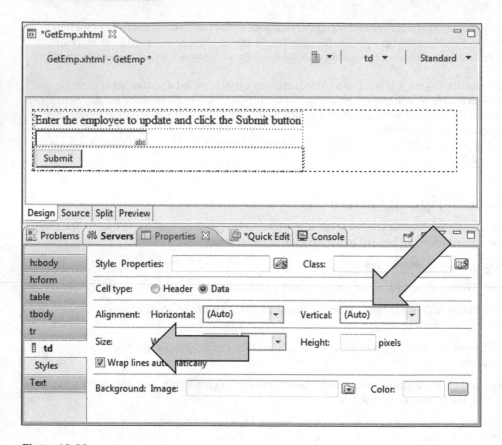

Figure 12-32.

8.   Center the button by clicking the Alignment Horizontal drop-down button and select Center from the options.

9.   Center the Input component (just as you centered the Submit button).

10.   In the Page Data view, expand Scripting Variables and then double click sessionScope (see Figure 12-33).

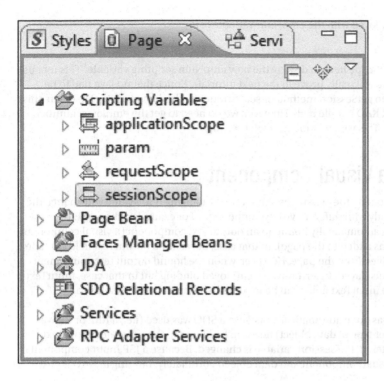

Figure 12-33.

The Configure sessionScope window will be displayed. To create a session variable we just need to specify a variable name and a type.

11. At the Configure sessionScope window, click the Add... button to display the Add Session Scope Variable.

12. Specify empNum as the Variable name, java.lang.String as the Type (see Figure 12-34), and click the OK button.

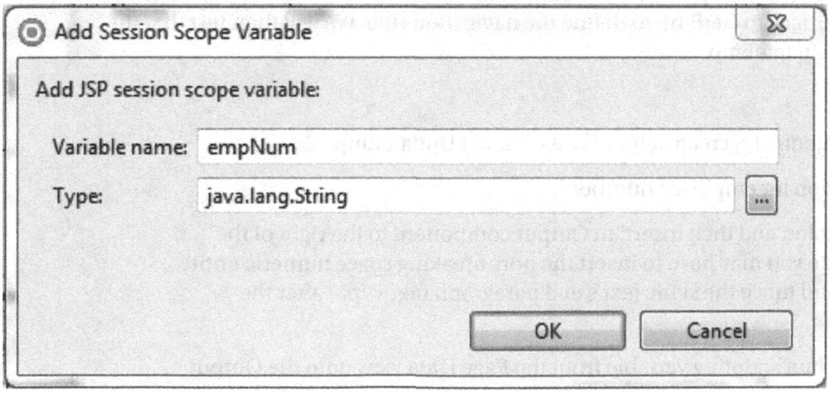

Add Session Scope Variable

Add JSP session scope variable:

Variable name: empNum

Type: java.lang.String

OK   Cancel

Figure 12-34.

The Configure sessionScope will be redisplayed with the empNum variable listed.

13. Click the Close button.

In the Page Data pane, expand the sessionScope item to display the new empNum scripting variable. This means that the session variable was created (which we will really prove in the next tutorial). Notice that no Java had to be entered (i.e., no **PageContext** object created, no getSession method or setAttribute method invoked, etc) to create this session-wide variable. The JSF framework and RAD handle it all. However, we do need to get the employee number from the input field into the scripting variable. This will be done through **binding**.

Binding a Data Object to a Visual Component

When a data object is bound to a visual component, they share the same value. Changing one's value will change the other's value. However, binding works differently with different visual components. For example, when AllEmps was created, each RRL field (i.e., a data object) was automatically bound to an outputText component (a visual component generated when the JSF Output component was added to the page). In that case, because an outputText field can't be changed by a user, the RRL field can't be modified from the page. However, when the bound outputText component is displayed, the value in the RRL field will be displayed. InsertEmp also employed binding but in that case, inputText components were bound to RR fields. Because inputText fields can be modified, this means the RR fields can be modified from the page.

In both these earlier examples, binding was done automatically because a SDO was used (i.e., a RRL or RR was used). In GetEmp, the session variable (another type of data object) needs to be bound to the generated inputText field so that when the employee number is entered, the session variable is changed. Because a JSF Input component is not an SDO, the programmer must bind the visual component and data object. Fortunately, binding in RAD is easy.

Tutorial: Binding

Let's try binding:

1. From the Page Data view, drag and drop the empNum variable onto the inputText component.

Yes, that is all it takes to bind. Notice that in the Properties view RAD put an EL statement into the value property and in Page Designer the variable name appears in the inputText component (within braces).

To finish GetEmp, we will define a navigation rule to run UpdateEmp when the Submit button is clicked. However, before the navigation rule is created, UpdateEmp should be created. We will create a very basic UpdateEmp (for testing purposes) and then come back to GetEmp to define the navigation rule. We will then test that the navigation rule works and complete UpdateEmp.

2. Save GetEmp.

3. In TutorialsJSF/WebContent/c12, create a new Facelet called UpdateEmp.

4. Insert the text "Information for employee number:".

5. Insert a space after the colon and then insert an Output component to the right of the space. (In the source code you may have to insert the non-breaking space numeric entity, , *after* the colon and move the static text's end paragraph tag, </p>, after the outputText tag.)

6. Drag and drop the empNum scripting variable from the Page Data view onto the Output component.

This binds the scripting variable to the outputText field. This also means that when the page is displayed, the scripting variable value will be shown.

7. Save UpdateEmp.

We will now define a navigation rule in GetEmp, then test that the empNum variable value is being set by GetEmp and displayed by UpdateEmp.

Navigation rules

Navigation rules are defined for a component(s) and, in this case, the component is the Submit button on GetEmp. A navigation rule dictates which resource to "go to" for the outcome of an action. You may be wondering, "What is an action?" In a Facelet, an action is simply a method in the RAD-generated pagecode class. The method (i.e., the action) is coded such that the method returns a string (i.e., an outcome), and the method name is doXXXAction, where XXX is the visual component name.

The method-naming convention must be followed because this is how the server knows which method in the pagecode class to execute when an event occurs to that visual component (e.g., the button is clicked). For instance, to define a navigation rule for button1 (the Submit button), a method called doButton1Action must be defined in the pagecode class. Inside of the doButton1Action method any Java statements can be entered; however, a **return** statement must be coded to return a string value. This returned value is the outcome of the method/action. Different outcome values (i.e., string values) can be returned based on the processing within the action (i.e., the method) and there can be many navigation rules, each based on a different outcome value.

As you probably suspect, RAD makes defining a default action easy. Default actions return an empty string as an outcome. (Yes, an empty string is a valid outcome!)

Tutorial: Defining a Navigation Rule

For this example, we will generate a success outcome and a single navigation rule.

1. In the Page Designer, click on GetEmp's Submit button.

2. Display the Properties View and scroll to the right to show the navigation rules table.

The Properties view should look like Figure 12-35. Before defining the navigation rule, however, the action (i.e., the method in the pagecode class GetEmp.java) must be created. The programmer can go directly into GetEmp.java and code the method, but RAD provides a much easier way to create the method.

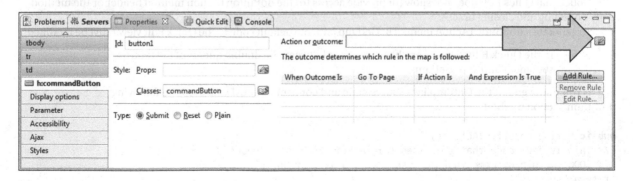

Figure 12-35.

3. Click on the "Select or code an action" icon (indicated by the arrow in 12-35) and from the shortcut menu choose "code an action."

This brings up the Quick Edit session for a small portion of code within GetEmp.java. The tabs along the left are options for the specific action/method to be created.

4. On the left of the Quick Edit view, click on the Command tab (indicated by the arrow in Figure 12-36) and then click anywhere in the source code (in the right of the pane).

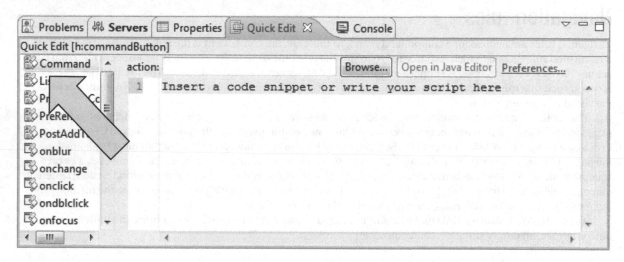

Figure 12-36.

Clicking the source code tells RAD to:

A. Create a doButton1Action method in the pagecode subclass (i.e., GetEmp.java)

B. Insert comments explaining the type of statements the programmer should enter

C. Insert a return statement for a null string

D. Start a Quick Edit session for the doButton1Action method

Notice that Quick Edit does not show (or provide access to) the doButton1Action method header or the method body's opening and closing braces.

To generate a doButton1Action method in GetEmp.java, the default code in the Quick Edit view must be modified.

5. In the Quick Edit view, insert the text success between the double quotes of the return statement and save GetEmp.

Scroll to the end of the GetEmp.java source code and confirm that RAD inserted the following doButton1Action method.

```java
public String doButton1Action() {
// This is java code that runs when this action method is invoked
// TODO: Return outcome that corresponds to a navigation rule
return "success";
}
```

For the time being, we will leave this very dull action as is.

6. Switch back to the Properties view for the Submit button and start defining a navigation rule by clicking the Add Rule... button.

The Add Navigation Rule window will be displayed. The only rule property that must be defined is the go to the page; however, we can also define the rule as a default. In other words, we can associate this rule with all components, pages, and/or outcomes. If there were several buttons on the page, the rule could be applied to all of them.

7. From the Page drop-down button, select /c12/UpdateEmp.xhtml.

We will not change any of the other options on this page. This means that any outcome of any component action on this page will result in the UpdateEmp Facelet being invoked. For instance, if there were multiple buttons, any action against these buttons would invoke this navigation rule.

8. Click the OK button.

The Properties View will be redisplayed and the rule will be shown in the navigation rules table. If you'd like to see the XML that was generated, double click the faces-config file in WEB-INF. Then in the FacesConfiguration Overview, click the Source tab and scroll to the end.

It is time to test the rule to see if it works and that the employee number is being set by GetEmp and being retrieved by UpdateEmp.

9. Run GetEmp.xhtml on the server.

GetEmp should be displayed in the browser.

10. Specify 8989 as the employee number and click the Submit button.

The browser should display the UpdateEmp page with the employee number 8989 (see Figure 12-37). Excellent!

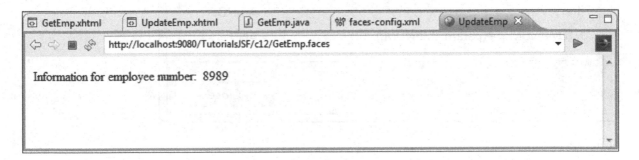

Figure 12-37.

Tutorial: Updating and Deleting Using a Relational Record

All we need to do now is change UpdateEmp so that it actually updates and deletes.

1. Close any open editing or browser sessions and open an editing session for UpdateEmp.jsp.

2. In Design view, click on a Relation Record item in the Data and Services drawer and then click beneath the existing text.

The Add Relation Record window will be displayed. As with AllEmps and InsertEmp, this window allows us to specify controls. Unlike earlier when we created display or create controls, UpdateEmp needs controls to both update and delete.

3. Specify empRRUpdate as the name and click the "Updating an existing record" radio button.

By choosing the update option, RAD will create buttons, methods, and variables for both the update and delete functions.

4. Click the Next button.

5. Make sure TNT_Employee_Con is specified as the Connection name.

6. Scroll down the tree diagram, expand TNTDB, click on Employee and then the Next button.

7. On the Add Relational Record pane, click on the Modify primary key link and specify the employee number field as the key.

8. On the Add Relational Record pane, click the Filter results option.

The Filters window will be displayed as shown in Figure 12-38. RAD automatically generates a condition that indicates a parameter called EMPNUM will determine which record will be displayed. We need to change this condition so that the scripting variable empNum determines the employee information displayed.

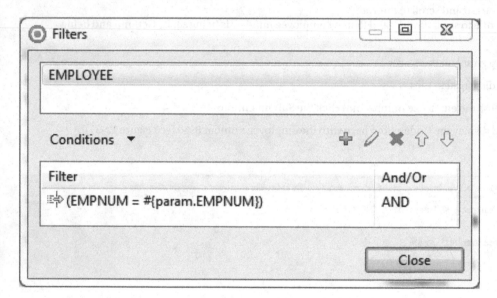

Figure 12-38.

9. Click on the filter condition and then the Pencil icon to edit the condition.

10. On the Conditions window, click the … button to the right of the Value field's drop-down button (indicated by the arrow in Figure 12-39).

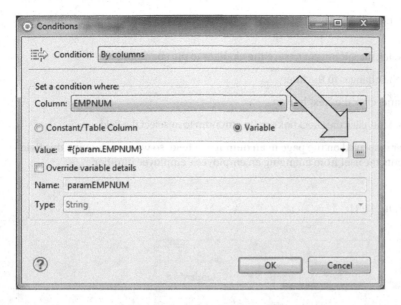

Figure 12-39.

11. On the Select Page Data Object window, expand the sessionScope item (in the tree diagram) and then click on empNum (see Figure 12-40).

Figure 12-40.

Notice that the Reference String field (toward the bottom of the window) now contains an EL statement that indicates the sessionScope variable.

12.   Click the OK button and then click the OK button to save the changes to the condition.

13.   Click the Close button to save the changes to the filter

14.   On the Add Relation Record pane, click the Next button.

15.   On the Configure Data Controls pane, click the checkbox next to empnum to unselect the field.

We already have the employee number displayed on the page in an outputText field, so we are removing this field from the Relational Record (this also prevents the user from changing an employee's employee number.

16.   Click the Finish button.

UpdateEmp.xhtml should look like Figure 12-41.

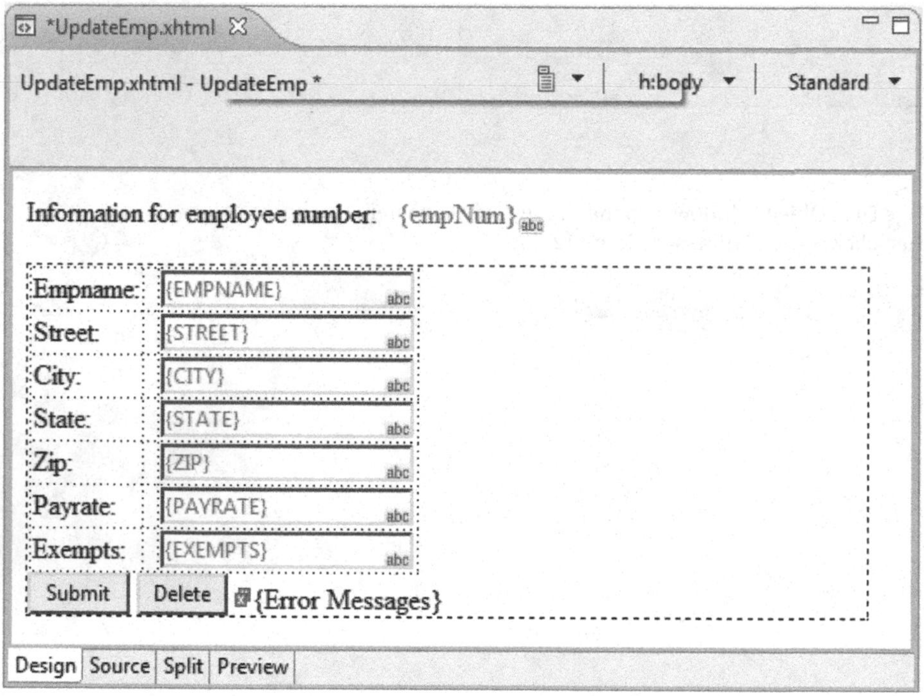

Figure 12-41.

Just like the insert page, RAD has created inputText components for each selected field in the database table and bound the fields to the RR data components. RAD has also created two buttons that will invoke the update and delete functions in the pagecode class (i.e., UpdateEmp.java). If you look at the UpdateEmp.xhtml source code, you'll see that the EL statement for each button's action parameter invokes a particular method in the bean/pagecode class (pc_UpdateEmp). For example, the Submit button invokes the doEmpRRUpdateUpdateAction method. Where did that method come from? RAD automatically generated these methods when the Updating option was selected in step 3.

Although RAD has done a wonderful job, the default text for the Submit button should be changed. Submit does not really describe what clicking the button will do, so we will change the text to Update.

17. Click on the Submit button and, in the Properties view, click the Display options tab.

18. Specify Update in the Button label field and save UpdateEmp.

Now we need to update the Employee Applications Web page to link to GetEmp.xhtml.

19. Start an editing session for EmpApps.html.

20. Highlight the Update An Employee text.

21. Click on Insert, Link, and then specify c12/GetEmp.faces as the URL.

22. Click the OK button, save EmpApps and UpdateEmp and close the edit sessions.

Test time.

Tutorial: Testing the Update and Delete Functions

Let's make sure it all works:

1. Run TNTApps.html on the server.

2. Click on the Employee Applications link.

3. Click the update link.

4. Enter 8989 as the employee number and click Submit.

UpdateEmp should be displayed with employee's 8989 information (see Figure 12-42).

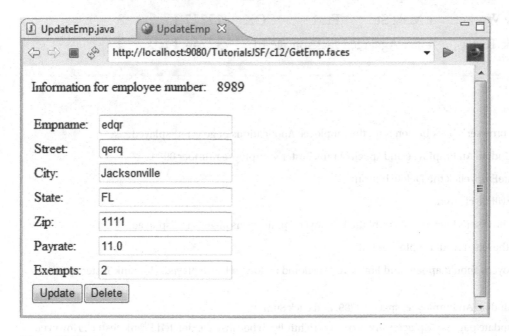

Figure 12-42.

5. Change the employee name to Frank Tester, the street address to 4 Try Again Rd, and Zip code to 32244, and click the Update button.

If you got error messages in the console when you clicked the Update button, it could be because the value entered is too big. If a database character field value is entered that is not the database field maximum size, many DBMSs will pad the value with spaces. For example, the employee name field was defined as 25 in length. When edqr was entered as the name, the DBMS may have put 21 spaces at the end of edqr. When the info for employee 8989 was displayed, the name displayed was actually edqr. If you replaced edqr with Frank Tester, the actual value in the field was 33 characters in length—the 12 characters that comprise the name plus the 21 blanks that the DBMS added.

You can prove this by clicking in the far right of any text field that contains character data that isn't the maximum field size. The cursor is placed after the spaces, well after the last visible character. So to get around the error, simply select the characters and the spaces in the text field then type the new information.

6. Click the browser's back button until the Employee Applications page is redisplayed.

7. Click on the Display All Employees link.

(If Frank Tester's info doesn't appear, refresh the page.) The browser should look like Figure 12-43.

Empnum	Empname	Street	City	State	Zip	Payrate	Exempts
333	Anne Analyst	4 Logic La	Jacksonville	FL	32233	22.0	1
222	Joe Programmer	2 Maple Ave.	Enid	OK	77777	19.0	2
111	Mary Worker	1 Main St.	Enid	OK	77777	17.5	3
8989	Frank Tester	4 Try Again Rd	Jacksonville	FL	32244	11.0	2

Figure 12-43.

8. Click the browser's back button until the Employee Applications page is redisplayed.

9. Choose Update An Employee and specify Frank Tester's employee number 8989.

10. On UpdateEmp, click the Delete button.

The input fields will be cleared.

11. Click the browser's back button until the Employee Applications page is redisplayed.

12. Click on the Display All Employees link.

Only three employees should appear and Frank Tester should no longer be displayed. (If Frank Tester appears, refresh the page.)

13. Choose Update An Employee, specify 8989, and click Submit.

Notice that the update page is displayed with no data (rightfully so because we deleted Frank Tester). However, the console is full of error messages with the originating message saying, "an index is out of bounds." Because there is no employee 8989, when the RR attempts to read the data from the DBMS there is an error. When there is no employee to update, the update page really shouldn't be displayed but unfortunately, this is not how the RR functions.

Building the update Facelet was remarkably easy; however, getting the RR to work with the DBMS was not, and the RR does not handle the "employee number not found" condition very well. SDOs are very powerful but, as mentioned, they often "do not play well" with non-SDO technologies. So in the next tutorial we will address some of these shortcomings.

Tutorial: Fixing the Application

There are several ways to fix the problems. The harder, but prettier way, is to change the pagecode classes associated with UpdateEmp (to trim off the spaces) and GetEmp (to check that the employee does exist in the DBMS). In addition, better navigation rules will be needed.

To check that an employee exists modify the GetEmp's doButton1Action to check to see if there is an employee record for the employee number specified. This would require importing DBAccess and Employee from TutorialsWeb/c11 into TutorialsJSF/JavaResources/src/pagecode. c12. (On the paste, RAD will change their package statements from c11 to pagecode.c12. Wasn't that nice of RAD!)

In doButton1Action, create an Employee object and then use the scripting variable to retrieve the record from the database. Remember, the Employee class **does not** throw an exception if no record is found so doButton1Action must check to see if employee information exists in the employee object. If there is an employee name, then a "success" outcome will be returned.

If there is no employee name, then employee number should be blanked out of the inputText field and an "employee doesn't exist" error message displayed on GetEmp.xhtml. To do this add a JSF Output field (which generates an outputText field called text2) to the page. In addition, create a sessionScope scripting variable (named msg) and bind it to text2. Then in doButton1Action, blank out the value in the scripting variable empNum. Because the scripting variable is bound to the text field, the text field will be blanked out also. Place the error message text in the scripting variable msg. Once again, because of binding the message will appear in the output field. Finally, we want to return an outcome of "failure".

The navigation buttons still need to be changed so that only when success is returned is UpdateEmp.xhtml displayed. On failure, GetEmp.xhtml will be redisplayed with the error message and the invalid employee number erased.

The following is the new doButton1Action method:

```
public String doButton1Action() {
    String Num = (String) getSessionScope().get("empNum");
    Employee emp = new Employee();
    emp.getEmpInfo(Num);
    getSessionScope().put("msg", "");
    if (emp.getEmpName().length() > 0) {
        return "success";
    } else {
        getSessionScope().put("msg", "Employee number " +
getSessionScope().get("empNum") +
" doesn't exist, please re-enter.");
        getSessionScope().put("empNum", "");
        return "failure";
    }
}
```

As mentioned, the old navigation rule must be changed so that it is not the default. This rule (displaying UpdateEmp.xhtml) should only be executed when the outcome is "success" (see Figure 12-44). Create a new navigation rule for the "failure" outcome that redisplays getEmp (see Figure 12-45).

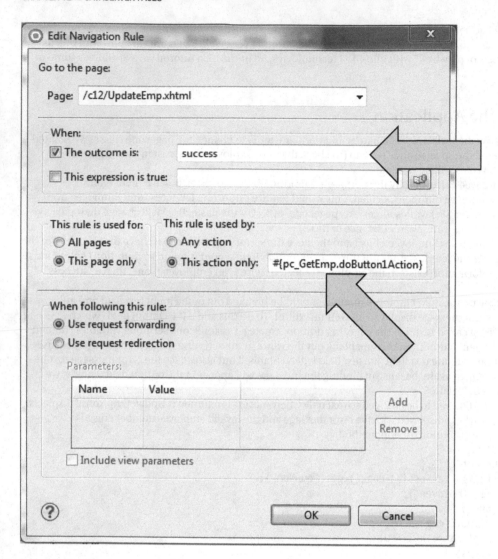

Figure 12-44.

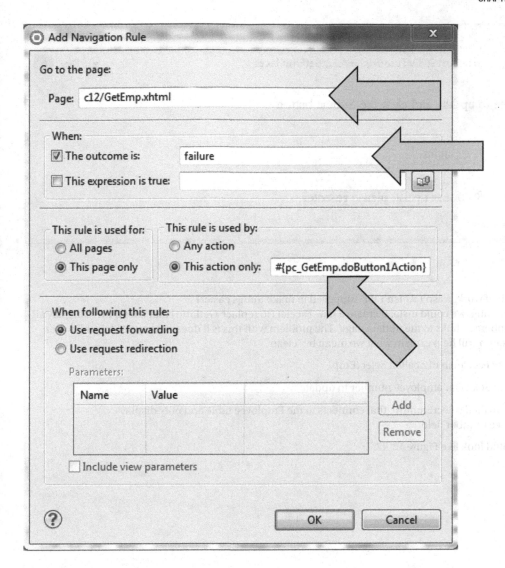

Figure 12-45.

1. Make the changes specified above.

2. Display GetEmp.xhtml, specify 8989, and click Submit.

The result should look like Figure 12-46.

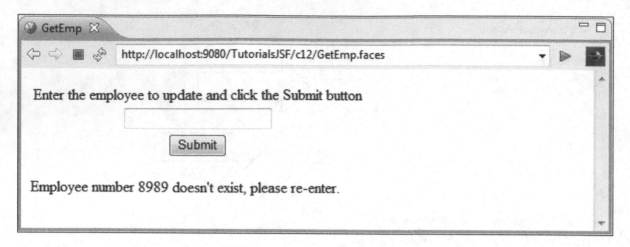

Figure 12-46.

That was quite a bit of work, wasn't it? Isn't JSF supposed to make things easier?

Instead of all that coding, we could instead create a new Facelet (to replace GetEmp) that uses a RR to display all the valid employee numbers as links to the update page. The problem with this is it does not have as "clean" a user interface. Seeing it in action will help explain what we mean by "clean".

3. Create a new Facelet in c12 called SelectEmp.

4. Add the text: Select an employee number to update.

5. Add an RRL called selectEmpRRL that connects to the Employee table and only displays the employee number field.

Page Designer should look like Figure 12-47.

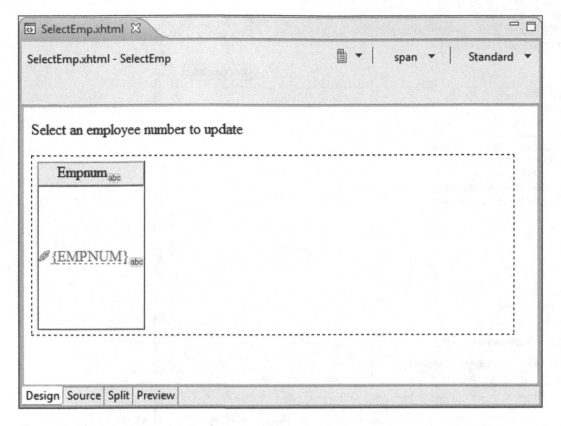

Figure 12-47.

6. In the Standard Faces Components tray, click Link and then click on the employee number outputText field.

7. In the properties view, add a navigation rule that specifies /c12/UpdateEmp.xhtml as the Page for any action and delete the Label text (i.e., Link).

When the link to UpdateEmp is executed, we will pass the selected employee number as a request parameter to UpdateEmp and have empRRUpdate use that value in the filter condition.

8. Make sure the link is selected and on the left of the Properties view, click the Parameter tab beneath the link tab.

9. Click the Add Parameter button and in the Name area specify employeeNumber.

10. Click the Value field to display the drop-down button and click the drop-down button to display the Select Page Data Object window.

11. Expand the selectEmpRRL items, choose the EMPNUM field (see Figure 12-48), and click the OK button.

Figure 12-48.

12.   Save SelectEmp.

UpdateEmp.xhtml must be changed to use the parameter when retrieving the employee data for update. When configuring the relational record, you must check the Reuse metadata definition checkbox before you can access the filter.

13.   Edit EmpRRUpdate's filter value to use the employeeNumber parameter (see Figure 12-49)
       and in the source code change the output text value to #{param.employeeNumber}.

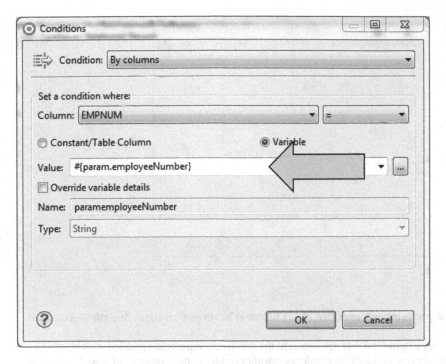

Figure 12-49.

14. Save UpdateEmp and run SelectEmp on the server.

The browser should look like Figure 12-50.

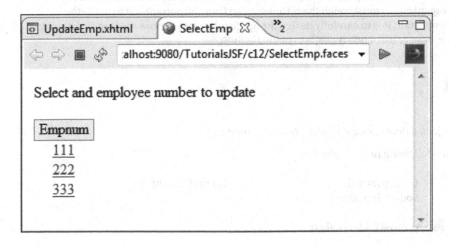

Figure 12-50.

15. Click on employee number 111.

16. Expand the browser window to display the full address as in Figure 12-51.

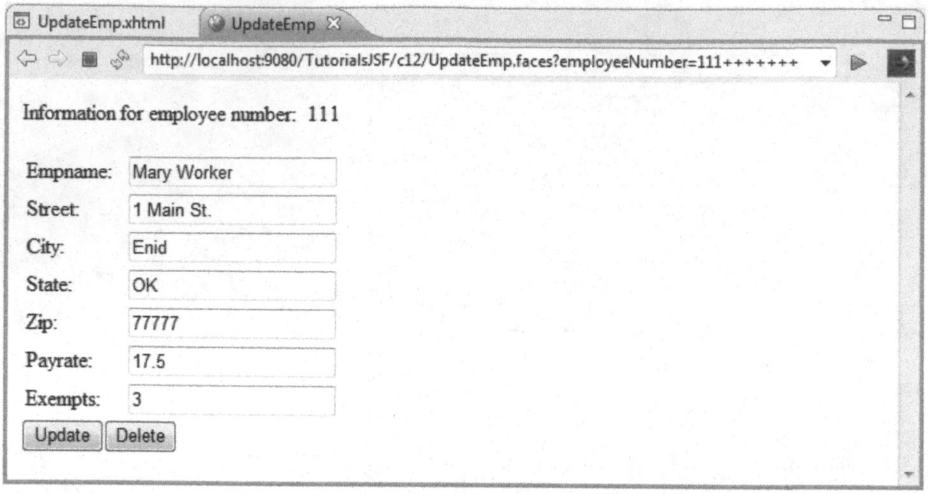

Figure 12-51.

Notice that the value for employeeNumber is specified as 111 followed by seven plus signs. Any guesses on what is going on?

Do you remember that earlier we discovered that the values in the text fields were being padded with blanks? In this case, because we bound the parameter to the RRL's employee number field, the parameter field was also padded with spaces (+ is the URL representation of a blank space).

Because it didn't require any coding, this solution (links and parameters) was much easier to implement. However, if there are many employees, users would have to scroll extensively to locate the desired employee number and SelectEmp would be very "busy" visually.

So which is the best solution? Unfortunately, there is no easy answer to the "which way is best" question. Using either technology (scripting variables vs. links and parameters) is viable. When making the decision on which technologies/solutions to use, an organization must weigh the business need (how important is it to make the application available) versus how important it is to carefully design the application and choose the best technology to maximize eye appeal, performance, ease of use, code reuse, and maintainability.

Results of the Tutorial

Let's look at the results:

1. In the TutorialsJSF project, a new package in WebContent named c12.

2. In WebContent/c12, the following new Facelet files:

    ```
    AllEmps.xhtml        GetEmp.xhtml              InsertEmp.xhtml
    SelectEmp.xhtml      UpdateEmp.xhtml
    ```

3. Inside of Java Resources: src, three folders called:

    ```
    com.ibm.faces.sdo      pagecode                  pagecode.c12
    ```

4. Inside of pagecode.c12, the following new Java files:

```
AllEmps.java        DBAccess.java       Employee.java
GetEmp.java         InsertEmp.java      SelectEmp.java
UpdateEmp.java
```

5. In the WebContent folder, two new Web pages called TNTApps and EmpApps (that provide links to the Employee functions) and page.jsp.

6. The employee JSF-based application can insert, display, and update employee information (using SelectEmp.jsp) in a database.

Review Questions

1. What is a pagecode class?

2. What is a framework?

3. Explain binding.

4. What are the advantages of a Facelet over a JSP?

5. What is a Service Data Object?

6. What is the purpose of a session scope variable?

7. What is the purpose of navigation rules?

8. In a JSF application, which components provide the model, view, and controller functions?

Review Exercise

You will create a Shipment application to insert, update, display, and delete shipment information in a DBMS using the JSF framework.

1. Create a new Dynamic Web Project, that is configured for JSF called ReviewExJSF and add it to a new EAR called ReviewExJSFEAR.

2. Copy the TNTApps and EmpApps Web pages from TutorialsJSF to ReviewExJSF.

3. Make a copy of EmpApps called ShipApps

4. On ShipApps, change the text to read Display All Shipments, Insert A Shipment, Update A Shipment.

5. On TNTApps, add a link to ShipApps.

6. In ReviewExJSF/WebContent, create a new folder called c12.

7. In c12, create a Facelet called DisplayShip.

8.   In DisplayShip:

   A.   Add a relational record list called shipRRL

   B.   Create a new database connection to the Shipment table called TNT_Shipment_Con
        and define TNT_Shipment_Con as the connection for shipRRL

   C.   Define the key of the table as shipment number

DisplayShip should have all the fields as in Figure 12-52.

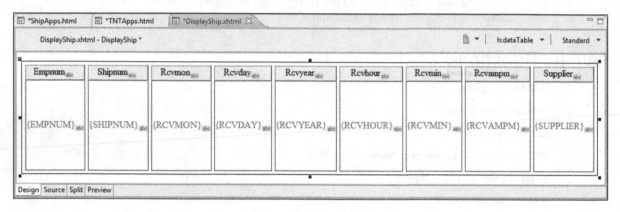

Figure 12-52.

9.   In c12, create a Facelet called InsertShip.

10. In InsertShip, add a relational record called shipRR that:

   A.   Has a control option for creating a new record

   B.   Uses TNT_Shipment_Con to connect to the Shipment table

   C.   Has a key defined as shipment number

InsertShip should look like Figure 12-53.

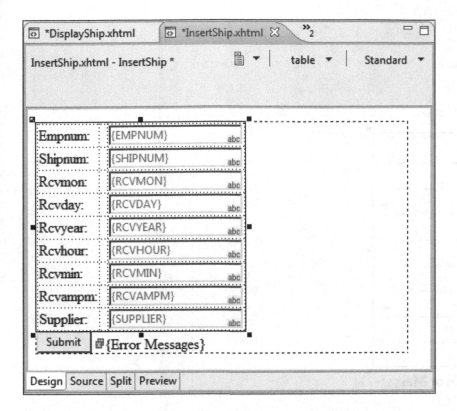

Figure 12-53.

11. In c12, create a Facelet called UpdateShip.

12. In UpdateShip, add a relational record called shipRRU that:

    A. Has control options for updating an existing record

    B. Uses TNT_Shipment_Con to connect to the Shipment table

    C. Has a key defined as shipment number

    D. Has a filter condition that uses a parameter called shipNum.

UpdateShip should look like Figure 12-54.

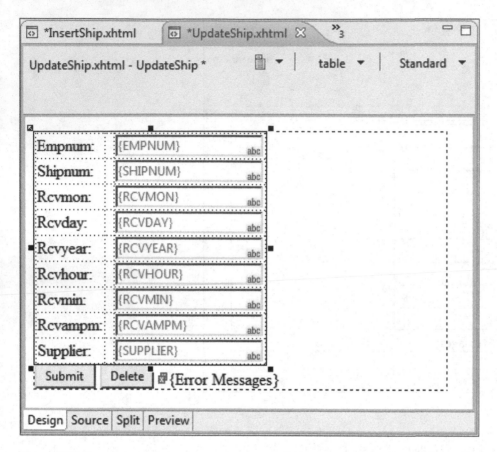

Figure 12-54.

13. In DisplayShip:

   A. Define a link to UpdateShip.xhtml for the shipment number field.

   B. Add a parameter to the link called shipNum.

   C. Specify shipRRL's shipnum field as the value of shipNum.

14. Define navigation rules for all buttons on InsertShip and UpdateShip, so that all outcomes go to DisplayShip.

15. On ShipApps, add a link to DisplayShip for the text Display All Shipments and Update A Shipment.

16. On ShipApps, add a link to InsertShip for the text Insert A Shipment.

17. Save all the source code.

Results of the Review Exercise

After the review exercise we have:

1. In the ReviewExJSF project, a new package in WebContent named c12 that has the following Facelet files:

   `DisplayShip.xhtml`   `InsertShip.xhtml`   `UpdateShip.xhtml`

2. Inside of Java Resources/src, a new folder called pagecode.c12 containing:

   `DisplayShip.java`   `InsertShip.java`   `UpdateShip.java`

3. Three new Web Pages called TNTApps, EmpApps, and ShipApps that provide links to the Shipment and Employee functions.

4. The JSF-based application can now insert, display, and update shipment information in a database.

Check that the Exercise Was Done Correctly

Finally, let's check it all worked:

1. Run TNTApps.html on the server and choose the Shipment Application option.

2. From the ShipApps page, select the insert option and insert the following information for a shipment:

   A. employee: 222

   B. shipment number: 1000

   C. the current date and time

   D. supplier: Fred Meyers

3. The DisplayShip page should be displayed with the shipment 1000 information.

4. Click shipment number 1000.

5. The UpdateShip page should be displayed with shipment 1000's information.

6. Change the employee number to 111 and click the Submit button.

7. The DisplayShip page should be displayed with the shipment 1000's employee number equal to 111.

8. Click shipment number 1000.

9. The UpdateShip page should be displayed with shipment 1000's information.

10. Click the delete button.

11. The DisplayShip page should be displayed without shipment 1000.

APPENDIX A

■ ■ ■

Installing a Java Application on a PC

In this Appendix, we will show you how to install an application onto a Windows PC from the RAD environment. The means explaining system environment variables and the software required to run a Java application on a PC. We will also explore PC batch (.bat) files and show how they make applications easier to use. Finally, we'll demonstrate how to import files into the RAD environment. The example assumes Chapters 1 and 2 have been completed.

Tutorial: Exporting an Application from RAD

Programmers use RAD to develop applications. Users do not have RAD. Therefore applications have to be installed onto user's computers. To install an application, the application's .class files must be moved from RAD onto the computer where they will be run. This is called exporting. In the process of installing a Java application, exporting is a relatively simple step. The more complicated steps involve installing a JRE and configuring Windows to enable Java applications.

In the example, the Employee application in myFirstPackage will be moved to a flash memory stick identified as the F: drive. We are putting the application on a memory stick so that it can be easily transported between computers. (If you don't have a memory stick, any storage media that has at least 150 megabytes of space is OK. For example, a zip disk can provide the needed space and portability. At worst, sacrifice portability and use the C: drive.)

1. In the Package Explorer, select MyFirstProject.

2. Click File, then Export.

The Export window will be displayed (see Figure A-1). Files can be exported in several different formats. For instance, there are ZIP and JAR format options for Java applications, as well as, WAR (Web Archive File) and EAR (Enterprise Archive File) options for exporting server-based applications. (In later chapters, the text will cover server-based applications and how to install them.) All of these formats compress the files. Usually these compressed formats are used when exporting and installing (rather than exporting the .class files directly) because of storage and transfer time efficiencies.

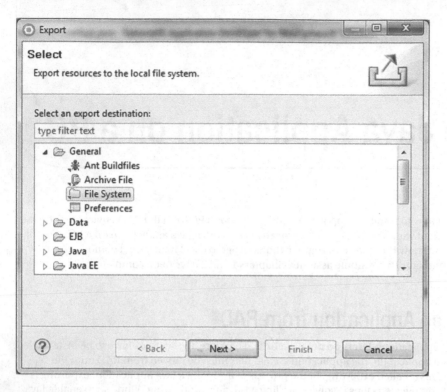

Figure A-1.

The application can also be exported in several different "ways." For instance, the FTP (File Transfer Protocol) option allows files to be sent to any computer that has a Web address (thereby helping with a remote application install). We are simply moving the application to a different location on the PC (i.e., from the RAD work space to the F: drive), so we will choose the File system option.

3. On the Export window expand the General item, click File System, then click the Next button.

The Export window will be displayed (see Figure A-2). Because we selected MyFirstProject for export, RAD assumes every folder and file will be exported. Because we are only going to run the application (not edit the source code) the .java files do not need to be exported.

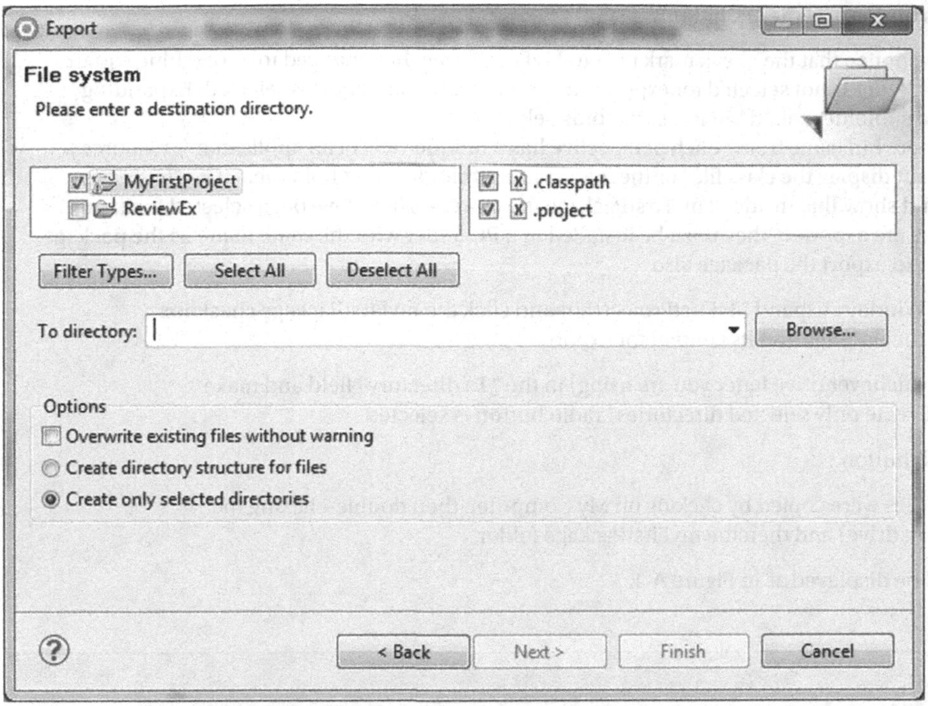

Figure A-2.

> **4.** Click the Filter Types. . . button.

The Select Types window will be displayed (see Figure A-3). As this window's name implies, files for export can be specified by their type (i.e., file extension). As an application gets more complex, it may be comprised of hundreds if not thousands of class files. Rather than specifically selecting each class, this enables you to specify all of them for export.

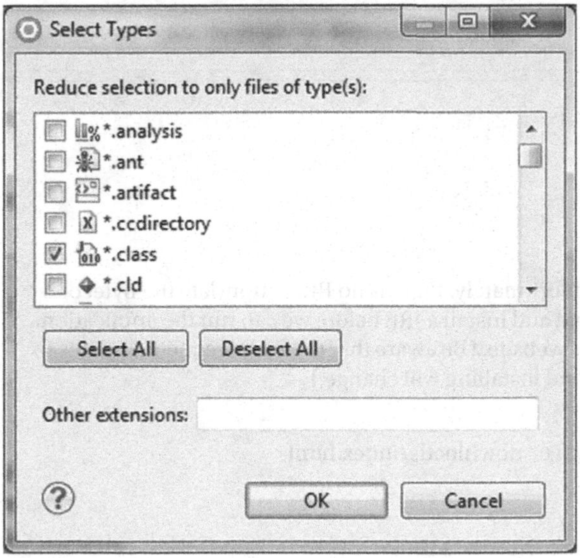

Figure A-3.

479

5. Click the .class option and the OK button.

On the Export window, notice that the check mark next to MyFirstProject has changed to a solid blue square. This means that the project folder is not selected for export but something in the project is selected. Expanding MyFirstProject shows that a subfolder called bin has something selected.

Are you wondering where bin came from? Each perspective has a unique view of an application's resources. The Java perspective does not display the class files or the folders and subfolders that hold them. Continuing to expand the subfolders would show that inside of myFirstPackage the two class files have been selected for export.

When files in a package are exported, they must be installed in a PC folder with the same name as the package. The easiest way to do this is to export the package also.

6. On the Export Window, expand MyFirstProject/bin and click the myFirstPackage checkbox twice to select the package and its content for export.

7. Specify F: (or whichever drive letter you are using) in the "To directory" field and make sure that the "Create only selected directories" radio button is selected.

8. Click the Finish button.

9. Verify that the files were copied by clicking on My Computer, then double-clicking the drive (e.g., the F: drive) and then the myFirstPackage folder.

The two class files will be displayed as in Figure A-4.

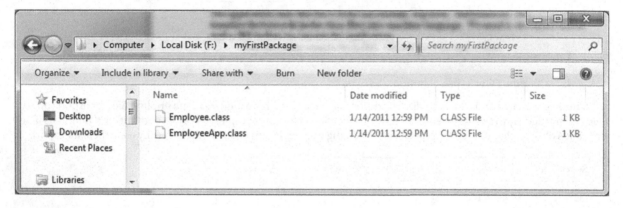

Figure A-4.

Tutorial: Downloading a JRE

The application class files have been successfully exported. Unfortunately, there is no JRE to translate the bytecode (in the class files) into machine language. We need to download and install a JRE before we can run the application.

There are many sources for a JRE. We will go to the Oracle website. (Be aware that there are frequent updates to the Oracle website and often the procedure for downloading and installing will change.)

1. In the Internet Explorer browser, specify
   http://www.oracle.com/technetwork/java/javase/ downloads/index.html

The download page will be displayed (see Figure A-5).

Figure A-5.

Oracle puts out new releases of the JRE quite frequently, so the download Web site address and page (as well as the documentation Web site) may change with different Java releases. In addition, the currently available JRE release you will download will probably be newer than JRE 6.23 shown in these figures.

2. Click on the JRE Download link (indicated with the arrow in Figure A-5).

The license agreement page will be displayed (see Figure A-6).

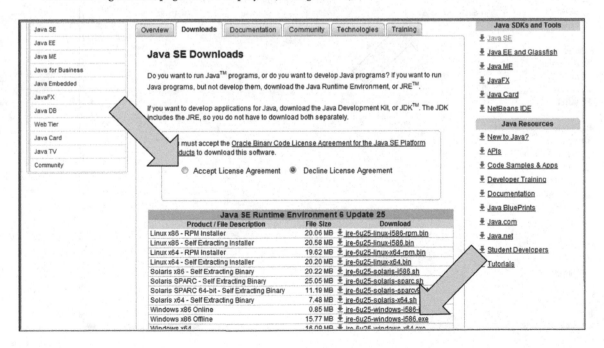

Figure A-6.

As mentioned earlier, there are many different JRE versions. Do you remember why?

Because the JRE must work with a specific operating system, there are different JRE versions for each operating system. (This is the same reason applications—like games, word processors, etc.—come in Windows and Apple versions.)

3.   Click the "Accept License Agreement" checkbox.

This activates the download links at the bottom of the page.

4.   If you are using Windows 7, you can click the Windows Offline Installation file link (as indicated by the arrow in Figure A-6).

The File Download window will be displayed.

5.   Click the Save button.

The Save As window will be displayed. The name of the file (jre-6u25-windows-i586-p.exe) will already be specified. (The name of the file will change with different releases, so do not worry if it is not exactly the same.) Make sure the correct drive is specified (i.e., F :).

6.   Click the Save button.

The file will be downloaded to the specified drive (i.e., F:).

7.   Click on My Computer and then double-click the F: drive icon to display the contents.

The newly downloaded Setup Launcher file and myFirstPackage folder will be displayed (see Figure A-7).

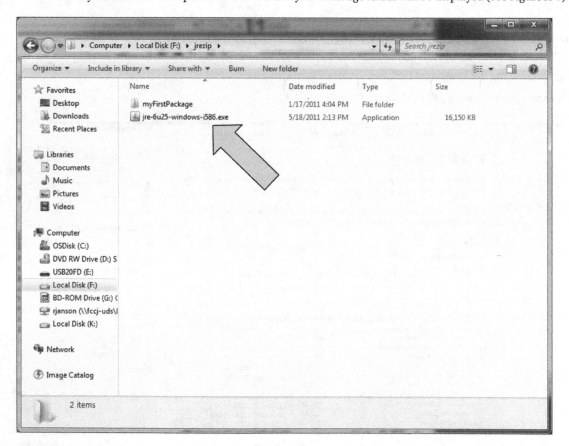

Figure A-7.

Tutorial: Installing a JRE

1. Double-click the Setup Launcher file (jre-6u25-windows-i586-p.exe) to run the install program.

The Java Setup – Welcome window will be displayed. The Typical setup puts the JRE on the computers default drive. Because we want to install to the F: drive, we will need to customize the setup option.

2. Click the "Change destination folder" checkbox and accept the license agreement by clicking the Install button (see Figure A-8).

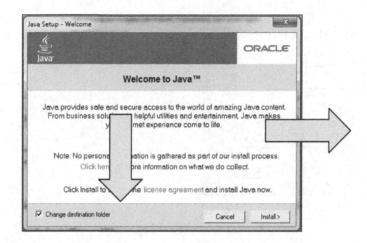

Figure A-8.

The "Java Setup – Destination Folder" window will be displayed (see Figure A-9).

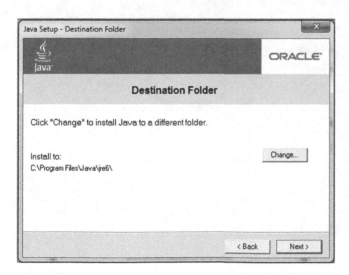

Figure A-9.

3. Click on the Change. . . button.

4. Click on the F: drive and click the Make New Folder button (see Figure A-10).

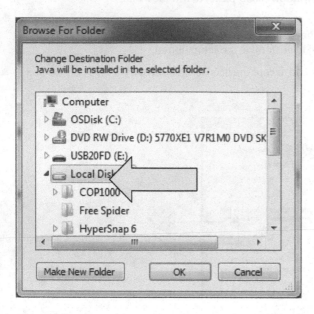

Figure A-10.

5. Type jre over the default name, New folder, and press the Enter key.

The folder will be renamed (see Figure A-11).

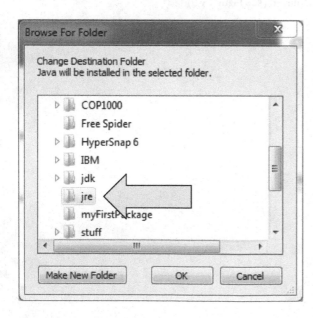

Figure A-11.

6. Click the OK button.

The "Java Setup – Destination Folder" window will be redisplayed with F:\jre specified as the destination.

7. Click the Next button.

A progress window is displayed as the installation is performed. This may take a while, depending on the speed of the computer and the media chosen for the install. In addition, if there are open browser sessions, you will be required to close them to continue the install. (There are other applications that you may also be prompted to close.)
Eventually, the "Java Setup - Complete" window will be displayed.
If the installation was successful, a folder named jre containing the JRE will be on the F: drive.

8. Verify that the JRE has been installed by double-clicking on My Computer, then double-clicking the F: drive icon to display the contents of the F: drive.

There should be a new folder called jre.

9. Double-click the F:\jre folder to display the contents.

The window should look like Figure A-12. (The contents of the folder may also change with new releases.) Most of the files contain general and legal information. The README file does contain a list of subfolders and files that are not essential for running Java applications. However, the entire jre folder is approximately 90 MB, so space should not be a problem.

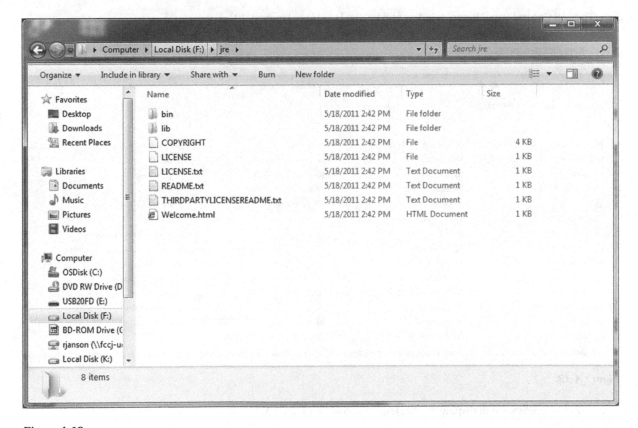

Figure A-12.

APPENDIX A ■ INSTALLING A JAVA APPLICATION ON A PC

More important are the bin and lib subfolders. The lib folder contains the JAR files that hold the core classes (e.g., **String**). For example, if you display the contents of lib, the rt.jar file can be seen. This file contains many of the core classes.

The bin folder holds many JRE functions. For instance, the file named java.exe in bin contains a program that allows you to run a Java application in the JRE. However, before that can happen Windows must be configured to find the Java support functions and core classes.

Tutorial: Environment Variables

There are many different Windows' environment variables, each with a unique name. Environment variables can be defined as system variables—meaning that they are universal for all applications on the PC. (It is like saying that a red traffic light is a national "driving environment variable" meaning **stop**. Regardless of where you are driving in the nation, a red traffic light means stop.) Environment variables can also be defined as user variables. User variables are only valid for a particular user of the computer. In addition, environment variables can be changed dynamically. This means that a user or an application can change them temporarily. When changed dynamically, the new values are only in effect for as long as that user or application continues processing. If another application or the same user starts up, the variables original values are used.

One way to change environment variables values is through the Control Panel.

1. Click the Start button and on the right side of the Start menu select Control Panel

The "All Control Panel Items" window will be displayed (see Figure A-13).

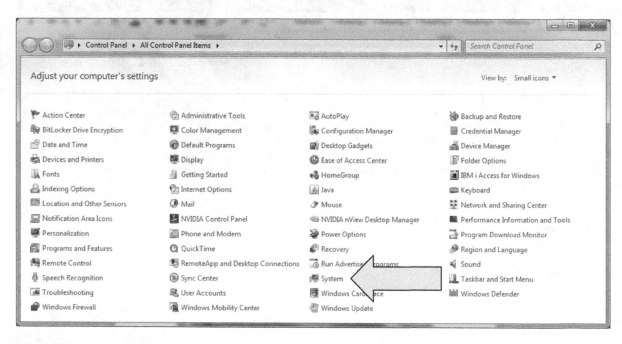

Figure A-13.

2. Click System to display the "System" window (see Figure A-14).

486

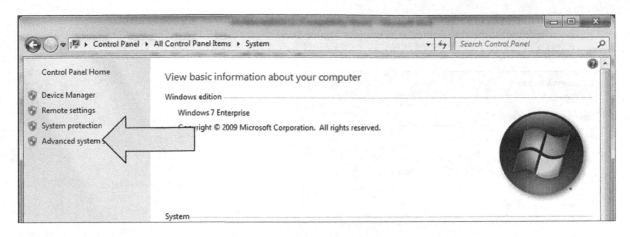

Figure A-14.

3. On the "System" window, click the "Advanced System Settings" button to display the "System Properties" window (see Figure A-15).

Figure A-15.

4. On the "System Properties" window, click the "Environment Variables" button to display the "Environment Variables" window (see Figure A-16).

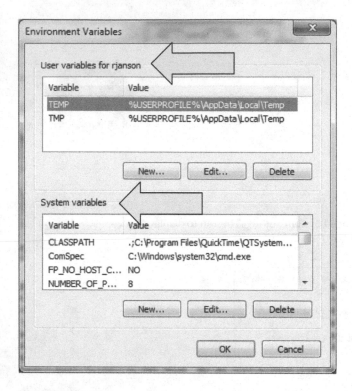

Figure A-16.

Notice that the environment variables are broken up in User and System variables. System variables are universal for all users on a computer. User variables are only valid for the particular user currently signed on to the computer. If there is a System and User variable with the same name, the User variable value will override the System variable value.

To understand the importance of Environment variables to Java we have to explain a little about how Windows (and many operating systems) "work". When a user clicks an icon or a menu item, they are telling Windows to do "something" (i.e., specifying a function/command) against "something" (i.e., a file). So clicking on the "Internet Explorer" icon or menu item means the user is specifying run (i.e., the command) the iexplore.exe file stored in C:\Program Files\Internet Explorer. This information was all specified when Internet Explorer was installed on the computer. Thank you, Microsoft!

Notice that Windows had to be told every little detail—like the exact location of the file to be run. This exact location and file name (C:\Program Files\Internet Explorer\iexplore.exe) is called a fully qualified file name. If a fully qualified name is not specified, Windows does not search the entire system to find the file. Instead Windows reads the environment variable PATH. PATH can hold many locations (separated by semicolons) and tells Windows where to search whenever an executable file (i.e., a command) is specified. The CLASSPATH variable tells Windows where to search whenever a Java class file is specified. As with the PATH variables, multiple path names (folders and subfolders) can be defined for the CLASSPATH variable. The "Environment Variables" window allows users to define a variable or edit an already existing variable.

In Chapter 2, you learned that Java source code has to be compiled (converted to bytecode) and interpreted (converted to machine language and run). Both of these functions are not standard Windows commands. If you tried to run a bytecode file, Windows would search the location in the PATH variable and not find the "run" command. In other words, Windows does not know anything about Java. Therefore, for a Java application to be executed, the PATH and CLASSPATH variables have to be edited to include the java command files location (i.e., in the JRE) and the location of the .class files.

If we modify the variables using the Environment Variables window, our application will only work for this computer. For example, if we took the memory stick (in the F: drive) to another computer, we would have to set that computer's environment variables to look for our class files and the JRE on the F: drive. This would have to be done for every computer we want to run the application on. To get around this problem, we are going to write a small batch program (and store it on the F: drive) that will set the PATH and CLASSPATH variables dynamically on whatever computer we want to run the application on.

If you have not programmed on a PC before this may come as a surprise, but all the functions performed from the Windows GUI (graphical user interface) can be performed with commands. For instance, the **dir** (directory) command lets a user display the contents of a folder or drive (the same function that the My Computer icon provides). In addition, there are **path** and **Set classpath** commands that can control the two environment variables we need to define. Our batch program will use these commands to configure the environment variables. In addition, we will include a JRE command to run our Java application.

Tutorial: Creating a Batch File

Windows commands can be stored in a file with an extension of "bat" (indicating that the file is a **batch** file). When a bat file is specified at the command prompt (or its icon is double-clicked), Windows will execute the commands contained in the file in sequential order. We will use the Windows Notepad utility to enter, and save the commands in a batch file called **Employee_Application.bat**.

1.   Click Start, All Programs, Accessories, and then Notepad (see Figure A-17).

Figure A-17.

Notepad will create an unnamed file and display a blank window indicating that the file is empty. Commands are entered by positioning the cursor and typing. The first command we want to enter is the path command.

2.   Type **path=f:\jre\bin** (see Figure A-17).

This will set the path to the bin folder that contains the JRE commands. The **java** command is needed to run the employee application in the JRE and is stored in the bin subfolder. (If you need proof, use My Computer to display the contents of the bin folder. You will see an "application" file called java. This program is run when the **java** command is issued.)

3.   Press Enter to add a new line.

4.   On the new line, type **Set classpath=f:**

This statement defines the classpath variable, which, essentially, tells Windows where to find our application classes (i.e., the package folders myFirstPackage). There must be at least one space between **Set** and **classpath**, and there are no other spaces in the command. Be careful: this must be coded exactly as shown. Common mistakes include using forward slashes instead of the back slashes, using colons for semicolons (and vice versa), and having an extra space at the end of a line.

5.   Press Enter to add a new line.

6.   On the new line, type **java myFirstPackage/EmployeeApp**

There must be at least one space after the **java** command and no spaces thereafter. When this command is encountered, Windows finds the **java** program (because of the **path** statement) and passes the name of our application (**myFirstPackage/EmployeeApp**) to the **java** program. Notice that when identifying the application both the package and class file names are needed and are separated by a forward slash. The **java** program then passes the bytecode (i.e., the class file) to the Java interpreter (i.e., the JVM) for translation into machine language and execution. The final code should look like Figure A-18.

Figure A-18.

7. In the Notepad window, click File, then Save As.

Notice that the default file save type is a text document (i.e., an extension of .txt). However, this file needs to be saved as a batch file (i.e., a file extension of .bat).

8. Click the "Save as type" drop down menu button and click on All Files.

The "Save as type" will change to All Files.

9. In the File name field, enter **Employee_Application.bat**

10. Change the location to F: and click the Save button.

11. In the Notepad window, click File, and then Print.

12. At the Print window, click the Print button.

A hard copy of the file contents will be printed.

13. Verify that the file was saved by selecting My Computer and display the contents of the F: drive.

The window will display the Employee_Application.bat file (see Figure A-19).

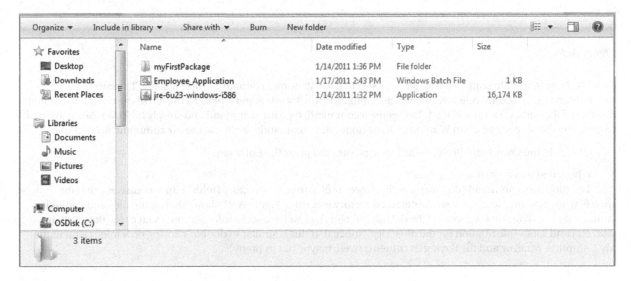

Figure A-19.

Tutorial: Running a Java Application on the PC

Let's run an application:

1. Click Start, All Programs, Accessories, and then Command Prompt.

If the Command Prompt option is not listing in the Accessories menu, you can click the Start button, and then in the "Search programs and files" text field, specify **cmd** and press Enter.

The "Command Prompt" window will be displayed with the computer's default directory (in this case, C:\Windows\system32 as in Figure A-20). The default directory can be changed, therefore it can be different for every PC, and so don't worry if yours doesn't match Figure A-20.

Figure A-20.

The "Command Prompt" window allows users to issue Windows commands interactively. The cursor (the blinking underscore) indicates where the commands will appear when typed. To the left of the cursor, the default directory followed by a > is displayed. To execute a command, type the command and simply hit Enter. As mentioned earlier, everything you can do in Windows can be done with commands. We'll use the **dir** command an example.

2.   In the Command Prompt window, type **dir**, and press the Enter key.

Whoa, that was a lot of information!

The directory command (**dir**) displays the contents of a drive or directory (folder). In this case, we did not specify what directory to display so the default directory was used. Figure A-21 shows that all the files and subfolders contained in C:\Windows\system32 (the default directory), as well as, some information about each (date and time, size, etc) and totals information for the directory. Notice that this is similar to double-clicking on a folder icon in the My Computer window and displaying its contents (well, maybe not as pretty).

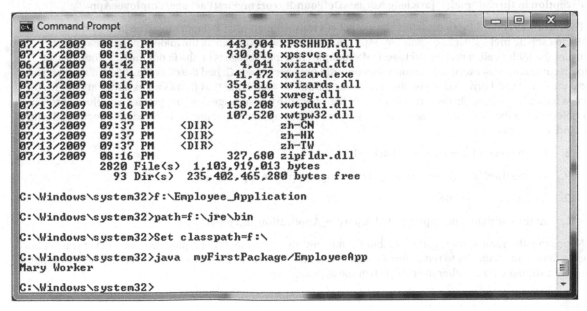

Figure A-21.

To run the Employee_Application batch file all you need to do is identify the file and press the Enter key. To identify a file specify where the file is located (the file's path) and the file name.

3. Type **f:\Employee_Application** and press Enter.

Because Employee_Application is a batch file, Windows knows to execute the commands contained within. Notice that the Command Prompt window (in Figure A-22) shows each of the three batch file commands and the result of the Java application.

```
07/13/2009   08:16 PM              443,904 XPSSHHDR.dll
07/13/2009   08:16 PM              930,816 xpssvcs.dll
06/10/2009   04:42 PM                4,041 xwizard.dtd
07/13/2009   08:14 PM               41,472 xwizard.exe
07/13/2009   08:16 PM              354,816 xwizards.dll
07/13/2009   08:16 PM               85,504 xwreg.dll
07/13/2009   08:16 PM              158,208 xwtpdui.dll
07/13/2009   08:16 PM              107,520 xwtpw32.dll
07/13/2009   09:37 PM    <DIR>              zh-CN
07/13/2009   09:37 PM    <DIR>              zh-HK
07/13/2009   09:37 PM    <DIR>              zh-TW
07/13/2009   08:16 PM              327,680 zipfldr.dll
              2820 File(s)  1,103,919,013 bytes
                93 Dir(s)   235,402,465,280 bytes free

C:\Windows\system32>f:\Employee_Application

C:\Windows\system32>path=f:\jre\bin

C:\Windows\system32>Set classpath=f:\

C:\Windows\system32>java   myFirstPackage/EmployeeApp
Mary Worker

C:\Windows\system32>
```

Figure A-22.

This may seem like a lot of work (for very little result). However, most of the work was one time, setup tasks. To rerun the application you only have to execute the java command again. No environment variables have to be reset, nor do you have to export the application again. However, if the application were modified, the classes would have to be reexported.

Tutorial: Breaking the Code

The batch file is very important to the successful installation of a Java application. Unfortunately, batch file mistakes are not easily diagnosed. We will create some of the most common mistakes and show their effects on running the application.

1. Start a Command Prompt session.

2. Start Notepad and open Employee_Application.bat.

3. On the first line change path=f:\jre\bin to path=f:\jre\Bin (i.e., change the b to upper case).

4. Save the source code.

5. At the command prompt, type **f:\Employee_Application** and press Enter.

The application worked! You are probably saying, "Hey, you said Java was case sensitive!" That's still true. However, Windows is not case-sensitive. If you reference files called Employee, employee, or EMPLOYEE, Windows will find the same file.

6. On the second line change the f to c (i.e., change the classpath).

7. Save the source code, go to the command prompt, type **f:\Employee_Application** and press Enter.

You will get the following (always frustrating) error message:

Exception in thread "main" java.lang.NoClassDefFoundError: myFirstPackage/EmployeeApp

The error was caused by an incorrect classpath. Let's walk through what is happening. The **java** command tells the JVM to execute myFirstPackage/EmployeeApp. The JVM searches through all the folders in the classpath (C:) looking for the folder called myFirstPackage. Unfortunately, myFirstPackage is on the F: not the C:. (Note, the set classpath command was executed, Windows not only did not check to see C: had the class file, it doesn't even check to see if the C: is a valid drive.) Because the application cannot be found, the JVM throws up its hands and issues the "No class found" message. This is a frustrating error to fix because the message does not provide any clues as to where the problem is. For example, this message is also generated if the application name is specified incorrectly in the **java** command. Let's prove it.

8. On the second line change C: back to F:.

9. On the third line, delete the last p (i.e., change EmployeeApp to EmployeeAp).

10. Save the source code.

11. At the command prompt, type **f:\Employee_Application** and press Enter.

Notice that the same error is generated, but the message says it cannot find EmployeeAp. Whenever you get the "No class found" message, try to remember that the JVM usually cannot find the class specified in the **java** command because of a simple typo in either the classpath or the application name.

12. On the third line, change EmployeeAp back to EmployeeApp.

13. On the first line, delete the e in jre (i.e., change path=f:\jre\bin to path=f:\jr\bin).

14. Save the source code, go to the command prompt, type **f:\Employee_Application** and press Enter.

You will get the following annoying error message:

'java' is not recognized as an internal or external command, operable program or batch file.

(If you do not get this error, the System32 folder contains the java.exe file. Go to the folder, rename the file, and do step 14 again. Don't forget to change the file name back to java after you are done with step 19.) This time the problem is with the path environment variable. Whenever you enter text at the command prompt, Window searches the directories in the path looking for a batch file, executable program file, or operating system command file with the same name as the text specified. In this case we specified an incorrect folder name (jr instead of jre) when we defined the path. Windows looked for the executable file called java (which contains the **java** command program) in the folders specified in the path. The file was not in any of those folders, so Windows could not find the **java** command (stored in the f:**jre**\ bin folder).

If you had specified **jave** instead of **java** in the third line, you would have gotten the same error but this time identifying **jave** as the unrecognized command.

15. In Notepad, click File, Print, and then the Print button to generate a hardcopy of the source code in the batch file.

16. On the first line, insert the e, and save the source code.

Just to emphasize how careful you need to be (or how picky computers are), we will create one last mistake.

17. On the first line, add two blank spaces to the end of the statement (i.e., change "path= f:\jre\Bin" to "path=f:\jre\Bin ") and save the source code.

18. At the command prompt, type **f:\Employee_Application** and press Enter.

You will get the "java command not recognized" error message again. Why? Because spaces are valid characters in a folder name, therefore a folder specified as "bin " is not the same as a folder specified as "bin." Yikes-a-hootie!! Isn't programming fun?

19. Delete the two spaces, save the source code, close Notepad, and close the command prompt session.

Tutorial: Stopping a Runaway Application in Windows

There will be occasions where you will write and/or run an application that never ends or "freezes up" (does not respond to the keyboard or mouse). On these occasions, you will want to end the application. The Windows Task Manager allows you to do this. (The Task Manager also displays performance information about the computer hardware, as well as, all active applications and processes.)

There are several ways to display the Task Manager. For instance, you can start the command prompt, type **taskmgr**, and press Enter. Alternatively, you can press the Ctrl, Alt, Delete keys simultaneously, and display the Windows Security window. The Windows Security window has a Task Manager option. Ctrl-Alt-Delete is used to regain control when the entire computer or all the applications are not responding.

However, it's easiest to simply right-click in an empty area of the task bar. The task bar is (usually) at the bottom of the screen and shows buttons for all of the applications that are currently running. You have probably clicked the task bar buttons to move between applications. However, right-clicking in an empty area anywhere to the right of the Start button, displays a shortcut menu and one of the options is the Start Task Manager.

1. Right-click in the far right of the Task bar.

2. Click the Start Task Manager option.

The Windows Task Manager frame will be display as in Figure A-23. In this example, there are twelve active applications and their names appear in the Applications view. (The applications would also appear in the task bar's application tray. Within each task bar icon would be individual items that are displayed in the task manager in Figure A-23.)

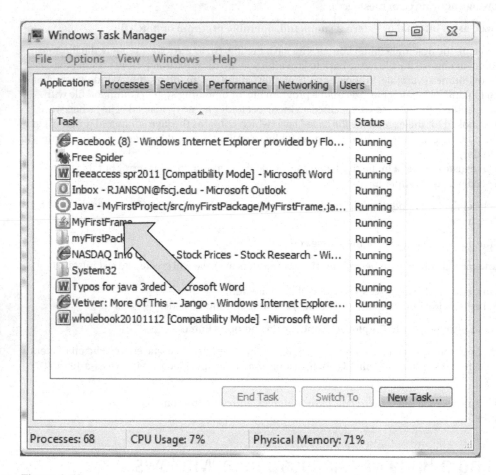

Figure A-23.

Java applications are identified with the "steaming cup of coffee" icon. In Figure A-23, the application My First Frame is a Java application. To end an application, first select the application by clicking its name and then click the End Task button.

Then "End Program – My First Frame" dialogue box will be displayed with a message saying that the application is not responding (Figure A-24). Of course, you would click the End Now button.

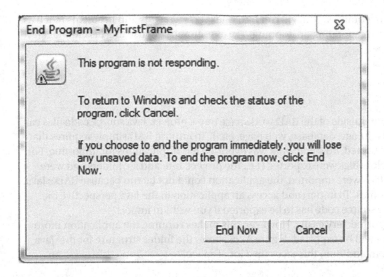

Figure A-24.

If you go back to the Task Managers Application list, you will see that the application name has been removed as in Figure A-25. (Sometimes this may take a second or two.)

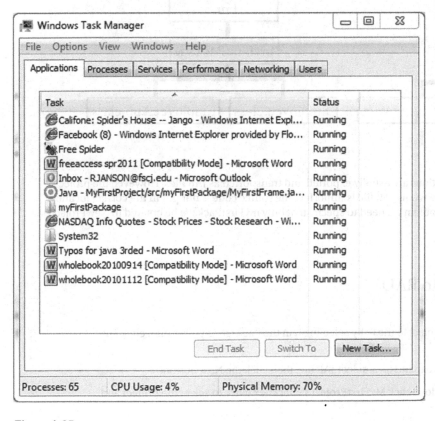

Figure A-25.

As the applications you write become more complex, you will run into unexpected results and problems (such as endless loops) that prevent the application from responding or stopping. Try to remember to use the Task Manager; it is your escape hatch from such problems.

Importing into RAD

Importing allows programmers to bring files from outside of the RAD workspace into a project. Java source code files can be imported, as well as, many other types of files (image, database, web page, etc.). To import, RAD simply requires that a project already exists. If an application were exported, how and what was exported has implications for importing. For example, earlier only myFirstPackage and the .class files were exported (i.e., the project, bin, and src folders and were not exported). If myFirstPackage and the .class files were imported, the application could not be run because RAD's Java perspective does not provide access to the .class files. To import and access an application in the Java perspective the source files have to be imported. This means the source code has to be exported if you want to import.

An entire project can be exported and imported very easily. However, this makes running the application more complicated because the entire folder structure will be exported. Figure A-26 shows the folder structure for the .java and .class files if the whole project is exported. In addition, this takes up a lot of space.

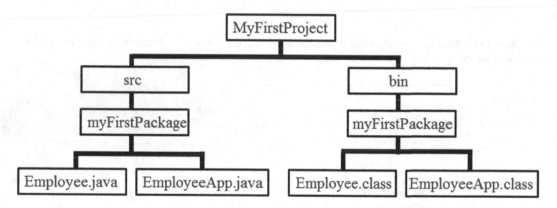

Figure A-26.

In the real world, Java applications are usually exported and transported as JAR files. However, the project structure is not preserved and if the whole JAR file is imported, the source code is not put in the correct location within the project. To avoid this problem we need to specify that only myFirstPackage be created in NewProject/src when importing.

Let's prove it.

Tutorial: Importing into RAD

Now let's import into RAD:

1. Export all of MyFirstProject to the F: by selecting it in the Package Explorer then click File and Export.

2. At the Export window, expand Java, select JAR file, then click the Next button.

3. At the JAR Export window, click MyFirstProject's checkbox twice to select the project and all its subfolders.

If you expand the tree and drill down into src/myFirstPackage, the .java files will appear checked in the right-hand pane. Even though all the folders, subfolders and java files are selected, the source code will not be exported. Exporting the source code must be explicitly specified.

4.　At the JAR Export window, click the Export Java source files and resources checkbox (see Figure A-27).

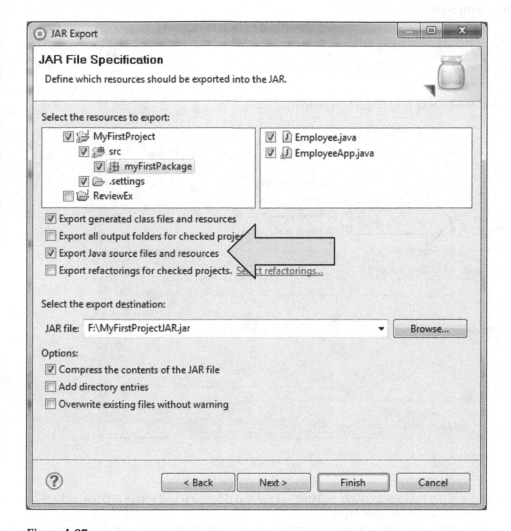

Figure A-27.

5.　In the JAR file text field, specify F:\MyFirstProjectJAR and click the Finish button. (If you get a JAR export warnings window, just ignore it by clicking the OK button.)

6.　Using My Computer verify that the jar file is on the F:.

Well that's great that we have a jar file but how can you tell what is in it? How about importing it into a new project?

7.　In RAD, create a Java project called NewProject.

8. In the Package Explorer, expand NewProject and click on the src folder.

9. Click File then Import and at the Import Window expand General and select Archive File.

10. Click Next and in the From archive file text field specify F:\MyFirstProjectJAR.jar.

11. Expand the tree diagram, unselect everything except myFirstPackage (see Figure A-28), then click the Finish button

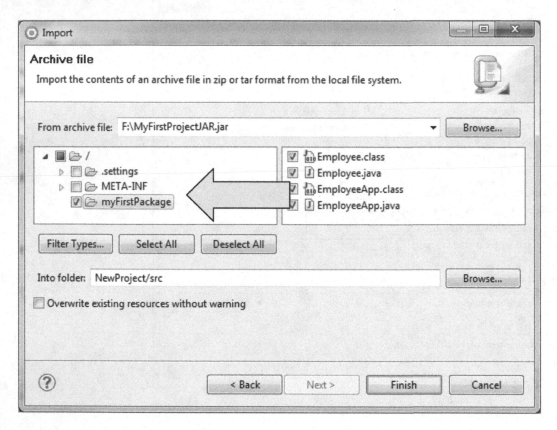

Figure A-28.

If you expand the src folder in the Package Explorer, myFirstPackage should appear and within myFirstPackage should be the two .java files Employee and EmployeeApp.

That seemed like a lot work. Let's show how easy it is to import if the entire project is simply exported to the file system.

12. Delete NewProject and all of its content.

13. Create a Java project called NewProject.

14. In the Package Explorer, click on MyFirstProject, then File and Export.

15. Expand the General item, select File System and click the Next button.

16. At the Export window, click the Finish button.

17. Using My Computer verify a folder called MyFirstProject is on the F drive and that the .class and .java files are in the correct subfolders per Figure A-27.

18. Now the easy part, select NewProject in the Package Explore, click File then Import.

19. Specify File System as the source and click the Next button.

20. Specify F:\MyFirstProject as the From directory, then in the tree click the MyFirstProject's checkbox and then click Finish.

21. At the Question window, click the Yes To All button.

Looking in NewProject should show that the myFirstPackage folder and its contents were imported. You can confirm that the import was successful by running EmployeeApp.

The "problem" with exporting the entire project is that structure the holds the package with the .class files is more complicated than the Tutorial example (which simply exported the package). This means that the classpath value has to be changed to point to this new location rather than the F: drive. If you are using the bat file, it must be modified to issue the correct set classpath command.

Results of the Tutorial

Let's check the results:

1. A new Java project called NewProject.

2. NewProject\src\myFirstPackage and F:\MyFirstProject\src\myFirstPackage each have two source files.

3. F:\myFirstPackage and F:\MyFirstProject\bin\myFirstPackage each have two bytecode files.

4. The JRE successfully installed and the Employee_Application.bat file created on the F: drive.

5. Two printouts of the commands in the Employee_Application.bat file.

Review Questions

1. What is the function of the JVM?

2. Which are executable: java files, class files, or both?

3. What does a batch file hold?

4. What is the classpath?

5. What is exporting?

6. What is the relationship between source code, machine language, and bytecode?

Review Exercise

You will export the shipment application to the F: drive and create a batch file to set the system variables and run the application. Because all the setup work has already been done, you will see how relatively easy it is to install the application.

1. Export the entire ReviewEx project (including the source code) to the F drive.

2. Start notepad and open F:\Employee_Application.bat.

3. Save the file as F:\Shipment_Application.bat. (This is a little tricky. If you are having problems, review the Creating a Batch File tutorial.)

4. Because ShipmentApp is in a different location than EmployeeApp, change the set classpath command to specify the correct location.

5. Change the java statement so that ShipmentApp in c2 is executed not EmployeeApp.

Results of the Review Exercise

The results are:

1. The two shipment class files are stored in F:\ ReviewEx\bin\c2.

2. The Shipment_Application.bat file is stored on the F: drive.

Check that the Exercise Was Done Correctly

Finally, let's check it was done properly.

1. Verify that on the F: the folders ReviewEx, bin, and c2 were created and that the two shipment class files are contained within c2.

2. Start a Command Prompt session.

3. Enter F:\Shipment_Application.bat (or substitute the correct drive letter for your computer) and press Enter.

4. Verify that the five shipment variables are displayed.

APPENDIX B

SQL

SQL is an industry-wide, standard set of relational commands that allows users to both define and manipulate data in a database. SQL has been adopted as the common interface for relational data definition and data manipulation functions on all major relational DBMS (Database Management Systems).

This chapter will introduce the reader to SQL and show how SQL commands can be used within a Java application.

After finishing this chapter, you will understand:

> The most commonly used SQL commands and their syntax

> The major SQL components

After finishing this chapter, you will be able to:

> Create schemas, tables, views, and indexes

> Manipulate and retrieve data using SQL

SQL and Relational Database Concepts

SQL uses schemas (also referred to as collections) and tables to store data. You can think of a schema as a folder. (In actuality, a schema is also comprised of journals, a catalog, and cross reference tables. However, these are things a beginning Java programmer does not have to worry about.) Database analysts use schemas to group tables that hold related data. The schema and its tables correspond to what we have been referring to as a database. SQL statements can be used in application programs to both create these SQL constructs and access and manipulate the data stored within. Using SQL within a program provides a big advantage because SQL statements reference the universally accepted SQL objects (e.g., schemas and tables) regardless of what the individual DBMSs call these objects. Because of this, the Java developers did not include any data manipulation keywords in the Java language. Instead they supplied Java classes (such as the **Statement** and **ResultSet** classes) to facilitate the use of SQL.

A table is a two-dimensional array of data in rows and columns. Rows are often referred to as records and columns as fields. Individual pieces of data are stored in a single column of a single row. If you are familiar with spreadsheets, this is comparable to a spreadsheet cell.

Within Java applications, SQL statements are passed to a **Statement** object for execution. For the purposes of initially learning SQL, all examples will only show the SQL commands and required syntax. The Database Access chapter will show how to integrate the commands into a Java class.

Creating

SQL commands are simple, but using them can be complex. For instance, to create a schema, use the keywords **create schema** followed by the name of the new schema. For example:

```
CREATE SCHEMA tntdb
```

Yep, that's all there is to it. SQL is not case sensitive (yay!) and very forgiving of extra spaces. For instance, specifying the command as follows is also correct:

```
CREATE        SCHEMA                         tntdb
```

However, SQL is not forgiving when you forget a space. The general rule is at least one space between keywords and/or parameters. So, the following statements would be incorrect:

```
CREATESCHEMA             tntdb
CREATE        SCHEMAtntdb
```

The SQL **create schema** statement is simple, but executing it is often not so simple. For instance, to create a schema you usually need a very high level of DBMS authority. Java programmers do not usually have that level of authority. In addition, simple DBMS such as MS Access do not allow you to create schemas from an application. So, if you try to use this command within a Java class, don't be surprised if it does not work. In addition, when you identify a table in an SQL command, you may or may not have to specify the schema. This depends on how the database connection was defined (which is partially dependent on the DBMS). For instance, MS Access requires the programmer to identify the schema in SQL statements regardless of the connection definition. An Oracle connection defined to a particular table, frees the programmer from specifying the schema in every SQL command. All examples will specify the schema, but if you are having trouble with the commands, try them without specifying the schema.

All DBMS, however, allow applications to create tables. You can probably guess that the first two keywords are **create table.** These keywords are followed by the name of the schema, the new table name, and definitions of each column/field in the table. When defining a column/field, you need to provide at least a name and the type of data that will be stored in the column. Depending on the data type specified, you may also be required to specify a field size. Unfortunately, the Java data types, the SQL data types, and the various DBMS data types are not the same. There is considerable overlap, however, and sticking with the basic types like **char**, **double**, and **int** will allow your Java applications to work with all DBMS.

The following is an example of a **create table** statement that will create a table called "employee" in the TNTDB schema.

```
CREATE TABLE tntdb.employee
       (empnum        char(10),
        empname       char(25),
        street        char(15),
        city          char(10),
        state         char(2),
        zip           char(5),
        payrate       double,
        exempts       int)
```

Notice that when defining a field as **char** (this corresponds to a Java **String**) a size was specified. This is not a requirement. If no size is specified, most DBMSs will create the field with a default length. The problem is that each DBMS can have a different default, so it is best to specify the length of character fields. Fields defined as **double** and **int** can't have a size because the sizes are predefined. The extra spaces and lines placed between the commands, keywords, and column names (to make the statement more readable) are helpful but not required. In fact, the command could be entered as a continuous character string on one line. Note that SQL, like Java, ignores the extra spaces.

Defining tables (and schemas) in an application is very unusual. These DB objects are usually defined once by a database analyst, not every time an application is run. Please remember that a table must be created in a schema before an application can access the table.

Manipulating Data in a Table

SQL has many commands to modify and format data in a table. We will concentrate on the four basic commands of **insert into**, **select**, **update**, and **delete**.

Use the SQL **insert into** command to enter a row of data into a table. The command is followed by:

> The name of the schema and table

> The **values** keyword

> The values to be inserted enclosed in parentheses with a comma separating each value

Additionally, character values must be enclosed in single quotes. As an example, the following statement would insert an employee row for Mary Worker:

```
INSERT INTO tntdb.employee
        VALUES('111', 'Mary Worker', '1 Main St.',
                'Enid', 'OK', '77777', 17.50, 3)
```

Remember to be careful about spaces, commas, parentheses, and quotes.

This example inserted data for every field. You can insert data for only some fields, but you must specify which fields (and the database has to be defined to allow partial records).

The following is an example of inserting a row with only four columns of data specified.

```
INSERT INTO tntdb.employee (empnum,empname,payrate,exempts)
            VALUES('222', 'Joe Programmer', 17.50, 2)
```

Notice that the column names are specified in parentheses, separated by a comma, and at least one space after the table name. There must also be at least one space separating the closing parenthesis and the **values** keyword.

The **select** command retrieves data from a table. The programmer can identify specific rows and or columns to be retrieved. The syntax of the **select** statement requires at least the **select** keyword followed by the column names to be retrieved (separated by commas, if individually specified), the **from** keyword, and the table name.

The following statement returns all rows and columns of the employee table:

```
SELECT * FROM tntdb.employee
```

The returned result set would look like the following:

```
111 Mary Worker 1 Main St. Enid OK 77777 17.5 3
222 Joe Programmer                           17.5 2
```

Notice that an asterisk was specified after the select keyword. This means that all columns should be retrieved. If the statement had only specified four fields as in the following:

```
SELECT empnum, empname, payrate, exempts
    FROM tntdb.employee
```

then only the four columns from each row would be returned as in the following:

```
111 Mary Worker 17.5 3
222 Joe Programmer 17.5 2
```

To retrieve only some rows, use the **where** keyword with a condition. A condition is comprised of two values and a comparison operation (=, >, <, >=, <=, etc.). The values can be a static value or the name of a table field. For instance, both of the following statements:

```
SELECT empnum, empname, payrate, exempts
      FROM tntdb.employee
      WHERE state = "OK"

SELECT empnum, empname, payrate, exempts
      FROM tntdb.employee
      WHERE exempts >= 3
```

return the following data:

```
111 Mary Worker 17.5 3
```

The first statement used the state field and a character string as part of the **where** condition. Notice that string (character) values must be enclosed in quotes (as in the first statement), but numeric values are not (as shown in the second statement's **where** condition).

SQL also provides data manipulation commands that allow users to modify data in a table, and the **where** keyword can be used with these statements to identify the particular rows to be manipulated.

Data Manipulation

Data manipulation is where SQL really shines. A single SQL **update** statement can modify many columns in many rows. The **update** statement syntax is the **update** keyword followed by:

```
The schema and table names
The set keyword
```

For each column to be changed the following three items must be included:

```
The column name to be modified
An equal sign
The column's new value
```

then:

```
The where keyword
A condition that identifies the row(s) to be modified
```

For instance, the following update statement would modify the "Joe Programmer" row by adding address information and changing the payrate column:

```
UPDATE tntdb.employee
SET street = '2 Maple Ave.',
 city = 'Enid',
 state = 'OK',
 zip = '77777',
 payrate = 19
WHERE empnum = '222'
```

If we ran the following statement to return all rows and columns of the employee table:

```
SELECT * FROM tntdb.employee
```

the returned data would be:

```
111 Mary Worker 1 Main St. Enid OK 77777 17.5 3
222 Joe Programmer 2 Maple Ave. Enid OK 77777 19.0 2
```

In this example, only one row was modified, however, a **where** condition can identify many rows. For instance, if the zip code for Enid changed to 77778, we could update all the Enid student records with the following single **update** statement:

```
UPDATE tntdb.employee
SET zip = '77778'
WHERE city = 'Enid'
```

Selecting all records and rows would return the following data:

```
111 Mary Worker 1 Main St. Enid OK 77778 17.5 3
222 Joe Programmer 2 Maple Ave. Enid OK 77778 19.0 2
```

Beware: if a **where** condition is not specified in an **update** statement, all rows will be changed. This is also true for all statements that support **where** conditions.

Of course, the ultimate modification to a row is to delete it. Deletions are performed by using the **delete from** keywords followed by the schema and table names and, optionally:

The **where** keyword, and
A condition that identifies the rows to be deleted.

The following statement would delete all rows from the table:

```
DELETE FROM tntdb.employee
```

but the following would only delete the Mary Worker row:

```
DELETE FROM tntdb.employee WHERE empName = 'Mary Worker'
```

Deleting all the rows from a table does not delete the table. For example, after deleting all the rows in a table, a new row could be inserted because the table (though empty) still exists. If you drop the table, all the rows are eliminated and the table is deleted such that no records can be inserted because the table no longer exists. The **drop** keyword is used to delete all database constructs. So for instance:

```
DROP TABLE tntdb.employee
```

would erase all rows from "employee" and delete the employee table. The following statement would delete the schema and all the tables in that schema:

```
DROP SCHEMA tntdb
```

Complex Conditions

Complex (or compound) conditions can be specified by using **and** and/or **or** keywords in a **where** condition. For instance, if we wanted to retrieve those employees who made less than $20 and had more than two exemptions, the following **where** condition would be specified in the select statement:

```
SELECT * FROM tntdb.employee
WHERE payrate<20 AND exempts>2
```

This would return only the "Mary Worker" row because only the "Mary Worker" row's payrate and exempts fields satisfy the conditions. If an **or** had been specified as follows:

```
SELECT * FROM tntdb.employee
WHERE payrate<20 OR exempts>2
```

both rows would be returned because an **or** only requires that one of the conditions be true for the row to be selected. In this case, Joe Programmer makes less than $20 per hour, therefore his record would be returned.

You can connect three, four or more conditions with **and**s and **or**s. However, the logic behind combining **and**s and **or**s is somewhat tricky. As a beginner, you should stick with either **and**s or **or**s and not combine them in one **where** condition.

Java was created to run on any type of computer and, therefore, to interface with many different types of databases. Because SQL is a nonspecific relational database language, SQL is a perfect fit with Java. This is why Java provides a rich set of classes to work with SQL. See the "Database Access" chapter for more information on how to use SQL in a Java application.

One last point of interest is the SQL error message "Token *blah blah blah* was not valid." This message will become etched into your brain because of its frequent appearance. Tokens are the individual components that comprise a command. In other words, the command, keywords, values, delimiters (parentheses, spaces, commas, single quotes, etc.) are all tokens. Whenever SQL encounters a syntax error (misspelled command, missing a parenthesis, etc.) the error will be "invalid token" with some portion of the command (the blah blah blah in the example) specified as the offending token. If a space or keyword is omitted, the message is somewhat misleading because the token identified as invalid could be a perfectly valid token. In this example, the token is "invalid" because SQL syntax requires a different token at that point in the command.

What the "invalid token" message really means is that the command syntax was correct **up to the token that is identified as invalid**. Keep this in mind when trying to decipher the messages. Also, the editor makes a "good faith guess" as to what should have been specified by displaying a "Valid tokens:" clause with a list of tokens that can be specified.

APPENDIX C

■ ■ ■

Installing a Java Application on WAS

In this appendix, you will learn what a JEE application server is and how to move a server-based application from RAD onto a WebSphere Application Server (WAS) using the WAS Administrative Console. In addition, you will learn about EARs (Enterprise Archive files) and WARs (Web Archive files) and how to export EARs and WARs using RAD. This appendix assumes that you have completed at least the JSP chapter but will demonstrate how to install and access the server-based applications created in Chapter 9.

Application Servers

What makes a computer an application server? The computer must have a communication line linked to a network, a network address, and, most importantly, be running application server software. Oracle dictates a set of rules called JEE (Java Enterprise Edition) that define how the Java application server must work. There are a variety of vendors who supply application server software, but all "JEE application servers" must follow Oracle's rules. (IBM's WebSphere Application Server (WAS) was one of the first certified JEE servers.)

For example, the JEE rules dictate where all the server-based application components are stored on the server. In other words, specific directories hold the various server-based application pieces (Web pages, Java classes, JSPs, etc.). Therefore, to publish a Web page or application to the Web, you need access to a computer that is acting as an application or Web server, and you need to know where to put the files. In the earlier days of server-side programming, the programmer had to move the files into the correct directories on the server. Fortunately, JEE also defines specialized files, EARs and WARs, to store all the application components in the correct directory structure.

Many years ago, Sun Microsystems defined the specifications for JARs (Java Archive Files). JARs are Zip files with a specific folder structure to hold multiple Java classes. JAR files are a very easy way to move and store many Java classes at once (just as Zip files are an easy way to move and store multiple PC files).

WARs and EARs are JAR files with extra information about the server-side application (i.e., a list of the class files and Web pages, security information, where the files are stored, etc.). Both WARs and EARs hold server-based applications, but EARs support very complex applications (e.g., applications that are installed across many servers, have client-based components, use application-wide database connections, etc.) In other words, EARs are more complicated than WARs. Fortunately, you don't have to worry about the internal structure of either of these files (and be happy you don't), because RAD creates EARs and WARs for you.

Tutorial: Exporting

Just as you must first export the PC-based application class files before installing them, the server-based components must be exported. As you may have noticed, the number of individual files in a server-based application can be quite large. Fortunately, RAD lets you export an entire project at once and if the project is exported as an EAR or WAR, RAD will maintain the correct directory structure.

1. In the Navigator pane select the TutorialsWeb project, then click File, and Export.

The Export window will be displayed.

2. Expand the JEE and Web items as in Figure C-1.

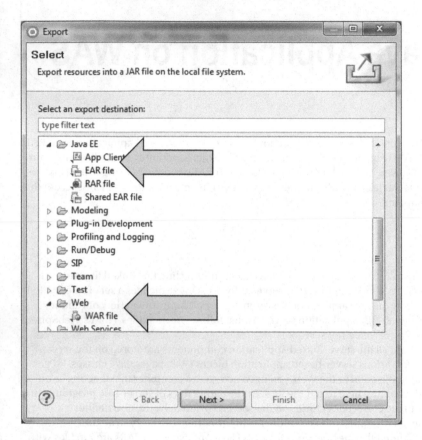

Figure C-1.

Notice that there are options to export as an EAR or a WAR. Because TutorialsWeb is not a very complex application, we do not need the added capability (and overhead) of an EAR file.

3. Select WAR file and click the Next button.

The "Export Resources to a WAR file" window will be displayed. At this window, you must specify where to store the WAR file. You can use the browse button to navigate to the location or simply specify the drive and path. In addition, you must give the WAR file a name.

Notice that there is also an option to export the source code. Generally, source code is not placed on the server. Because only programmers (not users) need access to source code, there is no good reason to store a copy on the server. In addition, having another copy of the source code could complicate future updates (e.g., which version of the source is the most recent?) and could pose a security risk if it fell into the wrong hands.

4. Specify a destination and deselect the Export source files option as in Figure C-2.

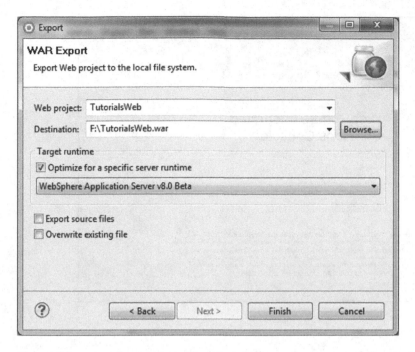

Figure C-2.

5. Click the Finish button.

6. Verify that the WAR file was exported by using My Computer to view the location.

Tutorial: Installing to a WAS

Amazingly, RAD and WAS make the process to install an application that encompasses hundreds or thousands of Web pages and Java classes as simple as installing a single Web page.

The first nice WAS feature we'll look at is remote installation. This means you do not have to physically access the server to load the WAR file and install the application. Instead, the server is accessed with the browser and the WAR file is transferred from the PC to the server. (Of course, this assumes you have the authority to install applications on the server.)

To perform the installation, first access the WAS Administrative Console page. This is done by starting a browser session and entering the URL or IP address of the WAS and specifying the admin directory. In this example, we use the host address of WAS-server. You will have to substitute your host IP address or URL in all the examples.

1. Start the browser and specify the following URL: `http://WAS-server:9061/admin/`

Notice that in addition to the host address, we specified a port number (9061). Multiple servers can be running on one host computer. The way the computer distinguishes between the various servers is by the port number. (A more user-friendly site would have created separate URLs for the various servers, thereby relieving the user of having to remember the port number.)

The WAS default is to run the administrative/technical functions on one port (9061) and the user applications on another port (9081). In addition, we must specify the admin subdirectory so that the Administrative Console logon window is displayed as in Figure C-3. (Again, your URL may have different port numbers and the console may be in a different subdirectory.)

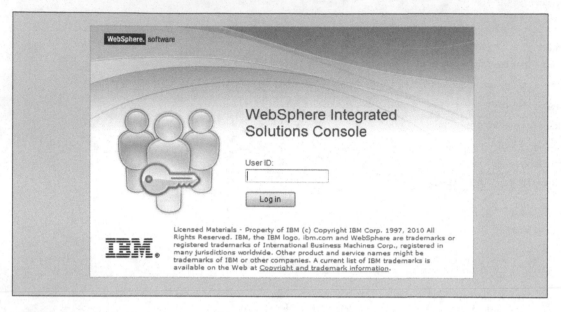

Figure C-3.

The logon screen may only require a user ID, but most "real world" sites will also require a valid password.

2. Specify valid logon information and click the Login button.

The Administrative Console home page is displayed. Notice that the left pane displays various function categories (servers, applications, security, etc.). Clicking an item will display a subtree of functions.
We must first install the application and then start it.

3. Expand the Applications options (as in Figure C-4) and click New Application.

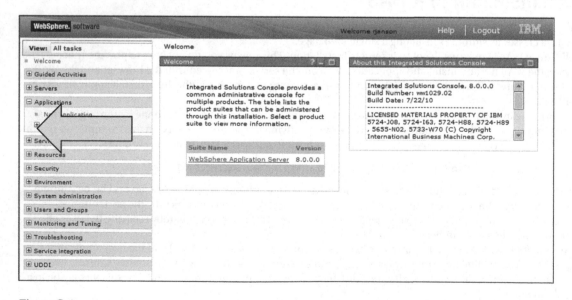

Figure C-4.

The new application pane will be displayed (as in Figure C-5). WAS allows many "enterprise applications" to be grouped into a "business level application." An application can also be added as an asset and then added to the business level application. Our simple application doesn't need a business level app, so we will simply add an Enterprise application. (WAS will actually create a default business application and add our enterprise application to it.)

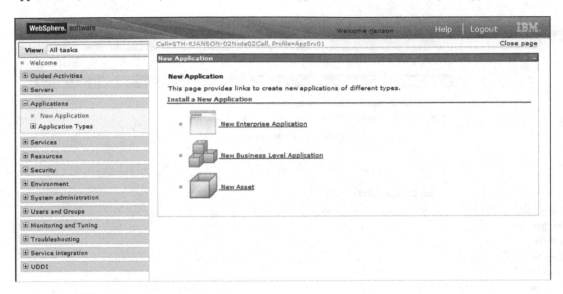

Figure C-5.

4. Click the New Enterprise Application link.

Installing the application begins with a one-step preparation that simple consists of identifying the WAR file.

5. In the Preparing for the application installation pane (see Figure C-6), specify the WAR file's local path (i.e., its location on the PC) and click Next.

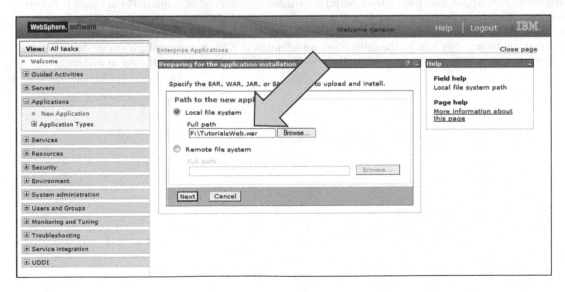

Figure C-6.

The How to install pane will be displayed (as in Figure C-7). There are two options for installing. The Detailed option results in an eleven step installation with all the sorts of configuration options. Although there are many important options in the detailed installation, our simple application can use the Fast Path method and its relatively simpler 5 step installation.

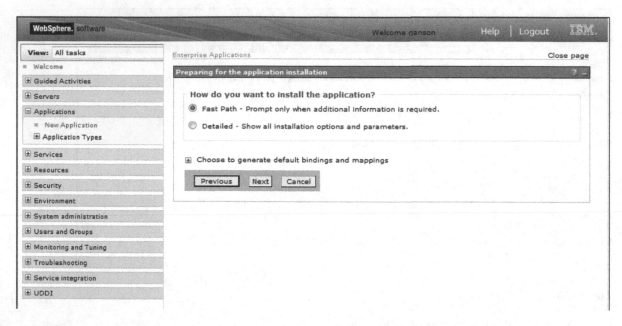

Figure C-7.

6. Leave Fast Path selected and click Next.

The first Install New Application page (Step 1: Select installation options) will be displayed as in Figure C-8. This page actually has a performance option where we will change the default. Usually the server waits until the first time a JSP is requested to convert the JSP to a servlet. As you know from running the JSPs in RAD, this can take a while. So instead of making the first user wait for the conversion, we will instruct WAS to convert all JSPs to servlets when the application is installed. This means that the installation will take longer, but no users will have to wait longer for pages.

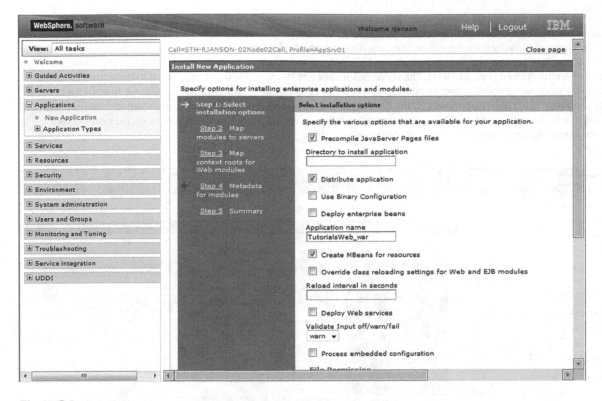

Figure C-8.

7. On the Step 1 page, click the "Pre-compile JSP" option (as in Figure C-8), then scroll down the page and click the Next button.

8. On the Step 2 page, click the TutorialsWeb checkbox (as in Figure C-9), then click Next.

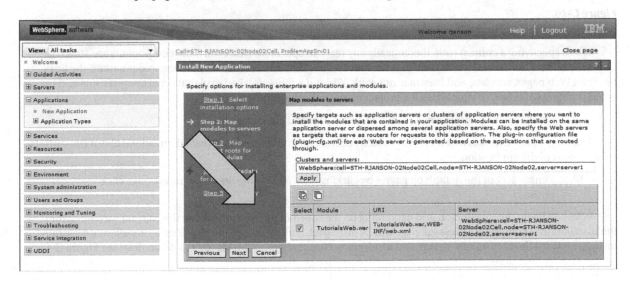

Figure C-9.

The Step 3 page (Figure C-10) requires that a context root be specified. The context root is part of the URL. Besides containing the host address (WAS-server:9060) and the particular page (Howdy.html), the URL often has a path. This path usually corresponds to the directories where the file being accessed is stored. However, instead of being restricted to the actual path (which can be very long and prone to typing errors), most servers allow you to define a context root (i.e., an alias). The server associates any requests for that context root to the actual location (directory path) of the application. For example, when we accessed the administrative console we specified a context root of *admin/*. This does not mean that the Web pages and classes that make up the administration functions are stored in a folder called admin. They are probably buried deep within folders and subfolders. So the context root admin simply makes it easier to specify the location.

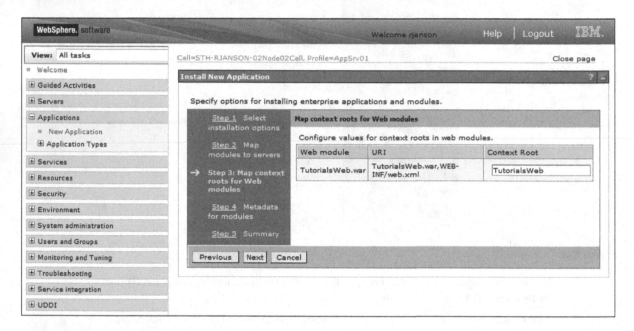

Figure C-10.

When specifying a context root, theoretically any text can specified. However, if the components are stored in a specific folder (like TutorialsWeb) and a context root is specified that is different from the folder names, the links between Web pages, servlets, and JSPs may not work. Without a more detailed explanation of context roots and how to avoid problems, it is best to simply use the project name as the context root.

9. On the Step 3 page, leave the default context root and click Next.

The Step 4 page controls whether WAS should generate default information (called metadata) about the various components of the application.

10. Simply accept the default on page 4 by clicking Next and on the Step 5 summary page click Finish.

WAS will begin the installation and depending on the speed of the host computer, this may take a while. After the installation is complete, a message page will be displayed. If all went well, there will be a "installed successfully" message toward the bottom of the page and a link to save the changes to the Master Configuration (see Figure C-11).

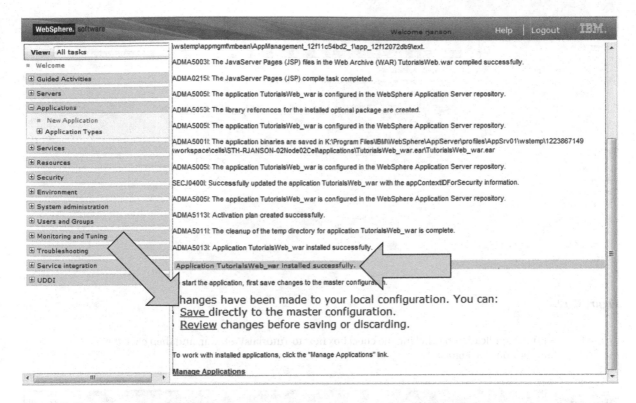

Figure C-11.

11. Double-click the "Save directly to the master configuration." link to save the changes and install the application.

The "Preparing for the application installation" page will be redisplayed. This means that the application was successfully installed and saved on the server. Now we need to start the application.

12. On the left of the "WebSphere Integrated Solutions Console" page, expand the Application Types item and the click the "WebSphere enterprise applications" link.

The Enterprise Applications page will be displayed (see Figure C-12). Notice that the TutorialsWeb application is listed but its status is stopped (indicated by a red "x").

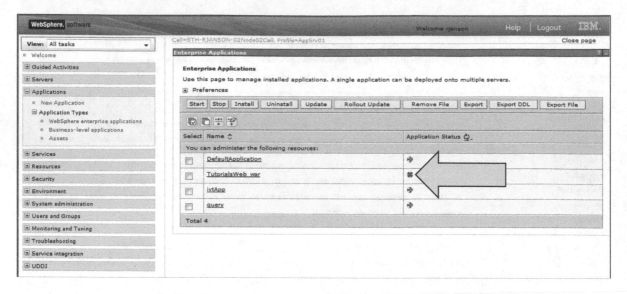

Figure C-12.

13. Start the application by clicking the checkbox next to TutorialsWeb.war, and then click the Start button (see Figure C-13).

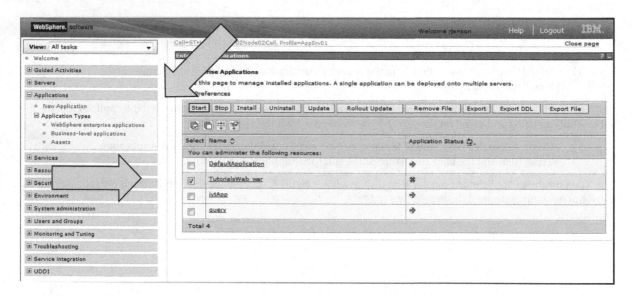

Figure C-13.

When the application is successfully started, a message will be displayed at the top of the page and the status will be changed to started (indicated with a green arrow where the red "x" was before). We will now verify that the application is available by using the browser to access some of the Web pages in the application.

Tutorial: Accessing a WAS Application

1. Start the browser and specify `http://yourhost:port#/TutorialsWeb/c9/HowdyJSP.jsp` (substitute your host address and port number for the text **yourhost:port#**).

The Howdy page created in Chapter 9 will be displayed as in C-14.

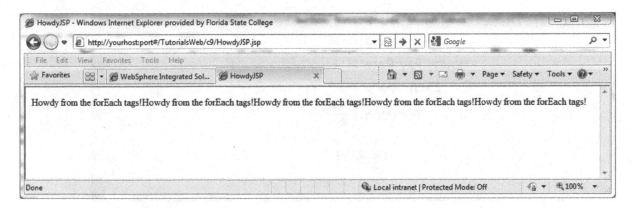

Figure C-14.

Yeeeeehaaaaaa! It works!

Note that a different port number is required for the application than for the administrative console. Usually the ports differ by 20. In other words, if the admin port was 9061 then the application server port is 9081.

Of course, one simple JSP does not an application make.

2. Display the EnterEmpInfoJSP from Chapter 9 by changing the URL to identify TutorialsWeb/c9/EnterEmpInfoJSP.jsp

3. In EnterEmpInfoJSP, specify the information as seen in Figure C-15, select Display as the function, then click Submit.

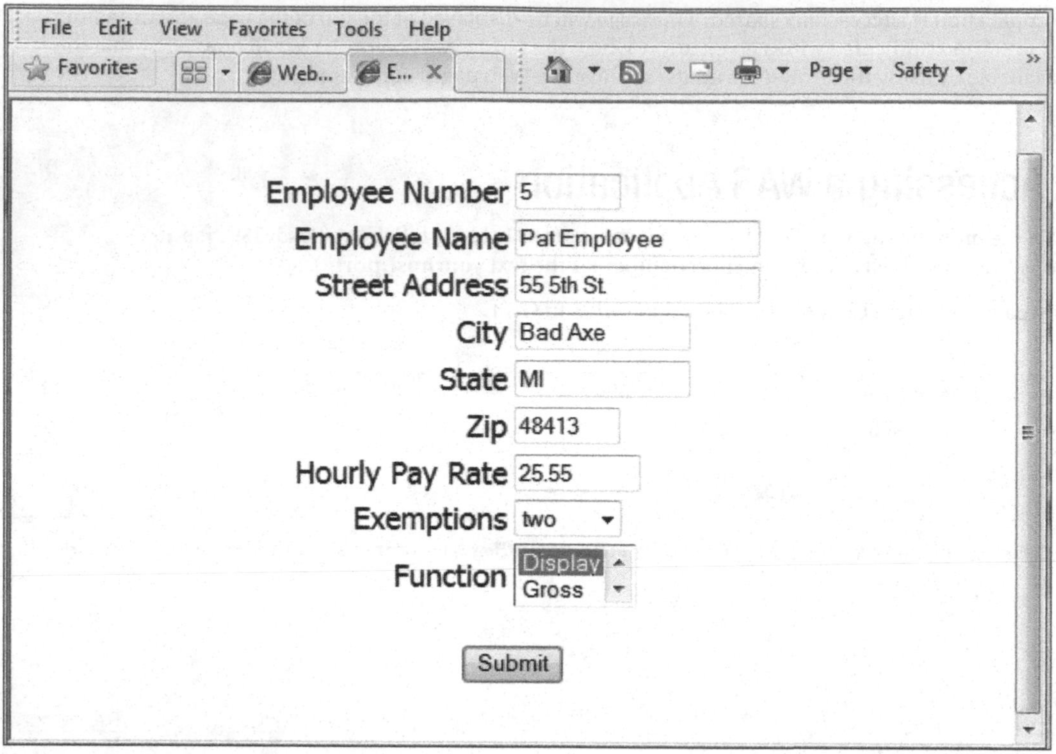

Figure C-15.

DispEmpInfoJSP will be invoked and the Employee information will be echoed back as seen in Figure C-16. Notice that the URL address in the browser identifies the page as Enter-EmpInfoJSP not DispEmpInfoJSP.

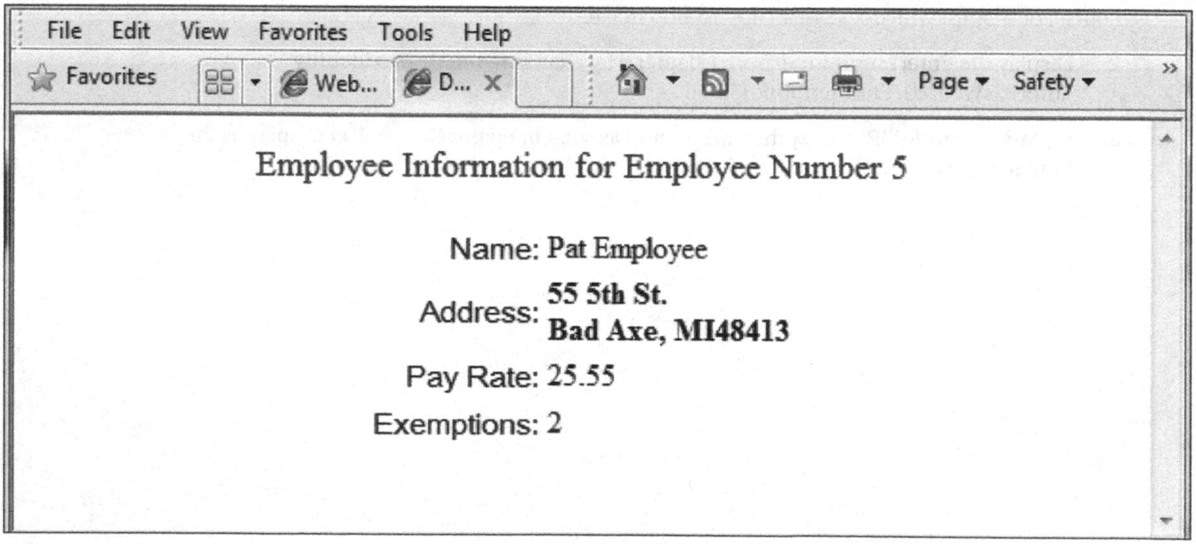

Figure C-16.

To thoroughly check the application, you should ensure that the correct JSPs and information are displayed for the Gross and TaxAmt functions.

Results of the Tutorial

1. The file TutorialsWeb.war is on the C: drive.

2. The TutorialsWeb project is successfully installed and running on the WAS.

Review Exercise

1. Export the ReviewExWeb project as a WAR to the C: drive.

2. Install ReviewExWeb.war on the WAS and start the ReviewExWeb application.

Results of the Review Exercise

1. The file ReviewExWeb.war is on the C: drive.

2. The ReviewExWeb project is successfully loaded and running on the WAS.

Index

■ J